Routledge Handbook of Graffiti and Street Art

Routledge Handbook of Graffiti and Street Art integrates and reviews current scholarship in the field of graffiti and street art. Thirty-five original contributions are organized around four parts:

- History, types, and writers/artists of graffiti and street art.
- Theoretical explanations of graffiti and street art/causes of graffiti and street art.
- Regional/municipal variations/differences of graffiti and street art.
- Effects of graffiti and street art.

Chapters are written by experts from different countries throughout the world and their expertise spans the fields of American Studies, Art Theory, Criminology, Criminal Justice, Ethnography, Photography, Political Science, Psychology, Sociology, and Visual Communication.

The Handbook will be of interest to researchers, instructors, advanced students, libraries, and art gallery and museum curators.

This book is also accessible to practitioners and policy makers in the fields of criminal justice, law enforcement, art history, museum studies, tourism studies, and urban studies as well as members of the news media. The Handbook includes 92 images, a glossary, and a chronology, and the electronic edition will be widely hyperlinked.

Jeffrey Ian Ross is a Professor in the School of Criminal Justice, College of Public Affairs, and a Research Fellow of the Schaefer Center for Public Policy, and the Center for International and Comparative Law, both at the University of Baltimore.

Routledge Handbook of Graffiti and Street Art

Edited by
Jeffrey Ian Ross

FOREWORD BY JEFF FERRELL

Routledge
Taylor & Francis Group

LONDON AND NEW YORK

First published 2016 by Routledge

2 Park Square, Milton Park, Abingdon, Oxfordshire OX14 4RN
52 Vanderbilt Avenue, New York, NY 10017

Routledge is an imprint of the Taylor & Francis Group, an informa business

First issued in paperback 2019

British Library Cataloguing-in-Publication Data
A catalogue record for this book is available from the British Library

Library of Congress Cataloging in Publication Data
   Routledge handbook of graffiti and street art/Edited by Jeffrey Ian Ross.
   pages cm
   Includes bibliographical references.
   1. Graffiti. 2. Street art. I. Ross, Jeffrey Ian, editor.
   GT3912.R68 2015
   751.7'3–dc23
   2015017717

ISBN: 978-1-138-79293-7 (hbk)
ISBN: 978-0-367-33597-7 (pbk)

Typeset in Bembo and Stone Sans
by Florence Production Ltd, Stoodleigh, Devon, UK

(Photo: Jeffrey Ian Ross, June 3, 2013)

To Francis T. Cullen, who has been an informal
mentor and supporter during my career

Contents

Contents

x

Contents

Figures

Tables

Contributors

Editor

Jeffrey Ian Ross, Ph.D., is a Professor in the School of Criminal Justice, College of Public Affairs, and a Research Fellow of the Schaefer Center for Public Policy, and the Center for International and Comparative Law, both at the University of Baltimore.

For over two decades, he has researched, written, and lectured primarily on corrections, policing, political crime (esp., terrorism and state crime), violence (esp., criminal, political, and religious), global crime and criminal justice, and crime and justice in American Indian communities. Ross's work has appeared in many academic journals and books, as well as popular media. He is the author, co-author, editor, or co-editor of several books.

Ross is a respected subject matter expert for local, regional, national, and international news media. He has made live appearances on Al Jazeera, CNN, CNBC, Fox News Network and MSNBC. Additionally Ross has written op-eds for *The (Baltimore) Sun, The (Maryland) Daily Record, The Gazette* (weekly community newspapers serving Maryland's Montgomery, Frederick, Prince George, and Carroll counties), the *Baltimore Examiner,* and the *Tampa Tribune.*

From 1995 to 1998, Ross was a Social Science Analyst with the National Institute of Justice, a Division of the U.S. Department of Justice. In 2003, he was awarded the University of Baltimore's Distinguished Chair in Research Award. During the early 1980s, Jeff worked almost four years in a correctional institution.

Ross is a former student of the Ontario College of Art. He has taught "Graffiti and Street Art" at the University of Baltimore and is currently taking classes through the Art League of Washington.

Contributors

Mona Abaza was born in Egypt and earned her Ph.D. in 1990 in sociology at the University of Bielefeld, Germany. She is currently Professor of Sociology at the American University in Cairo and former Chair of the Department of Sociology, Anthropology, Egyptology, and Psychology (2007–2009, 2013). Dr. Abaza was a visiting Professor of Islamology, Department of Theology, Lund University, Sweden for two years (2009–2011). She was a visiting scholar in Singapore at the Institute of South East Asian Studies (ISEAS 1990–1992), Kuala Lumpur 1995–1996, Paris (EHESS) 1994, Berlin (Fellow at the Wissenschaftskolleg 1996–1997), Leiden (IIAS, 2002–2003), Wassenaar (NIAS, 2006–2007) and Bellagio (Rockefeller Foundation 2005) and visiting fellow, at Morphomata, Cologne in 2014. Her books include: *The Cotton Plantation remembered,* American University in Cairo Press, 2013; *Twentieth Century Egyptian Art: The Private Collection of Sherwet Shafei,* The American University Press, 2011; *The Changing Consumer Culture* *of Modern Egypt, Cairo's Urban Reshaping*, Brill, Leiden/Cairo, American University Press, 2006; *Debates on Islam and Knowledge in Malaysia and Egypt, Shifting Worlds*, Routledge Curzon Press, U.K., 2002; *Islamic Education, Perceptions and Exchanges: Indonesian Students in Cairo*, Cahier d'Archipel, EHESS, Paris, 1994, and, *The Changing Image of Women in Rural Egypt*, Cairo Papers in Social Science, The American University in Cairo, 1987.

Joe A. Austin earned his Ph.D. in American Studies from the University of Minnesota, and is now an Associate Professor of History at the University of Wisconsin-Milwaukee. His research interests are in the post-1945 era of U.S. cultural and social history, with specialties in urban studies, youth, and popular culture studies. He is the co-editor of *Generations of Youth: Youth Cultures and History in Twentieth Century America* (with Michael Willard, NYU Press, 1998) and the author of *Taking the Train: How Graffiti Art Became an Urban Crisis in New York City, 1970–1990* (Columbia University Press, 2001). His recent publications include "More to See Than a Canvas in a White Cube: For An Art in the Streets" (*City*, vol.14, 2010). Austin is currently working on a book-length project on the social normalization of the "teenager" as a life-stage in the United States between 1940 and 1970, with a significant portion of this project focused on the formation of African American youth cultures in central cities, as well as the public sphere discussions of African American teenagers and criminality during this period.

J.A. Baird, Ph.D., FSA, is Senior Lecturer in Archaeology in the Department of History, Classics, and Archaeology at Birkbeck College, University of London. Her main interest is in the archaeology of everyday life, and she has published work on ancient graffiti, urbanism, housing, as well as archaeological photography, and the history of Classical archaeology. Her recent publications include *Ancient Graffiti in Context* (co-edited with Claire Taylor, Routledge, 2011), and *The Inner Lives of Ancient Houses: An Archaeology of Dura-Europos* (Oxford University Press, 2014).

Peter Bengtsen is an art historian and sociologist. He has been writing about street art since 2006 and is the author of the book *The Street Art World* (Almendros de Granada Press, 2014). This monograph is a result of a four-year research project carried out at the Division of Art History and Visual Studies at Lund University, Sweden. Bengtsen's most recent work has been focused on the connection between street art and spatial justice, and – as in the contribution to this volume – the collection of and trade in artworks taken from the street.

Stefano Bloch earned his Ph.D. in geography from the University of Minnesota and Master's in Urban Planning from UCLA. His dissertation, "The Changing Face of Wall Space" (2012), addresses illegally produced but tacitly tolerated graffiti-murals. Much of his data was gathered through participant observation and his in-depth access to the otherwise guarded L.A.-based graffiti, mural, and street art community of which Stefano was a member for over 20 years. His work has appeared in the *Radical History Review* (2012) and *City* (2013), and since 2014 Bloch has held a Mellon post-doctoral position with the Cogut Center for the Humanities at Brown University and is currently a Brown University Presidential Diversity Fellow in the Urban Studies Program where he teaches "Crime and the City" and "Bottom-up Urbanism."

Andrea Mubi Brighenti, Ph.D. in Sociology of Law, is Professor of *Social Theory* and *Space & Culture* at the Department of Sociology, University of Trento, Italy. His research topics focus on space, power and society. He has published *Visibility in Social Theory and Social Research*

(Palgrave Macmillan, 2010), *Territori migranti* (ombre corte, 2009), and *The Ambiguous Multiplicities* (Palgrave Macmillan, forthcoming, 2014). He is the Editor of *Urban Interstices. The Aesthetics and Politics of Spatial In-betweens* (Ashgate, 2013), *Uma Cidade de Imagens* (Mundos Sociais, 2012 – with Ricardo Campos and Luciano Spinelli), and *The Wall and the City* (professionaldreamers, 2009).

Besides various contributions to edited volumes, his articles have appeared in several Italian and international peer-reviewed journals, including *Theory, Culture & Society*, *Space and Culture*, *Urban Studies*, *Surveillance and Society*, *The Journal of Classical Sociology*, *European Journal of Social Theory*, *Thesis Eleven*, *International Journal of Law in Context*, *Critical Sociology*, *Etnografia e Ricerca Qualitativa*, *Quaderni di Sociologia*, *Current Sociology*, *Polis*, *Rassegna Italiana di Sociologia*, *Sociologia del diritto*, *Sortuz*, *The Canadian Journal of Law and Society/Revue Canadienne de Droit et Société*, and *Law and Critique*. He is the founder and editor of the independent online web journal *lo Squaderno* (www.losquaderno.professionaldreamers.net), and currently co-editor of the journal *Etnografia e Ricerca Qualitativa*.

Ricardo Campos is a social scientist and illustrator, born and living in Lisbon (Portugal). He holds a Graduation and Masters degree in Sociology and a Ph.D. in Visual Anthropology. Currently, he is postdoctoral research fellow at CICS.Nova – Interdiciplinary Centre of Social Sciences, Portugal. In the past fifteen years, he has been researching urban youth cultures and, particularly, the connections between youth and image. Dr. Campos has recently studied the graffiti community in the city of Lisbon for his Ph.D. thesis. Besides urban cultures, he has been studying and writing several articles and books – mainly in Portuguese – on topics such as visual methodologies, visual culture, art or education. His publications include *"Porque pintamos a cidade? Uma abordagem etnográfica ao graffiti urbano"* [Why do we paint the city? An ethnographic approach to urban graffiti] (Fim de Século, 2010) and *"Introdução à Cultura Visual. Abordagens e metodologias"* [Introduction to Visual Culture. Approaches and Methodologies] (Mundos Sociais, 2013). He has co-edited (with Andrea Mubi Brighenti and Luciano Spinelli) *"Uma cidade de Imagens"* [A city of images] (Mundos Sociais, 2011) and *Popular & Visual Culture: Design, Circulation and Consumption* (with Clara Sarmento, Cambridge Scholars Publishing, 2014). He is also one of the editors of the Brazilian academic journal *"Cadernos de Arte e Antropologia"* [Journal of Art and Anthropology] (www.cadernosaa.ufba.br).

Georgia Carragher (Ph.D., MSocSc, MSpEd, BArts Hon) is an experienced counselor and psychotherapist with a background in special education research. Currently Georgia is completing a B.A. in social work. Her particular field of research is adolescents with ADHD. Georgia also studies the impact of sexual abuse and family violence on children and young adults and how it affects their well-being and long term relationships. She also is interested in the way violence is portrayed by the media and the influence this has on young people and the general public.

Graeme Evans is Professor of Design and Urban Cultures in the School of Art and Design, Middlesex University, London. He also holds a chair in Culture and Urban Development at Maastricht University, The Netherlands and was founder-director of the Cities Institute (2003–12). Key publications include *Cultural Planning: An Urban Renaissance?* (Routledge) and *Designing Sustainable Cities* (Wiley) and he has published over a hundred articles and chapters and undertaken commissioned research for the U.K. Culture Ministry, Arts Councils, the OECD, and Council of Europe, particularly in the field of art and urban regeneration and cultural planning. He has led numerous research projects under Research Council and EU programmes including VivaCity2020, AGORA: Cities for People. He currently leads research projects funded by the Arts and Humanities Research Council on culture and sustainability.

Jeff Ferrell is Professor of Sociology at Texas Christian University, U.S.A., and Visiting Professor of Criminology at the University of Kent, U.K. He is author of the books *Crimes of Style*, *Tearing Down the Streets*, *Empire of Scrounge*, and, with Keith Hayward and Jock Young, *Cultural Criminology: An Invitation*, winner of the 2009 Distinguished Book Award from the American Society of Criminology's Division of International Criminology. He is co-editor of the books *Cultural Criminology*, *Ethnography at the Edge*, *Making Trouble*, *Cultural Criminology Unleashed*, and *Cultural Criminology: Theories of Crime*. Jeff Ferrell is founding and current editor of the New York University Press book series *Alternative Criminology*, and one of the founding editors of the journal *Crime, Media, Culture: An International Journal*, winner of the ALPSP 2006 Charlesworth Award for Best New Journal. In 1998 he received the Critical Criminologist of the Year Award from the Critical Criminology Division of the American Society of Criminology.

David Fieni is Assistant Professor of French at the State University of New York, Oneonta. He completed his Ph.D. in Comparative Literature at the University of California, Los Angeles, after which he was a Mellon Fellow in French at Cornell University. In 2014 he co-edited and contributed an essay to "The Global Checkpoint," a special issue of The Journal of Postcolonial Studies. He has published in PMLA on the Moroccan writer Abdelkebir Khatibi, and co-edited an issue of Expressions maghrébines about Khatibi. His article on graffiti in France, "What a Wall Wants, or How Graffiti Thinks: Nomad Grammatology in the French Banlieue," appeared in *Diacritics* in 2012. Fieni has published on topics as diverse as Algerian women writers and literary mourning (*Dalhousie French Studies*, 2014), the nexus between decadence and Orientalism in the French and Arab fin de siècle (Boundary 2, 2012), and the intersection of aesthetics and politics in the work of Jean Genet and Georges Bataille. *Empire of Language*, his translation of Laurent Dubreuil's book, was published by Cornell University Press in 2013.

Minna Haveri, DA, is an independent researcher and writer from Finland. She is currently a lecturer in the field of art education at Aalto University in Helsinki. She completed her doctorate at Aalto University School of Arts, Design and Architecture in 2010. Her dissertation *Nykykansantaide* on contemporary folk art investigated the various phenomena in Finnish visual folk art and the meanings attached to them. Haveri's current research interests include crafts-based art expression. Recently she has been actively writing on art by people with disabilities. Haveri is widely interested in the margins of art and social justice in visual art education.

Ronald Kramer, Ph.D. is a Lecturer in the Department of Sociology at the University of Auckland in New Zealand. He has conducted extensive ethnographic research on graffiti writing culture in New York City and published scholarly articles on the topic in various international journals, such as *Ethnography, Qualitative Sociology,* and *Critical Criminology*. He is currently working on two research projects. The first is a comparative analysis of official and public reactions to graffiti in New York City and Auckland. The second project explores the ways in which neoliberal inequalities are reconfiguring the practices and processes of criminal justice systems. This project grew out of recent fieldwork conducted inside a jail for young men participating in a cognitive treatment program. He has taught in the areas of sociological theory, research methods, political economy, crime and deviance, art and popular culture, and urban sociology.

John F. Lennon earned his B.A. from King's College and his Ph.D. from Lehigh University. He is an assistant professor at the University of South Florida where he teaches courses in 20th-century American literature and film with a cultural studies orientation. His research is principally concerned with how marginalized individuals exert a politicized voice in collectivized actions. His monograph, *Boxcar Politics: The Hobo in U.S. Culture and Literature, 1869–1956*, was published by UMASS Press in 2014, and his work has appeared in various edited volumes and journals including *Cultural Studies Review, American Studies, Rhizomes: Cultural Studies in Emerging Knowledge, Acoma*, and *Americana: Journal of American Popular Culture*. Lennon is currently at work on a new project examining conflict graffiti from a global perspective.

Nancy Macdonald, Ph.D., completed her Doctorate in 1997 at Brunel University in London. This was an ethnographic study of the illegal graffiti subculture in London and New York. Her work on this area was subsequently published as a book, *The Graffiti Subculture: Youth, Masculinity and Identity in London and New York* (Macmillan/Palgrave, 2001). She has contributed a chapter to *The Subcultures Reader* (Second Edition Routledge, 2005) on the masculine makeup of the subculture, and addressed the role of women in a foreword to the book *Graffiti Women* (Thames and Hudson, 2006). In addition, she has written course material for the Open University in Maybin. J (ed.) *The Art of English: Everyday Creativity* (Palgrave, 2006). She continues to write in the social/commercial research realm, publishing work on various subjects including ethnography, adolescent identity and youth subcultures. In her current role as a Social Research Director, Macdonald was named winner of the *AQR Prosper Riley Award for inno-vative research, MRS Financial Services Award in 2008*, for work conducted with the FSA on young people's financial management issues, and the *Marketing Week Engage Research Award* for multistage strategy work she conducted with Transport for London to address teenage road risk behaviours.

Favian Alejandro Martín is Assistant Professor of Criminology and Criminal Justice at Arcadia University, Metropolitan Philadelphia, PA. Dr. Martín earned his B.S. and M.A. in Criminal Justice from Pennsylvania State University and his Ph.D. in Criminology and Criminal Justice from Old Dominion University. His dissertation examined the perceptions of crime, violence, and justice among tribal police officers working in Indian Country. Dr. Martín's research interests are in the areas of race and crime, immigration, restorative justice, hate crimes, and social justice. He has published work in various academic journals such as *Critical Criminology, Journal of Criminal Justice, International Criminal Justice Review, Criminal Justice Policy Review*, and *Journal of Criminal Justice Education*.

Jessica Nydia Pabón is an Assistant Professor in the Women's, Gender, and Sexuality Studies Program at SUNY New Paltz where she is currently teaching Feminist Theory and Gender and Sexuality in Hip Hop Culture. She is an interdisciplinary feminist scholar with specializations in gender, hip-hop, latino/a, lgbtq, performance and visual studies. She has publications in *Women & Performance: a journal of feminist theory, Rhizomes: Cultural Studies in Emerging Knowledge*, and *TDR: the journal of performance studies*. Dr. Pabón was a Postdoctoral Fellow in the Arts and Humanities at New York University, Abu Dhabi from 2013–2014 and an American Association of University Women Fellow from 2012–2013. She is currently preparing her manuscript *Graffiti Grrlz: Performing Feminism in the Hip Hop Diaspora* for publication. Dr. Pabón blogs about her work at www.jessicapabon.com and tweets from @justjess_phd.

Rodney Palmer enjoyed research fellowships at the Istituto Italiano per gli Studi Filosofici, Naples, and World Art Progamme, University of East Anglia, U.K. With Thomas Frangenberg, Palmer has co-edited *The Rise of the Image* (Ashgate, London 2003) and *The Lives of Leonardo* (the Warburg Institute, London 2013). He is the author of *Street Art Chile* (8 Books, London 2008), its enlarged Chilean edition *Arte Callejero en Chile* (Ocho Libros, Santiago 2011) and *Murallas del Cono Sur de las Américas: Argentina, Chile, Paraguay, Uruguay* (Ocho Libros, Santiago 2015).

Julie Peteet is Professor of Anthropology and Director of Middle East and Islamic Studies at the University of Louisville. Her research has focused on Palestinian displacement and refugee camps in Lebanon and more recently the spatio-temporal dimensions of the policy and practices of closure in Palestine. She teaches classes on Mobilities, Middle East anthropology, Human Rights, and Refugees. She has authored three books: *Gender in Crisis: Women and the Palestinian Resistance Movement* (Columbia University Press, 1991), *Landscape of Hope and Despair. Palestinian Refugee Camps* (University of Pennsylvania Press, 2005), and *Space and Mobility in Palestine* (University of Pennsylvania Press, forthcoming 2015). She has published in a variety of journals including *Signs, American Ethnologist, Cultural Anthropology, Cultural Survival, International Journal of Middle East Studies, Third World Quarterly*, and *Middle East Report* as well as contributed numerous chapters in edited volumes. She was an editor of the six-volume *Encyclopedia of Women in Islam*. Her research has been funded by SSRC, Wenner-Gren, Fulbright, the Mellon Foundation, CAORC, and PARC.

Susan A. Phillips has studied gangs and the U.S. prison system since 1990. Phillips received her Ph.D. in anthropology in 1998 from UCLA, where she taught for four years before coming to Pitzer College. Her first book, *Wallbangin: Graffiti and Gangs in L.A.*, was published by the University of Chicago Press in 1999. Her second book, *Operation Fly Trap: Gangs, Drugs, and the Law*, was published in July 2012, also by Chicago. Phillips was named a Soros Justice Media Fellow in 2008, and received a Harry Frank Guggenheim research grant in 2005 to fund her fieldwork. Previous to that she was a fellow at the Getty Research Institute from 1996–1997, during the scholar year on Los Angeles. Phillips is interested in theories of violence, in the relationship between gangs and the state, and in utilizing academic writing and scholarship toward criminal justice reform. She currently directs community-based research programs in Ontario, California for Pitzer College and is a member of the Environmental Analysis field group, where she contributes curriculum on urban studies.

Doreen Piano is an associate professor of English and Interim Director of Women and Gender Studies at the University of New Orleans in Louisiana where she teaches undergraduate and graduate courses in writing, rhetorical theory, gender studies, and pedagogy. She has written popular and academic articles about the significance of DIY (do-it-yourself) culture in Third Wave feminism and most recently is documenting the recovery of the New Orleans post-Katrina through the aesthetic, collective, and political uses of public space by city residents. Her research about New Orleans dovetails with a growing interest in visual culture, rhetoric, and cultural geography and their intersection with critical literacy practices.

Julie Ann Pooley, Ph.D. is an Associate Professor and currently the Associate Dean of Teaching and Learning for the Faculty of Computing Health and Science at Edith Cowan University. Dr. Pooley leads the School of Psychology and Social Science's Lifespan Resilience Research Group and has been involved in teaching in both the undergraduate and postgraduate psychology programs and has been a recipient of a National Teaching Award and Citation by the Australian University Teaching Committee (2003, 2011). Her research focuses on resilience at the individual and community levels. Julie Ann has been involved in and directed many community based research consultancies, projects, and workshops and has been involved in the generation of many different community oriented reports for various cities and districts.

Rafael Schacter is an anthropologist, curator, and author from London. He has recently been made a British Academy Postdoctoral Fellow (2014–2017), based in the Anthropology Department and the Urban Laboratory at University College London. Schacter has been undertaking research on graffiti and street-art for almost ten years, culminating in the award of a Ph.D. at UCL in 2011. He is the author of *The World Atlas of Street Art and Graffiti* (Yale University Press, 2013), and *Ornament and Order* (Ashgate, 2014). Schacter has curated numerous exhibitions including the iconic show Street-Art at the Tate Modern in 2008 that he co-curated. He is currently curating a series of street-art and graffiti related exhibitions at Somerset House in London, including the recent and widely acclaimed Mapping the City exhibition. Schacter lectures widely around the world on street art and graffiti. In the last six months he has spoken at the Hermitage in Saint Petersburg, the Onassis Culture Centre in Athens and in other locations in the U.K., France, the Philippines, and the U.S.

Danwill Schwender is an Attorney at Foldenauer Law Group. He earned his Masters of Law degree in intellectual property law from The George Washington University Law School, received his Juris Doctor degree from the Thomas Jefferson School of Law, and earned a Bachelor of Science degree from the University of Utah. Mr. Schwender's legal practice focuses on the representation of individuals and companies in business disputes involving claims such as unfair competition, breach of contract, fraud, negligence, breach of fiduciary duty, intellectual property infringement, and trade secret misappropriation. Before returning to litigation, Mr. Schwender was the director of legal and business affairs for one of the largest distributors of action and outdoor sports films. Mr. Schwender has researched and written several articles, primarily in the field of intellectual property law. His papers have appeared in academic journals and books. His most recent effort, "If Reagan Played Disco: Rocking Out and Selling Out with the Talking Heads of Political Campaigns and Their Unauthorized Use of Music," was published in *Music and Law*, volume 18 of the series Sociology of Crime, Law, and Deviance (Ed. Mathieu Deflem, Emerald Group Publishing, 2013).

Yasumasa Sekine received his M.Engineering in Civil Engineering, Tokyo Institute of Technology and his Ph.D. in Social Anthropology at SOAS, the University of London, and is currently a professor of social anthropology at School of Sociology, Kwansei Gakuin University, Hyogo. He serves as president of the Japanese Society of Cultural Anthropology. Dr. Sekine's anthropological research started by intensively focusing on village lives in India and has gradually shifted to urban areas in India and later to Indians in U.K. and U.S.A. Dr. Sekine has continued to investigate theoretical implications of the living practices observed in subaltern situations for overcoming the neo-liberalist (neo-Orientalist) predicaments, which has been advocated as "Pollution" Theory and later as "Street" Theory. Over one decade, he has conducted the project on transnationalism and street phenomena and conducting research in the area of Street Anthropology. His numerous publications in English and in Japanese, include *From Community to Commonality: Multiple Belonging and Street Phenomena in the Era of Reflexive Modernization* (Seijo University, 2011), *Pollution, Untouchability and Harijan: A South Indian Ethnography* (Rawat Publications, 2011), *An Anthropology of the Street Vol. 1 & Vol. 2* (in Japanese, National Museum of Ethnology, 2009), *Exclusive Society and Receptive Society: Pollution Theory Today* (in Japanese, Yoshikawakōbunkan 2007), *Anthropology of Religious Conflicts and Discrimination* (in Japanese, Sekaishisōsha, 2006), *An Anthropology of "the Urban" in the Contemporary World* (in Japanese, University of Tokyo Press, 2004), *Anthropology of Pollution: The Life World of the South Indian Harijans* (in Japanese, University of Tokyo Press, 1995), *Theories of Pollution: Theoretical Perspective and Practice in A South Indian Village* (ILCAA Institute for the Study of Languages and Cultures of Asia and Africa, Tokyo University of Foreign Studies, 1989).

Gregory J. Snyder is a sociologist and ethnographer who studies subcultures. His research focuses on urban subcultures such as graffiti writers, hip-hop artists, musicians, and professional skateboarders, with an emphasis on subculture theory, urban space, and issues of social justice. His first book, *Graffiti Lives: Beyond the Tag in New York's Urban Underground*, (NYU Press, 2009) received critical acclaim in both the *New York Times*, and the *Journal of Contemporary Sociology*. Currently, Professor Snyder is working on his second book titled, *The Grind: Professional Street Skateboarding in an Age of Spatial Constraint*, (forthcoming NYU Press). Snyder is an Associate Professor at Baruch College, City University of New York.

Claire Taylor, Ph.D., is John W. and Jeanne M. Rowe Assistant Professor of Ancient Greek History at the University of Wisconsin-Madison. Her main interest is in the social and economic history of the ancient Greek world, particularly the lives of non-elite groups within classical Athens. She has published on ancient graffiti, political participation within Athenian democracy, and women's social networks. Her recent publications include *Ancient Graffiti in Context* (co-edited with J.A. Baird) and *Communities and Networks in the Ancient Greek World* (co-edited with Kostas Vlassopoulos (Oxford, Oxford University Press, 2015)).

Myra F. Taylor (Ph.D., M.Phil., MSocSc, DipSocSc, BGS, Cert Ed, JP) is a highly experienced Research Fellow in Edith Cowan University's School of Exercise and Health Sciences located within the Faculty of Computing Health and Science. Myra's research focus is on pathways into crime, adolescent subcultures, youth offending, interpersonal violence, substance abuse, domestic violence, and the effect that family dysfunction has on the cohesiveness of child, adolescent, parent, and grandparent relationships. This research builds on her extensive expertise in the area of child and adolescent emotional, behavioral and learning disorders. Myra is a published author with five books, and numerous book chapters and articles in these and related fields.

Adam Trahan, Ph.D. is Associate Professor in the Department of Criminal Justice at the University of North Texas. His research interests include capital punishment, jury behavior, and criminological and sociolegal theory. His most recent work examines the utility of frontloading mitigation in capital trials and the application of the 8th Amendment jurisprudence to current trends in the use of capital punishment. Dr. Trahan has also worked as a jury consultant on several capital cases assisting primarily with the process of voir dire and jury selection.

Minna Valjakka, Ph.D. is Researcher in Art History, University of Helsinki, Finland. During her Ph.D. and M.A. studies, Dr. Valjakka specialized in Chinese visual arts and culture. Currently, her research interests are broadening up to creativity and arts in urban public space in East Asia. In 2012–2015, she conducted a postdoctoral research project "East Asian Urban Art – self-expression through visual images in Hong Kong, Tokyo and Seoul", funded by the Academy of Finland. Besides publishing the results of the project in articles and edited volumes, Dr. Valjakka is also co-editing two special issues and a volume on arts and creativity in Asian cities and preparing a monograph focusing on the phenomenon in Hong Kong.

Anna Wacławek is the Department Coordinator and Affiliate faculty member in the Department of Art History, Concordia University, Montréal, Canada. Wacławek received her Ph.D. from Concordia's Interuniversity Doctoral Program in Art History (2009). She holds an M.A. in Modern Art Curatorship from the University of Sydney, Australia (2003), and a B.A. in Sociology and Art History from McGill University (2001). She began researching graffiti and street art in the mid-1990s, travelling extensively in Canada and the U.S.A. as well as Japan, China, Poland, Germany, the U.K., France and Spain to conduct first-hand analysis. Her Ph.D. dissertation, "From Graffiti to the Street Art Movement: Negotiating Art World, Urban Spaces, and Visual Culture c.1970–2008," explores how signature graffiti and urban painting contribute to the experience of the city and to the history of art. Wacławek's book *Graffiti and Street Art* (Thames amd Hudson, World of Art series, 2011), analyses the various functions of graffiti and street art in the urban environment and their increasingly important role in visual culture. As a guest lecturer, Wacławek frequently travels to participate in street art festivals worldwide.

Robert Donald Weide is an Assistant Professor in the Department of Sociology, California State University, Los Angeles. He is currently working on two books and a number of academic articles on racial conflict between Black and Latino gangs on the streets of Los Angeles and in California prisons. Having grown up in a marginalized community on the west side of Los Angeles, Robert is a nationally recognized icon in the North American graffiti subculture whose career as a graffiti writer spanned the better part of two decades. He has published in *CITY* journal with Jeff Ferrell on the graffiti subculture and has another book project in development on the freight train graffiti subculture.

Maia Morgan Wells, Ph.D., is a member of the faculty at Coastline Community College in Orange County, California, where she contributes to the success of students who may not otherwise have access to higher education. As a first-generation college student herself, Dr. Wells believes in the power of education to create an entirely different life path. The award-winning instructor's dissertation research focused on the development of a fine art market for graffiti and street art, and the final project explores sociological theories surrounding canonization of art, authenticity, aestheticism, valuation, identity, and property rights through the case study of graffiti. A recognized expert on subcultures and cultural movements, Dr. Wells also works as a marketing consultant for some of the world's largest brands, and develops digital content and strategies that attempt to connect authentically with audiences. Her website can be found at www.maiamorganwells.com.

Jacqueline Z. Wilson is a senior lecturer at Federation University in Victoria, Australia. She has a B.A. (Hons) in Sociology (La Trobe University), and a Ph.D. in History (Monash University). She has published extensively in the fields of Public History, Ethnography, Education, and Criminology, and is the author of *Prison: Cultural Memory and Dark Tourism* (Peter Lang: New York). Her research focuses on Australian historical sites of incarceration and institutionalization, and their role in the formalization and emergence of Australian welfare and justice systems. Jacqueline has amassed an extensive collection of prison graffiti and images of prison interiors photographed at various sites in Australia and internationally.

Hidetsugu Yamakoshi received his Doctor of Human Sciences from Waseda University, and is currently a part-time lecturer at Waseda University and Jichi Medical University. From 2011–2012, he was a student of Monterrey Institute of Technology and Higher Education (ITESM) in Mexico. He earned his M.A. in Human Sciences in Graduate School of Human

Science Waseda University in 2006. His present research focuses on "Youth Subculture in Tokyo," and "Political Street Art in Mexico," both of which examine the socio-political meanings of graffiti and street art. Ever since he wrote about graffiti culture in Japan for his graduation thesis, he has been researching to find out the mentality of youth through graffiti communication. From 2009–2013 he conducted investigations in New York City, Paris and Oaxaca (Mexico). His doctoral dissertation, "The Future of Indigenous Identity in Mexico: Recreation of the 'Indigenous' through the Street Art by ASARO" was completed in 2014. His articles have appeared in *General Human Science Research*, *Journal of Living Folklore*, *Journal of Public and Society*, and *Journal of Lifology*.

Editor's foreword

This handbook is the result of a number of experiences, many of which occurred prior to my entrance into academic studies.

Beginning in childhood and continuing during my high school years, I spent a considerable amount of time creating visual art – graphic design, painting, photography, and sculpture. Frustrated and/or disappointed with the quality of instruction in my public high school(s), I enrolled in and completed courses at the Ontario College of Art (now Ontario College of Art and Design) in Toronto. Later, I was accepted to the Central Technical School Commercial Art program, as well as the Photographic Arts program at Ryerson College (now University) (but chose not to attend).

I was impatient, unruly, and undisciplined. I craved excitement and an escape from the sanitized and stifling experiences of the suburbs where I had grown up and the mediocre public education system that I abhorred. I was attracted to the streets, the back alleys, and the persons who inhabited them. After two years as a courier, I got my taxi driver's license, and for two additional years, I drove nights in Toronto. The people who worked during those nocturnal hours, from the police officer to the nurse, to the waitress and bartender, fascinated me. Individuals going to parties and coming home from bars, small-time hustlers, prostitutes, johns, drug dealers, and victims of crime were my customers, and I was their conduit, if only temporarily. This was my life, and for the most part, I enjoyed it.

For a variety of reasons, I decided to complete a Bachelor's degree with a concentration in Psychology and Political Science. After working in a correctional facility for close to four years, and not content with my job prospects and level of education, I soon earned a Master's degree and a Doctorate, with a dissertation titled "The Politics and Control of Police Violence in Toronto and New York City." After two decades in academia teaching and conducting research in the fields of corrections, policing, political crime, violence, abnormal-extreme criminal behavior, and crime and justice in American Indian communities, I finally taught an undergraduate class on "graffiti and street art" at the University of Baltimore. Unexpectedly, this has become my favorite course.

In many respects, my study of graffiti and street art, and the content of this book represent a way of coming full circle. Moreover, the scholarly study of graffiti and street art deals with many subjects close to my personal interest areas, including codes, control, crime, criminal justice, deviance, gentrification, harms, illegalities, identity, state responses, power imbalances, protest, punishment, resistance, subjectivity, subterranean processes and networks, surveillance, urban incivility, and vandalism.

Why this book? Over time, as I started to read the body of work on graffiti and street art, I noticed that it was short on empirical scholarly analysis, was of uneven quality, and was distributed through a diverse number of scholarly venues. What was missing was a reference book that presented and analyzed the important research, theories, and ideas related to the field of graffiti and street art. I was determined to assemble a collection of original, well researched and written pieces created by experts on this subject under one literary roof. This handbook is the result of this effort.

Features of the book

The *Routledge Handbook of Graffiti and Street Art* (hereafter the *Handbook*) features current scholarship in the field of graffiti and street art. Thus, it avoids the nuts and bolts approach that one would find in a typical textbook. The *Handbook* consists of 35 chapters that focus on specific aspects of graffiti and/or street art. The book tackles each topic in as comprehensive a manner as possible by reviewing the causes, reactions, and challenges that have historically accompanied graffiti and street art. The contributors integrate a variety of methods (including, but not limited to, ethnography, discourse analysis, survey research, and content analysis) in their scholarly analysis and incorporate current events into their examinations by relying on information gathered through respected news and social media. The *Handbook* includes appendixes, which provide a glossary and a chronology.

In an effort to be as comprehensive as possible, the *Handbook* is organized around four principle themes:

- Definitions, History, and Types
- Theoretical Explanations of Graffiti and Street Art/Causes of Graffiti and Street Art
- Regional/Municipal Variations/Differences
- Effects of Graffiti and Street Art.

Introductions to the sections

Each part introduces the conceptual framework in which these studies are located. These explanations help the readers understand the structure of each subfield. The section introductions announce the theme of each section, discuss its importance and relevance to the field, and provide a preview of the selections included in each section. The section introductions, make broad observations about the field, and briefly analyze the various perspectives that are the most significant to understanding the subject matter at hand. The section introductions also provide an opportunity to discuss any material that may not have been included in the sections.

Disciplinary boundaries in the study of graffiti and street art

Although not a comprehensive list, the book includes chapters that draw from art history/theory, communication, criminology/criminal justice, social movements, subcultural studies, urban sociology/studies/planning, and youth studies. These components are reflected in the chapters throughout the *Handbook*. By utilizing these subject areas, not only do contributors report on how graffiti/street artists refer to their work, but they also convey to the reader the implied or actual meaning behind the art works. The contributors, through the lens of these subject areas are able to deconstruct the unfamiliar processes and practices that exist in the world of graffiti and street art, including expressions and neologisms used by graffiti/street artists.

Contributors

The chapters have been written by a diverse group of recognized world experts/scholars in the field of graffiti and street art, some of whom have or continue to be practicing graffiti writers and/or street artists. For one reason or another, however some specialists in this area were unable to participate. Thus not all aspects of graffiti and street art could be covered in a manner I would like. Nevertheless, more than half of the chapter writers come from countries beyond the United States and the United Kingdom. Indeed, the contributors are international in both their citizenship and scholarly foci. The nationalities/citizenship of the authors span a number of countries including:[1] Australia and New Zealand; Brazil; Canada; Egypt; Finland; Japan; Portugal; United Kingdom; and United States. More importantly, contributors to the handbook self-identify themselves with the fields of Anthropology, American Studies, Art History/Theory, Criminology, Criminal Justice, Ethnography, Geography, Law/Legal Studies, Literary Studies, Performance Studies, Photography, Political Science, Psychology, Sociology, Subcultural Studies, Urban Studies, and Visual Culture/Communications.

Having graffiti and street artists talk back to the *Handbook*?

Although it might be useful to have a separate section where graffiti/street artists could "talk back" or write about what they do (e.g. Macdonald, 2003), this approach would take the book in a different direction. In a perfect world, this would be good, but a considerable amount of resources would be required to locate graffiti and street artists that would be willing to participate in this kind of endeavor. At the same time, it was not clear why the book should privilege the voice of one particular actor (i.e. graffiti/street artist) over another. Thus, this idea, while interesting, was not pursued.

Photos

Various chapters in the collection include black and white photographs, and a handful of other illustrations (i.e. charts and tables). There is an average of about two images of graffiti and street art in each of the chapters, for a total of 92 for the entire book, but some chapters, particularly the city chapters, contain more photos than the other ones.

Audience

The *Handbook* is easy to read and designed to answer common questions asked by undergraduate and graduate students, as well as experts on graffiti and street art. This book is also accessible to practitioners (i.e. individuals working, or aspiring to work, in the fields of criminal justice, law enforcement, art history, museum studies, tourism studies, urban studies, etc.) and policy-makers in these fields, in addition to members of the news media covering stories on graffiti and street art. The analysis and writing is accessible to upper-level university students (i.e. typically referred to as juniors and seniors at American universities) and graduate students. This volume will also be useful for scholars and libraries, and can easily be utilized in the classroom context. A reference book of this nature will be of interest not only in the previously mentioned scholarly fields, but it will also be specifically relevant to those institutions that have programs in cultural studies, visual arts, tourism, and museum studies. Last but certainly not least, the *Handbook* will appeal to a wide international audience.

Note

1   Some of these individuals, like myself, have dual citizenship.

Foreword

Graffiti, street art and the politics of complexity

Jeff Ferrell

The publication of the *Routledge Handbook of Graffiti and Street Art* marks the next moment in the long, strange journey of graffiti and street art. As various chapters in this volume show, people have been regularly marking and drawing on public surfaces for centuries, from the wall inscriptions of Graeco-Roman antiquity to the monikers that hobos have inscribed on North American freight trains over the past 150 years. Over the past fifty years, though, graffiti, street art, and the issues surrounding them have become especially prominent. The new forms of graffiti writing and mural art that proliferated in Philadelphia and New York City during the 1970s soon enough went national and then global, and from the first began to spawn and spin off new styles of street art as well. As this U.S. graffiti style became global it in turn entangled with existing modes of graffiti and street art already flourishing in other world regions – and so, while the subcultural codes of U.S. urban graffiti were often reproduced with remarkable exactitude, the resulting work was shaped and reshaped by the distinct visual cultures of other locales. During the past few decades graffiti and street art have also coalesced into a definitive form of urban folk art, and a profitable form of commercial art as well, with graffiti and street art now moving back and forth from street to gallery to corporate advertising campaign. On the other hand, during this same period legal and political authorities in the U.S. and elsewhere have aggressively constructed graffiti as crime, characterizing graffiti and many forms of street art as harbingers of urban violence and decay, and launching high-profile campaigns to enforce harsh new anti-graffiti statutes.

In this sense a volume like the *Routledge Handbook of Graffiti and Street Art* is especially needed, and especially important – not only because graffiti and street art have now proliferated to the point of becoming the most visible forms of global urban culture and urban transgression (Bofkin, 2014), but because this proliferation has shaped graffiti and street art as ever more complex and confusing. On one level this confusion can be addressed and resolved by a volume like the present one, with the remarkable range and depth of the scholarship it assembles and its attentiveness to history and locale. On another level, though, I would argue that complexity and confusion are essential components of contemporary street art and graffiti – that street art and graffiti are today defined by the very impossibility of defining them. This is not a broad claim about the nature of reality or of knowledge, by the way; particular phenomena in particular periods can certainly be defined with some clarity. It is instead a specific statement about the status of graffiti and street art fifty years into their contemporary evolution – an evolution that has created endless complexity and contradiction regarding their status and meaning.

As largely urban phenomena, contemporary graffiti and street art derive a good bit of their contradictory complexity from two distinctive trajectories of urban life that have developed during roughly this same period. The first of these involves the steady growth of urban surveillance and policing regimes, risk management strategies, and restrictive environmental designs. Urban areas in the U.S., Europe and beyond are today awash in surveillance/CCTV cameras, sonic tracking devices, and motion sensors – and increasingly so. Those who engineer these hyper-surveilled urban environments justify them not only in terms of general public safety, but in terms of risk management, arguing that such environments enact a form of preventative policing that reduces risk and obviates the need for 'reactive' policing. Beyond surveillance cameras, this ideology is literally built into the urban spatial environment in the form of building sight lines, restricted passageways, closed public toilets, and other forms of CPTED – 'crime prevention through environmental design.' Providing the theoretical foundation for all of this – as well as a blueprint for everyday policing – is the neo-liberal logic of 'broken windows theory.' This approach proposes that acts of low-level urban disorder dispirit everyday urban citizens, embolden criminals, and thus inaugurate a downward spiral of urban violence and neighborhood decay. Given this, the approach argues, these low-level 'quality of life' crimes must be watched and policed aggressively if urban 'civility' is to be maintained and urban areas are to flourish.

The second urban trajectory points to a new political economy of urban life – a political economy that economic theorists call 'consumption-driven urban development' (Markusen and Schrock 2009). Under this model, the old industrial engines of urban growth are necessarily replaced by new forms of urban development based on privatized city spaces, cultural production, and the consequent creation of high-end, exclusive zones of consumerism and residence. At times this trajectory quite literally takes the emptied-out warehouses and factories of earlier industrial production and repurposes them as lofts, specialty shops, and restaurants; other times these old industrial zones and the working class neighborhoods that accompanied them are razed and replaced with gated communities or new retail/residential configurations. In either case, 'quality of life' for residents and retailers emerges as the marker of urban success, and the city becomes its own simulacrum, its image of urban hipness and exclusive metropolitan style now carefully manufactured and marketed to those whom city leaders hope to attract.

If is of course no accident that these two urban trajectories have emerged during the same period of urban history; while one centers on social control and the other on social class, in the contemporary practice of urban life the two are thoroughly intertwined. Regimes of risk management and surveillance are deployed to control those marginalized populations that would intrude on privatized consumption spaces, or more generally sully the city's manufactured image of itself. Likewise, the aggressive policing of low-level, 'quality of life' crimes under the broken windows model aims to erase unregulated urban interaction, and so to enforce the privileged urban lifestyle marketed to young professionals and other consumers of contemporary urban identity (Ferrell, 2001). Yet as regards urban graffiti and street art, the confluence of these two urban trajectories doesn't produce a consistent effect or response; instead it lays the foundation for many of the contradictions that animate the practice of street art and graffiti today. In this sort of urban environment, street art and graffiti can be defined as criminal threat, or as artistic undertaking and commercial opportunity. They can become markers of urban decay, or hip markers of vital urban culture. They can lead some of their practitioners to jail or prison, and others to the gallery or the design firm – with the first more likely to seek a good defense attorney, and the second a skilled copyright lawyer. Generally speaking, within the contemporary city the pervasive visibility of contemporary urban street art and graffiti can be attacked, eradicated, erased on the grounds of urban safety and quality of life – or it can be heightened, amplified, made all the more apparent and inescapable, as a sanctioned signifier of a new urbanism.

This contemporary urban context is certainly not the only factor that complicates street art and graffiti, and that spawns complexity and contradiction; as the chapters in this volume document, the sheer cultural and geographic range of contemporary street art and graffiti all but ensures a multiplicity of meanings, as do the uncertain situations of economic and political upheaval out of which graffiti often emerges (see for example Bushnell, 1990; Lennon, 2014). Still, it is the changing economic and political dynamics of the global city – put differently, the troubled conflation over the past half century of street art and graffiti with new forms of urban economy and control – that drive the confused status of graffiti and street art today.

Visibility and invisibility

As already suggested, graffiti and street art are in one sense among the most publicly visible forms of contemporary urban culture. In another sense, though, street art and graffiti have for the past half century consistently engaged a more subtle dialectics of visibility and invisibility, and increasingly so today. Within the subcultures of street art and graffiti, practitioners choose to paint in various sorts of 'spots' that embody widely different degrees of visibility and public access (Ferrell and Weide, 2010). At times secluded spots are chosen, with an eye toward creating a selective and appreciative audience or ensuring the durability of artwork well-hidden from legal authorities. At other times highly visible spots are preferred – sometimes physically high spots atop buildings or billboards – in the interest of increased public recognition or subcultural status. Still other spots for executing graffiti or street art are recognized for their cultural significance, or preferred for the particular sorts of cultural audiences they attract. Moreover, while the street art that inhabits these various spots may be visible, at least to some, its complex meanings likely remain invisible to most who witness it. Graffiti writers and street artists regularly paint in-jokes, aesthetic allusions, subcultural histories, street beefs, and other encryptions into their public art work. They are after all artists, at work within collective, street-level art worlds (Becker, 2008) that reproduce subtle aesthetic conventions and interpersonal dynamics just as other art worlds do – and so the chance that an uninformed outsider could 'see' these subtleties upon viewing a piece of street art is as unlikely as a first-time viewer seeing the history of impressionism in a single Monet. Pervasively visible, street art and graffiti are often invisible as well. As I've said elsewhere (Ferrell, 2013), borrowing from the brilliant subcultural analysis of Dick Hebdige (1988): street art and graffiti hide in the light.

Amidst all this there are other dynamics of visibility and invisibility at work as well. Among graffiti writers especially, subcultural status is negotiated and enforced in various ways, among them painting over the work of a rival writer, or a writer alleged to be inferior. Similarly, no matter how large the city, there are just so many spots that satisfy the criteria just noted – and consequently graffiti writers and street artists regularly paint over and replaced existing work as these spots evolve, even when no disputes over status are involved. Then there are the tireless efforts of the public and private anti-graffiti contractors and graffiti clean-up crews, well-funded and hard at work day after day as they go about buffing murals and painting over graffiti tags and throw-ups. Increasing urban surveillance, aggressive broken windows policing, and associated anti-graffiti campaigns over the past decades have had innumerable deleterious effects – on civil liberties and personal freedom, for starters – but among these effects has certainly been the wholesale destruction of urban graffiti and street art. Think about it: as pervasively visible as we take street art and graffiti to be, the vast majority of it that has been executed over the past half century is now distinctly and decidedly invisible; the street art and graffiti that we see today is but the latest layer in an ongoing urban palimpsest of spray paint and whitewash that hides away its own history. The very visibility of street art and graffiti enact their ultimate invisibility – unless, as we shall see, they somehow come to be preserved as image or artistic artifact.

Act and art

The terms 'graffiti' and 'street art' generally invoke an image – that is, a painted public surface of some sort. Yet graffiti and street art, by their very nature as public and often illicit productions, also incorporate a particular set of practices and experiences. To write graffiti or paint street art is to negotiate situations of vulnerability and risk far different than those inside the confines of the art studio or gallery, and often to do so in the company of other street practitioners. Because of this, graffiti writers and street artists not only produce distinctive forms of art that are governed by their own aesthetic and stylistic codes; they also engage distinctive if ephemeral artistic experiences and communities in the moments that they produce such art. Here the various accounts of graffiti writers and street artists themselves are instructive. Sound-One defines 'the act of doing graffiti' as a form of 'performance art,' and adds that 'the paint on the wall is purely an after-effect' (in Walsh, 1996: 28). Lister references the spontaneity of the action painting tradition in characterizing his work as 'an action painter's reflection painting, a combination of instinctual balance and mindful precision' (in Workhorse and PAC, 2012: 118). SheOne (n.d.; 2012) elaborates: 'I never really worry about the final image, I paint graffiti for the process, it is only important while I am actually making it . . . I paint walls for that exact moment of painting; I am interested in the direct experience of that timeframe and my own output as an abstract artist responding to a unique situation.' For its practitioners, the phenomenon under consideration is immediate act as much as eventual art.

This situated action nonetheless invokes dynamics that transcend the situation itself. As Lister's notion of 'instinctual balance and mindful precision' suggests, hard-earned practical and aesthetic skills are necessary pre-requisites for surviving the risky uncertainty of street art circumstances. To create art in such circumstance – amidst a jostling street crowd or alone in an abandoned building, navigating the darkness or dodging the lights of a police helicopter, atop a billboard or deep inside an abandoned subway station – requires a mix of project planning, physical prowess, and artistic training. In this sense graffiti writing and street painting can be thought of as forms of *edgework* (Lyng, 1990; Ferrell, 1996) – the fluid interplay of skill and risk in dangerous situations by which those involved are able to push out to the edges of human experience. For street painters and graffiti writers as for other edgeworkers, a mix of highly developed skills allows for success in situations of great risk, while such situations in turn polish and promote such skills – with both act and art in this way emerging as the unique products of the situations in which they are produced.

As such situations play out within the political economy of the contemporary city, further ironies and contradictions emerge. To begin with, these situations embody the very sorts of unregulated, precarious dynamics that regimes of urban risk management mean to eradicate. In this way legal and economic authorities find both the act and the art to be threats – the act in the realm of risky and illicit behavior, the art in the realm of appearance and urban image – and so redouble their efforts to eradicate graffiti and unsanctioned street art. Yet given that the situations that produce street art and graffiti are so often defined by the edgeworker's mix of skill and risk, and the addictive 'adrenalin rush' that comes from it, these aggressive anti-graffiti efforts often and predictably fail. Intending to erase the act and the art, they instead amplify the risk associated with them, thereby pushing practitioners to develop greater skills, and in turn to savor a heightened adrenalin rush that turns aggressive enforcement into illicit enjoyment (Ferrell, 1996). The alternative is no less contradictory. If graffiti writers and street artists are instead offered legal walls on which to paint, or avenues into legitimate artistic careers, they may or may not take them – but if they do, they will do so at the price of forfeiting the edgy situations and free-form experiences that define the art form for many practitioners. 'There is no substitute for the adrenaline and heightening of the senses that kicks in once you enter an illegal zone where you constantly have to watch your back,' says Haze. 'As the debate over what is graffiti or not heats up, I prefer to consider it more along these lines: it's not illegal – it's not graffiti' (in Workhorse and PAC, 2012: 20–21).

Ephemerality and elongation

The discussion so far would suggest that graffiti and street painting, as both act and art, are defined by their ephemerality. The risk, skill, and adrenalin of the act are embedded in the moments and situations of its execution; 'that exact moment of painting' that SheOne cherishes may last minutes or hours, but by way of completion, exhaustion, or police intervention, it is over soon enough. The art that remains behind is, by its public and often illicit nature, vulnerable to all sorts of erasure. Exposed to the elements, buffed into oblivion, gone over by other artists, or lost to changes in the built environment, it is unlikely to last. Graffiti writers understand this; when Rasta 68 argues that 'there is no respect in graffiti' (in Ferrell, 1996: 89), he is arguing that graffiti writers and street artists can harbor no reasonable hope that their work will endure the disrespect of weather, law, and economy. As Robert Weide's chapter in this volume shows, the emergence of freight train graffiti over the past few decades has if anything amplified this ephemerality; a freight car painted one day is generally gone the next, carrying away the artist's work to destinations unknown.

Increasingly, though, this ephemerality is countered by forces that elongate the experience of creating graffiti and street art, and that provide new sorts of aesthetic durability. These forces likewise liquefy the specific spatial physicality of graffiti and street art, moving them from the domain of particular city walls to the wider realm of circulating images. Central here is the digital camera and the cell phone. Once a camera was a hard commodity to come by among graffiti writers and other urban artists; now it is as common as a spray can. As a result, graffiti writers, street artists, and street art aficionados regularly photograph their own work and that of others, and then post these photographic images ('flicks') to photo sharing sites, blogs, graffiti web sites, magazines, and other media. With this process the ephemerality of executing street art in a particular situation can be elongated endlessly, in photographic or video terms at least, and the tag or mural eventually erased from a city wall can be granted eternal life. Taken as a whole, this process creates what anti-graffiti campaigns, urban redevelopment, and the ongoing vulnerabilities of the street take away: a vast visual archive of global graffiti and its history, spread across web sites and hard drives, and growing day by day.

Significantly, this widespread digitization of graffiti and street art does more than record actions and images, and elongate their presence; it feeds back into the very processes through which such actions and images unfold, and alters their essential meaning. Now conventions of style can be learned from websites as well as from local artistic communities; now fame can be calibrated on line as well as on the street, and graffiti writers, once intent on 'going citywide' with their work, can now go global. With graffiti and street art in this way coming unstuck from their situations of production, they become free-floating signifiers, increasingly available for inclusion in advertising campaigns, public service announcements, television shows, and films. Even these situations of production change as well; a graffiti 'spot' may now be chosen not for its immediate characteristics, but because of its utility in producing an image. As Snyder (2009: 148) says of the magazines or 'mags' devoted to graffiti, 'For some writers, the mags are not simply documents of achievement but have become the new fame spots. Writers don't have to consider the potential audience of the actual spot; they paint, take a flick, and send it off. . .to be seen by thousands'. To paraphrase Benjamin (1968), this is the work of the graffiti writer and the street artist in the age of digital reproduction, caught up in the liquidity of images that loop and spiral between one domain and another (Ferrell, Hayward, and Young, 2015). Still grounded in ephemeral experiences and street situations, graffiti and street art at the same time endure, and float beyond them.

Legality and illegality

A hallmark of criminological analysis is the notion that 'crime' is that which is constructed as so by the law and its enforcement; in particular historical periods, in particular places or situations, similar human activities come to be defined in vastly different legal terms. In the present urban and economic context – which, it will be recalled, mixes stringent surveillance and risk control with economies founded in urban imagery and consumption – graffiti and street art have emerged as exemplars of this criminological insight. While early, aggressive anti-graffiti campaigns carefully constructed graffiti and unsanctioned street art as crimes and as harbingers of further criminality, the past couple of decades have seen alongside these ongoing campaigns a growing embrace of street art and some forms of graffiti as valuable markers of urban desirability and vitality. As a result, and as many of the chapters in this volume demonstrate, contemporary graffiti and street art exist as both legal and illegal, crossing back and forth between the worlds of crime and of art alike. Were it not so consequential, this contradiction would sometimes seem almost laughably absurd. At one point in my life, for example, I was simultaneously an active graffiti writer, a published graffiti researcher, a convicted graffiti vandal, and an intermediary between a major U.S. city and its local graffiti underground, managing to broker the legal, city-funded painting of an immense downtown mural (Ferrell 1996). Or to cite a more recent example: Promoting high-end tourism as part of 'The Europe Issue' of its travel section, *The New York Times* highlights '12 Treasures' that the European traveler must experience. Alongside Copenhagen design and Brussels chocolate is another Continental treasure: the street art of Berlin, where 'elaborate murals still decorate firewalls' and 'images by sprayers and stencilers pop up everywhere else' (Bradley, 2014: TR8).

While regularly arrested and jailed under ongoing anti-graffiti campaigns, graffiti writers and street artists are nonetheless not simply passive victims of this legal contradiction; they are often well aware of it, and actively engaged in negotiating it. Some carefully carry with them explicit letters of permission from property owners, knowing that they still may be arrested even while painting a legal mural if they can't prove it to be so. Others carry with them fake letters of permission, seeing this bit of subterfuge as a safeguard if confronted while painting an illegal piece. On a far larger scale, street artists Workhorse and PAC organize a secret and thoroughly illegal two-year Underbelly Project in which they ferry some hundred street and gallery artists from around the world down into an abandoned New York City subway station, where the artists fill the space with graffiti, murals, stencils, installations, and artistic declarations. When they eventually reveal the project, *The New York Times*' front page coverage notes that the project 'defies every norm of the gallery scene' and 'goes to extremes to avoid being part of the art world, and even the world in general' (Rees, 2010: C1). Later on, though, the Underbelly Project does embrace the norms of 'the gallery scene' and the art world, as an Underbelly gallery show is staged at Art Basel in Miami, and a high-gloss photo book is published with art publisher Rizzoli (Workhorse and PAC, 2012). And the interplay of legality and illegality continues still; as Workhorse says, 'I think it's our goal for the future that each year we do two different Underbellies; one of them is legal, one of them is illegal. The sole point of the legal one is to finance the illegal one. So with Miami, that's essentially why we did that' (Ferrell, 2013).

The lives of street artists like PAC and Workhorse, and the complex trajectories of undertakings like the Underbelly Project, suggest yet another confounding of legality and illegality, this one based on the notion of *career*. Criminologists and sociologists talk about the deviant or criminal career – that is, the way in which the legal entanglements, periods of confinement, and social stigmas associated with an initial act of crime or deviance often spawn long-term involvement in criminal worlds and exclusion from mainstream society (Becker, 1963). This notion was invoked in some of the earliest academic research on contemporary graffiti and street art (Lachmann, 1988), and certainly the now decades-long campaigns of intense anti-graffiti enforcement have pushed many graffiti writers and street artists down this path. Yet as Snyder (2009) has carefully documented, early involvement in graffiti or illicit street art can, under present circumstances, also lead to a career in graphic design, gallery art, publishing, advertising, or tattooing. As the Underbelly Project suggests, illegal and legal careers can even unfold simultaneously, with artists moving back and forth from street to gallery, or more dramatically, from jail intake to art opening. In fact, not unlike the worlds of hip hop and other contemporary urban cultures, the skills honed while engaged in illegal street practices can underwrite legal careers, and the credibility that comes from illicit, street-level artistry can make for marketable artistic reputations. Certainly this was the case for artists like Keith Haring and Jean-Michel Basquiat in previous generations, and it seems even more the case now.

Banksy (2005) offers a particularly high-profile case study in this fluid interplay of legality, illegality, and career; so does ESPO. In fact, like Banksy, much of ESPO's work has engaged directly with this tension. A long-time Philadelphia graffiti writer and street artist with a college education in the arts, ESPO also founded and published *On the Go* magazine. *On the Go* originated as a counter to the Philadelphia anti-graffiti campaign's demonization of graffiti writers, and later developed into a commercial magazine devoted to graffiti and hip-hop culture. Moving his street art and graffiti writing to New York City, ESPO later concocted a plan by which he volunteered to paint over the clutter of graffiti that accumulated on the roll-down grates of businesses closed for the night – even rebranding ESPO to now denote 'Exterior Surface Painting Outreach' – but then, with a few quick lines, surreptitiously turned each grate he had cleaned into a giant ESPO throw up. Around this same time ESPO in addition published the book *The Art of Getting Over* under his given name, Stephen Powers (Powers, 1999). The book's ridicule of police officers and anti-graffiti campaigns, along with ESPO's public critiques of New York City's then-mayor Rudy Giuliani, led to ESPO's arrest and trial on serious legal charges; as Snyder (2009: 142) concludes, 'ESPO posed a threat because he proved to the public that graffiti writers could be positive, proactive members of the community and that not all graffiti is vandalism.' His illicit career now aborted by legal problems, ESPO/Powers turned to his emerging career as gallery artist and muralist, with which he has had continued success.

While still a New York City graffiti writer and street artist, ESPO painted one other notable piece. 'Greetings from Espoland, where the quality of life is offensive!' the piece said, but in a style that so perfectly mimicked vintage tourist iconography that this illegal piece appeared to be a legal billboard. Moreover, the 'quality of life' phrase referenced the low-order 'quality of life' crimes on which broken windows policing focuses – and to be sure the point was taken, ESPO even depicted these crimes in the piece itself (see Snyder, 2009: 73–74). Here, then, was a complex achievement: an illegal graffiti piece masquerading as a legal advertisement while questioning the process by which graffiti was deemed illegal and advertising not. A decade or so later, the question was repeated. When James Q. Wilson, one of the founders of the broken windows model (Wilson and Kelling, 1982), passed away in 2012, his front-page *New York Times* obituary highlighted his broken windows model and its unquestioned condemnation of graffiti as crime and crime progenitor (Weber, 2012). A few pages later in that same edition, though, there appeared a story about Kingston, New York, where illegally stenciled graffiti images had become so popular that the local newspaper endorsed them as 'a great symbol' and the mayor argued that they were 'good for Kingston's image' (Applebome, 2012: A15).

Illegal activity and basis for legal career, situated act and collective art, pervasively visible and invisible feature of everyday life, ephemeral urban residue and endlessly elongated image – the subject matter of this handbook would indeed seem to merit careful, thoroughgoing consideration. Little wonder that some three dozen chapters are included here – because as the following chapters show, in addition to these complexities there are issues of gender, ethnicity, spatial dynamics, global politics, and punishment interwoven with graffiti and street art as well. And that's the beauty of a comprehensive volume like the *Routledge Handbook of Graffiti and Street Art*: given its sweep and scope, it is able to capture the complexity of street art and graffiti while exploring the manifold contradictions that continue to shape them.

References

Applebome, P. (2012). "How Graffiti Goats Became a Symbol of . . . Something," *The New York Times* (3 March): A15.

Banksy. (2005). *Wall and Piece*. London: Random House.

Becker, H. (1963). *Outsiders: Studies in the Sociology of Deviance*. New York: Free Press.

Becker, H. (2008). *Artworlds*. 25th Anniversary Ed. Berkeley, CA: University of California Press.

Benjamin, W. (1968). "The Work of Art in the Age of Mechanical Reproduction," in Arendt, H (Ed.) *Illuminations* (pp. 219–253). New York: Harcourt, Brace and World.

Bofkin, L. (2014). *Concrete Canvas*. London: Cassell.

Bradley, K. (2014). "Berlin: Street Art," *The New York Times* (19 October): TR8.

Bushnell, J. (1990). *Moscow Graffiti*. Boston: Unwin Hyman.

Ferrell, J. (1996). *Crimes of Style*. Boston, MA: Northeastern University Press.

Ferrell, J. (2001). *Tearing Down the Streets*. New York: Palgrave/MacMillan.

Ferrell, J. (2013). "The Underbelly Project: Hiding in the Light, Painting in the Dark," *Rhizomes* 25, at www.rhizomes.net/issue25/ferrell/.

Ferrell, J., Hayward, K., & Young, J. (2015). *Cultural Criminology: An Invitation*, (2nd ed.) London: Sage.

Ferrell, J. & Weide, R. (2010). "Spot Theory," *City* 14(1–2): 48–62.

Hebdige, D. (1988). *Hiding in the Light*. London: Comedia.

Lachmann, R. (1988). "Graffiti as Career and Ideology," *American Journal of Sociology* 94(2): 229–250.

Lennon, J. (2014). "Assembling a Revolution: Graffiti, Cairo and the Arab Spring," *Cultural Studies Review*, 20(1), at http://dx.doi.org/10.5130/csr.v20i1.3203.

Lyng, S. (1990). "Edgework." *American Journal of Sociology* 95(4): 851–886.

Powers, S. (1999). *The Art of Getting Over*. New York: St. Martins.

Rees, J. (2010). "Street Art Below the Street and Out of Reach." *The New York Times* (1 November): C1, C5.

SheOne. (n.d.). "SheOne on Underbelly–Paris." Interview with Helen Soteriou, Modart, at www.modart.com/2012/01/24/sheone-on-underbelly-paris/, visited January 19, 2015.

SheOne. (2012). Interview with author (8 April).

Snyder, G. (2009). *Graffiti Lives*. New York: New York University Press.

Walsh, M. (1996). *Graffito*. Berkeley, CA: North Atlantic Books.

Jeff Ferrell

Weber, B. (2012). "Originated 'Broken Windows' Policing Strategy," *The New York Times* (3 March): A1, B8.
Wilson, J. & Kelling, G. (1982). "Broken Windows," *The Atlantic Monthly* (March): 29–38.
Workhorse & PAC. (2012). *We Own the Night: The Art of the Underbelly Project*. New York: Rizzoli.

Acknowledgements

No major project like this is done alone. To begin with, I want to thank Gerhard Boomgarden, Senior Editor at Routledge, who signed the project. Considerable help was also provided by Alyson Claffey, Assistant Editor, also at Routledge. Her guidance along the way was greatly valued.

Next, I want to extend my gratitude to my contributors for their excellent scholarship and incredible patience, for enriching my knowledge about graffiti and street art, and continuing the dialogue about this subject matter. As in any editorial enterprise, your timely and thoughtful responses to my numerous queries for clarification was deeply appreciated. Thanks to my colleague Jeff Ferrell for writing the foreword to this collection. Your friendship, scholarship, and good counsel throughout these years has been an inspiration to many, including myself.

Additionally, thanks go out to Rachel Hildebrandt for editing selected chapters that I wrote and to Stefano Bloch, Minna Valjakka and Ronald Kramer for their comments on a handful of chapters.

Also a big shout out goes to all of my visual arts teachers, too numerous to mention, from elementary to postgraduate studies, many of whom have been important influences in my understanding, production, and appreciation of art. This fact alone reinforces the long term effects that instructors can have on young formative minds.

Over the years a veritable army of colleagues have shaped my thinking about crime, criminals, the practice of criminal justice, not to mention graffiti and street art. These include, but are not limited to, Gregg Barak, James Conaboy, Francis T. Cullen, David O. Friedrichs, Peter Grabosky, Ted Robert Gurr, Mark S. Hamm, Chris Hart, Keith Hayward, Irving Horowitz, Mike (Lee) Johnson, Rick Jones, Victor Kappeler, Peter Manning, Ray Michalowski, Will H. Moore, Greg Newbold, Stephen C. Richards, Dawn L. Rothe, Marty Schwartz, Michael Stohl, Richard Tewksbury, Ken Tunnell, Austin T. Turk, Loïc Wacquant, Frank (Trey) Williams, Aaron Z. Winter, and Benjamin S. Wright.

I want to thank my sister, Karyn Groyeski, who encouraged me to pursue this project and finally, my immediate family – Natasha (my wife), and Keanu and Dakota (our children) – was incredibly encouraging at several points in time along the way. I would share with them, on a regular basis, my excitement with respect to how the book was coming together, and they helped to sustain my enthusiasm.

Introduction
Sorting it all out[1]

Jeffrey Ian Ross

Introduction

Graffiti has existed since the dawn of civilization (McCormick, 2011), however, since the mid-1980s, most large urban centers throughout the world have experienced an increase in unique styles of graffiti and street art (Ferrell, 1995). Naturally this has led to several efforts to understand this phenomenon. Indeed, the world of graffiti and street art is complicated and includes numerous subtypes and participants. Thus, it is not surprising that multiple, sometimes complementary and at other times competing, definitions and interpretations of what constitutes "graffiti" and "street art" exist. Much of this debate stems from the viewpoints by which practitioners, social control agents, and scholars examine and/or locate this phenomenon. The purpose of this introductory chapter is to briefly outline the definitional challenges of graffiti/street art, comment on the general state of scholarly research, and provide a brief history of graffiti/street art.

Definitional issues

Despite a tendency in some circles to ignore defining graffiti and street art, numerous definitions and attempts to define these phenomena exist (e.g., Lewisohn, 2008; Young, 2014). In general, there are approximately four interrelated contextual axes that one can use to identify, classify, and/or examine graffiti and street art (i.e., legal/sanctioned/authorized versus illegal/unsanctioned/unauthorized; content/aesthetic; perpetrator; and location). First, traditionally graffiti and street art have been seen as *illegal* actions. According to this perspective, graffiti typically refers to words, figures, and images that have been drawn, marked, scratched, etched, sprayed, painted, and/or written on surfaces where the owner of the property (whether public or private) has NOT given permission to the perpetrator. Likewise, street art refers to stencils, stickers, and noncommercial images/posters that are affixed to surfaces and objects (e.g., mail boxes, garbage cans, street signs) where the owner of the property has NOT given permission to the perpetrator (Ross, 2013). Thus, at a bare minimum, in most countries because of its illegal nature, graffiti and street art are *legally speaking* considered acts of vandalism.

Second, other scholars identify graffiti not based on the illegal/legal or sanctioned versus unsanctioned criteria, but on its *content, composition, and/or overall aesthetic*. For example, Bloch

(2012) identifies graffiti-murals as "those produced by self-described, acknowledged, and active members of the graffiti community in public view with, primarily, the use of aerosol spray paint. Graffiti-murals are also visually thematic in that they cover the entire surface of a wall with a balance of letters, characters, and/or images painted against fully painted backgrounds. Graffiti-muralists . . . are motivated to produce their work for the sake of fame and personal expression in addition to critical concerns for community and artistic concerns for aesthetics. Graffiti-muralists also work independently and illegally . . ." (p. 124).[2] Snyder (2009), who explores the burgeoning legal graffiti movement in New York City, states: "In the post-train era legal walls have become essential to the progression of the art form . . . many pieces done today are done on legal walls on which writers have been granted permission to paint by the building owner. Legal walls allow writers to take their time, and this results in some really good art" (p. 97). In this rendering of graffiti, the legal/illegal dimension is less important than the quality of the artwork. Building upon this notion is the idea of graffiti style, which can be extended to include the use of graffiti-like imagery on articles of clothing (e.g., shoes and t-shirts), in commercials, and on artwork that appears in galleries (Avelos, 2004).

In distinguishing graffiti from street art, Wacławek also relies upon the idea of content rather than issues of legality/illegality. According to her, the two styles differ in "visual and material terms (whereby one is focused on the rendition of the name sometimes with accompanying imagery and is most often executed in spray paint/markers, and the other is less concerned with letters/name and the abstraction of the alphabet and more with using recognizable/accessible imagery diffused in all manner of media). Typically then, I make the distinction between the two not only through a recounting of the movements' different histories/methodologies/ideologies, but also through the visual and material distinctions."[3]

Another form of graffiti/street art that highlights the importance of thinking about different types of content/aesthetic is knitting graffiti (also known as yarn bombing), which involves wrapping light poles, monuments, statutes, bicycle racks, street signs, and other public structures with wool/yarn. This practice does not involve damaging the object, but simply placing a more appealing/interesting covering on top of it.

An additional contextual issue is *who gets to define the perpetrators and practitioners of graffiti/street art*? Is it the state (via agents of formal social control – politicians, law enforcement), the local community, or the graffiti/street artists themselves? In other words, whose perceptions are being privileged? According to Snyder (2009), "There seems to be a consensus in the mainstream that graffiti murals are art while tags are just vandalism. Within graffiti culture itself, however, no such strict division exists between the various forms of contemporary graffiti. Pieces, throw-ups, and tags are all ways in which writers attempt to get their name seen for the purpose of achieving fame" (p. 47). On the other hand, "Anti-graffiti advocates attempt to separate the tag from other forms of graffiti by arguing that tags can never be art, only vandalism" (pp. 47–48).

Added to the mix are the numerous situations where the community eventually accepts works of graffiti and street art that were initially considered illegal, and thus unsanctioned, and become illegal but sanctioned. Bloch (2012), for example, outlines this dilemma in his description and discussion of the murals along Sunset Boulevard in Los Angeles that started to appear during the 1960s. Over time the community, with the assistance of a local Chicano activist and muralist, and the Los Angeles Department of Cultural Affairs, sought to protect this artwork.

Over the past three decades, graffiti by "artists" has eclipsed gang-based graffiti as a subject of scholarly study and news media attention. Thus, Bloch (2012) restricts graffiti to "systematic, stylistic, and name-based marking of infrastructure with implements such as markers and spray paint by acknowledged members of the graffiti community" (p. 125). Other scholars omit this restriction because this distinction clearly privileges one type of perpetrator/practitioner over another. In sum, there is considerable nuance of style and content that the untrained observer is not privy to with respect to the graffiti and street art world. And simple classification is extremely difficult (Taylor, Cordin & Njiru, 2010).

Finally, although graffiti and street art is more pervasive in some cities and neighborhoods than others, they are typically found on the walls of bathrooms (i.e. latrinelia), buildings, road and freeway overpasses, retaining walls of streets, and highways, as well as along train tracks. Graffiti and street art can also be placed on sidewalks, streets, floors, ceilings, light poles, billboards, and bus shelters. Not limited to physical structures, graffiti and street art can be placed on semi permanent and/or moveable items, like park benches, trash/garbage cans/bins, street signs, mail and newspaper boxes, and means of transportation, such as freight trains, metro/subway cars, buses, trucks, vans, and cars. Moreover, "with the proliferation of graffiti Websites and magazines and the emphasis on photographs of graffiti, writers can now go worldwide with their work as well" (Ferrell, 2013, p. 181).

Because both graffiti and street art are disproportionately done in public spaces (i.e., shared social space), graffiti and street art are considered a type of public art. In general, public art includes: "a vast assortment of art forms and practices, including murals, community projects, memorials, civic statuary, architecture, sculpture, ephemeral art (dance, performance theatre), subversive interventions, and, for some graffiti and street art. . . . [that] can be experienced in a multitude of places – parks, libraries, public squares, city streets, building atriums and shopping centres" (Wacławek, 2011, p. 65). Although much of this work is commissioned, unlike a museum or an art gallery that may require admission, these public spaces are freely accessible.

There is no easy way out of these conflicting/competing contextual definitions. Moreover, according to Weide, "Attempting to objectively define any of these terms is an exercise in futility. The various perceptions and uncertainty of their definition is in fact one of the most interesting things about them. I think that different people having different definitions add to the academic discourse, and any attempt to privilege any definition over any others is an uncritical abomination. I am vehemently opposed to any effort to arrive at any consensus definition."[4] Thus, this handbook allows contributors the latitude to explore the different meanings of graffiti and street art and reactions to this work, while understandably this kind of difficulty has resulted in numerous debates inside the practitioner community (see Figure I.1).

That being said, perhaps no other contemporary predominantly urban phenomenon is as misunderstood as graffiti and street art. Numerous articles, books, documentaries, websites, and blogs have been published and/or produced about the field. Not all of this work is of equal value/rigor. Some of it approaches the subject uncritically and from a romantic notion, ascribing all sorts of intentions and motivations to the perpetrators/practitioners of graffiti and street art. This is often done without interviewing or observing them. Other work use research methods that are ad hoc and unsystematic. And there are no shortages of so-called experts. Missing, however, is a sustained series of scholarly studies of graffiti and street art. The current collection goes beyond romanticization from a distance and questionable methods, and it approaches the subject from a more objective social scientific perspective.

Contemporary literature on graffiti and street art

Two basic types of literature on graffiti and street art have been published. One comprises the popular writing on graffiti and street art, while another is comprised of the scholarly work on graffiti and street art.

Figure 1.1 Street sign commandeered to explain differences between graffiti and street art

Popular literature

Over the past four and-a-half decades, a number of trade publishers have produced books that document examples of graffiti and street art, and those who create this work in various cities and countries. Some of these monographs have been general treatments (e.g., Reisner, 1971; Kurlansky, Naar, & Mailer, 1974; Reisner & Wechsler, 1980; Gastman & Neelon, 2010; Seno, 2010). Alternatively, almost each major city has a thriving graffiti and street art scene, and site-specific 'zines have been produced and books published documenting many of the artists/writers who have created the pieces that have appeared in these locations (e.g., Gastman, 2001; Grévy, 2007).

One of the results of this trend is that some graffiti and street artists have achieved celebrity if not cult-like status (e.g., Campos, 2013), becoming the focus of an array of publications. For example, not only has the Britain-based street artist Banksy released a series of bestselling books, including *Wall and Piece* (2006), showcasing some of his most infamous work, but he is responsible for directing a documentary,[5] *Exit Through the Gift Shop* (2010), which has had reasonable commercial and cult following success. Alternatively, one could mention Shepard Fairey, an American street artist, who originally focused his art on transforming the image of wrestler Andre the Giant into the pervasive OBEY icon, and helped turn the image of Barack Obama, a relatively unknown Senator from Illinois, into an aspiring presidential candidate and then into a worldwide figure.[6] The books focusing either on cities or artists predominantly include numerous photographs of the works with limited text by the graffiti or street artist, by selected contributors, and/or by the editor. These efforts may also include interviews with graffiti and street artists, and thus are celebratory in nature, seem to romanticize the graffiti and street artist's subculture (Campos, 2013), and are minimally interpretative.[7]

Scholarly literature

Since the mid-1980s, there has been a moderate amount of scholarly literature on graffiti and street art. Most of this has been in the form of articles published in peer reviewed and non-peer reviewed journals in a variety of social science and humanities disciplines. Although one academic journal published a special issue on graffiti,[8] no one scholarly venue specializes in publishing articles on graffiti and street art.[9] Some of that research has included ethnographies focusing on different cities, including Los Angeles (Philips, 1999) and Denver (Ferrell, 1996). One of the most popular urban locales for ethnographic study is New York City (NYC) (e.g., Lachmann, 1988; Austin, 2001; Snyder, 2009; Kramer, 2010). The NYC subway has been the source of numerous scholarly articles and books (e.g., Castleman, 1984; Austin, 2001).[10] These ethnographies typically include interviews with graffiti and street artists, observations of their work, and in some cases, participant observation. Some of the scholarly research is couched in the theories of youth subculture and/or psychosocial development (Lachmann, 1988; Snyder, 2009; MacDiarmid & Downing, 2012; Taylor, Marias, & Coltman, 2012), labeling (Lachmann, 1988), or masculinities (e.g., Macdonald, 2001). In this context, there is some attempt to understand the motivation of graffiti artists, seeing their work as a means of communication, attention-seeking behavior, legitimation among their subculture, or an avenue to develop important life skills.

Few studies focus exclusively on public or official reactions to graffiti/street art. Another rather underdeveloped area have been studies that looked at how graffiti and street art have been used and/or appropriated in other forms of popular culture (Alvelos, 2004; Ross, 2015). Finally some work has examined official reactions to the presence of graffiti/street art (e.g., Austin, 2001; Halsey & Young, 2002; Graycar, 2003; Iveson, 2010; Kramer, 2010; Taylor, Cordin, & Njiru, 2010; Taylor & Khan, 2013; Ross & Wright, 2014). For reasons that are not entirely clear, missing from this array are studies (e.g., surveys) that look at public reactions and business reactions to graffiti and street art.

Theoretical concerns

A number of relevant theoretical approaches can be examined in relation to graffiti and street art. One of them focuses primarily on the result, the graffiti and street art, in an attempt to deconstruct it. For example, Gottlieb (2008), building on Panofsky's model of iconographical analysis (1939/1972), has developed a classification scheme that categorizes different types of graffiti and street art. Taylor, Cordin, and Njiru (2010) have also developed a classification method that they argue would assist municipal authorities in making decisions about graffiti removal. Alternatively, the fledgling scholarly research on this subject, particularly the ethnographies, tends to see graffiti and street art as an expression of youth subculture (Ferrell, 1993). In this manner, graffiti and street art are intimately tied to juveniles' and young adults' desire to achieve "sneaky thrills" (e.g., Katz, 1988). The argument here is that their lives are otherwise boring and that engaging in low-level crime, in this case vandalism, gives them a rush that other age-appropriate activities cannot give them. Others have taken this idea one step further and argued that graffiti and street art are an expression of masculinity (Macdonald, 2001). Some of this work views graffiti and street art as a stage in an individual's development, whereby he or she graduates into other kinds of pursuits (Lachmann, 1988; Macdonald, 2001; Snyder, 2009). Still others (Taylor, Marias, & Coltman, 2002) argue that graffiti offenses are a step towards more serious kinds of criminal activity. Taylor (2012) sees the production of graffiti as an attempt, particularly amongst juveniles, to gain recognition among their peers. Finally, some researchers examine the political content of graffiti and see it as a form of resistance and/or political communication (e.g., Ferrell, 1996; Waldner & Dobratz, 2013).

Broad treatments

Despite the previously reviewed research, the field lacks a relatively comprehensive textbook, and/or a scholarly overview that does justice to the subject matter. Although there are a handful of compilations that primarily include photographs of graffiti and street art from well known locations around the world (e.g., Ganz, 2004; 2013; Seno, 2010; Deitch, Gastman & Rose, 2011; Schacter, 2013), no comprehensive works of an academic nature have been published.

Wacławek's book, *Graffiti and Street Art* (2011), which I use in my undergraduate "Graffiti and Street Art" class, is about the best comprehensive book on the subject. Wacławek introduces the subject and does a very good job in defining what both graffiti and street art are and describing their different types, before tracing the history of this unique art from its origins in New York City to other large cities around the world. In so doing, Wacławek locates graffiti in the framework of the hip hop culture that emerged in the Bronx during the 1980s and the struggles that New York City incurred trying to deal with graffiti in its subway system. The history is presented in an easy to understand, chronological order, outlining how graffiti has evolved as far as designs and meanings behind the work. She provides lots of examples to illustrate her points.

Wacławek also briefly reviews the commodification of graffiti. The author introduces us to the most well known graffiti and street artists, like Banksy and Shepard Fairey, and describes the meaning behind each artist's work. The book includes numerous color illustrations that help the reader to understand what the author is talking about. Wacławek tries to explain why artists choose particular locations for their works and the relationship between particular spaces and works of graffiti/street art.

Although this text is a relatively comprehensive treatment of the subject matter, Wacławek's approach is more useful to the field of artist history than to the social sciences. Despite its limitations, Wacławek's study offers a basis from which further advances can be made.

From gang graffiti to contemporary graffiti

The history of graffiti and street art is long, and has been explored in various forums, this book notwithstanding. It is a common misperception that urban street gangs produce the majority of graffiti and street art. Politicians, community activists, law enforcement and the mass media, in particularly the news media, have perpetuated this myth. Moreover, graffiti and street art are not only done by people trying to make a name for themselves (i.e. fame/notoriety), but by individuals who are passionate about art and who need an alternative place to channel their creative energies.

One additional false perception is that only select "celebrities" of the medium, like Banksy or Fairey, do graffiti and street art. Indeed some of the individuals who work in this medium have achieved cult like status, but there are numerous others who toil in the shadows who need the recognition they deserve. Since the original appearance of graffiti on the streets of Philadelphia and New York City, and its spread throughout major cities in the United States and the world, there have been subtle shifts among the writers/artists in their subject matter, techniques and the locations where they have chosen to do their work. Graffiti and street art, as this book suggests, is done by a wide variety of people or groups. The chapters contained in this book highlight these changes in greater detail.

Culture jamming/adbusting/subvertising

Although it is not covered in any great depth in this handbook, a relatively nuanced form of graffiti/street art should be mentioned. Starting in the 1980s, the number of independent clandestine protests, integrating elements of graffiti and street art, and drawing upon the long tradition of political graffiti increased. This was variably called culture jamming, adbusting, or subvertising (Dery, 1993; Klein, 2000). Although there are subtle definitional differences among the three terms, culture jamming typically refers to disruption, distortion, reconfiguration, subversion, and/or damage caused to publicly displayed cultural, religious, and political artifacts, icons, signs, logos, and images, including advertising, to create a different, sometimes humorous or mocking message. Adbusting, on the other hand, is a type of culture jamming where individuals or groups purposely distort and/or parody the advertised message of a business, corporation, or organization to create a different, sometimes humorous message. For example, sometimes words or images are added or removed from advertising slogans and images. Usually this is done on signs and billboards, but can also be accomplished with videos (e.g., posted on YouTube.com). Finally, subvertising usually involves making spoofs and parodies of commercial and political advertising. The resultant product looks as if it is the original advertisement, but on closer examination it is not. In short it has the look and feel of the original communication, but is changed in subtle and satirical ways

In this manner, the persons or groups engaging in these protest activities do not need to throw rocks, smash windows, or hack into a corporation's website, choosing instead to express their dissatisfaction with organizations (commercial or otherwise) through the techniques of graffiti and street artists (e.g., spray paint, paint, markers, etc.). So, why do people and groups do this sort of thing? They are often protesting against organizational power, in particular capitalism's dominance of public messages. These activities or "weapons of the weak," as Scott (1992) might call them, are a way for typically powerless individuals and groups to send a message to large corporations and the general public. The perpetrators might have problems with various products and services that are being manufactured and sold, because they may be unsafe and/or harmful to society. It is frequently the wish of graffiti and street artists who engage in this sort of activity that their actions may force those who view the adulterated images/messages to think about the negative effects of the original message, and perhaps be spurred into political action. Usually larger corporations do not want to sue the protesters because legal action would most likely draw negative publicity towards the products and services they would have to defend in a public forum.

The Internet and World Wide Web

Finally, the spread of graffiti and street art has been assisted through the development of the World Wide Web and the numerous social media that now exist.[11] There are both positive and negative implications for graffiti and street artists placing their material on the Web. On the positive side, the exposure can lead to more fame/notoriety. On the other hand, it can also result in a distancing from the subject matter, and the possibility that others may alter one's photo in ways that the original artist did not intend (Wacławek, 2011, pp. 178–180). Moreover, "What is online doesn't ever get to represent the actual situation on the streets. It's always a highly limited selection, esp. if you look any "global" platforms."[12] Clearly ownership is a contested subject matter. As Wacławek notes: "[t]he artists' sentiment is one echoed time and again by graffiti and street artists who simultaneously value the internet and criticize it for complicating, and at times trivializing these art forms" (p. 180). Today's Internet is clearly shifting the meanings of graffiti and street art in subtle ways.

Conclusion

The existing body of scholarly research on graffiti and street art forms a respectable base from which to grow. The study of graffiti and street art, however, lacks a consistent identifiable body of hypotheses/propositions, theories, and models. Although this is not necessary for studies in this field to progress, something of this nature is helpful to move beyond a field that is dominated by descriptive studies, and minimal theorizing supported with a paucity of data collection. A considerable number of untested and unquestioned assumptions about graffiti and street art exist, and are held not only by the public and agents of social control, but by graffiti and street artists themselves.

There are several ways we can improve scholarly research on graffiti and street art. First, it would be helpful if researchers had a better grounding in art, art history and aesthetic theory. Most researchers appear to be untrained in such areas and thus it is difficult for them to deconstruct the meanings of the work they observe. Visual analysis would help them and their audiences to understand the subtleties of the work and the creators they analyse. This includes the inside jokes and double entendres embedded in the work. Not only is a solid grounding in art important, but also because of the transgressive nature of graffiti/street art it would be helpful to get a better sense of the criminal justice system response to this body of work. Criminological theory might help shed light on practitioners/perpetrators motivations that underlie their choice of work.

In terms of ethnographies, more time should be spent with the graffiti/street artists during the times that they are not doing their work. Not simply ethnographies, but larger samples of graffiti/street artists followed would be helpful. As a method of enquiry, ethnographies are important to tease out these challenges and ideas, as is the systematic collection of data that are later subjected to critical analysis. Both of these approaches are in their infancy in the field of graffiti and street art. We must also acknowledge that, as subjects of study, graffiti and street art are moving targets. Practitioners are continuously exploring new techniques and surfaces, and we owe this development to both their creativity and to their adaptability against those who wish to control their efforts. There does not appear to be any upward bounds to their energy and tenacity, nor to the potential to create a social science of graffiti.

Not only can ethnographies be improved, but also so should surveys. These can include questionnaires administered to different segments of the public (e.g., retail store owners, landlords, etc.) to determine their opinions about graffiti/street art and solutions they propose. Likewise the integration of geomapping studies could help us understand the patterns of graffiti/street art dissemination (e.g., Megler, Banis, & Chang, 2014).

With respect to the wider public, including those who are responsible for monitoring or abating graffiti, they need to develop a greater literacy in graffiti and street art. If this was done perhaps there would be more acceptance of this work and more meaningful responses to this would develop.

As with all social science research, not to mention cultural studies approaches, it is important when conducting this analysis to keep an open mind and be as objective as possible. More research on culture jamming and adbusting, and their relationship to graffiti/street art, could be done in order to round out this body of work. Finally, this scholarship must be conducted in a manner that allows us to better understand graffiti/street art, especially its communicative and transgressive elements, not simply as another tool in eradications, abatement and desistance, but for the purpose of developing alternative, progressive approaches to the presence of graffiti/street art. This is a tough line to walk, and is no easy challenge.

Notes

1 Special thanks to Stefano Bloch, Rachel Hildebrandt, Ronald Kramer, and Minna Valjakka for comments.
2 Thus markings that appear on structures, such as houses in the wake of natural disasters, like "need food," or houses with the iconic X placed on them with spray paint, or markings left by utility companies on sidewalks are not graffiti. These are makeshift signs to expedite a process of aid, recovery, or prevent the cutting or disruption of utility lines.
3 Wacławek, personal communication, January 7, 2014.
4 Weide, personal communication, January 9, 2014.
5 Or mocumentary as some people have opined.
6 For a review of Fairey, see, for example, Daichendt (2014).
7 For current purposes, this review does not mention the numerous documentaries that have been produced on graffiti and street art. These, however, will be examined in one of the later chapters in the book.
8 See *City* (2010) *14*, 1-2. This issue also included feedback from graffiti practitioners.
9 In early 2015, *Street & Urban Creativity Scientific Journal* was formed with the express purpose of "publishing disciplines to discuss topics, research tools and methodologies used in advanced studies of the theme 'Street & Urban Creativity'" (http://www.urbancreativity.org/). Contributors to this journal may include scholars writing on graffiti and street art.
10 Included in this array is a comparative study of graffiti/street art in New York City and London (Macdonald, 2001).
11 As of this writing, popular social media include Facebook, Instagram, and Pinterest. Because of the rapidity of developments in this means of communication, by the time of publication of this monograph, this listing is most likely incomplete.
12 E-mail correspondence Minna Valjakka March 4, 2015.

References

Alvelos, H. (2004). The Desert of Imagination in the City of Signs: Cultural Implications of Sponsored Transgression and Branded Graffiti. In Ferrell, J., Hayward, K., Morrison, W., & Presdee, M. (Eds.) *Cultural Criminology Unleashed*, (pp. 181–191). London: The Glass House Press.
Austin, J. (2001). *Taking the Train: How Graffiti Art Became an Urban Crisis in New York City*. New York: Columbia University Press.
Banksy. (2006). *Wall and Piece*. London: Century.
Bloch, S. (2012). The Illegal Face of Wall Space: Graffiti-Murals on the Sunset Boulevard Retaining Walls, *Radical History Review, 113*(1), 111–126.
Campos, R. (2013). Graffiti writer as superhero, *European Journal of Cultural Studies, 16*(2), 155–170.
Castleman, C. (1984). *Getting Up: Subway Graffiti in New York*. Boston, MA: MIT Press.
Daichendt, G. J. (2014). *Shepard Fairey Inc.: Artist/Professional/Vandal*. Petaluma, CA: Cameron and Company.
Deitch, J., Gastman, R., & Rose, A. (Eds.). (2011). *Art in the Streets*. New York: Random House.
Dery, M. (1993). *Culture Jamming: Hacking, Slashing and Sniping in the Empire of Signs*. Open Magazine Pamphlet Series.
Ellsworth-Jones, W. (2012). *Bansky: The Man Behind the Wall*. New York: St. Martin's Press.
Fairey, S. (2009). *OBEY: Supply & Demand – The Art of Shepard Fairey – 20th Anniversary Edition*. Berkeley, CA: Gingko Press.
Ferrell, J. (1995). The World Politics of Wall Painting, in Ferrell, J. & Sanders C. R. (Eds.) *Cultural Criminology*. (pp. 277–294). Boston: Northeastern University Press.
Ferrell, J. (1996). *Crimes of Style: Urban Graffiti and the Politics of Criminality*. Boston: Northeastern University Press.
Ferrell, J. (2013). Graffiti, in Ross, J.I. (Ed.) *Encyclopedia of Street Crime in America*. (pp. 180–182). Thousand Oaks, CA: Sage Publications.
Ganz, N. (2004). *Graffiti World: Street Art From Five Continents*. New York: H.N. Abrams.
Gastman, R. (2001). *Free Agents: A History of Washington, D.C. Graffiti*. Bethesda, MD: R. Rock Enterprises, Inc.

Gastman, R. & Neelon, C. (2010). *The History of American Graffiti*. New York: Harper Design.

Gottlieb, L. (2008). *Graffiti Art Styles: A Classification System and Theoretical Analysis*. Jefferson, NC: McFarland.

Graycar, A. (2003). *Graffiti: Implications for Law Enforcement, Local Government and the Community*. Canberra, Australia: Australian Institute of Criminology.

Grévy, F. (2007). *Graffiti Paris*. New York: Harry N. Abrams.

Halsey, M. & Young, A. (2002). The Meanings of Graffiti and Municipal Administration, *The Australian and New Zealand Journal of Criminology, 35*(2), 165–186.

Iveson, K. (2010). The Wars on Graffiti and the New Military Urbanism, *City: analysis of urban trends, culture, theory policy action, 14*(1/2), 115–134.

Katz, J. (1988). *Seductions of Crime: Moral and Sensual Attractions in Doing Evil*. New York: Basic Books.

Klein, N. (2001). *No Logo*. Toronto: Macmillan.

Kramer, R. (2010). Moral Panics and Urban Growth Machines: Official Reactions to Graffiti in New York City, 1990–2005, *Qualitative Sociology, 33*(3), 297–311.

Kurlansky, M., Naar, J., & Mailer, N. (1974). *The Faith of Graffiti*. Westport, CT: Praeger.

Lachmann, R. (1988). Graffiti as Career and Ideology, *American Journal of Sociology, 94*(2), 229–250.

Lewisohn, C. (2008). *Street Art: The Graffiti Revolution*. New York: Abrams.

Ley, D. & Cybriwsky, R. (1974). Urban Graffiti as territorial Markers, *Annals of the Association of American Geographers, 64*(4), 491–505.

McCormick, C. (2011). The Writing on the Wall, In Deitch, J., Gastman, R., & Rose, A. (Eds.). (2011). *Art in the Streets.* (pp. 19–24). New York, Skira Rizzoli Productions.

MacDiarmid, L. & Downing, S. (2012). A Rough Aging out: Graffiti Writers and Subcultural Drift, *International Journal of Criminal Justice Sciences, 7*(2), 605–617.

Macdonald, N. (2001). *The Graffiti Subculture: Youth, Masculinity, and Identity in London and New York*. New York: Palgrave.

Megler, V., Banis, D., & Chang, H. (2014). Spatial Analysis of Graffiti in San Francisco. *Applied Geography, 54*, 63–73.

Philips, S. A. (1999). *Wallbangin': Graffiti and Gangs in L.A.* Chicago, IL: University of Chicago Press.

Reisner, R. (1971). *Graffiti: Two Thousand Years of Wall Writing*. Spokane, WA: Cowles Book Company.

Reisner, R. & Wechsler, L. (1980). *Encyclopedia of Graffiti*. New York: Galahad Books.

Ross, J. I. (2013). Street Art, in Ross, J. I. (Ed.) *Encyclopedia of Street Crime in America*. (pp. 392–393). Thousand Oaks, CA: Sage Publications.

Ross, J. I. (2015). Graffiti Goes to the Movies: American Fictional Films Featuring Graffiti Artists/Writers and Themes, *Contemporary Justice Review, 18*(3), 366–383.

Ross, J. I., & Wright, B. S. (2014). "I've Got Better Things to Worry About": Police Perceptions of Graffiti and Street Art in a Large Mid-Atlantic City, *Police Quarterly, 17*(2), 176–200.

Schacter, R. (2013). *The World Atlas of Street Art and Graffiti*. New Haven, CT: Yale University Press.

Scott, J. C. (1992). *Domination and the Arts of Resistance: Hidden Transcripts*. New Haven, CT: Yale University Press.

Seno, E. (2010) (Ed.). *Trespass: A History of Uncommissioned Urban Art*. Koln, Germany: Tashen.

Snyder, G. J. (2009). *Graffiti Lives: Beyond the Tag in New York's Urban Underground*. New York: New York University Press.

Taylor, M. F., Cordin, R. & Njiru, J. (2010). A Twenty-First Century Graffiti Classification System: A Typological Tool for Prioritizing Graffiti Removal, *Crime Prevention and Community Safety, 12*(3), 137–155.

Taylor, M. F., & Khan, U. (2013). A Comparison of Police Processing Reports for Juvenile Graffiti Offenders: Societal Implications. *Police Practice and Research, 14*, 371–385.

Taylor, M. F., Marias, I. & Coltman, R. (2012). Patterns of Graffiti Offending: Towards Recognition that Graffiti Offending is More than 'Kids Messing Around,' *Policing and Society: An International Journal of Research and Policy, 22*(2), 152–168.

Wacławek, A. 2011. *Graffiti and Street Art*. London: Thames & Hudson.

Waldner, L. K., & Dobratz, B. A. (2013). Graffiti as a Form of Contentious Political Participation. *Sociology Compass, 7*(5), 377–389.

Young, A. (2014). *Street Art, Public City: Law, Crime and the Urban Imagination*. New York: Routledge.

Part I

History, types, and writers/artists of graffiti and street art[1]

Jeffrey Ian Ross

Introduction

It is probably safe to say that graffiti has been around since the time that humans chose to live together in communities, and discovered the ability to translate their thoughts and ideas on to the surfaces of the spaces where they lived, worked, and travelled. Some experts consider the markings of cave dwellers the earliest form of graffiti (Brassai, 2002).

Others believe that the origins of contemporary graffiti can be traced back to gang graffiti. Readers must keep in mind that gang graffiti is only a small portion of all the graffiti that exists. Not only have the individuals, surfaces, and subject matter of graffiti changed since the time it was first used by street gangs, but gang experts/specialists have discovered that gang graffiti has decreased overall, and that it has been predominantly supplanted by art-related graffiti and street art.

It goes without saying that numerous types of graffiti and street art exist. In order to provide meaning to this body of work, this section of the *Handbook* provides in-depth descriptions and discussions of the prominent kinds of graffiti and street art that have emerged over time and in recent years. In addition, this section looks at the work and biographies of specific graffiti writers/artists.

Overview of chapters

This section consists of ten chapters. J.A. Baird and Claire Taylor offer the first contribution in the book. In their chapter "Ancient graffiti," they present the range and variety of the graffiti that existed in the ancient Mediterranean world (c. 700 BCE–500 CE). This chapter explores some of the disciplinary challenges in accessing, defining, and interpreting ancient graffiti, while also tracing the similarities and differences between ancient and modern graffiti trends. Baird and Taylor argue that contemporary paradigms which view graffiti as subversive or subcultural are misleading when applied to past societies. Ancient works of graffiti are important historical sources, contributing to a wide range of scholarly debates about the past, and they also prompt reflection on the interpretative paradigms used within studies of contemporary graffiti. Baird and Taylor reveal that graffiti, like most kinds of mark-making, are bound by convention, context, and performance, and as such, they are a form of cultural production in their own right. Viewing graffiti in this way ultimately raises questions about cultural value: Why are some graffiti preserved and studied, but others erased and vilified?

In Chapter 2, "Trains, railroad workers, and illegal riders: the subcultural world of hobo graffiti," John F. Lennon explains how hobo graffiti has a rich, mostly hidden, subcultural tradition. This particular graffiti form is rooted in the history of rail workers who chalked railroad cars for utilitarian purposes, writing instructions to other trainmen about which cars needed to be sided or rebuilt. While doing so, some trainmen also began placing their monikers on the cars, sending their messages and symbols throughout the country. Hobos, who physically shared the same geographic spaces as the rail workers (and were sometimes former railroad workers themselves), created a similar set of discursive emblems that were both practical and artistic. This graffiti expanded to all of the spaces in which the hobos congregated. Only those within the subculture could read – or even thought to look at – this graffiti. The means to decipher the graffiti was something taught from one hobo to another, as new riders became acquainted with more seasoned riders. In this way, graffiti was a way to link individuals, even though these people had no prior knowledge of each other and may not have ever met. Reflecting the individuality of the person, hobo markings and monikers were part of the shared language that helped bind together the geographically dispersed hobo subculture.

Next comes Robert Donald Weide's chapter, "The history of freight train graffiti in North America." This text examines the development of the freight train graffiti subcultural niche within the wider North American graffiti subculture, from its inception in the 1970s to the present day. The freight train graffiti subculture has yet to be examined systematically by scholars of the graffiti subculture. As a starting point for further scholarly research on this long-neglected topic, this chapter seeks to begin filling this void in the literature by offering a historical narrative of the emergence and proliferation of freight train graffiti in North America.

"Deconstructing gang graffiti," by Susan A. Phillips, reviews this variety of graffiti as a particular form of written and visual communication, utilizing three case studies from within the urban United States. The first case derives from Chicano gangs based in Los Angeles and California; the second case is provided by the Bloods and the Crips, African American gangs also located in Los Angeles; and the third case is offered by People and Folk, a loosely configured gang system based originally in Chicago. In each of these cases, gang members utilize complex semiotic systems to represent affiliation, enmity, and alliance. The written systems are situated both in place and out of place, moving between contexts of prison and the street. Gangs use graffiti to communicate at a distance, as placeholders that define neighborhood space. Phillips provides detailed examples from these three case studies in order to theorize about gang graffiti as a specific communicative genre.

In Chapter 5, "Prison inmate graffiti," Jacqueline Z. Wilson examines inmate-created graffiti in Australian, U.S. and U.K. prisons. Despite its unique nature, few studies of prison graffiti have been conducted. The scant existing literature in the area is reviewed to provide analytical context and highlight important differences between the varieties of "conventional" and inmate graffiti. A selection of examples accompanies the text, illustrating the styles, locales, and underlying motives discussed. A visual-ethnographic approach is employed to interpret the images' meanings and infer something of their creators' experiences. Inmates create graffiti for various reasons, not all congruent with those behind non-prison graffiti. While street graffiti, "paint-ups," "tagging," and so on are invariably rendered for public viewing, much prison graffiti is intended to remain hidden from anyone other than the graffitist. Inmate-graffitists' motives tend to reflect concerns arising from total, often dangerous, confinement. Thus their graffiti echoes prison-specific issues: Personal power relationships; sexual frustration and sexual aggression as self-assertion; resistance narratives against perceived oppression; or reactions to boredom. Some prison graffiti function as a form of personal diary.

Artistic creativity drives both clandestine and openly rendered graffiti. A variant form familiar to prison-museum tourists is the officially sanctioned "mural," often adorning major outdoor surfaces. These must be viewed as a category separate from the routinely prohibited "private" type commonly found inside cells. Wilson argues that the stylistic and motivational differences between inmate graffiti in private spaces and that found outside underscore the need for further research on prison graffiti, and scholarly acknowledgement of this subcategory's standing as a unique category of graffiti.

In "Ways of being seen: gender and the writing on the wall," Jessica N. Pabón explicates how female graffiti and street artists are marginalized by the gendered politics of visuality. She illustrates how the writing on the wall is assumed to be the work of a male who is a member of an urban, economically disenfranchised, ethnic minority – an assumption which makes women and girls invisible as participants. Pabón then offers an international sampling of contemporary female artists who are combating their social status through their art-making practices in Afghanistan, Australia, Brazil, Canada, Chile, Egypt, Japan, Mexico, South Africa, the U.A.E., and the U.S. This chapter is organized into six discussion points: "Gender Anonymity" allows graffiti writers and street artists to communicate and exercise their artistry without the stigma associated with their gender; "Gender Signification" directly combats the erasure of women in the subculture; "Hyperfeminine and Overtly Sexualized" graffiti and street art reclaims the imagery of girls' and women's bodies in public spaces; "Political and Cultural" artworks extend beyond the individual and the subcultural to provide a means to comment on political, social, and cultural environments; painting, graffiti, and street art "Collectively" invite girls and women into the culture and initiate a shift in women's minority status; and lastly, "Digital" frameworks enable artist/writers to identify themselves and one another, to build networks, and to make history. Overall, Pabón's analysis contributes to the literature on graffiti and street art by including girls and women, who challenge the conventional field of vision by demanding to be seen.

This chapter is followed by Adam Trahan's analysis of latrinalia (i.e. graffiti found in public bathrooms), "Research and theory on latrinalia." This contribution provides an overview of the major theoretical and empirical scholarship on latrinalia, which depicts latrinalia as a unique cultural form that, although similar in some fundamental ways to other types of graffiti and expression, is set apart by the nature of the space in which it is written and read. Public bathrooms are simultaneously "public" and "private" spaces that afford graffitists anonymity and segregate patrons by gender. These conditions give rise to graffiti that address a wide range of topics in a singularly direct and candid discourse. Latrinalia often prompts impassioned debates among multiple graffitists about identity, ideology, and the reproduction of the same.

Minna Haveri's chapter, "Yarn bombing – the softer side of street art," reviews the history and growth of this relatively new phenomenon. Already becoming an impressive part of the street art genre, knitting and crocheting, with a traditionally feminine material and techniques, are presented as an antithesis to traditionally masculine street art, especially graffiti art. Knitted street art has been called by many names, but the terms yarn storming in the U.K. and yarn bombing in the U.S. seem to have established themselves as the standard terms for visual expressions in the urban space that involve textile. Besides many names, yarn bombing also takes on many forms, but it generally involves wrapping hand-knitted or crocheted items around everyday objects, such as signs, poles, and streetlights, in city spaces. Creative and daring and getting in touch with environmental experiences, yarn bombing is related to social action.

For hobbyist knitters bored with only making socks and sweaters, it seems to be an alternative reason to use handicraft skills. It is appealing to knitters because it allows them to use their skills to do something beyond the functional. Despite its subversive nature, knitted graffiti is considered to make the environment feel inviting and cozy. This might explain the increasing interest of art institutions and different communities to organize yarn-bombing happenings.

Ronald Kramer's chapter, "Straight from the underground: New York City's legal graffiti writing culture," draws extensively from observations of and interviews with twenty New York City graffiti writers. Kramer rethinks the contemporary graffiti writing culture in two important respects. On the one hand, previous scholars have tended to explore graffiti writing as an illegal and/or criminalized (sub)culture. On the other, these same scholars have found it to be a practice that embodies a "critical" stance towards society. This chapter shows that, since 1990, a subset of graffiti writers who paint with permission has emerged. Furthermore, Kramer finds that those who produce legal graffiti tend to lead lives and espouse values that most would not hesitate to recognize as "conventional." The author concludes by suggesting that graffiti writing needs to be acknowledged as a multifaceted and historically fluid culture.

In "American Indian graffiti" (Chapter 10), Favian Martín uses the review of the current status of graffiti on American Indian reservations as an opportunity to engage in a public discourse on contemporary Indigenous social problems. He argues that American Indian graffiti exists as a form of resistance to the historical legacy of colonialism. In addition to this discussion, the chapter also investigates the criminal element of graffiti, which is associated with gang activities occurring in Indian Country. Lastly, the chapter surveys community-level initiatives to reduce the prevalence of graffiti within tribal communities.

Omissions

Despite the breadth of the work contained in this section, there are several notable omissions. One of these includes an analysis of *hate graffiti* (e.g. Sinnreich, 2004). This type of activity, clearly identifiable by its verbal and/or graphic content, appears all over the world. It is aimed at demeaning people based on their racial, ethnic, sexual, and national backgrounds. Like other types of hate crime, hate graffiti can take the form of racism, sexism, homophobia, or the targeting of specific groups based on their perceived deviation from the prevailing societal or moral norms. Hate crime is recognized by evocative graphic content, such as "general-purpose" symbols (e.g. swastikas) intended to convey hatred toward a range of targeted groups.

Also missing from this section is an in-depth analysis of *subway graffiti*, which exists throughout the world in cities that support a mass transportation system (e.g. Castleman, 1982; Cooper and Chalfant, 1988; Miller, 2002). The history of modern graffiti is intimately associated with "bombing" major subway systems (e.g. New York City, Paris, and London). Much of this literature approaches the artists and their work in a romanticized fashion, and little of it addresses the global aspect of this graffiti phenomenon.

Although the issue of gender has been examined in this section, as has Latino graffiti/murals and American Indian graffiti, a substantive analysis of *the role of race/ethnicity* has not been explored here in connection with graffiti/street art. This is a marked hole that future scholarship should attempt to fill.

Alternatively, although most contributors to this section and throughout this book note the political motivations and ramifications of graffiti/street art, a separate chapter focusing explicitly on *political graffiti/street art* is lacking. Such an analysis would go beyond reviewing the typical go-to personages of Banksy and Fairey, in order to incorporate lesser known purveyors of graffiti/street art.

Finally, *wartime graffiti and street art* is an especially important kind of work. As both Peteet and Palmer (this volume) suggest, graffiti/street art during political conflicts serve political propaganda purposes of all sorts, while simultaneously providing fertile communication channels for change, resistance, and protest. Wartime graffiti works are provocative and necessary parts of all political struggles, and Northern Ireland, Central America, and South America provide rich examples of this.

Despite these shortcomings, this section should assist the reader in understanding the distinct types of graffiti and street art that exist today. It is to be hoped that this will serve as a springboard for further studies of the differences and the commonalities between the various subtypes.

Note

1   Special thanks to Stefano Bloch, Rachel Hildebrandt, and Ronald Kramer for their comments.

References

Brassai. (2002). *Brassaï Graffiti*. Paris: Flammarion.
Castleman, C. (1982). *Getting Up: Subway Graffiti in New York*. Cambridge, MA: MIT Press.
Cooper, M. & Chalfant, H. (1988). *Subway Art*. New York: Holt Paperbacks.
Miller, I.L. (2002). *Aerosol Kingdom: Subway Painters of New York City*. Jackson, MS: University of Mississippi Press.
Sinnreich, H.J. (2004). Reading the writing on the wall: A textual analysis of Łódź graffiti. *Religion, State and Society*, *32*(1), 53–58.

1

Ancient graffiti

J.A. Baird and Claire Taylor

Introduction

Graffiti are commonplace within the urban cityscape, so much so that we easily think that this is a phenomenon of modern life. But graffiti are also found in many historical societies, both literate and pre-literate, from ancient Egypt to pre-Islamic Arabia to medieval Italy and beyond (Plesch, 2002; Macdonald, 2009; Bucking, 2012). Even though there is a wealth of information about – and interest in – graffiti from the past among different scholarly communities (i.e. historians, archaeologists and art historians), different disciplinary traditions have varying ways of understanding what 'graffiti' are and often use subject-specific terminology and definitions to understand the practice of making, preserving or 'reading' this material. Recently, however, work across historical studies (broadly defined) has made significant steps forward in broadening our understanding of different types of graffiti practices. Instrumental here is recognising the importance of the contexts in which graffiti are found and reflecting on the categories and assumptions that scholars use to interpret them (Baird and Taylor, 2011).

This chapter explores some important issues in the interpretation of historical graffiti by focusing on the cultures of the Graeco-Roman world in antiquity (c. 700 BCE–500 CE). Although graffiti also appears in other pre-modern historical societies, the use of the term 'ancient graffiti' in this chapter refers to material within this geographical and cultural context. The ancient Mediterranean world provides a good case study for a number of reasons. First, there is a lot of surviving evidence which provides a wide range of examples of graffiti from different chronological, geographical and typological contexts allowing historians to compare and contrast across time, space, production methods and material. Second, literacy in the past was widespread enough for large numbers of ordinary people to have access to the resources of writing whether they, or the marks they made, were literate or not. Third, the Graeco-Roman cultures of the Mediterranean world have been intensely studied for a number of generations which gives us good contextual material for interpreting different kinds of graffiti.

What are 'ancient graffiti'?

Graffiti are ubiquitous across the ancient Mediterranean. These markings are found from the beginning of the invention of writing, until the end of Antiquity. They appear in cities, in the countryside, at religious sites, both inside and outside houses, in public space and private. They are found on walls, columns, and other architectural forms, as well as in streets, market-places, on and in public and religious buildings and on moveable objects such as pottery. They include the written word (in multiple languages), pictures, pictograms and symbols. Some of the finest examples of graffiti survive in urban sites which are well preserved, for example Pompeii and Herculaneum in Italy (destroyed by the eruption of Vesuvius in 79 CE), Dura-Europos (a Roman fortress town in Syria), Aphrodisias, Smyrna and Ephesos (Graeco-Roman cities in modern Turkey), but they are also found in more remote regions and non-urban contexts too. It is reasonable to expect that a great deal has not survived, because they are most commonly found at sites with exceptional preservation contexts (e.g. those with standing walls and extant wall plaster).

In addition to appearing in a range of places in the ancient world, graffiti appear in a variety of media. They are incised in plaster, painted, scratched, charcoaled or inked on structures, as well as inscribed in stone, with survival often depending on local factors of production as well as preservation. Walls and floors generally were constructed out of stone or plaster which are relatively easy to mark, and graffiti also appear on objects such as pottery.[1] In terms of the practice of making graffiti, we might distinguish between those which remove material (by scratching with something sharp, hammering, chiselling or other means), and those which add it (with charcoal, ink or paint). The longevity of the mark is often related to the materials from which it was made, where it was made, as well as whether there was a desire to preserve it (or lack of desire to remove it). Additionally, there are the specific circumstances of archaeological preservation in which special archaeological environments preserve very ephemeral markings, for example dusty charcoal recording (perhaps) visitors to a house at Pompeii (Benefiel, 2011) or ink marks made in a collapsed basement at Smyrna (Bagnall, 2011: 6–26). Some forms of graffiti, such as those made on tree trunks, do not survive, but are known from ancient texts which mention them (Kruschwitz, 2010a). Graffiti could also be surprisingly tenacious, existing for years or even decades, and hence some graffiti could have a large audience over time.

Conventionally, the term graffiti is also applied by ancient historians to writing on objects such as pottery, incised or marked onto the vessel after firing. These include those which marked a particular owner of the object, or which provided information (such as price) related to the use of the vessel (Evans, 1987; Volioti, 2011). The distinction between these marks as 'graffiti' and others, including trademarks and *tituli picti* or *dipinti* (painted labels denoting content, volume, ownership or functioning as decoration), is a modern one. It is a distinction that relates to a temporal quality which scholars often implicitly use to define graffiti: They are marks made, which are not a part of the 'original' scheme of design, decoration or marking, whether on a wall or a pot (Chaniotis, 2011). One of the problems in the study of ancient graffiti is that such definitions and distinctions are not systematic and are complicated by different scholarly specialities, traditions and terminology that have evolved over time. For instance, short, ephemeral inscriptions made on fragments of broken pottery are conventionally known as their own class of material (*ostraca*) and not as graffiti, whereas some items which are sometimes labelled graffiti would probably surprise the general reader. This includes Roman election notices (*programmata*) painted onto the walls of buildings in Pompeii for example, but these are more akin to political campaign or advertising posters than might be initially assumed (Mouritsen, 1988). Deciding what is, or is not, 'graffiti' is often a necessary first step to interpreting this material.

In addition, specialists in different ancient disciplines have developed specific terminology to talk about graffiti, which can be confusing in itself, but also reveals some important – and problematic – ways in which this material has been conceptualised and categorised. Frequently this views graffiti as a sub-category of inscription, referring either to the place where they are found (parietal inscriptions, rupestral inscriptions), the manner in which they were written (Franklin, 1991; Mairs, 2011), or the type of mark (e.g. figural graffiti have often been collected separately from textual examples: Langner, 2001). This implicitly distinguishes graffiti from other forms of writing practice and often fails to acknowledge the temporal, spatial and cultural contexts in which they are found.

Partly because much of this material has traditionally fallen under the purview of those who study inscriptions (epigraphers), who are often more interested in the written word than in visual meaning or archaeological context, written texts have tended to have been recorded more frequently (and valued more highly) than drawings or other non-verbal or non-literate texts (i.e. those which communicate words and ideas with ideograms or symbols, often now undecipherable); indeed, entirely different groups of scholars have tended to work on this material. Thus graffiti have often been published either as examples of written *texts* within epigraphic corpora (i.e. with limited contextual or visual information) or as art-historical *images* (i.e. analysed only from a visual perspective) and have come off worse in both. The assumption that graffiti are subversive, unofficial or informal implicitly permeates contemporary definitions of graffiti with the effect that they have frequently been separated from what has been perceived as more 'formal' types of writing (on stone, papyri or parchment – the most common form of extant writing from antiquity) or more 'complex' styles of image production and (negatively) contrasted with them. On a conceptual level, this means that graffiti have (in some contexts) been constructed almost as an intrusive form and not held up to the same scholarly scrutiny as other evidence, and in a practical sense, examples of 'graffiti' are collected in a wide variety of publications using different terminology and classified according to typological, rather than historical, concerns. Only recently has work begun to bring together textual, pictorial and contextual information at specific sites which will be of huge benefit for researchers in the future (Benefiel and Sprenkle, 2014).

If the term 'graffiti' is sometimes problematic for describing the ancient material because of the breadth of the evidence to which it has been applied, 'street art' is even more so: Although there are some exceptions, much ancient graffiti do not appear in streets, they were only in some cases produced by or connected to any subculture (this cannot be assumed), and they were never associated with 'art' in the way that scholars of contemporary graffiti are often drawn into debates about (Deitch *et al.*, 2011). Similarly, defining ancient graffiti in terms of its relationship with the law (or other types of authority) or in terms of property ownership (Ross and Wright, 2014) can be misleading. What historians might identify as vandalism, illicit writing or defacement is often shown on closer inspection to be anything but. Much ancient graffiti appear inside houses and other buildings, often produced by, or with the tacit understanding of, the property owner (Benefiel, 2010, 2011; Baird, forthcoming). Graffiti are commonly found in sacred spaces too, but do not appear to be sacrilegious (Mairs, 2011; Stern, 2012, 2013). Assumptions about what graffiti are and what they do often need to be unthought and critically examined as part of the interpretation of this material.

Graffiti: ancient and modern

As can be seen from the brief overview so far, there are some important differences between ancient graffiti and modern graffiti. These are significant, but there are, of course, also some similarities. Like modern graffiti, there is a great variety of ancient graffiti. They appear on a range of surfaces in a variety of contexts and speak of a variety of topics. Some are mundane and even banal, such as simple names or quick calculations whereas others made literary allusions (Milnor, 2014), have a sacred or magical meaning (Baird, 2011), or have a pointed and resonant political message (Zadorojnyi, 2011). Some are deliberately humorous; others have serious points to make. There are clever word-plays (Bagnall, 2011; Benefiel, 2013) and crude sexual imagery (Levin-Richardson, 2011), pictures of people, animals and objects (Langner, 2001). They provide evidence for the presence of particular people and their use of spaces (Taylor, 2011), everyday life and colloquial language (Kruschwitz, 2010b), the ancient economy (Lawall, 2000) and belief systems (Chaniotis, 2002) not to mention the spread, as well as the uses, of reading, writing and non-literate communication (Franklin, 1991; Webster, 2008).

Graffiti in the ancient world frequently cluster together in particular locations, sometimes over a long period of time. Graffiti frequently appear to attract graffiti, so one useful interpretative tool is to consider the ways in which graffiti are in dialogue with one another as well as with their audience(s). In the well-preserved house of Maius Castricius, a wealthy Roman living in Pompeii, graffiti appear in the places of the house which had the most visitors. These include poetic exchanges between different writers engaging in literary one-upmanship as well as drawings of boats and people (Benefiel, 2010). Viewing the dialogues and conversations between graffiti has allowed historians to consider questions of temporality and spatiality, not only in terms of production or content, but in terms of audience and performance. Graffiti frequently 'talk' to one another, commenting on the message already present, sometimes responding in kind (some examples from Pompeii: 'Very many and continual greetings [from] Secundus to Onesimus, his brother', 'Onesimus to Secundus, his brother [greetings]', 'lots of greetings to Secundus, lovingly'), sometimes satirising them ('May he who reads this never have to read another thing in the future', 'May he who writes above never be well'). Some graffiti are knowing, asking to be read aloud ('I am amazed, O wall, that you have not fallen in ruins, you who support the tediousness of so many writers'), others memorialise the presence of the writer, or the text itself. Graffiti can map particular landscapes within the ancient city: Roman military graffiti in Dura-Europos shows not only where soldiers spent their time, but also delineates their relationships to each other and to the civilian community (Baird, 2011).

Graffiti have also been used to explore links between writing and identity more broadly, accessed via the analysis of language or the use of written space (Adams *et al.*, 2002; Adams, 2003; Mullen and James, 2012). The study of graffiti has been crucial to a range of historical debates, for example those about ancient literacy, education or bilingualism. They have helped historians to refine understanding of literate (and non-literate) cultures and provided a wealth of data on the practices of reading and writing throughout diverse populations. They have helped to elucidate knowledge of the education systems of the ancient world, of bilingual people and the presence of multilingual communities within different regions of the Mediterranean (Baird, 2011; Bucking, 2012).

When described like this, ancient graffiti seem familiar; they appear to be similar to those of the contemporary world. They define space, negotiate identity or demonstrate belonging, insult or admire people and deploy humour. However, the differences between ancient and modern graffiti are significant and there are dangers in interpreting the ancient material according to modern paradigms. Here we outline a few problems. As might be expected from the graffiti we see around us today, ancient graffiti are often found in public spaces – the public squares and market places of towns and cities, for example, are often good sites for writers (Langner, 2001; Hoff, 2006) – but we have to be cautious about making direct analogies when we are looking for the motivations behind this material. Ancient graffiti often have different functions from, and were received differently to, graffiti in modern urban or suburban contexts.

Frequently, modern graffiti are interpreted as a subcultural response to dominating power structures (see Ross, Campos in this volume). Political authorities frequently have criminalised graffiti-writing (to the extent of declaring war on graffiti) and taken 'zero-tolerance' approaches to those producing them, while the same work is valued by others for social messages or as art (Austin, 2002; Iveson, 2010). Others have viewed graffiti as a form of self-expression or a critique of authority (Abaza, 2013). It is seductive to take these paradigms and apply them to the ancient world, and certainly some examples of graffiti might well be best explained in these ways. However, a great deal of it cannot.

Take, for example, the graffiti which appears in late antique Aphrodisias (Chaniotis, 2011). This includes sporting slogans ('the fortune of the Greens [a chariot team] wins!'), acclamations of good governance of the local politicians ('you have earned fame') and acceptance of the authority of the Roman Emperor ('many years for the emperor!'). These appear in prominent public spaces, but they are not the voices of dissent. Quite the opposite: The political authorities certainly did not disapprove of such writing; they actively encouraged them. Many other examples across the ancient world show the same thing; graffiti are often produced by and for elites. It appears frequently *inside* their houses (Benefiel and Keegan, forthcoming).

We might also think of graffiti as a predominantly urban phenomenon, appearing in less-than-salubrious parts of town or as a way of marking territory. Graffiti do appear in ancient cities, and patterns of preservation ensure that these are common places in which they are found, but they are also found in non-urban contexts too. From remote mountainsides to deserts, graffiti attest to the use of writing, sometimes non-literate writing, as a means of communication. Made by travellers, pilgrims and nomads, this was a way to memorialise presence, to practice and demonstrate newly acquired skills, or to engage with others coming through a territory. The Safaitic graffiti in the Syro-Arabian desert, in particular, shows that graffiti in the ancient world are found in a very wide range of places. These are found almost exclusively in remote sites rather than settled villages, in places were nomads tended their pastures, and are often written in Greek as well as Safaitic, the authors' mother tongue (Macdonald, 2005). Similarly remote graffiti are also found elsewhere in the Mediterranean world (Langdon and van de Moortel, 2000; Mairs, 2011).

An important way to understand and explain these differences is to view graffiti simply as one aspect of the ubiquitous writing culture that appeared across the ancient Mediterranean. Walls, floors and potsherds were just another surface to write on and were often more available than papyri, wax or wooden tablets which might be expensive, inaccessible and not necessarily easy to use or familiar. In many places, the writing of graffiti did not require special tools: Scratched or incised graffiti requires only a sharp point such as a knife or a stylus. Inscribed graffiti in the marble at the theatre at Aphrodisias or in the Athenian town of Thorikos is surely related to the proximity of stone quarries to these places and the availability of stone carving tools to the general population there. Ancient graffiti are just one, of many, different forms of writing, which sometimes operated decoratively, and sometimes symbolically.

Historical approaches to graffiti

Interpreting graffiti, therefore, requires consideration of a number of issues. Most historians and archaeologists are interested in graffiti for what they reveal about life in the past, but some of their critical responses have resonance for the interpretation of contemporary graffiti. Ancient graffiti are not merely a pleasantly diverting curiosity, but instead they provide a means to think through some important issues of interpretation which apply to non-ancient contexts too.

Although we have outlined above some of the difficulties of ancient graffiti research, notably the question of definition and the lack of systematic approaches to recording, this downplays somewhat a vibrant, encapsulating and self-reflexive field which has much to offer those outside the discipline. Much exciting work has been done in the recent past and frequently this has deliberately engaged with other fields as well as with the general public. Researchers of the ancient world are well-placed to be at the centre of debates about graffiti since their work frequently lies at an intersection between different historical disciplines and they are well-trained in the close reading of both texts and images.

One of the most significant conclusions of the recent interest in ancient graffiti is that the context in which a graffito is found is crucial to our ability to interpret it; context(s) affect not only how the material is analysed, but how it is defined in the first place (Baird and Taylor, 2011). This means not only paying attention to the physical location of the text or image or its means of production, but also to its historical, social and cultural contexts, and the relationship to other graffiti and features in the landscape. One ramification of this is that the category of 'graffiti' itself should be seen as an umbrella term which encapsulates a wide variety of different practices, locations and social meanings.

Second, this research has shown that it is necessary to look past the stereotypes (popular and scholarly) about graffiti, whether these are assumptions that graffiti have an immediacy or truthfulness lacking in other texts, and so are 'unfiltered', or ideas that this form of writing has an immediacy which other forms lack. Both of these interpretations are fantasies that reflect unsophisticated assessments of the material. Graffiti, like most kinds of mark-making, are bound by convention, context and performance and as such are rarely as immediate or subversive as it might first be assumed. There is no unbroken link between a graffito on a wall in, say, Pompeii and the contemporary world, despite what we might like sometimes to think.

However, a third important conclusion, related to both of these, is that graffiti *can* be used to access otherwise 'invisible' historical groups. Although it should not be assumed that graffiti represent the unfiltered markings of the 'lower classes', as frequent interpretations have suggested, and we have stressed above that many graffiti reflect the thoughts and concerns of elites, in some contexts we can identify the writings and drawings of precisely this group of people. Drawing particularly on comparative approaches, close analysis of placement and content of graffiti has allowed the identification of marks likely made by children (Huntley, 2011; Garraffoni and Laurence, 2013), those made by slaves (Webster, 2008) or women's contestation of their normative sexual roles (Levin-Richardson, 2013). This has important ramifications for social history particularly in a field in which evidence for these groups (particularly the type of evidence which is produced by them) is extremely scarce. Comparative approaches like these open up many potential avenues of enquiry which have yet to be explored, and this promises to be a fruitful line of future research.[2]

Similarly, archaeological approaches, such as those which focus on materiality, have much to contribute to other graffiti studies (Frederick, 2014; Frederick and Clarke, 2014). Considering both graffiti and graffiti-making practices in this way poses questions not only about the techniques of production and the surfaces on which graffiti are found, but how these encourage or constrain human interaction (Tilley, 2007). They emphasise how the experiential qualities of writing and reading affect interpretation and how they are conditioned by our own cultural contexts. Viewing graffiti in this way has the potential not only of shifting our perceptions about the production, consumption and preservation of ancient material, but also encourages the recasting of contemporary graffiti outside of the illegitimate/illegal or vandalism/art paradigms. Instead it considers graffiti as cultural production in its own right which is situated in a variety of social, cultural and temporal networks. We all need to challenge the methodological assumptions which are rooted in our individual disciplines.

Perhaps most importantly, ancient graffiti raise questions of cultural value. As we have seen, the perception of (ancient) graffiti as something subversive, or as 'matter out of place' (in Mary

Douglas' famed formulation for 'dirt'),[3] has frequently led to their marginalisation as a historical source, but ironically such material is perceived as having greater cultural value than many contemporary graffiti. Generally, surviving ancient graffiti raise questions of preservation and vandalism, both in the ancient world and in the contemporary one; the former posing a historical problem and the latter an ethical one. The outcry in 2013 over a Chinese tourist writing his name on an Egyptian temple at Luxor reveals starkly divergent attitudes to graffiti – ancient and modern. The mark-making of ancient Greek, Roman or Coptic tourists visiting Egyptian sites is preserved, valued and studied (Adams, 2007; Bucking, 2012), that of a contemporary Chinese visitor considered as vandalism and removed. Press reports and social media were outraged by the actions of the teenager involved in this incident and considered them a form of defacement which 'ruined' the monument. He was hounded online and publically shamed. Much of the coverage of the incident employed negative ethnic stereotypes focusing on the writer's nationality (as opposed to his age) and depicting the Chinese abroad as 'uncivilised' and 'lack[ing] quality and breeding' (Pumin, 2013) as if Western tourists never engaged in such behaviour (that this is not exclusively the 'problem' of one group of people, see English Heritage, 1999). In contrast, the nineteenth-century graffito written by Lord Byron on the Classical Greek temple of Poseidon at Sounion, south of Athens, is considered a tourist attraction in its own right (Barber, 1999: 234). The intersection of race, class and cultural heritage are thrown into sharp relief through the production of graffiti. This highlights a temporal dimension to our analyses which plays into assessments of cultural value: Why are ancient graffiti preserved and studied but their modern equivalents at ancient sites erased and vilified (Frederick, 2009; Merrill, 2011)?

Conclusion

Historical approaches to graffiti are, therefore, not only useful for those interested in past societies, but also can provide interpretative paradigms for contemporary scholars in non-historical disciplines. Reading contemporary graffiti as historical data has distinct advantages; it prompts not only critical reading of the content of the graffiti but also shows how important various contexts might be. Since a contextual approach resists a one-size-fits-all interpretation, it encourages researchers to note the variety of material and develop a diversity of responses to it. Viewing contemporary graffiti in the *longue durée* of historical vision enables reflection and critique of culturally embedded patterns of interpretation rather than assuming a similarity. Instead of erroneously focusing of the perceived immediacy of the past, we can both expand and contract the distance between 'us' and 'them' as appropriate, and nuance our understanding of different types of writing and reading cultures in the past and in the present. Ancient graffiti resist monolithic interpretation. They are not a legal problem to be resolved, nor (necessarily) the marks of a subculture resisting authority, nor are they to be considered through the paradigms of defining what is, or what is not, a work of 'art'. Rather, ancient graffiti are examples of everyday writing that speak of a multitude of different and often competing concerns, contribute to numerous historical debates and reveal a tension between what is culturally valued and what is – and what will be – destroyed.

Notes

1 For discussion of the relationship between writing surfaces and texts, see, for example, Johnston (2013).
2 For instance, ancient and modern graffiti in places of confinement: Casella (2009).
3 See Douglas (1966).

References

Abaza, M. (2013). Walls, Segregating Downtown Cairo and the Mohammed Mahmud Street Graffiti. *Theory, Culture & Society 30*(1): 122–139.

Adams, C. (2007). Travel and the Perceptions of Space in the Eastern Desert of Egypt. In Rathmann, M. (ed.) *Wahrnehmung Und Erfassung Geographischer Räume in Der Antike* (pp. 211–220). Mainz: Philipp von Zabern.

Adams, J.N., Janse, M. and Swain, S. (eds) (2002). *Bilingualism in Ancient Society: Language Contact and the Written Word*. Oxford: Oxford University Press.

Adams, J.N. (2003). *Bilingualism and the Latin Language*. Oxford: Oxford University Press.

Austin, J. (2002). *Taking the Train: How Graffiti Art Became an Urban Crisis in New York City*. New York: Columbia University Press.

Bagnall, R.S. (2011). *Everyday Writing in the Graeco-Roman East*. Berkeley, CA: University of California Press.

Baird, J.A. (forthcoming). Private Graffiti? Scratching the Walls of Houses at Dura-Europos. In Benefiel, R.R. and Keegan, P. (eds) *Inscriptions in Private Places. Brill Studies in Greek and Roman Epigraphy*. Leiden: Brill.

Baird, J.A. (2011). The Graffiti of Dura-Europos: A Contextual Approach. In Baird, J.A. and Taylor, C. (eds) *Ancient Graffiti in Context* (pp. 49–68). London: Routledge.

Baird, J.A. and Taylor, C. (eds) (2011). *Ancient Graffiti in Context*. London: Routledge.

Barber, R. (1999). *The Blue Guide to Athens*. 4th edn London: A & C Black.

Benefiel, R.R. (2010). Dialogues of Ancient Graffiti in the House of Maius Castricius in Pompeii. *American Journal of Archaeology 114*(1): 59–101.

Benefiel, R.R. (2011). Dialogues of Graffiti in the House of the Four Styles at Pompeii (Casa Dei Quattro Stili, I.8.17, 11). In Baird, J.A. and Taylor, C. (eds) *Ancient Graffiti in Context* (pp. 20–48). London: Routledge.

Benefiel, R.R. (2013). Magic Squares, Alphabet Jumbles, Riddles and More: The Culture of Word-Games among the Graffiti at Pompeii. In Kwapisz, J., Petrain, D. and Szymanski, M. (eds) *The Muse at Play: Riddles and Wordplay in Greek and Latin Poetry* (pp. 65–79). Berlin: Walter de Gruyter.

Benefiel, R.R. and Keegan, P. (eds) (forthcoming). *Inscriptions in Private Places. Brill Studies in Greek and Roman Epigraphy*. Leiden: Brill.

Benefiel, R.R. and Sprenkle, S. (2014). The Herculaneum Graffiti Project. *ISAW Papers* 7(4). Online at: http://dlib.nyu.edu/awdl/isaw/isaw-papers/7/benefiel-sprenkle/.

Bucking, S. (2012). Towards an Archaeology of Bilingualism. On the Study of Greek-Coptic Education in Late Antique Egypt. In Mullen, A. and James, P. (eds) *Multilingualism in the Graeco-Roman Worlds* (pp. 225–264). Cambridge: Cambridge University Press.

Casella, E.C. (2009). Written on the Walls: Inmate Graffiti within Places of Confinement. In Beisaw, A.M. and Gibb, J.G. (eds) *The Archaeology of Institutional Life* (pp. 172–189). Tuscaloosa: University of Alabama Press.

Chaniotis, A. (2002). The Jews of Aphrodisias: New Evidence and Old Problems. *Scripta Classica Israelica* 21: 209–242.

Chaniotis, A. (2011). Graffiti in Aphrodisias. In Baird, J.A. and Taylor, C. (eds) *Ancient Graffiti in Context* (pp. 191–207). London: Routledge.

Deitch, J., Gastman, R. and Rose, R. (eds) (2011). *Art in the Streets*. New York & Los Angeles, CA: Skira Rizzoli; MOCA.

Douglas, M. (1966). *Purity and Danger: An Analysis of Concepts of Pollution and Taboo*. London: Routledge.

English Heritage. (1999). *Graffiti on Historic Buildings and Monuments – Methods of Removal and Prevention*. London: English Heritage.

Evans, J. (1987). Graffiti and the Evidence of Literacy and Pottery Use in Roman Britain. *The Archaeological Journal 144*(1): 191–204.

Franklin, J.L. (1991). Literacy and the Parietal Inscriptions of Pompeii. In *Literacy in the Roman World* (pp. 77–98). Ann Arbor, MI: Journal of Roman Archaeology.

Frederick, U.K. (2009). Revolution Is the New Black: Graffiti/art and Mark-Making Practices. *Archaeologies: Journal of the World Archaeological Congress 5*(2): 210–237.

Frederick, U.K. (2014). Shake Well Midden: An Archaeology of Contemporary Graffiti Production in Perth, Western Australia. *Australian Archaeology 78*: 93–99.

Frederick, U.K. and Clarke, A. (2014). Signs of the Times: Archaeological Approaches to Historical and Contemporary Graffiti. *Australian Archaeology 78*: 54–57.

Garraffoni, R.S. and Laurence, R. (2013). Writing in Public Space from Child to Adult: The Meaning of Graffiti. In Laurence, R., Sears, G. and Keegan, P. (eds) *Written Space in the Latin West, 200 BC to AD 300* (pp. 123–134). London: Bloomsbury.

Hoff, M.C. (2006). Some Inscribed Graffiti in the Roman Market in Athens. *Zeitschrift für Papyrologie und Epigraphik 155*: 176–182.

Huntley, K. (2011). Identifying Children's Graffiti in Roman Campania: A Developmental Psychological Approach. In Baird, J.A. and Taylor, C. (eds) *Ancient Graffiti in Context* (pp. 69–89). London: Routledge.

Iveson, K. (2010). The Wars on Graffiti and the New Military Urbanism. *City 14*(1–2): 115–134.

Johnston, A. (2013). Straight, Crooked and Joined-up Writing: An Early Mediterranean View. In Piquette, K.E. and Whitehouse, R.D. (eds) *Writing as Material Practice* (pp. 193–212). London: Ubiquity Press.

Kruschwitz, P. (2010a). Writing on Trees: Restoring a Lost Facet of the Graeco-Roman Epigraphic Habit. *Zeitschrift für Papyrologie und Epigraphik 173*: 45–62.

Kruschwitz, P. (2010b). Romanes Eunt Domus! Linguistic Aspects of the Subliterary Latin in Roman Wall Inscriptions. In Evans, T.V. and Obbink, D.D. (eds) *The Language of the Papyri* (pp. 156–170). Oxford: Oxford University Press.

Langdon, M. and van de Moortel, A. (2000). Newly Discovered Greek Boat Engravings from Attica. In Litwin, T. (ed.) *Down to the River to the Sea. Proceedings of the English International Symposium on Boat and Ship Archaeology, Gdansk 1997* (pp. 85–89). Gdansk: Polish Maritime Museum.

Langner, M. (2001). *Antike Graffitizeichnungen. Motive, Gestaltung und Bedeutung*. Wiesbaden: Ludwig Reichert.

Lawall, M.L. (2000). Graffiti, Wine Selling, and the Reuse of Amphoras in the Athenian Agora. *Hesperia 69*(1): 3–90.

Levin-Richardson, S. (2011). Facilis hic futuit: Graffiti and Masculinity in Pompeii's 'Purpose-Built' Brothel. *Helios 38*(1): 59–78.

Levin-Richardson, S. (2013). Fututa Sum Hic: Female Subjectivity and Agency in Pompeian Sexual Graffiti. *Classical Journal 108*(3): 319–345.

Macdonald, M.C.A. (2005). Literacy in an Oral Environment. In Bienkowski, P., Mee, C. and Slater, E. (eds) *Writing and Ancient Near Eastern Society: Papers in Honour of Alan R. Millard* (pp. 49–118). New York: T&T Clark.

Macdonald, M.C.A. (2009). *Literacy and Identity in Pre-Islamic Arabia*. Farnham: Ashgate.

Mairs, R. (2011). Egyptian 'Inscriptions' and Greek 'Graffiti' at El Kanais in the Egyptian Eastern Desert. In Baird, J.A. and Taylor, C. (eds) *Ancient Graffiti in Context* (pp. 153–164). London: Routledge.

Merrill, S.O.C. (2011). Graffiti at Heritage Places: Vandalism as Cultural Significance or Conservation Sacrilege? *Time and Mind 4*(1): 59–75.

Milnor, K. (2014). *Graffiti and the Literary Landscape in Roman Pompeii*. Oxford: Oxford University Press.

Mouritsen, H. (1988). *Elections, Magistrates and Municipal Élite: Studies in Pompeian Epigraphy*. Rome: L'Erma di Bretschneider.

Mullen, A. and James, P. (2012). Introduction. Multiple Languages, Multiple Identities. In Mullen, A. and James, P. (eds) *Multilingualism in the Graeco-Roman Worlds* (pp. 1–35). Cambridge: Cambridge University Press.

Plesch, V. (2002). Memory on the Wall: Graffiti on Religious Wall Paintings. *Journal of Medieval and Early Modern Studies 32*(1): 167–198.

Pumin, Y. (2013). Saving Face, Preserving Surfaces: Authorities and the Public Take Efforts to Maintain the National Image. *Beijing Review 24*, June 13. Online at: www.bjreview.com/culture/txt/2013-06/08/content_548038.html.

Ross, J.I. and Wright, B.S. (2014). "I've Got Better Things to Worry About": Police Perceptions of Graffiti and Street Art in a Large Mid-Atlantic City. *Police Quarterly 17*(2): 176–200.

Stern, K. (2012). Tagging Sacred Space in the Dura-Europos Synagogue. *Journal of Roman Archaeology 25*(1): 171–194.

Stern, K. (2013). Graffiti as Gift: Mortuary and Devotional Graffiti in the Late Antique Levant. In Satlow, M. (ed.) *The Gift in Antiquity* (pp. 137–157). London: John Wiley & Sons.

Taylor, C. (2011). Graffiti and the Epigraphic Habit: Creating Communities and Writing Alternate Histories in Classical Attica. In Baird, J.A. and Taylor, C. (eds) *Ancient Graffiti in Context* (pp. 90–109). London: Routledge.

Tilley, C. (2007). Materiality in Materials. *Archaeological Dialogues* 14(1): 16–20.

Volioti, K. (2011). The Materiality of Graffiti: Socialising a Lekythos in Pherai. In Baird, J.A. and Taylor, C. (eds) *Ancient Graffiti in Context* (pp. 134–154). London: Routledge.

Webster, J. (2008). Less Beloved: Roman Archaeology, Slavery and the Failure to Compare. *Archaeological Dialogues* 15(2): 103–123.

Zadorojnyi, A.V. (2011). Transcripts of Dissent? Political Graffiti and Elite Ideology under the Principate. In Baird, J.A. and Taylor, C. (eds) *Ancient Graffiti in Context* (pp. 110–133). London: Routledge.

2

Trains, railroad workers and illegal riders

The subcultural world of hobo graffiti

John F. Lennon

Introduction

Much as beat generation author Jack Kerouac attempted to do in literature, Harry Partch set out in music to capture a particular (masculine) spirit of America through experimental methods. One of the premiere composers of the twentieth century, Partch crafted his own instruments, threw out long sacred rules of compositional style and included within his text bawdy and personal conversations, all in a search of an authentic musical language. His inspirations – and conversations – often were realized on the road. And like Kerouac, Partch was fascinated with hobos.

Two of his major compositions, *Bitter Music* and *US Highball*, are specifically about his own hobo experiences during the early part of the twentieth century, highlighting the ways Partch played with language and tone to recreate an aura around this distinctly American tradition of traveling. *Bitter Music* explicitly details the loneliness of the hobo lifestyle, with its interspersed snatches of hobo conversations that expressed his alienating search for food, shelter, and sexual gratification in jungle camps and railroad yards throughout the country. *US Highball*, about a later hobo trip Partch embarked upon, is an aural montage of the protagonist Slim's hobo trip to Chicago. Slim's narrative interactions with other hobos and his crude and sometimes playful observations are distorted by Partch's compositional method, forcing the listener to consistently attempt to decipher the hobo argot. By experimenting with the sound of actual conversations he had with other hobos, or by creating songs around the graffiti he spotted and jotted down in his journals while shuttling around in boxcars, Partch's music taps into a refracted personal and national history.

Partch is interested in the tone of language – the way a hungry and tired hobo pronounces a certain turn of a phrase, or the comical inventiveness of a made-up word that a hobo uses to get his point across. Being accurate with these words and phrases was important to Partch but not in the same way a historian is beholden to his interviewees' words. Rather, he was attempting to tap into the hidden codes of the hobo parlance. The layers of meaning – of what words say and don't say – mattered to this composer and it is therefore no wonder that in the midst of his travels as a young man, he would find a specific interest in the graffiti of other transients.

Stuck in Barstow, California, in February 1940, he found eight different pieces of graffiti scratched into a railing that were, "eloquent in what it fails to express in words" (Gilmore 1998: 129). They were messages and complaints; seemingly simplistic offers of love and sex. They revealed a multitude of pressing desires, all dated and signed by different hands that were miles and perhaps years down the road. Hidden in plain sight, upon discovery, Partch was "thoroughly aroused by this sudden fountainhead of Americana." Referred by Partch as a "Hobo Concerto," the resulting musical work, *Barstow*, is sonically built by layering the graffiti messages, poetically arraigning the lived statements of everyday life from a certain segment of a hidden American populace (Gilmore 1998: 127–135).

I start off this chapter of hobo graffiti with a discussion of this "rebel composer" of American music for two reasons: When Partch sat shivering in boxcars, he took out a pen and wrote in his notebooks the words and symbols that he read because he knew that they were conduits into an American subcultural world that was consistently transforming. By recording them, he gave voice to forgotten men on the outskirts of society who marked their lives both materially and figuratively in the language and symbols that they used. But just as importantly, Partch knew that this subcultural world could never be fully revealed because it was also a ruse: the language, full of puns and made-up words, hid as much as they revealed. Partch, therefore, used the words of hobos (both written and spoken) not as a historical account, but as a musical platform to create an aura of hobo life. Hobos were an "invisible" subculture who survived by disappearing from sight in boxcars in one particular location before suddenly appearing in another part of the country. Their invisibility was the key to their movement and the graffiti on the walls of train cars, water towers or railroad towns speak of this transience. This graffiti is a testament to the everyday life of hobos that sometimes playfully and sometimes angrily reveals more about the instability and evolving nature of graffiti's symbolic power than the subculture itself. Referring to the graffiti he saw scratched along both asphalt and iron roads in his songs that challenge the listener into hearing the hobo language in new musical tones and arraignments, Partch did not create a myth around hobo graffiti. Instead, he laid bare the myth itself, showing the way this transient subculture can never be fully understood by those on the outside who only "know" hobos by examining the graffiti left behind.

To discuss hobo graffiti – and hobos themselves – one must, like Partch, also deflate the large myths surrounding this subcultural form of expression. Google "hobo signs," and webpage after webpage will reveal an intricate sign language system that hobos supposedly used. Like the symbolic, ubiquitous muted horn graffiti in Thomas Pynchon's *The Crying of Lot 49*, these signs supposedly mask a hidden, sophisticated subculture with a strong infrastructure and regulated foot soldiers. In my research on the hobo, however, I do not see conclusive evidence to support this idea. Hobos were transient working class men and women who traveled by train, looking for jobs and sustenance in the late nineteenth and early twentieth century. They were resourceful as they lived on the margins of society. Integral players in the political economy of the United States, they were needed when their labor power was in demand but quickly seen as dangerous and drains on society when they weren't. Like any subculture, they lived by their own rules and formed their own codes of conduct that were internally policed within jungles (hobo encampments) and boxcars. And hobos certainly did write graffiti – waiting in sidetracked train cars or passing the hours in jungles, graffiti relieved boredom and was an outlet for artistic, creative, and political expression. It was also a way to communicate with other hobos in rudimentary ways – much in the same vein that New York City subway writers in the 1970s communicated with each other when tagging trains (Austin 2001: 38–75).

The myth surrounding hobo graffiti as a sophisticated language system, however, must be carefully examined. For example, does a box with a line emerging from its side universally mean to hobos that "alcohol is in this town" as some have suggested (Wanderer 2002: 218)? In my research, I have found no evidence for this type of sophisticated symbolic language being used by a large swath of the hobo population. Hobo graffiti does not reveal an intricate symbolic language written by hobos during the Great Depression (and, conveniently, can be sold on t-shirts and hats on eBay in the present day). Instead, it helps us frame the working class politics of the hobo lifestyle within the narrative of graffiti history.

The hobo

A quick review of the hobo is needed before we can discuss the subculture's graffiti. The hobo figure originated from a specific set of economic and technological entanglements in the United States in the second half of the nineteenth century. The anxiety felt by the nation due to the new factory labor system, immigration, and increasingly vociferous underclass found symbolic embodiment in this itinerant figure (Phontinos 2007: 995). Many hobos, however, saw not villainy in this lifestyle, but a practical way to live. Most folk histories of the hobo begin with returning veterans from the Civil War who, after finding their homes in ruins, and having already been accustomed to traveling by train during the war, became itinerant agricultural laborers. Some stories suggest that these "hoe boys" did not like the derogatory nature of this term and combined the words, creating *hobo* for a more positive self-identity (Higbie 2003: 5). Although this origin story is somewhat suspect, this narrative does reveal a crucial identity marker for the hobo: they were workers. Reitman echoes many critics, scholars and other hobos when he categorizes the homeless into three groups: "The hobos who work and wander, the tramps who dream and wander, and the bums who drink and wander" (cited in Anderson 1923: 4). While traveling was connected to all three, according to this often used definition, what separated hobos from the rest of the homeless were their willingness to work. Unlike tramps and bums who avoided work, hobos prided themselves on their ability to find employment by illegally hopping trains to get from job to job (whether that job was in the next town, next state or across national borders in Canada or Mexico). There were two main aspects that made one a hobo: being a self-identified transient worker (even if the individual was without a job for long stretches of time) who travelled by illegally riding trains (Anderson 1923: 87–107). By the late 1890s, this new mobile working-class subculture had differentiated themselves from many other migrants who were part of what Schwantes describes as the "wageworkers' frontier" (1985: 150).

As "indispensable outcasts," the hobo was a member of a working-class subculture that was necessary, as Montgomery writes, "to nearly all forms of manufacturing, transportation and commerce" in the United States (1987: 60). Not mere vestiges held over from a preindustrial society, hobos fulfilled an essential economic requirement for the country. The railroad, steel and other major industries needed large amounts of laborers; the powerful trains advertised in glossy brochures would not move across the continent if itinerant manual laborers did not arduously strike the rails into the ground. Besides the rail industry, hobos were employed in a variety of agricultural and industrial jobs throughout the United States. Often times, laborers would quit their jobs in the steel mills in the East during the summer months and travel West to harvest wheat or beats only to return again East as the air turned cold, repeating the cyclical geographical traveling the following year (DePastino 2003: 59–85; Higbie 2003: 25–66; Montgomery 1987: 59–60).

But while hobos were part of the working class, there was an obvious difference between hobos following the spring harvests through Cedar City, Utah and generational steel workers in Bethlehem, Pennsylvania. An essential part of this difference was the way that hobos defined themselves. Not tied to one job or geographical area, many hobos thought of themselves as workers who picked up various employments along the way – as opposed to being defined by a particular job in a specific geographic locale – and therefore could move to a different locale or job whenever they wanted. (Anderson 1923: 107–125; Higbie 2003: 8). In 1,349 interviews conducted by McCook in 1889, Solenberger's data on *One Thousand Homeless Men* from 1900 to 1903, and Mills' 1914 investigation of seasonal labor in California, all three investigators concluded that a majority of transient workers (which would include members of the hobo subculture) articulated their ability to transition from job to job as a way to escape the confines of a stultifying industrial environment. Hobos saw themselves as workers, but their relationship to the work force was different from those who hitched plows on farms in Ohio or smelt iron in Pittsburg plants. The working class was not a monolithic entity and hobos were one subgroup; traveling from job to job in boxcars allowed hobos a particular labor vision that deviated from other working class individuals.

This ability to move made the hobo an object of study by those who were not hobos – resulting in draconian policies designed to keep the transient immobile (Creswell 2001: 48–87). There was generally a clear divide between the citizens of the town and the hobo who was traveling through their streets looking for jobs and sustenance. In national news, discussions of the itinerant worker were hyperbolic and often hysterical in nature and, as DePastino explains, this rhetoric highlighted many deep rooted socio-economic issues that had caused tensions in the decades after the Civil War including the socio-economic divides between the propertied and homeless over the use of public space and the rising numbers of transient workers converging in towns during the middle of the night (2003: 8). Hobos broke with official conventions of social, economic, and religious life and, like all homeless, were seen as pathologically harmful to their communities. Their poverty was explained as self-imposed rather than economic or political. Hobos were often viewed as suffering from "wanderlust" or other moral depravities and kept at arm's length; they were ostracized as voluntary dropouts from the working class rather than a vital subculture within it (Anderson 1923: 82–83).

The transcontinental railroads transformed the United States and are symbolic of American capitalism at the turn of the twentieth century. Described as a bully, the railroad is loud and overpowering (Lennon 2013; Schwantes and Ronda 2008; White 2011: 1–37). Hobos, however, did not try to stand up to the bully; rather, they stole from him by sneaking onto trains. To speak about hobos is to therefore speak about their connection to trains. This subcultural connection is literal and symbolic. Expanding on the view of Verstraete (2002: 145), who states, "systems of transportation and communication have been the site of fierce struggles for power among the nation-builders," the awesome technology that the train represents is also a site of struggle among those excluded from true citizenship. By hopping a train, hobos, whether they were members of the Industrial Workers of the World trying to cause revolution or distraught fathers trying to find money to send back home, were materially offering their bodies as resistance to the progress of an expanding capitalist society that the transcontinental railroad promised in its curling smoke and screeching wheels (Kornbluh 1988: 65–83; McGuckin 1987). The train is a powerful symbol and example of late nineteenth- and early twentieth-century American capitalism, and by physically stealing a ride, hobos were parasitic as they attempted to get to the next town, state, or nation. This materiality of resistance – of living the body politic – is crucial to understanding the hobo subculture. By hopping trains and disappearing into boxcars in one place and entering a new one the next day, hobos, consciously or not, were offering resistance, literally and symbolically, to the "progress" of the country underwritten by finance capitalism and embodied by the train. By stealing rides, hobos were parasitic to the life force of the train (and to the profit margins of the owner of these railroads), and like parasites circulating within blood, they sometimes went unnoticed, often caused minor ailments, and frequently had the potential to inflict serious illness (Lennon 2014).

Hobo graffiti

Since graffiti can be a resistive political act, it is not unsurprising that this medium fits well into the hobo lifestyle. Like TAKI 183, whose job as a messenger brought him into contact with all areas of New York City, hobos' jobs (and search for jobs) kept them in constant transit and the numerous boxcars they found themselves within offered plenty of canvases for their thoughts and messages (Austin 2001: 49). Produced before the era of aerosol cans, this graffiti was marked using oil based paints or carved into wooden boxcars (Burns 2005: 3). But a fascinating wrinkle into the complex world of hobo graffiti shows that much of the work often attributed to hobos actually did not come from them at all. Burns writes that train graffiti "inhabit[s] two specific worlds bound together by iron rails and wooden ties" (2005: 10). The first world is one of the railroad employees who were some of the most prolific train writers. Working in rail yards coupling cars together hours at a time, railroad workers were constantly in contact with trains. But while on duty, some rebelled against the rules of the company, painting train cars with their monikers – both hoboing and writing graffiti were illegal acts and therefore nicknames were often used (Burns 2005: 14; Gastman *et al.* 2006: 290–294). As one writer-employee succinctly stated about producing graffiti during company hours in Daniel's documentary of the subject, "They can't have all my time." Two of the most prolific writers of freight graffiti–*Herby* and *Bozo Texino* – worked in the train yards for the majority of their lives, producing tens of thousands of their monikers and drawings. These simplistic, easily reproduced graffiti would be sent zigzagging across the country; although the trainmen were stationary in their particular yards, these images shuttled over hundreds of thousands of miles (Ferrell 2006: 596–598; Gastman *et al.* 2006: 288–312). As another prolific writer showcased in Daniel's film, *The Rambler*, poignantly stated, "I'll never get [to far off places], might as well send something." Stealing company time to illegally mark their monikers on trains offered a creative outlet for these men who, unlike hobos, were rooted in particular places.

The second bounded world of hobo graffiti, according to Burns (2005), is the graffiti produced by hobos themselves. This work is extremely similar to the graffiti done by rail workers underlining the symbiotic relationship between the two worlds. An article in a 1939 issue of *Railroad Magazine* highlights this interrelatedness:

In addition to human faces and forms, students of boxcar calligraphy bump into figures of animals now and then, also pictures of trains and locomotives, but rarely any other type of machine. Most of these masterpieces are drawn by hoboes while they are waiting for freights or loafing around warehouses. Or, perchance, while enjoying free transportation at the company's expense. Other sketches are done by railroad men in terminal yards (Hecox 1939: 30).

As Hultkrins (2005) rightly points out when discussing this quote in the context of the world of hobo graffiti, there is a nonexistent divide between the world of the hobo and the world of the rail worker when it comes to producing graffiti – and "students of boxcar calligraphy" would be unable to tell which one was done by a hobo and which one was done by a rail worker. Standing on the sides of tracks, watching trains make their way past, the graffiti these observers would most often see would consist of an image or logo, a moniker, a date, and sometimes a particular location (Ferrell 2006: 597). The graffiti being produced could be read as both practical and political–it could be quickly reproduced train car after train car all the while declaring an illegal presence on the train for the writer. Both hobo and trainmen were part of the working class and their graffiti framed within the same hobo graffiti tradition that offered a physical announcement of the hidden, working lives of those that were intimately connected to trains. Frank Norris, a naturalist writer at the turn of the twentieth century, called the railroad conglomeration an Octopus who had a stranglehold of all the pieces of the political economy of the United States; by writing graffiti, hobos showed that these invisible voices were not completely choked off as they continued to leave markers of their presence on trains (Kornbluh 1988: 65–93)

Framing hobo graffiti

A 1972 ad for Heublein's "Hobo Wife" cocktail in *Life Magazine* tells the fictional story of J.B. King, a millionaire who inherited railroads, but was unsatisfied with his life and decided to become a hobo. But although he eschewed the money and comfort afforded to him from his class position, he did not give up on the memory of ownership and started doing graffiti "on all the cars I owned just to remind myself they belonged to me" (in Daniels 2008: 11). While this fictional ad campaign was designed to show the hidden regalness of a "full strength cocktail," it does tap into an idea popularized by many graffiti writers: writing your name implies a type of ownership (Gastman *et al.* 2006: 286). For J.B. King, it reminded him of actual ownership; for hobos, their names on the train symbolically rendered pieces of the train to them. Graffiti is one way for members of a disenfranchised subculture to claim a symbolic presence; by writing their monikers and symbols on train cars, these writers claimed their particular space on the train. If hobos were seen at inopportune times, they could be arrested or, worse, thrown out of train cars at high speeds; a great number of "tramp graves" throughout the United States speak of the dangerousness of being caught by railroad detectives "protecting" the property of their companies (Bailey 1973: 52–56; Barth 1969: 10; Black 1923: 62; Lawson 1980: 20). Being invisible was not only prudent, allowing hobos to get where they wanted to go, it was also a way to usurp the power dynamics as poor, homeless workers were able to escape from the watchful eye of the railroad companies (London 1907: 122–152). The cat-and-mouse game that hobos played "catching out" (hopping trains) and their lives hung in the balance, but by remaining unseen, the poor, penniless hobo beat the railroad company, parasitically stealing a ride. To be seen would invite potential grave danger, but their moniker placed on a train car stated their presence long after they had absconded.

Hobo graffiti can therefore be read in much the same way as reading New York City graffiti during the heyday of the subways – by placing their name on a train, writers were making their presence felt (Austin 2001: 38–75; Castleman 1982: 52–66). But while subway cars traverse a small geographic area, train cars could potentially travel over the whole continent – or across national boundaries into Canada and Mexico. Fame in NYC graffiti subculture was having your name seen in all the boroughs; fame in hobo community was having your name seen throughout the whole country or beyond (Ferrell 2006: 589–592). Hobo graffiti, therefore, is a subcultural reading and writing practice. Two short examples from a pair of famous hobos turned writers – Jack London and Jim Tully – will help explicate this particular type of communication system.

The man who would become a champion of the Socialist Labor Party of America (SLP) and tireless advocate for (white) workers anti-capitalism efforts was also a man who prided himself on being a premiere hobo. Jack London epitomized a specific subset of hobos: the individualistic rider who defined his self-worth by his train-hopping ability. It was a competitive individualist stance that placed him, at times, in competition with all members of society, including those within his hobo subculture (Lennon 2010). This competitive streak is epitomized in his graffiti as described in a tale from his book *The Road*. London's moniker was "Sailor Jack" which he was fond of carving into trains and water towers. While hopping trains throughout Canada, he saw the moniker of "Skysail jack." Perhaps because the name was too close to his own moniker, London then "chased clear across Canada over three thousand miles of railroad" following after the hobo (1907: 122). They never did meet but their race, described as a hyper-masculine competition where there were neither prizes nor even rules – just who could get farther ahead of the other – was marked by a trail of graffiti left in each other's wake. As London describes,

> I was a "comet" and "tramp-royal," so was Skysail jack; and it was up to my pride and reputation to catch up with him. I "railroaded" day and night, and I passed him; then turn about he passed me. Sometimes he was a day or so ahead, and sometimes I was (1907: 123).

They knew of each other's travels by watching the water towers and looking for their competitor's moniker and date notifying when the other had passed through towns. The names were easy to miss and there was little information conveyed; however, it allowed for these two hobos to form a competitive bond. London states that he encountered hundreds of hobos when traveling "who passed like ghosts, close at hand, unseen, and never seen" (1907: 122). By reading hobo graffiti, London was able to "see" others in his "invisible" subculture, allowing him the opportunity to mark his status in the hobo hierarchy. London prided himself on his position in the hobo subculture and graffiti allowed him to secure his spot.

Not all hobos, however, were as competitive as London. Jim Tully, a contemporary of London both as a hobo and writer, published over the course of ten years during the 1920s and early 1930s, the five books of the Underworld Series that detailed his early life and wanderings on the road, showcasing his distinct style of short, hard-hitting sketches of poor dispossessed individuals. At their best, these books reveal an underclass of forgotten, wandering men at the beginning of the twentieth century. Brimming with dark humor, an undercurrent of raw violence weaves itself throughout all the stories. Moving away from the naturalist mode of Frank Norris, Tully was a hard-boiled realist writer with a penchant for sharp phrases pulsing throughout these texts (Lennon 2013). *Beggars of Life* specifically details his life as a hobo and the value he recognized in hobo graffiti. In one episode, Tully finds himself in a boxcar with other men. Noticing a hobo carving his moniker into the train, Tully writes, "When he had finished, he stood up and admired it like an artist. An arrow was cut through the letters of his name. It pointed west, and denoted the direction in which he was traveling. The month and the year of the trip were cut beneath the name . . . form[ing] a crude directory for other tramps who might be interested in the itinerary of their comrades" (1924: 142). Here we see a symbolic communication system that uses the actual train itself to send and receive messages. Only those who are within the subculture, can read – or even think to look at – these systems embodied within the train. Learning to read graffiti is taught from one hobo to another as new riders become acquainted with more seasoned riders. In this way, graffiti is a way to link individuals, even though these people have no prior knowledge of one another and may not have even met. Reflecting the individuality of the person, these markings or monikers help to imaginatively suture the geographically disperse hobo subculture together.

What London's and Tully's retelling of their experiences with hobo graffiti shows is that these markings on the train represent a physical reminder of the illegal relationship that individuals shared with the subculture through their contact with the train. The railroad, as Verstraete states, is much more than a technology of transportation; it is also a technology of representation "about figuratively emplacing a specific citizenry" at the cost of others (2002: 150). But what this graffiti shows is that the displacement is never fully complete and individual hobos are (literally) leaving their marks on the train to be read by other members of a subculture who are parasitically appropriating the train. Hobo graffiti is a type of communication that had both practical and symbolic value for members of the hobo community.

Hobo graffiti is graffiti

Many experts assume that during the 1930s hobos developed a highly sophisticated pictorial language that became a "living, associative map keys for orienteering in strange places" for "hundreds or thousands" of the transient poor (Campbell 2001). Although many have repeated these stories as fact, there is no documented proof that exists to support these claims. Although it seems reasonable that some hobos could have used common symbols – especially in populated urban centers – to communicate certain information, my research has shown that hobo graffiti is comprised of much more basic materials: monikers, dates, and logos. The examples from London, Tully, and Partch remove hobo graffiti from a pedestal of a sophisticated language system that supposedly revealed a secret coded history of hobos. Instead, these writers' examples place hobo graffiti within the larger overall history of graffiti, where wall markings are about illegally emplacing a name on property, symbolically stating their presence as a member of minority subculture. As transient workers, hobos had only a fingertip grip on the bottom rung of the U.S. economy. But with their other hand free, many wrote their monikers on the trains, stating that, for a time at least, they had occupied a space on a train.

References

Anderson, N. (1923). *The Hobo: Sociology of a Homeless Man*, Chicago, IL: The University of Chicago Press.
Austin, J. (2001). *Taking the Train: How Graffiti Art Became an Urban Crisis in New York City*, New York: Columbia University Press.
Bailey, W. (1973). *Bill Bailey Came Home*, Logan: UT, Utah State Press.
Barth, C. (1969). *Hobo Trail to Nowhere*, Philadelphia, PA: Whitmore Publishing.
Black, J. (1923). *You Can't Win*, Oakland, CA: Nabat/AK Press.
Burns, M. (2005). We Were Here: Marks, Monikers, and the Boxcar Art Tradition, MA Thesis, Lehigh University.
Campbell, B. (2001). Signs of the Hoboes, *Canadian Geographic* 121(2); available online at http://canadian geographic.ca/vous_etes_ici-you_are_here/?path=english/nos_cartes-our_maps/signes-signs (accessed December 10, 2014).
Castleman, C. (1982). *Getting Up: Subway Graffiti in New York*, Cambridge, MA: MIT Press.
Cresswell, T. (2001). *The Tramp in America*, Clerkenwell, London: Reaktion Books.
Daniel, B. (2005). *Who is Bozo Texino?* Oakland, CA: AK Press.
Daniel, B. (2008). *Mostly True*, Bloomington, IN: Microcosm Publishing.
DePastino, T. (2003). *Citizen Hobo: How a Century of Homelessness Shaped America*, Chicago, IL: The University of Chicago Press.
Ferrell, J. (2006). Freight Train Graffiti: Subculture, Crime, Dislocation. *Justice Quarterly*, 15(4): 587–608.
Gastman, R., Rowland, D., & Sattler, I. (2006). *Freight Train Graffiti*, New York: Abrams.
Gilmore, B. (1998). *Harry Partch*, New Haven, CT: Yale University Press.
Hecox, A.W. (1939). Boxcar Art. *Railroad Magazine*, 26(2): 30–33.
Higbie, F.T. (2003). *Indispensable Outcasts: Hobo Workers and Community in the American Midwest, 1880–1930*, Urbana, IL: University of Illinois Press.
Hultkrins, A. (2005). Who is Bozo Texino? *Stim*; available online at www.northbankfred.com/p_bill.html (accessed December 11, 2014).
Kornbluh, J.L. (1988). *Rebel Voices: An IWW Anthology*, Chicago, IL: Charles H. Kerr Publishing.
Lawson, A. (1980). *Freight Trains West*, Sacramento, CA: Lucas.

Lennon, J. (2010). Can a Hobo Share a Box-Car? Jack London, The Industrial Army, and the Politics of (In)visibility. *American Studies*, 48(3): 5–30.

Lennon, J. (2013). The Polyphonic Boxcar: The Hobo Voice in Jim Tully's. *Beggars of Life. Midwestern Miscellany*, 41: 32–48.

Lennon, J. (2014). *Boxcar Politics: The Hobo in U.S. Culture and Literature, 1869–1956*, Amherst, MA: University of Massachusetts Press.

London, J. (1907). *The Road*, New York: Penguin.

McCook, J.J. (1893). A Tramp Consensus and Its Revelations. *Forum*, 15: 753–761.

McGuckin, H. (1987). *Memoirs of a Wobbly*, Chicago, IL: Charles H. Kerr Publishing.

Montgomery, D. (1987). *The Fall of the House of Labor: The Workplace, the State, and American Labor Activism 1865–1925*, Cambridge, MA: University of Cambridge Press.

Norris, F. (1901). *The Octopus: A Story of San Francisco*, New York: Penguin.

Partch, H. (2000). *Bitter Music: Collected Journals, Essays, Introductions, and Librettos*, Champaign, IL: University of Illinois Press.

Partch, H. (2003). *Harry Partch: U.S Highball*. Cond. Kronos Quartet. [CD]. New York: Nonesuch Records.

Phontinos, C. (2007). The Figure of the Tramp in Gilded Age Success Narratives. *The Journal of Popular Culture*, 40(6): 994–1018.

Pynchon, T. (1966). *The Crying of Lot 49*, New York: Harper Perennial.

Roy, W. (1997). *Socializing Capital: The Rise of the Large Industrial Corporation in America*, Princeton, NJ: Princeton University Press.

Schwantes, C. (1985). *Coxey's Army: An American Odyssey*, Lincoln, NE: University of Nebraska Press.

Schwantes, C. and Ronda, J. (2008). *The West the Railroad Made*, Seattle, WA: University of Washington Press.

Solenberger, A. (1911). *One Thousand Homeless Men*, New York: Charities Publication Committee.

Tully, J. (1924). *Beggars of Life*, Kent, OH: The Kent State University Press.

Verstraete, G. (2002). Railroading America: Towards a Material Study of the Nation. *Theory Culture Society*, 19(5–6): 145–159.

Wanderer, J. (2002). Embodiments of Bilateral Asymmetry and Danger in Hobo Signs. *Semiotica*, 142(1–4): 211–223.

White, R. (2011). *Railroaded: The Transcontinentals and the Making of Modern America*, New York: Norton.

Woirol, G. (1992). *In the Floating Army: F.C. Mills on Itinerant Life in California*, Urbana, IL: University of Illinois Press.

3

The history of freight train graffiti in North America[1]

Robert Donald Weide

Introduction

Since the collapse of the subway train era of graffiti in New York City in the 1980s, the modern freight train graffiti movement in North America has become an integral part of the overall graffiti subculture. Since the 1980s the freight train graffiti subculture within the wider graffiti subculture has been a primary medium for graffiti writers across the continent to establish subcultural identities for themselves and earn their status in the wider graffiti subculture. The freight train graffiti subculture is truly a subculture within a subculture. Not all graffiti writers participate in freight train graffiti, and many who do so only participate transiently. Conversely, many who do participate in the freight train graffiti subculture, commit themselves primarily to this particular graffiti medium and forego much of the street-level bombing and legal wall piecing, which other graffiti writers stake their subcultural reputations on. Some very few and extremely prolific graffiti writers do it all, excelling in every niche of the wider graffiti subculture.

Although freight train graffiti has become a very significant niche subculture within the overall graffiti subculture in North America, freight train graffiti has received surprisingly little attention from academic scholars of the graffiti subculture. This is due in part to the lack of access that scholars of the graffiti subculture have had to dedicated freight train writers, and partly due to the difficulty of studying a medium that is often gone and off to the next city before scholars are able to document it. This chapter reviews the existing scholarship on the freight train graffiti subculture and offers a social history of the freight train graffiti subculture, as a starting point for future scholarship on the freight train graffiti subculture.

Existing scholarship on freight train graffiti

Scholars of deviant subcultures have produced a remarkably thorough and coherent body of literature on the globalized graffiti subculture. Numerous books and academic articles have been published by scholars on the subject of the graffiti subculture from the 1970s onward, a timeframe that has coincided with an explosion in the popularity and proliferation of the graffiti subculture on a worldwide scale. Among the most notable and widely disseminated works on the graffiti subculture are books written by Abel and Buckley (1977), Castleman (1982), Ferrell (1995a,

1995b, 1996, 1998), Phillips (1999), Austin (2001), Macdonald (2001), and Snyder (2009). These and other authors, including Lachmann (1988), Conquergood (1993, 1997), Stewart (1997), Hutchison (1993), and Ferrell and Weide (2010), have also composed scholarship on the subject of graffiti. However, some of this work has been focused on gang graffiti and not on writer graffiti, which are completely separate subcultures (Hutchison 1993; Conquergood 1993, 1997; Phillips 1999). Other work has focused on the graffiti subculture in particular cities like New York City (Austin 2001; Macdonald 2001; Snyder 2009), London (Macdonald 2001), Los Angeles (Phillips 1999), and Denver (Ferrell 1996).

Despite this extensive academic literature on the graffiti subculture, only three scholars have offered any analysis of, or even mentioned, the freight train graffiti subculture (e.g. Ferrell 1998; Austin 2001; Snyder 2009). All other academic books and articles have been completely mute on this significant segment of the wider graffiti subculture. The first and most thorough of these contributions was by Ferrell (1998). Fascinated with the graffiti he saw on freight trains, Ferrell made an admirable attempt to research graffiti on freight trains through a sort of ethnography of images, by traveling from state to state, city to city, and town to town, to view and photograph freight trains with graffiti on them. Not knowing who had painted the graffiti he viewed, Ferrell was unable to interview any of the writers responsible, and was therefore unable to fully understand or comprehend the freight train movement he witnessed as an uninvolved observer. Little did he know that the graffiti he was observing was indeed the first "golden age" of the freight graffiti movement, when the painting of graffiti on freight trains became a widely practiced intercontinental phenomenon for the first time.

His analysis though, was nonetheless both insightful and sophisticated, given the limited contact he had with a subculture he did not have access to, within a wider subculture he did have access to (Ferrell 1996, 1998). Although he cannot be faulted for what he did not have access to, Ferrell neglected to recognize the subtle aspect that the freight train movement is indeed a subculture unto itself, within the wider globalized graffiti subculture, with its own set of rules, values, and practices. While my description and analysis of the freight train graffiti movement will explicate a number of the issues he could only wonder about, Ferrell nonetheless made a number of valuable insights and analyses that are worth reiterating here. The most basic of these is that the freight train graffiti movement is evidence of the success of the wider graffiti subculture in broadcasting itself to a widely dispersed geographic and subcultural audience. As Ferrell (1998: p. 9) stated, "Like other dimensions of the graffiti underground, freight train graffiti puts subcultural identities and images in motion, and shapes their meaning in transit." For writers who at one time could only conceive of their subcultural goals in terms of citywide recognition, freight trains provided the opportunity to display their work and their reputations to an intercontinental audience.

Ferrell (1996) situated his analysis theoretically in the postmodern and anarchist level of analysis that characterized his work at the time. Freight train graffiti was, as he perceived it, another example of subcultural usurpation of dominant authority and commercial paradigms of meaning, where graffiti writers had symbolically hijacked what were intended as vessels of intercontinental commercial transport, and reshaped them (aesthetically and symbolically, if not physically) into canvases of subculturally significant meaning, artistic prowess, and subcultural devotion. Through these rolling canvases, Ferrell suggested, writers deconstructed the everyday mundane meanings of physical representations of the capitalist system of commerce, and in the process, created new identities and demonstrations of subcultural status for themselves and their peers from the Atlantic to the Pacific Ocean. Shells of rolling steel hulks became the medium through which a certain segment of the wider graffiti subculture expressed the subcultural identities they had created for themselves.

Austin (2001: pp. 247–249), in his analysis of the graffiti subculture in New York City, dedicated only two paragraphs to freight train graffiti. Although this may not necessarily be due to oversight on Austin's part, but more likely on the small number of subjects he interviewed who had extensive involvement with the freight train graffiti movement. However, even in this short space, Austin made some particularly insightful points. Painting freight trains as opposed to subway trains, according to Austin, had a number of advantages. For one, freight yards are not fenced off the way subway yards are, or patrolled by security or police, protecting them against trespassers – making them easy targets for graffiti writers who don't want to go through the hassle of sneaking into a subway yard to paint clean trains. This is because due to their poor aesthetic exterior conditions, from weather, rust, and chemical stains, commercial freight companies are not particularly motivated to protect the aesthetic appearance of freight cars.

Furthermore, freight trains generally provide flat surfaces, which make a particularly convenient medium for graffiti writers to paint on. Although freight trains are not typically viewable by city residents who have no reason to go into freight yards to see them, freights do travel across the continent to other cities and states, where audiences unknown to the writers who painted them may view them. Austin points out that this phenomenon has led to widespread interest in freight train graffiti, even in rural areas where young people might not have any other opportunity to view graffiti painted by renowned writers from major urban areas, but have easy and unrestricted access to freight yards, where they can take the time to paint their own graffiti on freight trains, inspired by graffiti from writers in other parts of the continent they have seen on freight trains. According to Austin, freight train graffiti has thus contributed to the widespread proliferation of the graffiti subculture both to distant urban and rural areas across North America. Austin also included as an illustration, a black and white photograph of a closed top common hopper car (a common type of freight car used to carry grain products) painted by HUSH, provided by the artist.

Snyder (2009: pp. 31–32) also made passing reference to freight train graffiti, as one of a number of mediums certain graffiti writers have used to achieve citywide, national, and even international notoriety. As an example, Snyder included as an illustration a black and white photograph of a CSX boxcar with a piece by COLT .45, provided by the artist. The picture was reprinted in color and inserted in the middle of the book as well.

The pioneers of freight train graffiti

The emergence of the freight train graffiti movement began in earnest as a result of the end of the subway graffiti era in New York City in 1986, thanks to the implementation of a new kind of subway car in New York, which could easily be cleaned of any trace of exterior graffiti paint with a quick chemical wash. Another factor that resulted in the collapse of the subway train era was the implementation of drastically increased security measures at subway rail yards in New York City and zealous pursuit of graffiti writers who continued to paint the "clean trains" after they had replaced the old style subway cars. The golden age of subway graffiti had ended, but new subcultural niches blossomed in the graffiti subculture in North America as a result. Graffiti writers went from targeting transit trains to "bombing" streets and "piecing" yards, as well as painting on freight trains.

The first writers to paint freight trains did so in the early to mid-1970s, including but not limited to TRACY 168 and PNUT in New York, and SUROC and BRAZE in Philadelphia (Gastman *et al.* 2006). However, the practice of painting freight trains did not take off on a national scale until the mid-1980s when the subway graffiti subculture was laid to rest in New York City with the implementation of a new kind of subway car that could be easily wiped clean of external graffiti. New York writers, whose graffiti would no longer run on subway trains, eventually turned to what some of them saw as the next best thing, freight trains, which were trains after all, and were easily accessible and poorly guarded. While they did not at that time fully realize that the freight trains they painted would be seen by a national audience, since once the cars were pulled from the yard they never saw them again, some New York writers, including but not limited to, CAVS, KEY, SENTO, SANE (RIP), and SMITH, made a concentrated effort to paint freight trains in the 1980s. Fortunately many of these early freight train graffiti pieces were photographed, preserving them for posterity.

At the same time, from the mid to late 1980s, graffiti writers in Los Angeles and the Bay Area independently got the same idea, and began painting freight trains as well. These early west coast freight writers included RISKY, DREAM, POWER, FRAME and CHARLIE/ PORN/OCHO in Los Angeles, and CRAYONE, VOGUE, DREAM (RIP) and PICASSO in the Bay Area.[2] At that time, there were no websites or nationally distributed magazines through which writers in different cities could communicate, and unlike today, few writers were able to connect on an inter-city basis to know who had seen the trains they painted in other cities around the country. Some exceptions to this were RISKY, POWER, FRAME and CHARLIE/PORN/OCHO who traveled to New York City and discovered that New York writers they met there like CAVS and SMITH had seen their freights just as they had seen NYC writers' freights in LA (Gastman *et al.* 2006). That realization was an epiphany that ignited the proliferation of the freight train graffiti movement on both coasts. Friends told friends and in traveling to other cities writers began to realize that the freight trains they painted were being spotted across the continent and the movement spread across the continent like wildfire during a dry California summer.

However, it is worth noting that these early freight pioneers did not concentrate exclusively on painting freight trains as many of the big name freight writers of the last decade have. Freights were just another medium, another target, in their individual and collective mission to traverse the urban landscape and conquer every aspect of it by painting their assumed identities on anything and everything they possibly could. It was not until the early to mid-1990s that the freight train graffiti movement graduated into what could be truly considered the first golden age of freight train graffiti.

The first golden age of freight train graffiti

With the gradual accumulation of graffiti pieces on freight trains in North America, an increasing number of writers from all corners of the continent realized the potential fame that could be garnered by painting freight trains in a deliberate and concentrated manner. Although it seemed to many early writers of this period that once they painted a freight and the car got pulled from the yard, that it might never be seen again, many of them knew that other writers around the country would eventually see them and therefore committed themselves to painting as many freights with as high quality pieces as they could, thereby increasing the probability that other writers in different parts of the continent would see them. By the early to mid-1990s certain writers from every corner of the continent were fully committed to and involved in the systematic painting of graffiti on freight trains. This was truly the first golden age of the freight train graffiti movement, and many of today's most renowned writers, some of whom participated in this first golden age of freight train graffiti, found their inspiration in trains they saw that were painted during this time.

I myself painted my first freight train in 1994, at the age of sixteen. Driving my first car, a 1983 Oldsmobile Brougham, I was invited by some older writers I knew from AWR/MSK to go with them to the famed Woodman yard in the San Fernando Valley section of Los Angeles. It hadn't occurred to me at that age and at that point in my subcultural career that I was taking part in graffiti history, and consequently I didn't even think to take a picture of what I or anyone else that night had painted, but it is a memory I will always carry with me for the rest of my life. Many more hundreds and thousands of nights painting freights have long since been forgotten in a toxic fume of aerosol paint, marijuana smoke, and malt liquor, but that night will always stay with me.

During this time there were too many yards being painted, and too many writers and crews active across the country to name them all. However, I will make a modest attempt to name writers and crews from different parts of the country who I personally saw were active during that time. In Los Angeles, the most active writers not mentioned before whom I saw running on freight trains included, but were not limited to: SK8 CBS (RIP), MEK CBS, STRIP CBS, KRISES AWR/FK, LOOK FK, PHABLE AWR, BLES AWR, KEPT AWR, HAZE AWR, FATE AWR/MSK, SABER AWR/MSK, GKAE AWR/MSK, PUSH MSK, CHUNK MSK, BUS MSK, HAVOK MSK, BABA, JERO ICR, BLITS ICR, KOOLS ICR, KEYN AWR/ICR, PURE ICR (RIP), KICK TCS, BUDS, CHIL USC, BIG5 FU, SAHL COI, 125 CULT, UNIT, FEAR DCV, DOVE DCV, CHICO and BRUIN. From other areas of the west coast and the southwest, including the Bay Area, San Diego, and New Mexico, the most active writers not mentioned before whom I saw running on freight trains included, but were not limited to: JASE BA, KRASH TDK, POEM TDK, KING157, RASTA HS, HASH HS/TLT/RTM, FATE RTM, ZEN RTM, HIGH BA, FELON BA, NEON BA, ATOM BA, RENOS HTK, JALER TVC, ONOROK NG/LIES, 21 RAK NG, KAPER NG and SUG NG.[3]

Figure 3.1 Jase BA, Golden West flat boxcar, later re-stamped Southern Pacific, Oakland, CA circa late 1990s © the author

From the New York to Philadelphia eastern seaboard, the most active writers not mentioned before whom I saw running on freight trains included, but were not limited to: SIEN5 BFK, MONE BFK, PAVS, JENT, VISM BFK, CAMP, MILK TFP, STAK TFP, ZEPHYR, WANE, HUSH, IZ THE WIZ (RIP), FREE5, MUZE, PINK, TECK BS, NACE DF MAYHEM (RIP), NEWA MAYHEM, RIME KCW, SETUP KCW, CHIP 7 KCW/MAYHEM, CYCLE, KET MTK, DG NWC, KAWS, PRE/CRISPO, SACH and SOON. From Miami and Atlanta, the most active writers whom I saw running on freight trains included, but were not limited to: FAVES WH/FS/NETWORK, BASER FS/NETWORK, HARSH FS, DAKS FS/NETWORK, SB NETWORK, GSOUTH WH/FS/NETWORK, CHISME WH/FS/NETWORK, SMASH FS/NETWORK and CHROME MSG. Finally from Canada, the most active writers whom I saw running on freight trains included, but were not limited to: VIRUS AA, COSOE, SNEKE EDK, HEWS EDK, and WENT EDK. There are more writers from smaller cities or rural areas of North America whom I did not mention, but this list covers the majority of the active writers from that generation.[4]

Writers from that era painted at a number of locally and nationally known freight yards, including but not limited to: the Ghost Yard in Queens NY, the Sunset Park Ditch in Brooklyn NY, various layups in Bushwick Brooklyn NY, The Bronx Yard in the South Bronx NY, the GM Plant Yard in Elizabeth NJ, the Oakland Yards in the Bay Area, the Berkeley Layups in the Bay Area, the Budweiser Yard in LA, the Woodman Yard in LA, the LA River Yard in East LA, the Bandini Yard in LA, the Oxnard Yard north of LA, the Pomona Yard East of LA, and the Santa Fe Springs Yard in LA.[5] There are many more yards of course, but many of them are still active locations for graffiti painting, and I don't want to "burn" any of the few remaining spots left to those who still paint freights.

The first golden era in the freight train graffiti movement ended in the late 1990s, when railroad companies got fed up with writers painting in yards in broad daylight, leaving trash

Figure 3.2 Vism BFK, shortline boxcar, Bronx, NY circa late 1990s © the author

and empty paint cans in the yards, and acting recklessly, threatening the safety of both writers and train workers. One such event led to the death of LA graffiti icon SK8 CBS LOD (RIP), who at that time was the most renowned graffiti writer in Los Angeles. After painting freights in broad daylight at the Woodman yard in LA, he stepped back into the path of an active track to take pictures, and was clipped and dragged under a passing train, which shredded his body in the most gruesome manner possible. This occurred in the presence of his longtime girlfriend, BLOSM MTA, and a number of their friends who were also present. One can only imagine what impact this event had on their mental well-being.

In response to the safety concerns presented by graffiti writers painting trains in freight yards, the rail companies instituted a number of enforcement measures to prevent graffiti writers from freely painting graffiti in freight yards. The most significant practice was the use of law enforcement officers employed by the rail companies, commonly called "rail cops" or simply "The Bull," to patrol freight train yards in order to catch graffiti writers in the act of painting graffiti. Many rail companies including Union Pacific and Norfolk Southern employ both uniformed law enforcement officers, as well as investigative officers, to track, catch, and arrest freight train graffiti writers. Another measure that was taken to protect freight train yards from graffiti writers was the construction of fencing and barbed wire barriers in order to prevent writers from entering freight train yards. Rail companies also made a concerted effort to remove brush and trash from adjacent properties, so as to reduce the available areas that graffiti writers could hide in to avoid detection by rail cops.

The second golden age of the freight train graffiti movement

After the initial crackdown on freight train graffiti by the railroad companies and local law enforcement agencies in the mid to late 1990s, a number of writers gave up painting freight trains, either because they had been arrested for doing so, or friends of theirs had. The sudden threat of arrest for painting freight trains was a paradigmatic shift that produced such a degree of cognitive dissonance that many writers could not psychologically overcome it. Previously, they had perceived freights as a risk-free medium for painting graffiti, with the added bonus that someone in another part of the country might actually see what they had painted. When the threat of arrest came crashing down on yards across the country, many writers gave up painting freight trains altogether and declared to other writers that "freights are dead."[6]

Although some writers continued to paint trains through the late 1990s and at the turn of the millennium, the second golden age of freight train graffiti did not fully develop until a few years after the turn of the millennium. Two particular circumstances, contributed to the emergence of a second golden age of freight train graffiti. First, after police and railroad authorities began arresting writers at many of the popular yards that were painted in the 1980s and 1990s, writers stopped going to them. This resulted in a period of a number of years, depending on the yard, during which no one, or very few writers, dared to paint in those yards.

With the abandonment of yards by writers, rail cops eventually had no one left to arrest, and over the years more or less stopped checking yards for graffiti writers. Some very few clever writers realized this dynamic and took advantage of it to paint large quantities of freight trains in yards that were considered "burned" by most other writers. Without the competition and foot traffic that had previously burned yards, these writers were able to produce a massive quantity of graffiti in a relatively short period of time. When other writers saw these trains, and realized that people were painting freight trains in earnest again, the freight train graffiti movement took off all over again. However, this new generation of freight train writers, some of whom were pioneers of the freight train graffiti movement or had participated in the first golden age, modified their motivations and methods to match an elevated state of surveillance from railroad authorities and law enforcement agencies.

The second circumstance was the exponential increase in communication between writers in different parts of the country, facilitated in large part by the proliferation of graffiti websites like www.12ozProphet.com, which enabled writers across the continent and the world to contact and communicate with each other for the first time. Indeed, no single circumstance has contributed to the globalization of the graffiti subculture more than the advent of the internet (Austin 2001; Snyder 2009). For the first time, writers from all over the country were contacting each other, communicating and traveling to paint with each other across the continent; writers could see for themselves on the internet, or hear from friends and acquaintances on the phone, where and when freight trains they had painted had been spotted by other writers across the continent. Threads on certain websites like the Metal Heads blog on www.12ozProphet.com were dedicated solely to freight train graffiti, enabling writers to post pictures of their freights and those they had photographed in their yards on the internet for other writers the world over to view.

As a result of this increased communication and contact between writers from different parts of North America, for the first time writers started joining crews from other parts of the country in large numbers. Whereas members of graffiti crews during the 1980s and 1990s were typically all from the same city or area, in recent years, many crews have been made up of writers from multiple cities and regions across the country. Some of these crews are among the most prolific crews of the modern freight train graffiti movement, including but not limited to: A2M, FGS, FU, KYT/DTC, MAYHEM, NSF, TKO, WH, FS, NETWORK and DOS. The names of some of these crews reflect their dedication to primarily painting freight trains, including: Addicted

Figure 3.3 Chisme WH/FS/Network, UPFE refrigerated car, Miami, FL circa early 2000s © the author

2 Metal, Freight GangsterS, Freight Unit, and Freight Stars. The crew NETWORK took as their symbol a capitol N with a circle around it, which is a common marking on the wheel casing of freight trains. Although these nationwide crews were originally located in certain states or cities – A2M in Texas, KYT/DTC in the Bay Area, FGS and TKO in LA, WH and FS in Miami, and NETWORK in Atlanta – their members have moved throughout the country and new members from different parts of the country have been recruited. Furthermore, some of these crews have traded members, resulting in writers who are members of multiple crews from different parts of the country. The Weed Heads crew, originally from Miami is a prime example, including the following prolific freight train writers from the first and second golden ages of the freight train graffiti movement: GHOULS WH/A2M, WYSE WH/A2M, GSOUTH WH/TKO/FS/NETWORK, CHISME WH/FS/NETWORK, FAVES WH/FS/NETWORK, COLT .45 WH/TKO, MAD WH/NSF/ESC, AEST WH/DOS and LYES WH/DOS.

This second golden age of freight train graffiti has expanded the painting of freight trains exponentially from the last golden age, and there are far too many writers and crews to name who have made significant contributions to the freight train graffiti movement since the turn of the millennium. However, I will attempt to name as many of these writers who have not already been mentioned, as memory permits, for the purpose of this chapter, including but not limited to, and in no particular order: SIGH DOS, WORMS A2M, ERUPTO A2M, NEKST A2M, LEWIS A2M, CRAE A2M, VIZIE A2M, LEAD A2M, DEBT A2M, GLUE, UTAH, ZINE, PEPE, DECO TMB, CS TFK, KUMA, MOOSE, KERO, KWEST, EYE MAYHEM, NAVY8 MAYHEM, MET MAYHEM, MAD ESC, GESER 3A, KEM 3A, HENCE, SEAZ, KEMOS, DASAR MSP, CENSE MSP, PHONE WH/MC, VOICE WH, DIME WH, MECA WH, GUER WH/LD/TKO, OBCES LD/TKO, HOACS LD, GATES, SWEK, REGAL, SMASH FS/NETWORK, OILS WH/FS (RIP), DZ WH/KBT, SICKS WH/KBT, BASH WH/KBT, ZINK WH/TKO, ISTO, MENES, JEKA TM, ARYS TBK, MBER FS/HM, MUCH HM, SPEL HM, YEN HM, MONK SCA, JABER KYT, EATFUK KYT/DTC, VEKS KYT, KIRO DTC, DIAR DTC, SMOG KYT/DTC, ESKIMO KYT, BITER TBK, PIER TBK, TROUBLE TBK, CAMEO WCB, KAPUT WCB, NECS NSF, AREK NSF, REKE NSF, CON NSF, DRUGS TVC, FOKIS TVC/LTS, GESO IBD, BEGER FGS, APART FGS, ADGE FGS, PRAE FGS, KEB5 FGS, HATE FGS, PLEK FGS/WAI, KE42 FGS/TKO/WH, BUKET TKO/R10, RICKS TKO/SAC, SCAN 54 MDS, APES FCR, AROE, CLOWN TITS, MEWZ TITS, NECRO TITS, COUPE, CROW, SE ONE TA, MPOWER, DIET END, SICK156, SIZE 21, SINEK WA/FACT/WH, TOKEN WA/FACT/WH, TAKE5, AWE TCI, HEAT TCI, HYBRID TCI, MYTH WCB/TCI, SAMO WCB, EROS TCI, ICHABOD, JURNE YME, LEARN YME, and REMIO VTS. There are many more writers who have at some time painted freight trains, but these writers who have been mentioned are those who have made a significant commitment to systematically painting freight trains in as much quantity as possible.

The second golden age of the freight train graffiti movement has been on the decline for the past few years for a number of reasons. Principally among these is that it is a victim of its own success. As more and more younger, inexperienced "toy" writers around the country have been inspired by the work of the writers mentioned above, more and more toys have infiltrated freight train yards and "burned" them by painting over train markings, leaving trash and empty cans in the yard, day painting, threatening or assaulting train workers, writing on surrounding walls and areas around train yards, stealing from boxcars, crossing out or going over other writers' pieces, and other practices that are frowned upon by experienced freight train writers.

A second reason for the current decline is that as the popularity of the freight train graffiti movement increases, more writers want to paint trains. Therefore more writers are going to

Figure 3.4 Sigh DOS, Canadian Northern boxcar, artist from Richmond, VA, car painted in Los Angeles, CA circa mid 2000s © the author

train yards and "burning" them so no one can paint there. Consequently, security has again been increased by railroad companies, including regular patrols by rail cops; the installation of bright floodlights in most yards, which light up freight yards at night; and local law enforcement has once again become attentive to the painting of graffiti on freight trains in many jurisdictions. Many train yards that for a time were being painted regularly by experienced and prolific writers, are again the target of regular law enforcement sweeps, making them enticing locations for only the most novice of "toy" freight writers. Thus, the ebb and flow of vandalism, enforcement, vandalism and enforcement, continues.

A third reason for the decline of the second golden age of the freight train graffiti movement has been the proliferation of beefs between different crews of train writers. Whereas pieces and throw-ups on city walls that are dissed or gone over can be fixed, on freight trains, once a piece is dissed, the victim may never have the opportunity to fix his defaced piece. The problem has been exacerbated by novice "toy" writers who do not respect established writers and diss or go over their pieces in an attempt to get "cheap fame" by having beef with a known and respected writer. The result is a mess of dissed pieces, and poorly executed pieces done by novice writers on most freight trains today.

Conclusion

With this historical narrative, I have laid out the history of the freight train graffiti movement within the wider graffiti subculture. It is important to first consider the history of social phenomena before engaging in fieldwork to examine the various facets of those phenomena in order to best situate the data collected in fieldwork in its proper historical context. Without knowledge of the historical foundations of a subculture, examination and description of that subculture would be lacking. Therefore I offer this rather brief analysis of the history of the freight train graffiti subculture as a starting point for future research, and also to give credit where credit is due, to the writers who spent a considerable portion of their lives establishing and maintaining this particular niche within the wider graffiti subculture. Future research will expand on this foundation to examine and offer an in-depth examination of the various aspects of the freight train graffiti subculture, just as scholars like Castleman (1982), Ferrell (1995a, 1995b, 1996, 1998), Austin (2001), Macdonald (2001), Snyder (2009), and Ferrell and Weide (2010) have examined the graffiti subculture on subway trains and on the streets of our nation's cities.

Notes

1   Special thanks to FAVES WH/FS/NETWORK and GSOUTH WH/FS/NETWORK for their help in recalling the names of writers, magazines and videos in composing this chapter.
2   There were two different writers who wrote the name DREAM in Los Angeles and the Bay Area, respectively.
3   Some of these writers relocated to Northern California from places like the Washington DC/Baltimore area.
4   I apologize to anyone who I missed at any point in this chapter. Unlike other publications on the subject, the absence of anyone's name in particular is due to nothing other than my own lack of recollection. As proof, for anyone who knows my subcultural identity, I have included multiple names of writers with whom I have engaged in beefs with over the years. The absence of anyone's name in this or any other list in this chapter should not detract from the contributions they and others know they have made during their graffiti careers. Also, writers' crew affiliations in this section and throughout the chapter reflect their crew affiliations during the period being discussed. Many writers mentioned are no longer affiliated with crews they were with at one time.
5   Some of these yards do not exist as active rail yards anymore, the rest are usually very difficult to paint due to increased security since that time.
6   I recall being told this by CHUNK MSK and FATE AWR/MSK in the late 1990s, who had taken part in the first golden age of freight train graffiti.

References

Abel, E.L. & Buckley, B.E. (1977). *The Handwriting on the Wall: Toward a Sociology and Psychology of Graffiti.* Westport, CT: Greenwood Press.
Austin, J. (2001). *Taking the Train.* New York: Columbia University Press.
Castleman, C. (1982). *Getting up.* Cambridge, MA: The MIT Press.
Conquergood, D. (1993). *Homeboys and Hoods: Gang Communication and Cultural Space.* Evanston, IL: Center for Urban Affairs and Policy Research, Northwestern University.
Conquergood, D. (1997). "Street Literacy" in Flood, J., Heath, S.B., & Lape, D. (Eds) *Handbook of Research on Teaching Literacy Through the Communicative and Visual Arts.* (pp. 354–374). New York: Simon & Schuster MacMillan.
Ferrell, J. (1995a). "Urban Graffiti: Crime, Control and Resistance," *Youth & Society.* 27(1), 73–92.
Ferrell, J. (1995b). "The World Politics of Wall Painting" in Ferrell, J. & Sanders, C.R. (Eds) *Cultural Criminology.* (pp. 277–294). Boston, MA: Northeastern University Press.
Ferrell, J. (1996). *Crimes of Style.* Boston, MA: Northeastern University Press.
Ferrell, J. (1998). "Freight Train Graffiti: Subculture, Media, Dislocation," *Justice Quarterly.* 15(4), 101–122.
Ferrell, J. & Weide, R.D. (2010). "Spot Theory," *CITY Journal.* 14(1–2), 48–62.
Gastman, R., Rowland, D., & Sattler, I. (2006). *Freight Train Graffiti.* New York: Abrams.
Hutchison, R. (1993). "Blazon Nouveau: Gang Graffiti in the Barrios of Los Angeles and Chicago" in Cummings, S. & Monti, D.J. (Eds) *Gangs: The Origin and Impact of Contemporary Youth Gangs in the United States.* (pp. 137–171). Albany: SUNY Press.
Lachmann, R. (1988). "Graffiti as Career and Ideology," *American Journal of Sociology.* 94(1), 229–250.
Macdonald, N. (2001). *The Graffiti Subculture.* New York: Palgrave Macmillan.

Phillips, S.A. (1999). *Wallbangin': Graffiti and Gangs in LA*. Chicago, IL: The University of Chicago Press.

Sandmeyer, E.C. (1939/1991). *The Anti-Chinese Movement in California*. Urbana, IL: University of Illinois Press.

Saxton, A. (1971). *The Indispensible Enemy: Labor and the Anti-Chinese Movement in California*. Berkeley, CA: University of California Press.

Snyder, G.J. (2009). *Graffiti Lives: Beyond the Tag in New York's Urban Underground*. New York: NYU Press.

www.12ozProphet.com: Metal Heads thread. Accessed July 2014.

www.CSX.com: Accessed July 2014.

4

Deconstructing gang graffiti

Susan A. Phillips

Introduction

Gang graffiti is a longstanding form of graffiti production. With some traditions spanning over eighty years, gang graffiti's longevity is second in the United States only to hobo writing (Livingston, 1910; Daniels, 2008; also see Lennon, this volume).[1] Despite its substantial history, gang graffiti's marginality and connection to criminality and violence have resulted in relatively little academic analysis, disproportionately negative characterizations from popular media and law enforcement, and rampant misconceptions about its purpose and content.

This chapter begins with a brief introduction to gangs as social groups and provides some fundamentals for understanding gang graffiti by looking at law enforcement practices surrounding gang graffiti and scholarship on gang graffiti. I then turn to two case studies, both based in Los Angeles. A final section examines the entrance of the gang-related "cholo" style into global circuits of graffiti production.

Graffiti and gangs

Gangs are small-scale social groups associated with criminal behavior, violence, and drug dealing. Gangs operate in many countries, in contexts from first to fourth worlds. They have varying relationships to broader criminal enterprises, kinship systems, and cultural groups. Some gangs have arisen independently or in conjunction with transnational law enforcement patterns, such as deportation (Zilberg, 2011). The United States Federal Bureau of Investigation (FBI), a national security and intelligence organization, estimates that there are over 1.4 million gang members in the United States, with membership in 33,000 gangs.[2]

Associations between gangs and graffiti exist globally. In the United States, gang graffiti is associated with written systems of representation that appear in various media – on walls, on bodies, in dance, in speech, and, increasingly, on internet forums. Gangs use graffiti to define neighborhood space, to create lists of members, to signal affiliation, identity, enmity or alliance with other individuals or groups, and to create memorials. Gang writing usually carries cultural aspects of the broader social groups from which gangs emerge, as well as carrying symbolic representations of affiliation, enmity, and alliance with other groups (Vigil, 1988; Alonso, 1999; Phillips, 1999).

Several related factors fostered the development of gang writing in the urban United States. Hostilities in neighborhoods and in prisons, a lack of hierarchical communication, and the need to communicate neighborhood identity in absentia, all forced reliance on abstract messaging. As Jack Goody suggests, "writing represents not only a method of communication at a distance, but a means of distancing oneself from communication" (1986: p. 50).

In that sense gang graffiti acts as a semi-permanent alternative that represents neighborhoods without the risk of human presence. Graffiti is a particular written medium that helps gangs to define neighborhood space and infuse it with prideful or aggressive messages. Graffiti writing allows gang members to assert their identity despite tensions with warring groups or sanctions by law enforcement officials. In the process they have developed distinct styles and practices, and have made use of multiple media in which to express their messages.

Gang graffiti and law enforcement practices

In the United States, gangs have generated a significant amount of police interest since the early twentieth century. Police interpretations of gang graffiti range from being highly informed to laden with false assumptions. Informed practices involve police using graffiti to chart membership, map neighborhoods, and follow conflicts between individuals and groups.

More problematic interpretations involve a core assumption that aggressive graffiti leads to gang violence, a claim that has been contested in scholarly and activist arenas (Alonso, 1999; Phillips, 1999). The Los Angeles Police Department website, for example, states that, because gangs use graffiti to create intimidation, "innocent residents are often subjected to gang violence by the mere presence of graffiti in their neighborhood."[3] No statistical evidence, however, is offered for statements such as these, which rely on assumed linkages between gang graffiti and violence. Alonso (1999) offers a spatial analysis that de-couples graffiti from violent acts. Phillips (1999) reports that gangs will continue to cross out the names of enemies even if warfare between them is no longer active. Determining whether graffiti acts a driver of gang warfare in any neighborhood context requires more empirical data gathering and analysis.

Even when law enforcement minimizes direct links between graffiti and violence, gang graffiti is associated with "broken windows" policing, which posits that targeting smaller crimes, such as vandalism, will lead to the prevention of larger crimes. Though widely adopted as a law enforcement strategy, broken windows policing remains an unproven theory that has been debated in both law enforcement and academic circles (see, e.g. Harcourt, 2005).

In terms of legislation, penalties for gang-related graffiti may be subject to gang enhancements, which are legal mechanisms that provide lengthier sentences based on gang-related status. Gang enhancements may add time to graffiti vandalism sentences when the perpetrator is a gang member and/or when graffiti is shown to be in service of a gang. Gang enhancements added to vandalism charges can change the designation of a crime to a more serious misdemeanor or can convert a misdemeanor crime to a felony.

In California, graffiti and other forms of gang representation, such as handsigning, clothing, tattoos, or photography, comprise five of ten criteria that enable police to identify individuals as gang members. These criteria were established via California's 1988 Street Terrorism Enforcement and Prevention Act (STEP), state legislation designed to protect the public from the violence of gangs (Katz & Webb, 2006; Klein & Maxson, 2010). The ten criteria are as follows, with specific references to graffiti appearing in numbers six and ten:

1 Admits gang membership or association.
2 Is observed to associate on a regular basis with known gang members.
3 Has tattoos indicating gang membership.
4 Wears gang clothing, symbols, etc., to identify with a specific gang.

5   Is in a photograph with known gang members and/or using gang-related hand signs.
6   Is named on a gang document, hit list, or gang-related graffiti.
7   Is identified as a gang member by a reliable source.
8   Is arrested in the company of identified gang members or associates.
9   Corresponds with known gang members or writes and/or receives correspondence about gang activities.
10 Writes about gangs (graffiti) on walls, books, paper, etc.[4]

If individuals meet two of the ten criteria, they can be identified as gang members in a court of law and subject to the gang sentencing enhancements described above. (These were also established by the STEP Act). Meeting two of ten criteria also merits placement of individuals in the CalGang Database, a statewide database that tracks purportedly gang-related individuals for law-enforcement purposes.

Several activist and policy organizations, including the Youth Justice Coalition (YJC) and the Justice Policy Institute, have tracked use of the CalGang database, and have advocated ways in which youth can find out if they are on it, and can be removed from the list. The database is secret and can include minors. Most people are unaware that their names are included because they can be placed on it "without having been arrested or accused of criminal activity" (Muñiz & McGill, 2012: p. 4). The CalGang Database may be used further to determine who is served with gang injunctions – which are civil mechanisms that limit the freedom of gang-related as opposed to non-gang related individuals (Green & Pranis, 2007; Muñiz & McGill, 2012).

Given the role of graffiti and other expressive media in the ten criteria used to identify gang members, it is possible that at least some of the over 200,000 individuals in the CalGang Database have been placed there for representational reasons alone. Clearly more analysis of the CalGang Database is necessary, but only one group – the YJC cited above – has managed to access the data necessary for such analysis.

In 2012, the Los Angeles City Attorney's office used the gang injunction mechanism against members of a graffiti crew called Metro Transit Assassins (MTA) (Romero, 2012). The injunction prohibits members of MTA from being together in public or possessing graffiti tools. It also mandates individuals named in the injunction to obey an adult curfew. According to the YJC, many non-gang graffiti crews are also placed in the CalGang Database. Because of the close alignment of graffiti with the penalization of youth, the YJC recently worked to challenge a proposed citywide graffiti injunction (Muñiz & McGill, 2012).

Punitive graffiti-related policing strategies are intended to help stop graffiti writers from graduating to more serious kinds of crimes or gang related behavior. But there is no empirical evidence demonstrating the effectiveness of these tactics. Using gang-related policing tools against non-gang members, such as graffiti writers, confounds different kinds of graffiti writing groups and ultimately produces harmful youth-based profiling without substantive evidence.

Despite law enforcement knowledge of gang graffiti practices, even highly informed agencies such as the LAPD or the FBI regularly display ignorance of the distinction between gang writing and the graffiti of graffiti crews that stem from the New York tradition. Law enforcement agencies routinely place images of hip-hop style tags on their web site and other materials and mislabel these as gang graffiti. At best this practice demonstrates the lack of a holistic understanding of gangs that includes forms of representation. At worst such mistakes compromise law enforcement expertise regarding gang-related issues more broadly.[5]

Reading the walls can be an informative policing tool when law enforcement personnel minimize assumptions and maximize reliance on empirical data. Graffiti can tell police a great deal about the geography of gangs, their membership, and about ongoing rivalries. But the overreliance on assumptions rather than empiricism is widespread. This is in part because of how limited scholarship on gang graffiti has been. Of the few analyses conducted, an even smaller number carry an applied focus that might have resonance within policing arenas. Studies tend to remain buried in book chapters or journal articles whose content prioritizes academic issues. This work carries little relevance for policing practices both because of the weight given to theoretical concerns, and because findings are critical of policing practices to begin with.

As evidenced from the above discussion, analyses of power and injustice as related to gang identification, and the use of gang-related legal mechanisms against graffiti crews are critically important. Scholarship certainly has a role to play in terms of checking police strategies with regard to graffiti and gangs. But police officers in both rank-and-file and administrative capacities tend to ignore research that might be relevant unless it stems from academic criminology/criminal justice, a discipline that is perceived by some as already acting as a small arm of law enforcement.

Scholarship on gang graffiti

Despite its prevalence in urban landscapes, gang graffiti's study has been eclipsed by an overwhelming focus on contemporary street art and on graffiti styles that emerged from 1970s New York (see, e.g. Cooper & Chalfant, 1984; Austin, 2001; Grody, 2006; Ganz, 2009). A small number of scholars have focused on gang graffiti exclusively or as part of broader research projects. There are only two contemporary book-length treatments of gang graffiti (Phillips, 1999; Chastanet, 2009), as well as one book that folds graffiti into a surface-level treatment of gangs (Leet *et al.*, 2000). These works attempt to translate gang graffiti and symbols for a broader audience, link graffiti to other aspects of gang life, and examine the style and meaning behind graffiti for practitioners.

Though the study of gang graffiti is underdeveloped, case studies in Los Angeles, San Francisco, Phoenix, Chicago, and Philadelphia have resulted in two discernible threads of scholarly interest. These revolve around issues of language and representation, and territory and landscape, respectively. I return to the concern with style and aesthetics in a later section.

Scholarly interest in gang graffiti began with a 1974 landmark study conducted in Philadelphia by geographers David Ley and Roman Cybrwisky. Published in the *Annals of the Association of American Geographers*, "Urban Graffiti as Territorial Markers" is the first published article that takes gang graffiti as its primary topic. Ley and Cybrwisky mapped the spatial layout of graffiti in Philadelphia neighborhoods and distinguished between different kinds of graffiti and the role that these were playing. They noted the presence of "aggressive" or "affirmative" graffiti and mapped these in relation to other neighborhood boundaries.

Graffiti is one lens through which scholars continue to examine links between gangs and territoriality. Geographer Alex Alonso (1999) follows Ley and Cybrwisky's (1974) work in his work on Los Angeles gang graffiti. In this case their analysis of gang graffiti bleeds into or stems from broader discourses in human geography for people like Timothy Cresswell who theorize the place-making strategies of individuals and groups (Cresswell, 1996).

In one case, scholars have used graffiti as a "proxy for scent marking" to draw parallels between the territorial behavior of gangs and coyotes, wolves, or honeybees (Smith *et al.*, 2012). The work exhibits a fairly nuanced understanding of gangs. But the authors exhibit little awareness that comparing contemporary gang members to coyotes and wolves contributes to dehumanizing discourses surrounding those populations. In most cases, graffiti-based work on gangs counters facile law enforcement or popular beliefs that gang members act like dogs marking territories.

In the other cases, scholarly analysis feeds into examinations of social power, and relationships to dominant cultures, cultural formation, and social exclusion. Beginning in the 1990s, gang graffiti was included in several studies with a focus on sociolinguistics. These works expand ethnographies of literacy, examine the boundaries between oral and written communication, analyze overlap with other media such as tattoo, dance, clothing, and makeup (Mendoza-Denton, 2008), and query interrelationships between material expression and identity (Rymes, 1996; Phillips, 1999; Mendoza-Denton, 2008).

Rhetorician Ralph Cintron (1998) describes gang graffiti as repetitive semiotic indicators that communicate respect and identity in hostile conditions. He identifies four "negative morphemes" in Chicago-based gang expression. Cintron (1998) considers these negative morphemes to include reversed letters, inverted letters/symbols, the addition of the letter K, and "cracking," or crossing out. All mark disrespect for other groups, and allow gang members to use graffiti to engage in symbolic battles over respect and disrespect. For Cintron, studying gangs is part of a broader project regarding how people create respect in "situations of little or no respect." He offers that precise styles, neat and clean lettering counters neighborhood environments that are neither neat nor clean.

Where Cintron (1998) is interested in morphemes as akin to parts of speech, Adams and Winter (1997) position Phoenix gang writing as a "discourse genre," emphasizing its equivalence to speech acts. They analyze over 1500 instances of gang graffiti as "turns" and "utterances," viewing them as monologues and dialogues. Adams and Winter (1997) view intergang antagonisms on the walls as following explicit norms and conventions. They see gang graffiti as systematic and rule-driven and as an interactive, dialogic process.

Author of another Chicago-based case study, Dwight Conquergood (1997) describes how gangs use graffiti to navigate between invisibility and hypervisibility and in the process create complex symbolic and written performances that he describes as "gangster grammatology" (Conquergood, 1997: p. 358). He analyzes the complex lexicon of Chicago-based People and Folk gangs, which divide into two groups that take the numbers five and six, the five-pointed and six-pointed stars, and a host of other symbols associated with particular gangs. Phillips' (2009) work on Bloods and Crips, two well-known national gangs, also examines linguistic elements of gang expression in multiple media. Phillips describes different crossovers between graffiti, tattoo, speech, handsigning, and even dance.

As a whole, scholarly analysis counters the notion that gang graffiti is solely about marking territory. Academics show that gang graffiti is deeply social, based in communities, it represents interpersonal or intergroup relationships within neighborhoods, it plays in and out of related media, and it is about symbolic negotiations of power both within gangs and between gangs and the larger society. Rather than symbolizing control over turf alone, gang graffiti signals control over respect in neighborhoods.

Gendered analyses of gang graffiti remain under examined. While female gang members do write graffiti, they write with more frequency in indoor spaces or on notebooks. In addition to ignoring women's work, scholarship tends also to ignore explicitly masculinist components of writing and what gang writing means in terms of constructing masculinity.

Two case studies

I now turn to two case studies of gang writing in Los Angeles, California. The first introduces the basics of Chicano gang writing, and the second looks at the graffiti symbolism of African-American gangs called Bloods and Crips.

In Los Angeles, gang writing begins in Latino barrios in the 1930s and 1940s as a straightforward association of individual names with neighborhoods (see Figure 4.1). To some degree this system is based in an earlier tradition of hobo writing that dates back to the turn of the century

Figure 4.1 "Eddie DT" means that Eddie is from the neighborhood called Dog Town. Written in railroad tar and dated August 9, 1948. Permission of author

(see John Lennon's chapter on Hobo Graffiti in this book). At its most basic level, gang graffiti recalls Norman Mailer's quip that "the name is the faith of graffiti" (Kurlansky *et al.*, 1974).

For Eddie and others who wrote underneath the bridges around the L.A. River in the late 1940s, railroad tar was a key medium. Black tar would drip from passing freights, and kids would either put globs of tar onto fingers, or put the tar into a container to dab on with a stick. Several dozen instances of gang graffiti survive from this era.

Tar has a special longevity as a medium. Tar wins any war with spray paint. If whitewashed or written over, tar will soon reappear from underneath the paint. With time, tar will also etch into concrete, so that writing may survive in *bas* relief even after the tar falls off. Additional graffiti media from the early period of gang writing include chalk, railroad spikes or rocks on concrete, pencil, charcoal, lighters, and crayon. These are surprisingly durable, whereas spray paint will fade with time. Other media include shoeshine polish, paint and brushes, and flares. Most kids used what they had on hand or found along their journeys.

The 1940s aesthetic traditions included the use of quotations surrounding two or four corners of the composition, the use of crosses topping the compositions, the production of simple fonts usually in squared capital letters and sometimes including serifs, and a balance between compositional elements.

For Chicano gangs in Los Angeles, the basic association between neighborhoods, names, and dates eventually branched out to include expanding arenas of gang politics. By the 1990s these included age-graded cliques, streets, city or neighborhood names, regional divisions, the telephone area code, and a prison-based northern or southern designation (Phillips, 1999). This broader system remains the core, though not the sum total, of what gang members write (see Figure 4.2).

Figure 4.2 TxFlats, Goofy, Demon, Sparky, Sur 13. Permission of author

Figure 4.2 from the Tortilla Flats neighborhood demonstrates a telescoping process of representing identity. Several levels of affiliation are present in this composition. The top line reads "Goofy, Demon, Sparky," which are the names of individual gang members. Goofy, first on the list, is probably responsible for the composition. Below is a larger "TxFlats" for the Tortilla Flats neighborhood, with "x" being null space. Further below is the name of the clique to which those members listed belong: the Dukes. Cliques are smaller, subgroups of members who are usually the same age and from the same part of a neighborhood.

On the right side of the composition is a "Sur 13," a general proclamation of the South and a reference to the Eme prison gang. "M" is the thirteenth letter of the alphabet, and is shared as a symbol by some other groups, including bikers, because of its association with marijuana. Chicano gangs had long used the M to mean also *mota* (marijuana) or Mexican. By the 1990s, the 13/M was an exclusive reference to the Mexican Mafia prison gang, also known as *La Eme*, or "M." The 14/N developed later as a counter-reference to Northern California and the Northern prison gang, *Nuestra Familia*.

Prison gangs like *La Eme* extort taxes from street gangs, whose members must send a portion of profits from criminal activities to incarcerated members. Most gangs are beholden to this system for support. Use of the thirteen in gang names and compositions precedes *La Eme*'s control over this symbol, which is part of why it has been successful. Today usage of the thirteen in compositions – and gangs who claim "Sur" – are references to ties between prison and street gangs. In Figure 4.2, the "S" at the end of the word "Flats" serves as the first letter of "Sur," thus symbolically linking the two aspects of identity.

Missing from this image are references to the region (i.e. Harbor Area) and telephone area code. Although they sometimes appear in writing, region and area code are more commonly referenced in tattoos than graffiti. Both region and area code play into prison-based subgroups known as "cars." Broader than neighborhoods, cars are metaphorical vehicles in which people from the same areas "ride." These individuals may bunk together and spend time together on the prison yard or during meals.

Within Chicano gang writing, the individual name is anchored into a Durkheimian marriage of the gang social system and its collective representation. The writing in Figure 4.2 is a good example of the way Chicano gangs divide their social world in graffiti. Figure 4.3 is a more developed example of graffiti from an aesthetic perspective. Chicano gang members have historically placed significant interest in clean, crisp writing, in the development of specialized fonts, such as Old English or block lettering, and, by the 1990s, in the creation of monumental representations (see Figure 4.3). The section below on "Cholo Writing" goes into more detail regarding Chicano gang aesthetics. Figure 4.3 is an example of monumental block lettering from the "Santeros," or "Street Saints" gang in South Central Los Angeles.

For African-American gangs, the second case study, graffiti traditions followed the example of earlier Chicano gangs. African-American communities in Los Angeles did not develop gangs until the 1950s, when gang development was largely in response to pressure from white racist youth groups. The earliest African-American gang writing documented in L.A. dates from the mid-1960s (Phillips, 1999). An earlier system of African-American gangs was active in the 1950s, and included groups like the Ditalians, Slausons, or Businessmen. The widespread unity resulting from both the Civil Rights Movement and the 1965 Watts Rebellion brought a halt to overt gang warfare between these groups. Toward the end of the 1960s, gang unity was in part disrupted by the same law enforcement tactics, such as COINTELPRO, that disrupted Black Nationalist

Figure 4.3 Block lettering from the Santeros neighborhood, South Central Los Angeles.
Photo permission of author

movements as a whole. By 1969, a new generation of youth formed the Crips, which soon splintered into several groups. Several more groups, such as Brims and Pirus, consolidated to form the Bloods in the early 1970s.

Today African American diasporic linguistic traditions continue to inform African American gang writing. Like Chicano gangs, Bloods and Crips have developed a written system to represent social divides as well as collective power. Crips divide into various sub-categories (Neighborhood Crips, East Coast Crips, Compton Crips, Watts Crips, and so forth). Bloods break down into Bloods, Brims, and Pirus, which are all types of gangs that exist under the Bloods umbrella. Further divisions include the gang name, the names of street-based cliques, individual nicknames, listing of enemy names, and routine crossing out of enemy initials. Any of these categories may be represented in writing as series of words, initials, or numbers.

Gang communication with each other and among gangs is not restricted to graffiti. Within gangs, written conventions crosscut various media. Handsigning is a gang medium that originated in the African-American gang world, in which gestures and finger shapes represent particular letters, numbers, or insignia. Hands form the shapes of letters and are used in person-to-person communication, and also may be signified in graffiti and tattoo. Oral speech conventions also figure into gang writing. Avoidance of key enemy letters, crossing out, and different kinds of spellings represent basic affiliations or animosities and recall the "negative morphemes" Cintron discussed in relation to Chicago-based gangs. Avoidance and crossing out are evidenced in the image that follows.

Figure 4.4 is a composition by the 42,3 Gangster Crips based on 42nd and 42rd Streets in Los Angeles. The writer wrote the gang's initials vertically on the left facing side of the wall. This is partially obscured and reads "423G," with the "C" covered beneath a layer of paint.

Figure 4.4 Enemies of the 42,3 Gangster Crips neighborhood. Photo permission of author

This composition shows both generic and specific enemies of the gang. From left to right, the composition reads: "Fucc Piru Killa, Bloods Killa, and Avalon Killa's all day." Whereas Pirus and Bloods are generic group enemies, Avalon is a fellow Crip gang just west of the 42 Street neighborhood. The writer demonstrates enmity with all three groups and asserts identity in different ways. First is the color choice of blue, the Crips' signature color that stands in contrast to the red of Bloods. Second is avoidance of the initials "ck," which means "Crip Killa," in the word "fuck." By changing "ck" to "cc" the Crips avoid inadvertently denigrating themselves. This mirrors other linguistic strategies on the part of African American gangs. Gang members avoid using certain letter combinations in speech as well as in writing and made frequent use of "disnames," which are derogatory nicknames for enemies.

Next is the proclamation "Piru Killa," in which the "P" is also crossed out. In the word "Blood," not only the B is crossed out, but the two "o"s are also crossed out, as are zeros in the rest of the composition. Zeros are another category of Crips – enemies of this gang – named for streets whose numbers end in zero (30s, 60s, 90s, and so forth). Each A is also crossed out because it stands for 53 Avalon Gangster Crips, a key enemy of this gang.

African-American Crips in Los Angeles are frequently enemies with Bloods as well as with other Crip gangs. Bloods more commonly list Crip-only enemies unless there is active warfare with specific Bloods groups.

The examples from Los Angeles Chicano gangs and Bloods and Crips demonstrate how gangs use graffiti to create statements of pride, affiliation, enmity, and alliance. They demonstrate how gang members infuse graffiti with aesthetic and linguistic elements that often derive from their broader cultural groups. Some of these traditions have begun to find resonance in circuits of global graffiti production, which is examined in the next section.

The cholo style

Gangs have generally been excluded from conversations around street art and graffiti, as they occupy a more isolated social position that carries undercurrents of poverty, criminality, and violence. Despite problematic broader contexts, gangs exhibit an undeniably rich aesthetic heritage, have developed key styles, and perform the familiar work of claiming public space for youth-based expression.

The rise of interest in street art and graffiti globally has also seen an interest in the so-called "cholo style" of Los Angeles gang graffiti (Chastanet, 2009). Interest in this art world began in the 1970s with the explosion of gang writing in Chicano neighborhoods that saw the development of elegant, single-line scripts. Romotsky and Romotsky's (1976) *Barrio Calligraphy*, Cesaretti's (1975) *Street Writers*, and more recently Chastanet's (2009) *Cholo Writing* and Acker's (2013) *Flip the Script* are all interested in gang graffiti as a stylistic phenomenon.

Several key artists and exhibitions have brought this style to prominence and heightened its influence in street art circles globally. The cross-pollination between Los Angeles gang-influenced styles and graffiti/street art practices has brought recognition to Chicano communities as having produced a kind of "art world" (Becker, 2008). The production of lettering-based works by artists like Chaz Bojorquez, Cryptik, Prime, Sleep, Dufer, and Retna have begun to represent this work within regional and global circles of art collecting. Key exhibition venues have heighted the legitimacy of lettering styles that ultimately derive from gangs. In 2011, the Los Angeles' Museum of Contemporary Art mounted *Art in the Streets*, a major exhibition that included gang work in a broader range history of graffiti history (Deitch *et al.*, 2011). In 2013, *Alphabet Soup* was a smaller, more focused gallery exhibit with a focus on "hand styles" that stem from the *cholo* tradition (see Figure 4.5). The Getty-sponsored 2014 exhibit *Scratch* at the

Figure 4.5 Opening invitation to Alphabet Soup, Smogtown/Boat House at Plaza de la Raza. Photo permission of Rigoberto Jimenez

El Segundo Museum of Art and accompanying project *LA Liber Amicorum* also had a heavy presence of cholo-style lettering. The connection between art and gang worlds is based in Los Angeles and does not seem to have parallels in other gang-oriented cities.

Reference to "cholos" is in some sense a gloss away from the violence of gangs. It is a look back to the heyday of Chicano gang script styles in the 1970s and acts as a buffer from criminality by focusing on style instead of social context. This buffer is a construct linked to the fear that gang writing evokes – and the assumption referenced above about ties between gang graffiti and violence.

Additionally, relationships between gangs and other graffiti writers have often been hostile. Castleman writes of New York gangs hiring early graffiti writers for their artistic skills (Castleman, 1982). Since then gangs and writers have tended to have more antagonistic relationships. In the 1990s, the Mexican Mafia encouraged the beating or murder of graffiti artists or taggers who competed with gangs for neighborhood space and were assumed to be disrespecting gangs either directly or indirectly (Phillips, 1999).

Graffiti artists who utilize gang-related hand styles tend not to be actual gang members but rather members of communities where gangs are present. The artistic, archival, and academic work that focuses on *cholo* styles adds depth to the contemporary graffiti scene without embracing more problematic associations with gang lifestyles and criminality. But it also acts as an erasure of gang culture from the artistic innovations produced by gang members. This erasure plays into graffiti art markets by using style instead of social life to anchor the work of multiple artists.

Conclusion

Gang graffiti is a rich communicative medium whose analysis has enhanced understandings of subcultural social groups, symbolic production, and aesthetic practice. Clear emphasis on aesthetics as well as encoded meaning, are critical parts of gang compositions. Studying these trajectories through time is possible in cities with longstanding writing traditions.

The aesthetic quality and frequency of gang writing has decreased since the late-1990s. This is likely due to law enforcement success in dismantling street gangs, more frequent use of indoor spaces for recreation due to the digital revolution, social media, and cheap consumer goods, the migration of neighborhood artists into non-gang graffiti arenas, as well as the virulence with which cities have mounted graffiti erasure campaigns.

Through graffiti, gangs exhibit a fluidity of performance, a combination of orality and literacy, and a set of written conventions that have their roots in broader cultural traditions. Understanding gang social categories is critical in order to understand gang writing. While the representation of social categories is more insulated, the aesthetic traditions of some gangs have generated widespread recognition and subsequent adoption outside of gang culture. Because of persistent associations of gang graffiti with violence, how to navigate the entrance of gang styles into graffiti art worlds will remain an open question for some time to come.

Notes

1   Documented instances of hobo graffiti date to the end of the nineteenth century. While hobo writing continues now, the practice and style of the phenomenon have undergone radical changes and its associated cultural participants have diminished in number. Whether hobo writing traditions can be said to be continuous in nature it requires more research and documentation.
2   www.fbi.gov/about-us/investigate/vc_majorthefts/gangs.
3   www.lapdonline.org/get_informed/content_basic_view/23471.
4   List taken from Green, J. & Pranis, K. (2007). *Gang Wars: The Failure of Enforcement Tactics and the Need for Effective Public Safety Strategies.* A Justice Policy Institute Report. Retrieved at www.justice policy.org/images/upload/07-07_rep_gangwars_gc-ps-ac-jj.pdf.
5   Interestingly some gang books and policy reports also suffer from this same problem. See for example Justice Policy Institute's 2009 *Gang Wars*, cited above, which frames its book with a New York-style graffiti art piece. See also the FBI's website, found here, which shows "gang tags in Cincinnati," but which are actually the tags of a graffiti crew. www.fbi.gov/about-us/investigate/vc_majorthefts/gangs/gallery.

References

Acker, C.P. (2013). *Flip the Script: A Guidebook for Aspiring Vandals and Typographers.* Berkeley, CA: Gingko Press.

Adams, K. & Winter, A. (1997). Gang Graffiti as Discourse Genre. *Journal of Sociolinguistics, 1*(3), 337–360.

Alonso, A. (1999). *Territoriality among African-American Street Gangs in Los Angeles.* (Ph.D. diss., University of Southern California).

Austin, J. (2001). *Taking the Train: How Graffiti Art Became an Urban Crisis in New York City.* New York: Columbia University Press.

Becker, H. (2008). *Art Worlds.* Berkeley, CA: University of California Press.

Castleman, C. (1982). *Getting up: Subway Graffiti in New York.* Cambridge, MA: MIT Press.

Cesaretti, G. (1975). *Street Writers a Guided Tour of Chicano Graffiti.* Los Angeles: Acrobat Books.

Chastanet, F. (2009). *Cholo Writing: Latino Gang Graffiti in Los Angeles.* Arsta, Sweden: Dokument.

Cintron, R. (1998). *Angel's Town: Chero Ways, Gang Life, and the Rhetorics of Everyday.* New York: Beacon Press.

Conquergood, D. (1997). Street Literacy. In J. Flood, S.B. Heath, and D. Lapp, (Eds) *Handbook of Research on Teaching Literacy through the Communicative and Visual Arts* (pp. 354–375). New York: Taylor and Francis.

Cooper, M. & Chalfant, H. (1984). *Subway Art.* New York: Henry Holt and Company.

Cresswell, T. (1996). *In Place/Out of Place: Geography, Ideology, and Transgression.* Minneapolis, MN: University of Minnesota Press.

Daniels, B. (2008). *Mostly True: The Story of Bozo Texino.* Portland, OR: Microcosm Publishing.

Deitch, J., Gastman, R., & Rose, A. (Eds.). (2011). *Art in the Streets.* New York: Random House.

Ganz, N. (2009). *Graffiti World: Street Art from Five Continents.* London: Thames and Hudson.

Goody, J. (1986). *The Logic of Writing and the Organization of Society.* Cambridge, MA: Cambridge University Press.

Green, J. & Pranis, K. (2007). *Gang Wars: The Failure of Enforcement Tactics and the Need for Effective Public Safety Strategies.* A Justice Policy Institute Report. Retrieved at www.justicepolicy.org/images/upload/07-07_rep_gangwars_gc-ps-ac-jj.pdf.

Grody, S. (2006). *Graffiti L.A: Street Styles and Art.* New York: Abrams.

Harcourt, B. (2005). *Illusion of Order: The False Promise of the Broken Windows Theory.* Cambridge, MA: Harvard University Press.

Katz, C. & Webb, V. (2006). *Policing Gangs in America.* Cambridge Studies in Criminology. Cambridge: Cambridge University Press.

Klein, M. & Maxson, C. (2010). *Street Gang Patterns and Policies.* Oxford: Oxford University Press.

Kurlansky, I., Naar, J. & Mailer, N. (1974). *The Faith of Graffiti.* New York: Praeger.

Leet, D., Rush G. & Smith, A. (2000). *Gangs, Graffiti, and Violence: A Realistic Guide to the Scope and Nature of Gangs in America.* Independence, KY: Cengage Learning.

Ley, D. & Cybrwisky, R. (1974). Urban Graffiti as Territorial Markers. *Annals of the Association of American Geographers, 64*(4), 491–505.

Livingston, L. (1910). *Life and Adventures of A-No. 1, America's Most Celebrated Tramp.* Cambridge Springs, PA: The A-No. 1 Publishing.

Mendoza-Denton, N. (2008). *Homegirls: Language and Cultural Practice among Latina Youth Gangs.* New York: Wiley-Blackwell.

Muñiz, A. & McGill, K. (2012). *Tracked and Trapped: Youth of Color, Gang Databases, and Gang Injunctions.* A Report by the Youth Justice Coalition's RealSearch Action Center. Retrieved at www.youth4justice.org/wp-content/uploads/2012/12/TrackedandTrapped.pdf.

Phillips, S. (1999). *Wallbangin: Graffiti and Gangs in L.A.* Chicago: University of Chicago Press.

Phillips, S. (2009). Crip Walk, Villain Dance, Pueblo Stroll: The Embodiment of Writing among African American Gangs. *Anthropological Quarterly, 82*(1), 69–97.

Romero, D. (2012). Graffiti Crew MTA's Injunction is for Real. *L.A. Weekly*, November 8. Retrieved at www.laweekly.com/informer/2012/11/08/graffiti-crew-mtas-gang-injunction-is-for-real (date downloaded November 17, 2014).

Romotsky, J. & Romotsky, S. (1976). *Barrio Calligraphy.* Los Angeles, CA: Dawson's Books.

Rymes, B. (1996). Naming as Social Practice: The Case of Little Creeper from Diamond Street. *Language in Society, 25*(2), 237–260.

Vigil, J.D. (1988). *Barrio Gangs: Street Life and Identity in Southern California.* Austin, TX: University of Texas Press.

Zilberg, E. (2011). *Space of Detention: The Making of a Transnational Gang Crisis between Los Angeles and San Salvador.* Durham, NC: Duke University Press.

5

Prison inmate graffiti

Jacqueline Z. Wilson

Introduction

In the early 2000s I embarked on an ethnographic field trip to study decommissioned prisons across Australia that were, or were likely to become, prison museums. As a social historian with training in sociology and an interest in public history, I hoped to determine to what extent the former institutions I visited represented the lived experiences of those who had been incarcerated there. The project necessarily involved an investigation both of the sites as found and of their operational histories, plus a broad examination of the sociological and psychological nature of incarceration.

One of the methods I used in my efforts to glimpse, by inference, the narratives of the multitudes that had inhabited the sites was to photograph the abundant graffiti they left behind. This aspect of the work, which came to occupy a significant portion of my PhD and the resulting book (Wilson, 2008), was necessarily somewhat unstructured methodologically, reflecting in part the difficulties of doing research in some prisons – even decommissioned ones – arising from the obstructive influence of 'gatekeepers' among staff (Grimwade, 1999: 292–98; also Wilson, 2008: 19–20, 91), and also my intention to evoke from the sources primarily descriptive and qualitative discussion, rather than quantitative analysis.

This approach has some limitations from a social-science standpoint, and I applaud the work of others who both preceded and followed me for their more systematic approach (see, e.g. Klofas and Cutshall, 1985; Palmer, 1997; Dewar and Frederiksen, 2003; Yogan and Johnson, 2006; Casella, 2009; Johnson, 2009; Costanzo *et al.*, 2013; Ismail, n.d.). Yet my study was and (to my knowledge) remains the only nationwide study of prison graffiti across a range of prisons, and as such provides some basis for a generalised overview of the field. It also incorporated one of very few comparative studies of female inmate graffiti undertaken anywhere (Dewar and Frederiksen, 2003; Yogan and Johnson, 2006; Wilson, 2008: 91–114; Johnson, 2009), and the first study of racist prison graffiti in Australia (Wilson, 2008: 115–130).

The study of prison graffiti is an emerging field.[1] Compared to the abundance of research into graffiti created in the general urban environment outside prisons (which I will refer to as 'mainstream' graffiti), the prison variety has received scant attention. The earliest study of this subject was conducted by Klofas and Cutshall (1985). Their ground-breaking analysis of 2,765 items of graffiti extant in a decommissioned Massachusetts juvenile facility in the early 1980s, amply demonstrated the potential for graffiti to provide insights into the culture, social norms and inmate hierarchies within a carceral institution; however, almost no further work in the field was done until the mid-1990s. Only within the past decade has there been any sign of the field burgeoning significantly. As such, it is a forum of diverse and, to some extent, contested, methodologies and scholarly perceptions. This arises from two broad factors: Unresolved questions regarding just what constitutes 'graffiti' in the prison context; and an increase (albeit sporadic and piecemeal) over the past decade in the opportunities available to scholars to access the interiors of former prisons for the purpose of studying and recording surface texts and images left behind by inmates.

The nature of prison graffiti

The first aspect, regarding the nature of prison graffiti, mirrors the complex debate addressed elsewhere in this book, regarding the 'legitimacy' or otherwise of the various forms of mainstream graffiti. In step with official attitudes toward much mainstream graffiti, its equivalent within prisons and other carceral institutions has traditionally been viewed by custodial authorities as an illegitimate activity, subject to prompt eradication if found and deemed a breach of regulations leading to punishment. There are apparent exceptions to this; many examples have emerged from former prisons of inmate art, often in the form of highly elaborate murals, which were either informally sanctioned by prison officers on the grounds that they gave the 'crims' something to do (especially if the prison in question was destined for imminent de-commissioning), or were part of official programs aimed at rehabilitation. Thus, for instance, tourist visitors to Melbourne's Pentridge Prison after its closure in 1997 found the extensive exercise-yard walls of the notoriously harsh high-security discipline division, 'Jika-Jika', literally covered with full-colour, painted designs depicting a variety of non-prison-related subjects, and clearly created with the support of the Division staff.

This type of officially approved artistic endeavour, some of which may showcase examples of genuine talent, is of undoubted psychological value to the inmates who create it. In his study of what he famously termed the 'total institution', sociologist Erving Goffman dubbed such recreational-cum-rehabilitative pastimes 'removal activities' (1961: 69), in reference to the inmate's need for structured activity that enables him or her to temporarily forget the awful daily realities of incarceration. As such, the works produced may also be of value to the researcher seeking clues as to what interested the inmate. Whether such artworks qualify as 'graffiti', however, is another matter.

In the strict sense of graffiti as graphic or verbal matter painted, drawn, inscribed or sprayed onto surfaces not originally intended for the purpose, perhaps the Jika-Jika murals and their ilk do qualify; I do not propose to adjudicate with any pretence at authority or finality on this question, other than to say that, although of some interest, such 'authorized' works are very limited in what they can tell us about the thoughts, affect or outlook of the typical inmate. Apart from anything else, they are more likely than not created by inmates of an artistic bent, or at least hopes of such. Also, they are intended as unequivocally *public* works (in the context of the prison environment, that is), and therefore are more likely to exhibit the more 'assertive' aspects of the inmate/artist's persona.

The type of graffiti most likely to provide glimpses of the ordinary inmate's unguarded preoccupations, state of mind and/or personal narrative is that rendered transgressively and clandestinely, with no requirement for artistic skill or aspiration, in the form of graphic images, written texts or both. Nor, it should be noted, does it require even a modicum of literacy; prison populations tend to comprise a preponderance of under-educated people, and graffiti thus provides scope for those with few other avenues of self-expression. In this way, graffiti may be seen as a kind of 'natural idiom' of the prison.

Unlike approved artwork, the intended audience of transgressive graffiti is generally limited to other inmates, and as often as not, *no* audience is required other than the graffitist. This latter aspect – the occurrence of graffiti created and intended to be viewed entirely secretly – is unique to prison graffiti, and contradicts a seeming maxim of the field. As graffiti semioticians Bruner and Kelso (1980), speaking of mainstream graffiti, assert, 'To write graffiti is to communicate; one never finds graffiti where they cannot be seen by others' (p. 241). Likewise, criminologists White and Habibis (2005) state with equal certitude that 'whether written by pen, spray can, or paintbrush, it is always public and displayed on someone else's property' (p. 86).

Much prison graffiti is indeed found in communal spaces such as exercise yards, shower facilities, toilets and so on, that correspond to mainstream 'public' locations (although still mainly aimed at fellow inmates rather than staff). It is in such environments that we most often find examples of successive or competitive 'tagging,' for instance. But at least as much is found in the quasi-private environment of the cells, where it is sometimes openly displayed on walls (and even ceilings), but often has been installed in locations only visible if something more than a casual effort is made to find it – behind semi-fixed objects such as beds, or on the inside surface of doors that when open, face the wall and thus may escape the notice of custodial staff. Cell graffiti may be created as entertainment, in the form of visual and/or verbal humour, as cathartic declaration of anger, desire, vengeance and so on, or as personal 'diary'-style mementos – not necessarily in the serial form of a conventional diary, but rather as a sporadic, or even singular, record of whatever the inmate had on his or her mind at a given moment. In many cases they appear to be intended as straightforward affirmations of the individual's presence, in some ways akin to mainstream 'tagging,' but often showing less bravado. As we shall see, this impulse to spontaneously inscribe such immediate preoccupations seems to amount, in many inmates, to something akin to instinct.

Whether appearing in communal or 'secret' spaces, it is this transgressive graffiti with which I am mainly concerned here, and which I have made the subject of my research over the past decade. Graffiti of this kind can take many forms and display many categories of content, some seemingly congruent with mainstream graffiti, but more often expressing sentiments and thoughts very much peculiar to the day-to-day experience of the carceral environment.

Accessing prison graffiti

I noted above that two factors influence the nature of prison graffiti research. The second one concerns access to the venues in which the graffiti may be found – former sites of incarceration. As I mentioned, this aspect has shown signs of improvement over recent years, partly due to fortuitous timing, in that a large number of aging prisons have been decommissioned in the last couple of decades, and have thus become, at least notionally, open for research. Also, there seems to be a dawning appreciation of the potential historical, sociological, and/or criminological significance of inmate graffiti among some former prison staff and/or the custodians of decommissioned sites (very often the same people; see Wilson, 2008: 52, 55–63).

This represents a significant shift in attitude, as the norm among prison authorities has been not only to oppose the creation of graffiti during the institution's operational life, but also to eradicate it, or at least hide it from public view, after decommissioning. It is common for tourists at prison museums to hear from tour guides that the interior spaces they are viewing are in 'original condition,' just as the prisoners experienced them, without being told of the scrubbing and repainting that occurred after closure, in large part to expunge the graffiti

(Wilson, 2008: 68). Other sections sequestered from public view may still contain all or most of the graffiti, but the conservation of such areas is all too often neglected, with consequent deterioration of surfaces.

Prison graffiti research therefore often depends on an element of serendipity. Thus, for instance, criminologist Lee Johnson (2009: 10) recounts that he gained the opportunity to view the interior of a recently decommissioned jail, because the local police chief was impressed by the 'art' he found inside and took the trouble to call Johnson with an invitation to examine it. Johnson notes that the officer's motivation seemed to rest on a tacit distinction between illegal 'graffiti' and 'art' (2009: 10), and the resulting paper does indeed focus on a series of mostly pictorial renderings clearly not created with official approval (2009: 5–9, 13–14).

My own experience, although different, was no less accidental and was also heavily affected by official attitudes. As a social historian with an interest in institutions and sites of incarceration, I began a general study of the ways in which prison museums (and recently decommissioned prisons destined to become museums) across Australia represented the experience of imprisonment. After happening upon an example of inmate graffiti and musing upon both its 'implied narrative' potential and its obviously wilful inaccessibility – that is, a deliberate effort was made by curatorial personnel to conceal it (Wilson, 2008: 22) – I made a point thereafter of requesting access to the non-public areas, hoping to find and photograph more. In many prisons I visited, I was granted such access only grudgingly, and often under close and overtly disapproving supervision (Wilson, 2008: 24). Nor, I should add, was it 'just me'; my experience echoed that reported by media and art theorist Daniel Palmer when he made a study of graffiti in Fremantle Prison (Western Australia) in the mid-1990s (Palmer, 1997).

This is not to say that I received no cooperation at all regarding graffiti, nor that disapproval of graffiti is universal; curatorial staff at a number of prison museums I studied or corresponded with demonstrated far more progressive views (without need, it must be said, for the graffiti to be deemed 'art').[2] And as I noted earlier, there are signs that this is becoming more of a norm. Recent visual-ethnographic research by Costanzo, Bull and Smith (2013) into graffiti in Brisbane's Boggo Road Gaol, for instance, suggests that they met far less resistance from the Boggo Road personnel than I did ten years earlier, and their data reflects this in its scope and the systematic analysis they have been thus able to conduct. This shift in official attitudes is reason for a degree of optimism regarding the future of the study of prison graffiti, and hence increased insight into the nature of the experience of incarceration.

Interpreting prison graffiti

What, then does transgressive graffiti tell us about the inmate's 'unguarded preoccupations, state of mind and/or personal narrative'?

The individual's experience of incarceration is characterised by three main factors. The first, and most obvious, is deprivation of liberty, which of course constitutes the prison's raison d'etre. Second is a radical loss of personal autonomy, both in the sense of physical confinement – the effects of which can include intolerable boredom – and in the unbending requirement to conform to the institution's rules of operation. Third, and in many ways most confronting, is that the social environment of the prison is a 'closed system', in which rancorous and often violent encounters are the norm, and which fosters a sense of ambient menace that has been described as 'permeat[ing] every second of everyone's existence' (Heilpern, 1998: 86). As former inmate turned playwright Ray Mooney (1997) puts it, 'In [prison] there's no walking away from anything'.

It is therefore unsurprising that a great deal of prison graffiti, especially that rendered by male inmates, reveals a preoccupation with issues of personal power, violence and the means to inflict it, and/or the individual's identification or notional connection with power groups (on the masculinist imperatives underlying such preoccupations see, e.g. Denborough, 2001; Holmberg, 2001; Levit, 2001; Messerschmidt, 2001; Sabo, 2001; Jewkes, 2002). These expressions are often couched in terms that also affirm the individual's sense of self on more personal levels.

The descriptive analysis that follows mainly utilizes a selection of the prison graffiti I have observed in Australian prisons which in various ways address these issues. The examples are to an extent 'local,' but my discussion assumes certain universal, and globally ubiquitous themes regarding the subjective experience of imprisonment, in particular those concerning hierarchical power dynamics, preoccupation with and aggressive expression of sexual desire, racism, declarations of vengeance and violent intent. By and large, a perusal of the few international studies available confirms the validity of such assumptions: Firearms, swastikas, skulls, horrific and demonic images, visions of rape, sexist and misogynistic declarations of lustful intent and resistance, all abound in works on prisons in America (Klofas and Cutshall, 1985; Yogan and Johnson, 2006; Johnson, 2009), Malaysia (Ismail, n.d.), Britain (Commission for Racial Equality, 2003), and Ireland (Casella, 2009). However, some, possibly significant, differences also emerge, most notably the relative absence in Australian prisons of religious graffiti, compared to their American and Malaysian counterparts (Johnson, 2009; Ismail, n.d.), and the lack, also, of politically motivated resistance declarations, à la those found in Irish prisons (Casella, 2009).

Due to limitations of space, and the need to cover a representative range of examples, analysis of each graffito is necessarily brief and does no more than touch upon the thematic aspects. All the examples are found in Australian prisons except the first one, which is from the United Kingdom. The significance of this UK example lies in both the degree to which it conforms to the universal themes I have outlined, and the fact that it is one of the very few examples of transgressive prison graffiti to achieve public notoriety.

Memento mori

On 21 March 2000, Robert Stewart, a nineteen-year-old inmate of the Feltham Young Offenders Institution in London, bashed his twenty-year-old cellmate, Zahid Mubarek, to death as he slept. Mubarek was of Pakistani background; Stewart was white, and notorious for violent racism. Mubarek's murder became a prominent *cause célèbre* and led to a series of inquiries into the failings of the corrections system.[3]

The particulars of Stewart's terrible act and its legal and social consequences have been extensively dealt with elsewhere (see Keith, 2006a, 2006b; BBC, 2006). Of interest in the present context is an aspect of Stewart's behaviour which the reports note, but which has hitherto prompted only minimal commentary.

After the murder, Stewart was moved to a 'segregation' cell. There he used the edge of his boot-heel to graffiti the cell wall. Beginning with the single word 'Manchester', he then scrawled the stark admission 'Just killed me padmate'. This he followed with a crudely drawn swastika, and below that the letters 'RIP', then the cryptic sequence 'OV M1CR' (BBC, 2006).

Stewart was, presumably, expressing what was most on his mind at that moment. What we see here is a complex of impulses typical of much prison graffiti. The graffitist frames his action with a number of signifiers of personal identity, yet without actually naming himself. 'Manchester' is Stewart's home town; the swastika symbolises and is consistent with his previously avowed white-supremacist attitudes (he later admitted also authoring an earlier in-cell graffito, consisting simply of the letters 'KKK'; Keith, 2006a, 261); the letters 'RIP', which at first glance suggest a tincture of remorse or some acknowledgement of the gravity of his actions, in fact are far more assertive, in that they echo a self-drawn tattoo he had sported for some time on his forehead consisting of a small Christian-style cross topped with the letters 'R-I-P'. This tattoo has been interpreted as symbolising racist, National Front-style sentiments (Keith, 2006a: 218–220). The meaning of 'OV M1CR' is more arcane, and at this distance defies conclusive analysis beyond noting that 'M1' is the postcode of Central Manchester, and thus may well be a re-affirmation of the area with which Stewart most closely identified.

Stewart's graffito is of special interest as an example of non-artistic prison graffiti created by a known inmate which has, almost uniquely, gained a wide public audience. It is also of interest to the prison graffiti researcher, for its banal typicality – notwithstanding its horrific genesis. The urge to impose oneself on the fabric of the institution, in the form of fragmentary personal narrative, symbolic or verbal identifiers, expressions of group membership and/or solidarity and declarations of affect or intent, accounts for a majority of the topics and themes routinely addressed by inmates on their walls.

Racism

A significant number of those inmates have racist sentiments to express, and Stewart's graffito is of a piece with many I have observed. And as has been noted in other locales, the most aggressive racism tends to be expressed by white inmates (Klofas and Cutshall, 1985: 362–363). Swastikas, with or without commentary or slogans, abound on cell walls, as do affirmations of personal solidarity with the groups that regard such symbols favourably (there is evidence that the Ku Klux Klan have used prisons as recruiting grounds; Wilson, 2008: 122–123).

Figure 5.1, found in a cell of the former Melbourne City Watch House (MCWH), typifies this variety, in its graphic depiction of beleaguered yet indomitable Nazi ideology. Again, a Christian cross is juxtaposed with the racist symbol. The author's 'signature' suggests either that his own background is British, or that he wishes to be identified with the British 'bovver boys', or 'skin-heads', commonly associated with neo-Nazi groups.

The graffiti of Figure 5.2, decorating a cell door in Fremantle Jail, is even more unequivocal, and in this case combines neo-Nazi ideology with a notional 'resistance narrative' in the form of an anarchist symbol and slogan.

The graffitist's ideological allegiance and personal signifiers are trumpeted via cockily defiant symbols and slogans – some paradoxically juxtaposed. Nazism and anarchism have a long historical antipathy; their synthesis is a modern development signifying far-right nationalism combined with ultra-individualist antipathy toward authority. It is apparent that 'Cliffy' sees himself – or at least *represents* himself to himself – as a lone 'resistance warrior' standing against oppressive regimes within and outside the institution – 'FTW' is a common prison abbreviation for 'Fuck the World' – and against the racial element supposedly sullying the idealised nation.

Bad intentions

Notwithstanding the prevalence of racism in prisons, power-focused graffiti is by no means always ideologically or group-oriented; often it reflects nothing more than the values and lore of the underworld. A favoured category of image among some graffitists is the means of violent dominance.

Illicit weapons are, notoriously, ubiquitous in prison, but they are most commonly the stuff of close, face-to-face encounters. Yet knives and bludgeons – the kinds of close-quarters weapons most commonly found, in improvised form, inside – are in my experience rarely represented

Figure 5.1 'Keep the faith' © the author

Figure 5.2 'Up the Nazi Party' © the author

in graffiti. Far more likely to be rendered on cell walls, I found, are firearms, which, given their capacity to kill at a distance, are the antithesis of day-to-day prison life, which is an 'intensely organic world in which personal agency is achieved through nothing other than proximity' (Wilson, 2008: 75).

The shotgun in Figure 5.3 was drawn on the wall of a Boggo Road cell. Designed as a military/law-enforcement weapon, the SPAS 12's compactness and rapid-fire capacity make it ideal for certain kinds of criminal activity. Its depiction in a prison represents the epitome of unattainable desideratum, and in this it typifies the fantasy element underlying much of the violent intent expressed in prison graffiti. This is a key difference between the content of 'standard' prison graffiti and that rendered by Robert Stewart, for Stewart's graffito has the distinction of commenting on an accomplished deed.

Typical of power-focused prison graffiti, expressing fantasies of intended violence or vengeance is a succinctly eloquent message scratched into a wooden bench-seat in the male division of the MCWH: 'Jail makes good men bad, so now its revenge to the bent cunt who put me here – poetic justice'. This graffito may be read as a blend of self-pity and self-affirming bluster, and exemplifies a common theme among many inmates in the graffitist's attempt to lay blame for his physical situation, moral condition and notional future actions on agents outside his sphere of personal influence or responsibility.

The 'revenge' motif is common in prison graffiti, but is not always expressed in verbal form, nor is it always aimed at a specific individual or group; often it is graphically depicted, at times simply as an abstract idea. A cell wall graffito in Fremantle Jail typifies this 'pure' notion of revenge as ethos. A skull, an obvious symbol of death, has been drawn in marking pen, with

Figure 5.3 'Franchi shotgun' © the author

enough care to suggest that the graffitist aspired to a precisely crafted effect. Apparently copied from another source using a pencilled grid that remains faintly visible, it sports a number of generic, horror-themed features – three bullet holes in its forehead, crooked and discoloured teeth, jagged highlights within the pitchy depths of its eye-sockets. It is accompanied by a caption, 'Revenge is sweet motherfucker' rendered with similar care, and resulting in an arresting tableau that may or may not have a particular target. In withholding that information, the inmate projects a sense of controlled menace absent in the previous graffito, for although that message leaves no doubt as to the depth of hatred aimed at 'the bent cunt' supposedly responsible for the inmate's situation, his message serves more than anything to emphasise his incarcerated condition and therefore his current helplessness. The bullet-riddled skull and caption bespeak far greater self-assurance. This may be due in part to the relative equanimity arising from long-term residence in a cell, compared to the uncertainty inherent in the time spent in the MCWH, a temporary holding facility.

Sexual violence

One of the most feared and notorious aspects of prison life, and one which the curators of prison museums (in company with the legal system and the officialdom of operational prisons) tend to be least willing to acknowledge, is sexual violence (Heilpern, 1998). Inmate sexuality, practical expression of which is necessarily homosexual, is an incessant source of tension, reflecting as it does the 'precarious sense of masculinity' of men in prison (Richmond, 1978: 55; see also Kupers, 2001; Donaldson, 2001; Paczensky, 2001). This tension inevitably leads or contributes to much of the violence that accompanies or passes for sexual relations, and means, too, that a great deal of sexual activity in prison takes the form of rape. It is a short step from there to a mindset that equates rape with revenge.

Figure 5.4 shows a Fremantle Jail cell graffito, drawn in pencil, in which a newly freed prisoner orally rapes a policeman. The image is replete with pornographic rancour and perversity, its deviance radically compounded by the notion of inflicting the act upon 'Cunt-stable care'. This is an obvious reference to the mascot of the Constable Care Child Safety Foundation, a Western Australian police-community initiative begun in the 1980s to educate children about safety and crime prevention (Western Australia Police, n.d.). Thus the graffito's subtext includes connotations of the violation of innocence.

Despite engaging in a homosexual act, the rapist's heterosexuality is asserted through the homophobic condemnation he heaps upon his 'faggot' victim and the implied contempt shown for the victim's acquiescence. This aspect, an affirmation of the prison's 'exaggerated version of heterosexuality' (Jewkes, 2002: 18), is consistent with a norm of prison sexual violence that rape victims who take the path of least resistance in order to minimise the attendant violence often receive a bashing anyway, for 'wanting it' (Heilpern, 1998).

The notional rape of 'Cunt-stable care' is clearly far more an act of vengeful violence than of lust. It thus accords with the above observation regarding the nature of day-to-day personal power in prison, in that it almost invariably inheres in the proximate, in the inmate's capacity for direct contact. All violence in prison is intimate. In instances of rape such as that depicted (which, although fantastical in some particulars, certainly has a basis in the realities of prison life), the question of weapons becomes almost irrelevant, for the chief instrument of coercion and dominance is, in essence, the phallus.

Conventional expressions of heterosexual desire, most commonly in the form of crudely drawn pornographic pictures of naked women, are common graffiti subjects. (Very rarely does

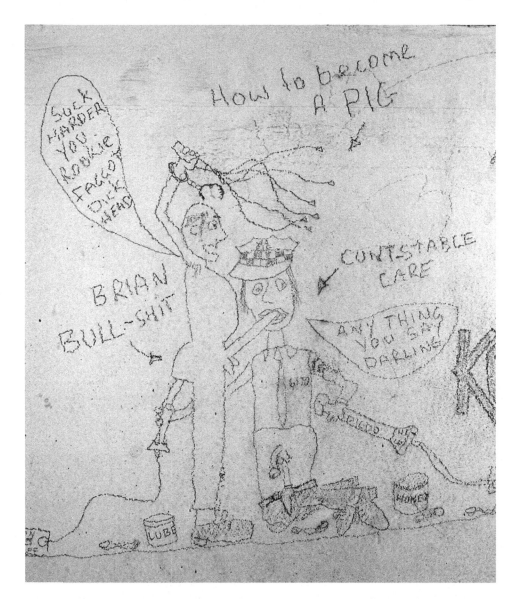

Figure 5.4 'How to become a pig' © the author

one find equivalent homosexual depictions.) Here, too, the prison's undercurrents of violence and rancour often surface, although sometimes in forms that may well have been intended as positive expressions of affection.

Figure 5.5, a graffito in the MCWH, is a small masterpiece of incongruity, given the juxtaposition of virulent misogyny in the inmate's declaration of intent and the conventional 'love-hearts' and paired names. In the process is epitomised the tension embodied in the prison's 'hyper-masculinist' environment.

Figure 5.5 'When I get out of here' © the author

Moral code

Even aside from their routine homophobia, prison inmates can be highly moralistic concerning what they deem unacceptable sexual transgression. This moralism, when combined with the prison's prevailing ethos of indiscriminate acrimony, can give rise to strikingly dramatic expressions of vilification. On a cell wall in Boggo Road I found the following invocation to an unidentified paedophile: 'This is a cell where every kidfucker hangs themselves. Do it dog. Ruff. Now. It's the least you can do'.

The text is printed in red marking pen, and is accompanied by a carefully drawn hangman's noose. The composition has then been framed with a border of brown pigment of uncertain origin, and below it in the same medium, as a kind of declarative coda, have been added the words 'You die dog'.

Paedophiles are reviled at least as much in prison as outside. We can only guess the circumstances behind the message; it may be directed at a cellmate, a speculative future resident or an individual in the graffitist's imagination or memory. The only certainty is the depth of condemnation expressed.

In an environment permeated with undifferentiated rancour, it is not a surprise to find expressions of hatred, frustration and fury that seem to be directed at no one in particular. Thus apparently random commands to 'Fuck off and die!' (in Gothic letters on a Boggo Road cell wall), and 'Up yours to all of you' (scratched into the paint of a lavatory door in MCWH women's division) are common; whereas 'Fuck this place forever' (Fremantle Jail cell) condemns the institution in toto.

'Time stops'

The latter two examples incorporate a fist with upraised middle finger. This defiant image, with or without accompanying text, is perhaps the most common graffito I observed in both male and female prisons across Australia. And at times, as in Figure 5.6 (Boggo Road cell wall), it represents a different but equally common motivation – the impulse simply to amuse.

Figure 5.6 'Santa' © the author

A straightforward need for entertainment or amusement, for anything at all to relieve the boredom, is also clearly behind the creation of graffiti such as a push-button drawn on a Fremantle cell wall and captioned 'Press for room service', or the cartoon-style faces, figures and creatures that typify the often darkly ironic style of facetiousness to be found in almost any prison.

Amusement-oriented graffiti also frequently depict a further ubiquitous theme of prison life: illicit drug use and drug paraphernalia. These can range from jocular depictions of the drug experience, to items such as water-pipes, bongs and hypodermic syringes, to elaborate psychedelic montages.

Whether the graffito in Figure 5.7 was influenced in its creation by drug use is impossible to say, but its hallucinatory qualities certainly make such a suggestion plausible. An imposing cell mural in Fremantle executed in red and black pencil, ink and crayon and occupying the entire upper half of one wall, it is emblematic of many of the emotional and psychological aspects of the prison experience, with its personification of Death, demonic icons of hellfire and attendant naked woman. The agonising timelessness of incarceration is poignantly represented by the handless clock face with its redolent caption.

The size, deliberateness and complexity of this graffito make it, of course, a far cry from the modest and most often clandestine texts I defined in my introduction as central to my study of prison graffiti. It might seem more of a piece with the 'legitimate' mural works which, I argued, fail to provide us with candid glimpses of the inmate sensibility. I suggest, however, that by virtue of its location, lack of inhibition in execution and spectacular embracement of the transgressive, it is the antithesis of the officially sanctioned works the touring public views as 'inmate art'.

The key factors in this judgement are its unabashed candour, its bleakly solipsist tone and the fact that its prime intended audience could not have been other than its creator. Having adorned his 'bedroom' – his sole quasi-private space – with this nightmarish vision, the inmate was apparently content to live with it. We must assume it went some way toward relieving the boredom.

Figure 5.7 'Time Stops' © the author

Needless to say, such a work could not have actually remained *secret*; cells are routinely accessed by prison officers. But there is evidence that in some cases they turned a blind eye to what inmates got up to, especially in the latter years of institutions leading up to decommissioning. It is in graffiti produced during those transitional periods that we sometimes encounter texts of a didactic purport – messages to future outsiders. This seems to be the case in the brief message from a Fremantle cell reproduced below. It was not written by the creator of 'Time stops', but I believe it is instructive to consider it with that vision in mind.

> Sixteen hours a day
> We are locked in here
> With the cockroaches and rats
> And with our shit bucket
> Could you handle it?
> How would it change you?

Conclusion

The above selection of images provides a glimpse into the subjective condition of imprisonment. Inmates create graffiti for a range of reasons, and to express a range of sensibilities, in the main radically unlike the feelings and perceptions that motivate the mainstream graffitist. Life inside the total institution has a banal intensity that impels, and may well compel, the expression of immediate experiences on the nearest available surface

As I have said, the study of prison graffiti is a young field, and as yet it lacks the 'critical mass' needed to bring scholars together easily, to facilitate collaboration and sharing of information, and thus to provide the researcher with a sense of what areas need attention, what questions need to be addressed. A comparative smattering of publications worldwide comprise the sum total of relevant scholarship. Indeed, a search of the Internet using keywords such as 'prison graffiti', 'prisoner graffiti' or 'inmate graffiti' is likely to glean more web pages advertising graffiti eradication services than sites on graffiti created by inmates. Compounding the problem is the inter-disciplinary nature of the field (the works cited here have been produced by academics working in criminology, art theory, social history, archaeology, museology, architecture and sociology). This fragmentation will, I believe, ultimately prove one of the strengths of the field, but at this early stage it tends to result in a lack of cohesion among researchers – there is not yet a global scholarly 'community' of prison graffiti researchers.

Both the similarities and the differences between culturally disparate samples of inmate graffiti may provide a direction for researchers. A comparative global study of inmate graffiti, not only across national borders but also looking at that produced in the many different types of carceral institutions, may also prove fruitful. It is beyond the scope of this brief survey to do more than raise a few suggestions. The field is wide open.

Notes

1   The term 'prison graffiti', if taken literally, is problematic, and is employed here as a matter of convenience. In using it I refer to graffiti created by those confined in all forms of carceral institutions, including temporary police lockups, mental asylums and youth detention centres. A more precise term, which I use intermittently in this chapter, is 'inmate' graffiti. Likewise, the terms 'prison' and 'jail' are used indiscriminately to mean any site of legal imprisonment.
2   Old Adelaide Gaol makes a feature of some of its graffiti, and the management of the MCWH have taken considerable trouble to preserve the site's abundant collection and make at least some available for public viewing.

3   The Mubarek case spawned a series of inquiries, culminating, in 2004, in the independent inquiry by High Court Justice Brian Keith, whose report (Keith 2006a, 2006b) stands as the most complete account of the affair. A useful summary of his findings is available from BBC (2006).

References

BBC. (2006). Mubarek inquiry: Key findings. *BBC news*. Available: http://news.bbc.co.uk/2/hi/uk_news/5129660.stm (accessed 22 January 2014).

Bruner, E. and Kelso, J. (1980). Gender differences in graffiti: A semiotic perspective. *Women's Studies International Quarterly*, *3*(2–3): 239–252

Casella, E.C. (2009). Written on the walls: Inmate graffiti within places of confinement. In A. Beisaw and J. Gibb (eds), *The archaeology of institutional life.* (pp. 172–186). Tuscaloosa: Alabama University Press.

Commission for Racial Equality [UK]. (2003). Racial equality in prisons: A formal investigation by the commission for racial equality into HM prison service of England and Wales (Part 2). Available: www.statewatch.org/news/2003/oct/crePrisons.pdf (accessed 18 February 2014).

Costanzo, B., Bull, M., and Smith, C. (2013). If these walls could speak: A visual ethnography of graffiti at Boggo Road Gaol. *Queensland Review*, *20*(2): 215–230.

Denborough, D. (2001). Grappling with issues of privilege: A male prison worker's perspective. In D. Sabo, T.A. Kupers, and W. London (eds), *Prison masculinities.* (pp. 73–77). Philadelphia, PA: Temple University Press.

Dewar, M. and Frederiksen, C. (2003). Prison Heritage, public history and archaeology at Fannie Bay Gaol, Northern Australia. *International Journal of Heritage Studies*, *9*(1): 45–63.

Donaldson, S. (2001). A million jockers, punks, and queens. In D. Sabo, T.A. Kupers, and W. London (eds), *Prison masculinities.* (pp. 118–126). Philadelphia, PA: Temple University Press.

Goffman, E. (1961). *Asylums: Essays on the social situation of mental patients and other inmates.* Garden City, NY: Anchor Books.

Heilpern, D. (1998). *Fear or favour: Sexual assault of young prisoners.* Lismore NSW: Southern Cross University Press.

Holmberg, C.B. (2001). The culture of transgression: Initiations in the homosociality of a midwestern state prison. In D. Sabo, T.A. Kupers, and W. London (eds), *Prison masculinities.* (pp. 78–92). Philadelphia, PA: Temple University Press.

Ismail, K.A. (n.d.). *Pudu Jail's graffiti: Beyond the prison cells.* Draft conference paper. Available: www.inter-disciplinary.net/wp-content/uploads/2011/04/ismailexpaper.pdf (accessed 6 May 2014).

Jewkes, Y. (2002). *Captive audience: Media, masculinity and power in prisons.* Cullompton, Devon: Willian.

Johnson, L.M. (2009). Jail art and public criminology. *Research and Practice in Social Sciences*, *5*(1): 1–21.

Keith, Mr Justice B. (2006a). *Report of the Zahid Mubarek inquiry* (vol. 1), London: UK Government. Available: http://image.guardian.co.uk/sys-files/Guardian/documents/2006/06/29/volume_one.pdf.

Keith, Mr. Justice B. (2006b). *Report of the Zahid Mubarek inquiry* (vol. 2), London: UK Government. Available: http://image.guardian.co.uk/sys-files/Guardian/documents/2006/06/29/volume_two.pdf (accessed 18 February 2014).

Klofas, J. and Cutshall, C. (1985). Unobtrusive research methods in criminal justice: Using graffiti in the reconstruction of institutional cultures. *Journal of Research in Crime and Delinquency*, *22*(4): 355–373.

Kupers, T.A. (2001). Rape and the prison code. In D. Sabo, T.A. Kupers, and W. London (eds), *Prison masculinities.* (pp. 111–117). Philadelphia, PA: Temple University Press.

Levin, B. (1979). *Taking sides.* London: Pan Books.

Levit, N. (2001). Male prisoners: Privacy, suffering, and the legal construction of masculinity. In D. Sabo, T.A. Kupers, and W. London (eds), *Prison masculinities.* (pp. 93–102). Philadelphia, PA: Temple University Press.

Messerschmidt, J.W. (2001). Masculinities, crime, and prison. In D. Sabo, T.A. Kupers, and W. London (eds), *Prison masculinities.* (pp. 67–72). Philadelphia, PA: Temple University Press.

Mooney, R. (1997). Bluestone shadows. *Sunday Age* (Melbourne) Agenda. 14 September.

Paczensky, S.V. (2001). The wall of silence: Prison rape and feminist politics. In D. Sabo, T.A. Kupers, and W. London (eds), *Prison masculinities.* (pp. 133–136). Philadelphia, PA: Temple University Press.

Palmer, D. (1997). In the anonymity of a murmur: Graffiti and the construction of the past at the Fremantle Prison. *Studies in Western Australian History*, *17*: 104–115.

Richmond, K. (1978). Fear of homosexuality and modes of expression of sexuality in prisons. *Australian and New Zealand Journal of Sociology: Symposium on Deviance, Crime and Legal Process*, *14*(1): 51–57.

Sabo, D. (2001). Doing time, doing masculinity: Sports and prison. In D. Sabo, T.A. Kupers, and W. London (eds), *Prison masculinities*. (pp. 61–66). Philadelphia, PA: Temple University Press.

Western Australia Police (n.d.). *Constable care*. Available: www.police.wa.gov.au/YoungPeoplesZone/Youth programs/ConstableCare/tabid/1577/Default.aspx.

White, R. and Habibis, D. (2005). *Crime and society*. Melbourne: Oxford University Press.

Wilson, J.Z. (2008). *Prison: Cultural memory and dark tourism*. New York: Peter Lang.

Yogan, L. and Johnson, L. (2006). Gender differences in jail art and graffiti. *The South Shore Journal, 1*: 31–52.

6

Ways of being seen
Gender and the writing on the wall

Jessica N. Pabón

Introduction

Be it a wheat-pasted character complimented by a confrontational political message, an indecipherable name spray-painted in 3D puzzle-piece letters, or a stenciled silhouette of a familiar pop culture icon – without an explicit identifier, the "writing on the wall" is assumed to be the work of an unfailingly gendered, raced, and classed subject. The process of a viewer's visual and cognitive perception replaces anonymity with biases and stereotypes of the subject held responsible and/or given credit for the public act. This subject is likely assumed to be urban, economically disenfranchised, and a racial or ethnic minority. Moreover, the writer/artist is invariably assumed to be male. Under the conditions of this particular gaze, girls and women who write graffiti or make street art are not visible.

Contemporary street art descended from what is now classified as Hip Hop graffiti – a kind of writing that emerged in the post-Civil Rights era of the United States, pioneered by mostly African American and Latino youth living in Philadelphia and the Bronx in the mid-1960s. Hip Hop graffiti writing changed everything we knew about "graffito" (an inscription or drawing on a surface) from cave paintings, to hieroglyphics, to freight train monikers, to gang symbols, and declarations of love on bathroom stalls. Also known as spray can or aerosol art, graffiti is widely understood as an anarchic aesthetic of communication and rebellion against political disenfranchisement and social invisibility. Sometimes referred to as "post-graffiti" by art critics and art historians, street art is comprised of a wide range of mixed media imagery affixed to public surfaces such as posters, stickers, stencils, video projections, and yarn, which differs from graffiti in that it is not centered around the repetitive production of a tag name (Wacławek, 2011). Graffiti writers "bomb the system" with their tags, performing an identity they have created as opposed to the one that appears on their birth certificates. In contrast, street artists may or may not use aliases and therefore the artwork itself may or may not reflect that alias, and the central visual will instead be a character, a landscape, a statement, a symbol, etc. Despite differences in method and medium, as aesthetic descendants of Hip Hop graffiti, other forms of street art contain the seed of sociopolitical communication and rebellion, but are generally understood to be less "risky," less physical, less dangerous, and therefore, less "masculine."

Early studies and reports established the overwhelmingly sexist ideological conventions that would shape the subcultural and mainstream imaginary in regards to *how* we see the writing, and *who* we see as the doer of the writing – especially when framed alongside other elements of Hip Hop such as dancing, rapping, and deejaying (Mailer & Naar, 1974 [2009]; Banes, 1981 [2004]). Graffiti history was not written from (or even inclusive of) the perspective of girls and women, nor did it consider the condition of gender difference within the subculture. There were exceptions who instead of being marginalized, were tokenized as unique representatives in canonical works. The earliest women on record to write graffiti include Lady Pink, Abby, Lady Heart, Barbara 62 and Eva 62, Poo-ni 167, Charmin, Gidget, Stoney, Cowboy, Grape, Kivu, Suki, Chic SS, Bambi, Anna, Dawn, and Kathy – each to individual acclaim (Castleman, 1982; Cooper and Chalfant, 1984; Chalfant and Prigoff, 1987; Siegel, 1993; Guevara, 1996; 149St Staff, 2002; Miller, 2002; Pabón, 2014a). Despite these exceptions, our ways of seeing the writing on the wall remain heavily influenced by hegemonic Western gender norms.

Scholars and documentarians of graffiti writing and street art have noted that more women tend to participate in street art (Ganz, 2006), rather than graffiti writing, because of the following: The juridical designation of street art as "art" versus graffiti as vandalism (the assumption being that women are less likely to participate in criminal behavior); the preparation of stickers, stencils, and posters in the private domain prior to being affixed to public surfaces (the assumption being that women are naturally inclined to be more comfortable in the safety of the private sphere); and the lack of an investment in "making masculinity" (the assumption being that women do not have the desire to exercise masculine behaviors) (Macdonald, 2001).

These ideas, developed over time and in relationship to graffiti writing/street art history, have exacerbated the numerical minority status of female participants and grossly underestimated and over generalized their realities, desires, and potential: Realities faced by writers like Utah who was went to jail for a year (six months in NYC, six months in Boston) and yet can still be found blogging about her graffiti exploits throughout Asia at www.utahether.com (UtahEther, 2008; Irving, 2009; ClawMoney, 2010; Turco, 2010; TEDx Talks, 2012; Sherman, 2009); desires for writers like ClawMoney, who began tagging in the late 1980s and over the years has turned her iconographic "claw" logo into an internationally known retail brand (www.clawmoney. com); she also became the first woman to design the paint scheme for a Nascar fleet in 2012 – activating the potential in her artistry (ClawMoney, 2007; Turco, 2012).

Graffiti writers/street artists construct, deconstruct, and subvert the social mechanics of representative identity through their ephemeral public artworks – sometimes consciously, sometimes not. But women, because they are not the presumed doers, have to decide whether or not to make their gender difference visible, and if so, how to accomplish that task. Signaling yourself as "woman" automatically makes your artwork susceptible to judgments based on your gender rather than on your skill: "That's good for a girl," and "her boyfriend must have done that for her," are standard responses. The paradox is that for the gender signification to perform – to do the work of identification and representation – it must utilize the very same gender conventions that have traditionally worked to suppress them. The following contributes to the literature on graffiti and street art by offering an international sample of how girls and women from around the world navigate the politics of visuality.

Ways of being seen

Gender anonymity

Sensing that her male peers were likely to evaluate her graffiti writing as "girl graffiti," Jerk chose a tag name that concealed her gender identity within a word implicitly identified with men (Swenson, 2013). Jerk is a Chicana graffiti writer from Los Angeles, California who began tagging the concrete flood-control channels of the L.A. river as a teenager in the mid-1990s – about a decade after Hip Hop graffiti gained popularity on the West Coast, in contrast to territorial gang graffiti in style and purpose (Phillips, 1999). "Vandals" in California risk violating the "inscribed material" penal codes, being arrested, charged, and convicted of vandalism, and depending on the offense, subsequently sanctioned to community service, fines, county jail time of six months to one year (the latter is a felony), or counseling (Anon, n.d.). Despite these risks, Jerk has been bombing the system for over twenty years and represents the CBS crew out of Hollywood. Her style varies, but she favors plump, crisp, legible throwies and elongated, serpentine wildstyle letters – all of which can be seen on the freight trains, walls, and highway barriers of her city (www.facebook.com/Jerk.LA213). Through her dedication and "ups" she has now gained fame and her gender identity is no longer hidden.

Choosing a pseudonym that signaled her desire, Free was the first girl to start writing *pixação* in São Paulo. Pixação (to trace or stain) emerged in Brazil in the mid-twentieth century as a form of political protest against years of dictatorial rule (Coelho, 2011). Free and her peers, respectfully referred to as "G8" or Generation 80s, revived the form but replaced the direct political activism with self-empowerment and subcultural recognition. Characterized by cryptic monochrome letters resembling runes (ancient characters used in Northern Europe), during that time pixação appeared mostly on bridges and at street level. Pixação was the anarchic and exceptionally criminalized precursor to – the decriminalized – Brazilian Hip Hop graffiti, which intensified in popularity at the turn of the millennium (Pardue, 2011; Dixon, 2014). Free chose her tag name to signal the importance of independence and to celebrate the affective significance of taking the streets when she felt powerless and invisible as a young girl in a patriarchal society.

Figure 6.1 JERK LA, 2012, Northeast Los Angeles, California. Photo courtesy of Jerk

She was determined to "burn [her male peers] on the walls" – she wanted to do the best and the most pixação in her city (Pabón, 2012). She built her reputation before other pixadors knew she was a girl, but once her gender became common knowledge she became a model for up and coming female street artists.

Motel7 is a graffiti writer from Cape Town, a member of the notable graffiti crew 40HK, and one of the first white (of Norwegian-English ethnic heritage) women to paint graffiti in post-apartheid South Africa (www.motelseven.com). Black South Africans, by and large, were the first to embrace Hip Hop culture through political/conscious rap and dance for two decades before "non-political" graffiti popularized in the late 1990s (Marco, 2011). When she started painting in 2003, she chose the tag name Misty to highlight her "female identity," but she soon adopted the name Motel7. Oftentimes feeling like a social "misfit," graffiti subculture became the world in which she explored herself with indulgence and without explanation (Du Plessis, 2009). Motel7's brightly colored geometric letters are deconstructed to the point of animation; they are sometimes accented with a goofy character bringing humor and accessibility to the image. Cape Town became the site of South Africa's first anti-graffiti by law in 2010, which states that any "mural art applied to a wall facing the street requires permission by the City" (Council, 2010). Painting walls *with* permission has meant painting less frequently for Motel7, but her legacy as a prolific female writer who claimed unbridled self-expression through graffiti art remains.

The utilization of a gender-neutral tag name like Free, a "masculine" name like Jerk, or an androgynous one like Motel7, allows graffiti writers and street artists to communicate a message, and/or exercise their artistry without the stigma associated with their gender in everyday life. It is important to note that the decision regarding gender visibility or invisibility affects graffiti writing women more than street artists because the tag name is the central component of the work for the former. Further, because of the stakes of representation, and the number of girls and women who choose anonymity as a negotiation strategy, the "real" numbers of participation will never be known. Against those artists/writers choosing various forms of gender anonymity, we can juxtapose artists/writers who choose to publicize their gender specifically through signification.

Gender signification

Since 1998, NYC's Miss17 has been writing graffiti on every single surface she can and in every single city she visits (www.facebook.com/miss17nyc). Regardless of the "miss" in her tag, which signaled her gender from the start, her peers uniformly recognize her as a "king" – the highest status one can attain in graffiti subculture. Making her mark in a matter of moments, her graffiti style is more often than not "gritty and raw." She is probably best known for her throw-ups appearing alone or in a "family" and for popularizing the vertical tag. Miss17 registers her complaints about social conformity by scrawling her name on every surface she comes across – not just walls, but also objects that circulate through everyday life like dollar bills and postcards. In 2011, Miss17's lawyer estimated that she was wanted for over $600,000 worth of damages to NYC alone, a city notorious for its anti-graffiti laws and task force (Austin, 2001). The intensity with which she approaches her work makes hers a loud, present voice in graffiti (Lennon, 2009). Miss17's tags and throwies draw an alternative map of each city she visits. For those in the know, or for those who pay attention, she makes streets familiar; she makes cities feel differently. The "miss" in her tag modifies, if temporarily, the gendered sense of belonging to, safety in, and ownership of public space influenced by architectural features and urban planning (Pabón, 2013f).

Hailing from Sydney, Australia, Ivey's tag name comes from the DC comic book super villain "Poison Ivy" who exploits the ideological boundaries of conventional femininity to her

Figure 6.2 King Robbo Tribute, Steffi Bow, Leake Street, London, 2014 © Steffi Bow

advantage. Ivey's pieces are embellished with cartoon figures, elements from tattoo culture, and sometimes a provocative catch phrase. Her letters are old school (1970s NYC), funky yet legible, and always finished with some combination of bubbles, bows, or stars – elements that immediately signify her gender if perhaps her name doesn't. In 2012, Ivey painted a bubble letter piece with a band across the middle bottom half that read: "Real chicks paint, fake chicks talk." In this one piece, she identified herself, her expectations for other "chicks" who write, and claimed the sub-cultural value of her act. In 2008, Sydney's local government officials moved from an unsystematic effort to remove graffiti to a zero-tolerance policy akin to former New York City Mayor Rudolph Guiliani's 1990s support of zero-tolerance policing, making the consequences of being a "real chick" in Sydney that much more relevant (Giuliani, 2012; McAuliffe, 2012).

In Dubai, UAE, where there is a small but lively Hip Hop scene pioneered by the Deep Crates Cartel (DCC), Bow (herself a DCC crew member, and a British expat) has emerged as the first female street artist in the UAE and one of the foremost in the region (DtNews, 2014). She began stenciling little bows around East London in 2008, and after moving to Dubai began honing her craft into freestyle graffiti flavored "fa-BOW-lous" images (Pabón, 2014b). Mostly painting in the Arts District of Dubai, which is located in the industrial area known as Alserkal Avenue, Bow and her crew paint live, in public, and with permission (http://syabow.tumblr.com; Olson, 2013). The arguably Western notion that street art/graffiti writing is only (sub-culturally) legitimate if it is legally or socially transgressive does not hold because the context of the scene's emergence is radically different. Street art in major cities actively developing their arts and culture sector – like Dubai – emerged *because of* the gradual legitimatization and cultural currency of street art and graffiti as opposed to an emergence as a mode of sociopolitical resistance. Within this context, Bow is a highly visible female street artist motivated to develop a scene where there simply isn't one, a scene with women at the forefront.

The historical marginalization of women street artists/graffiti writers has consequently produced an aesthetic hierarchy whereby imagery, lettering, and approach characterized as "feminine" is degraded – tacitly informed by the notion that only men are capable of producing graffiti/street art with "masculine" characteristics. As an active deconstruction of a sexist value structure, a way to bring gender equity to these value systems, and/or as a nonchalant rejection of them, graffiti writing and street art making women mark their letters with embellishments (bows), popular culture references (Poison Ivy), and titles (Miss). Others revel in overt female sexuality and hyperfemininity through characters.

Hyperfeminine and overtly sexualized

DanaPink is a writer from Santiago Chile who began painting in 1999 and settled into her subject matter of choice – children, animals, and flowers – after joining Chile's first all-female graffiti crew, Crazis Crew (Pabón, 2013a). While Dana certainly paints her fair share of graffiti pieces, she is known for her wide-eyed *muñecas* (little doll-like girl figures), which don dresses, carry dolls, eat lollipops, and are accompanied by animals. Signifying her gender in name and aesthetic, she asserts her difference by valorizing and valuing an aesthetic often deemed "less than" in graffiti conventions – cuteness. Dana favors all shades of pink and purple; she exploits the highly gendered nature of these colors purposefully because she knows without marking her gender in some way, her graffiti could be attributed to someone else. She refuses invisibility with cute, pink, youthful, joyful characters and letters. She also refuses to subjugate her desires to paint in this way in order to match up to a North American or European aesthetic ideal and instead embraces the long history of muraling and public art in Latin American culture.

Shiro is a Japanese writer from Shizuoka, intermittently living in the United States, who has been writing graffiti since 1998 (www.bj46.com). Her tag name translates to "white" in English from Japanese, and for her that signals a kind of blank slate from which she can just be herself. The exploration and expression of one's self, in Shiro's graffiti, means the exploration and expression of one's selves – multiple and ever changing in terms of visuality, yet somehow remaining the same: voluptuous and flirtatious (Pabón, 2013b). Her "Mimi" characters are hypersexual Barbie-like figures whose features are modified depending on place, theme, and purpose, but they always maintain the basic contours of the Mimi. She signifies her Asian ethnicity acronymically by tattooing her mimi's with "BJ46," big jade 46; the numbers and letters in her tag also locate her within Hip Hop graffiti specifically. Partaking in a visual tradition of sultry and playful female characters initiated by street artists including Miss Van and Fafi in the mid-1990s – both from Toulouse, France – sexualized characters like Mimi often come under scrutiny for the presumed reliance on beauty ideals and the male gaze (Fafi.net; missvan.com). Why would a female graffiti writer/street artist reproduce imagery that sexualizes and objectifies women? Shiro creates her Mimi characters as agents of communication between women of varying identities and experiences – not as passive objects to be gazed upon.

Painting on the categorical boundaries between street artist and graffiti writer, Brazilian artist Injah faces similar scrutiny with her figures. Using a tag name that reflects her spiritual commitments (in jah, in God), she's been using street art and graffiti to communicate her sex-positive feminist politics in Rio de Janeiro since 2005 (Pabón, 2013a). Injah's nude female figures are meant to inspire liberation of women's sexuality from morally inflected social conventions. She sometimes punctuates her imagery with a short phrase relative to the content of the piece (i.e. liberate yourself). In terms of medium, Injah tends to use stickers and posters because she is hesitant to stay in dark alleys, under bridges, and in hidden places for too long. For women, painting at night – often alone – can be dangerous at the outset. When the imagery one is putting on the wall is *specifically* about sex and sexuality, the threat of rape and sexual harassment is magnified. Her characters spread their legs, touch themselves, and gaze directly at the viewer; they float through the air, hair down, unencumbered and delighting in their sexual indulgence.

Whether it is through cuteness or sexiness, graffiti writers/street artists like DanaPink, Shiro, and Injah reclaim and revalue the presence of girls' and women's bodies in public spaces. Taking strength from claiming their ethnic and gender difference, they manipulate the stereotypes and expectations that would otherwise subordinate them subculturally, socially, and historically. There are graffiti writers/street artists whose work is political because of what it is (mode of resistance) and what it does (change public perspectives, communicate messages, etc.), but there are also street artists whose work is primarily politically and/or culturally oriented.

Political and cultural

Starchild Stela, a queer Québécoise feminist street artist from Montréal, Canada redefined her sense of "being a girl" through criminal behavior (the fines and penalties for vandalism in Quebec vary by municipality; www.facebook.com/starchildstela). She began making stickers and painting on the street and on freight trains in 2006, and after some on and off activity settled into her "Stela" moniker (Pabón, 2013d). Mostly, she paints only the torsos of fairytale-like characters, some of which are part-animal (cat, specifically) and others with bouffant hairstyles in a pastel color palette; she makes them fierce with the addition of thought bubbles or captions in a curvilinear handstyle that generally include an explicative diminishing heterosexist patriarchy. Her textual and figural spray paint street art is a kind of visual consciousness raising initiative. Marking her gender (and her gender politics) through name, message, and imagery, she uses

Figure 6.3 Starchild Stela, 2014, Photo Courtesy Laurence Philomene

her painting to cope with everyday life and to inspire others to "think critically or die trying" – to resist the social order of things particularly in relationship to gender inequality and oppression.

Faith47 is a world-renowned street artist living in Cape Town, South Africa who was introduced to graffiti in 1997 (www.faith47.com), just three years after the end of apartheid. Sharing a common sentiment among women who write graffiti or paint street art, Faith does not want to be known specifically as a "female artist," to be compared to male artists but rather as an artist in her own right (Pabón, 2013e). The themes of her artwork tend to focus on concerns such as equality, poverty, liberty, and justice – as her tag name suggests, she has faith that one day civil liberties and justice will overcome. Often, the central figure of Faith's piece is a woman: An angel, lady liberty, or an African mother with child on her back. The messages communicated through these pieces are related to motherhood, the feminization of poverty, and women's place in the world. Her imagery – spray painted, wheat pasted, or posted – is visually light, but conceptually heavy. With the simple but elegant placement of a word ("libre"), or a phrase with a corresponding figure, she breathes profound life into decaying objects like cars, rusty gates, and decrepit walls. Faith's street art touches spectators affectively, without a visually aggressive message.

Japanese street artist Lady Aiko signals her gender and her status with her title: "Lady" (www.ladyaiko.com). She's been developing her Pop-influenced street art style since she moved from Tokyo to New York in the 1990s (JapanSocietyNYC, 2013). She uses her artwork to delve into topics such as heritage, preservation, and place as a Japanese woman living in the United States and traveling all over the world (MOCATV, 2013). Aiko's feminine female figures often gracefully occupy painstakingly collaged mixed-media landscapes complete with butterflies and flowers, bringing to mind those eighteenth-century Japanese woodblock prints she pulls inspiration from and gives a contemporary twist to by adding a bit of sexual energy in the figures' pose. In 2012, she became the first woman to paint the legendary Keith Haring Wall in Manhattan at Houston and Bowery (Leon, 2012). For days, she plotted the space, taped the stencils, sprayed the paint, repositioned the stencils, and re-sprayed the paint – creating layers and balancing negative and positive space with an extreme attention to detail.

Stela, Faith, and Aiko all create works for a purpose that is different from the proliferation of an individual tag name, or the social recognition of their presence in a subculture. Their oeuvres extend beyond the individual and the subcultural – by broadcasting their commentary, they respond to their personal, political, social, and cultural environments. A growing trend, which responds particularly to the social/subcultural male-dominated environment in street art/graffiti writing, is the formation of all-female collectives and crews. More often than not, the aesthetic choices in relation to gender representation differ among individual members, but as a whole they "represent" one another and they do so in full view of the public – bringing a new level of visibility and recognition for girls and women.

Collectively

Rede Nami is a feminist urban arts collective, founded by graffiti writer Anarkia Boladona aka Panmela Castro in 2010 that made use of the 2009 decriminalization of street art in Brazil (www.panmelacastro.com). Anarkia cites TPM (*Transgressão Para Mulheres*/Transgression for Women), Rio's first all-female crew, as Nami's inspiration; TPM was active from 2003–2007 and founded by semiretired writer Prima Donna (Pabón, 2013a). Nami concentrates on girls and women living in the favelas of Rio de Janeiro and teaches them how to paint street art and graffiti while educating them on reproductive rights, domestic violence, and sociopolitical empowerment (www.redenami.com). The themes of their murals reflect their politics and praxis, providing information to onlookers (such as how to call for help in a domestic violence situation). In addition, a structural part of the organization is to employ trained members to recruit and train other girls and women in their communities. Nami is also empowering these women economically. The groups' magnetism and influence is such that in just three years the collective expanded from a grassroots organization with 20–30 members, to an NGO with over 200 members ranging in age from adolescents to elders (Lavoie, 2014).

Few & Far is an US-based collective of graffiti writers/street artists founded in 2011 by Californian graffiti writer Meme, which includes skater girls, deejays, photographers, and jewelry makers (www.facebook.com/FewandFargirls). They are the only all-female graffiti/street art collective in the US, and because of their productions at high art events like Art Basel: Miami Beach, they are making history with themes including "Queen Bees" and "Women Warriors" (McCorquodale, 2012). Painting as a collective of self-identified and proud women is a striking act in a sexist subcultural (and indeed, mainstream) environment where doing so is perceived as too political or too ghettoizing. When the members of Few & Far paint together they are generally in a public setting where spectators can witness and participate in the support network they have built (TheSlashskateboards, 2011; Ironlak Films, 2012; Bazookafilms77, 2014). As a collective, they make it a point to give each individual the safe and supportive space to paint whatever she wants to, trusting that her work will contribute to the overall piece.

Women on Walls (WOW; ستات حائط) is a loose network of over sixty street/visual artists, founded in Cairo, Egypt, after the January 2011 people's revolution in Tahrir Square by photographer/author Mia Grondahl and activist/journalist Angie Balata (http://womenonwalls.org; www.facebook.com/RevolutionGraffiti.StreetArtEgypt). The 2011 revolution sparked a surge of street art: Egyptians have taken their political fight to the walls and thus WOW employs street art as a medium to organize and empower women in that fight, articulating social and political resistance during a period of precarious national transformation (Pabón, 2013c; see http://suzeeinthecity.wordpress.com). The grassroots feminist art network launched their first national campaign in 2013, during which time they traveled to Alexandria, Cairo, Luxor, and Mansoura writing their feminist revolution on the walls – visually inhabiting each city (www. facebook.com/womenonwalls.WOW). In January 2014, WOW completed Phase 2 of their initiative by painting a 40-meter long wall addressing the problems women in public spaces face in the Arab world; also they transformed a parking garage in downtown Cairo into a kind of urban gallery (Bajec, 2014). WOW reclaims public spaces with street art that is particular to women's empowerment in general, and with specific reference to pivotal moments in the revolution: From stenciled images of stoic female figures in gas masks to blue bras (citing the Muslim woman stripped of her veil and beaten by police in Tahrir Square; Amaria, 2011). In the autumn of 2014, WOW expanded their work by inviting twenty-five street artists from the Middle East to Amman, Jordan, where they painted the longest wall in support of women and women's rights in the region.

All three collectives use an art form that does not "belong" to them – per the gender conventions described in the introduction – in order to invite more girls and women into street art and graffiti culture by staking their claim to belonging *as* girls and women. The gradual, but certain, subcultural shift in the active presence of girls and women in street art/graffiti writing is not only linked to all-female crews and collectives, but also to the power of digital culture. Similar to how painting as part of an all-female crew at a public event changes the condition and consequences of anonymity for women, going online changes the anonymity and the ephemerality of the art work in such a way that enables artist/writers to identify themselves and one another, to build networks, and to participate in the project of memory making and

Figure 6.4 "We are discussing the man who sits at the café and harasses women in the street. We tried to reflect the negative effect of this harassment on the female, even after she's entered the private space of her home." Indoor parking lot Sitt Naguiba's Garage, Nour Shoukry, Ahmed Nour, and Sad Panda, 2014, Cairo, Egypt. Photo by Mia Gröndahl © Mia Gröndahl

history writing. Digital culture offers countless means to subvert erasure, invisibility, and impossibility (Sweza, 2009).

Digitally

Predated by the now inoperative, but still significant, websites *GraffGirlz.com* and *CatFight Magazine.com* (F. Lady, 2007), since 2006 Kif, a graffiti writer from Guanajuato, Mexico, has been managing the website *LadysGraff* (http://ladysgraff.blogspot.com). LadysGraff is a Spanish language site where Kif continues in the tradition of the aforementioned sites by bringing the work of female artists to light through interviews and sharing photos. She has been writing graffiti since 2001 and is part of the IKS crew (Insane Kings Crew). Her graffiti sensibilities tend toward gender-neutral, legible, crisp letters consistently including multidirectional arrows on legal walls. She is not what one would conventionally consider a bomber because when she started writing graffiti in 2001, the laws against graffiti were not enforced because a tradition of socially acceptable writing on walls such as murals and *bardas de baile* (dance party advertisements) existed (Heller, 2013). In 2004, that dynamic changed as Mexico City began to implement zero tolerance policies and practices (Grillo, 2004). Nevertheless, Kif builds graffiti community in her city and online – making it a point to create online communities specifically and exclusively for graffiti writing women not only through her blog, but also on social media platforms like Facebook.

Shamsia Hassani's arts practice merges street culture and digital culture in a novel way (Graham-Harrison, 2012; Radio Free Europe, 2012). An Afghanistan-based artist, she began experimenting with graffiti and street art in 2010 after attending a workshop sponsored by the Commbat Comms. Though graffiti is not illegal in Afghanistan, Hassani finds that the socially conservative and politically tumultuous circumstances make painting in Kabul extremely dangerous. As a coping technique, she created a form of graffiti that would enable her to paint the city and feel safe simultaneously (Pabón, 2014c). At first deeming her practice of superimposing images on buildings through graphic design software as "digital graffiti," she now considers her work "dreaming graffiti" and has taken to painting on photograph prints with acrylics. Living in Kabul, and working as a lecturer in the Department of Fine Arts at Kabul University, Hassani's portraits of Muslim women in burqas are more like block letters than figural bodies; they are usually engulfed by, or producing, arabesque color streams. Her art is her contribution to rebuilding the city with a particular eye to the conditions of women before, throughout, and after the war (www.facebook.com/pages/Shamsia-Hassani/252100761577381).

Conclusion

The graffiti writers/street artists cited here negotiate, manipulate, exploit, and reject the ways in which the writing on the wall is seen, particularly in relation to gender representation. They do so by: Using the possibilities of anonymity to negate the sexism within graffiti writing and street art culture; developing a value system unaffected by the conventional aesthetic hierarchy dependent on the gender binary; celebrating women's sexuality and women's bodies through a mode of sexualization that does not subordinate or dominate; using art to share and provoke cultural critique; painting in groups, in public, and in front of an audience; inviting, training, and mentoring other girls and women into street art and graffiti culture; and accessing the power of digital culture to connect across borders and time zones, to make history where girls and women are a part of the story (FemaleCaps, n.d.). The hopeful intention behind their cultural work is that the sexist and bigoted generalizations about the graffiti/street art "doer" will fade in favor of a realization that all writers/artists are individuals with the potential to expand the aesthetic diversity of the writing on the wall (Turco, 2012; McCorquodale, 2012; Harrington and Rojo, 2013; Wyatt, 2013).

References

149St Staff. (2002). Female Writers [Internet]. *At149st.com*. Available from: www.at149st.com/women.html [Accessed April 15, 2014].

Amaria, K. (2011). *'Girl In the Blue Bra' Symbol of Egypt's Ongoing Strife* [Internet]. Available from: www.npr.org/blogs/pictureshow/2011/12/21/144098384/the-girl-in-the-blue-bra [Accessed April 17, 2014].

Anon. (n.d.). *California Penal Code Section 639–653.2* [Internet]. Available from: www.leginfo.ca.gov/cgi-bin/displaycode?section=pen&group=00001-01000&file=639-653.2 [Accessed March 19, 2014].

Austin, J. (2001). *Taking the Train: How Graffiti Art Became an Urban Crisis in New York City*. New York: Columbia University Press.

Bajec, A. (2014). Can Graffiti Remake Egypt? *Daily Beast-Women in the World* [Internet]. Available from: www.thedailybeast.com/witw/articles/2014/02/19/can-graffiti-remake-egypt.html [Accessed April 29, 2014].

Banes, S. (1981; 2004). Physical Graffiti: Breaking Is Hard to Do. In R. Cepeda (Ed.). *And It Don't Stop: The Best American Hip-Hop Journalism of the Last 25 Years* (pp. 7–11). New York: Faber & Faber.

Bazookafilms77. (2014). *Few and Far Women* [Online Video]. January 29. Available from: http://vimeo.com/85340528 [Accessed April 15, 2014].

Castleman, C. (1982). *Getting Up: Subway Graffiti in New York*. Cambridge, MA: The MIT Press.

Chalfant, H. & Prigoff, J. (1987). *Spraycan Art*. New York: Thames & Hudson.

ClawMoney. (2007). *Bombshell: The Life and Crimes of Claw Money*. New York: powerhouse Books.

ClawMoney. (2010). Utah: The Interview [Internet]. *Blogue*. Available from: http://blogue.us/2010/02/10/utah-the-interview [Accessed May 5, 2014].

Coelho, G. (2011). *Luz, Câmera, Pichação* [Online Video]. Available from: www.imdb.com/title/tt1841730 [Accessed April 13, 2014].

Cooper, M. & Chalfant, H. (1984). *Subway Art*. New York: Holt, Rinehart and Winston.

Council. (2010). *City of Cape Town Graffiti By-Law 2010* [Internet]. Available from: www.capetown.gov.za/en/Lawenforcement/Pages/Grafittiunit.aspx [Accessed March 19, 2014].

Dixon, C. (2014). Painting the Town Yellow, Green, and Blue: Street Art in Rio de Janeiro, Brazil [Internet]. *Global Site Plans*. Available from: www.globalsiteplans.com/environmental-design/painting-the-town-yellow-green-and-blue-street-art-in-rio-de-janeiro-brazil [Accessed March 19, 2014].

DtNews. (2014). *Writing on the Walls: Sya and Steffi Bow Unveil the Secret of Street Art* [Internet]. Available from: http://dt.bh/writing-on-the-walls [Accessed April 17, 2014].

Du Plessis, A. (2009). Motel7: Tears and Castles. *34 Long Fine Art*. Available from: http://vgallery.co.za/34long/img/motel7/motel7_cat.pdf [Accessed March 19, 2014].

F. Lady (2007). *Catfight Magazine*. Available from: www.catfightmagazine.com [Accessed March 19, 2014].

FemaleCaps. (n.d.). *Female Caps* [Internet]. Available from: http://femalecaps.tumblr.com/?og=1 [Accessed April 17, 2014].

Ganz, N. (2006). *Graffiti Women: Street Art from Five Continents*. New York: Abrams.

Giuliani, R.W. (2012). What New York Owes James Q. Wilson [Internet]. *City Journal*. (Spring). Available from: www.city-journal.org/2012/22_2_james-q-wilson.html [Accessed April 14, 2014].

Graham-Harrison, E. (2012). Art in the streets of Kabul [Internet]. *The Guardian*. February 24. Available from: www.theguardian.com/world/2012/feb/24/graffiti-street-art-kabul [Accessed March 27, 2014].

Grillo, I. (2004). Mexico City Cracks Down on Graffiti [Internet]. *Houston Chronicle*. January 31. Available from: www.chron.com/news/nation-world/article/Mexico-City-cracks-down-on-graffiti-1959318.php [Accessed March 27, 2014].

Guevara, N. (1996). Women Writin' Rappin' Breakin'. In W. Perkins (Ed.). *Droppin Science: Critical Essays on Rap Music and Hip Hop Culture* (pp. 49–62). Philadelphia, PA: Temple University Press.

Harrington, S. & Rojo, J. (2013). Women Rock Wynwood Walls at Miami Art Basel 2013 [Internet]. *Huffington Post*. Available from: www.huffingtonpost.com/jaime-rojo-steven-harrington/wynwood-walls_b_4416142.html [Accessed December 15, 2013].

Heller, S. (2013). *The Writing on Mexican Walls Isn't Graffiti—It's 'Vernacular Branding'* [Internet]. Available from: www.theatlantic.com/entertainment/archive/2013/08/the-writing-on-mexican-walls-isnt-graffiti-its-vernacular-branding/278116 [Accessed April 17, 2014].

Ironlak Films. (2012). *Few & Far at Primary Flight – Miami, 2011* [Online Video]. February 28, 2012. Available from: www.youtube.com/watch?v=Eq8yDrZDiIg&feature=youtube_gdata_player [Accessed October 30, 2013].

Irving, S. (2009). *Issue 28: 'En Route' Feature – UTAH & ETHER MUL* [Internet]. Available from: www.acclaimmag.com/arts/issue-28-en-route-feature-utah-ether-mul [Accessed April 9, 2014].

JapanSocietyNYC. (2013). *Edo Pop – AIKO: The Making of Sunrise* [Online Video]. March 7. Available from: www.youtube.com/watch?v=qru9U1fdj2U&feature=youtube_gdata_player [Accessed March 12, 2014].

Kif. (n.d.). *Lady s Graff* [Internet]. Available from: http://ladysgraff.blogspot.ae [Accessed April 17, 2014].

Lavoie, A. (2014). Un féminisme mur à mur avec les reines du graffiti [Internet]. *Métro*. Available from: http://journalmetro.com/monde/392720/un-feminisme-mur-a-mur-avec-les-reines-du-graffiti [Accessed April 29, 2014].

Lennon, J. (2009). 'Bombing' Brooklyn: Graffiti, Language and Gentrification [Internet]. *Rhizomes*. (19). Available from: http://rhizomes.net/issue19/lennon/index.html#_ednref1 [Accessed April 25, 2014].

Leon, S. (2012). *Bowery Mural Wall: Lady Aiko Takes over Space from RETNA* [Internet]. Available from: www.huffingtonpost.com/2012/07/09/lady-aiko-mural-new-york-photos_n_1659610.html [Accessed April 14, 2014].

McAuliffe, C. (2012). Graffiti or Street Art? Negotiating the Moral Geographies of the Creative City. *Journal of Urban Affairs*, 34(2), 189–206.

McCorquodale, A. (2012). *Few And Far Graffiti Collective Paint Miami's Largest All-Female Mural* [Internet]. Available from: www.huffingtonpost.com/2012/03/02/few-and-far-all-women-gra_n_1316217.html [Accessed November 21, 2013].

Macdonald, N. (2001). *The Graffiti Subculture: Youth, Masculinity and Identity in London and New York*. New York: Palgrave Macmillan.

Mailer, N. & Naar, J. (1974; 2009). *The Faith of Graffiti*. New ed. New York: It Books.

Marco, D. (2011). Rhyming with 'Knowledge of Self': The South African Hip-Hop Scene's Discourses on Race and Knowledge. *Muziki*, 8(2), 96–106.

Miller, I.L. (2002). *Aerosol Kingdom: Subway Painters of New York City*. Jackson: University Press of Mississippi.

MOCATV. (2013). *Global Street Art – Tokyo – Art in the Streets – MOCAtv* [Online Video]. July 4. Available from: www.youtube.com/watch?v=fGeWIT1JYks&feature=youtube_gdata_player [Accessed March 12, 2014].

Olson, M.L. (2013). *Dubai's Steffi Bow is a Girl with a Graffiti Habit* [Internet]. Available from: www.thenational.ae/arts-culture/art/dubais-steffi-bow-is-a-girl-with-a-graffiti-habit [Accessed April 14, 2014].

Pabón, J. (2012). Interview with Free! *BUSTOLEUM* [Internet]. Available from: http://jessicapabon.com/2012/09/13/interview-with-free/.

Pabón, J. (2013a). Be About It: Graffiteras Performing Feminist Community. *TDR: The Journal of Performance Studies*, 59(219), 88–116.

Pabón, J. (2013b). Shifting Aesthetics: The Stick up Girlz Perform Crew in a Virtual World [Internet]. In J. Lennon & M. Burns (Eds). *Rhizomes*, 25. Available from: http://rhizomes.net/issue25/pabon/index.html [Accessed April 17, 2014].

Pabón, J. (2013c). *Wipe It off and I Will Paint Again: An Interview with Blogger Suzeeinthecity* [Internet]. Available from: http://muslima.imow.org/content/wipe-it-and-i-will-paint-again [Accessed April 17, 2014].

Pabón, J. (2013d). Interview with Stela. *BUSTOLEUM* [Internet]. Available from: http://jessicapabon.com/2013/03/21/interview-with-stela.

Pabón, J. (2013e). Let's Be Clear: Aiko and Faith47 ARE NOT 'Female Banksys' [Internet]. *BUSTOLEUM*. Available from: http://jessicapabon.com/2013/10/22/lets-be-clear-aiko-and-faith47-are-not-female-banksys.

Pabón, J. (2013f). Following Carmen Sandiego..er Miss17 Around Athens. *BUSTOLEUM* [Internet]. Available from: http://jessicapabon.com/2013/10/24/following-miss17-around-athens/.

Pabón, J. (2014a). Interview with AbbyTC5: A Pioneering 'HomeGirl' in Hip Hop Herstory. *Women & Performance: A Journal of Feminist Theory*, 24(1), 8–14.

Pabón, J. (2014b). Notes on Street Art Night in Dubai. *BUSTOLEUM* [Internet]. Available from: http://jessicapabon.com/2014/01/25/notes-on-street-art-night-in-dubai/.

Pabón, J. (2014c). Digital Interview with Shamsia Hassani, 'Dreaming Graffiti' in Kabul Afghanistan. *BUSTOLEUM* [Internet]. Available from: http://jessicapabon.com/2014/04/19/digital-interview-with-shamsia-hassani-dreaming-graffiti-in-kabul-afghanistan/.

Pardue, D. (2011). *Brazilian Hip Hoppers Speak from the Margins: We's on Tape.* Palgrave Macmillan, New York.

Phillips, S.A. (1999). *Wallbangin': Graffiti and Gangs in L.A.* Chicago, IL: University Of Chicago Press.

Powers, S. (1999). *The Art of Getting over.* New York: St. Martin's Press.

Radio Free Europe. (2012). *Female Graffiti Artist Struggles to Make a Mark In Kabul* [Online Video]. Available from: www.rferl.org/media/video/24660846.html [Accessed March 18, 2014].

Sherman, W. (2009). UTAH Faces Graffiti Charges in Queens Court. *ANIMAL* [Internet]. Available from: http://animalnewyork.com/2009/utah-faces-graffiti-charges-in-queens-court [Accessed April 9, 2014].

Siegel, F. (1993). Lady Pink: Graffiti with a Feminist Intent. *MS. Magazine*, 3(5), 66–68.

Swenson, E.M. (2013). *Jerk: Female Graffiti Legend* [Online Video]. December 28. Available from: www.youtube.com/watch?v=5wWEGGrPARA&feature=youtube_gdata_player [Accessed March 19, 2014].

Sweza (2009). *GRAFFYARD* [Internet]. Available from: http://sweza.com/graffyard [Accessed April 17, 2014].

TEDx Talks. (2012). *Feminism on the Wall: Jessica Pabón at TEDxWomen 2012* [Online Video]. December 4. Available from: www.youtube.com/watch?v=z_4JOexUj0M&feature=youtube_gdata_player [Accessed March 20, 2014].

TheSlashskateboards. (2011). *Few and Far all Female Skate Jam* [Online Video]. October 20. Available from: www.youtube.com/watch?v=pX0eFfped3s&feature=youtube_gdata_player [Accessed April 15, 2014].

Turco, B. (2010). UTAH Is Free. . .To Release Photos, Discuss Graffiti [Internet]. *ANIMAL.* Available from: http://animalnewyork.com/2010/utah-is-free-to-release-photos-discuss-graffiti [Accessed May 5, 2014].

Turco, B. (2012). CLAW's Graffiti Inspired NASCAR Truck [Internet]. *ANIMAL.* Available from: http://animalnewyork.com/2012/claws-graffiti-nascar-truck [Accessed April 21, 2014].

UtahEther. (2008). *UTAH & ETHER* [Internet]. Available from: www.utahether.com/about [Accessed April 21, 2014].

Wacławek, A. (2011). *Graffiti and Street Art.* New York: Thames & Hudson.

Wyatt, D. (2013). *In Search of a Female Banksy: Aiko and Faith47 Take on a Male-Dominated Street Art World* [Internet]. Available from: www.independent.co.uk/arts-entertainment/art/features/in-search-of-a-female-banksy-aiko-and-faith47-take-on-a-maledominated-street-art-world-8882082.html [Accessed April 14, 2014].

7

Research and theory on latrinalia

Adam Trahan

Introduction

Latrinalia, also known as bathroom graffiti, may seem like an odd topic for serious scholarship. Some of what we read on the bathroom walls, like the infamous "for a good time call . . .," is so ostensibly mundane that it seems better off ignored. Some of it is so obscene that it seems better off unspoken. However, it is these very characteristics that make latrinalia such an intriguing and important topic of study. According to Schottmiller, "It is precisely because latrinalia seem so mundane, that it is so powerful. When the seemingly trivial is overlooked by serious scholarly analysis, it becomes normalized, and when scholars overlook this normalization, they become complicit in its reproduction" (2009: 4).

Closer inspections have shown that latrinalia goes far beyond the stereotypes we associate it with (Cole, 1991). People often mark the walls of public bathrooms with thoughtful commentaries and critiques of political, social, cultural, and economic issues to name a few. These graffiti often spark impassioned and ongoing debates between multiple authors. People also frequently write about deeply personal issues that confront them. Dermakardijian (2008: 12) stated that latrinalia is often a site for "secret sharing and confessions." In short, the walls of public bathrooms contain discourse about a full range of topics, from broad social commentary to specific challenges in the lives of individuals.

These messages are also compressed and compact due to the characteristics of the space in which latrinalia are produced (Islam, 2010). Put simply, there is a limited amount of space and arguably time available to work with. Graffitists are thus forced to get straight to the point, so to speak. This establishes latrinalia as a uniquely direct form of expression (Ferem, 2006, 2007). It is highly unlikely that the messages contained on the walls of public bathrooms would appear in other spaces or types of discourse. For these and other reasons, many consider latrinalia to be a rich cultural form that can provide great insight into the psyches of those who write on the walls and the societies in which they live (Bartholome and Snyder, 2004; Ferem, 2006, 2007; Islam, 2010). For instance, Ferem (2006) considers latrinalia to be the "last strong hold of pure self-expression." The following sections review the major themes of the current theoretical and empirical literature on latrinalia.

Public vs private

Do latrinalia constitute a public or private form of expression? Coming to some sort of under-standing about this is potentially important. It could certainly influence the content of what people write on the walls. People may share very different attitudes and opinions in private than in a public forum. Moreover, public commentaries (can) serve a very different purpose than our private sentiments (Habermas, 1991). Indeed, it seems odd to even discuss the *social* and/or *cultural* significance of something that is quintessentially private. The answer to this question ultimately lies in whether the bathrooms that contain latrinalia are public or private spaces.

Theory and research on the public-private nature of bathroom graffiti have been guided in large part by Margaret Kohn's (2004) cluster concept of public space. The cluster concept is a model that Kohn developed to measure the extent to which any given space is essentially public or private. It is comprised of three factors – ownership, accessibility, and intersubjectivity. Each of these factors is placed along a continuum with one side representing entirely public space and the other representing entirely private space.

Ownership literally refers to who owns the space. Kohn specifies three primary types of ownership – private people, corporations, and the government. She posits that spaces owned by private people are the most private, and those owned by the government are the most public. Accessibility refers to the ability for anyone to enter the space and travel freely within it. A space in which a large number and wide variety of people are allowed to enter and traverse is much more public, Kohn argues, than a space that restricts all but a few peoples access to it. These first two factors – ownership and accessibility – are frequently interconnected. Our homes would be high on the private side of the ownership scale because they are owned by private individuals. Because we own them, access to our house is limited to us and to anyone we choose to allow inside. Conversely, government property, such as a public park, is often accessible to virtually anyone precisely because it is owned by the government.

Intersubjectivity is certainly the most nebulous of the three factors. It refers to how people are positioned in any given space and whether that positioning fosters interaction. Ultimately, spaces in which there is a high degree of interaction between people are considered public whereas places that mute interaction are more private. Kohn offers movie theaters as an example of private space because they position people in such a way as to undermine the likelihood that they interact. Spaces that position people to face each other, such as parks, are considered more public because they foster interaction.

Two notable and recent studies of latrinalia have attempted to situate public bathrooms along the private-public continuum using Kohn's cluster concept. Young (2009) examined the private-public nexus in both men and women's bathrooms by analyzing the content and dialogue present in latrinalia at Miami University. Although Young never explicitly states where along the spectrum his findings would situate public bathrooms and latrinalia, his discussion seems to suggest that he considers them somewhere in the middle. He explains that 40 percent of the latrinalia he recorded were part of a dialogue between multiple people and therefore bathroom graffiti are public (interactive) phenomena. However, many of these discussions centered around very personal issues that suggest privacy is a functional element to the production of latrinalia.

Sawka (2012) recorded graffiti twice a day for one week from eight heavily trafficked women's restrooms at the University of Winnipeg. After analyzing the physical structure of the bathrooms as well as the spatial distribution of the latrinalia and their content, she ultimately concludes that "women's public washrooms are slightly more public than private" (p. 22). It is important to note, however, that Sawka's conclusion may not pertain to men's bathrooms. If women do indeed interact more often than men in public bathrooms, women's bathrooms will thus rank higher on the intersubjectivity component in Kohn's model.

These studies have yielded valuable information about the "public vs private" nature of restrooms and the latrinalia contained therein. However, attempting to identify a specific point along a continuum may be akin to splitting hairs. That is, public bathrooms and latrinalia are clearly both public and private, and understanding the interaction between these domains is arguably more beneficial than attempting to ascertain which is (slightly) more prominent in the production of latrinalia. Haslam (2012: 114–115) states that public bathrooms offer graffitists a unique mix of privacy and publicity. He states,

> All graffiti writing requires a certain amount of secrecy, and bathroom stalls are more private than the spaces where other forms of graffiti are produced, allowing wall-scribblers more time and leisure to compose their messages . . . Public bathrooms are also in some sense more public than other shared spaces, offering graffiti-writers a confined and captive audience with whom to communicate.

Islam (2010) argues that latrinalia are both public and private because the graffiti are written in private but become public shortly thereafter, at least until their abatement. Moreover, the interaction between public and private elements seems to influence the form and function of latrinalia. As Taylor (2010) explains, public restrooms are simultaneously public and private, and that latrinalia "grow out" of the characteristics of this context. The public and private nature of the space allows individuals unique opportunities for deviance and self-expression. The privacy afforded by closed stalls permit us to voice attitudes and ideas that we may not express in purely public settings (Ferem, 2007). Conversely, the public elements of bathrooms allow us to express our sentiments to a potentially limitless array of different people. An interesting question to ponder is – why do we not write these statements on the walls of our home or private bathroom? We write them on the walls of public bathrooms, in part, because we know people will read them. The statements become public the second we vacate the stalls.

The privacy afforded in public bathrooms seems to influence the spatial distribution of latrinalia. Studies have shown that latrinalia tend to be heavily concentrated in particular places within public bathrooms. An overwhelmingly large proportion of all bathroom graffiti are written inside the toilet stall farthest from the door. For instance, Sawka (2012) showed that 89 percent of the latrinalia in her sample were found inside the stall that was located farthest from the door to the bathroom. Moreover, each stall that was closer to the door contained, on average, progressively less latrinalia. This spatial trend suggests that privacy is a powerful force in the production of latrinalia. People seem to seek out privacy or at least are more likely to write graffiti when their perceptions of solitude are at their highest.

Anonymity

The privacy of the stalls create a context for another essential characteristic of latrinalia – anonymity. Although privacy and anonymity are highly related, they refer to somewhat different elements that influence the production of bathroom graffiti. Privacy refers to the freedom from observation. Put simply, no one is watching when people write on the walls of a closed toilet stall. Anonymity on the other hand refers to the freedom from identification (Sawka, 2012). Latrinalia, and many other forms of graffiti, typically do not contain any identifying information and therefore cannot be tied to any individual. The most straightforward way to consider the relationship between privacy and anonymity in the context of latrinalia is that privacy provides the opportunity for but does not require anonymity. Behind the locked door of a bathroom stall, free from observation, people can and sometimes do choose to attach themselves to what they write on the wall. Studies have found that "tags" – markers of group or individual identity – are not entirely uncommon among latrinalia (Ferem, 2007). For instance, Young's (2009) analysis of latrinalia at Miami University found that 15 percent of bathroom graffiti contained expressions of identity. Research on latrinalia has however unequivocally shown that most graffitists seize upon the opportunity for anonymous expression (Nwoye, 1993). The majority of comments found on bathroom walls appear without any way to identify who inscribed them.

Dermarkardijian (2008) refers to anonymity as a "defining characteristic" of latrinalia. Indeed, anonymity itself affects the form and function of latrinalia in several important respects. The absence of individual or group identification means that "readers" can only view what was written, not who wrote it. Rodriguez and Clair (2009) argue that this establishes latrinalia as "free and open discourse." That is, all the hierarchies that privilege some members of our society and their voices are suspended within latrinalia. The advantages of wealth, power, and status that can lend power to some people's opinions in wider society are quite literally irrelevant among the anonymous markings on bathroom walls. Who we are and where we come from has no impact on the potency of our sentiments. As such, Rodriguez and Clair argue that latrinalia represents an "equal opportunity rhetorical form." They also state that latrinalia is the only rhetorical form that affords such virtues.

This unique privacy-anonymity nexus also influences the content of latrinalia. Free from judgment and ridicule, people often choose to write about deeply sensitive personal information (Sawka, 2012). This is particularly true of latrinalia in women's restrooms. Dermakardijian's (2008) study of women's latrinalia suggests that latrinalia often consists of secret-sharing and confessions. Other studies have shown that women often use latrinalia to share and solicit advice regarding personal problems in their lives (Green, 2003). Cole (1991) reports one lengthy exchange in which the author began with "people, help me with my problem." This person then discussed sexual problems she was having in a relationship and how they were exacerbated by having been raped earlier in her life. Several responses advised the author of the original statement to seek counseling, offered suggestions on how to proceed in her relationship, and ultimately wished her luck.

Anonymity does not always influence the content of latrinalia in an explicitly positive, supportive, or pro-social manner. Many people, both men and women, often use latrinalia as an opportunity to direct antagonism toward other people and groups. Some of this "anonymous negativity" that appears on bathroom walls is relatively minor. For instance, one common theme among bathroom graffiti in University settings is facetious antagonism between members of different fraternities and non-fraternity students (Young, 2009). However, some latrinalia contains malicious attacks of different people and groups. It is not uncommon to read unapologetically racist, sexist, and homophobic content on bathroom walls. Privacy and the anonymity it affords play a key role in the production of malicious latrinalia (Young, 2009; Trahan, 2011). It's highly unlikely that the authors of these graffiti would express the same sentiments in any other setting where they might be held accountable for their spite.

Content

Research on latrinalia content has generally involved creating taxonomies and classifying graffiti in an attempt to identify and explain exactly what people tend to write on the walls of public bathrooms. Before discussing the findings of this research, it is important to note that analyzing the latrinalia content is a much more precarious exercise than it may at first appear. The difficulty lies in deciding what and how many categories to create, and determining which category any given graffito belongs in.

Many of the markings commonly found in public bathrooms can fit into multiple categories (Haslam, 2012). For instance, graffiti that is explicitly sexual also frequently contain attempts at humor. It is not uncommon to read comments that poke fun at sexual conquests or genitalia. Latrinalia such as this could quite accurately be classified as "sexual" or "humorous" and might be classified differently from one study to the next. Some studies that have attempted to manage these complexities have ultimately constructed over a dozen categories (Anderson and Verplanck, 1983; Bartholome and Snyder, 2004). This of course makes interpreting the research somewhat challenging. However, given that there have been a relatively large number of studies on the content of latrinalia, convergent findings and trends across the literature make it possible to reach some conclusions about what exactly we tend to write about in the bathroom (Whiting and Koller, 2007).

Sexuality

Studies have consistently found sexuality to be the most common topic of latrinalia. In part because of the frequency of sexual latrinalia, these graffiti include a wide variety of different types of messages. Many researchers have chosen to divide sexual latrinalia into heterosexual, homosexual, and homophobic subcategories to account for the differences in their content. Findings are somewhat conflicted as to which subcategory – homosexual or heterosexual – is most common. Some studies have shown that homosexual graffiti outnumber heterosexual inscriptions (Abel and Buckley, 1977). This is particularly true of latrinalia in men's bathrooms (Haslam, 2012). For instance, Liu's (2008) analysis of 135 homosexual inscriptions in public bathrooms found that only 3 (2.2 percent) appeared in women's bathrooms. The remaining 132 were distributed across various men's bathrooms. He concludes that the prevalence of homosexual latrinalia in men's bathrooms acts as a challenge to the heteronormativity of public spaces (i.e. the socio-cultural establishment of heterosexuality as "normal" and "right"). Latrinalia allows men to covertly resist the cultural milieu of hypermasculinity and heterosexuality as the projected way of life. Homosexual latrinalia frequently consists of simple jokes about sex, solicitations and desires for sex, and statements about the authors' orientation and the challenges they face in wider society (Innala and Ernulf, 1992).

Although some homophobic latrinalia are written as solitary messages, they often appear as part of a dialogue with homosexual markings. That is, statements of hostility toward homosexuality are often written in response to homosexual graffiti and vice versa. This can prompt a back-and-forth response set among multiple authors. These "response chains" frequently become quite hostile as people infuse their religious and ideological orientations into what they write on the walls: "Homosexuality is a sin. [Response] Fuck all you homophobic discriminatory males." (Trahan, 2011),

Heterosexual latrinalia are also composed of a wide variety of different messages. People write about their desires, brag about their bodies and conquests, and joke about sex acts: "Sex is like a snow storm. They never know when they'll get it, or how many inches they'll get." (Bartholome and Snyder, 2004).

Religion

The abundance of religious graffiti that have been found in public bathrooms suggests that, as one graffitist stated, "God *is* everywhere, even here [in the toilet stall]." Religious latrinalia often appear as announcements of religious affiliations. Simple declarative statements such as "Christian and proud," "Jesus is lord," and other personal affirmations of religiosity appear frequently (Islam, 2010). There is also evangelism among religious latrinalia. Studies have found that people prescribe their own religious beliefs and attempt to convert others on the walls of public bathrooms: "Without Jesus you'll be in *hell*." (Trahan, 2011).

The last form that religious latrinalia often takes is what might best be described as anti-religion. These graffiti decry religious beliefs and the people who subscribe to them. Some anti-religious graffiti also promote atheism, humanism, and non-spiritual belief systems in much the same way as their religious counterparts prescribe their own beliefs (Trahan, 2011).

Political

Latrinalia frequently includes expressions of political ideology and opinions of specific political issues, elections, and politicians. Studies suggest that political latrinalia is especially common in university bathrooms (Haslam, 2012). Olusoji (2013: 6) analyzed bathroom graffiti in two college campuses and concluded that "the content of information provided … suggests that no national affair escapes the students' attention." Moreover, political latrinalia varies from short, facetious comments to more extensive and serious debates about contentious issues. For instance, Bartholome and Snyder (2004) found a lengthy debate about abortion in the women's restroom.

Humor

Bathroom graffiti is often funny, or at least attempts to be. Humorous latrinalia may suffer more than any other category from the challenges to classifying graffiti noted above. Specifically, latrinalia in other categories, especially sexual and political, regularly contain jokes: "Sex is like a bridge – if you have a good hand you don't need a partner." (Bruner and Kelso, 1980). "If you voted for Clinton, you cannot sit here because your asshole is in Washington, DC" (Bartholome and Snyder, 2004). It can be easy to shrug off humorous latrinalia as less significant than some other content. However, studies have found several intriguing aspects of humorous graffiti. First, humorous latrinalia often pokes fun at the physical environment of the bathroom. For instance, one recently observed graffito was written below a hook for hanging coats or bags and advised "do *not* use as a prostate massager, although it would be a great one." Second, a prominent sub-category of humor is scatology, which includes jokes about excretion and urination: "Here I sit all broken-hearted. Tried to shit and only farted." (Gonos *et al.*, 1976).

These latrinalia may simply represent juvenile attempts at humor, but there is also evidence that they act to minimize both the author's and audience's discomfort with public bathrooms and what takes place therein (Trahan, 2011).

Love and relationships

Graffiti concerning love and relationships are much more common in women's bathrooms than men's. For instance, Batholome and Snyder (2004) found that love/relationship ranked thirteenth among sixteen categories in terms of frequency among men's latrinalia. It was the second most common topic of women's latrinalia in their sample. An interesting facet of graffiti in this category is that they are frequently conversational and involve advice seeking and giving. That is, graffitists, typically women, often describe their problems with relationships or desires for love which then sets off response chains. Others may give advice, whether solicited or not, which can be supportive or disparaging (Rodriguez and Clair, 2009).

Hostility

As an antithesis of sorts to the graffiti about love and relationships, some latrinalia express insults and hostility toward other people or groups. Some hostile latrinalia includes general insults directed toward almost any reader (Bartholome and Snyder, 20014). Other comments are directed toward specific groups of people. Common among hostile latrinalia are racial and ethnic derogations as well as comments that may overlap somewhat with other categories, such as hostile comments toward homosexuals and religious believers. For instance, Rodriguez and Claire (2009) found that women frequently use latrinalia to denigrate each other for supposed promiscuity and homosexuality. Studies suggest that the anonymity available to bathroom graffitists influence both the frequency and form of hostile latrinalia. People are afforded opportunities to express frustrations and opinions that they cannot in other social settings without having to confront the consequences of their hostility (Haslam, 2012).

Gender differences

Exploring the differences between graffiti in men and women's public bathrooms is by far the most common focus of the existing scholarly literature on latrinalia. This should come as no surprise. Gender is, in a sense, fundamental to the organization of public bathrooms. They are one of the last remaining spaces in which people are conspicuously segregated. There are separate rooms, often situated right next to each other, for men and women and we are instructed which room we belong in by the signs and symbols that are centered on the front of the door. Put simply, public bathrooms make biological sex prominent and significant. Studying latrinalia as a social and cultural phenomenon necessitates an understanding of gender differences.

There is also an interpersonal element regarding gender and public bathrooms that may influence (and be reflected in) latrinalia. We patronize public bathrooms solely with members of the same gender as ourselves. As such, people who write graffiti on the walls of public bathrooms likely do so with an awareness that only members of the same gender will read what they write. These factors, combined with the anonymity available to graffitists in public bathrooms, may lead to the exaggeration of "maleness" and "femaleness" in latrinalia (Green, 2003). It is plausible then that latrinalia represent a unique and fruitful source of intra-gender discourse and identity (Schottmiller, 2009). Indeed, some of the earliest and oft cited studies of latrinalia analyzed differences in the quantity and content of graffiti in men's and women's bathrooms, and these studies shaped much of the later research on latrinalia.

One of the first empirical studies of latrinalia appeared in Kinsey and colleagues' (1953) now infamous *Sexual Behavior in the Human Female*. They recorded latrinalia in over 300 public restrooms, both male and female. After systematically comparing men and women's graffiti, they found two patterns that would become the focus of latrinalia research on gender differences for the next half-century. First, they found that men produced more latrinalia overall than women. Second, men's latrinalia was markedly more sexual than women's. A full 86 percent of men's latrinalia contained erotic content compared to only 25 percent of women's. They found that women more often wrote comments about romantic love. In an attempt to explain these disparities, Kinsey and his colleagues argued that women wrote fewer latrinalia generally and sexual comments specifically because they are more committed to moral codes and social conventions. Studies that followed continued to find that women produced less latrinalia overall and proportionately less sexual content than men (Dundes, 1966; Landy and Steele, 1967; Peretti *et al.*, 1977). Explanations for these differences continued to echo stereotypical gender roles, such as greater adherence to social conventions and conservative sexual mores among women. Reisner (1971) went so far as to suggest that women are less likely to make markings in the bathroom because they place a greater value on clean walls due to the fact that they are usually the ones to clean them.

Research on gender differences in latrinalia stagnated until experiencing a resurgence beginning in the 1980s. A primary driving force behind this resurgence was a suspicion that women's liberation movements throughout the late 1960s and 1970s might have caused a shift in women's latrinalia. That is, if liberation loosened women's commitment to social conventions, especially those regarding sexuality, then women might be expected to produce more latrinalia and that the content of their latrinalia would be proportionately more sexual. The findings of this research are considerably mixed. Some studies found that the gender disparities in latrinalia were shrinking (Bates and Martin, 1980; Grant, 1993). Others continued to find differences in the quantity and proportionate sexuality between men and women's latrinalia (Bruner and Kelso, 1980; Loewenstine et al., 1982). In one of the most seminal studies of this period, Arluke et al. (1987) directly examined whether the differences in men and women's latrinalia had narrowed overtime. They found that the content of women's latrinalia was less sexual than men's. They concluded that liberation movements had little effect on women's tendency to produce latrinalia, particularly of a sexual nature.

A bevy of recent research has produced a relative consensus regarding the quantity and sexuality of men and women's latrinalia. Taken as a whole, the literature seem to suggest that Kinsey's first finding – that women write less frequently on bathroom walls – may no longer be true (Haslam, 2012). While some studies have continued to find less latrinalia in women's restrooms (Liu, 2008), other studies have found the opposite – that women produced an equal or even greater amount of bathroom graffiti than men. For instance, Bartholome and Snyder (2004) collected 269 latrinalia over a two week period and found that women produced slightly more (52 percent) latrinalia than men (48 percent).

Kinsey's second finding – that men's latrinalia tends to be more sexual in nature than women's – has better stood the test of time (Green, 2003; Haslam, 2012; Olusoji, 2013). For instance, Matthews et al., (2012) conducted a sophisticated analysis of 1,201 graffiti recorded in the men's and women's bathrooms of nine bars. They found that men produced more sexual graffiti than women. Women composed more messages about romantic love and authored more insults. Olusoji (2013) found that, although sex was the most common topic among both, men wrote proportionately more about sex than women (46 to 37.5 percent).

Many recent analyses have gone beyond the somewhat narrow "quantity and sexuality" focus and discovered a host of other differences in men and women's latrinalia. Findings show that men's latrinalia tends to be more hostile and derogatory, including racist and sexist comments. Men's latrinalia has also been found to be more argumentative, competitive, and generally conflict-oriented. Lastly, men's latrinalia has been found to contain more humorous and political comments (Whiting and Koller, 2007). Conversely, women's latrinalia is generally more conversational, friendly, and confessional. Women tend to discuss romance and relationships as well as offer support and express solidarity (Fisher and Radtke, 2014; Green, 2003).

Modern explanations of these sex differences focus on gender socialization and its influence on the ways that men and women view the public restroom. Gadsby (1995: 49) posits that women tend to view public restrooms as a "sanctuary, a safe retreat from a hectic world . . . a place to talk and put on make-up." For men, public restrooms are functional spaces that are not for socializing. Young (2009) argues that interaction in men's restrooms is intentionally subdued. Men abstain from conversation and avoid even having to acknowledge each other's presence. The argument goes that these conditions lead to conversational, friendly, and supportive latrinalia among women due to their positive impressions of public bathrooms as a space for interaction. Men's co-presence in public bathrooms is a source of angst and discomfort, and their deleterious comments develop out of these conditions. Whether and to what extent these are plausible explanations or a reiteration of gender stereotypes is debatable.

Conclusion

Many of the new directions of latrinalia research resemble the current trends in criminology and social science generally. For instance, several recent studies have explored different intersections of race, gender, and sexual orientation and their influence on latrinalia (see, e.g. Liu, 2008). This approach is based on the recognition that isolating these identity characteristics does not reflect the reality of people's lives and backgrounds. For instance, past research isolated biological sex from, say, race, and sexual orientation and essentially placed all graffiti and their authors into two categories – men and women. From there, sweeping generalizations are made about the distinctions, or lack thereof, between what men and women write on the bathroom walls. This type of approach essentially ignores the fact that the people within each group derive from various different social locations. Women who produce latrinalia may be homosexual, heterosexual, bisexual, and transgendered. Women's latrinalia contains messages written by and from the perspective of black, white, and Hispanic people. Some of the authors of bathroom graffiti are young and some are old. The combination of these identity characteristics may well influence what and why people write on the walls.

In one of the most sophisticated intersectional studies of latrinalia to date, Rodriguez and Clair (2009) analyzed how biological sex and sexual orientation shape latrinalia at a predominantly black university. Among the many intriguing facets of their research, they found that expressions of homosexuality were met with singular hostility. This ardent homophobia, they argue, reflects the general resentment of homosexuality in the black community at large. Even in university settings then, which are often considered epicenters of liberal thought and progress, marginalized people engage in derisive communication and further abuse and marginalize each other. This discourse functions to perpetuate the status quo and maintain current hierarchies of privilege. Findings such as this cannot derive from research that isolates one characteristic (e.g. biological sex) at the expense of other important aspects of our identities and backgrounds.

Research should also take into account the different settings and environments that bathrooms are located in. To date, the literature is comprised of research on latrinalia in a variety of different settings. Bartholome and Snyder (2004) analyzed latrinalia in a Bar-B-Que restaurant. Islam (2010) collected latrinalia from bathrooms in coffee shops. Matthews et al., (2012) used nine local bars. The most common site for latrinalia research is University bathrooms. The prevalence of Universities as sites for latrinalia research is likely due to several factors. Latrinalia are common to University bathrooms and they often contain a wide range of different messages. Thus, the quality and quantity of latrinalia in University bathrooms make them fruitful sites for latrinalia research. There is also a "convenience sampling" factor at play – scholars have relatively easy access to large samples of latrinalia in the Universities where they work. Despite a basic recognition among latrinalia scholars that, as Taylor (2010: 44) stated, "place is important" there exists no systematic theoretical or empirical mechanism for distinguishing between settings.

It is entirely plausible that the general environments and the peculiar characteristics have an impact. For instance, the restaurant in which Batholome and Snyder (2004) collected data invited patrons to write on the bathroom walls. In this particular context, people may produce latrinalia of a different quantity and content than in other settings where latrinalia represents an act of transgression. Moreover, the qualities of latrinalia may vary across different regions. This is particularly plausible given that latrinalia has been found to reflect local political, social, and cultural values.

Research and theory would also benefit from exploring the similarities and differences between latrinalia and other forums. One that is particularly ripe for comparative analyses is the internet (Dermakardijian, 2008). Chat rooms, blogs, comment sections, and various messaging systems provide opportunities for expression that share some of the core characteristics of latrinalia. The most essential shared characteristic is that both afford people anonymity. By using screen names or other monikers, people can post almost anything without fear of reprisal. There is evidence that opportunities for anonymous expression on the internet lead to content that is similar to latrinalia. People often post political opinions, seek support, and antagonize each other (Johnson, 2000).

There are, however, several important distinctions between the internet and latrinalia as modes of expression. First, the internet is not segregated by gender. Second, public bathrooms are unique environments. Internet postings can be written virtually anywhere, but writing on bathroom walls requires occupying a toilet stall (Dermakardijian, 2008). It would be intriguing to say the least to explore the similarities and differences between virtual self-expression and the age-old act of writing on the bathroom wall. Doing so may shed light on how different and emerging modes of social interaction influence self-expression.

References

Abel, E.L. & Buckley, B.E. (1977). *The handwriting on the wall: Toward a sociology and psychology of graffiti.* Westport, CT: Greenwood Press.

Anderson, S.J. & Verplank, W.S. (1983). When walls speak, what do they say? *The Psychological Record, 33*(3), 341–359.

Arluke, A., Kutakoff, L., & Levin, J. (1987). Are the times changing? An analysis of gender differences in sexual graffiti. *Sex Roles, 16*(1/2), 1–7.

Bartholome, L. & Snyder, P. (2004). Is it philosophy or pornography? Graffiti at the Dinosaur Bar-B-Que. *The Journal of American Culture, 27*(1), 86–98.

Bates, J.A. & Martin, M. (1980). The thematic content of graffiti as a nonreactive indicator of male and female attitudes. *The Journal of Sex Research, 16*(4), 300–315.

Bruner, E.M. & Kelso, J.P. (1980). Gender differences in graffiti: A semiotic perspective. *Women's Studies International Quarterly, 3*(2/3), 239–252.

Cole, C.M. (1991). 'Oh wise women of the stalls. . .' *Discourse & Society, 2*(4), 401–411.

Dermakardijian, A.G. (2008). *Beyond "a good bathroom read": A Bakhtinian study of the gendered carnival in women's latrinalia* (Master thesis). Retrieved from ProQuest. (UMI Number: 1458369).

Dundes, A. (1966). Here I sit: A study of American latrinalia. *Kroeber Anthropological Society Papers, 34*, 91–105.

Ferem, M. (2006). Latrinalia: It's all in the head. *50mm Los Angeles.* Retrieved August 24, 2014 from www.50mmlosangeles.com/viewStory.php?storyId=226

Ferem, M. (2007). *Bathroom graffiti.* New York: Mark Batty Publisher.

Fisher, M.L. & Radtke, S. (2014). Sex differences in the topics of bathroom graffiti. *Human Ethology Bulletin, 29*(2), 68–81.

Gadsby, J. (1995). *Taxonomy of analytical approaches to graffiti.* Retrieved August 21, 2014 from www.graffiti.org/faq/appendix.html

Gonos, G., Mulkern, V., & Poushinsky, N. (1976). Anonymous expression: A structural view of graffiti. *Journal of American Folklore, 89*(351), 40–48.

Grant, E. (1993). Writing on the wall: The wit and wisdom left on the stalls of higher learning at the University of California. *Playboy, 40*(2), 82–83.

Green, J.A. (2003). The writing on the stall: Gender and graffiti. *Journal of Language and Social Psychology, 22*(3), 282–296.

Habermas, J. (1991). *The structural transformation of the public sphere: An inquiry into a category of bourgeois society.* Cambridge, MA: MIT Press.

Haslam, N. (2012). *Psychology in the bathroom.* London: Palgrave Macmillan.

Innala, S.M. & Ernulf, K.E. (1992). Understanding male homosexual attraction: An analysis of restroom graffiti. *Journal of Social Behavior and Personality, 7*(3), 503–510.

Islam, G. (2010). Backstage discourse and the emergence of organizational voices: Exploring graffiti and organization. *Journal of Management Inquiry, 19*(3), 246–260.

Johnson, D. (2000). Anonymity and the internet. *The Futurist, 34*(4), 12.

Kinsey, A.C., Pomeroy, W.B., Martin, C.E., & Gebhard, P.H. (1953). *Sexual behavior in the human female.* Philadelphia, PA: W.B. Saunders.

Kohn, M. (2004). *Brave new neighborhoods: The privatization of public space.* New York: Routledge.

Landy, E.E. & Steele, J.M. (1967). Graffiti as a function of building utilization. *Perceptual and Motor Skills, 25*(3), 711–712.

Liu, E.Y.L. (2008). *Neo-normativity, the Sydney gay and lesbian mardi gras, and latrinalia: The demonstration of a concept on non-heterosexual performances* (Unpublished doctoral dissertation). University of New South Wales, Sydney, Australia.

Loewenstine, H.V., Ponticos, G.D., & Paludi, M.A. (1982). Sex differences in graffiti as a communication style. *Journal of Social Psychology, 117*(2), 307–308.

Matthews, N., Speers, L., & Ball, J. (2012). Bathroom banter: Sex, love, and the bathroom wall. *Electronic Journal of Human Sexuality, 15*(17), 1–11.

Nwoye, O.G. (1993). Social issues on walls: Graffiti in university lavatories. *Discourse and Society, 4*(4), 419–442.

Olusoji, O.A. (2013). Graffiti as a tool of students' communication. *International Review of Social Sciences and Humanities, 5*(2), 1–11.

Peretti, P.O., Carter, R., & McClinton, B. (1977). Graffiti and adolescent personality. *Adolescence, 12*(45), 31–42.

Reisner, R. (1971). *Graffiti: Two thousand years of wall writing.* Chicago, IL: Henry Renery.

Rodriguez, A. & Clair, R.P. (2009). Graffiti as communication: Exploring the discursive tensions of anonymous texts. *Southern Communication Journal, 65*(1), 1–15.

Sawka, M. (2012). This is weird...people do this?: Locational aspects of women's latrinalia at the University of Winnipeg. *Prairie Perspectives: Geographical Essays, 15*, 19–24.

Schottmiller, C.D. (2007). *If these stalls could talk: Gendered identity and performativity through latrinalia* (Unpublished master thesis). University of California, Berkeley.

Taylor, N. (2010). *On the poises of latrinalia* (Master thesis). Retrieved from ProQuest. (UMI Number: 1479303).

Trahan, A. (2011). Identity and ideology: The dialogic nature of latrinalia. *The Internet Journal of Criminology*, 1–9. Retrieved August 12, 2014 from www.internetjournalofcriminology.com/

Whiting, S. & Koller, V. (2007). Dialogues in solitude: The discursive structures and social functions of male toilet graffiti. Working paper 126, Centre for the Study of Language in Social Life, Lancaster University.

Young, J.C. (2009). Restroom politics: Voices in the stalls. *Lethbridge Undergraduate Research Journal, 4*(2), 1–10.

8

Yarn bombing – the softer side of street art[1]

Minna Haveri

Introduction

The new alternative craft movements have moved traditional craft techniques from the home environment to public Internet blogs, to art worlds and to street art. The ties of tradition have given way to free creativity in amateur crafts, which allows the expression of thoughts and feelings, and can be political or critical as well.

Yarn bombing is one form of craft-based artistic expression. It is a field where amateurs and professionals, traditions and the contemporary culture cross. Yarn bombing is based on handicraft skills, but it operates using strategies familiar in street art. Like traditional graffiti, knitting graffiti can be playful creation or considered as a political and subversive medium of communication. The concept of urban knitting is far more complex than the innocent appearance of these street knits might at first suggest.

Re-crafting the past

The new alternative craft scene has been flourishing in the past decade. Many artists and craftspeople are using traditional craft techniques, like knitting and crocheting, but in a contemporary and unconventional way (Levine, 2010). According to Orton-Johnson (2014), knitting in particular has enjoyed revived popularity and this popularity has been associated by a growing presence of knitters on the web.

The Internet is brimming with knit blogs, and young people are gathering to knit in public or at special knit cafes. Crafts are not a trend, because trends are related to the sense of transience. Handicrafts are something permanent with a long history. Without the slightest doubt, crafts will also be made in the future.

Crafts are strongly related to traditions, and techniques carry a long history. Crafts are something that connects different generations. Figuratively speaking crafts are loaded with tacit knowledge that speaks to us through our hands and touches us. They have a special ability to reach our personal thoughts, our emotional memory.

In Western culture, males have traditionally dominated art history. By contrast, craft culture is markedly feminine. It is associated with women so self-evidently that it is often left unquestioned (Parker and Pollock, 1987; Parker, 2011). Women have traditionally been responsible for the household and clothing. Female textile crafts became an extension of that everyday work. Handicrafts have always been associated with care and maintenance. Craft products come close, even on the skin, like domestic textiles, such as bedding, towels and clothes. The handicraft products, like sweaters and woollen socks, have been used and touched, but not necessarily paid particular attention to (Ihatsu, 2005). A distinction between 'craft products' or 'applied arts' and 'works of art' still persists in the Western world. Handicrafts are considered to be the results of skilful work, whereas art is seen to be an expression of individual creativity. When handicrafts are historically made for use, fine art is mainly made to be seen.

Despite the long tradition, crafts and especially knitting are being renewed and converted all the time (Strawn, 2007). Nowadays crafts have a new role in our society. Greer (2008) says that before the year 2000, the term *knitting* evoked many thoughts about grandmothers, the home district and all pastoral and definitely non-radical things but thanks to the recent resurgence of crafts, the new generation of knitters have redefined crafts and the homemade in a way that better reflects the current view of feminism and domesticity.

In the contemporary knitting circles, the ties of tradition and utility have loosened and given way to artistic expression and free creativity (Haveri, 2013). These new articulations have brought handicrafts from private homes to the public areas of city spaces and the Internet.

Even in a new environment, crafts are still a medium with a meaning. According to Searle (2008) the versatility of knitting appeals to artists who may use the craft to honour the history and tradition of women's work or to raise questions about gender and domesticity. Knitting can evoke associations with adornment and the body, and memories of comfort, warmth and caring. It can also raise questions about time and productivity and how these are valued in our society.

Knit graffiti revolution

Our urban landscapes are filled with government and corporate sponsored public sculptures and monumental architecture, the embodiments of power and cultural memory. By contrast, street art has come to populate certain cities. For many people street art seems to be almost a synonym for graffiti. The graffiti culture is a very complex subculture. Graffiti is an urban and artistic way of influencing the visual surroundings, but on the other hand it could be seen as vandalism. Nowadays some art museum exhibitions consider graffiti as 'real art', but at the same time the mainstream news inform us that cities have paid enormous sums to clean sprayed paintings from public spaces.

Contrary to traditional graffiti and street art, newer kinds of street art can increase the attractiveness of the city space without leaving permanent marks on property. In recent years these kinds of urban art forms, for example guerrilla gardening, reverse graffiti and yarn bombing, have gained favourable attention. The main idea of this alternative graffiti genre, raised in the 2000s, is to make a statement with positive activism, not with disobedience and anarchism.

Knitting, with a traditionally feminine material and technique, is presented as a much-needed antidote to traditionally masculine street art, especially graffiti art (Macdonald, 2001), and its rebellious and destructive undertones. Yarn bombing is still quite a new phenomenon, but it has already become an impressive part of the street art genre. Graffiti knitting, as we now know it, began in 2005 with Austin-based self-taught knitter, Magda Sayeg. She didn't have a strong background in knitting, but in 2005, she decided to knit a door pull to warm up the storefront of her women's clothing boutique in Houston (Harper, 2010).

According to Moore and Prain (2009) this first knitted graffiti was just a tiny rectangular strip out of blue and pink acrylic yarn, but from the very beginning the response was surprisingly strong. People came inside the shop to ask what it was and were stopping their cars to take photos. So, Sayeg invited her friend to join her and they started to tag the city with knitted items. Together they, using pseudonyms PolyCotN and A Krylik, formed the first yarn graffiti crew called Knitta. In the following years, the knitting crew grew and also other groups started to emerge.

As a crew they were able to realise large projects and gain more attention with their knitted pieces. Photographs of this new form of street art spread online around the world and also other knitters got excited and started to follow their lead. By 2008, yarn bombing, also known as the textile graffiti revolution, became an international phenomenon, mostly because of the Internet. Besides individual knitters, many knitting crews and collectives were founded, for example Masquerade in Stockholm, Ladies Fancywork Society in Denver and Knit the City in London.

In recent years, many books have introduced the works of the international yarn bombing movement. The publication *Yarn Bombing: The Art of Crochet and Knit Graffiti* by Mandy Moore and Leanne Prain in 2009 has been a kind of manifesto for the movement. The book is partly a reference book about creative yarn bombs from all over the world and partly tutorial with tips and patterns for knit bombing.

The very first knitting crew founded by Sayeg has already dwindled, but for Sayeg knitting became her full-time profession. Thanks to yarn bombing, she is a well-known textile artist with assistants knitting, running her websites and coordinating project logistics (Wollan, 2011). She has said that by her knitting she has questioned the assumptions of knitting as well as those of graffiti (Harper, 2010).

Over her knitting career, Sayeg has covered all kinds of objects from signposts to cars (most of them on commercial purposes) and to an entire bus, which she did in Mexico City in 2008. These tremendous yarn installations consist of hundreds of knitted pieces. In her works she prefers hand-knitted pieces, but also uses loom to make the process quicker (Harper 2010; Wollan, 2011), On her webpage, Sayeg (2014) tells that she continues to lead community-based projects and works on commission around the world with many international companies. She is seeking ways to expand her boundaries by experimenting new mediums and techniques, such as the usage of lighting with knitted material.

Softer side of street art

Knitted street art has been called by many names, for example, guerrilla knitting, urban knitting and graffiti knitting, but the terms *yarn storming* in the UK and *yarn bombing in the US* seem to have established themselves as the standard terms for visual expressions in the urban space that involve textile. According to Björk (2012), yarn bombing

> is an allusion on the graffiti term *bombing*, originating in the 1980s New York graffiti scene, where it meant writing one's *tag* all over a subway train car. Tagging, which in the graffiti tradition is about a crew name written with a felt pen, is also widely used as a term in knitting graffiti.

When the London based movement Knit the City was established in April 2009 by Lauren O'Farrell, she renamed her group's activities *yarn storming*, because it 'sounds more creative than bombing, which is destructive' (Costa, 2010). The FAQs on the Knit the City webpage (2014) tell the story:

> Being of a gentler disposition the Yarn Corps feel a bit sheepish about being labelled as astardly yarn terrorists. We live in a city where "bomb" is possibly not the best word to bandy about, even if it is woolly. We're not blowing things up. We're creating a bit of handmade chaos.

Besides many names, yarn bombing also takes on many forms, such as tree wears or arigurumi creatures, but it generally involves a gesture of wrapping a hand-knitted or crocheted item around everyday objects, such a signs, poles and streetlights and in city spaces. Warmly wrapped poles, fences and traffic signs, called *cosies*, are thought to make the streetscape, dominated by steel and concrete, softer and more pleasurable. These yarn installations can be large-scale pieces covering cars or public monuments or just very small and simple knitted strips (Moore and Prain, 2009; Werle, 2011).

Like all forms of street art, yarn bombing is related to social action, being creative and daring and getting in touch with environmental experiences (Malinen, 2008). Yarn bombing is illegal if it has been done without the permission of the property owner, and it could be considered vandalism or littering. However, knitters rarely run into trouble with the law. Like Sayeg said in an interview: 'You'd have to be the most bored police officer to want to arrest me' (Costa, 2010).

The concrete reason why the police and security guards tolerate the woollen version of graffiti better than painted graffiti is that yarn graffiti is gentler than its hard counterpart. The removal of painted graffiti is expensive and fraught with obstacles, whereas knitted graffiti is easily removed: A pair of scissors or even a firm tug is enough to detach yarn bombs without a trace. Its impermanent nature allows the practitioner to produce impressive street art without damaging public property (Moore and Prain, 2009).

Knitted graffiti is considered to make the environment feel inviting and cosy. This might explain the increasing interest of art institutions and different communities to organise yarn-bombing happenings. During the early years of yarn bombing, Sayeg was identified with under-ground graffiti artists, but nowadays the authorities she feared to get in trouble with are inviting her to work for them (Wollan, 2011).

Although the yarn sculpted personal statements do not cause a great risk to be arrested, they still evoke excitement – not because of breaking the law, but breaking invisible and non-verbal norms. McGovern (2014a), who has interviewed yarn bombers, describes:

> Yarn bombers get a kick from participating in something a little bit rebellious; and this subversion occurs on a number of levels. They may be subverting norms about knitting and how it should be employed and enjoyed. Equally, yarn bombers may be about subverting ideals of the feminine and women as homemakers. They may even be seeking to subvert ideas about the space in which yarn bombing installations occur.

Street art is outside the institutional art world, and in many cases graffiti art has been made without permission. From that perspective we cannot be sure that everything that looks like yarn bombing really is part of the graffiti culture. Nowadays many established artists do huge yarn installations with permission from property owners or on their request. These artists are not necessarily considering themselves as knit bombers. For example, Agata Oleksiak aka Olek, who is one of the best-known yarn installation artists at the moment, sees the city space as an extension of the gallery and announces: 'I don't yarn bomb, I make art' (Wollan, 2011).

Towards a softer world

Crafts are traditionally made in the middle of daily routines. They are engaged with everyday life. Even when they move to the world street art, they still have that humble nature. Soft art offers a contrast to the masculine and massive public art. The impermanence of crocheted and *knitted artworks* set against the infinity of these art monuments.

The popularity of knitting is changing the face of the craft, but some crafters go further and also see knitting as a way to change the world. Because of the softness, it may be difficult to see a connection between knitting and anarchy, but yarn craft and activism have a long history. For example, yarn craft played an important role in numerous 1970s and 1980s political actions (Parker and Pollock, 1987; Robertson, 2011).

Betsy Greer (2008) has created the term *craftivism* for the point where crafts and activism meet. According to her, craftivism is a way for knitters to voice their opinions through creativity. Yarn bombing can be seen as one of the many forms of craftivism (Greer, 2014). It is anonymous, non-commercial and unauthorised. It is something that is born to communicate with the living and changing environment. Nowadays many crafters regard the act of creating something with their hands as a stance against mass-production, the consumer culture and corporate values (Greer, 2008; Tapper, 2011). They are making something themselves rather than just consuming what has been given by the big suppliers. And when they do something, they usually choose something to recycle, renew and reuse.

With the knitted graffiti the medium is the message. Yarn bombing brings soft human values and an ecological approach to replace the hard technologies of our time. The hectic rhythm of everyday life has given rise to cultural phenomena that emphasise slowness. There are concepts, such as *slow food, slow design, slow cities* and, of course, the super-ordinate term *slow life*. The growing popularity of crafts is related to this phenomenon. It challenges us to ask what good life is and what is valuable, real and enduring. Yarn bombs in are telling this message.

Many yarn bombing crews have been known to base their activities on activist ideas. They use their needles to do good by collecting money and knit woollen socks and warm blankets for charity. In many cases craftivism has been used as a way to a peaceful protest that could centre on a political statement, feminist ideas or anti-consumerist sentiments (McGovern, 2014b).

It seems that for many yarn bombers it is very important to include a message in their actions. The main reason for yarn bombing, however, is probably the opportunity to beautify the surrounding environment, to give the sterile urban space a personal and cosy touch (McGovern, 2014a).

Creating a connection

The important learning environment for traditional handicraft skills has been the home, where skills have been passed on from the mother to the daughter and from the father to the son – from the older generation to the younger ones. This home learning has ensured the continuity of tradition and the constancy of folk aesthetics. The Internet, however, has revolutionised informal learning (Bal *et al.*, 2014).

The Internet is a place where everyday do-it-yourself (DIY) creativity has been flourishing in recent years (Gauntlett, 2011; Ratto and Boler, 2014). It has opened up a world of imagination and participation where users create content and messages. The Internet is a platform where crafts have had the opportunity to renew their nature and attitudes towards them. Knitting instructions and patterns can be found on the Internet, and cultural influences are no longer confined to national borders.

Partly caused by the new communication strategies of social media on the Internet, the status of hobbyist handicrafts has changed. Instead of being associated with diligence and utility, knitting has become an instrument of self-expression and activism. 'For guerrilla knitting communities and activist groups, blogging, vlogging and representing material practices in online spaces to a global audience is a vital part of the acts of citizenship and resistance that they are engaged in' says Orton-Johnson (2014: p. 143). She argues that online spheres have made the often private and domestic knitting visible, and social networking and the related activities have enriched the experience of knitting and provided new ways of constructing the maker's self.

It is not surprising that crafters have been so keen to communicate and share their knowledge and creations via new social networks. For centuries ordinary people, especially women, have been denied the ability to share their craft-based creations with the audience (Parker, 2010). Previous research on self-taught art (Haveri, 2010) shows that even outside of the art world people are rarely satisfied doing their art just for themselves. Sharing is the basic nature of all kinds of artistic actions, regardless of education, techniques or art world connections. Artistic creativity cannot be a monopoly of those who are the educated insiders of art.

Making handicrafts creates social interaction when crafters are developing skills by co-operating with others. We could say that also the heart of the new wave of crafts is the community. In the contemporary craft culture and the global Internet networks, sharing the same interests have replaced locality, which was typical for earlier folk crafts. In these new collaborations local and global participants are able to share a sense of community and connectivity (Orton-Johnson, 2014). Despite the distances, the Internet has made the existence of craft communities possible. Crafters have set up online galleries to present their works to the public. In web blogs crafters can discuss the meanings of handicrafts, their experiences and share ideas and encouragement, as well as work instructions and patterns (Vartiainen, 2010; Levine and Heimerl 2008). Like Greer (2008) says, knitting is a common language. For craft makers the community and the whole international phenomenon of the new craft movement are inspiring and empowering (Waterhouse, 2010).

The Internet has also played a key role also in craft communities' off-line real-world activities (Levine and Heimerl, 2008). For the knitters it has provided a tool for communication and opportunities to create networks and organise happenings. Using Internet connections, knitters are able to find other people sharing the same passion and interests. Many local, national, and international knitting events have been organised through the Internet. These craft meetings can be regarded as the contemporary counterpart of sewing clubs.

One of the biggest events for knitters and crocheters is the annual International Yarn Bombing Day, which is organised every year in June, all around the world. The day 'calls crafters to unite in the goal of covering the world in yarn' (Faces, 2014). The originator of the first Yarn Bombing Day in 2011 was Joann Matvichuk, from the Canadian province of Alberta. For that purpose she set up a Facebook group that in 2014 had more than 5,800 followers from all over the world.

Act locally to be seen globally

An important channel of expression for today's crafters is web blogs, where they can share images and stories about their own aesthetic activities with the public in a large online community. In addition to self-expression, the aim of craft blogging is the social status. It is a way to make one's life and oneself more 'visible'. That recognition is shown as the number of visitors and comments.

Craft blogs are part of the DIY culture, which seeks to resurrect traditional handicrafts and are spreading through the Internet as a global phenomenon and have increased the appreciation and popularity of handicrafts (Oakes, 2009). These blogs combine a sense of community and individualistic aesthetic experiences, with all meanings.

Blog keeping is an essential part of yarn bombing. Knitters encourage visitors to read their blogs by attaching the blog address to the graffiti. From the blogs those interested can find more information about the piece, maybe a map telling how to find more works, or an opportunity to discuss and comment on knitted art.

The blog culture gives folk aesthetics a channel to mutate and regenerate. On the other hand it eliminates the local influence typical of knitting and harmonises the style. Though yarn bombing blogs the pictures, new ideas and patterns spread all over the world have been fast adopted by other knit bombers. This has made it as an expression of handwork truly international, so that the bloggers' nationality shows rather in the location of the knit graffiti than in the knitted piece itself.

In graffiti knitting it is almost impossible to recognise the knitter's individual needlework. The cosies (i.e. covers for teapots) made by different knitters may look the same which can be explained by the fact that they are possibly made according to same knit patterns. For bombers, however, blogs offer a possibility to distinguish themselves from others as artists and at the same to keep a log of their knitted works.

Lauren O'Farrell (2014) aka Deadly Knitshade, argues on her webpage called *Whodunnknit* that there are mainly two kinds of graffiti knitting: Cosies that are basically handmade covers for street items and stitched stories. According to her: "The Stitched Stories style of graffiti knitting moved on from 'cosies' to artists using amigurumi (knitted toys) and other styles to add a theme or story to their installation. It gave the woolly street art a bit of a voice." Yarn bombing blogs, however, reveal that even tiny 'cosies' can have stories to tell. Stories can be related to the location and remind of some life experience that happened there, or they can be expressed through material (Prain 2014) with, for example, recycled meaningful textiles as parts of the graffiti. These hidden stories only become relevant for the audience through blogs.

Reasons for graffiti knitting

Isn't it a bit of a waste of yarn? I mean shouldn't you be knitting for homeless pre-mature penguin babies with TB? I always find this question oddly narrow minded. Would you tell a painter or sculptor to use their materials for something more practical? "Hey, Michelangelo! What do you think you're doing carving a giant naked chap when you could be making a nice functional bathroom set for your local hospice?"

(O'Farrell, 2014)

The common attitude towards crafting and especially knitting is slowly changing, but it is still surprisingly usual to consider yarn bombing as a waste of materials and time. Because textiles have traditionally been only seen as functional, it can be difficult to accept other uses for one's skills, time and expensive yarns. There are great examples of charity knitting, but it cannot totally explain why the waste of resources is not criticized in art generally, only if art pieces are made of yarn. It seems that the strong utilitarian background still speaks to us through knitted pieces. For knitting and crocheting, the long tradition is not only a strength but also a weakness.

Dissanayake (1995) argues that people have a biological need to make something with their hands. This explains why there is such enjoyment in making and creating something new.

Creative activities increase mental and even physical well-being, and crafting can be a tool for a better life and greater self-appreciation (Pöllänen and Kröger, 2000). Many yarn bombers say that they are knitting graffiti because it is fun (Moore and Prain, 2009). This does not mean, however, that yarn bombing is merely meaningless entertainment.

Crafting could be seen as a way to belong to a tradition and community. It is as a life-style and an active form of existence. Gauntlett (2011) suggests that the rise of the craft culture could be one step from the 'sit back and be told' culture towards a more active 'making and doing' culture. According to him, in our institutionalised schooling system, learning has been a process directed by the teacher and our media and consumer culture has also supported passive receiving. It is a pity that so many people have learnt to spend their leisure time lodged on the sofa instead of going out and doing things. A growing engagement with making crafts rejects the passivity and seeks outlets for creativity, social connections and personal growth.

According to Eija Vähälä (2003), who has studied the health effects of knitting, the process of crafting combines skills, meditation and emotions. The colours, materials and knitting motion give the feeling of pleasure. Vähälä investigated the connection between well-being and making things with one's hands by doing physiological tests during the crafting work. She argues that the creative craft process can be used to achieve a relaxed and meditative state that slows the heart rate and provides an intense feeling of happiness. This, however, only relates to the knitting part of yarn bombing. When the knitted piece is ready, it needs to be exhibited somewhere in the city environment. The bombing is the part that many knitters find exciting and a little bit rebellious (McGovern, 2014a).

Knitters also have more practical reasons to relish yarn bombing (Moore and Prain, 2009). Yarn bombs are usually rather small, or even large installations comprised of many pieces, so that the works are portable and easy to do whenever and wherever. Small projects are not expensive or time consuming. Moreover, yarn bombs offer knitters a good way to test and practise new techniques and patterns.

For hobbiest knitters bored with only making socks and sweaters, yarn bombing seems to be an alternative reason to use handicraft skills. It is appealing to knitters because it allows them to use their skills to do something beyond the functional. For some knitters the thrilling part of urban knitting is to show and place their makings in the city sphere. Besides yarn bombing, there is also guerrilla kindness, which in this context means that the crafter has left something handmade, like socks or maybe a crocheted flower, in a public place for strangers to find and take away. Lothian (2014: p. 15) describes that 'guerrilla kindness work is about extending your community. It's about reaching out your hand to a stranger and using your skills to make someone's day brighter. It's a handcrafted, joyous experience for the maker and the finder'.

Urban knitters are using their time and money to do something they do not get any profit for. They are not after fame either because in many cases they stay anonymous. They do their art entirely on their own good will or because they have an acute need to express themselves. Traffic signs do not necessarily need legwarmers, but the knitted piece of art could warm the heart of someone passing by.

Calm after the yarn storm

Yarn bombing is a relatively new phenomenon, less than a decade old. In short time it has become a significant form of street art in the United States, Canada, Australia and many European countries. However, it seems that the hype around urban knitting is slightly fading. The feedback from the public at large has been so positive that many museum pedagogues and art teachers have taken yarn bombing to be part of their educational programmes. It is considered a great creative activity and an excellent way to improve environmental awareness and handicraft skills. On the other side, yarn bombing is already so well-known that the element of surprise is no longer effective. It can be a challenge for the street credibility of yarn bombing that even grannies are knitting graffiti.

Note

1 The chapter is an extension of the seminar paper presented at the Cumulus Northern World Mandate Conference, in Helsinki 2012. It is based on the author's current research, in which she examines the use of traditional craft techniques in artistic expression, and on qualitative interview data from Finnish yarn bombers involved in local and international knitting networks.

References

Bal, A., Nolan, J. and Seko, Y. (2014). Mélange of Making: Bringing Children's Informal Learning Cultures to the Classroom. In Ratto, M. and Boler, M. (Eds) *DIY Citizenship: Critical Making and Social Media*. (pp. 157–168). Cambridge, MA and London: The MIT Press.

Björk, H. (2012). *Yarn Maters*. In Mustekala Kulttuurilehti [on-line cultural magazine]. Retrieved 16 October 2014. www.mustekala.info/node/35777.

Costa, M. (2010). The Graffiti Knitting Epidemic. *The Guardian*, 10 October 2010. Retrieved 16 October 2014. www.theguardian.com/artanddesign/2010/oct/10/graffiti-knitting.

Dissanayake, E. (1995/1992). *Homo Aestheticus: Where Art Came From and Why*. Seattle, WA: The University of Washington Press.

Faces/The Fiber Arts Center of the Eastern Shore. (2014). *International Yarn Bombing Day*. Retrieved 16 October 2014. www.fiberartscenter.com/international-yarn-bombing-day/.

Gauntlett, D. (2011). *Making is Connecting: The Social Meaning of Creativity, From DIY and Knitting to YouTube and Web 2.0*. Cambridge and Malden, MA: Polity.

Greer, B. (2008). *Knitting for Good! A Guide to Creating Personal, Social, and Political Change, Stitch by Stitch*. Boston, MA and London: Trumpeter.

Greer, B. (2014). *Craftivism: The Art of Craft and Activism*. Vancouver, WA: Arsenal Pulp Press.

Harper, M. (2010) Artist Adds Color to City's Fabric. *Statesman*, 21 April 2010. Retrieved 16 October 2014. www.statesman.com/news/lifestyles/fashion-style/artist-adds-color-to-citys-fabric/nRsDk/.

Haveri, M. (2010). *Nykykansantaide* [In Finnish] [Contemporary Folk Art]. Helsinki: Maahenki.

Haveri, M. (2013). Neulegraffiti – ITE-taiteen kaupunkilaisserkku [In Finnish] [Knit Graffiti – The Urban Cousin of Contemporary Folk Art]. In Haveri, M. (Ed.) *ITE Kaakossa*. (pp. 20–25). Helsinki: Maahenki.

Ihatsu, A-M. (2005). *Käsityö suomalaisessa kulttuurissa*. [In Finnish] [Handicrafts in the Finnish Culture]. In Kaukinen, L. and Collanus, M. (Eds) *Tekstejä ja kangastuksia: Puheenvuoroja käsityöstä ja sen tulevaisuudesta*. Artefakta 17. (pp. 19–30). Helsinki: Akatiimi.

Knit the City. (2014). Knit the City -Website. Retrieved 16 October 2014. http://knitthecity.com.

Levine, F. and Heimerl, C. (2008). *Handmade Nation: The Rise of DIY, Art, Craft, and Design*. New York: Princeton Architectural Press.

Lothian, S. (2014). Guerilla Kindness. In Greer, B. (Ed.) *Craftivism: The Art of Craft and Activism* (pp. 11–15). Vancouver, WA: Arsenal Pulp Press.

McGovern, A. (2014a). Knit One, Purl One: The Mysteries of Yarn Bombing Unraveled. *The Conversation*, 5 March 2014. Retrieved 16 October 2014. http://theconversation.com/knit-one-purl-one-the-mysteries-of-yarn-bombing-unravelled-23461.

McGovern, A. (2014b). Crafting for Good: Why We All Want to Knit for Penguins. *The Conversation*, 18 March 2014. Retrieved 16 October 2014. http://theconversation.com/crafting-for-good-why-we-all-want-to-knit-for-penguins-24291.

Malinen, P. (2008). "Spraycan Leads" – the Urban Paradox of Graffiti: An Art Teacher Studying a Subculture. In *Synnyt* 4/2008. (pp. 40–51). https://wiki.aalto.fi/download/attachments/70792370/malinen.pdf?version=1.

Moore, M. and Prain, L. (2009). *Yarn Bombing: The Art of Crochet and Knit Graffiti*. Vancouver, WA: Arsenal Pulp Press.

Oakes, K. (2009). *Slanted and Enchanted: The Evolution of Indie Culture*. New York: Henry Holt and Company.

O'Farrell. (2014). *Whodunnknit*. Retrieved 16 October 2014. www.whodunnknit.com/.

Orton-Johnson, K. (2014). DIY Citizenship, Critical Making, and Community. In Ratto, M. and Boler, M. (Eds) *DIY Citizenship: Critical Making and Social Media*. (pp.141–156). Cambridge, MA and London: The MIT Press.

Parker, R. (2011/1984). *The Subversive Stitch: Embroidery and the Making of the Femine*. London and New York: I.B. Tauris.

Parker, R. and Pollock, G. (1987). *Framing Feminism: Art and the Women's Movement 1970–1985*. London: Pandora.

Pöllänen, S. and Kröger, T. (2000). Käsityön erilaiset merkitykset opetuksen perustana. [In Finnish] [The Different Meanings of Handicrafts as the Basis of Teaching] In Enkenberg, J., Väisänen, P. and Savolainen, E. (Eds). *University of Joensuu*. Retrieved 20 January 2012. http://sokl.uef.fi/verkkojulkaisut/kipinat/kansi.htm.

Prain, L. (2014). *Strange Material. Storytelling Through Textiles*. Vancouver: Arsenal Pulp Press.

Ratto, M. and Boler, M. (2014). *DIY Citizenship: Critical Making and Social Media*. Cambridge, MA and London: The MITT Press.

Reynolds, R. (2009/2008). *On Guerrilla Gardening: A Handbook for Gardening Without Boundaries*. London: Bloomsbury.

Robertson, K. (2011). Rebellious Doilies and Subversive Stitches: Writing a Craftivist History. In Buszek, M.E. (Ed.) *Extra/Ordinary: Craft and Contemporary Art*. (pp. 184–203). Durham and London: Dyke University Press.

Sayeg, M. (2014). *Magda Sayeg*. Retrieved 16 October 2014. www.magdasayeg.com/about.

Searle, K. (2008). *Knitting Art: 150 Innovative Works from 18 Contemporary Artists*. Minneapolis, MN: Voyageur Press.

Strawn, S. (2007). *Knitting America: A Clorious Heritage from Warm Sosks to High Art*. Minneapolis, MN: Voyageur Press.

Tapper, J. (2011). *Craft Activism: People, Ideas, and Projects From the New Community of Handmade and How You Can Join in*. New York: Potter Craft.

Tracey, D. (2007). *Guerrilla Gardening: A Manualfesto*. Gabriola Island: New Society.

Vähälä, E. (2003). *Luovan käsityöprosessin yhteydet psyykkiseen hyvinvointiin – käsityön aikana koettujen itseraportoitujen emootiokokemusten ja fysiologisten vasteiden väliset yhteydet*. [In Finnish] [The Relationship Between the Creative Handicrafts Process and Mental Well-Being – the Connection Between Self-Reported Emotional Experiences and Physiological Responses.] University of Joensuu.

Vartiainen, L. (2010). *Yhteisöllinen käsityö – Verkostoja, taitoja ja yhteisiä elämyksiä*. [In Finnish] [Handicrafts and a Sense of Community – Network, Skills and Shared Experiences] Joensuu: University of Eastern Finland.

Waterhouse, J. (2010). *Indie Craft*. London: Laurence King Publishing.

Werle, S. (2011). *Urban Knits*. Munich, London and New York: Prestel.

Wollan, M. (2011) Graffiti's Cozy, Feminine Side. *The New York Times*, 18 May 2011. Retrieved 16 October 2014. www.nytimes.com/2011/05/19/fashion/creating-graffiti-with-yarn.html.

9

Straight from the underground

New York City's legal graffiti writing culture[1]

Ronald Kramer

I can take two, three, four days, a week, or a month to do a piece on a wall. On the walls you get to do your piece a fairly nice size and then if you want to add background and characters and all that stuff you could. On the train, your piece was constricted because of the next guy's piece. Now, the thing about walls is they became big murals. In the early to mid-1990s you had a lot of people going from one aesthetic to another.

(NIC ONE)[2]

Introduction

By the mid-1970s a particular form of graffiti, distinguished by its emphasis on highly stylizing an individual's name, emerged as the dominant form of public writing in New York City. Referred to over the years as "subway art" (Cooper and Chalfant, 1984; Stewart, 1989), "spray can art" (Chalfant and Prigoff, 1987), and "hip-hop graffiti" (Phillips, 1999), this variant of graffiti has been analyzed by academic discourse in more ways than one. On the one hand, there is a tendency to situate what I will call "graffiti writing culture"[3] as a small fragment within broader cultural formations, such as "hip-hop" (Hager, 1984; Rose, 1994; George, 1998; Chang, 2005) or gang culture (Phillips, 1999). On the other hand, some accounts treat graffiti writing culture as demanding study in its own right. In these cases, analysts have tended to focus on graffiti as it existed in New York City during the 1970s and 1980s (Lachmann, 1988; Austin, 2001; Miller, 2002) or on emergent graffiti writing cultures that, although in different geographic regions, took their inspiration from what was happening in New York City (Ferrell, 1993; Macdonald, 2001; Rahn, 2002).

Although this latter approach has innumerable strengths and has contributed greatly to our understanding, it tends to prioritize illegal graffiti. In doing so, it generates an image of graffiti writing culture that is no longer complete. Drawing from over five years of ethnographic fieldwork incorporating interviews, observations and document analysis, I explore the post-1989 era of graffiti, a time in which many graffiti writers not only turned to legal modes of graffiti production, but also sought social acceptance for their practice and creative outputs.

Graffiti as "generalized lawlessness" and an "art of rebellion"

Most accounts of graffiti tend to take its illegality for granted (Mailer, 1974; Castleman, 1982; Stewart, 1987; Lachmann, 1988; Spitz, 1991; Ferrell, 1993; Austin, 2001). Of course, given that graffiti is often produced in direct violation of the law and accompanied by auxiliary criminal activities, such as the stealing of spray paint and breaking into train yards, this is not surprising. In many accounts, especially those with a tendency to romanticize the practice, the focus often turns towards how graffiti is over criminalized. Such criminalization is usually motivated by political and economic ends, and occurs by investing "graffiti" with negative meanings, and via the introduction of stricter legislation (see especially Castleman, 1982; Ferrell, 1993; Austin, 2001 on this point).

In other accounts, illegality functions as an essential element in theorizing graffiti writing culture. According to Nancy Macdonald (2001: 126), the illegality of graffiti constitutes "the subculture's backbone" because it allows for the construction of a masculine identity or character. As she puts it, "This subculture must be acknowledged for what it is . . . an illegal confine where danger, opposition and the exclusion of women is used to nourish, amplify and salvage notions of masculinity" (Macdonald, 2001: 149).

For Janice Rahn (2002) illegality does not so much ensure a space in which a sense of masculinity can be developed, but one in which autonomy from dominant social groups can be found. Insofar as this autonomy is achieved through illegality, the latter becomes an ethic among graffiti writers and something that needs to be preserved

> The community's ethics concerning graffiti's illegal status ensures that it cannot be entirely co-opted. As it becomes popularized, writers seem to push their art back to the margins of a clearly distinguishable underground culture. Members are dedicated to their own code of ethics . . .
>
> (Rahn, 2002: 162)

The illegality of graffiti often paves the way for further explorations of how graffiti writers violate the law in other respects. When, for example, Castleman explored graffiti writing culture in the early 1980s, theft was so common among writers that it could be said to constitute a "tradition" (1982: 46). On occasion, this proclivity for theft even led to the commission of burglary

> Another spectacular rack-up . . . was not the result of chance discovery . . . [T]hree writers carefully planned and executed a late-night robbery at a warehouse in the Bronx, getting away with more than 2000 cans of spray paint. Only Rustoleum and Red Devil paint, the brands most preferred by writers, were taken.
>
> (Castleman, 1982: 47)

In Austin's account the theft that constitutes a tradition for Castleman becomes a "virtue" that, if followed dutifully, establishes a writers "street cred" and commitment to the subculture's "ethical code." "Since the quantity of paint needed for a piece was beyond the economic means of most writers, necessity was made a virtue, and theft or swapping was considered the only ethical means of acquiring paint" (2001: 65).

Alongside the focus on graffiti writing's illegal aspects, one is also likely to find the notion that it embodies a critical or oppositional stance towards the dominant society in which it is located. Based on an analysis of the graffiti scene in Denver, Colorado during the late 1980s and early 1990s, Ferrell (1993: 172) finds that "the politics of graffiti writing are those of anarchism." As he ultimately concludes, graffiti "stands as a sort of decentralized and decentered insubordination, a mysterious resistance to conformity and control, a stylish counterpunch to the belly of authority" (1993: 197).[4]

More circumspect in his approach, Ivor Miller (2002) draws from research conducted on New York City's graffiti writing culture during the 1970s and 1980s to argue that graffiti is an "intrinsically rebellious" public art that addresses "race" and class tensions. In relation to the former, Miller argues that graffiti constitutes a cultural response to "the imposition of the European colonial masters' culture" upon those of non-European descent (2002: 33). In relation to class tensions, Miller claims that graffiti writers "combat the impositions of a consumer society by reshaping the alphabet to redefine their own identities and their environment" (2002: 85). Furthermore, insofar as graffiti writers make their art free to the public, Miller argues that writing culture defies a "system that put[s] a price tag on everything" (2002: 154).[5]

Following the "cultural turn," Janice Rahn (2002) finds that graffiti is an "adolescent obsession" (2002: 210) that speaks less to class and/or "race" tensions than to regimes of "knowledge and power" (2002: 137). For Rahn, the specific power/knowledge regimes in question are those that surround "adulthood." In this context, graffiti is said to afford adolescents an opportunity to express disdain for the normalization and disciplinary processes that can be associated with one's teenage years and presuppose the transition to adulthood (Rahn, 2002: 143).

Finally, Nancy Macdonald (2001: 154) refrains from framing graffiti writing as resistance altogether. Instead, she finds it to represent a deliberate quest for social and cultural isolation. By creating a gulf between themselves and the broader society, graffiti writers can confound and frighten outsiders – a pastime from which they supposedly derive great pleasure. "The greatest satisfaction comes when graffiti does not just confound, it frightens. To many, graffiti is sinister and threatening, and this gives writers something of an upper hand" (2001: 158).

This brief analysis reveals the existence of a diversity of findings concerning the relationship between graffiti writing culture and the society in which it is embedded. Yet these differing interpretations all emphasize illegality and suggest that the relationship between graffiti writing culture and society is one marked by discordance. For the most part, graffiti writing culture is postulated as a critical force that challenges society.

In the post-1989 era, however, graffiti writing experienced a profound transformation in its norms and practices. Due to prolonged state opposition in New York City, graffiti writers were squeezed out of the subway system and went above ground. Those interested in painting elaborate graffiti works started seeking out permission from property owners to paint their walls. This occasionally led to opportunities to paint commissioned works for private and business clients (e.g. business owners requesting store fronts to be painted in graffiti style fonts).

To be sure, "commercial" and "legal graffiti" did exist prior to 1990, but it was much less common than it is today. After 1989, the production of legal graffiti quickly came to dominate the subculture. And, although some graffiti writers continue to paint illegally or work on both sides of the fence (MacDiarmid and Downing, 2012), the most prominent graffiti writers in the world focus overwhelmingly on legal work.

While it is difficult to quantify these changes, my fieldwork suggests that the "career" of the illegal graffiti writer, especially when compared to writers of earlier eras and those who paint with permission, is generally one of short duration. After a year or two, perhaps after as little as six months, the majority of those who paint illegally either retire or, if they are committed to the aesthetics of graffiti, begin to pursue legal domains in which to paint. There are, of course, some exceptions to this rule, such as JA, DRO, and FEC, who are known for painting illegally for well over a decade. Nevertheless, beyond a small handful of writers, there are not too many in New York City that could be recognized for painting illegally for a prolonged period of time. In light of such transformations, the portrayal of graffiti writers as "outlaws" and "revolutionaries" may be historically accurate, but it only provides a partial image of contemporary graffiti writing culture.

The production of legal graffiti in New York City

Throughout the 1970s and 1980s, the location most favored by graffiti writers in New York City for plying their craft was the subway system. After numerous outbreaks of "moral panic," new policies, and massive financial expenditures, the city officially declared that the subway was "graffiti free" in 1989 (Schmidlapp and Phase2, 1996: 112). This declaration, however, hardly constituted an accurate assessment of the aesthetic order of things. While the city was, and remains, preoccupied with keeping subway graffiti out of the public's view, graffiti writers simply adapted to new conditions.

They did so in three main ways. First, some remained committed to the subway. Second, a portion of writers went "above ground" and started focusing their energy on buildings, highway embankments, signs, storefront gates, freight trains, and anything else they could possibly write on. Third, some writers started seeking out legal avenues in which to pursue their craft. This third adaptation is an important, albeit often overlooked, development within graffiti writing culture. It could easily be said that enough graffiti writers have crossed the line that distinguishes illegal from legal graffiti, such that it is possible to categorize "legal graffiti artists" as a distinct coterie within graffiti writing culture. To put it another way, if during the 1970s and 1980s graffiti writers painted subway trains and, at best, occasionally ventured out to produce legal graffiti, since 1989 a portion of writers have focused exclusively on the production of legal graffiti. This shift in the "mode of production" seems to have paved the way for the development of a new ideological standpoint among those who produce graffiti with permission.

The vast majority of legal graffiti in New York City is found on the exterior sidewalls of small businesses, large factory walls in the outer boroughs, schoolyard walls, and sometimes on vans and trucks. In order to produce legal graffiti murals, graffiti writers must seek out and obtain written consent from property owners. For the most part, writers simply ask property owners if they will grant permission to paint murals on their wall space. These negotiations are often facilitated by the graffiti writers leaving business cards and, sometimes, portfolios of their work with property owners.

Most legal graffiti writers do not seek financial rewards from property owners and most will paint for free provided they are able to retain control over the creative process. The shunning of material rewards does not necessarily reflect the belief that to exchange creative services for money somehow compromises the artist and renders what they produce "inauthentic." Rather, money is shunned because graffiti writers ultimately seek a Hegelian mutual recognition from their peers, most of whom will view the work on the Internet or perhaps in magazines after it has been documented (cf. Halsey and Young, 2006: 279–280 and Snyder, 2009 who report similar findings). In this context, it is not money that is necessary, but *wall space*, which affords the opportunity to paint on a large scale.

A single artist or many artists working in collaboration may produce legal works of graffiti. Occasionally, graffiti writers acquire permission to paint on surfaces that can accommodate up to, if not in excess of, twenty artists. But more often than not, murals are painted by three to five artists. The amount of time spent working on a mural varies. Not taking into account weather conditions, artists capable of painting fast can cover relatively large walls in a single day; but sometimes walls take months to complete due to the detailed work involved. Generally speaking, however, most large-scale murals are completed over the course of two to four days.

Most works of legal graffiti contain "pieces," which emphasize through highly stylized lettering the "tag" names of artists, and a "background," which usually takes the form of some kind of visual scenery. A work that incorporates pieces and a background is referred to as a "production" (Snyder, 2009). Prior to and during painting the artists working on a mural will discuss it in great detail. The themes and concepts to be explored in the background, the composition and location of "pieces," the size of imagery and letters, the colors to be used, the style in which things are to be painted ("photo-real" versus "illustrative," for example), will all be discussed at length. Graffiti writers will also work out who is doing what and when. Occasionally, detailed sketches are produced in advance and then reproduced on the wall. More often than not, however, the artists will be accustomed to working as a group and will develop a set of creative ideas during the painting process.

The seriousness with which graffiti writers approach their aesthetic production is further reflected in the concern they display with the materials they use. Much in the same way a "fine artist" primes a canvas, legal graffiti writers will use regular household paint to roll or "buff" the surfaces on which they will be producing murals. They may spend anywhere from 20 to 100 dollars on the paint required to prepare a wall in this manner. Some, in order to make the process of priming walls much more time efficient and less labor-intensive, have invested several hundred dollars in air compressors and spray guns.

Graffiti writers, however, are most fussy when it comes to the aerosol spray paint cans that they use. Since the early 1990s, graffiti writers in European cities have worked with spray paint manufacturers to create an aerosol that can be specifically designed to meet their needs. In fact, it could easily be said that there now exists something of a "graffiti industry." Aside from the well over 1,500 colors supplied by new companies, the most important development in terms of aerosol paint was the introduction of low-pressure cans. These aerosol cans release paint at a much slower and "softer" rate, which allows graffiti writers to shade in ways almost impossible with the technology that was available during the 1970s and 1980s. But it is not only the cans that have advanced. There is also an extensive market for the caps that dispense the paint from the spray can when depressed. Caps allow a writer to vary the width of spray. By the mid-1990s, technology along these lines had advanced so far that a writer could make lines the width of a pencil to lines three inches thick.

For a variety of reasons, such as new anti-theft technologies, these products cannot be stolen and therefore cost money. A good quality can of aerosol spray paint costs approximately eight US dollars. Any given cap costs about fifty cents and, given that some caps clog fairly easily, it is not unlikely that an artist will need to use three to four caps per can. This means that every high quality can of spray paint used comes at a cost of approximately ten dollars. In light of this booming graffiti industry, the American paint brands that Castleman's graffiti heroes held in high esteem, and which presently cost less than half as much as the new paints available, have been disavowed by legal graffiti writers. Today's legal graffiti artists not only refrain from stealing their paint, they also insist on spending more than twice as much in order to work with the best materials.

To be sure, all these costs add up. A legal graffiti writer is not unlikely to use at least five cans of paint in order to produce a decent "piece."[6] The amount of paint required for the "background" of a legal mural, although it varies depending on the kind of detail involved, will require at least another five to ten cans of spray paint. Thus, a work of legal graffiti that includes five pieces and a background involves an expenditure of several gallons of house paint and at least thirty cans of spray paint. In short, stealing relatively cheap American brands of spray paint and then illegally painting subway trains is no longer the only method that is available and perceived as acceptable for the production of graffiti. A portion of today's graffiti writers actively seek permission from property owners in order to *spend* close to, if not more than, 350 dollars on murals that will appear on walls and other publicly visible surfaces that they do not own, and from which they will not derive any direct material advantages.

"Conventional" lives, "conventional" values

Contrary to popular (and academic) belief, much contemporary graffiti is not produced by "youth." To be sure – and this consistent with the findings of Snyder (2009) – many of the legal graffiti writers that I have met over the years did start their "careers" during their teenage years by painting illegally. However, as they began to reach their twenties and as the trains were no longer viable as surfaces to paint, they transitioned to legal graffiti work. Once they had made this transition, they tended to remain on the permissible side of the border that divides legal from illegal graffiti. It would seem that with the occupying of a financially rewarding position within the economic structure, mortgage payments, family, and other responsibilities, illegal graffiti quickly comes to be seen as an unnecessary risk to one's career and lifestyle.

Legal graffiti writers range in ages from twelve to fifty years. Although the majority of graffiti writers are men, they come from a variety of class and ethnic backgrounds. They display great occupational diversity and may work as graduate students, corporate employees, teachers, fine artists, professional graphic designers, or pursue creative careers, such as interior design. Ironically perhaps, I met several writers in New York who work for the Metropolitan Transport Authority (MTA) or other city agencies. A handful even work in various branches of law enforcement. Many of the older graffiti writers that I have met are in stable family environments, often raising children with their partners.

This relatively "conventional" material existence is often accompanied by an embracing of hegemonic values and a desire to participate in society. Perhaps the best way to demonstrate this is by directing attention towards some of the moments during interviews where it was particularly evident and, to be frank, somewhat surprising.

Opposing vandalism, concern over the aesthetics of space, and "public art"

I asked my interviewees to reflect on some of the contemporary forms of illegal graffiti, such as scratchiti and etch bombing. I was expecting to hear a variety of rationalizations for such practices. However, most of my respondents voiced a strong opposition to "graffiti vandalism" and displayed a tendency to sympathize with the owners of private property. BEEN3 and EMA acknowledged the clarity of the laws in New York City regarding illegal graffiti writing and their overall legitimacy.

> The vandalism, if you get caught, you got caught man. Don't bitch and moan about it . . . You got caught doing something you weren't supposed to do – you painted somebody's property. (BEEN3)

[It's] against the law to write on someone's door. You don't ask for permission so you have to deal with the consequences. And that's something I'm really surprised with graffiti writers sometimes because they don't accept that. (EMA)

SONIC articulated an ethic of graffiti writing which involves showing respect for some forms of private property. He stated,

[You] have the new guys that are out there and they don't know what they're doing. They're writing on people's garages, they're writing on people's cars and vans and they're writing on people's gates. I don't appreciate that. If you're gonna get into graffiti, you better learn the rules of graffiti . . . (SONIC)

Related to this ethic, writers also displayed a genuine concern for the appearance of their neighborhoods. This was often accompanied by efforts to work in ways that benefit the city and the public square. In talking about legal walls, BEEN3 said,

[With] the walls, we are not doing anything illegal. We are asking for permission. We are paying for all our own supplies, which is helping the city because we are paying taxes on it of course. Everything they [the city] need is being done: They don't have to pay to maintain it because we're maintaining it. They don't have to worry about cleaning it anymore. And a couple of other things: It makes the neighborhood look better than just having it destroyed.

If the words of other graffiti writers are anything to go by, it would seem that the general public does indeed appreciate the work. Although, admittedly, I have heard one or two stories in which some members of the public do not appreciate legal graffiti art, legal graffiti writers overwhelmingly report positive feedback from the public. They say,

We have never had a bad comment from the general public ever. In fact, we were doing a wall with a big demon on it and he's coming out of the ground. We didn't realize it, but this was across the street from a church. We were doing the wall and we turn around and a nun comes walking across the street. Me and MUSE are just like, "oh man, she's just gonna lay into us." She came over and said, "I see your guys work around. I love it. Could I have one of your cards in case we ever need anything done?" So that's the type of thing we get from the public. (DEMER)

I have had mostly really beautiful encounters with the public in New York City and all over the world. People are often very thankful for the work we do. They offer food, music, drinks . . . (CERN)

You know, I've never had so much flattery in my life. I don't consider myself a talented guy or anything like that. I just do what I like to do. And the response I've gotten has been really, really positive. (JUSE ONE)

In some of the above quotes we have seen how writers acknowledge the legitimacy of law and display a genuine concern for the aesthetics of shared public spaces. This embracing of established social institutions and respect for public space only became clearer when I asked about the MTA's *Art for Transit* program, which, by working with artists, seeks to beautify an otherwise fairly bleak subway environment. After approximately twenty years of fighting subway graffiti and removing any type of unauthorized public art – for example, the MTA routinely erased Keith Haring's now famed chalk drawings – the MTA now invites artists into the subway system on a regular basis.

In asking graffiti writers about the *Art for Transit* program, I was expecting to hear anger and resentment directed against the MTA for their willingness, after a long history of animosity towards graffiti writing, to work with more conventional artists. However, all of the writers I interviewed voiced support for public arts projects and some of them expressed an active desire to participate in such projects. They have said,

> The Arts for Transit program is cool. I wish they would try to find a balance with [graffiti] writers . . . I hope the generations that take control of these institutions aren't so closed minded. (CERN)
>
> I myself can adapt to different mediums. I could deal with something like [the Arts for Transit] program, especially if there is a little money involved or some exposure. It's just another outlet. (PART)

The desire for social acceptance: a new argot, cultural inclusion, selling one's "skillset"

That many writers have begun to see themselves (and their art form) as legitimate participants within the public square can be seen in changes in their vocabulary and when asked what kind of place in society they would like to see writing culture occupy. In the 1970s and 1980s writers would describe their painting expeditions as "bombing," "hitting," or "killing." In the 1990s, with the transition to legal walls, writers now got together to "paint." If the previous vocabulary suggested aggressive or antagonistic action, the new vocabulary was suggestive of a peaceful and harmless process. As previously noted, the final works became known as "productions." While writers have a long tradition of working together, the notion of "production" is important insofar as it acknowledges that creating graffiti is now dependent on successful co-operation with people from outside the writing community, such as property owners.

When asked about the kind of place in society they would like to see writing culture occupy, writers are consistent in emphasizing the importance of seeing it acknowledged by mainstream society. From here it often follows that writing culture should be actively incorporated by social institutions, such as schools and cultural arenas. Graffiti writers told me,

> I'd like to see it everywhere. I teach. Graffiti helps me with the kids. The minute they know I paint, it's like 'oh, can you do my name?' I tell them, 'no, but *you* can do *your* name and I can just help you along with it.' And now these kids are more into learning because I'm one of them now. It's like, 'oh, he writes. He's not a regular teacher. Look at the work he does.' I bring my portfolio into work all the time. They love it . . . Museums. More where they're teaching you about the culture, where it started, how it started, things that it has gone through, the political aspects – everything. (BEEN3)
>
> I'd like to see it in schools so kids could actually learn about graffiti. Because once they learn about it in schools, then they're not going to want to go outside and vandalize because they know what it is. If you learn it in school you would want to do it in the positive form. (SONIC)

I'd like to see it occupy a space in fine arts. Graffiti to move into fine arts, absolutely, because it is that. I'd also like to see it grow in public art realms. There are those traditional mural companies that think painting with brushes is the only way of creating murals. And by now we've got a 30-year old tradition of painting murals around the world too with spray paint. (LADY PINK)

Finally, utilizing the increasing use of graffiti within advertising as a pretext, I have often asked graffiti writers to reflect on the nexus firmly solidified during the early to mid-1990s between the aesthetics associated with graffiti writing culture and the sphere of commodity exchange. While several scholars, most notably Hebdige (1979: 92–99; but see also Spitz, 1991: 34), have suggested that the absorption of emergent cultural forms by the realm of commercial exchange signifies the dissolution of their critical potential, my fieldwork suggests a strikingly dissimilar view is warranted. Among the graffiti writers with whom I have spoken, the issue is not one of maintaining a position that is independent of consumer culture and therefore one from which a "resistant" standpoint can somehow be secured, but a matter of establishing *connections with* those who control capital in order to ensure that any possible economic gains go to graffiti writers and/or graffiti writing culture.

I think it's a real good thing when we can get in and work with people outside of the culture. The problem is that outside entities come into our culture, they look at the way we do certain things, then they go paying some other people top dollar and they cut us out. You'll see a lot of computer generated illustration and graphics that are graffiti based. And if you're from the graffiti world, you'll sit there and say, 'Yo, a graffiti writer had to have something to do with that.' And, yeah, a graffiti writer had something to do with that, but not necessarily created it for them. (NIC ONE)

When it comes to having real graffiti writers do these advertisements and getting paid good money for it, it's all great. I'm happy to see graffiti writers make money for it. [Advertisements show that] graffiti is a big part of America. And they use it to advertise their multi-million dollar business and their products . . . [But] for someone who never did graffiti, yet actually take the style and use it and make money of it, there's a problem there . . . I don't dig that too much. (SONIC)

When you have a graphic designer trying to imitate graffiti I think it's wrong. If graffiti writers can get paid and be involved in it, then I'm definitely all for it. People say it's 'selling out' – I think that's a ridiculous term. If you love what you're doing and you can get paid to do it, there's nothing better than that. (DEMER)

It would seem, then, that producers of legal graffiti lead lifestyles and hold to values that many people would consider "conventional." Many of them are career and family oriented individuals who spend their spare time creating paintings within the urban environment. More often than not, the artists absorb the costs involved in producing legal graffiti. The writers see themselves and their art as contributing to communities in ways that are beneficial and it would appear that portions of the general public are appreciative of the work that they do. (To be sure, much of the general public enjoys the more elaborate forms of illegal graffiti too.) When possible, graffiti writers try to work not against, but as NIC ONE might well put it, "with people outside the culture." Almost needless to say, this is not the type of imagery that comes to mind when one usually thinks of "anarchists," "rebels," or those who revel in their "outlaw" status.

Conclusion

Drawing from ethnographic fieldwork, I have suggested that a portion of graffiti writers in New York City do not reflect, at least in two important respects, the image created of them in previous academic accounts. Whereas previous research tended to focus on illegal graffiti and often saw in this illegality some form of "resistance," it would appear that since 1990 some graffiti writers have not only become adamant about seeking out and acquiring permission in order to produce graffiti, but have also attempted, in various ways and at various levels, to become a part of the society in which they find themselves embedded.

Of course, this should not be taken to mean that we can go too far in the opposite direction and begin to imagine graffiti writing culture as something that always operates on the permissible side of legality. Nor should we simply imagine graffiti writers as philanthropic altruists free from egoistic impulses. To do so would amount to over emphasizing a particular segment or "region" of graffiti writing culture at the expense of others.

However, in light of how graffiti has adapted to a shifting political context, it is clear that writing culture cannot be reduced to a singular entity that is united through a shared disregard for the law. To be sure, previous scholars did explore tensions among graffiti writers, but they did not explore the differences (and/or similarities) between those who produce graffiti with and without permission in much detail. This, of course, did not generally occur because, until the 1990s, such a tension was difficult to discern given the ways in which the painting of graffiti was historically practiced. It is, however, becoming apparent that graffiti writing needs to be recognized as a culture that has expanded and become more complex, and is likely to continue to do so with time. I suspect that this is due to a variety of reasons, such as the movement of its practitioners through the life course, and through times and spaces regulated in fluid ways by powerful actors such as the state.

Our understanding of graffiti would be enhanced by further research that consults a greater diversity of graffiti writers, that is, those who paint with and without permission, and works towards the development of a descriptive account that more adequately reflects the heterogeneity of contemporary graffiti writing cultures. Future research could also address explanatory and policy concerns. In relation to the former, one important question revolves around the causes and mechanisms that shape the choices of individual graffiti writers in terms of how and what type of graffiti they will want to produce. In relation to the latter, future research could explore the policy implications of legal graffiti at the city level. Should urban political elites, for example, reconsider current policies that attempt to suppress graffiti and, instead, work to incorporate legal graffiti writers into civic life?

Notes

1 Special thanks to Jeffrey Ian Ross for thoughtful comments and feedback on this chapter. This chapter builds upon my article "Painting with permission: Legal graffiti in New York City", *Ethnography*, *11*(2), 235–253.

2 This quote, and all of the subsequent quotes from graffiti writers that appear in this chapter, are taken from in-depth interviews conducted by the author from 2006 through to 2008. After acquiring consent from study participants, all interviews were audiotaped and transcribed as part of a larger ethnographic research project.

3 I prefer the term "graffiti writing culture" over "aerosol art" and "hip-hop graffiti" as this appears to be the convention used most widely among graffiti writers. While this type of graffiti was firmly established by the early to mid-1970s, it is important to note that it has its origins in the late 1960s (Powers, 1999). It then appeared throughout New York City's subway system during the 1970s and 1980s before finding new spaces in which to exist during the 1990s (Murray and Murray, 2002; Ganz, 2004). Although slightly anachronistic, it is generally acknowledged to consist of three main forms:

"Tags," "throw-ups," and "pieces." In my view, on the basis of the (sub)cultural context in which it is produced and its stylistic regularity, this type of graffiti is to be sharply distinguished from political graffiti, racist graffiti, and so on. In what follows, I am not concerned with these latter forms, but only with "graffiti writing culture."

4   For variations on the graffiti-as-resistance theme that take their lead from psychoanalytic perspectives, see the brief essays of Spitz (1991: 44, 55) and Mailer (1974: np).
5   For a comparable view concerning the relationship between graffiti and consumer society, see the brief analysis offered by Stewart (1987: 174–176).
6   Halsey and Young (2006: 278, 290) also found that graffiti writers – even those who paint illegally – will spend approximately 50 dollars to produce a "piece."

References

Austin, J. (2001). *Taking the Train: How Graffiti Art Became an Urban Crisis in New York City*. New York: Columbia University Press.

Castleman, C. (1982). *Getting up: Subway Graffiti in New York*. Cambridge, MA: MIT Press.

Chalfant, H. & Prigoff, J. (1987). *Spraycan Art*. London: Thames and Hudson.

Chang, J. (2005). *Can't Stop Won't Stop: A History of the Hip-Hop Culture*. New York: St. Martin's Press.

Cooper, M. & Chalfant, H. (1984). *Subway Art*. London: Thames and Hudson.

Ferrell, J. (1993). *Crimes of Style: Urban Graffiti and the Politics of Criminality*. Boston, MA: Northeastern University Press.

Ganz, N. (2004). *Graffiti World: Street Art from Five Continents*. New York: H.N. Abrams.

George, N. (1998). *Hip Hop America*. New York: Viking.

Hager, S. (1984). *Hip Hop: The Illustrated History of Break Dancing, Rap Music, and Graffiti*. New York: St. Martin's Press.

Halsey, M. & Young, A. (2006). 'Our Desires are Ungovernable: Writing Graffiti in Urban Space,' *Theoretical Criminology 10*(3), 275–306.

Hebdige, D. (1979). *Subculture: The Meaning of Style*. London: Routledge.

Kramer, R (2010). Painting with Permission: Legal graffiti in New York City, *Ethnography, 11*(2), 235–253.

Lachmann, R. (1988).'Graffiti as Career and Ideology,' *American Journal of Sociology 94*(2), 229–250.

MacDiarmid, L. & Downing, S. (2012). 'A Rough Aging out: Graffiti Writers and Subcultural Drift,' *International Journal of Criminal Justice Sciences 7*(2), 605–617.

Macdonald, N. (2001). *The Graffiti Subculture: Youth, Masculinity and Identity in London and New York*. Hampshire: Palgrave Macmillan.

Mailer, N. (with photographs by Mervyn Kurlansky & Jon Naar). (1974). *The Faith of Graffiti*. New York: Praeger.

Miller, I.L. (2002). *Aerosol Kingdom: Subway Painters of New York City*. Jackson, MS: University Press of Mississippi.

Murray, J. & Murray, K. (2002). *Broken Windows*. Corte Madera, CA: Gingko Press.

Phillips, S.A. (1999). *Wallbangin': Graffiti and Gangs in L.A.* Chicago, IL: University of Chicago Press.

Powers, S. (1999). *The Art of Getting over: Graffiti at the Millennium*. New York: St. Martin's Press.

Rahn, J. (2002). *Painting Without Permission: Hip-Hop Graffiti Subculture*. Connecticut: Bergin and Garvey.

Rose, T. (1994). *Black Noise: Rap Music and Black Culture in Contemporary America*. Hanover, NH: Wesleyan University Press.

Schmidlapp, D. & Phase2. (1996). *Style Writing from the Underground: (R)evolution of Aerosol Linguistics*. Terni, Italy: Stampa Alternativa/IGTimes.

Snyder, G.J. (2009). *Graffiti Lives: Beyond the 'Tag' in New York's Urban Underground*. New York: New York University Press.

Spitz, E.H. (1991). *Image and Insight: Essays in Psychoanalysis and the Arts*. New York: Columbia University Press.

Stewart, J. (1989). 'Subway Graffiti: An Aesthetic Study of Graffiti on the Subway System of New York City, 1970–1978.' Unpublished doctoral dissertation, New York University.

Stewart, S. (1987). 'Ceci Tuera Cela: Graffiti as Crime and Art,' in Fekete, J. (Ed.) *Life After Postmodernism: Essays on Value and Culture* (pp. 210–231). New York: St. Martin's.

10

American Indian graffiti

Favian Martín

Introduction[1]

Historically, American Indians rely on art to "express their connection with the sacred earth and the plants and animals with which they share it" (Zimmerman, 2008: 70). To draw this analogy into the present, we find American Indians using graffiti to illustrate their connection with society (Berkhofer, 2011; Rader, 2011).[2] For many American Indian artists, their art creates a forum to discuss contemporary indigenous social problems. With the use of vibrant colors and indigenous cultural symbols, American Indian graffiti also emerges as a form of resistance to historical trauma and cultural oppression, which is traced to the legacy of colonialism (Snipp, 1992; Blades, 2011). Despite the positive influence of graffiti in promoting indigenous advocacy, American Indians also engage in graffiti, which has been linked to gangs operating Indian Country (Major *et al.*, 2004; Hailer, 2008; Smith, 2012).[3] Given the criminal element found in gang-related graffiti, many tribal communities view this type of graffiti as having a destructive influence on their tribal culture (Hailer, 2008). As a result, many tribal governments have established programs to address gang-related activities that lead to graffiti within these communities.

Although the native and nonnative public perceives most graffiti as a type of vandalism, scholars suggest that the appearance of graffiti creates "arenas of contest in which they [are] a vehicle or an agent of power" (Peteet, 1996: 140). Contemporary research on graffiti asserts that this art form provides individuals with a sense of empowerment. As Ferrell (1995: 77) argues, "kids (and others) employ particular forms of graffiti as a means of resisting particular constellations of legal, political, and religious authority." Perhaps this line of thought can explain the American Indian use of graffiti. Historically, the United States government adopted a paternalistic approach to handling American Indian affairs. Given that American Indians (as a collective group) lack political clout (Henson, 2008), their social problems are largely ignored and often fall on deaf ears. For some American Indians, the use of graffiti provides a platform to educate the general population about their marginalization within society. Indeed, American Indians view art as a source of empowerment and advocacy (Mihesuah, 2003; Berkhofer, 2011; Rader, 2011). Although some American Indians engage in graffiti, the scholarship on this topic is severely limited, and as a result, much of the information on this type of art emerges from social media sites and the news media. The purpose of this chapter is to provide a broad overview about American Indian graffiti, which is found in both Indian reservations and urban areas. Before discussing the dynamics behind the creation of American Indian graffiti, it is important to acknowledge the socio-historical legacy of American Indians as it is related to this type of art form.

Historical background

Early precursors to American Indians graffiti can be traced to early indigenous cave paintings (pictographs) and carvings (petroglyphs), which were used to record their history (Waldman, 2006; Zimmerman, 2008; O'Brien, 2009). Aside from recording their tribal history, these individuals also painted and carved illustrations that represented their culture and religion. In fact, archeologists have found depictions of mythical creatures (i.e. thunderbirds and serpents) associated with various indigenous groups in cave dwellings scattered across the United States (Zimmerman, 2008; O'Brien, 2009). Referring back to the early use of art to chronicle early indigenous history, archeologists found petroglyphs from the sixteenth century in Canyon de Chelly in Arizona, which documented the first encounter between Spanish conquistadors and the local indigenous population (Zimmerman, 2008). Colonialism greatly changed the social dynamics among American Indians. For example, the colonists and the indigenous population had two distinct views on land ownership. The colonists believed in private property and landownership, whereas the indigenous population did not believe in these concepts and felt that the land was a shared commodity. With the colonization of the Americas, early indigenous culture and art underwent great changes as American Indians were forced to assimilate into the dominant Anglo culture. For example, early Spanish colonists forced southwestern indigenous groups to destroy art that was related to their religion. In response to colonialism, American Indian art grew into a hybrid medium containing elements of indigenous and European art (Thomas, 1999). Therefore, a discussion pertaining to the social ills of colonialism is needed as it relates to contemporary American Indian graffiti.

Colonialism

Colonialism devastated the American Indian population in the United States. Generally, colonialism is defined as "nations [that] incorporate new territories or peoples through processes that are essentially involuntary, such as war, conquest, capture, and other forms of manipulation" (Blauner, 1972: 53). Colonialism also shifts the cultural and structural status of indigenous groups as European colonists establish a caste-like system, which allows them to be economically and politically superior over the indigenous population. After being relegated to a lower class status, the indigenous population is forced to adhere to the dominant group's culture, norms, rules, and religion. As a result, colonialism also negatively impacted the indigenous population. Before the European colonization of the Americas, an estimated 15 million indigenous individuals inhabited North America (Sale, 1990); however, by the late 1890s, the American Indian population was substantially reduced to 250,000 (Healey, 2003). This substantial decline in the American Indian population was due to a wide array of causes ranging from genocide to forced relocation (Snipp, 1992; Salisbury, 1996; Smith, 2005). As Zimmerman (2008: 126) notes, "the disruption wrought by Europeans and their American successors was violent, far-reaching and often very sudden . . . within less than a generation, people's way of life could change radically." More important, colonialism is widely recognized to be a source for many contemporary American Indian social problems.

Current status

Official data suggest that there are over 5 million American Indians in the United States, which comprises about 1.7 percent of the general population (Norris et al., 2012). Nearly half of these individuals live within a tribal community located in Indian Country.[4] Many individuals living on Indian reservations are plagued with social problems, such as high rates of poverty (United

States Department of Commerce, 2009), lack of employment opportunities (Sandefur, 1989; Henson, 2008), suicide (Garroutte *et al.*, 2003; Vigil, 2006; Indian Health Service, 2008; Centers for Disease Control and Prevention, 2011), substance abuse (Howard *et al.*, 1999; National Institute on Drug Abuse, 2003; Wahab and Olson, 2004; National Congress of American Indians, 2006; United States Bureau of Indian Affairs, 2006; Yuan *et al.*, 2006; Substance Abuse and Mental Health Services Administration, 2010), and high rates of crime and victimization (Greenfeld and Smith, 1999; Perry, 2004). Given these harsh realities, some American Indians turn to graffiti as both a coping mechanism and to provide a public outlet to educate individuals about indigenous social problems.

Indigenous advocacy through graffiti

Although American Indians experience a myriad of social problems, most of the general population remains unaware about these issues (Perry, 2009). As a consequence of this ignorance, there appears to be a lack of discourse pertaining to American Indians in society (Smith, 2005; Henson, 2008; Perry, 2009). In rare instances when a discussion on American Indians occurs, it is often distorted by negative stereotypes (Churchill, 1997; Henson, 2008). For example, the general population "question about whether all Indians are getting rich on gambling or whether it is 'really Indian' to run businesses or governments" (Henson, 2008: 2). Taken together, the ignorance about indigenous social problems and misrepresentations about these individuals has propelled many American Indians to "set the record straight" about their existence within society. With that being said, many American Indians turn to address these problems and to overcome negative stereotypes.

Scholars assert that graffiti is often used to address a range of issues ranging from promoting a social movement to supporting gang activities (Castleman, 1984; Ferrell, 1993; Austin, 2001; Macdonald, 2001; Rahn, 2001; Sanders, 2005; Halsey & Young, 2006; Chmielewska, 2007; Iveson, 2007, 2010; Dickens, 2008; Schacter, 2008; Brighenti, 2010; Nierhoff, 2014). With respects to American Indian advocacy graffiti, the focus tends to be on responding to historical trauma and cultural oppression that is traced to the effects of colonialism. For many tribal communities, they continue to experience mistreatment and oppression, which obstructs their ability to maintain their cultural heritage. That is to say, American Indian advocacy graffiti serves a two-fold purpose: preserve the indigenous culture and expose the general population to the social injustices that are experienced among American Indians. With respects to preserving the cultural identity, American Indian art is "rooted in history, tradition, experience, yet often incorporate new messages" (Henson, 2008: 299). Drawing upon cultural symbols and motifs, American Indian artists create innovative methods to draw attention to indigenous social problems. With that being said, such cultural images and symbols were used during an American Indian social movement to protest the mistreatment of the indigenous population in San Francisco, California.

Alcatraz occupation graffiti

On November 20, 1969, a group of American Indians formed the Indians of All Tribes organization (IAT), which sought to raise awareness about indigenous problems by occupying the abandoned federal penitentiary on Alcatraz Island in San Francisco Bay (Johnson and Fixico, 2008; Zimmerman, 2008; O'Brien, 2011). The organization cited a clause in the 1868 Treaty of Laramie, which stated that abandoned federal land should be returned to American Indians (Johnson & Fixico, 2008; Zimmerman, 2008). With regard to the penitentiary, the federal government considered the property as a federal surplus shortly after the facility closed on March 21, 1963. Therefore, the IAT argued that the abandoned island should be returned to the American Indian community. During the two-year occupation, "hundreds of Indians traveled back and forth to Alcatraz . . . which empowered them with a sense of accomplishment and the desire to make conditions better for Indian people throughout the country" (O'Brien, 2011: 213). From the island, the IAT issued the Alcatraz proclamation, which listed a series of grievances and the mistreatment of American Indians by the federal government. Believing that their actions were symbolic, the IAT felt that their occupation would achieve social justice for American Indians.

In addition to the proclamation, the IAT members also relied on pro-indigenous rights graffiti to express their frustration about the oppression of American Indians. In fact, several of the historic buildings on the island were vandalized with pro-Indian messages. For example, members wrote "yata hey," which is a Navajo greeting on one of the buildings (Johnson, 1996; Johnson & Fixico, 2008). The protestors spray-painted other sayings throughout the island such as "peace and freedom," and "this is Indian Land." The protestors also made reference to the ill-fated attack by George Custer in the Black Hills in the late 1890s, by painting the words "Custer had it coming" (Johnson & Fixico, 2008). The occupation of Alcatraz Island garnered considerable media attention as several celebrities, including Jane Fonda and Marlon Brando, visited the protestors to lend their support in the movement (Johnson, 1996). Although the occupation was initially successful in raising awareness about American Indian social problems, the occupation experienced a series of setbacks, which resulted in the protesters vacating the island in 1971. Despite the controversy surrounding the occupation, the movement is generally viewed as being successful in educating the public about indigenous social problems (Johnson, 1997; Johnson & Fixico, 2008) and empowering American Indians (Johnson, 1996).

Realizing the historical significance of the occupation, the federal government has allocated resources to protect and maintain the pro-American Indian graffiti on the island. One of the most visible signs of the occupation is the graffiti on the ten-storied water tank with the words, "Peace and freedom welcome home of the free Indian land" (Nolte, 2013: 1). Over the decades since the occupation, the graffiti and the water tower had deteriorated to the point where the words were barely legible (Sankin, 2012: 1). With guidance from the American Indian Movement and the Indian Treaty Council, the National Park Service initiated a $1.5 million project to restore the water tower and the graffiti to its original state during the protest action on the island (Wollan, 2012). According to the National Park Service, the restoration project is seeking to honor the legacy of the occupation as it promoted the advancement of indigenous rights. As David Dusterhoff, a project manager for the restoration states, "we all agreed we were doing the right thing. We were honoring an important part of the island's history" (Pfeiffer, 2013: 1). To further educate the public about the occupation and the pro-Indian graffiti, the National Park Service also established a display chronicling the events surrounding the occupation. For many visitors to Alcatraz Island, they are largely unaware of the graffiti that is associated with the occupation. As revealed by Marcus Koenen, the site supervisor for Alcatraz Island, "it is not something that people expect to see . . . when you see this graffiti when you walk off the boat, it opens your eyes to the Indian story of the island" (Nolte, 2013: 1). Indeed, the occupation of Alcatraz ushered a new sense of American Indian empowerment, which pressured the United States government to enact the Indian Self-Determination Act of 1975 (Johnson, 1996; Johnson & Fixico, 2008). The use of graffiti to advocate indigenous rights extends beyond Alcatraz Island to other areas of the country. Although graffiti is used to advocate indigenous rights, many Indian gangs operating in Indian Country are also relying on graffiti for communication purposes.

Gang-related graffiti

Although research is limited, the available scholarship on American Indian graffiti tends to associate this type of art with gangs. With regard to gangs in Indian Country, many tribal communities have become greatly concerned about their presence. Perhaps this is for good reason considering that tribal communities experience a high rate of gang-related activity (Hailer and Hart, 1999; Joseph and Taylor, 2003; Pridemore, 2004). As Carmen Smith, the Warm Springs Tribal Police Chief suggests, "these criminal organizations are growing in Indian country at an alarming rate" (Millman, 2009). Official rates substantiate her claims as there are over 400 gangs with over 4,500 members operating in or in close vicinity of tribal communities (Pridemore, 2004). Unfortunately, the presence of gangs in Indian Country also impacts the rates of crime and violence within these communities. According to the U.S. Department of Justice, "anecdotal reports and official records from juvenile justice officials (i.e. tribal courts and probation and/or law enforcement officers) in a number of Indian country communities indicate increased levels of crime associated with youth gangs" (Major, et al., 2004). Similarly, over 20 percent of American Indians claim that their community experience gang-related property crimes such as vandalism and graffiti (Major et al., 2004). More importantly, "gang members most often were said to be juvenile, male, and involved in property crimes such as vandalism and graffiti" (Flores, 2004: 14). With that being said, graffiti appears to be strongly associated with gangs operating in Indian Country. Interestingly, these gangs emulate images and attitudes from gangs found in urban areas. As Grant (2013: 17) notes,

> When gangs form in tribal communities, it is not unusual for the individuals involved to identify by a unique, localized name (i.e., Odd Squad, The Boyz, Red Nation Klique, etc.). However, the usual trend in most tribal communities involves the gang identifying with, and adopting the names and symbols of, major urban gangs (i.e. Native Gangster Bloods, Native Gangster Crips, Native Gangster Disciples, Native Latin King).

Indeed, Indian gangs are largely influenced by urban gangs. Similar to urban gangs, Indian gangs also rely on graffiti to communicate their organization's activities and goals (Hutchison and Kyle, 1993; Klein, 1995; Weisel, 2004). Gang-related graffiti often serve as symbols to "mark claimed gang territory, list gang members, show the colors and images with which the gang identifies, and challenge rival gangs and law enforcement personnel" (Armstrong et al., 2002: 34). Additionally, gang graffiti has also been used to "insult or taunt rival gangs" (Short, 1996: 7). In conjunction with urban gang symbols, many Indian gangs also draw upon their own tribal symbols to communicate the gang's activities. Irrespective of the meanings associated with Indian gang-related graffiti, there have been several reports of tribal buildings and homes being defaced by this type of vandalism.

Gang-related graffiti and vandalism appears to be an everyday occurrence for tribal members living on the Pine Ridge Indian Reservation. Local authorities have recognized several Indian gangs that are responsible for graffiti and tagging tribal buildings and homes with their gangs' insignia (Eckholm, 2009; Smith, 2012). For example, the Indian gang "Wild Boyz," which is comprised of Lakota Indians, have been responsible for tagging buildings with a symbol of a bear claw with "Wild Boyz forever" alongside the illustration (Hailer, 2008; Eckholm, 2009). In some cases, buildings have been found with the letters "WBZ" spray painted, which serves as an acronym for the gang's name (Hailer, 2008). In a recent report, researchers found that a significant portion of police calls-for-service was related to graffiti and vandalism within the tribal community (Eckholm, 2009; Smith, 2012). Indian gang graffiti extends beyond Pine Ridge Indian Reservation to other tribal communities.

Local authorities in Coville Indian Reservation in Washington found that graffiti and vandalism was being traced to both Indian and non-Indian gangs. Recent gang trends suggest that urban gangs are increasingly conducting their organization's business within the confines of Indian reservations. Due to the disjunction between federal and tribal court systems, many gangs realize that there is little risk of punishment. As a result, "reservations from Arizona to Idaho have watched gang activity evolve from graffiti to assaults to drive-by shootings, as gangs spread from their traditional urban confines into rural Indian Country" (Ogburn, 2006). With respects to the Coville Indian Reservation, local law enforcement found graffiti connected to gangs such as Native Gangster Bloods, Barrios Los Padrinos, and East Side Bloods (Thomas, 2009). Given the high volume of gang activity on the reservation, many residents reported a wide array of gang insignia and symbols spray painted throughout the community. For example, law enforcement found spray painted "187," which represents the California penal code for murder along a road barrier within the reservation (Rodriguez, 2010). Similarly, the Ute Mountain Ute Indian Reservation in Colorado, has experienced tagging from two outside gangs such as Sureño 13 and the Crip Killing Society (Thomas, 2009). Unfortunately, tribal governments have also reported gang-related graffiti and vandalism on indigenous cultural and historical landmarks in Indian Country.

Within the past several years, indigenous cultural sites have been defaced by gang-related symbols and slang. For example, gangs have been responsible for defacing the Petroglyph National Monument in New Mexico by spray painting graffiti on boulders that lead to the entrance of the park (Associated Press, 2007). Park authorities reported that the tagging on the boulder read "TSK," which is an abbreviation to "Too Sick Krew." The tagging was believed to be part of an inter-gang turf-war among several local gangs in the area (Associated Press, 2007). Non-gang affiliated graffiti has also been found on other indigenous ancestral sites. For instance, Jamestown S'Klallam authorities found that someone painted "I (heart) Miranda" on Tamanowas Rock, which has a sacred meaning for the local tribal community (Smillie, 2014). The site has long been used among the Salish Indians for ceremonial rituals (Associated Press, 2014). Although gang-related graffiti appears in Indian Country, there have been several reports of anti-Native graffiti within tribal communities.

Hate crime graffiti

American Indians frequently find themselves as victims of hate crimes. According to the Department of Justice, "American Indians are more likely than people of other races to experience violence at the hands of someone of a different race" (Perry, 2004: iii). In fact, nearly 70 percent American Indian victims reported that their perpetrator was a non-American Indian (Perry, 2004). Given these realities, many hate crimes against American Indians occur within reservation communities. As Raymond Foxworth, an administrator for the American Indian College Fund observes, "just as some areas of the South remain hotbeds of racism because of the history of slavery and discrimination, the same can be said of areas where there are large Indian populations" (Buchanan, 2006: 1). Hate crimes can be defined as "acts of violence and intimidation that are not always technically criminal in nature, and that are usually directed towards already stigmatized and marginalized groups" (Perry, 2008: 11). In her research on hate crimes against American Indians, Perry (2008: 80) suggests that "regardless of the region, or town, or tribal community, there was a very strong sense among the people interviewed that racial violence – hate crime – is endemic." Additionally, she also argues that hate crimes serve as "a mechanism of power, intended to reaffirm the precarious hierarchies that characterize a given social order. It simultaneously recreates the hegemony of the perpetrator's group and the subordination of the victim's group" (Perry, 2008: 11). For many American Indians, they are subjected to intimidation through racially charged graffiti that is often found in tribal communities. For example, tribal members living in Coeur d'Alene Tribe in Idaho experience anti-Native graffiti on tribal buildings and property. In one particular incident, local authorities found the words "white power" on an historical marker. Additionally, "die . . . Indians" and swastikas were also found painted on the sign. The vandalism is likely to be connected to the hate group "Lone Wolves," which is headquartered within proximity to the reservation (Mischke, 2014). Indeed, several hate groups have been responsible for spreading intimidation and fear through the use of graffiti throughout Indian Country. Irrespective of the type of graffiti found in in Indian Country, there are community programs designed to remove this type of vandalism.

Community response to graffiti

To address unwanted graffiti and vandalism in Indian Country, many tribal communities have enacted programs and policies to reduce the appearance of graffiti, especially gang-related graffiti. For some tribal police departments, failure to remove gang-related graffiti will exacerbate violence and crime within the tribal community. For example, the Puyallop Tribe of Indians Police Department strongly encourages tribal members to report and document any instances of graffiti. According to their website, "Graffiti should be removed to reduce the likelihood of continued violence. Gang graffiti left unchecked can be dangerous. Remember it can communicate an outright threat against an opposing gang or person." (www.puyallup-tribe.com/law-enforcement).

In response to the threat associated with gang-related graffiti, some tribal communities have created specialized task forces to remove graffiti. For instance, the Western Navajo-Hopi Meth Task Force and the Coconino County District Attorney's office collaborated to eradicate graffiti from tribal buildings and property. David Rozema, the county attorney, asserts that "graffiti is vandalism and it harms the heart of the community. We started our graffiti removal efforts two years ago and we are committed to fighting against it" (Navajo-Hopi Observer, 2011). Indeed, several tribal communities recognize graffiti as having a negative influence among tribal members. As a result, some tribes have offered monetary rewards to assist in apprehending individuals who are responsible for graffiti. In 2011, the Eastern Band of Cherokee Indians in North Carolina offered a $1,000 reward for tips that will lead to the arrest of an individual who has been tagging various tribal buildings on the reservation (McKie, 2011). Other tribal communities have implemented programs to address some of the social problems that may facilitate graffiti. Recognizing the need to address Native youth involvement in Indian gangs, the Navajo Nation has implemented programs to create opportunities for at-risk youth to deter them from participating in gangs and reduce their involvement in graffiti. Navajo Nation leaders created a series of community service projects, which had the juveniles repairing buildings and assisting the elderly within the reservation (Armstrong et al., 2002). The leaders believed that these projects allowed the juveniles to develop a sense of community pride which would prevent them from participating in gang-related activities such as graffiti.

Conclusion

In closing, this chapter provides a broad overview on American Indian graffiti. Although there has been a lack of scholarly attention to this subject, the limited research has shown that American Indian graffiti is used to advocate the rights of American Indians and raises awareness about their social problems, which may serve to educate the general population. For some American Indian artists, it also offers them the ability to achieve social justice. As Jaque Fraque states,

> From now on when people pass this wall they will understand that we as Indigenous beings are still here and that we are actively decolonizing the culture, the art, and the community. We will not tolerate violence, injustice, nor division any longer. Please help us to bridge the gaps and push towards the peace we all seek.

(www.fragua.com)

In doing so, it also reclaims their cultural identity by expressing their thoughts through their own cultural legacy. While graffiti is viewed as promoting the American Indian community, it (more specifically gang-related graffiti) is considered harmful to those living in tribal communities. As a result to this threat, many tribal communities have enacted policies and programs to eradicate gang-related graffiti from their communities. Unfortunately, this type of art will continue to appear in Indian Country if the structural conditions remain unchanged.

Notes

1 The author wishes to thank Alese Wooditch from George Mason University for her helpful comments on earlier drafts.
2 Although American Indians engage in graffiti and street art, the literature on American Indian street art is extremely limited. With that being said, the focus of this chapter is American Indian graffiti.
3 Indian Country refers to land held in trust by the federal government for American Indian use.
4 Indian Country refers to land held in trust by the federal government for American Indian use.

References

Adams, K.L., & Winter, A. (1997). Gang Graffiti as a Discourse Genre. *Journal of Sociolinguistics* 1(3), 337–360.
Alonso, A.A. (1999). *Territoriality among African-American Street Gangs in Los Angeles*. Master's thesis, University of Southern California.
Armstrong, T.L., Bluehouse, P., Dennison, A., Mason, H., Mendenhall, G., Wall, D., & Zion, J. (2002). *Finding and Knowing the Gang Nayee – Field Initiated Gang Research Project: The Judicial Branch of the Navajo Nation*. Unpublished final report, Washington, DC: United States Department of Justice, Office of Juvenile Prevention, OJJDP.
Armstrong, T.L., Guifoyle, M.H., & Melton, A.P. (1992). *Native American Delinquency: An Overview of Prevalence, Causes, and Correlates, and Promising Tradition-Based Approached to Sentencing*. Office of Juvenile Justice and Delinquency Prevention. Washington, DC: National Institute of Justice.
Associated Press. (April 2007). Petroglyph Monument Tagged with Gang Graffiti. Available at www.abqjournal.com/news/state/aptagged04–25–07.htm (accessed September 13, 2014).
Associated Press. (July 2010). Update: FBI offers $10,000 Reward in Train Track Vandalism on Cattaraugus Indian Reservation. Available at www.syracuse.com/news/index.ssf/2010/07/seneca_nation_marshals_investi.html (accessed September 13, 2014).
Associated Press. (July 2014a). Historic Marker Defaced with Racist Graffiti on CDA Indian Reservation. Available at www.krem.com/news/regional/Historical-CDA-Tribe-marker-defaced-with-graffiti-267059261.html (accessed September 13, 2014).
Associated Press. (August 2014b). Ancient Native American Site Desecrated. Available at www.cbsnews.com/news/ancient-native-american-site-desecrated-with-i-hearts-miranda/ (accessed September 13, 2014).

Austin, J. (2001). *Taking the Train*. New York: Columbia University Press.

Beauvais, F., & LaBoueff, S. (1985). Drug and Alcohol Abuse Intervention in American Indian Communities. *International Journal of the Addictions 20*(1), 139–171.

Beauvais, F., Oetting, E.R., & Edwards. R.W. (1985). Trends in the Use of Inhalants among American Indian Adolescents. *White Cloud Journal of American Indian Mental Health 3*(4), 3–11.

Beauvais, F., Oetting, E.R., Wolf, W., & Edwards, R.W. (1989). American Indian Youth and Drugs, 1976–87: A Continuing Problem. *American Journal of Public Health 79*(5), 634–636.

Berkhofer, R.F. (2011). *The White Man's Indian: Images of the American Indian from Columbus to the Present*. New York: Random House.

Blades, M. (December 2011). The Black Hills Are Not for Sale: The Mural Is up in Los Angeles. Here's How it Got There. Available at www.dailykos.com/story/2011/12/04/1042350/-The-Black-Hills-Are-Not-for-Sale-The-Mural-Is-Up-in-Los-Angeles-Here-s-How-It-Got-There# (accessed September 13, 2014).

Blades, M. (September 2012). Sioux Are Victorious in Effort to Restore Black Hills Land to the Tribes. Fund-Raising Continues. Available at www.dailykos.com/story/2012/09/03/1127342/-Sioux-are-victorious-in-effort-to-restore-Black-Hills-land-to-the-tribes-Fund-raising-continues (accessed September 13, 2014).

Blauner, R. (1972). *Racial Oppression in America*. New York: Harper and Row.

Blauner, R. (1994). Talking Past Each Other: Black and White Languages of Race. In F. Pincus & H. Ehrlich (Eds), *Race and Ethnic Conflict: Contending Views on Prejudice, Discrimination, and Ethnoviolence* (pp. 27–34). Boulder, CO: Westview Press.

Bohn, D.K. (2003). Lifetime Physical and Sexual Abuse, Substance Abuse, Depression, and Suicide Attempts among Native American Women. *Issues in Mental Health Nursing 24*(3), 333–352.

Bond-Maupin, L., GoodTracks, T.X., & Maupin, J.R. (2006). Research on Juvenile Delinquency in Indian Communities: Resisting Generalization. In J.I. Ross & L. Gould (Eds), *Native Americans in the Criminal Justice System* (pp. 187–196). Boulder, CO: Paradigm Publishers.

Brave Heart, M.Y.H. (2003). The Historical Trauma Response among Natives and Its Relationship with Substance Abuse: A Lakota Illustration. *Journal of Psychoactive Drugs 35*(1), 7–13.

Brighenti, A. (2010). At the Wall: Graffiti Writers, Urban Territoriality, and the Public Domain. *Space and Culture 13*(3), 315–332.

Buchanan, S. (January 2006). Violence against American Indians Is a Pervasive Problem. Available at www.splcenter.org/get-informed/intelligence-report/browse-all-issues/2006/winter/indian-blood (accessed September 15, 2014).

Burnett, S. (2006). Ute Homicide Rate Soars. *The Rocky-Mountain News*. Available at www.rockymountainnews.com/com/news/2006/Nov/25/ute-homicide (accessed September 20, 2014).

Carrington, V. (2009). I Write, Therefore I Am: Texts in the City. *Visual Communication 8*(4), 409–425. Los Angeles, CA: Sage Publications.

Castleman, C. (1984). *Getting up: Subway Graffiti in New York*. Cambridge, MA: MIT Press.

Centers for Disease Control and Prevention. (2011). *National Center for Injury Prevention and Control. Web-Based Injury Statistics Query and Reporting System (WISQARS)*. Atlanta, GA: Centers for Disease Control and Prevention.

The Cherokee One Feather. (May 2011). Reward Being Offered for Graffiti Crimes Info. Available at http://theonefeather.com/2011/05/reward-being-offered-for-graffiti-crimes-info/ (accessed September 22, 2014).

Chmielewska, E. (2007). Framing [Con]text: Graffiti and Place. *Space and Culture 10*(2), 145–169.Churchill, W. (1997). *A Little Matter of Genocide: Holocaust and Denial in the Americas 1492 to the Present*. San Francisco, CA: City Lights Books.

Churchill, W. (2004). *Kill the Indian, Save the Man: The Genocidal Impact of American Indian Residential Schools*. San Francisco, CA: City Lights Books.

Danver, S. (2011). Alcatraz Island Occupation. In *Revolts, Protests, Demonstrations, and Rebellions in American History an Encyclopedia*. Santa Barbara, CA: ABC-CLIO.

Deloria, V. (Ed.). (1985). *American Indian Policy in the Twentieth Century*. Norman, OK: University of Oklahoma Press.

Dickens, L. (2008). Placing Postgraffiti: The Journey of the Peckham Rock. *Cultural Geographies 15*(4), 471–496.

Eckholm, E. (December 2009). Gang Violence Grows on an Indian Reservation. Available at www.nytimes.com/2009/12/14/us/14gangs.html?pagewanted=2&_r=0 (accessed September 9, 2014).

Ferrell, J. (1995). Urban Graffiti: Crime, Control, and Resistance. *Youth & Society* 27(1), 73–92.

Fragua, J. (July 2014). Decolonize and Keep Calm, and We Are Still Here, Los Angeles, CA. Available at http://fragua.co/ (accessed September 9, 2014).

Garroutte, E.M., Goldberg, J., Beals, J., Herrell, R., & Manson, S.M. (2003). Spirituality and Attempted Suicide among American Indians. *Social Science & Medicine* 56(7), 1571–1579.

Gomez, M. (1993). The Writing on Our Walls: Finding Solutions through Distinguishing Graffiti Art from Graffiti Vandalism. *Journal of Law Reform* 26, 633–707.

Grant, C.M. (1996). Graffiti: Taking a Closer Look. *FBI Law Enforcement Bulletin* 65(8), 11–15.

Grant, C.M. (2013). *Native American Involvement in the Gang Subculture: Current Trends & Dynamics.* Community Corrections Institute Bureau of Justice Assistance, Office of Justice Programs, Washington, DC: U.S. Department of Justice.

Greenfeld, L.A. & Smith, S.K. (1999). *American Indians and Crime.* United States Department of Justice, Bureau of Justice Statistics. Washington, DC: U.S. Government Printing Office.

Hailer, J. (2008). *American Indian Youth Involvement in Urban Street Gangs: Invisible No More?* Doctoral Dissertation. University of Arizona.

Hailer, J.A., & Hart, C.B. (1999). A New Breed of Warrior: The Emergence of American Indian Youth Gangs. *Journal of Gang Research* 7(1), 23–33.

Haining, R., & Law, J. (2007). Combining Police Perceptions with Police Records of Serious Crime Areas: A Modeling Approach. *Journal of the Royal Statistical Society* 170(4), 1019–1034.

Halsey, M., & Young, A. (2006). Our Desires Are Ungovernable: Writing Graffiti in Urban Space. *Theoretical Criminology* 10(3), 275–299.

Healey, J.F. (2003). *Race, Ethnicity, Gender, and Class: The Sociology of Group Conflict and Change.* Thousand Oaks, CA: Pine Forge Press.

Henson, E.C., Taylor, J.B., Curtis, C.E.A., Cornell, S., Grant, K.W., Jorgensen, M.R., Kalt, J.P., & Lee, A.J. (2007). *The Harvard Project on American Indian Economic Development. The State of the Native Nations Conditions under U.S. Policies of Self-Determination.* New York: Oxford University Press.

Honor The Treaties: Facebook Page. (n.d.). Available at www.facebook.com/HonorTheTreaties (accessed September 25, 2014).

Honor The Treaties: Website. (n.d.). Available at www.honorthetreaties.org (accessed September 25, 2014).

Indian Country Today Media Network. (December 2012). Alcatraz Occupation Graffiti. Available at http://indiancountrytodaymedianetwork.com/2012/12/06/alcatraz-occupation-graffiti-preserved-146159 (accessed September 9, 2014).

Indian Health Service. (2008). *Indian Health Service Introduction.* U.S. Department of Health and Human Services. Rockville, MD: Department of Health and Human Services.

Iveson, K. (2007). *Publics in the City.* Oxford: Wiley-Blackwell.

Iveson, K. (2010). The Wars on Graffiti and the New Military Urbanism. *City* 14(1–2), 115–134.

Johnson, T. (1996). *The Occupation of Alcatraz Island: Indian Self-Determination and the Rise of Indian Activism.* Urbana: University of Illinois Press.

Johnson, T. (1997). *Indian Land Forever: The Indian Occupation of Alcatraz (We Hold the Rock) 1969 to 1971.* San Francisco: Golden Gate National Parks Association.

Johnson, T., & Fixico, D.L. (2008). *The American Indian occupation of Alcatraz Island: Red Power and Self-Determination.* Lincoln: University of Nebraska Press.

Joseph, J., & Taylor, D. (2003). Native American Youths and Gangs. *Journal of Gang Research* 10(2): 45–54.

Kent, J. (April 2013). Graffiti Art Brings Hope to Reservation. Available at http://listen.sdpb.org/post/graffiti-art-brings-hope-reservation (accessed September 9, 2014).

Macdonald, N. (2001). *The Graffiti Subculture.* New York: Palgrave Macmillan.

Major Jr., A.K., Egley, A., Howell, J.C., Mendenhall, B., & Armstrong, T. (2004). *Youth Gangs in Indian Country.* U.S. Department of Justice Office of Juvenile Justice and Delinquency Prevention, Office of Justice Programs. Washington DC: U.S. Government Printing Office.

Mihesuah, D.A. (2003). *Indigenous American Women: Decolonization, Empowerment, Activism.* Lincoln: University of Nebraska Press.

Millman, J. (November 2009). Mexican Pot Gangs Infiltrate Indian Reservations in U.S. Available at http://online.wsj.com/news/articles/SB125736987377028727 (accessed September 5, 2014).

Mischke, N. (July 2014). Coeur d'Alene Tribe Reports Graffiti. Available at www.kulr8.com/story/2601 4757/coeur-dalene-tribe-reports-graffiti (accessed September 6, 2014).

National Congress of American Indians. (2006). *Methamphetamine in Indian Country: An American Problem Uniquely Affecting Indian Country.* Arlington, VA: National Congress of American Indians.

National Institute on Drug Abuse. (2003). *Drug Use among Racial and Ethnic Minorities*. U.S. Department of Health and Human Services: National Institute of Health. Washington, DC: U.S. Government Printing Office.

Navajo-Hopi Observer. (October 2011). County attorney and Meth Task Force continue Graffiti Fight. Available at http://nhonews.com/main.asp?SectionID=1&SubSectionID=795&ArticleID=13992 (accessed September 6, 2014).

Nierhoff, A. (August 22, 2014). How Street Art Hopes to Save the World. Available at www.dw.de/about-dw/who-we-are/s-3325 (accessed September 5, 2014).

Nolte, C. (January 2013). Alcatraz Pays Tribute to Indian Occupation. Available at www.sfgate.com/bayarea/article/Alcatraz-pays-tribute-to-Indian-occupation-4191169.php (accessed September 6, 2014).

Norris, T., Vines, P.L., & Hoeffel, E.M. (2012). *The American Indian and Alaska Native Population: 2010*. U.S. Census Bureau. Washington, DC: U.S. Government Printing Office.

O'Brien, G. (2011). *Chronology of Native American*. London: Amber Books.

Ogburn, S. (August 2006). Tribes Tackle Taggers. Available at www.hcn.org/issues/328/16475 (accessed September 10, 2014).

Ogunwole, S.U. (2006). *We the People: American Indians and Alaska Natives in the United States*. U.S. Census Bureau. Washington, DC: U.S. Government Printing Office.

Perry, B. (2008). *Silent Victims: Hate Crimes against Native Americans*. Tucson, AZ: University of Arizona Press.

Perry, B. (2009). *Policing and Place in Indian Country*. Lanham, MD: Lexington Books.

Perry, S.W. (2004). *American Indians and Crime*. U.S. Department of Justice, Bureau of Justice Statistics. Washington, DC: U.S. Government Printing Office.

Peteet, J. (1996). The Writing on the Walls: The Graffiti of the Intifada. *Cultural Anthropology 11*(2), 139–159.

Pfeiffer, E. (January 2013). Federal Government Restores Native American 'Occupation of Alcatraz' Graffiti. Available at http://news.yahoo.com/blogs/the-sideshow/federal-government-restores-native-american-occupation-alcatraz-graffiti-201458906.html (accessed September 14, 2014).

Phillips, S. (1999). *Wallbangin': Graffiti and Gangs in L.A.* Chicago: University of Chicago Press.

Pridemore, W.A. (2004). Review of the Literature on Risk and Protective Factors of Offending among Native Americans. *Journal of Ethnicity in Criminal Justice 2*(4), 45–63.

Puyallup Tribal News. (July 2007). Task Force, Police Step up Anti-Gang Efforts. Available at www.puyalluptribalnews.net/news/view/task_force_police_step_up_anti-gang_efforts/ (accessed September 9, 2014).

Puyallup Tribe of Indians. (n.d.). Gang Awareness: Information Directory. Available at www.puyallup-tribe.com/law-enforcement/gang_awareness/ (accessed September 20, 2014).

Rader, D. (2011). *Engaged Resistance: American Indian Art, Literature, and Film from Alcatraz to the NMAI*. Austin: University of Texas Press.

Rahn, J. (2001). *Painting without Permission*. Basingstoke: Palgrave.

Riviere, M. (2005). The Dynamics of a Canvas: Graffiti and Aerosol Art. *Public Art Review 17*(33), 24–27.

Robinson, J. (July 2014). Idaho Tribe Seeks Information on Vandals Behind 'White Power' Message. Available at http://nwnewsnetwork.org/post/idaho-tribe-seeks-information-vandals-behind-white-power-message (accessed September 22, 2014).

Rodriguez, D. (2010). *Northwest High Intensity Drug Trafficking Area*. Seattle, WA: Washington State Gang Intelligence Bulletin 2010.

Sale, K. (1990). *The Conquest of Paradise: Christopher Columbus and the Columbian Legacy*. New York: Knopf Publishing.

Salisbury, N. (1996). The Indians' Old World: Native Americans and the Coming of Europeans. *The William and Mary Quarterly 53*(3), 435–458.

Sandefur, G.D. (1989). American Indian Reservations: The First Underclass Areas? *Focus 12*(1), 37–41.

Sanders, B. (2005). *Youth Crime and Youth Culture in the Inner City*. London: Routledge.

Sankin, A. (December 2012). Alcatraz Water Tower Graffiti Restored, Preserving Memory of Historic Native American Occupation. Available at www.huffingtonpost.com/2012/12/03/alcatraz-water-tower_n_2234876.html (accessed September 16, 2014).

Smillie, J. (August 2014). Native Americans' Sacred Tamanowas Rock Desecrated with an 'I ♥' tag. Available at www.peninsuladailynews.com/article/20140803/NEWS/308039977/native-americans-sacred-tamanowas-rock-desecrated-with-an-i (accessed September 9, 2014).

Smith, A. (2005). *Conquest: Sexual Violence and American Indian Genocide*. Cambridge, MA: South End Press.

Smith, A. (February 2007). Soul Wound: The Legacy of Native American Schools. *Amnesty International Magazine*. Available at www.amnestyusa.org/node/87342 (accessed September 7, 2014).

Smith, S.J. (November 2012). Street Gangs Gain Foothold on Native American Reservations. Available at http://thegrio.com/2012/11/23/street-gangs-gain-foothold-on-native-american-reservations/ (accessed September 8, 2014).

Snipp, C.M. (1992). Sociological Perspectives on American Indians. *Annual Review of Sociology 18*(1), 351–371.

Substance Abuse and Mental Health Services Administration, Center for Behavioral Health Statistics and Quality. (2011). *The NSDUH Report: Substance Use among American Indian or Alaska Native Adolescents*. Rockville, MD: Substance Abuse and Mental Health Services Administration. Available at www.samhsa.gov/data/2k11/WEB_SR_005/WEB_SR_005.htm (accessed September 12, 2014).

Substance Abuse and Mental Health Services Administration, Office of Applied Studies. (2010). *The NSDUH Report: Substance Use among American Indian or Alaska Native Adults*. Rockville, MD: Substance Abuse and Mental Health Services Administration. Available at www.samhsa.gov/data/2k10/182/American Indian.htm (accessed September 1, 2014).

Thomas, K. (July 2009). Tribal Leaders Seek Help with Indian Gang Activity. Available at www.newsday.com/tribal-leaders-seek-help-with-indian-gang-activity-1.1338887 (accessed September 12, 2014).

United States Bureau of Indian Affairs. (2006). *BIA Funded School Adequate Yearly Progress 2004–2005*. Washington, DC: U.S. Government Printing Office. Available at www.oiep.bia.edu/ (accessed September 4, 2014).

United States Department of Commerce. (2009). *Census Bureau, Decennial Census, 1990 and 2000*. Washington, DC: U.S. Government Printing Office.

Vigil, D. (2006). *Division of Health Programs, White Mountain Apache Tribe. Oral Testimony Offered to the U.S. Senate Committee on Indian Affairs. Hearing: Indian Youth Suicide*. Washington, DC: U.S. Government Printing Office.

Wahab, S., & Olson, L. (2004). Intimate Partner Violence and Sexual Assault in Native American Communities. *Trauma, Violence, & Abuse 5*(4), 353–366.

Wollan, M. (December 2012). Antigovernment Graffiti Restored, Courtesy of Government. Available at www.nytimes.com/2012/12/25/us/alcatraz-american-indian-occupation-graffiti-preserved.html?_r=1& (accessed September 6, 2014).

Yuan, N.P., Koss, M.P., Polacca, M., & Goldman, D. (2006). Risk Factors for Physical Assault and Rape among Six Native American Tribes. *Journal of Interpersonal Violence 21*(12), 1566–1590.

Zimmerman, L. (2008). *Native North American: Belief and Ritual*. London: Duncan Baird.

Part II

Theoretical explanations of graffiti and street art/causes of graffiti and street art[1]

Jeffrey Ian Ross

Introduction

In the social sciences, we care about numerous processes. The most dominant questions revolve around the primordial who, what when, where, how, and why of activities deemed important and relevant. This is the perpetual causal question – the one in which many scholars invest numerous resources in their attempts to tease out the contributing variables/factors and to understand how numerous inputs interact with each other. The field of graffiti/street art is no different in this respect.

In the contemporary history of graffiti/street art, the reasons why individuals engage in this activity has been ascribed to numerous causes, including but not limited to disaffection felt by lower class and/or unemployed or underemployed Latino/Hispanic and African-American youth, gang members staking out their territory, art students trying out new techniques, artists/writers trying to make names for themselves, and hedonistic tendencies. Indeed, there is some truth to these claims, but rarely are these processes examined in a systematic fashion as could be provided by an objective scholarly approach.

Over the past three decades, a handful of scholars have conducted ethnographies, and these individuals have studied graffiti and street art practitioners in order to analyze their actions and motivations. The results have proven to be nuanced and sophisticated in their conclusions.

Overview of chapters

A total of six chapters are featured in Part II. This section of the book begins with Rafael Schacter's "Graffiti and street art as ornament," which selectively explores where graffiti/street art fits into art history and art theory. This chapter claims that graffiti and street art are a form of contemporary ornamentation. Corresponding with the two formal defining aspects of ornament-as something attached to a surface and as something providing embellishment, Schacter argues that the power and messages embodied in graffiti and street art emerge, in a large part, as a result of this ornamental essence. Schacter further maintains that an entrenched relationship exists between (architectural) ornamentation and (social) order. It is the fact that ornament *creates* order, rather than merely reflecting it, that gives graffiti and street art the capability to radically overturn the idea of the city, and to disturb and disavow the norms of contemporary city life.

In "Graffiti, street art and the divergent synthesis of place valorisation in contemporary urbanism," Andrea Mubi Brighenti argues that over the last decade, street art has moved much closer to the core of the contemporary art system, at the same time that graffiti has received unprecedented attention from mainstream cultural institutions. Albeit to different extents and not without contradictory or even paradoxical outcomes, both graffiti and street art have been increasingly associated with thrilling lifestyles, urban creativity, fashionable outfits, and hip neighborhoods. A radical transformation has followed concerning the impact these practices have on the value attributed to certain urban places. Rather than the value-neutral (invisible) or value-detracting (supravisible) functionalities that existed previously, now graffiti – and even more pronouncedly street art – seems to be value-bestowing (visible) in its essence. Visibility means that these activities have turned into recognizable and much sought-for items in the urban landscape.

In this context, Brighenti examines recent graffiti and street art events in the context of urban transformation trends. Although such events have popped up almost everywhere in the world, especially in Western countries, the author uses examples from Italy, where in the last five years he has been collecting a series of detailed field observations. Brighenti grapples with the social and cultural significance of graffiti and street art in the changing cityscape and the unfolding urban process. By doing so, the author questions the economic process of *place valorization* in the current transformations of capitalism. Finally, the author places these concerns in the framework of the new political processes of disciplination and urban governance.

"Graffiti art and the city: from piece-making to place-making," by Graeme Evans, suggests that a graffiti "art-vandalism" dialectic in cities contributes to the increasing emphasis on place-making. In particular, the trend towards embracing and valorizing different forms of graffiti as destination markers and public art, in both mainstream and off-beat locations – and as local and visitor attractions – is discussed. This visual culture forms part of the wider urban design impetus, resulting in the re-imaging of and new theoretical approaches to the post-industrial city. The place and role of graffiti artists is, however, ambiguous as an informal activity, which has developed as an oppositional and illegitimate practice. Evans presents examples of graffiti, and its celebration and controversy in place-making and creative city efforts, including its adoption in cultural tourism itineraries and city branding initiatives.

It has been over a decade since Nancy Macdonald's groundbreaking ethnography *The Graffiti Subculture: Youth, Masculinity and Identity in London and New York* (2001). In this exploration of the dynamics of illegal graffiti, Macdonald focused largely on understanding the unmistakable male dominance of the subculture. Exploring the interplay between graffiti's illegality and risk, she argued that graffiti is a resource that young men can use to construct masculine identity. In her contribution to this *Handbook*, "Something for the boys? Exploring the changing gender dynamics of the graffiti subculture," Macdonald briefly summarizes the arguments she put forward in her book, and analyzes and integrates the scholarship on masculinities and crime/graffiti which has been published since 2001. Macdonald also reexamines the changing gender dynamics of the graffiti subculture since the proliferation of the "street/stencil graffiti" posts (ca. 2000). This alternative subcultural branch has now brought more women into the fold. Macdonald, thus, asks if her gender/masculinity thesis is still relevant, and where should future scholarship on this topic go?

In "The psychology behind graffiti involvement," written by Myra F. Taylor, Julie Ann Pooley, and Georgia Carragher, we learn why adolescents and young adults who have become marginalized from their mainstream peers or from society are motivated to join the graffiti subculture. The authors argue that through risk-taking, these youth can acquire peer recognition and subcultural respect via their graffiti involvement. The researchers strive to address the following question: What does the graffiti subculture provide that keeps young people involved in graffiti? The answer would seem to be that admittance into a small graffiti crew provides marginalized members with the social capital support resources that are missing from their daily lives. These support resources help the crew's membership to bond together, and in doing so, facilitate both the individual member's and the crew's sense of place, belonging, community, and connection. However, as the graffitists mature, they are faced with the life-course dilemma of whether to leave the graffiti culture and conform to society's social mores, to remain a graffitist, or to morph from a graffitist into an urban artist. This chapter closes by revealing that the urban artist pathway back into mainstream inclusion is, in itself, not without controversy.

This section of the *Handbook* is rounded out with "Graffiti and the subculture career" by Gregory J. Snyder. Based on a decade of ethnographic research among graffiti writers in New York City, Snyder highlights the impact that this youth culture has had on the adult lives of its practitioners. This chapter features a descriptive account of the contemporary forms of graffiti writing, and shows that those who are successful graffiti writers are able to turn their subcultural capital into actual capital. Snyder maintains that graffiti writers, contrary to classic subculture theory, do indeed create subculture careers. These careers are facilitated by subculture media, which create a need for the documentation and dissemination of subcultural content. This, in turn, generates career opportunities within the subculture that can often be transferred into other careers, such as magazine editing, graphic design, fine art, tattooing, and youth marketing. This chapter addresses the classic subculture theory of the Birmingham School, as well as the contemporary genre known as post-subculture studies. Snyder also argues that graffiti is a subculture that requires further theoretical accounting, because rather than symbolic resistance, economic co-optation, or post-modern identity formation, graffiti writers use their graffiti experience to help make successful lives for themselves.

Omissions

A handful of appropriate subtopics did not make it into this section. One of them concerns the *longstanding connection between graffiti and hip-hop music* (e.g. Chang, 2007). Graffiti folklore is intricately intertwined with the narrative of hip hop, most popularly consisting of "four elements," including DJing, emceeing (rapping), break dancing and the art of graffiti. What many observers of graffiti and street art do not realize is that this intertwining of activities is disputed (e.g. *Just to Get a Rep*). Graffiti, as a practice and an art form, was established long before hip-hop music emerged in the South Bronx, and many of its practitioners do not identify with the music or its subculture at all. Writers are a much more diverse set of people than most realize, and even though graffiti has been adopted as part of the hip hop culture and has grown aesthetically because of this association, it is not necessarily intricately linked with hip hop.

Another cause that was not directly addressed in this section is *the relative contribution that gentrification has on graffiti and street art*. In many urban neighborhoods, a dialectic exists between graffiti/street art and property development. Some observers have argued that gentrification can lead to graffiti/street art. Dilapidated and abandoned buildings waiting to be renovated, rehabilitated, or torn down are magnets for all sorts of activities, including temporary shelters for homeless people, drug sales, and use (e.g. shooting galleries, crack houses, etc.), and places where graffiti/street art are placed. Other scholars have suggested that graffiti/street art can be an engine for tourism, helping improve the aesthetic quality of otherwise drab or dull parts of a city.

Although other causal dynamics could be examined, the chapters in this part of the *Handbook* should provide a well-rounded introduction to the complexity of causal explanations for graffiti/street art.

Note

1   Special thanks to Stefano Bloch, Rachel Hildebrandt and Ronald Kramer for their comments.

References

Chang, J. (2007). *Can't Stop Won't Stop: A History of the Hip-Hop Generation*. New York: Macmillan.
Macdonald, N. (2001). *The Graffiti Subculture: Youth, Masculinity and Identity in London and New York City*. New York: Palgrave/Macmillan.
Just to Get a Rep. Directed by Peter Gerard, 2004.

11

Graffiti and street art as ornament

Rafael Schacter

Introduction[1]

In both the popular and media imagination, graffiti[2] and street art[3] have come to be related to a set of binary oppositions that serve to narrow rather than expand our comprehension of these complex forms. Broadly outlined through pairings which I shall here term 'creativity vs criminality' and/or 'art vs vandalism', these oppositions stifle debate over a pursuit which is, most likely, one of the most practiced forms of visual culture today. Moreover, they reduce topics of discussion to artless concerns over graffiti and street art's legal permissibility rather than more pertinent questions regarding its basic materiality. While proponents of the form (from lay practitioners to design aficionados) may claim that graffiti and street art exist on the former side of these couplets, as truly inventive, regenerative, expressive acts, its opponents (from police authorities to property owners) place them firmly as examples of defacement, destruction, and disfigurement. Much effort has been spent on this debate, a debate which is unwinnable, subjective, and overwrought.

This chapter, however, will attempt to sidestep this clash and, instead, present an alternative perspective on the topic. Seeing both graffiti and street art as forms of contemporary (if insurgent) ornamentation, I will take very seriously the suggestion by architectural theorist Jonathan Hill (2006) that '[g]raffiti and sgraffito ornament a building', that graffiti is, in its purely material state, an 'additive rather than reductive' practice (p. 176): As artefacts that are both adjunctive (a thing added) and decorative (a thing embellished), graffiti and street art will hence be explored through their status as quite classical, literal, rather than metaphorical, ornaments. Yet this designation as ornament will be seen to bestow as much power as peril upon them, as well as placing graffiti and street art within the wider debates (and wider anxieties) over ornament in the architectural canon as a whole. Examining these illicit objects through this lens I then hope to reveal an understanding of graffiti and street art that rejects the attempt to either promote them as 'art' or to demote them as 'vandalism'. And rather it will be the material nature of these artefacts which will be explored here, the markedly ornamental characteristics graffiti and street possess which will come to provide us with a valuable insight into the idiosyncratic status of these visual forms.

Adjunctive and decorative

Be it an acid etching[4] or a multi-coloured mural, a scratched insignia or a stencilled ideogram, the products of graffiti and street art exist within the dense medium of the street, amidst the dirt, the noise and the concrete of the city walls. They are not produced on a neutral surface (on a pristine canvas or from virgin clay), nor are they formed from scratch, or out of nothing. These images are not created within a separated studio space, nor are they constructed within the detached passive milieu of the gallery. These are visual forms that are engraved, embedded, embossed onto the very surface of the city and affixed onto previously constructed forms. Whether spray paint on the outer surface of a train, or a scratching incised into stone, both graffiti and street art can only ever function upon, within, attached, or fixed to a secondary surface.

In this manner, all of these works – and graffiti and street art as a whole – come to comply quite succinctly with the first part of the Oxford English Dictionary's definition of ornament, functioning as an 'accessory or adjunct' – a secondary element on a primary surface, an auxiliary element on a customarily architectural surface. As 'graffito' (etymologically originating from the Italian graffito, a 'little scratch'), these objects can only ever be apprehended in connection to what they are scratched upon, in connection to what they exist *within*. The 'what' of the image, as Hans Belting terms it (2005) – the graffiti or street art image itself – is hence 'steered by the how in which it transmits its message' (p. 304), through the how of their having been scored, stamped and situated onto the architectural body of the city.

Rather than describing a particular style or particular aesthetic, to ornament, as Grabar (1992) has suggested, must simply be understood as the 'act of putting something on something else', rather than describing the specific 'nature of what is put' (p. 22). And graffiti and street art can be seen as precise material examples of this. They are images placed upon supplementary surfaces.

Figure 11.1 Neko, Untitled (acid etching in process – etchings also visible in surround), Madrid, Spain, 2010 © the author

Figure 11.2 3TTMan, Viva la Calle Libre, Madrid, Spain, 2010 © the author

They are inscribings or engravings placed upon the architecture of the city, irrespective of their precise nature. And they are thus objects that cannot be understood outside of their necessarily additive status. Consequently, what I will first be arguing within this chapter is that both graffiti and street art must be understood to be fundamentally ornamental in their primary adjunctive, additional sense – as objects added to a surface, as supplements to a further medium; they are works which can only exist through the body of a secondary medium and are hence activated and enabled though the 'how' of the city itself.

Furthermore, be it concrete 'scratchitti'[5] or a wheat pasted poster, futuristic wildstyle[6] or a retro tag, these artefacts all function within the sphere of the decorative, within the realm of the beautiful or what David Brett (2005) has termed 'visual pleasure'.[7] Working through a physical sensuousness that can act as a marker of 'social recognition, perceptual satisfaction, psychological reward [or] erotic delight' (Brett 2005: 4), through a mode of material communication that can express both social and intimate themes, these artefacts engage the power of the visual to captivate and gratify their viewers and their makers in equal measure. Whether in their most overtly aggressive or 'vandalistic' form – such as the aforementioned acid etching – or in their most apparently amicable or 'decorative' state – such as an elaborate, colourful mural – all of these artefacts are created through a complex tradition of visual dexterity and physical skill. They are all objects that contain a quite defined notion of aesthetic value and beauty at their core, even if a naturally *subjective* notion of beauty. Formal qualities such as 'order or unity, proportion, scale, contrast, balance and rhythm' (Moughtin *et al.* 1999: 3) – elements understood as key principles of decorative production – are basic tenets in the production of all these designs, basic formulae from which they materialise. Even if elements established only so as to later defile – used to form a contrast to, rather than coherence with their architectural surroundings – the basic structure of all graffiti and street art can only become visible through working with these underlying decorative principles. These are decorative criteria meant to make an object 'selectable, meaningful, affective and complete' (Brett 2005: 64). They are qualities meant to enliven, to enrich the objects on which they appeared. And what I will thus secondly argue within this essay is that all graffiti and street art are, in this exact manner, produced specifically to 'decorate, adorn, embellish [and/or] beautify' their surfaces, and hence all comply quite faithfully with the second half of the Oxford English Dictionary's definition of ornamentation.

But how can we see the additive status of graffiti and street art (its status as a supplement to a surface) as well as its decorative position (its standing as an embellishment or beautification) working in practice? If we take as an example the commonplace practice of tagging – not only one of the most prominent examples of graffiti and street art but one often thought of as the least artistic and most vandalistic[8] by non-practitioners – we can see how this practice is entirely homologous with calligraphy, one of the most classical forms of ornament. Emerging through both the formal as well as conceptual characteristics graffiti and calligraphic cultures embrace – through the clear attempt by both practices to supplement and embellish standardised typography, to amend and adorn it through their loops, serifs and cusps; emerging through the crucial elements of unity, proportion, scale, contrast, balance and rhythm that are paramount to the production of both scripts (and elements used to judge the perceived *qualities* of each example); emerging through the subcultural linguistic discourse each practice contains, the layered terminology and descriptive categories each utilise; emerging through to the legendary ancestors and masters that both groups reify – these two forms of 'beautiful writing' can in truth be seen to be fundamentally indistinguishable, only their *legality* and *locality* differentiating them.

Taking this line of reasoning further however, tagging can not only be seen to be ornamental through its status as an addition and adornment of our writing system: It can in fact be seen to be supplementing its material surroundings as much as the very letters which it transforms. It supplements and embellishes the wall and the word, the alphabet and the architecture. Tagging must therefore be seen as *doubly* ornamental, the 'what' of the image – the written name – guided by the 'how' of the city and the 'how' of the letter at the same time. Moreover, the very fact that tagging is often deemed (or derided) as incomprehensible can be seen to be the fate, almost the *requirement* of all calligraphy. Beautiful writing can be, as Grabar pronounces (1992), 'meaningful in a different way from the one in which is it legible' (p. 117). Viewers can be attracted not by what is literally read but rather by the sensory pleasure that visual complexity provides. The commonly pronounced indecipherability of tagging is thus, perhaps surprisingly, a direct link toward, rather than a barrier against, its ascription as calligraphy, and lack of comprehension no reason to dismiss its status as ornament. And as an indisputable accessory, as a clear embellishment to a base structure, tagging must therefore be understood as a fundamentally ornamental form.[9]

Not only tagging, however, but also all the artefacts which come under the umbrella of graffiti and street art must be seen as prime examples of ornamental forms. Whatever their shape or their size, they all function as the 'applied decoration' that Brett (2005) argues is at the essence of all ornament (p. 4). They all work through the basics of 'form, line, tonality, material, disposition [and] colour', they work through 'asserting surface', through enriching their recipients 'with a secondary potential of light and shade' (Phillips 2003). Whatever their 'meaning' or even their intentions, they all function as intermediaries, as agents through which 'messages, signs, symbols and even probably representations are transmitted [. . .] in order to be most effectively communicated' (Grabar 1992: 227). And this, therefore, is the key proposition that I want to make in this chapter: *whether 'constructive' or 'destructive', graffiti and street art are both decorative and adjunctive, they are accessories to a primary surface, forms of embellishment upon a secondary plane and hence objects with a fundamentally ornamental status.*[10]

Figure 11.3 Nano4814, Untitled, Vigo, Spain, 2009 © the author

This understanding of graffiti and street art as ornament does a number of things. First, it helps to remove the practices from the tropes habitually brought up in their discussion – from the debates over creativity and criminality, of art and vandalism as mentioned above. Second, and perhaps more significantly, it can come to expose the source behind the corresponding potency and anxiety that graffiti and street art so commonly incorporate. And what I now want to move to argue is that it is the very ornamental condition of graffiti and street art that creates much of the fear (and passion) that they draw to the surface. Rather than it simply being due to their illegality, due to the campaigns and 'wars' against graffiti undertaken over the last thirty years, it is the fundamentally decorative and adjunctive status of graffiti and street art which I believe causes much of the friction and fervour which they so clearly elicit. And while today the epithet 'mere' has become as if almost affixed to the term ornament (perhaps as a way to diminish its potentiality), the strange power that it seems to contain, its capability, as with the iconoclash which Bruno Latour and his colleagues has famously discussed (2002), to 'return again, no matter how strongly one wants to get rid of them' (p. 15), is something which now must be explored. So what is it that makes ornament so strangely irrepressible, which makes graffiti so tenacious even in the face of its common abhorrence?[11] Why is ornament subject to as much condemnation as devotion, subject to, as Frank Lloyd Wright put it (2005 [1932]: 348), 'ornamentia' (the love of ornament) and 'ornaphobia' (the fear of it) in equal measure? And how did this seemingly innocuous artefact, this object that can take, in effect, practically any form (as long as both adjunctive and decorative), come to exist within this complex state?

Agency and unease

Although architectural modernists – most famously epitomised by Adolf Loos (2002) – claimed that ornament was dangerous due to its 'falsity' (its failure to represent true order) or due to its defilement of the 'pure' (its failure to reconcile form and function), the true grounds for the perils and passions ornamentation invokes centres, in the view of the anthropologist Alfred Gell (1998), on the notion of *artefactual agency* – the power of objects to act with as much intentionality as their human counterparts. While, as he says, the 'most committed aesthetes are far from keen on riotous decoration' (whether this be a decorated cigarette case or a graffiti covered city wall), it can be understood to have survived and prospered, 'even in the face of aesthetic condemnation from on high, because it is *socially efficacious*' (p. 82, emphasis added). As a 'social technology', surface decoration was believed by Gell to produce a vigorous 'attachment between persons and things' (p. 74), an attachment bound through the *social*, as much as the *physical* complexity of these artefacts. Art objects, and likewise ornamental artefacts, were thus understood to act as material indicators of their producer's agency, 'vehicles' of their 'personhood' (p. 81). They were believed to behave in many quite logical ways *as* the person who formed them (as Gell explains through examples as diverse as anti-personnel mines and the oeuvre of Marcel Duchamp). As 'fragments of *primary* intentional agents in their *secondary* artefactual form' (p. 21), they could act as physical traces of persons, and as a method of binding disparate individuals through the transference or simple viewing of these highly dynamic, almost living objects. Actors were hence compelled to 'load surfaces with decoration' in order to 'draw persons into worldly projects' (p. 82). They were compelled to ornament, to embellish, in order to 'mediate social agency back and forth within the social field' (p. 81). Akin to Gottfried Semper's suggestion that by 'adorning anything, be it alive or inanimate, I bestow upon it the right of individual life' (Semper in Collins 1998: 124), the agency of decorative technologies was grasped by Gell to emerge through the webs of relationality these forms create, through their ability to become part of the social field in ways very similar, if not identical, to human actors themselves.

Figure 11.4 The agency of the image: Madrid 'window' of fame, 2010 (image includes tags by Buni, Hear (Alone), Ring, Spok, Nano4184, Neko, Dier, Remed, Shit, Garr (Garrulo – Koas), Parse, Suee, Til, Tonk, Los del rodillo and unknown others) © the author

Not only materialising through this indexical status however, the ability of the decorative was further understood to emerge through what Gell calls the 'pleasurable frustration' of our being trapped within a rhythmic, patterned surface (Gell 1998: 80). The animation of design functioned as a 'mind trap', a technology of enchantment which comes to obstruct our ability to intellectually reconstruct a pattern, leading us to be 'held inside it, impaled, as it were, on its bristling hooks and spines' (p. 76). Our captivation and fascination with decoration is thus understood to be formed through our inability to 'mentally rehearse' their productive origins, our inability to 'follow the sequence of steps in the artist's "performance"' (p. 81). It is the commonly felt impossibility of untangling the maze that the image presents us with, the impossibility of comprehending how these works came into existence that enchants us. And this creates what Gell terms 'unfinished business', a 'delay or lag, between transactions' meaning the object is 'never fully possessed' but always 'in the process of *becoming* possessed' (pp. 80–81 my emphasis). It forms an uneven exchange in which the viewer is forever entangled in its materiality, not only meaning that it remains out of our grasp, but that it forms an inexhaustible bond between index and recipient, object and beholder. As Wigley continues (2001), just to 'look at decoration is to be absorbed by it. Vision itself is swallowed by the sensuous surface' (p. 132). Merely resting our eyes on these visual forms is hence a profound danger. We become captivated by the magical power of the image, entrapped in its physical form.

This Gellian way of comprehending patterned form can, I believe, start to explain the deeply phobic, deeply iconoclastic attitude so often displayed toward ornament. It can start to explain the iconoclastic attitude not only towards Art Nouveau and the decorative, rather than *fine* arts, but that displayed toward the graffiti and street art of today. It is the agency and animation of these images, the stigma of personhood and their status as in some way alive which produces this fear of the decorative, the relationship formed between object and viewer which generates the pollution which they are so often believed to contain. As previously discussed in Schacter (2008), the way both producers and consumers understand these images, the metaphors used as well as the reactions prompted, consistently return to the living qualities of these supposedly inanimate objects.[12] They constantly return to the status of these objects as not merely likenesses, not merely representations, but as living relations, as offspring or replications of their selves. The personhood invested within these ornaments is what creates this (often unwanted) relation. Their ability to trap our eyes, to weave us into their histories, their ability to force us into an exchange and to undertake communion with them. And that the word 'tacky', as Gell continues, was chosen by 'severe modernism to condemn the popular taste for riotous ornament' (and is equally a term often placed before street art and graffiti itself) can hence be seen to be quite elucidating, 'tactile adhesiveness' being something which attacks the 'body/world boundary' (pp. 82–83), which contains a viscosity, an adhesion, literally attaching the material world to ourselves. Ornamentation, as Grabar continues (1992), cannot therefore simply be understood as a 'category of forms or of techniques applied to some media' but rather must be seen as an 'unenunciated but almost necessary manner of compelling a relationship between objects or works of art and viewers and users' (p. 230). It is the agency of the decorative which creates their fierce ability to attach. It is this agency that creates the fear that so clearly surrounds them. It is the 'wanton subjectivism' (Foster 2002: 17) of these artefacts, their personhood and literal vivacity which can thus be understood to stand at the centre of this ornaphobia. It is their inherent personhood that necessitates their removal from sight.

The unease and angst that emerges at the mere witnessing of graffiti and street art can hence be understood to emerge not simply through their contravention of legal codes. It can be understood to emerge through their providing evidence of an embedded form of sociality, expressing the evident 'personhood' of their producers, eliciting an evidentially animative quality. Through 'tattooing walls', as Jean Baudrillard remarked (1976/1993), graffiti 'free[s] them from architecture and turn[s] them once again into living, social matter' (p. 36); it turns each tag, each mural, each marking in the city into a material marker of an *individual*, a personhood revivifying a physical space. The very function of these decorative markings is to attract, is to entice us within their web. They are produced explicitly for this purpose, not only providing clear evidence of an individual (as clear with a graffiti-artist's tag as a street-artist's icon), but at the same time embedding a form of sociality within the wall they touch. They open a network between objects and persons, between writer and reader, producer and consumer of the work. And the decorative nature of ornament, the 'what' of the image, can thus be seen to be as powerful as it is pollutive (as following Mary Douglas 1966), to have an ability to attack and repel, to attract and disgust in quite equal measure. It can be seen to trap and captivate its recipients, to draw them into their visual and social world irrespective of their viewers' desires.

The parerga and the quasidetached

Ornament's anxiety-producing yet simultaneously attractive status can also be understood to emerge through its confusing position in *physical* terms (literally confusingly, from its Latin root *confundere* to 'mingle together'), through its placement both *attached* and *detached* from the integrity

Figure 11.5 Graffiti as parerga, frame and content in the same moment: Vova Vorotniov, Spray as Index 1, Warsaw, Poland, 2011 © the author

of its 'primary' structure. As the archetypal *parergon* – a Greek term whose literal meaning is 'beside', or additional to the 'work' (famously illustrated by Kant by the frame of a painting, but also by clothing or architectural columns), and yet a term which Jacques Derrida (1987) has explained must always be understood through its *relation* rather than *separation* to the *ergon* – ornament is seen by Derrida to be 'neither inside or outside, neither above nor below' (p. 9) but to exist as both constitutive and peripheral in the same moment.

> The natural site chosen for the erection of a temple is obviously not a parergon. Nor is an artificial site: Neither the square, nor the church, nor the museum, nor the other surrounding works. But drapery or the column, yes. Why? Not because they are easily detached; on the contrary, they are very difficult to detach. Without them, without their quasidetachment, the lack within the work would appear or, what amounts to the same, would not appear. It is not simply their exteriority that constitutes them as parerga, but the internal structural link by which they are inseparable from a lack within the ergon. And this lack makes for the very unity of the ergon. Without it, the ergon would have no need of a parergon. The lack of the ergon is the lack of a parergon, of drapery or columns which nevertheless remain exterior to it.
>
> (Derrida, 1979: 24)

It is ornament's status of 'quasidetachment', the inherent impossibility of disengagement or disconnection while appearing to be both engaged and connected, that makes the *parergon* so fascinating. It is ornament's position as inseparable, rather than severable, that bring so much power. It is its quasidetachment that means it acts not only as the supplement, the addition, but as that which exposes the lack within the interior, the surplus which reveals the inadequacy of the surface itself. Working in accordance with the general principle of supplementarity as explained by Derrida in *Of Grammatology*, 1998 [1967]), ornament can be understood to expose the shortcomings of the whole as well as the natural deficiencies of its own form. It can expose the fact that its surface is both vulnerable and insufficient in the same moment.

This, then, is ornament's inherent paradox, its status, as Mark Wigley (1992) has suggested, as something that 'destabilises the very structure that it at once supplements and makes possible' (p. 1014), something that disrupts what seemed to be the very clear distinction between *ergon* and *parergon*, between structure and ornament. Much like a tattoo then (an artefact seen as one of the primary, originary forms of ornamentation), we can see ornament as both on the body and yet external to it, integral to the structure while simultaneously extraneous. Yet, if it is separated or detached, the ornament, the tattoo no longer remains what we understand it to be; the structure, the body, must be destroyed. 'Lodged on the border between inside and outside, the tattoo', as Juliet Fleming notes (2001), 'occupies the no-place of abjection' (p. 84); like all ornament (and like, as she contends, medieval graffiti), it is a 'creature of', as it is a 'disturbance to', its very surface (p. 85); like all ornament it is a substance that is both in and out of place, included and excluded, within and without. It is a substance that can be defined, in fact, by the inherent difficulty of identifying its boundaries.[13]

From this perspective then, ornament can only ever be understood through the tense relationship to its 'other'. It can only ever be seen as the 'outsider that "always already" inhabits the inside as an intrinsic constituent', the 'subversive alien', the 'foreign body that already inhabits the interior and cannot be expelled without destroying its host' (Wigley 1987: 160). Like the fetish, it is thus 'first and foremost a question of place', only existing 'as such when it both occupies and veils a space not properly its own' (Wigley 1992: 103). And the ornament hence 'territorialises, unsettles, displaces and reaffirms' its surroundings, it comes to both 'fix and unsettle borders', confounding 'clear-cut boundaries among things and between persons and objects'

(Spyer 1998: 2–3). As with frames and fetishes, tattoos and graffitos, it acts both as a part of the whole and *a*part from it, blurring the boundary between interior and exterior, licit and illicit, primary and secondary, inside and out. The ornament is thus a border rather than boundary – not 'a limit' but an edge, a site which does not simply *de*limit, but which is 'porous and resistant', which enables and constrains in the same moment (Sennett 2008). It is a material status that creates a friction, a danger that acts as an external threat to its own internal purity.

The deep-seated iconoclash we find present within the history of ornament, within the aesthetics of graffiti and street art, can thus be seen to emerge through its curious ability to destabilise the distinction between primary and secondary, *ergon* and *parergon*. The very bond made between structure and ornament, between wall and pigment creates the near impossibility of ever separating the two. Once applied to its surface (again, much like a tattoo) paint can only be removed through harming, disfiguring the primary surface itself, being blotted out entirely by anti-graffiti advocates and thus creating what has often been called accidental or abstract graffiti (the erased markings of graffiti which often occur in a different colour to the wall itself), as well as commonly returning to haunt their sites through the failure of the overpainting to entirely hide the original mark (in what are commonly termed graffiti 'ghosts', instances when the original marking bleeds through the paint which attempted to remove it). It is the ornaments' simultaneous fixity and flux that causes this (dis)comfort, this (dis)pleasure. Paint not only lies on the surface of the wall, it embeds itself deep within it and infuses into its surface. And each marking not only makes the innate porosity of the wall clear. It displays its primary lack, its double-bind as both perfectly in, and perfectly out of place, its ability to entirely transform the nature of the ergon, to allude toward another order existing within the city.

Every example of graffiti and street art can hence unveil the deep 'lack' of its surface; its lack of protection, its lack of pattern, its lack of personhood. Each example of graffiti and street art can come to function to disrupt the master/slave, structure/ornament dynamic of the urban realm. The bare wall thus begs to be etched upon. The bare surface calls out for its ornamentation, a horror vacui, or, as Gombrich notes (1984), an *amor infiniti* (p. 80), that only ornamentation will relieve. It reveals a cenophobia, a fear of the empty, that only decoration will alleviate. The ornament thus not only implies a constitutional deficiency within the ergon but at the same time in some way satisfies that lack, re-establishing a harmony within the whole. As Boris Groys notes (2010), every 'act of aesthetisation' is 'always already a critique of the object of aesthetisation simply because this act calls attention to the object's need for a supplement in order to look better than it actually is' (p. 42). It makes clear that structure has failed, that it is alienating, vulnerable, and insufficient. It points toward the originary want that the supplement fills while destabilising the very notion of primary and secondary, supplement and structure, ornament and order. And, as Roland Barthes so beautifully outlined (1991 [1979]), what can be understood to 'constitute' graffiti is thus 'neither the inscription nor its message but the wall, the background, the surface (the desktop); it is because the background exists fully, as an object which has already *lived*, that such writing always comes to it as an enigmatic surplus: What is *in excess*, supernumerary, out of place' (p. 167). What can be understood to constitute graffiti is thus not the image itself, not the materials used, not its illicitness or transgression. It is the *medium* which is the key. It is its status as ornament which is crucial. And it is because they are parerga, because they confuse the dynamic between primary and secondary, that these artefacts contain so much inherent potential.

Ornament and order

The uproar graffiti and street art so often arouses is not simply due to their illegality, to their status as a material form which contravenes the laws of public space. It is, I contend, their

Figure 11.6 Remed, Untitled, Leon, Spain, 2011 © the author

fundamentally ornamental nature that causes much of the anxiety which surrounds it, their ornamental nature that is at the root of the iconoclash in which they exist. The decorative and thus agentic nature of graffiti and street art (the adjunctive, and thus parergonic status), act as the causal factors, provoking the fear of these urban ornaments, their tactile adhesiveness and lack of fixity provoking unease. And while of course I would not contest the fact that some amount of fear is generated by the basic illegality of many of these ornaments (due, most likely, to their recurrent linkage to more violent or invasive crimes by the now widely discredited Broken Windows theory of Wilson and Kelling 1982), this simply does not explain why other illicit aspects of our visual environment (such as bill posters, or the vast amount of public advertising hoardings which are illegally erected) do themselves not generate the level of fear and loathing graffiti and street art are subject to.[14] It is the tension between the ornament and the architecture which bestows the concomitant vitality and vilification[15] upon graffiti and street art. It is its decorative, sticky agency which grants it the power to both bind and repulse.

For all these reasons then, ornament, as Wigley has argued (1988), has always been 'conceived of as potentially dangerous', as 'potentially chaotic' by those who design our built environments, something which must be made 'servile to structure precisely because [it] lies in the dangerous realm of representation and can mislead us, take us away from the natural presence of harmony and order' (p. 52). Architects have thus habitually attempted to 'tame ornament', to make it 'represent' and 'articulate structure' (p. 52), to prevent it from running wild: They have used it to reaffirm rather than interrogate, to placate rather than activate. And this, I believe, leads us to the critical point, to the punch-line of this piece. Ornament, as earlier mentioned, is never merely 'mere'. Rather it is its ability to produce social as much as structural formations which is so significant. It is the power of ornament to not simply reflect but to *create* order which we must now take into consideration. Whether taking on harshly repressive configurations then (such as the Haussmannisation of Paris or within Jeremy Bentham's infamous panoptican), or richly emancipative ones (such as within Yona Friedman's *Ville Spatiale* or Ebenezer Howard's garden-city), the material body of the city has always been able to effect the material body of the person in very real ways. And this is what makes ornament such a crucial issue. This is what makes it something not only good to think *with*, but something that in fact affects the very way we think in itself. Our built environment must be seen to not simply '*involve* argument' but to be, at its core, '*about* argument' (Fleming 1998: 147), to have the capacity to both 'enable and constrain' it, to mould both 'the production and reception of social discourse' (p. 148). And the *insurgent* ornamentation of our urban realms, the grassroots ornamentation of the city 'coming from outside the official institutionalised domain of urban planning and urban politics' can then come to embody, as Groth and Corijn (2005) suggest, a 'different notion of "urbanity" from that which is evident in planned developments' (p. 506). Graffiti and street art is such a non-institutional practice. It is a practice questioning, subverting 'the conventions, codes and "laws" of architecture' (Hill 1998: 36), a practice, like all illegal architecture, as Hill terms it, which emerges through the 'public domain of the street rather than the private realm of a familiar building site' (p. 11). It is a practice in which pleasure can be 'derived from the misuse of form' (p. 48), an 'insurgent architecture' that can create 'alternative visions as to what might be possible' (Harvey 2000: 237), that can act as a 'critique of structure' from within structure, that can act as an 'interrogation of structure' (p. 52) from within the physicality of structure itself.

Not only coming to create a form of voluptuousness in the midst of cultural aridity, fashioning a form of embellishment which can counterpoint a dominant set of signs, graffiti and street art can be seen to have the ability to construct a new sense of order within the city, to be able to physically score an idea, a concept of civility onto its material surface. It not only confronts us, provokes equal fear and adulation, but evidences and engenders a way of thinking

Figure 11.7 Goldpeg, Untitled, Vigo, Spain, 2008 © the author

about the city contrary to the norm, not simply containing a 'second-order significance as a mere reflection of some other more important determinant' but having clearly 'agentive and transformative' abilities (Pinney 2002: 134–35). As ornament, graffiti and street art remodel our physical environment. They reconstruct an understanding of the world itself. And just as tattooing can work, as Alfred Gell has again shown (1993), as an influential form of bodily practice, as a mode of 'honourable degradation' (p. 207), so too these ornaments which tattoo the skin of the city can work as an influential form of *social* practice, a means of re-forming the city, re-negotiating the symbolic and formal expressions of built form, re-framing the very meaning of the space they inhabit. Their supplemental nature can expose the immanent tensions within our metropolitan environments, the double-bind encased within the concrete walls of the city. It can expose the various conflicts around notions of public and private space, of use-value and commercial rights. Their status as embellishment signalling a life, a personhood, a social relation within the stone. Revealing a human touch within our increasingly depersonalised, increasingly reconstructed urban landscape. Its ornamental logic demonstrating the shortcomings of structure, while, at the same time, in some way completing it.

Notes

1 Sections of this chapter are taken from my monograph *Ornament & Order: Graffiti, Street Art and the Parergon* (2014).

2 In very general terms, graffiti will here be understood as a practice of image making (often thought to focus on text over image – these being the chosen pseudonyms of their producers), created using spray cans, markers or various other tools of inscription, and undertaken illicitly within our urban environments. It is a very baggy, promiscuous term however, one with as many meanings as practitioners. Yet what will be crucial in the utilisation of the expression here however is that the

labelling of an image as graffiti is inextricably dependent on its site of application, this being the public space of the city itself. So called 'graffiti' on canvas, for example, will thus be considered as spray can art, calligraphic art, whatever art its medium obtains, but will not work within the designation graffiti itself. And only images found in the public realm, in the unbound space of the commons, will thus here be classed within the term graffiti.

3 Likewise, and again in very general terms, street art will here be understood as a practice of image making (often thought to focus on image over text – these being the iconic symbols of their producers), created using either spray cans, stencils, posters, or a number of further techniques of composition, and undertaken illicitly within our urban environments. It is a very baggy, promiscuous term however, one with as many meanings as practitioners. Yet what will again be crucial in the utilisation of the expression is that the labelling of an image as street art is inextricably dependent on its site of application, this being the public space of the city itself. As such, 'street art' on canvas, for example, will be considered as stencil art, poster art, whatever art its medium obtains, but will not (unsurprisingly considering its very name), work within the designation street art itself. And only images found in the public realm, in the unbound space of the commons, will thus here be classed within the term street art.

4 A design produced onto glass with the use of an acid solution or paint stripper.

5 A design, often a tag, scratched into a surface.

6 A multi-coloured, large-scale graffiti design based on the producers chosen name, often so complexly designed to be illegible to non-practitioners.

7 Not in the purely scopophilic sense meant by Laura Mulvey (1975), however.

8 This negative appreciation of tagging could be argued to be due in main to the innate lack of curatorial delimitation within graffiti and street art; the sheer fact that the work of the neophyte and the expert is equivalently available to public results in a difficulty distinguishing between 'good' and 'bad' work, the viewer simply overwhelmed with quantity and thus being unable to define quality. The specialist, as in any aesthetic discourse of course, is able to filter out works almost immediately, however.

9 Grabar's beautiful description of calligraphy (1992) can in fact be seen as an almost perfect elucidation of tagging: 'Letters can be modified, extended, looped, shortened, thickened; dots and diacritical marks float around letters rather than help fix their specificity . . . while 'correct' orthography is frequently violated for the sake of the composition' (p. 106). There cannot be a more consummate portrayal of the richness of tagging than this.

10 This connection between ornament and graffiti is also supported by a number of other theorists. While I have earlier noted Jonathan Hill's argument, the architect Robert Venturi and Ben-Amos (2004) has also suggested that 'graffiti on ordinary – or, let's say, 'generic' buildings – can be richly decorative . . . We finished a campus center at Princeton, the Frist Campus Center, and on the walls inside we have what we call 'ornamental graffiti'. These are sayings by famous Princeton graduates – John Adams, Woodrow Wilson, people like that. That's a form of graffiti that's valid. There's a tradition of classical buildings having words on their façades'. While Venturi does not explain exactly why this 'ornamental graffiti' is more 'valid' than more commonplace graffiti (and perhaps he would backtrack from these comments if pressed), the linkage between decoration, ornamentation and graffiti is made quite clear. In more overtly supportive terms, the renowned British artist Tom Phillips has claimed (in his 'treatise' on the subject), that the 'often ephemeral' work of 'graffiti artists' must be considered as quintessentially ornamental; 'The use of calligraphy in ornament is as old as writing itself and the graffiti artists of the late twentieth century especially in New York brought calligraphic expression to a new height comparable with the best of Islamic letter-based art or mediaeval illumination'. Phillips provocative hypothesis (perhaps unsurprising from an artist who has often worked within the public sphere) will be, I hope, fully born out within this chapter.

11 As Brett has argued (2005), 'the impulse to decorate and to find sensuous pleasure in materials cannot be denied; IT WILL BREAK OUT, COME WHAT MAY' (p. 208).

12 A quote recently found in the film *Kings and Toys* by British graffiti writer Prime underscores this fact again: Discussing his many tags, he suggests that 'it's almost like I have agents working for me and I put them in different places round the city, and they stand there and pose for me, and everyone walks by and says "yeah, that's me, that's Prime".'

13 The similarity between these two ornamental forms is further reinforced by the extremely high proportion of graffiti artists who have gone on to become professional tattoo artists.

14 One could also suggest that it is the non-instrumental, aneconomic nature of these works that cause discomfort, going so clearly against the neo-liberal understanding of the city as a location for consumption.

155

15 On the occasions that graffiti and street art *does* become venerated on a more popular level, however, I would argue this often has much to do with perceptions of wider market value than any aesthetic value per se.

References

Barthes, R. (1991 [1979]). Cy Twombly: Works on Paper. In *The Responsibility of Forms: Critical Essays on Music, Art, and Representation.* (pp. 157–176) Howard, R. (trans.). Berkeley: University of California Press.

Baudrillard, J. (1993 [1976]). *Kool Killer. Les graffiti de New York ou l'insurrection par les signes.* Available at: www.lpdme.org/projects/jeanbaudrillard/koolkiller.zip.

Belting, H. (2005). Image, Medium, Body: A New Approach to Iconology. *Critical Inquiry. 31*(2): 302–319.

Brett, D. (2005). *Rethinking Decoration: Pleasure and Ideology in the Visual Arts.* New York: Cambridge University Press.

Collins, P. (1998). *Changing Ideals in Modern Architecture, 1750–1950.* Montréal: McGill-Queens University Press.

Derrida, J. (1998 [1967]). *Of Grammatology.* Spivak, G.C. (trans.). Baltimore: Johns Hopkins University Press.

Derrida, J. (1981 [1972]). *Dissemination.* Johnson, B. (trans.). Chicago: University Press.

Derrida, J. (1987). *The Truth in Painting.* Benington, G. and McLeod, I. (trans.). Chicago: University of Chicago Press.

Douglas, M. (1966). *Purity and Danger: An Analysis of Concepts of Pollution and Taboo.* New York: Praeger.

Fleming, D. (1998). The Space of Argumentation: Urban Design, Civic Discourse, and the Dream of the Good City. *Argumentation. 12*(2): 147–166.

Fleming, J. (2001). *Graffiti and the Writing Arts of Early Modern England.* Philadelphia: University of Pennsylvania Press.

Foster, H. (2002). *Design and Crime: And Other Diatribes.* London: Verso.

Gell, A. (1993). *Wrapping in Images: Tattooing in Polynesia.* Oxford: Clarendon Press.

Gell, A. (1998). *Art and Agency: An Anthropological Theory.* Oxford: Clarendon Press.

Gombrich, E.H. (1984 [1979]). *The Sense of Order.* Oxford: Phaidon.

Grabar, O (1992). *The Mediation of Ornament.* Princeton, NJ: Princeton University Press.

Groth, J. and Corijn, E. (2005). Reclaiming Urbanity: Indeterminate Spaces, Informal Actors and Urban Agenda Setting. *Urban Studies. 42*(3): 503–526.

Groys, B. (2010). *Going Public.* Berlin: Sternberg Press.

Harvey, D. (2000). *Spaces of Hope.* Berkeley: University of California Press.

Hill, J. (1998). *The Illegal Architect.* London: Black Dog Publishing.

Hill, J. (2006). *Immaterial Architecture.* London: Routledge.

Latour, B., Weibel, P., Boltanski, L., Gamboni, D., Ristelhueber, S., Mondzain, M-J., Sloterdijk, P., Belting, H. and Obrist, H-U. (2002). *Iconoclash: Beyond the Image Wars in Science, Religion, and Art: Exposition, ZKM, Center for Art and Media, Karlsruhe, du 4 mai au 4 août 2002.* Karlsruhe: ZKM.

Loos, A (2002 [1908]). Ornament and Crime, in *Crime and Ornament: The Arts and Popular Culture in the Shadow of Adolf Loos.* (pp. 29–36) (eds) Miller, B and Ward, M. Toronto, ON: YYZ Books.

Moughtin, C., Oc, T. and Tiesdell, S. (1999). *Urban Design: Ornament and Decoration.* Oxford: Architectural Press.

Mulvey, L. (1975). *Visual and Other Pleasures.* Houndmills, Basingstoke, Hampshire: Palgrave Macmillan.

Phillips, T. (2003). *The Nature of Ornament: A Summary Treatise.* Available at: www.tomphillips.co.uk/publications/item/5311-the-nature-of-ornament-a-summary-treatise.

Pinney, C. (2002). Creole Europe: The Reflection of a Reflection. *Journal of New Zealand Literature: JNZL, 20*: 125–61.

Schacter, R. (2008). An Ethnography of Iconoclash. *Journal of Material Culture. 13*(1): 35–61.

Schacter, R. (2013). *A World Atlas of Street Art and Graffiti.* New Haven: Yale University Press.

Schacter, R. (2014). *Ornament & Order: Graffiti, Street Art and the Parergon.* Farnham: Ashgate.

Sennett, R. (2008). *The Craftsman.* New Haven: Yale University Press.

Spyer, P. (1998). *Border Fetishisms: Material Objects in Unstable Spaces.* New York: Routledge.

Venturi, R. and Ben-Amos, A. (2004). 'Venturi and Scott Brown'. *The Philadelphia Independent.* p. 3.

Wigley, M. (1987). Postmortem Architecture: The Taste of Derrida. *Perspecta*. 23: 156–172.

Wigley, M. (1988). The Displacement of Structure and Ornament in the Frankfurt Project: An Interview. *Assemblage*. (5): 51–57.

Wigley, M. (1992). 'Theoretical Slippage'. in *Fetish*. (eds) Whiting, S. et al., Princeton, NJ: Princeton Architectural Press.

Wigley, M. (2001). *White Walls, Designer Dresses: The Fashioning of Modern Architecture*. Cambridge, MA: MIT Press.

Wilson, J.Q. and Kelling, G. (1982). Broken Windows. *Atlantic Monthly*. *249*(3): 29–36, 38.

Wright, F.L. (2005). *Frank Lloyd Wright: An Autobiography*. Petaluma: Pomegranate.

12

Graffiti, street art and the divergent synthesis of place valorisation in contemporary urbanism

Andrea Mubi Brighenti

Place valorisation and divergent synthesis

What is the role and function of graffiti and street art in the context of larger contemporary urban transformations? In the course of the last fifteen years or so, graffiti art has received unprecedented attention from mainstream cultural institutions, ranging from local municipality arts services and grant schemes to major contemporary arts museums. At the same time, street art – or what is sometimes referred to as 'post-graffiti' (Manco 2002) – has moved closer than before to the contemporary art system. To various extents and not without contradictory or even paradoxical outcomes, both graffiti and street art have been increasingly associated with thrilling lifestyles, urban creativity, fashionable outfits and hip neighbourhoods. The value attributed to these expressions as well as the urban places where they occur has changed accordingly (e.g. Dickens 2010). Rather than merely value-neutral (invisible) or necessarily value-detracting (supravisible) as before, now graffiti and even more pronouncedly street art can be value-bestowing (visible). Visibility means they have turned into recognisable and in some cases much sought-for items in the urban landscape. Yet, because visibility is never straightforwardly linked to value (Brighenti 2010a), some additional considerations are needed to make sense of the dynamic at stake.

The notion of 'place valorisation' could be usefully developed. Valorisation is the process whereby entities – places included – are bestowed a certain *value*. This notion can be traced back to Marx, who employed the term *Verwertung*. In the first volume of *The Capital*, Marx (1867: §§3–7) outlines three different money-commodity (M-C) circuits, namely C-M-C, M-C-M and M-C-M'. While the first circuit represents pre-capitalist economy (i.e. money only appears as a link between commodities: One sells a commodity only to purchase another one), the second represents early modern mercantilism (money frees itself from any absolute dependence on commodities and turns into a universal circulatory medium, into 'exchange value'). But, Marx notices, from the point of view of the merchant who buys and sells, it would not make sense to let money go into a purchase if not in order to have it back in *increased measure* through a sale. This realisation (the coming about of the third circuit, where M' > M), marks precisely, passage to actual capitalism. For Marx, the exchange-based view of classical economic theory cannot really explain what he calls the 'trick' of value increase entailed by M-C-M'. The circulatory exchange paradigm fails to explain the creation of value because it is inherently based on a principle of generalised equivalence, while in fact value is created in 'the background' of circulation, that is, in the process of *production*.

Two essential ideas can be retained from Marx in this regard: First, value *changes*, and cannot but change (prices, incomes and profits go up and down); second, value *metamorphoses*, and cannot but metamorphose (even bare economic value always necessarily incorporates additional social dimensions, such as labour). What the above points to, is that *value* functions as a 'polymorphous magical substance' – to borrow a phrase Michael Taussig (2009: 40) uses to elaborate an anthropological take on *colour*. Although the economic side of value is the easiest to grasp, the anthropological phenomenon of value is far from being a merely economic one. In fact, there cannot be a valorisation which is only economic. Valorisation processes are complex, multifaceted, inherently unstable dynamics of *production, circulation and transmutation*. In the case of urban places, the sheer economic side of value (building prices and land revenue) actually precipitates and condenses a number of scattered, *convergent or divergent*, social forces which include discourses, repertoires, representations, imaginaries, reputations, judgments, position-takings, conflicts, negotiations, resistances, justifications and so on. In the valorisation of a place such as a neighbourhood, a square, a park, a building, an alley or a metro station, the production, circulation and transmutation of all these items is as important as the production, circulation and transmutation of material commodities in the analysis carried out by Marx in the mid-nineteenth century.

'Convergent or divergent' is an essential qualification, too. Indeed, at the outset, an apparent progressive 'integration' of graffiti and street art into the mainstream has been highlighted. But this is at best only part of the story. More precisely, the hypothesis I am submitting is that, presently, with graffiti and street art we are facing different, *incompossible (i.e. mutually exclusive) yet simultaneous* processes of place valorisation. The notion that may help to understand this is 'disjunctive synthesis' (Deleuze 1969). Perhaps, the term *diavolution* (Brighenti 2008) could also be employed, although it would call for a longer explanation which is not possible to unfold here. In his 'logic of sense' Deleuze observes that we usually imagine disjunction as merely negative, that is, as synonymous with the reciprocal exclusion of the alternatives. This is because we associate affirmation with identity and the suppression of difference. But, Deleuze suggests, *affirmation* may also proceed *through difference*, that is, without being subsumed under identity. In this case, we do not have simply a coincidence of the opposed terms (*coincidentia oppositorum*), rather,

> we are faced with a positive distance of different elements [*des différents*]: no longer to identify two contraries with the same, but to affirm their distance as that which relates one to the other insofar as they are different [*ce qui les rapporte l'un à l'autre en tant que « différents »*]. The idea of a positive distance as distance (and not as an annulled or overcome distance) appears to us essential, since it permits the measuring of contraries through their finite difference instead of equating difference with a measureless contrariety, and contrariety with an identity which is itself infinite [*une identité elle-même infinie*].
>
> (Deleuze 1969: 202; English ed. 1990: 172–73)

Instead of ruling each other out, assimilation and deviance proceed hand in hand, precisely thanks to a sort of 'positive distance' – where 'positive' carries no moral or axiological signification and rather hints at a certain possibility of practical commensuration. Applied to social reality, the disjunctive synthesis stands in opposition to what is usually referred to as 'integration', regardless of whether we understand it as social (agent) or system (structural) integration (Archer 1996). The disjunctive synthesis, in other words, excludes the 'measured' yet for some reasons insipid and unsatisfactory recipe of integration – insipid and unsatisfactory according to current social practice, not to the theorist's taste. Properly speaking, graffiti and street art are not being integrated, tolerated, accepted or recognised by the cultural and economic establishment. Rather, integration is surpassed in both opposite directions, i.e. simultaneously towards expulsion *and* capture, or re-inscription.

Expulsion, capture, re-inscription: urban eventfulness as a counter-measure of valorisation

On the one side, attention on the part of cultural institutions such as museums and festivals has not turned graffiti into an accepted practice. Quite on the contrary, in many instances graffiti continues to be banished from the range of acceptable conducts. This is particularly evident if we consider teenage graffiti writers and the production of a series of 'excessive events' (Pavoni 2013).[1] Since the mid-2000s, for instance, emergency brake graffiti writing 'attacks' on metro and commuters trains have appeared and risen. These actions, carried out by teenager crews have spread all over the world by copycat effect – from Melbourne, through Moscow, to Milan (e.g. Kobyscha 2013; Ten News 2013; Santucci and Stella 2014). Such spectacular actions performed by stopping trains in operation with passengers on board can be even watched online, filmed as they are by writers themselves or captured by CCTV security systems and leaked to the media. The hedonistic thrill of emergency-braked train writing would be framed by criminologists as a 'seduction of crime' (Katz 2008), or as 'ungovernable desires' (Halsey and Young 2006). Meanwhile the mainstream media present the perpetrators as 'extreme vandals', if not 'enemies of society'. It is noteworthy that these actions are met not only with the usual indignation traditionally raised by graffiti, but with an outspoken hatred which makes the 1980s–1990s US climate of the 'war on graffiti' (Austin 2001) now understandable to the European public. The language used in the news media coverage of these events not only includes words like 'hooligans' and 'gangs', but stretches to the paramilitary 'commando'. In Italy, the politically-charged term 'squadrismo', with reference to the punitive squads of early 1920s Fascism, has been evoked by media commentators (even though these writers do not have explicit political motivations whatsoever, and the content of their graffiti is not at all political, least right-winged). In Germany, to provide another example, the pragmatic attitude of Deutsche Bahn, Germany's national railway company, has been to apply a warfare frame, testing flying drones capable of catching train writers on the spot (BBC News 2013).[2]

On the other side, as anticipated, street art – or 'post-graffiti' as it is sometimes referred to, remarking its descent (albeit a nonlinear one) from traditional graffiti – is increasingly ingrained in the official presentation of urban places. London for instance can no longer be imaged globally without Banksy. Not only have this artist's images become an unmistakable component of tourist paraphernalia, but his actual artworks have undergone instant museification (the artist, who is a communication genius, has also played skilfully with this). As well documented by Alison Young (2014: 147–50), Banksy stencils on the street have been put under Plexiglas to shield them, stolen from their original locations (sometimes removing the whole wall, as one would do in the case of an ancient fresco) only to be sold illegally on eBay and/or at art auctions, and even in some cases restored *qua* common heritage. From this point of view, the relation London entertains with Banksy is not so dissimilar from the relation Padua entertains with Giotto. Even market targets need not be different, considering that street art tours appear to have turned into a settled form of 'territorial marketing'. Additionally, cities around the world have sanctioned street art with festivals, urban events, special projects, exhibitions, calls, collections, conservation programmes and so on. To mention just one case, a graffiti collection is present at the recently inaugurated Mediterranean Civilisations Museum in Marseille which, as the website proudly states, was started 'before the market craze of art [*sic*] for this type of works' (Mucem 2013).[3] Even apart from devoted collections, increasingly major contemporary art museums have at least one piece of street art in their collections.

How can we explain the coexistence of such synthetically diverging valorisation circuits? The 'positive distance' between the two circuits can be related to a certain entwinement of *excess* and *measure* that is inherent in current valorisation processes. In the early 2000s, for instance, the excitement about the latest generation of street art – the one that actually 'made it' out of the underground – was due to its being unexpected, provocative, disordered, proliferating. Like graffiti in the early 1970s, early 2000s street art positioned itself and was received as an 'excessive event' capable of changing the established measure of urban space. Graffiti was excessive because it refused to be contained within the allotted places for art (Austin 2001). But, excess also appears to be a more general feature of contemporary urbanism (Pavoni 2013). Taking capitalist production and consumption into account may explain why. Following Deleuze and Guattari (1972), capitalism works on the *fringe of decoding* where previously coded social relations are untied and made immanent.[4] It is from this point of view that excess holds a function and has a place in the valorisation process. In its attempt to attain always higher quantities of profit and attest always new levels of valorisation, the capital must also pass through a series of trans-mutations. In the terms introduced above, (quantitative) change cannot happen without (qualitative) metamorphosis. Excessive disorder manifests one such metamorphosis. Consequently, there exists an undistinguished zone between the imperative of 'performativity', the rhetoric of the 'cutting-edge', the celebration of 'urban creativity', the aesthetic of the 'gritty' or 'dodgy' area, the flow of 'grime' music[5] and the alternative aesthetic of 'subversion'. Clearly, these phenomena are different: There is a positive distance between them. Yet, simultaneously, it is impossible to draw a sharp line between them. Precisely, they form the environment or milieu of a divergent synthesis.

The 'event' embodies a challenge to established social relations and, inherently, lies at the origin of every valorisation, due precisely to the metamorphic nature of value described above. In the case of urban space, street art can be seen as a movement that has inscribed such 'eventfulness' into the city. The specific territorialisation processes at play can be observed only through in-depth ethnographic studies. With their 'spot theory', Ferrell and Weide (2010) have captured perfectly the logic of visibility that regulates the micro-spatial choices of writers and artists. Similarly, street art aficionados are sensitive to the specific location and emplacement of the pieces. For instance, Young (2014: 96–97) has described beautifully the sense of loss she felt when she realised that a specific situational artwork she was heading to had been buffed. She states:

> Several years later I'm still struck by the depth of the loss I experienced. It was more than a momentary than a momentary flicker of disappointment, more than a sense of annoyance at my objective being thwarted. I actually felt quite disoriented – I found myself looking around, as though the image might have migrated somewhere else. I felt saddened by its disappearance, and the same feeling resurfaces now, when I think about those blank panels.

The situatedness of street art, its 'territoriality' (Brighenti 2010b), turns the modern city into a multiplicity of unique intensive encounters. Nonetheless, place valorisation applies to not only the specific spots where graffiti is placed. Just like in the case of music scenes, when it comes to the larger valorisation circuit, the concerned spaces involve those streets, neighbourhoods and districts perceived as the 'authentic places' of the movement. Eventually, these areas tend to coincide with the places where street art shops, cafes, gatherings and venues are. In the mid-term, one might expect that the zones valorised as street art districts are not necessarily those where cutting edge street art pieces currently are. The networked online circulation of images also contributes to such multiplication of territories. In this sense, Zukin (2010) has outline a 'paradox of authenticity': It is the yearning for authentic places – often identified with 'original' places endowed with strong local identity, a 'hip' or even 'gritty' aesthetic and a specific 'vibe' – that leads to 'upscaling', the rise of local real estate prices, the progressive eviction of earlier inhabitants and, ultimately, to a radical transformation of the neighbourhood itself – that is, to the destruction of its original 'soul'. But before such paradoxical effects become fully visible, authenticity functions as a means to up the value and attractiveness of certain neighbourhoods, usually former working class, immigrants or minorities areas whose local culture had been shaped through economic hardship and the experience of domination. The progressive colonisation by artists, cultural entrepreneurs and young audience attracted by the phenomenon progressively turns those places into recognised tourist attractions for the Lonely Planet guide, showcasing major fashion stores and food chains.

Chiasm points: some cases . . .

Contemporary graffiti and street art provide us with a number of 'points of reversal' in the divergent-synthetic field of urban authenticity. We might also call these 'chiasm points', where convergent series begin to diverge and vice versa. Since the 1985 death of graffiti artist Michael Stewart on a Manhattan subway platform by the hand of police officers (Austin 2001), similar utterly nonsensical episodes have been sadly recurrent across the world, despite the fact that graffiti prevention might not be a real priority form the point of view of the police (Ross and Wright 2014). In 2011, in Bogotá, for instance, Diego Felipe Becerra, a young graffiti artist, was shot dead by a patrol policeman while he was tagging his Felix-the-cat signature in an underpass (Brodzinsky 2013). The 'enemies of society' frame seems to be fully working. In this specific case, not only did the civil society and the local community react loudly, but a police cover-up attempt to portray Becerra as a suspected armed robber was also discovered, and two police officers were arrested. Such was the popular outrage that the whole municipal policy with respect to graffiti changed dramatically. In February 2013, the mayor of Bogotá, Gustavo Petro, issued a decree to promote graffiti and street art as valuable artistic and cultural expression, while a spatial plan to identify tolerated and interdicted façades was released. In the Guardian article covering this story, a key informant enthusiast about this alleged sea-change is the Bogotá-based street artist DJ Lu. In fact, however, one cannot overlook that the fifteen-year-old Diego Felipe Becerra was drawing pretty conventional hip hop graffiti, while DJ Lu is a representative of much more refined and stylish stencil art. Under the new policy which seems to have turned the city of Bogotá into a Mecca destination for street artists from all over the world, it is both city authorities and street artists who are caught in a divergent-synthetic situation. As DJ Lu himself admits, 'being told where you can paint goes against the spirit of graffiti'.

The point is that the 'spirit of graffiti', just like the spirit of capitalism, has uncertain edges. And it is not to demonise street art recognising that these two spirits may overlap. In this sense, more successful and commercially-oriented street artists who have devoted themselves to extensive merchandising of their 'products' (as their artwork is referred to on their very websites) have but brought to the linear consequences a specific 'alignment' in the 'event of street art'. Such a trend belongs to a series that neatly diverges from that of the unlucky Diego Felipe Becerra. A successful artist like INSA, for instance, presents himself as follows:

> [INSA] has done work on commission for such famous companies as Sony and Nike [. . .] The store is a reflection of INSA's best known 'Heels' image that merges black and white patterns that wave and distort the space, causing the viewer to question today's popular culture of consumerism.
>
> (INSA 2013)

One might wonder how an artwork commissioned by Nike or Sony can lead anyone to question consumer culture. Especially if compared with traditional graffiti writers and their focus on a certain minimalism of means (graffiti is based on limited technical equipment and a well-defined set of techniques), a widespread characteristic among contemporary post-graffiti artists seems their extremely *eclectic* approach (including a multiplication of styles and techniques). And a similar 'eclectic' attitude might be detected as concerns ethics. The fact that street art turns into a profession and that, as every other profession, it activates a whole economy, is certainly not scandalous (contrary to the Romantic myth portraying the artist as an exceptional human being who is severed from everyday matters). Nonetheless, reading several biographies of street artists, one cannot escape the impression that, for some reasons, street artists cannot content themselves with just being 'integrated professionals', as Becker (1982: 232) would call them – that is, established professional artists who dominate the scene by producing large amounts of conventional artworks everyone from the audience can understand and appreciate.

There seems, in other words, to be a deliberate attempt on the part of street artists – or, on the part of the authors of such biographies, perhaps art critics or gallerists – to establish a certain 'street credibility'. In other words, their valorisation circuit is tied to their being 'street', and therefore necessarily 'excessive' vis-à-vis the image of the integrated professional artist. Unsurprisingly, it is rather uncommon to find a bio profile which reads: 'X is a street artist and has never made an illegal piece in the streets', although such a description would fit for several street artists currently displaying their work in galleries, given that those who have a background in graffiti are only a part of those who are into post-graffiti nowadays. This proves that the *Verwertung* in street art still hinges upon a type of transgressive and unsettling attitude which is the original mould of graffiti culture, illegality being the 'zero degree' of graffiti writing (Brighenti 2010b). In this sense, the legal graffiti group documented by Kramer (2010), that only paints 'with permission' (or maybe even 'by commission'), is really a street art avant-garde. When graffiti is reduced to urban 'decoration' it turns into something 'decent' which has lost its peculiar street resonance.[6] Recent heated debates within the street art community are illuminating in this respect. For instance, an insider to the culture and prolific blogger, DJ Rushmore (2013) has commented:

> There's a nagging suspicion floating around that all of this work supposedly made for people walking down the street is really just being used in a massive game of who can get the most hype for their next print release, and that the importance of nonpermissioned interventions in public space has been diminished.

In this vein, and even more radically, the French artist Christian Guémy (2013) has lamented that the new generation of street artists (since the 2000s) has sold out the original spirit of graffiti:

Nowadays, the substance and form of 'street art' are conditioned by the standards of the Internet and its new modes of cultural diffusion. So, these new street artists have borrowed the graffiti form and transformed it [*en la détournant*] to better spread it on the Internet, their own sites, specialized blogs and, ultimately, social network audience.

Statements like these testify to the presence of an inner tension that shapes two radically divergent series inside the practice of street art (let's not forget that Guémy a.k.a. C215 is a renowned stencil artist). Certainly, the legal/illegal code alone is insufficient to understand the complex topologies of valorisation at play. In the 1950s, the situationists contemptuously labelled as 'recuperation' all the forms of co-optation of countercultural practices into the system. Their method consisted in exactly the opposite: Take fragments from the mainstream and reassemble them so as to turn them into subversive messages. Such a technique they called *détournement*. But, as noted with bitterness by Guémy himself, street artists are now doing a double *détournement* to re-inscribe their work into the art system.

To social scientist, however, it is likewise insufficient to oppose good old-time original graffiti writers on the one hand and bad bamboozling sell-out street artists on the other.[7] A poignant example of the complexities associated with the positioning of contemporary graffiti and post-graffiti in the cultural economy is the European Central Bank (ECB) case (Neate 2013). In 2012, during the construction of its new €1bn headquarters in Frankfurt, the ECB/EZB bank supported a number of graffiti artists to 'decorate' the building site fence. The event organiser, Stefan Mohr, who is a Frankfurt social worker, made a point of honour in securing for the artists' absolute freedom as concerns subjects. This almost reads as an answer to Guémy's concern about self-censorship and compromising choices. Indeed, the final pieces have been described as 'highly political, [including] caricatures of ECB president Mario Draghi and German chancellor Angela Merkel'. The evil face of money and how capitalism has spoiled the earth and bred the current economic crisis feature prominently among the subjects of this wall. Also, the shift from social work to urban art appears fluid since Stefan Mohr, who was initially only looking for a recreational activity for kids in a context were almost no legal graffiti spots had remained in town, 'had no idea that some of the world's most famous graffiti artists would help turn the fence into one of Frankfurt's biggest tourist attractions' (Neate 2013). As a result, the EZB fence has turned into a *Freiluftgalerie* (open-air gallery) ingrained in the official presentation of the city of Frankfurt. The fact that the largest majority of pieces are actually by graffiti writers,[8] only a tiny minority of which are represented by art galleries, problematizes a bit Christian Guémy's trenchant reconstruction.[9] On the top of it, several of the fence pieces containing derogatory representations and anti-capitalist visual stories have been bought by banks and money managers. We tend to assume that to portray contemporary, crisis-ridden capitalism as, say, two cocks fighting is defiant or oppositional; but maybe bankers actually like to picture themselves this way, or in any case they don't see this as particularly harmful to business.

Conclusion

The Frankfurt EZB headquarters case contains a number of thorny issues concerning graffiti and post-graffiti urban valorisation processes, beginning from the position of cultural producers. Certainly, the image of the artist who works in freedom and isolation from the market is a myth inherited from Romanticism, as well as reconstructed by art historians Kris and Kurz (1981). But the kids who originated hip hop graffiti in the North American inner city in the 1960s did not study art history, nor were they asking for permission to write on walls – least looking for galleries to represent them. Despite socio-economic hardship, or maybe because of that hardship, they managed to start something new. Simultaneously, their position – precisely due to lack of educational and career options – was easier than that of subsequent artists who grew up in the graffiti culture and contributed to develop it. The latter have found themselves operating in a different topology of valorisation and, as seen above, in an uncomfortable position vis-à-vis the figure of the integrated professional. It is as if they still need to keep an – albeit implicit – association with the packs of emergency brake vandals because, despite the great diversity of means and ends, their own valorisation hinges on that environment and attitude.

Today, the urban visual ecology is tied to a whole economy of visibility crossed by complex valorisation circuits, in which not only artists, but virtually all citizens are caught up in. Everyone who, in various ways, makes uses of public space (prototypically, the street) is affected by the coming about of synthetic-divergent series of expulsion, capture and re-inscription of cultural productions – graffiti and street art representing just one case among others, albeit a very peculiar one. Consequently, to social scientific analysis, the point is not so much to tell who gains and who is fooled at the graffiti game, as it is to trace the dynamics of production, circulation and transmutation of value that emerge through the entwinements of excess and measure in contemporary urban space. To understand which urban spaces are valorised, which valorisation circuits are activated, with which outcomes, this text has submitted the hypothesis that value is not only an economic phenomenon, rather, a phenomenon that enables acts of creation and conversion across different social domains (or fields, or subsystems). The task for future social research is to draw the maps of the new valorisation trajectories and circuits as they are not simply projected onto pre-existing space but, in turn, topologically shape it. Because, as observed, valorisation operates at the level of places which may not correspond to (post-) graffiti spots themselves, the mismatches illuminate larger urban trends. Similarly, the temporal scale matters, given that for instance a building site functions like a 'temporal interstice' which will eventually disappear. In this case, *where* precisely the produced value ends up, remains to be ascertained. In conclusion, the economic process of *place valorisation* in the current transformations of capitalism needs to be studied in conjunction with the social and cultural *significance* of graffiti and street art in the changing cityscape and the unfolding urban process, the new political processes of urban *governance*, control and discipline as well as, ultimately, the new emerging measures and political models of *citizenship*.

Notes

1   More precisely, Pavoni's argument is that all urban events are in some ways excessive. While accepting his argument in full, we do not think it rules out the possibility of some events being more *visibly* excessive than others.
2   On the other hand, New York street artist Katsu has designed a drone that *paints* graffiti (Wainwright 2014). This opens the chance that graffiti wars evolve into drone wars.
3   The Martin Wong Graffiti Collection at the Museum of the City of New York is another obvious case. In 2014, the exhibition, *City As Canvas* has presented 'over 150 works on canvas and other media, along with photographs of graffiti writing long erased from subways and buildings' (MCNY 2014).
4   Deleuze and Guattari (1972: 170; Eng. Ed. 1983: 153) write that capitalism is '*the negative* of all social formations'. Perhaps, 'the obverse' would be a more accurate term for the dynamic they describe. The idea that capitalism begins with a generalised deterritorialisation is a motif in Marx, although Deleuze and Guattari's discussion also engages anthropology and psychoanalysis.
5   Style initially made popular in the East End of London.
6   'Decoration' derives from the Latin impersonal verbal form *děcet*, 'to be appropriate', from which the term 'decency' also comes. Decoration cannot simply be defiant.
7   On the other hand, Guémy's declaration helps explaining at least why several cutting-edge street artists have more or less implicitly disassociated themselves from such a label. The quintessential global iconic

Andrea Mubi Brighenti

street artist Banksy, for instance, consistently defined himself 'graffiti artist', while the Italian Blu laconically stated 'I make walls', thus siding with muralists.

8 With the notable exception of Andreas von Chrzanowski a.k.a. Case, an aerosol artist who however has a most respectable graffiti pedigree from Maclaim Crew.

9 More generally, in his critique of subcultural theory, Gregory Snyder (2009) has rejected the image of graffiti culture as a purely symbolic form of 'resistance through rituals' and as necessarily disconnected from all sorts of economic valorisation and career opportunity: 'What – he has asked – if today's subcultures are a path toward future success?' (Snyder 2009: 165).

References

Archer, M. (1996). Social integration and system integration: Developing the distinction, *Sociology*, *30*(4): 679–99.

Austin, J. (2001). *Taking the Train. How Graffiti Became an Urban Crisis in New York City*. New York: Columbia University Press.

BBC News. (2013). German railways to test anti-graffiti drones, 27 May, retrieved at www.bbc.com/news/world-europe-22678580 (accessed 1 July 2013).

Becker, H.S. (1982). *Art Worlds*. Berkeley, CA: University of California Press.

Brighenti, A.M. (2008). Revolution and diavolution. What is the difference? *Critical Sociology*, *34*(6): 787–802.

Brighenti, A.M. (2010a). *Visibility in Social Theory and Social Research*. Basingstoke: Palgrave.

Brighenti, A.M. (2010b). At the wall. Graffiti writers, urban territoriality, and the public domain, *Space and Culture*, *13*(3): 315–32.

Brodzinsky, S. (2013). Artist's shooting sparks graffiti revolution in Colombia, *The Guardian*, 30 December, retrieved at www.theguardian.com/world/2013/dec/30/bogota-graffiti-artists-mayor-colombia-justin-bieber (accessed 1 January 2014).

Deleuze, G. (1969). *Logique du sens*. Paris: Minuit.

Deleuze, G. and Guattari, F. (1972). *L'Anti-Œdipe*. Paris: Minuit.

Dickens, L. (2010). Pictures on walls? Producing, pricing and collecting the street art screen print, *City*, *14*(1): 63–81.

Ferrell, J. and Weide, R.D. (2010). Spot theory, *City*, *14*(1): 48–62.

Guémy, C. a.k.a. C215. (2013). Graffiti, street art, muralisme. . . Et si on arrêtait de tout mélanger?, *Rue 89/Le Nouvel Observateur*, 11 November, retrieved at http://rue89.nouvelobs.com/rue89-culture/2013/11/06/graffiti-street-art-muralisme-si-arretait-tout-melanger-247235 (accessed 1 January 2014).

Halsey, M. and Young, A. (2006). 'Our desires are ungovernable'. Writing graffiti in urban space, *Theoretical Criminology*, *10*(3): 275–306.

Katz, J. (2008). *Seductions of Crime. Moral and Sensual Attractions in Doing Evil*. New York: Basic Books.

Kobyscha, V. (2013). Encounter with Graffiti: Breach and Normalization. Paper presented at conference, *Street Art in the Changing City: Theoretical Perspectives*, Moscow, 7–8 June.

Kramer, R. (2010). Painting with permission: Legal graffiti in New York City, *Ethnography*, *11*(2): 235–53.

Kris, E. and Kurz, O. (1981). *Legend, Myth, and Magic in the Image of the Artist*. New Haven, CT: Yale University Press.

INSA – Indian National Science Academy. (2013). Artist profile, retrieved at www.stencilrevolution.com/profiles/insa (accessed 1 July 2013).

Manco, T. (2002). *Stencil Graffiti*. New York: Thames & Hudson.

Marx, K. (1867). *Das Kapital. Kritik der politische Oekonomie. Erster Band*. Engl. edn *Capital: A Critique of Political Economy*, 1st edn, London: Penguin, 1992.

MCNY – The Museum of the City of New York. (2014). City as canvas, retrieved at www.mcny.org/content/city-canvas (accessed 1 June 2014).

Mucem – Musée des civilisations de l'Europe et de la Méditerranée. (2013). General presentation, *Mucem Collections*, retrieved at www.mucem.org/en/collections/general-presentation (accessed 1 July 2013).

Neate, R. (2013). Graffiti makes an art world sensation of the ECB's Frankfurt building site, *The Guardian*, 29 December, retrieved at www.theguardian.com/business/2013/dec/29/european-central-bank-graffiti-project (accessed 1 January 2014).

Pavoni, A. (2013). *Exceptional Tunings: Controlling Urban Events*. PhD Dissertation. Westminster University (London).

Ross, J.I. and Wright, B.S. (2014) "I've got better things to worry about": Police perceptions of graffiti and street art in a large Mid-Atlantic City, *Police Quarterly*, *17*(2): 176–200.

Rushmore, R.J. (2013). Viral Art, online release available at: http://viralart.vandalog.com/read/ (accessed 1 July 2013).

Santucci, G. and Stella, A. (2014). Assalto dei writer stile Far west. Metrò bloccato e botte, *Corriere della Sera Milano*, 8 May, retrieved at http://milano.corriere.it/notizie/cronaca/14_maggio_06/writer-assaltano-treno-corsa-aggrediscono-macchinista-3f9985f2-d50d-11e3-b55e-35440997414c.shtml (accessed 15 May 2014).

Snyder, G. (2009). *Graffiti Lives. Beyond the Tag in New York's Urban Underground*. New York: New York University Press.

Taussig, M. (2009). *What Color is the Sacred?* Chicago, IL: The University of Chicago Press.

Ten News. (2013). Emergency brake action in Melbourne, 5 December, retrieved at www.kimmatthiesen.dk/graffsite/2013/emergency-brake-action-melbourne/ (accessed 1 January 2014).

Wainwright, O. (2014). Spraycopter: The drone that does graffiti, *The Guardian*, 21 April. www.theguardian.com/artanddesign/architecture-design-blog/2014/apr/21/drone-does-graffiti-street-art

Young, A. (2014). *Street Art, Public City. Law, Crime and the Urban Imagination*. Abingdon: Routledge.

Zukin, S. (2010). *Naked City: the Death and Life of Authentic Urban Places*. Oxford: Oxford University Press.

13

Graffiti art and the city
From piece-making to place-making

Graeme Evans

Introduction

Graffiti and street art have received varying research treatment from artist, subcultural, ethnographic and crimogenic perspectives which are reflected in the literature on individual graffiti and street artists, gangs and genres, with a growth in art monographs and coffee table style pictorials. As Irvine observes: 'street art is. . .defined more by real-time practice than by any sense of unified theory, movement, or message' (Irvine, 2012: p. 235). The productionist dialectic between graffiti as vandalism and as 'art' (including in galleries) has not considered the wider aspects of the role and place of graffiti and street art in the city; responses from city authorities, local communities, visitors and property owners; and how different places and city cultures receive and react in different ways, including graffiti and street art now used in place-making, branding and destination strategies. This includes the growth of graffiti and street art commissioning agencies and organisations, often established by former graffiti and street artists employed by clients (e.g. retail, advertising firms, local authorities) and legitimised spaces and walls for safe experimentation. The cultural content of graffiti and street art also reflects local conditions and contexts, whether protest/political, territorial, vernacular (e.g. local events, history) or playful in nature.

Graffiti and street art now occupies an enduring place in the image of the city and our urban heritage:

> The tour bus picked us up outside of the designer-hotel in Manhattan. Commuting office and shop workers, tourists, police and road diggers mingled in the chaos of downtown traffic. Across the Williamsburg Bridge we stopped to pick up our tour guide for the day, Angel Rodriguez, from an unsalubriousinsalubrious building covered in layers of posters, graffiti and grit. He was a Latino musician, a salsa drummer from the Bronx who proceeded to give the tour group the background to the area – 'Bronx is burning' (arson attacks on tenement blocks by landlords), old jazz and dance club haunts, Fort Apache –'the movie' – the now rebuilt district police station self-styled to defend itself against the 'natives', (i.e. black/Hispanics), graffiti art of local rap stars (Figure 13.1), the massive American Mint building covering four blocks, where two thirds of all US dollar notes were once printed

and now housing two community schools, artist studios and employment schemes; the local penitentiary with twelve year olds kept in shackles – before arriving at our destination, *The Point*. Here the graffiti boys' operation base – once the crew that covered the New York subway trains and led to the mayor's zero tolerance regime – have now gone 'legit', working for large advertising firms and department stores in Manhattan on large-scale shop displays and billboard art.

(Evans, 2007: p. 35)

Graffiti has thus come a long way from its modern roots in the 1960s ethnic ghettoes of New York and Los Angeles, signalling perhaps a commodification of this activity, as well as a widening of graffiti into other cultural forms such as music (e.g. rap/hip hop), fashion (e.g. street artist Mau Mau graduated from T-shirt design to graffiti art), film (e.g. animation, pop videos) and architecture/urban design, which collectively have extended its shelf life. Early forays of artists who first worked 'on the street' and in 'street style' into art galleries, such as the late Basquiat, has had less success, despite the rapid valorisation of particular artists' work in recent years, notably Banksy, whose distinctive stencil murals have fetched over $500,000 (often to US buyers and celebrities). This reached a nadir in 2014 – from Banksy's street-cred perspective – in an unauthorised retrospective of 1970 'works' by the international auction house Sotheby's in London.

Here however, the work has been first validated in situ (a fundamental element in its value and authenticity), and then removed, much like a historic mural, into a (private) collection.

Figure 13.1 Big Pun 'memorial', The Bronx, New York © the author

Graffiti has therefore largely resisted (art) museum-ification and thrives primarily in a museum-without-walls – but very much 'on' a city's walls. The varying treatment and cultural significance of graffiti was also observed by Walter Benjamin, in his essay on the walls of 1920s Marseilles:

> Admirable, the discipline to which they are subject, in this city. The better ones, in the center, wear livery and are in the pay of the ruling class. They are covered with gaudy patterns and have sold their whole length many hundreds of times to the latest brand of aperitif, to department stores, to the 'Chocolat Menier', or Dolores del Rio. In the poorer quarters they are politically mobilized and post their spacious red letters as the forerunners of red guards in front of dockyards and arsenals.
>
> (1999: p. 135)

Indeed, it was the appropriation of the post-industrial city's walls by what are perceived as undemocratic and unwanted advertising images that has provided the political impetus for contemporary graffiti artists such as Banksy.[1]

Graffiti as vandalism

Until recently official responses to graffiti have placed it squarely in the criminal 'vandalism' sphere and early commentators fuelled this view: 'graffiti disrespects private property and official notions of order and aesthetics' (Lachmann, 1995: p. 100 on Ferrell, 1993). Early responses to the graffiti 'epidemic' in New York and Los Angeles saw criminal sentences increase and special tasks forces established, claiming that the order of the landscape had been disrupted, and clean-up costs were rising: more than $50m a year in both cities by the late-1980s. Today in the UK, clean-up of graffiti is estimated to cost £1 million per year and in Chicago alone $6m (see graffitihurts.org). English Heritage estimates that 70,000 heritage buildings and monuments are vandalised and defaced by graffiti while Network Rail spends £5m and London Transport £10m a year on graffiti clean-up. In 1960s/1970s New York, gang graffiti-ists were also enabled by the subway system that took their tags across all of the city's boroughs and away from their local territories, with large 'pieces' covering whole carriages. (Transport police advise operators to take trains out of commission quickly to reduce this incentive). While the New York subway was successfully cleaned-up, transport still remains a key site for graffiti – attractive for its wide availability and high audience potential. For visitors to many cities, whether by road or rail, the first visual sign they will see is graffiti and tags along motorway walls and bridges, and on the approaches to railway stations. Despite the advent of CCTV and other surveillance, stations and bus stops receive both unwanted as well as commissioned artworks and tagging, for example in Stockholm Art on the Underground (Figure 13.2) and in London, an on-going programme of Art posters and Poetry on the Underground commissions.

Graffiti and street art have therefore been faced with a dual onslaught from different dominant cultures (police/city politicians and art curators/galleries) to remove or restrict its practice and impact. However, despite this, or perhaps spurred on by this marginalisation, counter-hegemonic discourses have emerged which in some senses have kept graffiti alive as both a cultural concept and a practice that is now evident in many forms internationally – that is, graffiti is now global cultural force. Lachman's observation in 1988 is therefore still valid today: 'Graffiti in some forms can challenge hegemony by drawing on particular experiences and customs of their communities, ethnic groups and age cohorts, thereby demonstrating that social life can be constructed in ways different from the dominant conceptions of reality' (1988: pp. 231–32).

Figure 13.2 Art on the Underground, Stockholm; graffiti on Madrid Underground station and Amsterdam bus shelter © the author

This challenge is evident in artists' response to the art market itself, in the case of Banksy's 'mockumentary' film *Exit Through the Gift Shop* (2010). Here a fictional filmmaker pursues the underground art scene in Los Angeles, New York, London and Paris, assuming the role of self-styled street artist hyping his avant garde 'show' in LA and creating an art world/underground buzz for the lucky few who could take part. Banksy thus,

> pokes fun at the contemporary art world and its hunt to unearth and exploit underground art scenes. The willingness to validate recycled art and popular cultural symbols, which are rendered empty if not meaningless, is revealed as undiscerning and opportunistic . . . whereby social critique is downplayed in the pursuit of print, poster, and postcard sales.
>
> (Birdsall, 2013: p. 116)

The mobile value of his own street art has however fuelled a destructive market (another form of vandalism) which sees 'public' works cut from walls to disappear then reappear via auction. These sites continue to attract viewers and subsequent graffiti responses, and place branding through graffiti can therefore persist (including in memory) despite the absence of the artwork itself (Hansen and Flynn, 2014).

Mixed messages

Today, this duality (vandalism or art) continues, reflected in prohibitory sentences – in the UK up to ten years imprisonment where criminal damage by an adult (18+) exceeds £5,000, and detention/training order of up to two years for 12–17 year olds. For 'minor offences', sentences are much lower and fixed penalty charges can also be issued (£80) without court proceedings, so there is some discretion over the response if found guilty/'caught in the act'. At the same time, art museums and galleries engage with graffiti as an international art form. For example, in 2008, Tate Modern's Street Art commission and exhibition brought together six internationally-acclaimed artists whose work is linked to the urban environment. Sponsored by the Japanese car firm Nissan, this was the first major public display of Street Art in London. In order to give it artistic validation, 'good' street art in this case was distinguished from the more low-brow graffiti and tagging, thus seeking to 'insert graffiti into its proper place and rob it of its denaturalising power' (Creswell, 1996: p. 55). The link with sponsor Nissan was also significant since the Qashqai car it launched the year before utilised striking street art in its adverts. This also provides a clue to the current ambiguous place and relationship between graffiti/art and the city. In one sense this reflects the consumption and visual culture prevalent in the contemporary city environment – the merger of commerce and culture in highly visualised form. As Chang maintains, 'saturated by images, the contemporary city has been theorised as a site legislated by the eyes' (2013: p. 216), while street art today in Irvine's view 'is a paradigm of hybridity in global visual culture' (Irvine, 2012: p. 235).

Lombard goes further in response to the question, has the governance of graffiti changed since its more reactive origins? She uses the concept of governmentality (Lombard, 2013) ('conduct of conduct' – Gordon, 1991) to analyse how graffiti is currently controlled, arguing that while there appears to be a softening of policy and responses towards graffiti, this does not mean that there is less governance, but that this marks a greater acceptance of graffiti due to the effects of a neo-liberal form of governance. Chang also notes the emergence of the counterveilling terms: post-graffiti and neo-graffiti, 'signalling some kind of qualitative and stylistic shift in modes of inscribing the city. Encompassing multiple forms or urban inscription like murals, postering and sculpture that move beyond written text . . . [which] mark the spectacular nature of urban space' (2013: p. 217). Here she critiques the work of artist Blu, who painstakingly paints and photographs over existing graffiti (representing a single film frame) then turns these into remarkable street life animations (see www.blublu.org). This is one example of graffiti being transformed into moving image while drawing and building on its everyday street art nature. This also represents an important cultural practice of capturing as well as creating graffiti art in a different non-ephemeral form – important with so much street art being time-limited and subject to clean-up, defacing and deterioration due to the weather etc. Archives of graffiti art also seek to document this work alongside publications and films, in a variety of media (DeNotto, 2014).

A governmental response to the 'demand' for graffiti by young people is also seen in various schemes which seek to offer a safe (from prosecution) opportunity for budding Banksy's to practice their art with impunity. For example in Wales, the Heritage Graffiti Project helps young offenders 'learn valuable lessons from their heritage'[2] by introducing them to archaeological artefacts and explaining what they mean to the people who used them (e.g. Roman soldiers, miners, canal boaters). A mural was created: 'Our Wales', by the young people depicting their interpretation and experience that was documented and opened to the public. In the DPM Park in Dundee, Scotland, the longest legal graffiti wall in the UK (110 metres) is open for all to use at any time, and the council-run project holds workshops for local kids. How far these participants subsequently refrain from illegal graffiti activity is not however clear.

Attitudes of city residents towards graffiti and street art are also changing and ambiguous. These not surprisingly also vary within cities, with some neighbourhoods, sites and buildings treated differently in terms of surveillance, prosecution, protection – and celebration. For example, in the Colombian capital, Bogota, following the death of a young street artist shot by police in 2011, a new tolerance of street art has emerged. The city mayor issued a decree to promote the practice of graffiti as a form of artistic and cultural expression while at the same time defining surfaces that are off limits, including monuments and public buildings. City grants are available for selected artists with two, three and even seven-storey walls provided along the main thoroughfares as their canvases. The result is colourful displays with political and social messages. Everyday graffiti has also spread under this liberal regime including on buildings prohibited from writing. This indicates the difficulty of controlling graffiti in this way without rules being observed, and the appeal to marking untouched surfaces and public spaces. Lisbon is another city that has embraced street art, as it tries to move out of austerity and recession (GAU, 2014). Large scale pieces and murals adorn public buildings and industrial districts (Figure 13.3), which range from artistic to protest images and messages.

Local artists such as Vhils (Alexandre Farto) are celebrated and combine the aesthetics of vandalism with social comment. Rather than spray can and stencil, Vhils carves into the render

Figure 13.3 Street Art, Lisbon © the author

of the walls of buildings using electric drills to produce large scale portraits, often of local community members, and also works on utility installations. As a sign of his acceptance into the city art establishment, his inaugural exhibition was held at the opening of a new art museum based in a converted electricity station, 'Museu Da Electricidade' (Figure 13.4). Lisbon University also hosted the first international conference on Street Art and Urban Creativity between 3 and 5 July 2014 (www.urbancreativity.org) with an extensive programme of papers from academics, curators and doctoral students.

Figure 13.4 Electricity museum and storage tank graffiti – launch of Vhils 'Dissection' exhibition, Lisbon, 4 July 2014 © the author

Elsewhere, commissioning of young artists to adorn corporate buildings presents an alternative to the usual public art installation. In Frankfurt, the European Central Bank HQ, a forty-five-storey building under construction is surrounded by a high protective fence. A local social worker approached the bank that agreed to allow him and the 'troubled' young children he works with, to spray paint a wooden fence that they erected around the site (costing €10,000). The graffiti depicts caricatures of ECB President and Chancellor Merkel (60 per cent of the works reflect the Eurozone crisis), to fighting cocks that will be displayed within the building when it opens this year.

Several of the graffiti artworks have been purchased (via the Under Art Construction programme), ironically, by bankers, although remaining works are not, apparently, for sale. The city mayor has called on other construction sites to emulate this project. Other 'meanwhile' sites are also the subject of sanctioned graffiti since these can on the one hand animate otherwise ugly hoardings and also prevent/dissuade opportunistic graffiti, as well as divert attention from permanent structures. For example in Madrid and in Amsterdam (Figure 13.5) where the former Royal Dutch Shell European HQ building awaits redevelopment and temporary occupation by dance event organisers. This northern part of the city known as Amsterdam-Noord also represents a new creative quarter, served by frequent free ferries from behind the main station, where a cluster of digital media workshops and arts and entertainment venues has replaced this industrial complex and working class district. In this case, graffiti art signifies transition, fun, creativity – rather than degradation and social unrest, as it would have done in the past.

The dichotomies between, *crime-art, control-tolerate* in practice are therefore played out in a continuum along which city authorities, the public, and graffiti and street artists move, as taste, opinion (including local and national media), city branding and development shift over time. This can represent a hardening as well as a softening and instrumental use of street art, as we have seen, increasingly used in city branding and place-making efforts and strategies. The public is of course no longer homogenous as major cosmopolitan cities and historic towns mix tourists and a range of business, education and leisure visitors with residents and commuting workers from many countries with differing aesthetic and moral positions. The perspective of a say, an overseas tourist to street art/graffiti may be one of attraction, branded image, signifier of a cool place – or one of fear, decline and poor aesthetic value/appeal. To a resident, the same images may form part of their everyday experience, represent local identity (theirs or others – good, bad or indifferent), or even align with the visitors view.

Figure 13.5 Construction hoarding, Madrid; Graffiti art on base of former Shell HQ, Amsterdam © the author

It is more likely, however, that the local resident will engage in a deeper, knowing way, depending on the length of time the graffiti has been there, where it is placed (i.e. on what type of building/structure) and its meaning to them, if any. Graffiti and street art are certainly increasingly identified with a 'sense of place' than was the case before – aside from the previous tags and territorial/gang variety which are more likely to be cleaned up by city authorities. The attraction of place to graffiti artists is reciprocal. Cities in flux such as post-reunification Berlin are perceived as a 'graffiti Mecca of the urban art world . . . the most "bombed" city on Europe' (Trice, in Arms, 2011). Here its acceptance/condonement has been associated with Berlin's designation as UNESCO City of Design and as a growing cultural tourist destination, which is in part fuelled by this urban image of street creativity. This includes international artists, including graffiti artists whose work moves from street to gallery to street and of course, via social media. In cities such as Sydney, the creative class discourse (Florida, 2005) and policies towards public art has also provided 'opportunities to resignify graffiti as productive creative practice' (McAuliffe, 2012: p. 189).

Place branding

Models of city and place branding generally draw their references from product and corporate branding as an extension of marketing strategies that address the product life cycle decline-renewal challenge (Butler, 1980). In this sense, towns and cities, and specific areas felt to be in need of regeneration and renewal that face post-industrial or other structural socio-economic change, have been presented with the branding option as a response to the competitive-authentic city dialectic. How this is achieved and sustained is the stuff of city branding literature with results reflected in proprietorial branding and related indices, league tables and measurement formula.

Here the various models attempt to disaggregate or 'reverse engineer' the key factors that provide the brand (marketing) mix – the elements that together present the brand value and power of a place. These combine hard and soft infrastructure with historical and cultural amenities and qualities – which themselves are hard to quantify and ascribe values to – values that also vary according to the viewpoint of resident, visitor, investor, media and politician. As Zenker maintains (2011), place identity (a wider concept than the 'brand') influences the perception of the target audience, however prior perceptions (and their historic and contemporary sources) also influence the identity of a place as seen both internally and externally, and these are often reinforced through images of cityscapes, including graffiti. In urban space, and therefore in place-making efforts, the 'social production' that Lefebvre conceived (1974) also stresses the essential experiential nature of the relationship with our everyday environment, and our identification with discrete places and spaces. In this sense we do not 'use' space or our urban environment as 'consumers' (e.g. of branded products), but we experience it individually, productively (i.e. work) and collectively, albeit with diminishing influence over the (re)construction of the public spaces we inhabit – including the presence of graffiti.

In city branding models, the cityscape (or 'urban landscape') is characterised in several ways, as 'place physics' (Anholt, 2006) and 'spatial picture' (Grabow, 1998). Kotler *et al.* (1999) prioritise design ('place as character') as distinct from 'attractions' in their place marketing approach, while Ashworth and Voogd (1990) first proposed a 'geographical marketing mix' to capture the 'whole entity of place-products' (Kavaratzis, 2005) with 'spatial-functional' measures one of four instruments in this mix. However, despite the physical imagery and changing cityscapes strongly associated with city and place branding and destination marketing, it is interesting to note that in Zenker's analysis of eighteen place branding studies between 2005–10 (2011), architecture, buildings and city spaces were largely absent in the brand elements cited. The surveys on which these studies were based tended to focus on generalised or intangible associations (culture, historical, buzz etc.) rather than specific physical or spatial attributes. What is becoming evident however is that graffiti and street art have become established visual forms which cities both adopt and project as part of their destination marketing mix. Street art is now an emerging strategy for place-making and branding particular areas, which takes it out of its crimogenic roots. An example of newly-branded creative industry quarters in London are therefore described here (and see Evans, 2014) – where street art both defines a particular district and destination and reveals its importance in effectively showcasing a range of graffiti artists.

Place-making through graffiti art

Digital Shoreditch, London

The pattern of technology districts adopting the prefix 'Silicon' has accelerated over the last decade. This is a case of place and 'hard branding' (Evans, 2003) through the hope value associated with emulating Silicon Valley or 'Silicon Somewheres' (Florida, 2005). Unlike the microchip and hardware manufacturing sectors however, these new media clusters are a digital-creative hybrid producing the cultural content that drives the numerous online platforms, web-based services and mobile devices. Clusters that have evolved more organically, to those envisioned through government investment and development areas, can be seen at various scales – both regional and in highly concentrated spatial geographies. Examples include Silicon Fen (Cambridge, UK) and Silicon Glen (Dundee, Scotland), to local hubs where ICT firms often co-locate with creative and other advanced producer and financial services. Examples of the latter include Silicon Sentier, Paris; Silicon Allee, Berlin; Silicon Alley, New York – and Silicon Roundabout or Digital Shoreditch, in East London. This latter creative-digital district (Foord, 2013) presents an interesting city branding case, located in a city fringe area historically non-descript, with a low income/deprived resident community, essentially a working area of the city untouched by the visitor economy or more conspicuous cultural consumption. Its cultural workspace tradition dates back several centuries to crafts (jewellery, metalwork), printing and publishing, and fashion and textile sweatshops, with an established artist community occupying cheaper studio spaces.

This low cost cultural economy provided crucial elements in the area's transformation to one of the most vibrant creative quarters in the world. This now contains a high concentration of new media and digital firms, alternative clubs and venues for music, art and independent retail outlets and a high concentration of digital creatives. This profile and reputation has created a demand for hosting key design and digital events and festivals from the London Design Festival to the week-long annual Digital Shoreditch Festival which was first held in 2011 attracting 2,000 participants/visitors rising to 15,000 in 2013. The image of this neighbourhood combines post-industrial use of workshops and factories, with small crafts and retail outlets, social and warehouse loft apartments and extensive graffiti art on this historic mix of buildings and walls. This has offered an effective graffiti street laboratory within which aspiring artists such as Banksy and Stik have first experimented (Figure 13.6).

A new 'destination' has thus been created – several boutique hotels have opened in recent years including the ACE hotel, the first outside of the USA (originating in Seattle), designed with materials produced locally from specialist bricks, tiles to lighting and with photographic references in bedrooms to the building's music hall past. As an indication of the importance of street art, several companies provide guided Shoreditch Street Art tours, with online galleries and listing of artist/artwork profiles: 'in Shoreditch art is an open air affair. From huge murals

Figure 13.6 'Digital Shoreditch' – Stik, Banksy and Dscreet © the author

Figure 13.7 'Bees', Shoreditch © the author

on buildings [see "Bees" Figure 13.7] to tiny stickers you'll spot everywhere, the streets are fair game. Who knows, you might even spot a new Banksy' (Shoreditch Urban Walkabout, May– November 2014).

Specialist galleries and agencies also provide commissioning services for clients wishing to hire graffiti and street artists for temporary or permanent work – such as Graffiti Life and Graffiti Kings. The emergence of the professional graffiti artist has therefore arrived. The strategic importance attached to this sub-regional cluster and its role in the new digital industries was also recognised in 2010 when the UK government designated the wider area anchored in the city fringe by this creative industries quarter, as 'Tech City' – a swathe connecting this quarter further east to the Olympic Park, representing the physical the legacy from the London 2012 Summer Games. The event site, now designated the Queen Elizabeth Olympic Park which re-opened in Spring 2014, is spatially and socially divided between the new Stratford International City quarter leading to the Olympic stadia and newly landscaped park, and its canalside neighbour, Hackney Wick, a former industrial workshop district with social housing and waterside heritage.

Hackney Wick, London

At Hackney Wick, a high concentration of practicing artists work from studios, among temporary gallery spaces and a cluster of industrial buildings and canal infrastructure. This concentration has been accelerated as studios have been demolished to make way for the Olympic facilities and park and new housing in the post-event legacy phase, and as the cost of workspace has increased in other parts of east London (priced out by commercial housing and hi-tech markets) – including Shoreditch. This landscape and industrial canvas has provided an opportunity for graffiti artists to create large scale works and also to express their displeasure at the gentrification of this neighbourhood, which may also lead to their eventual displacement (Figure 13.8).

The area hosts an annual arts festival, Hackney WICKed, and is promoted as a visitor destination by the local authority, the Canals and Rivers Trust, and the Olympic Park authority, who see their mission as 'stitching together' these divided neighbourhoods and communities: 'through design quality to create a unique and inspiring place for events, leisure, sport and culture, a hub for enterprise and innovation, and diverse sustainable communities' (LLDC, 2014: p. 5). The agencies that control and legitimise this newly promoted district have also commissioned graffiti artists to adorn local buildings as part of a curated[3] project which engaged international (as opposed to local) artists – for example the Canal Project[4] (Figure 13.9)

This project was however met with outrage by local (graffiti) artists and residents, following what had already had been a graffiti clean-up of the area prior to the 2012 Olympics. To add insult to injury, several artists from Brazil, The Netherlands, Sweden and Italy were funded to produce artworks on these same buildings. In the words of the funding agency: 'we unashamedly wanted to showcase the best international artists and transform this part of the canal into a destination for street art – I hope people will come on boat tours to see the work'. But as local graffiti artist Sweet Toof says: 'with the commercialisation of street art it's becoming pay-as-you-go wall – every surface sold off to the highest bidder' (Wainwright, 2013). Place-making which adopts graffiti as a distinction and vernacular expression will therefore need to develop strategies which treat such work as part of the area's built heritage and community culture,[5] as Smith observes: 'It's as if the street art has been given the responsibility of preserving the Wick's

Figure 13.8 Graffiti art, Hackney Wick © the author

Figure 13.9 Canal Project-commissioned graffiti art (2011), Hackney Wick © the author

soul as it's squeezed on all sides by colossal tectonic pressures of redevelopment' (Introduction, in Lewisohn, 2013: p. 5).

Conclusion

Graffiti and Street art has a complex and ambiguous place in the city. Clearly a duality now exists between 'high' street art and '(un)popular' graffiti. Technically an illegal activity unless fully commissioned and authorised by property owners and other stakeholders (e.g. transport and local authorities), condonement of street art is evident in cities and areas of a city where either control has diminished or a general laissez faire situation exists. This is evident currently in cities where economic decline and socio-political fragmentation has reduced the power and resources for clean-up or enforcement (e.g. Athens – see Avramidis, 2012, and Madrid). Here the vacuum this has created is also fuelled by political response/resistance to the governance deficit and economic impacts, (e.g. unemployment, debt, cuts in services). Other cities equally affected by the severe economic recession have adopted a more creative approach, such as Lisbon, reviewed earlier.

Attitudes of local police are also variable and their stance on graffiti and street art can be determined by a number of factors. In the USA, research on a mid-Atlantic police department found that the race of police officer and the shift (e.g. night) effected the attitude towards graffiti crime, and therefore towards perpetrators and enforcement (Ross and Wright, 2014). Safety Neighbourhood Teams in London also follow a priority crime regime, as a form of resource efficiency and policy/political targeting (e.g. burglary, mugging), leaving graffiti deprioritised unless literally 'caught in the act' or in response to complaints. This contrasts with the British Transport Police who operate a zero tolerance regime, recording and attributing tags/pieces to identify subsequent offences and provide evidence to support prosecution of what they term 'serious vandals'.[6] However, in areas undergoing transformation or interstitial zones (often post-industrial), where landowners are distant or unconcerned (and property values not threatened), graffiti and street art flourishes, as in Hackney Wick, London. More cosmopolitan neighbourhoods such as Beyoğlu in Istanbul also provide a concentration of street art in a more liberal, if contested, area than permitted elsewhere in the city (Erdogan, 2014). In other cities, areas such as Amsterdam's main university district, is subject to extensive graffiti, indicating a combination of tolerance, complacency and place-making by its student residents. This is also evident in more protest-oriented university zones in cities such as Athens, but this also extends to areas around government buildings and conflict zones, including sites where the death of protesters has occurred (Avramidis, 2012). Elsewhere, street art is seen in commercially-driven commissioning, installations and contemporary art interventions in downtown, retail and in other locations undergoing regeneration (e.g. Dumbo, Brooklyn, New York), particularly in temporary sites. Graffiti still persists however, as a dominant image in derelict sites and in 'accessible' transport facilities, and is associated in this case with decline and redundancy. In other areas, street art reflects a creative quarterisation of a neighbourhood and effectively helps to add value to its image and distinctive brand.

Street art has thus on the one hand joined the canon of contemporary art, and the art market (if treated with caution by graffiti artists themselves – Brighenti, 2010) and been appropriated in commercial advertising and media, and on the other hand graffiti in its basic form, continues to inhabit the everyday city environment as a low level 'noise' and nuisance for many, as well as an endless canvas for its producers. An indication of graffiti and street art's arrival and enviable status is provided by established contemporary British artist, Grayson Perry, on the launch of the *Art Everywhere* scheme which seeks to place selected artwork images over 30,000 billboard and poster sites across the UK: 'given that street art was everywhere these days, it was nice to put gallery art on the streets' (Brown, 2014: p. 11) – or if you can't beat them, join them.

Notes

1   Cronin suggests that outdoor advertising and graffiti should be studied together, in terms of their ubiquity and visual impact (2008).
2   Heritage Graffiti Project http://cadw.wales.gov.uk/learning/communityarchaeology/heritage-graffiti-project/?lang=en. Accessed 5 April 2014.
3   The curator of the Canal Project was Cedar Lewisohn, who also curated the 2008 Tate Modern Graffiti Exhibition.
4   www.canalrivertrust.org.uk/art-and-the-canal-and-river-trust/the-canals-project-street-art-on-the-waterways. Accessed 3 August 2014.
5   Merrill goes further, suggesting that graffiti and street art should be perceived as an example of 'alternative heritage' whose authenticity might only be assured by avoiding the application of official heritage frameworks (2014).
6   www.btp.police.uk/advice_and_info/how_we_tackle_crime/graffiti.aspx. Accessed 3 August 2014.

References

Alonso, A. (1998). Urban Graffiti on the City Landscape. Paper to *Western Geography Graduate Conference*, San Diego State University, 14 February.
Anholt, S. (2006). *Anholt City Brand Index: "How the World Views Its Cities."* Bellvue, WA: Global Market Insight.
Arms, S. (2011). The Heritage of berlin street art and graffiti scene. Art, inspiration, legacy, *Smashing Magazine*, July 13. London, 1–16. www.smashingmagazine.com/2011/07/13/the-heritage-of-berlin-street-art-and-graffiti-scene/.
Ashworth, G.J. and Voogd, H. (1990). *Selling the City: Marketing Approaches in Public Sector Urban Planning.* London: Belhaven Press.
Avramidis, K. (2012). 'Live your Greece in Myths': Reading the Crisis on Athens' walls. professionaldreamers working paper no. 8 www.professionaldreamers.net/_prowp/wp-content/uploads/Avramides-Reading-the-Crisis-on-Athens-walls-fld.pdf.

Benjamin, W. (1999). *Selected Writings, Volume 2: 1927–1934*. Cambridge, MA: Belknap/Harvard University Press.

Birdsall, C. (2013). (In)audible frequencies: sounding out the contemporary branded city. In C. Lindner and H. Hussey (eds), *Paris-Amsterdam Underground* (pp. 115–131). Amsterdam: Amsterdam University Press.

Brighenti, M. (2010). At the wall: Graffiti writers, urban territoriality, and the public domain. *Space and Culture, 13(3)*, 315–332.

Brown, M. (2014). Gormley and company send art all over the place. *The Guardian*, 17 July, London, 11.

Butler, R.W. (1980). The Concept of the tourism area life cycle of evolution: Implications for management of resources. *Canadian Geographer, 24(1)*, 5–12.

Chang, V. (2013). Animating the city: Street art, blu and the poetics of visual encounter. *Animation, 8(3)*, 215–233.

Creswell, T. (1992). The crucial 'where' of graffiti: A geographical analysis of reactions to graffiti in New York. *Environment & Planning D: Society and Space, 10(3)*, 329–344.

Creswell, T. (1996). *In Place/Out of Place: Geography, Ideology and Transgression*. Minneapolis: University of Minnesota Press.

Cronin, A.M. (2008). Urban space and entrepreneurial property relations: Resistance and the vernacular of outdoor advertising and graffiti. In A.M. Cronin and K. Hetherington (eds), *Consuming the Entrepreneurial city: Image Memory, Spectacle* (pp. 65–84). New York: Routledge.

DeNotto, M. (2014). *Street art and graffiti. Resources for online study*. C&RL News, April, 208–211.

Erdogan, G. (2014). Mapping Street Art in the Case of Turkey, Istanbul, Beyoglu Yuksek Kaldirim. Paper to *Lisbon Street Art & Urban Creativity International Conference*. Lisbon University, 3–5 July.

Evans, G.L. (2003). Hard branding the city of culture: from Prado to Prada. *International Journal of Urban and Regional Research, 27(2)*, 417–440.

Evans, G.L. (2007). Tourism, creativity and the city. In G. Richards and G.J. Wilson (eds), *Tourism Creativity & Development*. London: Routledge, 35–48.

Evans, G.L. (2014). Place branding and place making through creative and cultural quarters. In M. Kavaratzis, G. Warnaby and G.J. Ashworth, (eds) *Rethinking Place Branding – Critical Accounts*. Vienna: Springer (forthcoming).

Ferrell, J. (1993). *Crimes of Style: Urban Graffiti and the Politics of Criminality*. New York: Garland.

Florida, R. (2005). *Cities and the Creative Class*. New York: Routledge.

Foord, J. (2013). The new boomtown? Creative city to Tech city in East London. *Cities, 33*, 51–60.

Foucault, M. (1991). Governmentality. In G.Burchell, C. Gordon and P. Miller (eds), *The Foucault effect: Studies in Governmentality* (pp. 87–104). London: Harvester Wheatsheaf.

GAU (Galeria De Arte Urbana). (2014). Vol. 03. www.facebook.com/galeriadearteurbana.

Gordon, C. (1991). Governmental rationality: An introduction. In G. Burchill, C. Gordon and P.Miller (eds) *The Foucault Effect: Studies in Governmentality*. (pp. 1–51). London: Harvester Wheatsheaf.

Grabow, B. (1998). Stadtmarketing: Eine Kritische Zwischenbilanz. *Difu Berichte, 98(1)*, 2–5.

Hansen, S. and Flynn, D. (2014). "Bring Back our Banksy!" Street art and the Transformation of Public Space. Paper to *Lisbon Street Art & Urban Creativity International Conference*, Lisbon University, 3–5 July.

Irvine, M. (2012). The work on the street, street art and visual culture. In B. Sandywell and M. Heywood (eds), *The Handbook of Visual Culture* (pp. 235–278). New York: Berg.

Kavaratzis, M. (2005). Place branding: A review of trends and conceptual models. *Marketing Review, 5*, 329–342.

Kotler, P., Asplund, C., Rein, I. and Haider, D.H. (1999). *Marketing Places Europe: Attracting Investments, Industries, Residents and Visitors to European Cities, Communities, Regions and Nations*. London: Pearson Education.

Lachmann, R. (1988). Graffiti as career and ideology. *American Journal of Sociology, 94(2)*, 229–250.

Lachmann, R. (1995). Review: Crimes of style: Urban graffiti and the politics of criminality (Ferrell, J., 1993). *Journal of Criminal Justice and Popular Culture, 3(4)*, 98–101.

Lefebvre, H. (1974). *The Production of Space* (trans. Nicholson-Smith, D.). Oxford: Blackwell.

Lewisohn, C. (2013). *The Canals Project Fanzine*. London.

Lombard, K-J. (2013). Art crimes: The governance of Hip Hop Graffiti. *Journal of Cultural Research, 17(3)*, 255–278.

McAuliffe, C. (2012). Graffiti or street art? Negotiating the moral geographies of the creative city. *Journal of Urban Affairs, 34(2)*, 189–206.

Merrill, S. (2014). Keeping it real? Subcultural graffiti, street art, heritage and authenticity. *International Journal of Heritage Studies*, *21(4)*, 369–389. DOI: 10.1080/13527258.2014.934902.

Ross, J.I. and Wright, B.S. (2014). "I've got better things to worry about": Police perceptions of graffiti and street art in a large Mid-Atlantic city. *Police Quarterly*, *17(2)*, 176–200.

Vermuelen M. (2002). *City Branding. Image Building & Building Images*. Rotterdam: NAI.

Wainwright, O. (2013). Olympic Legacy murals met with outrage by London street artists, *The Guardian*, 6 August. www.theguardian.com/artanddesign/2013/aug/06/olympic-legacy-street-art-graffiti-fury. Accessed 3 August 2014.

Zenker, S. (2011). How to catch a city? The concept and measurement of place brands. *Journal of Place Management and Development*, *4(1)*, 40–52.

14

Something for the boys?

Exploring the changing gender dynamics of the graffiti subculture

Nancy Macdonald

Introduction

It has been fifteen years since I researched and wrote my ethnography exploring the illegal graffiti subculture in London and New York (*The Graffiti Subculture: Youth, Masculinity and Identity in London and New York*, Palgrave Macmillan, 2001). In this, I focused largely on understanding the subculture's unmistakable male dominance. As a feature which had long been overlooked by other studies of subcultural groups generally, I chose to problematise graffiti's masculine bias. Why were young men so drawn to this? What did they get out of it, and what features of the subculture enabled this gratification? Exploring the interplay between graffiti's illegality and risk, and the warrior style meanings writers attach to their activities, I presented graffiti as a resource which young men can use to construct and validate youthful masculine identity. I also looked at how male writers marginalise and exclude women writers and, with this, their emasculating threat.

In this chapter, I want to take a look back and evaluate whether this argument in understanding the activities of this subculture's members is still relevant or indeed valid. A great deal has changed over the years since my research. First, the Internet, especially the World Wide Web, is now accessible to the masses, and has taken hold as a major influence within the graffiti subculture and its practices today. The proliferation of smart phones that allow graffiti writers to share their work almost immediately, and the development of social media are also important catalysts. Second, a new arm to the graffiti scene has emerged in the form of street art. This adopts the practice of writing in public places, mainly illegally. However, it is far less prescriptive than graffiti, enabling its artists to use different tools such as stencils, stickers and posters to create works which deviate from graffiti's more traditional sprayed or written tag name. So have these major developments changed anything regarding the makeup of graffiti writers? Have they softened the boundaries of the subculture and invited more women to enter and participate? And has this, in turn, impacted its observed use as a site for the construction of masculine identity? In order to address these questions, I want to first revisit my original thesis, and understand how illegal graffiti can function as a constructive identity resource.

Using illegality and danger to create "men's" work

For the graffiti writer quoted below, the rewards of involvement in this illegal subculture are clear and unambiguous: "It was wanting to belong to something that I thought was creative and dangerous. It helped me build my masculinity" (Iz, as quoted in Macdonald, 2001: p. 133). The vast majority of graffiti (that is found on the streets and transport system) is illegal, and a multitude of deterrent measures, both physical and judicial, have been implemented by the authorities to discourage individuals from participating. Those who persist therefore have to confront a multitude of hazards in their quest to earn fame and respect from their peers. These include the threat of arrest, falling from vast heights as they scale buildings or bridges to write their tags or construct their pieces, the dangers of oncoming trains and, perhaps most importantly, dodging the electrified third rail which powers these on the subway and under-ground system. To most outsiders just the thought of spending hours out on the cold, wet, dark streets doing graffiti would be enough to truncate a budding graffiti career. To a dedicated graffiti writer with something to prove, however, these risks and dangers are all important: "If it was legal, there'd be no threat; graffiti would be a waste of time. I do graffiti for the excitement, it's like I get a big adrenalin rush out there" (Col, as quoted in Macdonald, 2001: p. 126). Illegality introduces threat and this, in turn, provides the "buzz" that, as any illegal graffiti writer will tell you, transforms a writer's artistic quest into an important test of their bravery and resolve:

> It comes down to keeping grace under pressure. You know, you have trains burrowing down on you, cops chasing you, you have different gangs in there, you don't know what's going to happen and when you finish and you come up . . . you're walking through some ghetto, which makes you feel kind of manly anyway, and you're thinking, "Yeah I did it". So there's a certain sense to the illegality.
>
> (Freedom, as quoted in Macdonald, 2001: p. 103)

This illegal graffiti subculture embraces a doctrine of confrontation and achievement (Gilmore, 1990) and defining elements of graffiti writers' masculine identities; resilience, bravery and fortitude are all achieved by confronting and overcoming these associated risks.

As Freedom, the writer mentioned later recognises, the nature of this challenge and the masculine qualities which enabled it to be completed are authorised by the adopted tag or signature a graffiti writer uses. This forms the basis of all that they write and paint and its prominence is all important:

> If your name rode by on a train . . . that implies that you ran up a train tunnel, probably late at night, left your parents, faced the gangs and everything else and wrote your name on it. So that's what it was about and the better you did it then the more it implied, like, you stayed there longer, you did it better, you know.
>
> (Freedom, as quoted in Macdonald, 2001: p. 104)

By writing his name on a train or in an illegal area, the graffiti writer effectively says, "I was there and it was my courage and resilience which got me there". In this context masculinity is very much a *homosocial* enactment. Writers write graffiti, not only for themselves, but, most importantly, for their subcultural audience – other men. The respect and acknowledgment graffiti writers gain from others for "proving themselves" in this way completes the final and, perhaps, most significant part of this process. Indeed, writers will usually cite earning respect as their main reason for doing graffiti. Its centrality is also evidenced in the subculture's hierarchy which positions writers very much in these terms; the greater the danger and risk and thus associated daring and bravery, the greater the respect, the greater the status, the greater the man.

From writing to warfare

It is not just graffiti's physical and legal risks which serve as an identity resource. The antagonistic relationship graffiti writers share with their "enemy"; for example the British Transport Police in the UK or the Vandal Squad in New York City's Police Department (NYPD), remains a significant feature of this subculture, and another means of constructing a masculine narrative. The many militaristic metaphors which abound, testify to the symbolic significance of this conflict, as well as its desired presence: "The crew or platoon I currently paint for is KIA, Killed In Action, a crew consisting of various artists and vandals from the city who come together to form an understanding. We shall overcome" (Popz – *Londonz Burning* 1, as quoted in Macdonald, 2001: p. 112). Graffiti writers' terminology is drenched in combative imagery, tone and meaning, and this, in turn, transforms the writer, his/her quest and, indeed, their spray can into a symbolic weapon of war:

> Through this, the writer fires "hits" (tags) like bullets. Unlike the "tag" (writer's written name) which declares "I'm here", "hits" proclaim, "I'm here and I have the power to wreak havoc and destroy". Although "bombing" involves the same action as "tagging", the emphasis on the name is overshadowed by destructive intentions . . . In the same way, pieces are "dropped", like missiles, to "burn", "kill" and "destroy" the trains and walls they land upon.
>
> (Macdonald, 2001: p. 109)

This is warfare in writers' minds. Accordingly, the fences, laser beams, cameras, security guards, patrol dogs and multitude of other obstructions imposed by their enemy cease being deterrent measures and are reconstructed, instead, into an overt invitation to do battle:

> We have just recently come through a huge onslaught of action by the British Transport Police graffiti squad, one, it must be said, we didn't even see coming. Admit it, we lost that battle, [. . .] So wake up Britain, the war is on again after the recent heavy defeat at the hands of the graffiti squad in our last battle. Don't deny it, face the facts, learn the relevant lessons, re-arm, re-group and analyse strategy, for this war is far from over.
>
> (Drax – *Londonz Burning* 2, as quoted in Macdonald, 2001: p. 122)

Indeed, the authorities have not always worked to dampen this fervour. As Cavs, a writer in New York, explained to me:

Cavs: See this piece here, it got crossed out. See the "V", the cops crossed it out. They do "VS" for the vandal squad. They do that "V" and then they circle it. By crossing my piece out, that's like a warning, you know.

Nancy:	Does that say toy [incompetent writer] there?
Cavs:	Yeah, the cops did that. Yeah, they know all about it, they know everything, that's their job, you know . . . See all the V's, they ragged [messed up] our whole car. Look at this beautiful whole car and the cops crossed it out. You know why? Because that's disrespecting us.

(Cavs, as quoted in Macdonald, 2001: p. 120)

By using writers' own adopted terminology, creating their own distinctive tag or marking and crossing out writers' work to disrespect them in their own terms, the New York Vandal Squad remove their "official" mask and effectively escalate the fervour of this conflict. Their fight becomes less an official body opposing a group of writers – and rather a battle between two rivals of equal status.

In rewriting the script in this way, graffiti writers have transformed their subculture into a militaristic world of machismo. And, as Morgan (1994) attests, "of all the sites where masculinities are constructed, reproduced, and deployed, those associated with war and the military are some of the most direct . . . the warrior still seems to be a key symbol of masculinity" (Morgan, 1994: p. 165). Here, a graffiti writer dodging the beam of police headlights and fighting for control of the transport system is no longer merely a tough and courageous writer. Rather, he becomes an intrepid and valiant soldier; potentially even a war hero. Illegality and the militaristic relationship this has engendered between writers and the police injects a huge measure of perceived machismo into writers' already "masculine" actions. Importantly, it also works to amplify the exhilaration and fun that can be had in the process: "It's a lot more exciting . . . for the sake of playing the old cops and robbers kind of thing. You get to run and hide and the rush of getting away with it, so it's more like a game" (Pink, as quoted in Macdonald, 2001: p. 115).

Viewed from this angle, graffiti ceases to be a helpless gesture of frustration or alienation. Likewise, graffiti writers cannot be seen as propelled into this crime through forces beyond their control. Rather, my research in the 1990s presented these individuals as coming together to create and collectively celebrate the construction of a very much desired "outlaw" identity:

It's against the law, you know at that time when you're growing up it's like you're just an outlaw, you know. You don't have a horse, but you can be like an outlaw, you're out in the Wild West . . . The whole thing about graffiti is being an outlaw.

(Sae 6, as quoted by Macdonald, 2001: p. 127)

One of the boys? Graffiti writing as a woman

Traditionally, outlaws have been men. Not many books or films depict women as the type of outlaw Sae 6 alludes to above. So how then do the women who enter and participate in this subculture (as it stood back in the 1990s) impact this construction? To understand this we need to appreciate just how important "maleness" actually is to this exercise. As Prime, as quoted in Macdonald (2001: p. 101), explains it:

Nancy:	Why do you think blokes are so into it?
Prime:	It's part of the image. There's the macho thing to it, the Superman, superhero thing is very much prominent, "No one can do what I can do, no one can go through what I've gone through".

If Superman status depends on no one being able to "do what you can do", then other men, let alone women, plausibly have the capacity to diminish its potency.

Academics have been slow in recognising the "subculture", graffiti or otherwise, as a site of masculine formation. Consequently, they have been slow to observe the related implications of the female member's absence or indeed the inferior role she usually occupies when she is present in male dominated subcultures such as these. I started my research for my book in the early 1990s and at that time female writers were extremely hard to find. There were a few well-known names, but nothing like the numbers of men writing. That is not to say women were not present. They were many within the periphery of the scene, but they tended to be graffiti writers' girlfriends, as opposed to writers in their own right. I quickly got the sense that this is the role male writers expected of women generally.

I did finally manage to find and talk to three women – all highly active within the illegal graffiti scene. Despite living in different cities and being involved in the subculture for different lengths of time, all of them shared very similar experiences. I summarise these here to illustrate two things: the apparent threat they represent as women, and the different ways male writers deal with and try to deflect this.

Lady Pink, a long time graffiti writer from New York, recalls the response she would usually get when she asked to go with other male writers to paint subway trains:

> They didn't take me seriously, some little girl like, "Take me to the train yard, take me to the train yard", and they wouldn't have anything to do with it . . . I got the things, "Oh you'll scream, we'll have to protect you" . . . I couldn't go off and cry and scream and carry on like a girl because that's what they expected. I had to prove myself too, that I wasn't a wimp.
>
> (Pink, as quoted in Macdonald, 2001: p. 129)

Women who start writing graffiti appear to be attributed an automatic and tainted set of stereotypical feminine qualities by their male counterparts. These present her as a trembling, timid little thing with no capacity to confront the rigours underpinning her craft. Accordingly, while male writers work to prove they are "men" using the constructive processes outlined above, female writers must first strive to demonstrate that they are not "women" – that is indicate that they have the same stamina and resilience as their male peers:

> Guys can't lose face by wimping out in front of a girl, I couldn't do that either. I couldn't go off and cry and scream and carry on like a girl because that's what they expected, so I can't do that. I had to prove myself too, that I wasn't a wimp and I could carry my own paint thank you.
>
> (Pink, as quoted in Macdonald, 2001: p. 130)

Unfortunately, the female writer's ability to demonstrate this is obstructed by a number of strategies designed to prevent her from fully realising her competitive force. The first centers on the issue of accountability. Male writers, whether inexperienced or not, are generally expected to prove themselves by their own merits alone. They are rarely helped, and must stand on their own two feet as "men". In contrast, female writers claim that they frequently experience other male writers' attempts to support or aid them – either physically while out painting, or technically in terms of their writing skills. While this chivalrous gesture might be just that, accordingly to the women writers I spoke to it is also commonly used as a way to attribute her achievements to whoever helped her. Both Lady Pink and Claw work hard, deflect such measures and position themselves as responsible for her their own work and associated credit: "I went piecing deliberately with different groups so that everyone could see I could actually paint this stuff and I'm not having some guy do it for me" (Pink, as quoted in Macdonald, 2001: p. 144). "When people try to help me do my piece, I get really, 'No, no, no, I have to do it, don't, I'm doing it', because I don't want anybody to, you know, say, 'Oh, I saw Divo do her piece'" (Claw, as quoted in Macdonald, 2001: p. 144).

The sexual rumours that typically circulate about women within graffiti can serve to distract from her achievements in a similar way. While male writers are recognised for what they do with their spray can, greater interest is often shown in what the female writer does (or not as the case may be) with her body:

> I've heard the maddest stories I'm supposed to have done. I'm supposed to have fucked this writer and that writer I don't even know. I'm supposed to give any writer a blow job, give me a can of hammerite and I'll do anything and all this kind of stuff, just the maddest things. And it's just been like this constant battle where I've got to try and prove myself that I'm not a slag, I'm not out to fuck writers, you know what I mean?
>
> (Akit, as quoted in Macdonald, 2001: p. 147)

Unlike a girl, a male writer's reputation or identity rests upon his writing, not his sexual activities, his demonstrations of masculinity, not his passive physicality.

Female writers who battle on through this adversity still have one more sizable challenge to confront – that is proving she is dedicated to graffiti and, thus, an "authentic" writer who is loyal and "true". This is where life as a female graffiti writer probably gets its hardest. Through no fault of her own, a woman's unusual subcultural status means her journey to prominence is both quicker and easier than her male counterpart's. Because she is a novelty, her actions are more likely to be noticed, spot lit and discussed, and her journey to fame is fast tracked as a result. While this short cut may look like a bonus, in reality it is a severe impediment. Writers are legitimised by the hard work and effort they put in, and the female writer's quicker rise to fame removes her ability to satisfy this. She does not benefit from her greater profile, she suffers. She gets fame without having to put in equivalent effort and this stops her from enjoying "true authenticity" in other writers' eyes.

As these obstructive measures serve to illustrate, this subculture's values and standards make it very difficult for women to be fully recognised. The male writer occupies a sphere which grants him a presence and, thus, competitive force. All he has to do is work hard and prove himself. In contrast, a woman's contribution is often minimised by focusing instead on her sexual exploits and/or questioning her dedication and accountability. In effect, attention is shifted away from her achievements and the challenge she may represent, and her emasculating potential is diminished as a result. In the past, the inferior position women have tended to occupy in other subcultures has been understood as a reproduction of the subordinate status women occupy in wider society (Brake, 1985; McRobbie and Garber, 1991). However, located within a setting centered on the construction of masculine identity, it is perhaps better understood as a position that has been pushed upon her by men who are trying to protect their masculine credibility. "If women can do what 'real men' do, the value of the practice for accommodating masculinity is effectively challenged" (Messerschmidt, 1993: p. 132). A woman achieving in the same way as her male peers has the power to silence their masculine commentary. Unless, that is, she is consigned to a place where her actions have no volume; a woman on the subcultural sidelines is going to have very much less to say than a woman on the pitch.

The influence of the Internet on women's participation and experience

The first major development since I conducted my research was the birth of the internet. In the early 1990s, online access and the communication advantages it afforded were not accessible to most people, including those writing graffiti. To communicate and share news and events, graffiti writers depended largely on their own generated print media. Photographs were taken and then sent off to individuals publishing fanzine style magazines for dissemination. This lack of instant and immediate access made the different graffiti scenes around the world more insular. And, while many writers travelled, day to day awareness of who was doing what in other cities or, indeed, countries, was often absent. Today, the internet has dissolved such boundaries. Writers from all corners of the globe can communicate, share, debate and even fight. Likewise, writers' crews (an allied band of writers) are now being formed between like-minded peers regardless of where they reside.

Jessica Pabon's recent work on female graffiti writers seeks to understand how technology and the internet has impacted how women approach and participate in this subculture. As she recognises, prior to 2000 women writers were all but invisible. In the last decade, however, we have seen a dramatic increase in female representation here. Whether this is due to their numbers swelling or their previously shadowed visibility being enhanced – either way Pabon (2013) puts this firmly down to the role of the internet:

> The shift to the Internet is definitely reordering the dynamic of participation and visibility for female graffiti writers. With the availability of the Internet, female graffiti writers are not only performing their countercultural identities and demonstrating their belonging, but they are also building and sustaining their communities and crews through the openness enabled precisely by the technology itself.
>
> (Pabon, 2013)

As Pabon (2013) suggests, the impact of the Internet on women's involvement is multi-faceted. The exposure of her graffiti work and activities online does not just afford the female writer greater profile, presence and visibility. Most importantly, it affects how she orientates herself; enabling her to derive community, support and encouragement from other women who are also writing. Pabon (2013) elaborates on this in reference to SUG, an all-female global graffiti crew:

> By building an all-female crew in a manner which makes the individual writers and the crew as a whole visible to the public, SUG is proclaiming something about the potentiality of familial ties between female writers that is, to this day, a unique phenomenon.
>
> (Pabon, 2013)

The power of these "familial ties" to a woman writing graffiti cannot be underestimated. Their experience within this subculture is both harsh and isolating, and banding together with those facing similar difficulties can lend succour and an encouraging rally cry to others to persevere. Interestingly, the increased visibility of her work may also be inspiring other women to compete. Initiating the challenge and competitive dialogue which was previously lacking, could the internet, as Pabon (2012) suggests in her TED Women lecture, be inciting more women to get involved and get competitive with each other?

However the internet has benefited women writing, it is ultimately going to benefit male writers too. By showcasing women's capacity and dedication, eventually, Pabon (2013) asserts, men will be forced to reappraise their collectively shared sexist beliefs regarding women's lack of courage, dedication and ability. In this way, the internet may not just be working to address the subculture's gender membership, but ultimately its values and principles too: "The reordering of habits, routines and relations because of graffiti culture's online presence manifests itself by challenging the patriarchal order, breaking down sexist boundaries and building new relationships among those formerly marginalized writers" (Pabon, 2013).

The rise of street art and the increase in women's participation

Born around 2000, the street art scene, a new arm to the urban art movement, has been developing steadily. With the likes of Banksy and other notable street artists selling works at auction and displaying their art in museums, street art is now a high profile global move-ment. It sits alongside graffiti, sharing in its motives the use of the street as a canvas. Its work is illegal (mainly), but unlike graffiti, this is more a consequence of its placement, rather than its central focus. Street artists may enjoy the mystique and, often humour which accompanies the placement of their work in public and proscribed locations, but the motivation to overtly fight the Transport Police or Vandal Squad through this act is comparatively lessened.

Perhaps its' most important deviation from traditional graffiti lies in its subject matter and the materials street artists use to create their work:

> Over the past few years, graffiti artists have been using a wider scope of expression. Personal style is free to develop without any constraints, and stickers, posters, stencils, airbrush, oil-based chalk, all varieties of paint and even sculpture are used. Most artists have been liberated from relying solely on the spray can.
>
> (Ganz, 2009: p. 7)

Street art frees its artists from graffiti's more prescriptive lean towards the written tag name and the use of the spray can. And many see this to be a key reason for the much greater representation of women within its boundaries. Mad C, a female street artist, upholds this creative freedom as the main reason for her involvement within this arm of the subculture: "It broadens the realms of possibility. There isn't the restriction of letters and added characters . . . there are simply so many more techniques and materials than in the graffiti field" (Mad C, as quoted in Ganz, 2006: p. 11).

Perhaps female street artists have less to earn from the written name and thus gravitate to the wider creative realms of street art instead? In my original thesis I presented the tag name as not just a creative product but, importantly, an authorisation of the actions which underpin that creation; actions which, within illegal graffiti certainly, generally involve risk, danger and, with this, the display of perceived masculine qualities. While street art can also place its artists at risk and in danger, less emphasis on the name would suggest less need to be immediately recognised and validated for this commentary on "masculine" endeavour. Focus is more commonly placed on the art or the statement it makes, rather than physical and legal risks the, often unnamed street artist, took to complete it.

These wider creative boundaries also provide female street artists much greater opportunity to perform and explore femininity through her craft – not something that was apparently permissible in the traditional graffiti subculture back in the 1980s and 1990s. Freedom, an American graffiti writer, recounts the reaction that followed Lady Pink's foray into more stereotypical feminine subject matter back in the day:

> *Freedom:* It's unfortunate that Pink's earlier work was as feminine as it was because I think that turned off guys. Guys wanted to paint guy stuff.
>
> *Nancy:* Right, and if she was going to be part of this then she would have to paint like a guy?
>
> *Freedom:* Yeah, and she wanted to paint flowers.
>
> (Freedom, as quoted in Macdonald, 2001: p. 130)

With a male majority dictating what is "graffiti" and what is not, female graffiti writers have far less permission than female street artists to take their art down alternative avenues. And this, ultimately, makes the street art scene an easier place for women artists to reside. With less emphasis on performing masculinity, male street artists appear to be more supportive and embracing of the contributions women make here and the community feels more balanced and bonded across gender lines as a result (Ganz, 2006).

Conclusion

The last fifteen years have seen an enormous degree of change occur within the graffiti subculture. We have moved from a pre to a post internet world and, for graffiti at least, this development has substantially transformed its community's practices. Writers are able to make greater and broader connections with each other, and their activities now enjoy immediate global exposure. Likewise, and possibly because of this, we have seen much greater experimentation and development to the art form itself in the guise of street art. Using the streets as their canvas, street artists are expanding their subject matter beyond the more traditional tags and name focussed pieces and a much more open and permissive arm to this subculture is developing as a result.

The upshot of both of these events is that women are finally making a more significant appearance on this subcultural stage. The "familial ties", support and competition needed to spur greater numbers of women to participate and persevere in graffiti is being enhanced by female writers' online visibility (Pabon, 2013). Likewise, the creative freedom and comparatively greater acceptance that the street art scene offers its members also appears to be swelling the numbers of women looking to get involved. On both counts, then, this subculture and its offshoots do appear to be moving towards more balanced gender membership – albeit one where men do still represent the overwhelming majority.

The question then remains, has this increase in female participation (or visibility) impacted this subculture's role as a site for the construction of masculine identity? Is a masculinity thesis still relevant in understanding the dynamics of this subculture fifteen years on? Given the fact that most recent scholarship has swung, quite rightly, towards bolstering our understanding of the experiences of women and other neglected aspects of our subcultural understanding, this is hard question to answer definitively. However, one recent article, "Boys Doing Art"

(Monto *et al.*, 2012), provides us with a clear sense of the continued relevance of this analytic angle. Presenting its interpretation along exactly these lines, this ethnographic study of an illegal American graffiti crew in Portland, Oregon in 2012 argues that the "outlaw" status of graffiti, alongside other aspects of the lifestyle, serve as resources for constructing masculinity. Furthermore, recognising the subculture's additional female membership, they go on to state that "this does not necessarily undercut the argument for the connection between graffiti and outlaw masculinity" (ibid.: p. 285). Indeed, despite these changes or developments, the authors claim the "graffiti scene of today has been and continues to be shaped by its outlaw status" (ibid.: p. 286), and thus continues to provide powerful opportunities for masculine construction.

It would seem that boys will be boys, and the need for accessible resources with which to build gender identity at a time in life when such options may be lacking, is abiding. For male writers, at least, masculine construction would appear to continue to define graffiti's deeper role regardless of any gender related changes that may be occurring. In light of this, it would be interesting to explore how this apparent gender co-existence continues to develop in the future. As the subculture adapts to greater female representation within its boundaries, will we begin to see male writers actually appreciate and celebrate the endeavours of their female counterparts without feeling the need to exclude or tear them down? Can masculinity be constructed alongside women writers without the need to physically and symbolically exclude their presence? Conversely, perhaps things will swing entirely the other way. As more women start to participate, could we see male writers work even harder to salvage their male only "retreat" and the masculine narratives which are supported by this? As opposed to coming together, will we begin to see even greater resistance and attempts to foreclose women's place and legitimacy within graffiti moving forward? In many ways, such responses could be mediated by the age of the subculture's respective scenes. With the birth of the internet, graffiti has travelled and embedded in an increasing number of locations, with more recent graffiti scenes emerging and developing. Studies exploring how gender relations develop within these more nascent and potentially balanced scenes could provide us with an interesting comparison to the dynamics which shape those where women have traditionally been a distinct minority.

References

Brake, M. (1985). *Comparative Youth Culture: The Sociology of Youth Cultures and Youth Subcultures in America, Britain, and Canada*. London: Routledge.

Ganz, N. (2006). *Graffiti Woman: Graffiti and Street Art from Five Continents*. London: Thames & Hudson.

Ganz, N. (2009). *Graffiti World: Street Art from Five Continents*. London: Thames & Hudson.

Gilmore, D. (1990). *Manhood in the Making: Cultural Concepts of Masculinity*. New Haven, CT: Yale University Press.

Macdonald, N. (2001). *The Graffiti Subculture: Youth, Masculinity and Identity in London and New York*. Basingstoke, Hampshire: Palgrave Macmillan.

McRobbie, A. and Garber, J. (1991). Girls and Subcultures, in A. McRobbie (ed.), *Feminism and Youth Culture: From 'Jackie' to 'Just Seventeen'* (pp. 1–15). London: Macmillan.

Messerschmidt, J. (1993). *Masculinities and Crime: Critique and Reconceptualisaion of Theory*. Lanham, MD: Rowman & Littlefield.

Monto, M.A., Machale, J. and Anderson, T.L. (2012). Boys Doing Art: The Construction of Outlaw Masculinity in a Portland, Oregon Graffiti Crew. *Journal of Contemporary Ethnography*, 42(3), 259–290.

Morgan, D. (1994). Theatre of War: Combat, the Military and Masculinities, in H. Brod and M. Kaufman (eds), *Theorising Masculinities: Research on Men and Masculinities* (pp. 165–182). London: Sage.

Pabon, J. (2012). Feminism on the Wall, *TED Women Talk*.

Pabon, J. (2013). Shifting Aesthetics: The Stick up Girlz Perform Crew in a Virtual World, in J. Lennon and M. Burns (eds), *Rhizomes.net/issue 25*, Available from: http://rhizomes.net/issue25/pabon/index.html (accessed: 17 April 2014).

15

The psychology behind graffiti involvement

Myra F. Taylor, Julie Ann Pooley, and Georgia Carragher

Introduction

A person's sense of belonging within society has been described as being a convergence of cognitions, behaviours and emotional affect as well as an environmental experience (Pretty *et al.*, 2003). Moreover, the desire for a sense of place belonging within society is not constricted by age, gender, ethnicity or economic status. For, as Antonsich (2010) points out, both society's 'insiders' and 'outsiders' have an inherent longing to claim bodily, temporal and/or ephemeral ownership of a place within society. Once they have located this place, their sense of belonging is realised through their physical or cognitive occupation of that space. Such occupation may be permanent (i.e. residential) or, transitory in nature (Grillo *et al.*, 2010). To identify with their selected place within society it is commonplace for insiders and outsiders to use language markers to indicate their occupancy of that space to other members. In the case of society's insiders these markers typically include such things as residential addresses, business cards and clothing/accessories emblazoned with a club, church or organization's logo. In contrast, society's outsiders (e.g. graffiti crew members) often resort to monikers (e.g. cryptic tags) to inform fellow outsiders of their sense of place, belonging, or identity affiliations. For example, graffiti crews regularly use zip or postal code numbers (e.g. 5163) to identify their suburb of origin or tagging territory and letters to denote their place location (e.g. HU – Hills Unit; WC – Wanneroo Crew; AB – Aus[tralian]-Boys), tagging range (e.g. A2M – Ashfield-to-Midland; ACK – All-City-Krew; UTB – Up-Town-Boys), cultural origins (e.g. BP – Black Power; BWC Black-and-White-combined; ABC – All-Black-Crew), identity (BB – Bowl Boys; SK8S – Skaters; BK – Bike Krew), tagging times (ANC – All-Night-Crew; DNK – Day-Night-Crew; M2K – Morning-to-[K]night) and focus activity (FNC – Fun-Not-Crime; DF – Drunken Fools; DK – Dope-Krew; LBB – Lone-Bum-Boys; NSH – Non-Stop-Havoc; SDC – S[e]Duce-Crew) to name just a few. Such monikers demonstrate that while the crew's tags can appear to be 'mindless scribble' to those outside of the graffiti subculture, to those within the graffiti sub-culture they are well known and informative.

Clearly, spoken, written and cryptic language markers hold explicit and implicit meanings that are understood and conveyed to those who use or observe them. Thus, societal insiders and outsiders have their own means of distinguishing themselves from other non-occupiers of their selected place. In doing so, they generate a within group sense of identify which further contributes to their sense of place (Antonsich, 2010; Taylor and Khan, 2014). This chapter examines the psychological motivations of graffiti writers for initially selecting a societal 'outsider' (but graffiti subcultural 'insider') graffer social identity within the broader context of the psychological conceptualisations of people's sense of place belonging, subcultural sense of place, sense of community and sense of connection.[1] The chapter concludes by highlighting the motivations behind sanctioned graffiti artists' drive for social inclusion (i.e. transitioning from a societal outsider to a societal insider).

A sense of place belonging

A sense of place belonging is used as a synonym for 'identity' and relates to the emotional feeling of being connected to a place and, by extension, feeling supported and included within the sub/cultural group, community or population cohort who also frequent that same space (Antonsich, 2010). In contrast, a lack of a sense of place belonging generates feelings of loneliness, isolation and societal alienation. The types of close links that facilitate a sense of place belonging occur in sub/cultural groups, communities or population cohorts wherein the membership share parallel interests or hold similar personal, religious, environmental, cultural or political values (Pretty *et al.*, 2003). The 'cementing' of these place belonging links typically occur as a result of the trust bonds that form between members, for mutual trust is a major determinant in deciding who belongs (i.e. are insiders) and who does not belong (i.e. are outsiders) within any given sub/cultural group, community or population cohort (Antonsich, 2010).

Adolescence is a critical period for the development of a sense of place belonging because during this time young people attempt to differentiate themselves from their parents and find their place within the peer-group with which they wish to identify. Consequently, adolescents spend a large amount of time at this juncture in their life associating with and socialising with their peers (Dallago *et al.*, 2009). Within the child development field, it is widely recognised that while no pathway is absolute or totally predetermining adolescents who come from stable family backgrounds and have parents who project mainstream beliefs and values tend to select a conforming social identity albeit somewhat differentiated from that of their parents (Carroll *et al.*, 2009; Taylor, 2011; Wilkinson-Lee *et al.*, 2011). Conversely, it is also acknowledged that adolescents, originating out of dysfunctional families and who have parents who hold beliefs and values that are not consistent with those of mainstream society, tend to emulate their parents' non-conformity and, also tend to gravitate towards the company of other similarly situated youth (Taylor *et al.*, 2010). To attract the attention of these non-conforming peers, the aspirant adolescent according to reputation enhancement theory (see Carroll *et al.*, 2009) will often go to great lengths to be noticed. In this regard, adolescents seeking admission into one of the most readily accessible non-conforming youth cultures, the graffiti subculture, will place their 'tag' (i.e. a two to five letter moniker) in a place of visual prominence so as to maximise their potential for recognition. By doing so the aspirant youth announces their presence, provides proof of their audacity and stakes a momentary ownership claim of the place they tagged (Taylor, 2011).

The adrenaline 'rush' experienced from the risk-taking involved in completing such a tag without being caught accentuates the aspirant youth's determination to continue with their attention-seeking tagging practices (Taylor, 2012). Once the aspirant youth has attained a certain level of visual recognition and gained a degree street kudos for their daring, they typically will be invited by an established graffer to join (dropped into) one or more graffiti crews. According to Taylor (2013), graffiti crews differ in size and purpose with large, to very large crews (i.e. crews with 20–50 and 50–100+ respective members) tend to be loose configurations that typically engage in mass graffiti 'bombing' activities (i.e. blitzing an area with tags) and small graffiti crews (i.e. crews with 2–5 members) in contrast tend to be bound together by bonds of trust and camaraderie (Taylor *et al.*, 2010; Taylor, 2013).

Hence, aspirant graffitists need to prove their value to a small crew before they are trusted, nominally accepted and included in all the crew's machinations and activities. To gain this trust, an aspirant member is often set a graffiti task to complete. This task often involves a degree of law breaking (e.g. stealing paint, trespass, property damage). Indeed, it is through the act of proving their daring and commitment to the crew that aspirant young members gain full acceptance as well as in time the highly prized youth non-conforming 'graffer' (as opposed to 'toy' [learner]) street social identity. In order to increase their recognition within the graffiti crew as well as the wider graffiti subculture, newly accepted members as well as established graffers will endeavour to maintain or enhance their street cred by engaging in acts of increasing daring (e.g. tagging high or dangerous places or moving objects) (Taylor *et al.*, 2012).

The awarding of a graffer identity and the obtaining of full acceptance within a graffiti crew and the wider graffiti subculture, however, is not readily given and as such aspirant members are required to prove themselves to be trustworthy. This proof is considered essential, given that if apprehended any 'disclosure' (ratting) by an untrustworthy new crew member to the police of the other crew members' names has serious financial and imprisonment ramifications for the named members. Hence, there is often a process of negotiated deliberation that goes on between crew members while a new member's trustworthiness is being assessed (Croucher, 2003).

Once a newly admitted member has proved themselves and has cemented their place within a graffiti crew, they then develop a sense of belonging to the crew. A strong sense of within crew belonging is associated with the ability of individual members to amass sufficient social capital resources so as to then be able to support the crew in times of collective adversity (e.g. a brawl with a rival crew) or individual need (e.g. police summons). Conversely, a poor sense of crew belonging is associated with the failure of individual members to amass sufficient levels of social capital resources so as to support the crew in times of collective adversity or individual need. (Social capital resources in the graffiti crew context being defined as individual members sustained access to the types of sociological support networks that glue the crew's members so tightly together that they become so strongly bonded they develop such a sense of trust and collective wellbeing they are able to function effectively as a unit) (Rankin *et al.*, 2000; Smith, 2011; Taylor, 2013; Taylor *et al.*, 2014). Thus, it is plausible to assume that the receipt of social capital support resources not only enhances crew members' sense of place affinity and sense of belonging, but also their psychological sense of wellbeing. Specifically, by providing the archetypical types of social capital support resources (e.g. reciprocal trust, information sharing, social engagement networks, camaraderie and protection) crews provide their members with an increased sense of purpose, self-worth and group identity (see Seamon, 1979; Hagerty *et al.*, 1996; Warin *et al.*, 2000; Steger and Kashdan, 2009; Smith, 2011). Acceptance over time facilitates the establishment of an emotional attachment to the crew and cements the crew members' sense of place belonging.

Although the terms 'sense of belonging' and 'sense of place affinity' remain definitionally vague and indeterminable in relation to whether a sense of belonging is the basis for a sense of place affinity or vice versa, however, both terms encompass the emotional dimensions of attachment and identity status (Antonsich, 2010). Attachment, being conceptualised as the facet of feeling 'at home' and feeling 'safe' within a given place, because these feelings are engendered by insider members of a sub/cultural group, community or population cohort, then these feelings typically generate a belief among insider members that this is the place where they belong (Yuval-Davis, 2006; Antonsich, 2010). Safe, in the physical sense of the word, relates to the protective social capital support resource of knowing that another crew member will literally 'have your back' in a fight and, in the cognitive sense of feeling secure in the knowledge that if a member of your graffiti crew is apprehended by police, then the unwritten code of silence that binds the crew together will prohibit the apprehended member from informing on the rest of the crew (Taylor, 2013).

A feeling of being safe and at home within a crew is not just a personal issue, but is also a whole crew membership issue. For the social capital support resource of providing members with social networks, allows members to establish and sustain strong friendship connections. In doing so the former non-conforming adolescent outsider becomes both an accepted crew and subculture insider. The immediate mental health benefit of this crew acceptance is it provides graffers with a supportive and disclosing environment in which to discuss personal, relational, sexual and monetary issues, and, thus, relieves their latent anxieties. However, acceptance within a graffiti crew and the wider graffiti subcultural community comes at a cost. For, in hanging out with crew members who through their engagement in illegal graffiti writing consistently break trespass and property damage laws, the chances that the newly admitted members will emulate their mates' illegal acts is greatly increased (Taylor et al., 2012). This likelihood is enhanced in crews that operate under a hierarchical leadership system for in such instances coercion is often used as a means of maintaining control. Indeed, the use of coercive control is not restricted to the leaders of graffiti crews for aggression and violence are commonplace in many subcultural entities where there is an unequal power distribution (Nijhof et al., 2010; Van Ryzin and Dishion, 2013; Taylor et al., 2014).

Individual members of a sub/cultural group, community or population entity as well as the group itself benefit too from the admittance of new members as each new member broadens and strengthens the entity's collective skill set. As mentioned in the previous paragraph, this membership comes with the reciprocal expectation that individual members as well as the collective entity will adhere not only to the micro group's mores of behaviour, but also those of the overarching sub/cultural group (Newman et al., 2007; Jack, 2010; Taylor et al., 2010). In relation to the micro (small) crews, their adherence to the wider graffiti subculture's more of behaviour reinforces both the individual member's and the crew's sense of identity and place belonging (Putnam, 2000; Barry, 2006; Deuchar, 2009; Taylor et al., 2014).

A subcultural sense of place

When people attach an emotional meaning to a place, then they make sense of the larger undifferentiated space that surrounds that place (Jack, 2010). A sub/cultural group, community or population cohort's sense of collective belonging is conveyed by a collection of people occupying a shared physical or ephemeral place, as well as the entity's collective identity as being the users of that space. Moreover, through claiming temporary ownership of a place, the occupiers further reinforce their collective sense of 'us' the insiders and the 'we' who belong to this place and, conversely the notion of 'them' the outsider 'others' who do not belong. By tagging surfaces with their own and/or their crew's moniker graffitists affirm on three levels (i.e. affective [emotional], conative [behavioural] and cognitive [perceptual]) that the tagged place belongs to 'us' for 'we' have claimed transient ownership of this space (Smith, 2011). When a tagger develops such a three tier attachment to a place, then during the time they occupy that space they typically experience a sense of oneness with both the place and the people who co-tag that space. This sense of oneness facilitates interactions between graffers and creates a group sense of identity and dependence which are the foundation blocks for developing a sense of community (Pretty *et al.*, 2003).

As alluded to earlier, the term 'sense of place' is not necessarily location limited, the term also captures the intangible and symbolic personal, social and cultural experiences which people have as a result of their interactions with their selected place (Pretty *et al.*, 2003) and the behavioural desires they associate with their occupancy of that space (Stedman, 2003). Place attachment or place identity is a process of developing both a sense of self in relation to place as well as a communal social identity. Collectively, over time and with repeated positive interactions with a place, people develop a sense of affection for that place and, in the process become bonded to it (Dallago *et al.*, 2009). It is this bond that anchors a person's self-identity and feelings of place belonging (Morgan, 2010). However, just as people change over the course of their lifetime so too can their sense of place belonging and their sense of community.

Sense of community

According to Gusfield (1975), a sense of community occurs on two dimensions, the first being relational (i.e. the sense of belonging) and the second territorial (i.e. sense of place). Whereas, previously a community was considered to involve some form of physical interaction between members (Chavis *et al.*, 1986), since the advent of new online social networking sites the physical requirement to meet is redundant as communities can now form and engage in cyberspace. Indeed, graffitists have embraced social networking and as a result the subculture has morphed into a global community.

Once people see themselves as belonging to a community, they form ties and interact socially with other people within the community. In this way, they become an integral and functioning part of the community (Kissane and McLaren, 2006). While no clear conceptualisation or construct of sense of community exists (Reich, 2010) within the field of Community Psychology, Sarason's (1974) definition of sense of community is broadly accepted as being a shared perception of similarity among the community's members, an acknowledgement of their interdependence, and a realisation that the coherence of the entity (and the social capital resource that it dispenses) is only maintainable by the insiders adherence to the structures which bind the entity together. In other words there is a united belief among the community's members that they belong together and that they will join together to support each other in times of adversity (Hodgetts *et al.*, 2010; Tonts and Atherley, 2010; Smith, 2011). A strong sense of community typically is comprised of a number of interrelated micro, meso, exo and macro social systems which when they work together optimise the entity's members' sense of satisfaction, wellbeing and efficacy (Sum *et al.*, 2009; Huitt, 2009; Smith, 2011). Indeed, the term 'sense of community' encompasses the common interests, cultural values, affiliations and the multiple (micro, meso, exo and macro) associations which bond a group or groups of people together.

One mark of a bonded community (i.e. a community where members benefit from the cooperation and assistance of its members) is that the individual members or groups who have the greater abilities and stocks of social capital resources support those with lesser abilities (Semenza and March, 2009; Lewicka, 2010). When this interdependent sense of community exists, characteristically community members (individuals and groups) hold an expectation that their needs will be met and that they will receive the social capital support resources they require (Pretty *et al.*, 2003). As a result there is an incumbency on the part of the person or group receiving the support resources to invest in the entity by contributing to the community's cohesivity and wellbeing. This cohesivity usually is built on trust and cemented by adherence to the community's mores of behaviour (Hosmer, 1995; Das and Teng, 2004; Mannarini and Fedi, 2009). Within the graffiti community, the predominant more that binds graffers, crews and the wider graffiti community together is the subculture's strict 'no snitching' street code of silence (Taylor, 2013). This no snitch code of silence is embedded within the hip-hop gangsta rap music genre, whose lyrics not only glorify criminality and hegemonic violence, but also instruct listeners to not 'snitch' on each other and furthermore, exhort its devotees to exact retribution on those individuals who do 'rat' (inform) on their mates (Anderson, 1999; Kubrin, 2005; Taylor, 2013). As a consequence, orchestrated retribution has become a common means by which street communities brutally enforce their 'no snitch' code of silence (Harris, 2007; Taylor, 2013). Indeed, within the graffiti community crew members are under no misconception whatsoever that if they are found to have collaborated with police and ratted (i.e. informed) on their fellow graffers, they will be labelled an informer, ostracised, and on their release from police custody will be subjected to (often violent) retribution (Tafler, 2000; Taylor, 2013).

Communities are not static entities, people join and people leave, so their membership is in a state of continual change and renewal. A tipping point for graffitists in terms of their willingness to remain part of the graffiti community typically arrives around the time they enter adulthood. For it is at this stage that young people begin to contemplate their future. A future that is comprised of adult responsibilities; for example, obtaining a source of income to pay for their living costs and fulfilling the time requirements and personal commitments that are needed to foster and sustain intimate partner relationships. Added motivational clarity to change their life-style also comes from the increasingly harsh adult financial and penal penalties that many governments put in place to deal with what their mainstream populace deems to be acts of graffiti vandalism (i.e. the unauthorised and illegal written, scratched, marked, sprayed or affixed defacement of property) (Taylor et al., 2012). Hence, during early adulthood some graffitists leave the graffiti community to resume a life within the mainstream, others with limited artistic talent and limited scholastic skills gravitate towards a life of un/under employment or criminality. However, for those graffers with street honed artistic skills, a third option has in recent years opened up, namely, the chance to adopt the more publically palatable and 'legitimate' identity of a sanctioned graffiti artist, an identity which attracts a degree of mainstream community respect along with a potential source of income (Taylor, 2012). Some graffitists making this re-entry into mainstream society choice though appear to oscillate for a period of time between the illegal graffiti community and the sanctioned graffiti artist community. In some cases, their willingness to re-enter the mainstream community and abide by its laws is contingent on the sanctioned graffiti artist gaining the respect, mentorship and financial support that they are seeking from mainstream society (Taylor, 2014). For if they are 'dissed' or rebuffed, or unable to secure a financial reward for their artwork then these transitioning young adults will return to the security and camaraderie of the illegal graffiti community. The choice to remain within the illegal graffiti community or to become a mainstream sanctioned graffiti artist is further complicated by some subcultural graffitists' belief that by selling graffiti to mainstreamers sanctioned graffiti artists are also selling out the very essence of the graffiti subculture, namely, that of being an art form which challenges society's mores.

The conundrum for mainstream society is that in recognising sanctioned graffiti artists as respected members of the mainstream community and providing them with the necessary social capital support resources and financial rewards, they need to sustain their sanctioned artwork, then they evoke the ire of the citizenry opposed to graffiti. For such individuals are quick to point out that in paying sanctioned graffiti artists you are rewarding them for the years of illegal graffiti they wrote on the streets while they were honing their present artistic skills. Thus, solving this conundrum is not easy. What is clear though is that in order for former graffitists to make the switch to legal sanctioned graffiti society needs to help foster a connection between them and the mainstream community if a compromise to this conundrum is to be found (Newman *et al.*, 2007). This is no easy task given that a sizeable proportion of mainstream society resents the presence of graffiti on the streets and questions why taxpayer dollars should be spent on legitimising graffiti under the banner of urban or street art. Thus, a major challenge for society is how to build links between the sanctioned graffiti artist and the anti-graffiti lobby, sanctioned graffiti artists and youth mentors as well as put in place pro-social legal pathways into sanctioned graffiti art for disenfranchised youth. This pathway has to be inclusionary for it is competing with an illegal, but cohesive crew subculture, which is able to provide disenfranchised graffitists with the social capital support resources that they need to deal with their non-conforming lives.

Sense of connection

Social cohesion among the occupiers of a physical, online or ephemeral place occurs when collectively a group of insiders establish a sense of solidarity with their co-occupier of that space and with outsiders (Goodenow, 1993; Steger and Kashdan, 2009). When a sense of connection and a sense of place belonging co-occur, then a sense of wellness develops and it is this sense of connection with others that provides the types of mental health benefits which contribute to psychological well-being (Cemalcilar, 2010). Indeed, Cemalcilar suggests that the mental health benefits of achieving a sense of connection with others is a lower internalised sense of alienation, loneliness and hostility, which in turn helps generate positive attitudes, pro-social behaviours, interpersonal associations and enduring friendships. These positive attributes act as a buffer (particularly among young people) against negative life experiences (e.g. criticism, bullying, rejection), and generate the emotional capacity and resilience young people need individually and collectively to deal with life's challenging or adverse events (Ladd *et al.*, 1997; Ladd and Troop-Gordon, 2003; Walker *et al.*, 2014). Although, with the growth of the Internet concerns have been raised as to whether a virtual online sense of connection is fostering in the I-Generation a greater sense of individualism as opposed to the traditional sense of collective community (Reich, 2010). Thus, further research is needed to examine both young people's conforming and non-conforming sense of community.

Summary

Seeking an adult identity, a sense of personal belonging, place and community with others typically begins around the onset of adolescence. At this stage, the socially conforming or non-conforming identity that the adolescent chooses in many ways orientates their future life trajectory (Pereira and Pooley, 2007). Providing sanctioned graffiti art pathways back into the mainstream community for graffitists is one way young people with demonstrable art skills and proven tenacity of spirit can enrich society. The adoption of such a social inclusion pathway is less costly to society than the alternative pathway of graffiti removal, policing, prosecution and incarceration costs, graffiti-related injury health costs and arguably the lost taxable income on artwork that if written legally could have possibly been sold. Although others may argue that mainstream societal support resources are better spent on providing assistance to adolescents when they first show signs of ostracising themselves (or being ostracised by their peers) from the mainstream school community and start seeking a sense of identity among the cohort of non-conforming street youth. What is clear, however, and needs to be kept in mind by politicians, lawmakers and other agents and institutions of social control, is that non-conforming young people involved in the graffiti subculture are no different from their mainstream conforming age-mates in so far as they too desire a sense of place, belonging, community and connection within and to society.

Note

1   Although this discussion can probably be applied to street artists, the focus here is on graffiti writers.

References

Anderson, E. (1999). *Code of the street*. New York: W.W. Norton and Company.
Antonsich, M. (2010). Searching for belonging: An analytical framework. *Geography Compass* 4(6): 644–659.
Barry, M. (2006). *Youth offending in transition*. Oxon: Routledge.
Blanchard, A.L. (2007). Developing a sense of virtual community measure. *Cyber Psychology and Behaviour* 10(6): 827–830.
Carroll, A.M., Houghton, S., Durkin, K. and Hattie, J. (2009). *Adolescent reputations and risk*. New York: Springer-Verlag.
Cemalcilar, Z. (2010). Schools as socialization contexts: Understanding the impact of school climate factors on students' sense of school belonging. *Applied Psychology* 59(2): 243–272.
Chavis, D., Hogge, J., McMillan, D. and Wandersman, A. (1986). Sense of community through Brunswick's lens: A first look. *Journal of Community Psychology* 14(1): 24–40.
Croucher, S.L. (2003). *Globalization and belonging: The politics of identity in a changing world*. Boulder: Rowman and Littlefield Publishers.
Dallago, L., Perkins, D.D., Santinello, M., Boyce, W., Molcho, M. and Morgan, A. (2009). Adolescent place attachment, social capital, and perceived safety: A comparison of 13 countries. *American Journal of Community Psychology*, 44(1–2): 148–160.
Das, T.K. and Teng, B.S. (2004). The risk-based view of trust: A conceptual framework. *Journal of Business and Psychology*, 19(1): 85–116.
Deuchar, R. (2009). *Gangs, marginalised youth and social capital*. Stoke-on-Trent, UK: Trentham Books.
Goodenow, C. (1993). The psychological sense of school membership among adolescents: Scale development and educational correlates. *Psychology in the Schools* 30(1): 79–90.
Grillo, M., Teixeira, M. and Wilson, D. (2010). Residential satisfaction and civic engagement: Understanding the causes of community participation. *Social Indicators Research* 97(3): 451–466.
Gusfield, J.R. (1975). *The community: A critical response*. New York: Harper & Row.
Hagerty, B.M., Williams, R.A., Coyne, J.C. and Early, M.R. (1996). Sense of belonging and indicators of social and psychological functioning. *Archives of Psychiatric Nursing* 10(4): 235–244.
Harris, L.V. (2007). See no evil, speak no evil: In hip-hop and beyond, telling the police what you've seen is a high crime itself: Silence shouldn't be golden. *The Atlanta Journal-Constitution*, 20 May.
Hodgetts, D., Stolte, O., Chamberlain, K., Radley, A., Groot, S. and Nikora, L. (2010). The mobile hermit and the city: Considering links between places, objects and identities in social psychological research on homelessness. *British Journal of Social Psychology* 49(2): 285–303.
Hosmer, L. (1995). Trust: The connection link between organizational theory and philosophical ethics. *Academy of Management Review* 20(2): 379–403.
Huitt, W. (2009). A systems approach to the study of human behaviour. *Educational Psychology Interactive*. Valdosta, GA: Valdosta State University.
Jack, G. (2010). Place matters: The significance of place attachments for children's wellbeing. *British Journal of Social Work* 40(3): 755–771.
Kissane, M. and McLaren, S. (2006). Sense of belonging as a predictor of reasons for living in older adults. *Death Studies* 30(3): 243–258.
Kubrin, C.E. (2005). Gangstas, thugs and hustlas: Identity and the code of the street in rap music. *Social Problems* 52(3): 360–378.
Ladd, G., Kochenderfer-Ladd, B. and Coleman, C. (1997). Classroom peer acceptance, friendship and victimization: Distinct relational systems that contribute to adjustment. *Child Development* 68(3): 1181–1197.

Ladd, G. and Troop-Gordon, W. (2003). The role of chronic peer difficulties in the development of children's psychological adjustment problems. *Child Development* 74(5): 1344–1367.

Lewicka, M. (2010). What makes neighbourhood different from home and city? Effects of place scale on place attachment. *Journal of Environmental Psychology* 30(1): 35–51.

Mannarini, T. and Fedi, A. (2009). Multiple senses of community: The experience and meaning of community. *Journal of Community Psychology* 37(2): 211–227.

Morgan, P. (2010). Towards a developmental theory of place attachment. *Journal of Environmental Psychology* 30(1): 11–22.

Newman, B.M., Lohman, B.J. and Newman, P.R. (2007). Peer group membership and a sense of belonging: Their relationship to adolescent behaviour problems. *Adolescence* 42(166): 241–263.

Nijhof, K.S., Scholte, R.H., Overbeek, G. andEngels, R.C. (2010). Friends' and adolescents' delinquency: The moderating role of social status and reciprocity of friendships. *Criminal Justice and Behavior* 37(3): 289–305.

Pereira, A.J. and Pooley, J.A. (2007). A qualitative exploration of the transition experience of students from a high school to a senior high school in rural Western Australia. *Australian Journal of Education* 51(2): 162–177.

Pretty, G.H., Chipuer, H.M. and Bramston, P. (2003). Sense of place among adolescents and adults in two rural Australian towns: The discriminating features of place attachment, sense of community and place dependence in relation to place identity. *Journal of Environmental Psychology* 23(3): 273–287.

Putnam, R. (2000). *Bowling alone.* New York: Simon and Schuster.

Rankin, L.B., Saunders, D.G. and Williams, R.A. (2000). Mediators of attachment style, social support, and sense of belonging in predicting woman abuse by African American men. *Journal of Interpersonal Violence* 15(10): 1060–1080.

Reich, S.M. (2010). Adolescents' sense of community on MySpace and Facebook: A mixed-methods approach. *Journal of Community Psychology* 38(6): 688–705.

Sarason, S.B. (1974). The psychological sense of community: Prospects for a community psychology. San Francisco: Jossey-Bass.

Seamon, D. (1979). *A geography of the life-world: Movement, rest, and encounter.* New York: St. Martin's.

Semenza, J. and March, T. (2009). An urban community-based intervention to advance social interactions. *Environment and Behavior* 41(1): 22–42.

Smith, K. (2011). *The relationship between residential satisfaction, sense of community, sense of belonging, and sense of place in Western Australian urban planned community.* Unpublished doctoral thesis: Edith Cowan University, Western Australia.

Stedman, R. (2003). Is it really just a social construction? The contribution of the physical environment to sense of place. *Society and Natural Resources* 16(8): 671–685.

Steger, M. and Kashdan, T. (2009). Depression and everyday social activity, belonging, and wellbeing. *Journal of Counselling Psychology* 56(2): 289–300.

Sum, S., Mathews, R.M., Pourghasem, M. and Hughes, I. (2009). Internet use as a predictor of sense of community in older people. *Cyber Psychology & Behaviour* 12(2): 235–239.

Tafler, S. (2000). The code of silence: Replacing the 'rat' mentality. *The Globe and Mail*, 31 March, A15.

Taylor, M.F. (2011). Hanging with the Hoodies: Towards an understanding of the territorial tagging practices of prolific graffiti writers seeking an adolescent non-conforming social identity. *International Journal of Child & Adolescent Health* 4(3): 223–232.

Taylor, M.F. (2012). Addicted to the risk, recognition and respect that the graffiti lifestyle provides: Towards an understanding of the reasons for graffiti engagement. *International Journal of Mental Health and Addiction* 10(1): 54–68.

Taylor, M.F. (2013). Towards understanding the street code of silence that exists among prolific graffiti offenders. *Victims and Offenders* 8(2): 185–208.

Taylor, M.F., Deuchar, R. and Van der Leun, J. (2014). 'Out on the street it's like a brotherhood of sorts': Violent Scottish and Australian troublesome youth groups. In M. Taylor, J.A. Pooley and J. Merrick (eds), *Adolescent domain: Places and spaces.* (pp. 121–132). New York: Nova Science.

Taylor, M.F., Houghton, S. and Bednall, J. (2010). Friendship and peer socialization practices among skateboarders and graffiti writers. In F. Columbus (ed.), *Friendships: Types, cultural variations and psychological and social aspects.* New York: Nova Science.

Taylor, M.F. and Khan, U. (2014). What works and what does not work in reducing juvenile graffiti offending? A comparison of changes that occurred in the frequency of persistent graffitists' patterns of offending following the announcement of two successive initiatives aimed at reducing graffiti proliferation. *Crime Prevention & Community Safety* 16(2): 128–145.

Taylor, M.F., Marais, I. and Cottman, R. (2012). Patterns of graffiti offending: Towards recognition that graffiti offending is more than 'kids messing around'. *Policing and Society: An International Journal of Research and Policy* 22(2): 152–168.

Tonts, M. and Atherley, K. (2010). Competitive sport and the construction of place identity in rural Australia. *Sport in Society* 13(3): 381–398.

Van Ryzin, M.J. and Dishion, T.J. (2013). From antisocial behavior to violence: A model for the amplifying role of coercive joining in adolescent friendships. *Journal of Child Psychology and Psychiatry* 54(6): 661–669.

Walker, A., Taylor, M.F., Caltabiano, N. and Pooley, J.A. (2014). Creating friendship networks, establishing a social identity, developing a sense of belonging, meeting new people, and building connections with the community: The social capital support health benefits to be derived from skateboarding in skate-parks. *International Journal of Child Health and Human Development* 7(2): 2–12.

Warin, M., Baum, F., Kalucy, E., Murray, C. and Veale, B. (2000). The power of place: Space and time in women's and community health centres in South Australia. *Social Science & Medicine* 50(12): 1863–1875.

Wilkinson-Lee, A.M., Zhang, Q., Nuno, V.L. and Wilhelm, M.S. (2011). Adolescent emotional distress: The role of family obligations and school connectedness. *Journal of Youth and Adolescence* 40(2): 221–230.

Yuval-Davis, N. (2006). Belonging and the politics of belonging. *Patterns of Prejudice* 40(3): 197–214.

16

Graffiti and the subculture career[1]

Gregory J. Snyder

Introduction

My initiation into the world of graffiti writers began in the fall of 1995. I was riding my bike over the Williamsburg Bridge in Brooklyn, New York and was overwhelmed by a large and colourful graffiti painting. The piece said 'Sento' and each letter had a different style, and twisted into the next producing a wholeness that was readable even to my novice eyes. Various greens melding into blues, twisting back into the forest green background, yellow highlights orange accents, light blue shading and white outlined letters 'S E N T O'. Although surrounded by graffiti in New York City, it had finally penetrated my indifference. This was the first time I had really looked at it as something to be seen, instead of just white noise, something to be overlooked and avoided. I relayed my bridge incident to a co-worker who I had overheard was involved with graffiti. He lent me his copy of the classic book, *Getting Up: Subway Graffiti in New York*, by Craig Castleman (1982).[2] The book told the story of the New York City graffiti scene during the 1970s, albeit one of graffiti's most colourful periods, but since then not a single text had been written about the graffiti that I had seen on the bridge and I badly wanted to know more.

I would spend the next decade studying graffiti subculture. I established entrée in the graffiti community by asking writers to piece words in a 'blackbook',[3] and I would then interview the writers based on the words they chose. As time went on my knowledge of the culture grew which increased my ability to establish relationships with more accomplished writers. I spent years hanging out with writers such as VERT, ESPO, AME, PSOUP, AMAZE, MEK, CRO, HUSH, RELS, KR, DES, KEST, EARSNOT, ZER, KEZAM, COLT[4] and others, who taught me about their world. In these participant observation settings, I often played the role of lookout and documenter, and once even proudly assisted ESPO in the painting of one of his murals (Snyder, 2009).

The beginning

TAKI 183 was the first New York writer to recognise that the purpose of writing your name was to produce fame. A 1971 *New York Times* article, 'Taki Spawns Pen Pals', inspired many youth all across the city to begin writing. In just a short time, the culture progressed from scribbled signatures to elaborate masterpieces, or 'pieces', done with multiple aerosol colours on the sides of New York City subway cars. Soon thereafter, the best writers would paint pieces that covered an entire train, or the 'whole car'. Writers whose names were up the most were called 'Kings' and they were exalted by their peers. By 1974, BLADE was doing conceptual pieces in which an octopus held up each letter in his name. By 1977, LEE and members of his FAB 5 crew painted an entire train, a total of ten cars, over the period of two nights. Other superstars from this period include STAY HIGH 149, HURTZ, SLUG, SLAVE, DOC, MONO, VULCAN, and BAMA.

This activity got considerable attention throughout the world, and while the reaction from the public was often positive (Goldstein, 1980), the response from city hall was not. Both John Lindsay and Ed Koch, mayors during the 1960s and 1970s respectively, implemented wars on this new form of writing, which they called graffiti (Austin, 2001). Meanwhile, gallery owners and art collectors at home and abroad, were treating some writers like artists and paying them for their work. This was their first glimpse that they might be able to have a future of their own making.[5]

While New York City's mayors were busy leading their war on urban youth, gallery owners at home and abroad were inviting talented writers like DONDI, ZEPHYR, PINK, CRASH and others to exhibit their work on canvas. The first show was in the Bronx, in 1978 at the Fashion Moda gallery. Then in the spring of 1980, ZEPHYR and FUTURA developed a relationship with Samuel Esses, an art collector. In an effort to preserve graffiti art, Esses, along with ZEPHYR and FUTURA, invited writers into his studio to do aerosol on canvas. It was here that writers learned that they could successfully translate some of their creative ideas to a new medium.

In 1983, Dutchman Yaki Kornblitt invited DONDI and others to show their work in his gallery. Later that year these writers, who at home were being treated like criminals by the mayor, showed their work at the Boymans Van Beuningen Museum in Rotterdam, Amsterdam.

When I began my research, the academic literature on contemporary graffiti was slim. Craig Castleman's *Getting Up* (1982) was seminal in its exploration of the train era, while cultural criminologist Jeff Ferrell's (1993) *Crimes of Style* explored the graffiti scene in Denver, Colorado. That, along with Richard. Lachman's article 'Graffiti as Career and Ideology', (1988), was it.

In the new century, graffiti's popularity within the academy increased rapidly. Nancy Macdonald argues in *The Graffiti Subculture* (2001) that graffiti is a site for the formation of male identity. Joe Austin's *Taking the Train* (2001) is the seminal historical account of the social construction of graffiti as a crime in New York City.

Ivor Miller's (2002) *Aerosol Kingdom* is a reflexive attempt at interpreting the cultural roots of graffiti. Miller suggests a cultural continuity between the African orisha Ogun – the god of iron – and African-American, Caribbean-American and Puerto-Rican-American youths' application of aerosol to the iron sides of subway cars. Other notable scholarship includes, Brewer and Miller (1990), Kramer (2010), Ferrell and Weide (2010) and Alvelos (2004).

In 1989, the New York City train era officially came to a close. When city officials refused to put painted trains into service, graffiti on the subways no longer produced fame. So writers took to the streets, and continued to progress the form. This move freed writers from underground tunnels and forced them to become experts of urban exploration in cities all over the world. (Some writers still paint clean trains for the thrill and the 'flicks' (i.e. photos), although the trains are never put into service.)

The idea of graffiti names on canvas lost much of its momentum, but in the mid-1990s the next generation of writers, many of whom were art school graduates, forced their way back into galleries to do installations. TWIST (Barry McGee) was a pioneer in this direction and his success created opportunities for others. Fellow former writers, ESPO (Steve Powers), REAS (Todd James) and so many others have moved beyond piecing with spray cans to conceptual pieces that deal with signage, commercialism, fame and urban aesthetics. This artistic work is not graffiti, but it is clear by their use of letters, graphics and sometimes aerosol paint, that each of these artists' vision was developed in conversation with the cities' built environment.

There are also writers who have turned their youthful graffiti success into other adult careers. There are writers like the members of TATS CRU who are muralists for hire, tattoo artists like VERT, graphic designers like DES and numerous magazine publishers.

Graffiti is not a monolithic culture. Writers are white, brown, light and dark skinned; they are rich, poor, smart and dumb; most are male; some are militantly opposed to social norms, some are quiet conformists, while others are practical political activists; they span a broad range of ethnic groups; they come from the cities, from the suburbs and some from the country and they are from cities which include, New York, Philadelphia, Atlanta, Houston, Los Angeles, San Francisco, Washington, DC, Paris, Berlin, Stuttgart, Amsterdam, Tokyo, Sao Paulo and Santiago.

The culture of writers is not bound together by appearance, language, birthplace, or class. Although many recognise and respect these differences, what binds them is the history of graffiti and the process of doing it. Writers are a multi-class, race, ethnic, religious and lingual culture of younger and older people who define themselves not on what they look like or what language they speak, or what clothes they wear, but on what they do. Their identities are as writers first, and as ethnic, religious etc. -writers second. I am not trying to claim that writers never experience or evince the racism, classism, sexism, and homophobia that is typical in our culture but it is important to understand that writers' identities are largely constructed from their achieved status as rather than from an ascribed status imposed upon them by the larger society.

Many of the original pioneers of the graffiti movement, like DONDI, DEZ, KASE 2, SKEME, STAN 152, STAY HIGH 149 and FUTURA, were black, also many like, SEEN, PJAY, MIN and CAP, were white. Over the last fifteen years, however, graffiti writing has become less popular among black kids, and more popular among white kids. As hip hop grew and progressed, many talented African-American youth chose rap over writing because of the possibility of monetary reward. However, the ubiquity of white kids writing graffiti is not the same as white kids playing the blues, or rapping. White kids writing graffiti should not be construed as an act of cultural thievery or imitation. Graffiti writing – unlike most indigenous forms of American music is not specifically steeped in African-American cultural traditions – white kids, black kids, brown kids, rich kids and poor kids have all participated in the creation and perpetuation of graffiti culture from the beginning.

The explanation as to why so many white kids write graffiti, however, does perhaps follow class lines. Graffiti is not part of the sports and entertainment industrial complex; there is no dream of huge monetary rewards that will offer a way out of impoverished circumstances. Since race continues to limit access to opportunity in this country, kids of colour are more likely to be poor, and hence, more inclined to focus their talents on more lucrative endeavours, like academics, sports or music. White kids practice graffiti because they can afford it. Meaning they can afford to do something in which the monetary rewards are not immediate. I am not trying to claim graffiti for white boys, or even to somehow suggest that white privilege does not operate in graffiti, but it is the case that this subculture is primarily a meritocracy.

Although a minority, women have participated in writing culture since the beginning. Writers like BARBARA and EVA 62, were famous for tagging the Statue of Liberty, and GRAPE and STONEY were prominent in Brooklyn. PINK was one of the few subway superstars, and her work inspired a new generations of 1990s writers including, BLUE, MUK, DONA, HOPE, JAKEE, DIVA and SARE.

While graffiti talent is not gendered, graffiti writers must literally fight for their reputations and this fighting tends to turn off many women, who often concentrate on legal walls. But there are the exceptions. PINK wrote right along with the boys during the train era in the 1980s and has achieved legendary graffiti and artistic fame. CLAW, who describes herself as a nice middle class Jewish girl (Ashman, 2007), has been a dedicated street bomber (illegal graffiti writer) since the mid-1990s with pieces, throw-ups and tags all over the city. Today her fame is everywhere. She is the subject of a book, *Bombshell: The Life and Crimes of CLAW MONEY*, is featured in the Doug Pray film, *Infamy*. She runs her own business, a successful clothing line that features her iconic claw with the three finger nails (Ashman, 2007).

Very often women team up with men for protection and comradeship and this was the case with CLAW who bombed NYC in the 1990s with MQ of DMS crew. However, more recently she has taken young, up and comer MISS 17, as her partner in her PMS (Power, Money, Sex) crew. These women are no doubt tough, and while they are less likely to be roughed up or harassed by cops, or male writers, women have had their share of beefs (disputes) with other writers. Nevertheless, women face enormous challenges negotiating dangerous streets alone at night. The street, in many ways, is a place for maleness, but these women and many like them have braved the night and demanded inclusion. While female writers have no doubt experienced sexism from their male counterparts, their accomplishments are duly noted and respect is given if they have put their names up and are 'all city', a term used to describe writers who have saturated the city with their names.

Anyone who can get large quantities of paint, is able to fight, and is willing to break the law, can become a graffiti writer. In theory, writers are not even excluded from the subculture for lack of artistic talent, what writers call 'style'. To be sure, novice writers with bad style and poor technique are ridiculed by their peers, and often quit, but with proper instruction and practice even people who cannot draw can develop an adequate tag and throw-up, and after writing their names thousands of times, they get good. The task of writing is to saturate the city with your name and any writer who does this will get fame and respect from fellow graffiti writers, regardless of style, race, gender, class, age, nationality or sexuality. In its purest form, graffiti is a democratic art form that revels in the American Dream. With desire, dedication, humility, courage, toughness and most of all hard work, anyone can potentially become a successful graffiti writer, and maybe even make a life as a result.

As the decade wore on, politicians continued to wage war on graffiti writers and the novelty of graffiti on canvas for outside collectors began to wear off. By 1989, the public art show that had run on New York City subways had ceased and the gallery opportunities, especially in the US, were also drying up.

But writers kept writing, and they were good. On walls, on clean trains that never ran, and in secret tunnels, they continued to progress the form. Many of these writers had become excellent self-taught artists and were encouraged by some sympathetic adults (high school counsellors) to put portfolios together with photos and sketches of their graffiti work and apply to colleges.

This is a significant point that receives little or no attention. Many of the first and second generation of post-subway graffiti writers like ESPO, KR, VERT, AME, PSOUP, KEST, DES, AMAZE, CYCLE, HUSH, and KAWS, all went to college. There they expanded their repertoires and learned many of the skills that would help them to start magazines, retail businesses, and/or become fine artists. All of which increased the career options for adults who were successful graffiti writers as youth.

Gregory J. Snyder

Graffiti magazines

Although in the post-train era writers quickly began to paint on walls all over the city, there were no longer central locations, like the so-called Writers Bench at the 149th and Grand Concourse subway station, where writers could view passing graffiti on the trains. The movement, though, found a new medium for producing fame: the photograph. Photographs made ephemeral graffiti pieces permanent, allowing writers to study the work of others without attachment to a specific place or time.

Initially, graffiti was documented by sympathetic outsiders, many of whom became advocates for the art and the artists. Henry Chalfant and Martha Cooper's classic photographic study *Subway Art* (1984), and Chalfant and Prigoff's *Spray Can Art* (1987), showcased some of the world's very best graffiti art, and along with the films *Wild Style* (1982) and *Style Wars* (1985), fuelled the dissemination of graffiti culture beyond New York City.

However, as photographic and publishing technology became more affordable, writers began to actively document their own subculture. This began with the simple trading of photos,[6] but quickly evolved into magazines and videos. This transition also allowed writers to take control over the representation of their subculture, as well as to reap possible financial rewards.

The *International Graffiti Times* (IGT) was the first graffiti magazine and was established in 1983 by legendary pioneer PHASE 2 and editor/graffiti-advocate David Schmidlapp. Originally done in black and white in a fold-out, subway map format, IGT was one of the first instances where graffiti wasn't exclusively about public space. This development was significant, as it created solidarity among writers who became both producers and consumers of graffiti related material.

Anti-graffiti campaigns, in which 'moral entrepreneurs' insisted that graffiti is always vandalism and never art, did not go unnoticed by graffiti writers, who saw the them as opportunistic and hypocritical – especially given the fact that artists, collectors, critics, journalists and even some corporations, were defining graffiti as a legitimate artistic pursuit, and one that, at times, could generate considerable money. Experienced graffiti writers responded by creating their own subculture media to combat the perception that they were in ESPO's words 'immoral idiots ', and his magazine *On the Go* offered intriguing art, hip hop journalism and thoughtful critical analysis.[7] Other important graffiti magazines include: *12oz. Prophet, GSXL, Can Control* and later *While You Were Sleeping.*

The writers who started magazines were also influenced by the DIY ethos of punk zines. Duncombe (1997) argues that zinesters, as he calls them, create a subculture of both readers and writers who find solace in an anonymous collectivity and the expression of middle class ennui. While Atton (2002) suggests that a commitment to political activism is at the core of alternative media, his definition focuses on the collective activities involved in the production of alternative media, from researching and writing, to making copies and finding outlets for distribution. He argues that through working together to put out alternative media, individuals feel a sense of collective power that is in the end political.

The subcultures that Duncombe and Atton describe come about through the process of making media, zinesters and alternative media activists do not document a subculture, but create one. Cultural Studies scholar Paul Hodkinson (2002) uses the term 'subculture media' to describe media which is produced by members of existing subcultures with the intent of serving the needs of that subculture. The creation of such media comes after the creation of the subcultural form, and in many ways expands the reach of the subculture beyond geographic and physical space. This, I argue, is the critical component in understanding how contemporary subculturalists make careers out of their subcultural pursuits. Graffiti magazines showcase the very best graffiti and therefore produce subcultural capital for writers, who often turn this subcultural fame, into actual capital.

The one requirement for those in the production of graffiti magazines however, is status as a current or former graffiti writer. These magazines report on illegal activities and often use illegal graffiti tactics to market themselves, all of which require the skills and interpersonal trust developed by graffiti writers. The production of magazines on a larger, more professional scale has also had the effect of providing jobs, and for some like Roger Gastman careers, in the publishing industry (Gastman, 2001; Pressler, 2006).

For the most part graffiti magazines have run their course, as most folks have turned to the internet and social media to showcase graffiti writing. The first graffiti web site, Art Crimes (www.graffiti.org), now showcases graffiti from all over the world and offers links to hundreds of graffiti sites with photos and articles, as well as providing links to spray paint manufacturers. These sites are forging closer and closer ties among a vast population of underground illegal artists, who continue the process of turning illegal fame into legitimate, if alternative, adult careers.

The creation of subculture media is the key to understanding the subculture career. Modern day subculture participants, like skaters, bmx street bikers, bike messengers, parkour practitioners, street racers and so many others, use digitally documented evidence, disseminated to a world-wide audience to increase their subcultural reputations which are then translated into real capital, both inside and sometimes even outside of the subculture itself.

Subculture theory

Graffiti writers are not a spectacular subculture in the tradition of mods or punks; they do not have a style of dress that announces to the larger society that they are part of a subculture. In fact, writers are cautious and try to remain anonymous around outsiders and have the option of choosing how and when to reveal their secret identities.[8] Graffiti writers were one of the first global subcultures, yet they have been largely ignored by modern and even post-modern subcultural scholars (Hall and Jefferson, 1975; Hebdige, 1979; Muggleton, 2000; Hodkinson, 2002). Subculture theorists focus almost exclusively on participants' style of dress and musical tastes.

In *Resistance Through Rituals*, Hall and Jefferson argue that subculture participation is merely symbolic resistance; it does not have actual effect on the lives of the participants because they can never escape their class position. They write:

> The problematic of a subordinate class experience can be 'lived through' negotiated or resisted; but it cannot be resolved at that level or by those means. There is no 'subcultural career' for the working class lad, no 'solution' in the subcultural milieu, for problems posed by the key structuring experiences of the class.
>
> (Hall and Jefferson, 1975: 47)

They argue that being punk, while interesting for a time and resistant for a moment, is ultimately tragic because participants cannot escape working class oppression. Hence, even though they had spectacular youths, their adult lives, will in all likelihood, be similar to their parents'; rife with occupational boredom and class exploitation.

The Birmingham School also anticipated that the culture industry would quickly market punk style as a commodity for mass consumption (Hebdige, 1979), which meant that subculture resistance was futile and led to the so-called 'death of punk' (Clark, 2003). Clark argues however, that this death also led to punk's rebirth, where new followers are in a constant dialogue with the forces of commodification. He argues that the commodification of stylistically resistant punk, led to the politicization of punk whose consequent forms of resistance were no longer merely symbolic. As Clark writes, 'contemporary punk has forgone these performances of anarchy and is now almost synonymous with the practice of anarchism' (Muggleton and Weinzierl, 2003: 233).

Much like graffiti writers who responded to media criticism by making their own media, Clark argues that punk's experience of witnessing the commodification of their own subculture, politicized them to the point where the spectacular was replaced actual political activism.

Early in the twenty-first century, a new generation of UK scholars, many of whom had subcultural experiences (Hodkinson, 2002; Muggleton and Weinzierl, 2003), reassessed subcultural theory from a post-modern perspective. These 'post-subculturalists' took many of the Birmingham tenets to task; specifically the notion of class homogeneity, and symbolic resistance. However, their focus remains almost exclusively on music subcultures in which participants signal their membership through their style of dress. Subculture studies is still mostly concerned with young people playing dress up, and researchers have for the most part neglected subcultures that do not revolve around a specific type of music.

While contemporary scholars have done an excellent job of dragging subculture studies into the post-modern era, even these conceptions cannot account for cultures like graffiti. Most subculture literature focuses on passionate fans who consume a style of music and dress to identify themselves as such.

While Angela McRobbie (1988; 2002) often gets less credit than her Birmingham colleagues, she has consistently defended young peoples' attempts to make their own lives. Rather than claim an authentic political purity, she argues that subcultures have an 'entrepreneurial dynamic [that] has rarely been acknowledged' (Gelder and Thornton, 1997: 197). This was a fact that most of her colleagues denied or ignored because they were beholden to a political ideology in which any sort of commercialism was evidence of capitalist co-optation. McRobbie takes seriously young peoples' ambitions and desires for success '*on their own terms*', against those who want to judge young people for their complicity with capitalism and consumption (McRobbie, 2002: emphasis added).

It turns out that McRobbie was right about the lasting impact of subculture. The 'entrepreneurial dynamic' has in fact sustained them over the past thirty years and can be attributed in part as a reaction to the boring career choices many young people face. (Thornton, 1996; McRobbie, 2002) While not every subculturalist achieves upward social mobility, it is equally narrow minded to assume that those who do have material success, should be deemed selfish, complicit, apolitical or amoral.

Further, many scholars (Hogan and Astone, 1986; Furstenberg *et al.*, 2004) take it as a given that subculture is something that one leaves as one ages. While many have argued about the significance of subcultural style, whether as symbolic resistance or as a facilitator of post-modern identity, few have theorised the impact that youth subculture participation has on the members themselves as they move into adulthood. Most scholars assert that subculture membership will cease as one gets older, or will lead to more serious forms of criminality, or that these youths will become simply, ordinary, working class adults.

Although success in a subculture leads to increased status within the subculture, my experience with graffiti has shown that kids who write graffiti, and are good at it, have a very good chance of becoming successful adults. There are many reasons for this, from the psychological benefits of fame and respect, to the way in which writing and writers teach each other about art, or the way in which clever young people understand that there is a market for their transgressive activity.

Though it may be an over-simplification to assess subculture on a normative level, subculture scholars from Chicago to Birmingham, all predicted that bad things were going to be in store for these bad kids and this is simply not the case. I have witnessed kids in their teens and twenties going 'wild in the streets' only to become, successful adults. In the literature, this issue is usually framed in terms of co-optation and selling-out, but I would argue that even the Birmingham School would find it difficult to criticise the success of these completely self-made young people.

There are trace elements in the deviant literature of the understanding of subcultures leading to careers (Lachmann, 1988) however, few, if any, have described the impact of youth culture into the adult years. While this may not have had the political impact that Birmingham scholars had hoped for, it is the case that many kids found creative ways to thrive as adults.

While understanding the complexities involved in this foray into consumer culture, I do not intend to suggest that any of these graffiti careerists have sold out graffiti culture. In fact, they are better understood as pioneers who created greater awareness of the power of their medium and the ultimate result may be more opportunities for more young people and less hassle from the police and politicians.

Coda

Stephen Powers (ESPO) made a very successful transition into the art world. He has generated both critical acclaim and financial stability, but he would balk at the notion that he is a street artist.

These days VERT goes by the name Timmy Tattoo. He owns and operates his own tattoo shop in Huntington, Long Island, following a path from graffiti to tattooing, pioneered by early legends like SEEN.

AME, the incredible graffiti talent, is long gone. Matt's transitions were made through some very tumultuous college years. He switched from graphic design, to painting, to sculpture where he excelled. Matt's biggest accomplishment through this time was winning his battle with depression. He completed a two year course in toy design at the Fashion Institute of Technology in New York City, but still has problems with the compromises involved in commercial success.

All in all, the real discovery of this research is that many graffiti writers find ways to make adult careers out of their participation in the graffiti subculture. As the research grew, so did my contacts, and as they aged, they began to focus less on illegal graffiti and more on how to turn their graffiti success into an adult, income generating career.

Notes

1   To all the writers, past and future, thank you for your patience, tolerance and everything that you've taught me. I am humbled by this culture and am honoured to have had the opportunity to tell a bit of your story.
2   The book was listed as 'missing' from most New York City libraries.
3   Writers carry sketchbooks that they call blackbooks which they use to practice outlines and to get autographs from other writers.
4   It is common practice in graffiti magazines to write a writer's name in ALL CAPS, and this practice is repeated here.
5   For more on the early phases of the gallery scene see Witten and Whites (2001: 146–180).
6   In the early 1980s in New York there was a group that called themselves the Photo Kings, who encouraged the trading of flicks with kids in other cities. (ESPO interview, 1996)
7   Author interview, summer 1997.
8   This insight came about through a series of prodding questions from Tony Jefferson at the 'On the Edge: Transgression and the Dangerous Other' conference, John Jay College, August 2007.

References

Alvelos, H. (2004). The Desert of Imagination in the City of Signs: Cultural Implications of Sponsored Transgression and Branded Graffiti, in J. Ferrell, K. Hayward, W. Morrison and M. Presdee (eds), *Cultural Criminology Unleashed* (pp. 181–192). London: Glasshouse.

Ashman, A. (2007). Claw Money Honey: A legendary Graffiti Artist Turned Fashion Designer Cashes in Her Street Cred. *Village Voice*. 27 February, www.villagevoice.com/2007-02-27/art/claw-money-honey/

Atton, C. (2002). *Alternative Media*. London: Sage.

Austin, J. (2001). *Taking the Train*. New York: Columbia University Press.

Becker, H. (1963). *Outsiders: Studies in the Sociology of Deviance*. New York: The Free Press.

Brewer, D. and Miller, M. (1990). Bombing and Burning: The Social Organization and Values of Hip Hop Graffiti Writers and Implications for Policy. *Deviant Behavior*, *11*(4): 345–369.

Brown, D. (2002). *NOV York: Written by a Slave*. New York: Xlibris Corporation.

Castleman, C. (1982). *Getting up: Subway Graffiti in New York*. Cambridge, MA: MIT Press.

Chalfant, H. and Prigoff, J. (1987). *Spraycan Art*. London: Thames and Hudson.

Cooper, M. and Chalfant, H. (1984). *Subway Art*. London: Thames and Hudson.

Duncombe, S. (1997). *Notes from Underground: Zines and the Politics of Alternative Culture*. New York: Verso.

Ferrell, J. (1993). *Crimes of Style: Urban Graffiti and the Politics of Criminality*. New York: Garland Publishing.

Ferrell, J. (1998). Freight Train Graffiti: Subculture, Crime, Dislocation. *Justice Quarterly*, *15*(4): 587–608.

Ferrell, J. and Weide, R. (2010). Spot Theory. *City Journal*, *14*(1): 48–62.

Furstenberg, F., Kennedy, S., McLoyd, V.G., Rumbaut, R.G. and Settersten, R.A. Jr. (2004). Becoming an Adult: The Changing Nature of Early Adulthood. *Contexts*, *3*(3): 33–41.

Gastman, R. (2001). *Free Agents: A History of Washington D.C. Graffiti*. Bethesda, MD: R. Rock Enterprises.

Gelder, K. and Thornton, S. (eds) (1997). *The Subcultures Reader*. New York: Routledge.

Goldstein, R. (1980). In Praise of Graffiti: The Fire down below. *Village Voice*, 24 December, p. 58.

Goldstein, R. (1998). Generation Graff: Branded as Young Vandals, Young Graffiti Writers Bomb on. *Village Voice*, 20 January, p. 59.

Goldstein, R. (1999). The New Real Thing: Barry McGee Throws up in Soho. *Village Voice*, 13 April, p. 41.

Goldstein, R. (2000). The Joy of Bombing: Graffiti's Next Generation Gets up by Any Means Necessary. *Village Voice*, 28 November, 38–40.

Hall, S. and Jefferson, T. (eds) (1975). *Resistance through Rituals: Youth Subcultures in Postwar Britain*. London: Hutchinson.

Hebdige, D. (1979). *Subculture: The Meaning of Style*. London: Routledge.

Hodkinson, P. (2002). *Goth: Identity, Style and Subculture*. Oxford: Berg.

Hogan, D. and Astone, N. (1986). The Transition to Adulthood. *Annual Review of Sociology*, *12*: 109–130.

Katz, J. (1988). *Seductions of Crime*. New York: Basic Books.

Kramer, R. (2010). Moral Panics and Urban Growth Machines: Official Reactions to Graffiti in New York City, 1990–2005. *Qualitative Sociology*, *33*(3), 297–311.

Lachmann, R. (1988). Graffiti as Career and Ideology. *American Journal of Sociology*, *94*(2): 229–250.

Macdonald, N. (2001). *The Graffiti Subculture: Youth, Masculinity and Identity in London and New York*. London: Palgrave.

McRobbie, A. (ed.) (1988). *Zoot Suits and Second Hand Dresses: An Anthology of Fashion and Music*. Boston: Unwin Hyman.

McRobbie, A. (2002). Clubs to Companies: Notes on the Decline of Political Culture in Speeded up Creative Worlds. *Cultural Studies*, *16*(4), 516–531.

Miller, I. (2002). *Aerosol Kingdom: Subway Painters of New York City*. Jackson, MS: University Press of Mississippi.

Muggleton, D. (2000). *Inside Subculture: The Postmodern Meaning of Style*. London: Berg.

Muggleton, D. and Weinzierl, R. (eds) (2003). *The Post-Subcultures Reader*. London: Berg.

Phillips, S. (1999). *Wallbangin': Graffiti and Gangs in L.A.* Chicago: University of Chicago Press.

Powers, S. (1999). *The Art of Getting over: Graffiti at the Millennium*. New York: St. Martin's Press.

Pressler, J. (2006). Remember Zines? Look at Them Now. *New York Times*, 7 May, p. 14.

Rose, A. and Strike, C. (eds) (2004). *Beautiful Losers: Contemporary Art and Street Culture*. New York: Iconoclast.

Schmidlapp, D. and Phase 2. (1996). *Style: Writing from the Underground, (R)evolutions of Aerosol Linguistics*. Terni, Italy: Stampa Alternativa in Association with IGTimes.

Snyder, G. (2009). *Graffiti Lives. Beyond the Tag in New York's Urban Underground*. New York: New York University Press.

Stewart, J. (1989). Subway Graffiti: An Aesthetic Study of Graffiti on the Subway System of New York City, 1970–1978. Ph.D Dissertation, New York University.

Sutherland, P. (2004). *Autograf: New York City's Graffiti Writers*. Text by REVS. New York: Powerhouse Books.

Thornton, S. (1996). *Club Cultures: Music, Media and Subcultural Capital*. Cambridge, UK: Polity Press.

Walsh, M. (1996). *Graffito*. San Francisco, CA: North Atlantic Books.

Wimsatt, W. (1994). *Bomb the Suburbs*. Chicago, IL: Subway and Elevated Press.

Witten, A. and White, M. (2001). *DONDI, Style Master General*. New York: Harper Collins.

Part III

Regional/municipal variations/differences of graffiti and street art[1]

Jeffrey Ian Ross

Introduction

Graffiti and street art appear in different regions, countries, and cities. What does this mean? Not all graffiti and street art is the same, nor are the people who engage in this activity, the dynamics among them, their influences, subject matter, and places where they pursue their work. In short, considerable variability exists. In order to get as comprehensive a picture of graffiti and street art throughout the world as possible, it is important to review who the major players in the local graffiti and street art scene are or were. It is also useful to have a sense of the dominant images, symbols, and icons employed by the writers/artists. In many cases, each city has a set of particular norms that are shared among local graffiti/street artists. In the instances of variations from these norms, this section's contributors speculate as to why these differences have developed.

Although graffiti/street art is a worldwide phenomenon, some regions and continents appear to play more prominent roles than others in terms of the proliferation of this particular art form/vandalism. The regions that the contributors see as being of great importance to the proliferation of graffiti/street art are North America, Western Europe, South America, Eastern Europe, and Australia/Oceana. In regions such as Africa, Asia, the Middle East, and Southeast Asia, however, graffiti/street art appears to be less prominent.

Although examining countries or regions as a whole is a worthwhile point of comparison, few scholars of graffiti/street art examine these activities on a country or regional basis, and most ethnographies of graffiti/street art look at the city as the unit of analysis.[2] This is perhaps because of the primacy of ethnography as a research tool in this subject area. In general, it is very difficult to perform a competent ethnography on graffiti/street art in a region larger than a single city.

Overview of chapters

This part of the book consists of eleven detailed studies of graffiti and/or street art in major international cities and/or contexts. Similar to the work of Ferrell, Kramer, Macdonald, and

215

Snyder, these chapters review the history, locations, major writers/artists/crews, content, and responses by various communities. These responses include but are not limited to artists, writers, galleries, the wider public (especially moral entrepreneurs actively working against the production of graffiti and street art), local/municipal politicians, departments of public works, law enforcement, criminal justice practitioners, the art world, and local businesses. With few exceptions, the city chapters will cover the time span of the 1980s to present. These chapters selectively integrate various social scientific theories and the authors' own ethnographic research. The chapters do not focus on specific graffiti/street artists/crews or neighborhoods.

In "From the city walls to 'Clean Trains:' graffiti and street art in New York City, 1969–1990," Joe A. Austin argues that although graffiti and street art both have complex origins in multiple locations, New York City (NYC) was the key site for their emergence in the U.S., and as a "world city," NYC was also an important spring board for the global spread of graffiti/street art after the mid-1980s. Graffiti art's characteristic typographic conventions and forms of social production developed in the NYC subway yards during the early to mid-1970s, and were significantly influenced by city government suppression and removal strategies in the "war on graffiti." As city efforts to keep graffiti art off of the subways became effective in the mid-1980s, artists turned to new spaces (streets, walls, and freight trains) and innovated new forms (stickers and "productions"). A growing graffiti media presence circulated the work worldwide, and important new centers of production appeared on the U.S. West Coast and in Europe. By the end of the 1990s, NYC had become a leading member in a global graffiti art network. The established example of graffiti art, as well as NYC's post-WWII status as the "Art Capital of the World," were important contexts for the emergence of street art in the city during the 1980s. Graffiti artists joined urban "outsider" artists and traditionally trained gallery artists in experimenting with new forms of "unauthorized" art in the city's public spaces. By the turn of the century, graffiti/street art had become iconic elements in the struggles over NYC's neoliberal development strategies (e.g. gentrification), while also gaining a level of legitimacy that renewed debates about the unsteady connections between political struggle and artistic production.

"'Boost or blight?' Graffiti writing and street art in the 'new' New Orleans," by Doreen Piano, examines graffiti/street art's role in the renewal of public culture in post-Hurricane Katrina New Orleans, by examining how public space has been contested in the aftermath of disaster. The author investigates how the multiple responses to and uses of graffiti within New Orleans have been situated within larger debates over the city's future. Through descriptive analysis, Piano illustrates how the street art/graffiti culture has become what *Times-Picayune* art critic Doug MacCash called "the most vital art movement of the past decade in New Orleans." Additionally, Piano's case study points to how social media has become an essential tool for graffiti writers/street artists to create informal networks and engage with global audiences.

Anna Wacławek's chapter, "Pop culture and politics: graffiti and street art in Montréal," traces the history of Montréal's signature graffiti writing culture, which emerged in the early 1990s when a couple of French tourists introduced the city to tagging. A few years later, the "second wave" of the Montréal scene, characterized by painting in makeshift spaces physically and ideologically removed from the cityscape's visual culture, was in full effect. Abandoned warehouses and factories, as well as highways and train yards were among the breeding grounds of local hand styles and letterforms. These sites became emblematic of what it meant to write graffiti in Montréal during this period; far removed from the city center, a subculture was brewing. These developments eventually led not only to the creation of "Under Pressure," the largest international graffiti festival in North America, but also to the creation of numerous impressive commission, permission, and legal walls. As the subculture blossomed within the downtown core and in various other neighborhoods, participation grew and the city began enforcing stricter penalties for graffiti writing. At the same time, street artists, whose practices are universally more tolerated and enjoyed by the general public than by municipal authorities, were transforming the local scene both visually and politically as Montréal residents began opening up the age-old debate of art vs. crime. In this chapter, the specificities of urban painting in Montréal are explored with regard to local politics, visual culture, and socio-cultural particularities as formative factors in the city's distinct graffiti/street art scenes.

In Chile, unsanctioned open-air propaganda painting has been a political tool since the 1960s. Hip-hop graffiti writers, who emerged during the latter part of Chile's military dictatorship (1973–1990) and whose work took off during the first decades of Chile's interminable "transition" to a fully democratic system, had a different audience and objectives from political mural groups to the extent that both sides recognize that there was an "abyss" between their respective subcultures. Their only shared aim was to illegally appropriate prominent public spaces; their common enemy was government-backed erasures. The hub of activity was the capital, Santiago, through which the Mapocho River flows as a main artery. Rodney Palmer's chapter, "The battle for public space along the Mapocho River, Santiago de Chile, 1964–2014," gives an historical perspective to the left-wing protest murals, anarchic graffiti, and the fusion of the two impulses in the international twenty-first-century phenomenon of the "graffiti mural." Palmer also addresses the censorship of all kinds of libertarian art and its impact on Chile's chronically polarized socio-cultural front lines.

"London calling: contemporary graffiti and street art in the UK's Capital" by Jeffrey Ian Ross examines why London has become a magnate for graffiti and street art, and the people who engage in this kind of activity, and profit from it. Although graffiti and street art is found in most parts of London, the chapter outlines the three principal locations in the U.K. capital; Camden, East London and Leake Street in Waterloo. Additional factors such as the legal context, and how graffiti and street art is tolerated by some councils and not by others is discussed. The chapter continues by examining the paucity of existing scholarship on this topic including the 2002 report commissioned by the London Assembly. Notable London-based graffiti and street artists such as Solo One, Banksy, King Robbo, and EINE are described. The chapter finishes by providing a brief history of contemporary graffiti and street art in London, including the increasing acceptability and recognition of the importance of this type of vandalism and art for its' aesthetic and economic benefits it provides.

Shifting over to the continent, the Parisian graffiti scene was born long before the contemporary graffiti crossed the Atlantic Ocean, coming from the United States. During the early 1930s, Brassaï was already taking photos of the graffiti he saw all over the city to track the urban changes. May 1968 remains another key cultural moment in this history, when student protestors expressed their often surrealist demands in the form of graffiti (e.g. "Beneath the paving stones, the sea"). In the 1980s, hip-hop related graffiti arrived in Paris, also helped by some American writers, such as Jonone from the crew 156 All Starz, who fixed residence in the city. In "Graffiti and street art in Paris," written by David Fieni, the author traces the origins of this contemporary work over the years, the locations where it has occurred and some well-known writers and artists, such as Bando, Blek le Rat, Mode 2, Invader, Skii, Ash.2, OENO, Miss.Tic, Dja'louz, Septik, El-Seed, l'Atlas, Monsieur Chat, Seth, Levalet, and Mygolo 2000. Fieni focuses his overview on three key relationships: that between the city of Paris itself and the outlying suburbs and housing estates; the fluid lines between the categories of graffiti and street art; and the way that the axes of illegality and aesthetics have intersected and informed the production of graffiti in the context of Paris.

In "From Marx to Merkel: political muralism and street art in Lisbon," Ricardo Campos provides an analysis of the post-revolutionary period following the Carnation Revolution of

1974, when the walls of Lisbon became the repository for many political murals made by various political parties, particularly from the left wing. At the time, this was a socially accepted way of political communication. Therefore, Marxist and Maoist iconography was very present in the urban visualscape. These murals slowly vanished, giving way in the 1990s to American-inspired graffiti. Driven by a globalized hip-hop culture particularly present in the media, tags, throw-ups, and masterpieces gradually acquired a significant place in the metropolitan area of Lisbon. These visual expressions were present not only on city walls, but also on trains and subway carriages, following the most relevant North American graffiti tradition. The spread of legal and illegal graffiti in the 2000s slowly generated a public reaction of discomfort, particularly because of the street bombing in the central and historical quarters of Lisbon. Subsequently, a graffiti abatement program was established and an overall increased control over graffiti was put in action. It soon became apparent that graffiti/street art was now considered a kind of urban blight. In recent years, two phenomena are noteworthy. On the one hand, the non-sanctioned, unofficial political mural produced by graffiti writers and street artists has reemerged because of the severe economic and social crisis affecting Portugal, and, on the other hand, there has been official consecration and legitimation of many Portuguese street artists through promotion by public entities, cultural entrepreneurs, museums, and art dealers. This chapter seeks to provide a description of the historical evolution of these expressions in Lisbon, analyzing the social, cultural, and urban impact of these changes. The data presented is based on ethnographic research conducted by the author and on several projects carried out on this topic over the last decade.

Graffiti and street art have figured prominently in pre- and post-revolution Egypt. In "The field of graffiti and street art in post-January 2011 Egypt," Mona Abaza describes and analyzes this expansion in terms of artistic networks mobilizing for complex projects, mediating events that prompted new cycles of graffiti, and changing techniques that made street art more democratic in the propagation of downloadable stencils and, at the same time, more refined. In 2012, several formally trained artists shifted the canvas of their work to prominent walls in Cairo, Alexandria, Mansoura, Luxor, and Ismailia, and this work came to be perceived as part of the broader public art movement, folding back into the significance of artistic networks and common points of entry for broad participation. The tension between "high" and "low" painting techniques and imagery – allegory and freehand painting versus tagging and stencils – remains an ongoing debate, though it productively enriched the range of styles seen in Egyptian street art and fostered the perception that fine art belonged to the Egyptian people rather than to the gallery elites. In keeping with the temporal horizons of revolution that shaped the post-January 25 street art, Abaza discusses several pivotal events that led to the rapid organization of work in response to state violence, martyrdom, and elections. She focuses specifically on the roles of two groups that have been underrepresented in the literature on Egyptian street art: the Ultras and women. The Ultras are a highly organized group of soccer/football fans that have engaged in revolutionary protests over the last three years, actions that are in keeping with their strident, pre-revolution stance against the police state. Their influence on the graffiti scene in Egypt is significant, though under-documented. In addition, Abaza analyzes the role of women as iconic representations and as artists. Representations of women are critical components of most Egyptian street art images, and they are often related to the specter of abuse and gendered violence. In reaction, female artists have been involved in generating new work and posing questions about "space claiming" and female representation, both of which have traditionally been biased toward masculinist markings of domains and themes. Women are now presenting alternative modes of space-claiming and thematizing, and Abaza explains the factors responsible for expanding the participation of women in street art. She concludes her contribution by addressing the recent criminalization of street art, punishable by fines and imprisonment, and the ways that the law has been applied selectively in order to target work that criticizes the military regime. The distinction between the broad criminalization afforded by legal changes and criminalized critique is significant, and can be traced through patterns of arrests and shifts in subject matter.

Also in the Middle East, the Palestinian-Israeli conflict has inspired considerable graffiti and street art. In "Wall talk: Palestinian graffiti," Julie Peteet reviews the current state of graffiti from the Palestinian perspective. In the wake of the First Intifada (uprising) against the Israeli occupation of the West Bank and Gaza, the author published an article on the then-ubiquitous graffiti dotting the built environment in Palestine. Graffiti continues to proliferate, as do large, colorful murals painted by Palestinians, as well as foreigners, including most famously, work by Banksy. In the aftermath of the Second Intifada, continuing occupation and dispossession, and most significantly, the construction of the 24-foot high cement wall that snakes through the West Bank, graffiti and murals convey a markedly different message. In the First Intifada, before the advent of cell phones and the Internet, graffiti was a means of circumventing Israeli censorship of Palestinian expression and communicating directives, as well as proclaiming opposition to the occupation. Most graffiti was written in Arabic and signed by various political parties. More recent graffiti is in languages other than Arabic, particularly English, and much of it is written by foreigners and is personal in its commentary. The West Bank wall serves as a canvas, a sort of international bulletin board, on which Palestinians and foreigners proclaim opposition to Israeli actions, solidarity with the Palestinians, and commentary on the wall. Political affiliations are less pronounced in their presence. With the Israeli policy of separation, the writing on the walls elicits little Israeli response, unlike in the First Intifada when jeeps rushed to blacken out graffiti or residents were compelled to paint over it.

Next, "Graffiti/street art in Tokyo and surrounding districts" (Chapter 26) by Hidetsugu Yamakoshi and Yasumasa Sekine, argue that this movement began during the 1970s, when Rocco Satoshi, one of the originators of street art in Japan, began to draw murals on the walls of Sakuragi-cho district in Yokohama (near Tokyo). During the 1980s, others imitated his style. In the 1990s, the first generation of Japanese graffiti writers travelled to the United States to learn about graffiti. Thereafter, graffiti writing spread among the youth who did their work on the walls of Sakuragi-cho, transforming this area into a "graffiti and street art sanctuary."

From the 1990s through the 2000s, graffiti culture developed considerably in Japan. In 2005, the first large scale exhibition "X-Color/Graffiti in Japan" was held. As graffiti and street art proliferated, it sometimes caused conflicts between artists and the local governments. In the mid-1990s, for example, Junichirou Take, a well-known street artist, was arrested for protesting local government efforts to chase homeless people out from the Shinjuku station yard in Tokyo.

In order to deal with difficult situations like this, the Non-Profit Organization "KOMPOSITION" started to mediate between the local municipal administrations and the graffiti writers/street artists. However many writers/artists refuse to cooperate, because they want to draw freely and that the essence of graffiti/street art is about acting illegally. Under the strengthening tendency of "societies of control" in Deleuze's sense, the battlefield of writers and street artists are marginalized and cornered spatially and temporally but it does not mean their activities are diminishing or inactive. They are continuously searching the edge of the governing system and there unchangingly working is the iron law that new creativities are born only in the liminal domain of predicament.

Next, in "Claiming spaces for urban art images in Beijing and Shanghai," Minna Valjakka challenges the prevailing assumption that because contemporary graffiti/street art trends are global and transcultural, they are similar and homogenous around the globe. When Zhang Dali first brought graffiti to Beijing in the mid-1990s, he did not put up his name with alphabetic letters, but instead, by spraying an outline of his profile. Later, he modified his work by chiseling a hole shaped like his profile into the walls of buildings slated to be demolished. Neither of Zhang's markers fit into the common Euro-American understanding of graffiti as form of vandalism based on writing one's name with spray paints or marker pens. Nonetheless, Zhang claims he is the first graffiti writer in Mainland China. Evidently, the notions of graffiti (tuya), graffiti art (tuya yishu), and street art (jietou yishu) vary greatly from one creator to the next, and do not always correspond to the Euro-American perceptions.

As John Clark (1998) has shown, the transfer of a visual system from one cultural area to another is essentially based on adaptation and cannot be regarded as mere imitation. When visual systems are transferred from one cultural area to another, the complex process depends on varying modes of transfer. Even the intentions of the visual system can be changed. Indeed, Valjakka illustrates how local creators in Beijing and Shanghai have challenged, adapted and modified the transcultural norms and features for their own, indigenous needs. In order to assist a more open minded study of this visual phenomenon in mainland China, Valjakka applies the broader concept of "urban art images" to denote creative action that leaves a visible imprint, even a short-lived one, on public urban space. Inspired by James Elkins' (1999) suggestion of a trichotomy of an image, Valjakka regards urban art images as reproductions that can include writing (in any language), pictures and three-dimensional objects – or any combination of these – as the most appropriate approach to the complex scenes today. The reproductions can be legal or illegal, commissioned, or voluntarily made, resulting from private or collective actions. Valjakka's contribution suggests that the close analysis of the urban art images in terms of Chineseness depends primarily on the nationality/ethnicity of the creator, the language, content, visual signifiers, and site-responsivity of the urban art image.

Finally, "Contesting transcultural trends: emerging self-identities and urban art images in Hong Kong," also by Minna Valjakka, argues that the first known tags appeared in Hong Kong in the 1980s and were created by foreigners. Despite this early appearance, it was not until the late 1990s that the first local crews emerged. Hong Kong is known as a hectic business city, where new forms of visual arts around the globe intersect and mutate. The foreign creators of urban art images, whether they were living in or passing through the city, have left their marks on the walls and inspired collaborations with local creators. How have the locals shaped their own identity and self-expression as Hongkongnese in this on-going transcultural interaction? How do the local creators interact with Mainland Chinese creators? What kind of visual signifiers of Hongkongness are employed in the urban art images? Based on extensive fieldwork periods in 2012–2013, thousands of photographs, and information derived from ongoing communication with over sixty creators, this chapter examines the main characteristics of the urban art scene in Hong Kong compared with mainland China. The main focus is on the question of Hongkongness, and how it is expressed in the perceptions of the creators and the urban art images.

Omissions

Missing from this collection are analyses of a handful of cities with established graffiti/street art traditions. At the very least, this list includes cities such as *Barcelona, Berlin, Bologna, Buenos Aires* (e.g. Kane, 2009), *Frankfurt, Johannesburg, Madrid, Melbourne* (e.g. Young, 2010), *Miami, Milan, Moscow* (e.g. Bushnell, 1990), *Perth, São Paulo, Sydney* (e.g. Mcauliffe, 2012), and *Toronto* (Bowen, 1999).[3] That being said, adding more cities raises the possibly unanswerable question of how many cities are necessary in order to provide a comprehensive treatment. Despite these omissions, the work contained here should give the reader an ample idea of the range of work and reactions to graffiti and street art in the localities reviewed in this section.

Notes

1 Special thanks to Stefano Bloch, Rachel Hildebrandt and Ronald Kramer for their comments.
2 An alternative unit of analysis could be "scenes" or intention (e.g. political, agnomen, art for art's sake, etc.) as a valid basis of comparison.
3 The listing of citations in this section is meant to be illustrative and not comprehensive.

References

Bowen, T.E. (1999). Graffiti art: A contemporary study of Toronto artists, *Studies in Art Education*, 41(1), 22–39.

Bushnell, J. (1990). *Moscow Graffiti*. Boston, MA: Unwin Hyman.

Kane, S.C. (2009). Stencil graffiti in urban waterscapes of Buenos Aires and Rosario, Argentina, *Crime, Media, Culture*, 5(1), 9–28.

Mcauliffe, C. (2012). Graffiti or street art? Negotiating moral geographies of the creative city, *Journal of Urban Affairs*, 34(2), 189–206.

Young, A. (2010). Negotiated consent or zero tolerance? Responding to graffiti and street art in Melbourne, *City*, 14(1/2), 99–114.

17

From the city walls to 'Clean Trains'

Graffiti in New York City, 1969–1990

Joe A. Austin

Introduction

In general, graffiti is an unauthorised text comprised of images and pictures inscribed, written, drawn and/or painted within easily visible, densely populated urban public spaces. This very broad categorisation is complicated by its multiple and contested points of production across time, incorporating the entire multi-millennial history of human cities. Have scholars of 'graffiti' been studying the same objects and practices? Art historian Jack Stewart pieced together an extensive classification of graffiti from prior academic studies and concluded that the New York City graffiti of the early 1970s, called *writing* by its early creators, was significantly different from any other type scholars have observed across human history, citing its repetition and ubiquity across urban space, the size of individual works and its aesthetic intentions (Stewart, 1989). Based on Stewart's research on past scholarly categories of the '[human-made] scratchings on the wall', and for the purposes of this chapter, I will adopt the term 'graffiti art' to describe this new phenomenon (Lefebvre, 1968; Kofman and Lebas, 1996; Austin, 2010). Although 'graffiti art' appeared first in Philadelphia sometime around the mid-1960s (Stewart, 1989; Powers, 1999), it was 'from New York City' (with much thanks to the city's global media hub) that the wider world became aware of graffiti art and observed the first public and municipal actions taken in response as it developed over time.

The New York City graffiti art scene has reproduced itself for almost a half-century, and has served as the primary site for several of the existing book-length, English language academic histories and ethnographies on graffiti art (e.g. Castleman, 1982; Stewart, 1989; Austin, 2001; Macdonald, 2001; Miller, 2002; Snyder, 2009), as well as numerous participant and observer reports on its development across time (e.g. Fedorchak, 2005; Cooper, 2008; Felisbret, 2009; Farrell and Pape, 2010). In order to better understand some of the origins of modern day graffiti, this chapter covers the main developments within the New York City graffiti art scene from its beginnings in the late 1960s until the early 'clean train era' in the 1990s.

From graffiti to writing

New York City was by no means the first city on the planet to host a self-organized youth graffiti scene (Levitt, 1965, 1987; Ley and Cybriwsky, 1974; Cesaretti, 1975). There are reliable records of graffiti traditions among urban young people since at least the nineteenth century (Sheon, 1976). Even within New York City, there were local graffiti practices among young people well before its new forms appeared (Phase 2 and Schmidlapp, 1996; Austin, 2001) and these are important precursors since there is no evidence that graffiti art or artists migrated from Philly until after the scene was well established in NYC. Educator Hebert Kohl observed a thriving neighbourhood graffiti tradition in New York City's Spanish Harlem during the mid-1960s that had existed long enough to produce 'layers of graffiti' in local alleyways (Hinton and Kohl, 1972). Almost all of the contenders for the title of the first graffiti artist in New York City cite a predecessor as their inspiration. Most origin stories of graffiti art in New York City (as narrated by early participants) begin in upper Manhattan or the Bronx in 1968 or 1969 (Phase 2 and Schmidlapp, 1996; Fedorchak, 2005; Felisbret, 2009), but each account also reflects experiences within a particular neighbourhood or city area. This geographic specificity suggests that the new graffiti in NYC had multiple, independent points of origin that coalesced into a common social phenomenon at some later point.

By 1970, a significant number of young people were *writing* 'tags', most using ink markers, in shared public spaces along their daily pathways as they travelled to their jobs, schools, shopping and socialising. Invariably this carried them across the city. New *writers* joined the practice through imitation and association, and a cross-borough peer network developed, along with an evolving set of shared norms (Ehrlich and Ehrlich, 2007). The new graffiti art was based on the repeated and stylised presentation of an invented name, something akin to both the signature and the advertising logo. Creativity in the design of the name was highly valued, as was its repetition and unexpected placements within urban space (Castleman, 1982; Stewart, 1989). Three of the early artists' norms remained relatively stable for the first two decades: A *writer* did not adopt the name of another *writer* without a significant distinguishing feature; a *writer* did not write over the name of another unless the underlying name was fully covered or as an intentionally provocative act; and all paint and markers had to be stolen (although these materials might be swapped or sold among graffiti artists after their initial shoplift). Since most of the early *writers* were junior high/middle school and high school students, their choice of surfaces were made with a youth audience in mind.

Buses and bus stops, stairwells, signs along the sidewalks, ice cream trucks and the inside surfaces of subway cars were early favourite spots (Ferrell and Weide, 2010). One of the goals of the activity was to have one's name become famous but otherwise be disassociated with the individual who wrote it, a careful balance between visual ubiquity and personal anonymity (Austin, 2001; Shuterlan, 2004, Campos, 2012). Within the early peer culture of *writers*, of course, the individual sought respect, and a social hierarchy formed. Status could be negotiated around the social scenes at particular locations, most notably the Writers Corner at 188 St. and Audubon Avenue in Manhattan that was tended by STITCH 1, and a bit later, the Writers Benches at the 149th Street and Concourse subway station in the Bronx and the Atlantic Avenue station in Brooklyn (Miller, 2002). As the status system among the new graffiti artists formed and developed, on the lowest end were 'toys', the term attached to inexperienced or poorly-performing writers, who were assumed to lack talent or seriousness and devotion to the art. At the highest status positions were 'kings' whose ubiquity within a particular space (e.g. particular bus lines, subway lines, neighbourhoods) and distinctiveness in design and/or location were widely admired and whose valued contributions to *writing* had reached a broad consensus (Castleman, 1982; Stewart, 1989).

Graffiti art, the public sphere, and the 'war on graffiti'

In 1971, a *New York Times* journalist tracked down and interviewed TAKI 183, a prominent graffiti writer, for an article, which included a substantial photograph of his tag amidst a host of others on a neighbourhood door. TAKI 183 may not have been the first graffiti artist in the city, and was perhaps more noticeable to the public than most other writers because his job – a messenger – carried him to areas of the city where few other writers commonly travelled. He particularly concentrated his *writing* on buildings and walls that might be passed by the city's media and advertising professionals. It worked. The early *Times* article initiated the graffiti artists' long lasting attention to the news media's pages, screens and cameras for evidence of their work, which suggested that city dwellers more generally, not just youth, were interested in the graffiti artists' work as well. This development was a key turning point in most of the academic and vernacular histories of graffiti art, and many claim that the number of new *writers* exploded soon after (Castleman, 1982; Austin, 2001).

By 1972, graffiti art was perhaps better described as a citywide youth subculture than a peer network, with specific centers of production and recognisable stylistics developing within the boroughs of Manhattan, the Bronx and Brooklyn. The ink marker was increasingly supplemented by the spray paint can as the artists' works increased in size. The artists began to collectively map out and explore the Metro Transit Authority's (MTA) extensive subway car storage system to gain access to the exterior surfaces of the cars during the late evening hours and weekends. The works on the outside of the subways were larger and more aesthetically elaborate as the artists gained control of their painting technique and their collective work developed new motifs and typographies (Stewart, 1989). While New Yorkers might have been able to mostly ignore the tags on the walls and the buses, the increasing size of the works on the outside of the subway trains were unavoidable, visible on the elevated lines from a distance and often covering over the windows and making it difficult for riders to see out and inside the cars (Farrell and Pape, 2010). The surfaces of the subway system – mostly underground, mostly late at night – became hotly contested spaces for both the MTA and the graffiti artists, with the City of New York and the MTA declaring 'war on graffiti' within six months after the TAKI article in the *Times*. Both municipal organisations now sought out and competed for the attentions if not the approval of the subway riders, the various media that observed and represented the city, and with varying degrees of awareness, a wider national and global audience (Austin, 2001; Greenberg, 2008).

The subway era

The New York City subway system – the major transportation artery of the city- covered more than 750 miles and flowed through multiple lines into four city boroughs, transporting almost four million people a day through a city with a residential population of more than seven million during the first two decades of graffiti art history. The circulation of the trains was an ideal broadcast system for the large, mural-sized works that graffiti artists painted on the trains. The trains circulated new and existing works among the artists, and were also frequently addressed to the city at large, as well as any camera that turned that way. Several of the key and most prolific writers have claimed that they were both talking *to* other New Yorkers, as well as talking *as* New Yorkers promoting their hometown. Graffiti art thus developed as a movement in dialogue with the real and imagined City, and many of its most ferocious critics (e.g. Mayor John Lindsay, Mayor Ed Koch, sociologists Nathan Glazer, the *Times* editorial staff) were most appalled by the way they understood graffiti art to be representing the city (Brooks, 1997; Austin, 2001; Greenberg, 2008).

As the art developed in size and sophistication on the outside of the subway cars, the artists developed a vocabulary to classify their works, distinguishing the smaller 'tag' from the larger 'piece', and then further classifying pieces by the spaces they covered on the sides of a standard train car (e.g. 'window down', 'ends', 'whole car'), as well as the lettering style (e.g. inflated 'softie' letters, sharp-edged '3-D') and motif (e.g. 'clouds', 'shines'). Aesthetic innovation continued to progress as writers learned from each other and gained experience controlling the paint spray and also experimenting with replacing the original paint nozzles ('caps') with those from other products, like spray starch or oven cleaner, to create new effects (Castleman, 1982; Stewart, 1989). With each innovation, the standards for fame within the subculture rose, and mastery of a substantial body of subcultural knowledge was necessary to successfully compete at the highest levels (Becker, 1982; Austin, 2001; Campos, 2012).

Organizational innovations developed alongside increasing size and aesthetic sophistication of the works. New York City graffiti art appeared during the apex of territorial street gangs (youth subcultures enforcing exclusive claims to some social and criminal resources within a bounded neighbourhood 'turf'; see, e.g. Ley and Cybriwsky, 1974; Hazlehurst and Hazlehurst, 1998, and some of the first writers' organisations were borrowed from the street gang model, with the EX-VANDALS and THE EBONY DUKES among the most well-known. These early graffiti gangs were noticeably more efficient in covering the city with their individual and collective names, but their successes also attracted the attention of territorial gangs, and most artists were not looking for a life of fighting; many had explicitly taken up graffiti art as an alternative to the local territorial gang (Hager, 1984; Stewart, 1989). These early *writing* gangs dissolved into smaller 'crews', usually ten members or less, and this remains the basic productive organisation for most graffiti artists to this day. Individual graffiti art works commonly incorporate the artist's crews' initials (usually two or three letters) into the work or are placed nearby. In the 1970s, The Fabulous Partners (TFP), Three Yard Boys (3YB), Independents (INDS) and The Crazy 5 (TC5) were among many famous crews (Chalfant and Cooper, 1984; Fedorchak, 2005).

Crews served a multitude of functions, including friendship, protection and back-ups during fights, lookouts for cops, art teachers and art critics. Like a winning sports team, a crew gained fame from the collective glow of its members. A novice might be brought into a crew in any number of ways, e.g., as a kind of apprentice or protégé to a more experienced writer, or introduced through a social connection with one of the members or for having established a bit of fame as an individual prior to joining the crew. In this capacity, the novice received advanced instruction in the locations of the car storage lots, the various entrances and exits (often holes cut into surrounding fences), how to navigate the electrified 'third rail' that powered the trains, how to steal paint, visual design elements, and how to manipulate the can and the paint spray successfully (Becker, 1982; Castleman, 1982; Austin, 2001; Bengtsen, 2014). Although the artists' status system made 'biting' another writer's style (appropriating without permission) a constant point of contention (sometimes addressed through fighting), the competition among artists was balanced against the common endeavour in advancing the art and outfoxing the authorities. Cooperation, technique sharing and constructive criticism were more common than fisticuffs, particularly in the first several years as the *writers'* culture was taking shape (Castleman, 1982; Stewart, 1989).

Who became a graffiti artist in New York City? There is some consensus on broad generalities, and some reliable individual and small group case studies, but otherwise we have only anecdotes and partial perspectives. We know that individual writers wrote for varying lengths of time and with differing commitments (not always continuous), and the names and identities of most 'toys' (low-status novices, the vast majority of artists) are not part of the scene's long-term collective memory; artists recalling 'the early days' are much more likely to report on those who (eventually) gained fame or were part of an important crew, and these 'famous' individuals form the basis for their memories of 'writers' in a general sense. It appears that most of the early graffiti writers were from working class origins, with the majority (but by no means all) of them being kids of colour, and that most of them were young men, aged about twelve to eighteen years. We cannot be certain of how many young people were actively *writing* at any one time, but it appears that their numbers grew rapidly until about 1973, and after that time may have stabilised at a significantly lower number. Young women participated in the early years, including several key figures (e.g. Barbara 62, Eva 62, Charmin 65, Lady Heart, Stoney, Z-73). Stewart identifies 123 females among the more than 2900 graffiti names in his appendices, with estimates of around 5–10 per cent of all graffiti artists being women. Many of these young females did not follow when the graffiti scene moved almost exclusively onto the subway trains after about 1973, and it appears that the subway scene did not encourage or support their participation, with a few notable exceptions (e.g. Lady Pink). Several observers note 1973–1974 as a transition period when some of the 'first generation' of artists retired and many of the less-committed novices left the scene (Castleman, 1982; Stewart, 1989).

The 1973 repainting and the origins of the throw-up

Although the *Times* article that solidified the fame of TAKI 183 in graffiti art history had been relatively amused and sympathetic in tone, the MTA and NYC Mayor John Lindsay, then running for presidential nomination, were not pleased. Subsequent reporting on graffiti in the *Times* described it as a 'plague' on the city, and tended towards a demonization of the artists that attempted to incite a moral panic. The city government called for a 'war on graffiti'. While the general phenomenon of these 'wars' is covered in a separate chapter in this handbook, the topic is important in the history of New York City because the early attempts to 'wipe out' graffiti became historic opportunities for innovation and expansion within the graffiti art world. Initially only garnering a reprimand from a municipal judge, the city and the MTA police force collaborated on new punishments, including 'Saturday train cleaning duty'. These collectivised punishments had the ironic effect of bringing writers together from all over the city, creating social spaces for new graffiti art collaborations as well as exchanges of technique and other useful knowledge. Piecemeal attempts to paint over the works had proven inadequate – the 'work ethic' of graffiti artists was no match for the MTA before the system's technological improvements in the early 1980s. With no real understanding of the subculture and its collective motivations, the MTA attempted, during the last few months of 1973, to rapidly repaint the entire fleet of more than 7000 cars, assuming this massive undertaking to obliterate the existing history of graffiti art would demoralise the artists and discourage new artists from beginning. There are some suggestions that the repainting may have depressed the overall number of graffiti artists, although equally viable alternative explanations for the drop have been proposed. Of particular note, MCing, DJing and breakdancing coalesced into a new Bronx party culture around this time (later called hip-hop), and provided another, less criminalising and more social, creative gathering for youthful energies (Hager, 1984; see below).

The repainting effort solved the subculture's problem of space, since the outside of the trains had been saturated. An earlier 'spatial fix', the 'cloud' motif which both covered over any underlying works and served as a 'background' for a new writer's work, became less acceptable as the scale of the art works on the trains moved towards the 'whole car'. The MTA's 1973 repainting effort supplied more than 14,000 new 'blank' surfaces (two 'whole cars' per individual subway car) and this opportunity allowed writers to jump the usual scale of their work, with whole-car works becoming increasingly common. Writers also took the MTA's repainting as a direct challenge to their work ethic, and immediately set about retaking the trains. In this effort, a new form was developed and perfected, the 'throw-up', a quickly-executed two-letter abbreviation of the writers name usually in a lighter coloured 'bubble letter' style, outlined in a darker colour. An accomplished graffiti artist could produce a creditable throw-up in less than thirty seconds, and thus could write their name hundreds of times in a short evening's endeavour. Masters of this form, such as IN, are reputed to have created more than 10,000 works in less than four years (Castleman, 1982; Stewart, 1989; Austin, 2001).

The golden age of graffiti art on the subways

The period from about 1975 until about 1982 is considered by many to be the 'golden age' of graffiti art on the subways of New York City. By the mid-1970s, a significant number of talented writers had mastered their skills and formed productive crews, something akin to rock and roll's 'super groups'. The whole car masterpiece emerged as the favoured format for the best work, and linked, multiple-car works appeared more frequently. Some artists took an abstract turn in their typographic stylistics, and many of the most impressive works were no longer readable to the untrained eye. At the same time, other writers built on earlier figurative drawing to develop fully rendered characters. Advertising, psychedelia, album cover art as well as superhero and countercultural comic books were common cultural materials of urban youth cultures of these times, and it was from these sorts of resources that graffiti artists borrowed, and then reassembled them into the subcultural productions of the early New York graffiti art scene (Chalfant and Cooper, 1984; Austin, 2001; Campos, 2012). New York subway graffiti during this period could be understood as a running comment on what was culturally important among a segment of the city's youths.

Graffiti art aesthetics in some ways divided into multiple trends. Tagging and 'getting up' continued as a saturation technique. Some artists perfected the throw-up as a massive saturation/coverage genre at a larger scale. Some artists focused on large or whole-car works with stylised but readable letters and 'characters' from commercial popular culture. Others crushed, twisted and distorted the alphabet into complicated but beautiful swirls of interconnected visual fragments and patterns. While the 'readable' styles could and did directly address the general population, and the complicated stylistics of the unreadable pieces seem to be more directed towards the internal hierarchy of the subculture, most artists claimed an intention to beautify a dilapidated and troubled city for the benefit of all citizens. Distinctions can be justifiably drawn between differing genres and styles, but most writers practiced the entire range – tagging, throw-ups, readable pieces, 'character' drawing and 'wild style' alphabetics – and often during the same evenings work.

The buff

The infrastructural problems of New York City during the mid-1970s were a world event, as a global financial hub teetered on municipal bankruptcy. Several scholars have argued that the attempts to resolve the city's financial problems were a key event in the rise of neoliberalism and an early rehearsal for austerity within the welfare states of the developed world that would become more common in the next century (Harvey, 2007; Greenberg, 2008). City services were cut back and unemployment among young people soared above 75 per cent. High crime rates inspired popular films like *Death Wish* (1974), *Taxi Driver* (1976), *The Warriors* (1979) and

Escape from New York (1981), which imagined the city falling into a lawless social chaos. Despite these frugal times, the MTA, undeterred by their failures in their war on graffiti thus far, developed a 'car wash' for trains that sprayed paint solvents. Dubbed 'the Buff' by the artists, the project was a disaster in several ways. A number of workers died or were injured by exposure to the solvents, which were blown into the air and nearby public areas (Chidakel, 1977; 'Fume Fears Halts Graffiti Work', 1977; 'Graffiti Solvent', 1977; Dwyer, 1989). The Buff did not always effectively remove the paint, and often simply smeared and degraded the images, so the exteriors had neither the 'authorised' visual organisation that the MTA intended nor the 'unauthorised' visual dynamics of the writer's works, but a dull smudge that could only attest to the struggle for visual dominance. Writers quickly determined that some brands of spray paint were more resistant to the Buff solvents than others, and shifted their preferences accordingly. The solvent also corroded the electrical wiring in the cars, leading to even more frequent train failures and evacuations in a system that was being threatened by a shutdown by the National Transportation Association. Although the Buff did not completely remove the writers' works, it did spoil them, and this, in turn, opened up more space for new works. While the Buff introduced an unpredictable randomness into the writer's collective judgments of the merits of works – the MTA made no distinction between an outstanding and innovative whole-car masterpiece and a novice's tag – it also facilitated a continual supply of new available surfaces. As the work became more ephemeral, it also became more sophisticated and spectacular, and more photographers and videographers turned to document the works (Chalfant and Cooper, 1984; Austin, 2001).

As New York City began to slowly regain some of its financial stability in the late 1970s, the subway system continued to decline. Removal of graffiti art from the cars was posed as a major test for the MTA (and the city government) to demonstrate that it could rehabilitate the city's image and effectively govern. Sociologist Nathan Glazer admitted that graffiti artists' crime was 'relatively trivial', but opined that their 'aggregate effects on the environment of millions of people are massive' (Glazer, 1979). For Glazer, graffiti was a main culprit in the city's image problem. Building on these and other neoconservative ideas from criminology and social policy (Feiner and Klein, 1982; Wilson and Kelling, 1982), Koch and the MTA used their access to news media to publicly justify a huge expense to address a minor surface problem on the nation's largest subway system during a period when the entire system was near collapse. The *New York Times* seemed particular eager to help in this public relations effort (*New York Times* Editorial Staff, 1980, 1981a, 1981b). As part of an overall rehabilitation of the crumbling subway system, the MTA rebuilt and significantly enhanced the fences around the subway car storage yards, using razor wire extensively to make cutting or crossing the fences difficult and dangerous; the perimetres of many of the storage yards came to resemble medium security prisons (Stewart, 1989; Austin, 2001). New trains were purchased and added to the fleet (replacing some trains that were more than fifty years old) and a 'clean car' program was implemented incrementally across the system, which held any newly-painted train out of circulation until it had been 'cleaned'. The MTA adopted the language of counterinsurgency and approached the task with a new seriousness bolstered by a substantial increase in the 'vandal squad' of the Transit Police and maintenance crews in the yards, and a commitment to withhold any 'clean' train from circulation in the system until new graffiti was removed, even if that meant a less reliable transportation schedule. By 1984, the MTA was noticeably removing the art works from the subways faster than the artists were replacing them (Austin, 2001; Cavalieri, 2011). Over the next few years, entire subway lines were rendered 'graffiti free', although the MTA's claims of complete control over the visual order of the trains were, and are, somewhat overstated.

In the gallery

During the first two decades of the New York City graffiti art's existence, there were at least two major eras in the attempts to divert graffiti writers to work as mainstream gallery artists and commercial graphic designers. In the first era, Hugo Martinez, a sociology student, organised United Graffiti Artists (UGA) in 1972 with the goal of rechannelling the writers' talents toward a standard art career, and had significant successes, including a show favourably reviewed by renowned *New York Times* art critic Peter Schjeldahl, several purchases by collectors, and invitations to exhibit at galleries and museums in other cities. During the 'crisis' of New York City, the group failed to maintain its prominence and develop an identifiable art market trend, although many of the artists continued to produce works on canvas (Schjeldahl, 1973; Castleman, 1982; Stewart, 1989).

A second 'wave' of interest in graffiti art emerged in the early 1980s from the art markets. This move towards the galleries was part of a wider phenomenon of cultural revival taking place in New York City during the late 1970s and early 1980s as the city's financial outlook improved. The East Village scene coincided and sometimes intersected with the emergence of punk rock, but for graffiti art it was more often with 'hip-hop' music and dance that had been developing in the Bronx during the previous eight years. A few artists were represented by well-established galleries and were heavily promoted, with a significant 'Post-Graffiti' exhibition in 1983 (Hager, 1986; Thompson, 2009). Although some artists sold paintings on canvas for art world prices during this period, others felt that the commercial art world's values, including its aesthetic judgments, were far below those upheld within the artists' own self-managed art world. Many left in disgust at the exploitation and disrespect shown to the artists. It should be noted that there is no evidence that the move towards the galleries in the 1970s or the 1980s significantly diminished the illegal works on the trains; most of those that participated in UGA and the 1980s gallery scene were also illegally painting trains at night (Chalfant and Cooper, 1984; Hager, 1984; Austin, 2001).

On the screens and in the pages: mediation and new forms of graffiti art

Alongside the East Village art scene and the emergence of hip-hop were movies, documentary films, and books on hip-hop that appeared in the first half of the 1980s. As hip-hop moved downtown and began to attract significant local and then national music and dance audiences, graffiti art became associated with this new performance culture, although *writing* predated hip-hop and had developed independently. Although some graffiti artists were hip-hop fans, dancers and musical artists (and vice versa), these crossovers were by no means the majority. The contemporary presumption that graffiti art is the 'fourth element' of hip-hop is operative only after the early 1980s; for more than a decade, graffiti art developed with only marginal affiliation to MCing, DJing, and breakdancing (Phase 2 and Schmiddlapp, 1996; Austin, 2001).

Henry Chalfant and Martha Cooper's collection of photographs of the artists' works on the trains, *Subway Art*, was published in 1984, and the book sold well across the nation. *Subway Art* has since become the global 'old school bible' of graffiti style and its narration is frequently the 'history' that most contemporary graffiti artists know of the first fifteen years of the art. *Subway Art* was preceded by a popular movie, *Wild Style* (1983), which wrapped scenarios and characters from hip-hop, the East Village scene, and punk rock around a romantic drama involving two of the major graffiti artists of the era, LADY PINK and LEE. *Wild Style* was among the first of several commercial films attempting to promote and exploit hip-hop, and its distribution in other nations was another of the global introductions of the new graffiti art. Chalfant and filmmaker Tony Silver also released their documentary *Style Wars* (1983) during this period, which featured not only photographs of the trains with a hip-hop soundtrack, but also extensive interviews with the artists, their parents, MTA officials, but also footage of the writers painting. The documentary travelled on the film festival circuits and was broadcast on PBS in the US and several stations in Europe. Between *Wild Style*, *Style Wars* and *Subway Art* (and several other hip-hop themed films), New York City graffiti art opened up to the rest of the world, and new scenes began to emerge in cities across the planet. Ironically, just as these developments were bringing global admiration and imitation to the cultural productions of New York City's youth, Mayor Edward Koch and the MTA's war on graffiti was nearing its endgame (*Wild Style*, 1983; *Style Wars*, 1983; *Beat Street*, 1984; Chalfant and Cooper, 1984; Gablik, 1984; Hager, 1984; George *et al.*, 1985; Hager, 1986; Butterfield, 1988; Austin, 2001).

As writers came to understand the MTA's new effectiveness in removing their works from the trains, a number of new developments began. As the trains became less reliable as a way of circulating works and the MTA became more determined to capture and prosecute writers for serious federal and state property crimes, some writers moved onto the streets and began to paint the roll-down gates of businesses, alley and parking lot walls, handball courts and the areas under public infrastructure, like bridges, and in abandoned buildings. By the late 1980s, there was more graffiti art visible within New York City public spaces than perhaps ever before, as writers were pushed off the trains and into the streets.

After the subways

On the streets, new graffiti formats appeared. Tags and throw-ups increasingly became the dominant forms, in part because the city streets were more open-range and visible to passers-by and authorities, and thus the several hours that the subway yards had afforded to produce works were reduced significantly, often to a matter of minutes. In line with quicker works, writers began to develop stickers with their tags (US Postal Service mailing labels were favoured), which allowed a writer to walk around the city and discretely slap up sticker tags in broad daylight. Some of the new street writers also began to interact with the emerging street artists and put up wheat-pasted Xerox posters. COST and REVS were key innovators in this form (Cooper, 2010). They were also part of a move towards 'roller tags' in which writers would use paint roller brushes with long handles to recreate huge linear works on the sides of buildings. Some areas of the city were more graffiti-friendly than others, and some crews began to work as advertisers and muralists, creating massive 'legal walls'.

Others pressed forward in the 'war' and painted 'clean trains', videotaping their exploits and then circulating the footage (see Greg Snyder's chapter in this Handbook), even though the painted subway train may not have ever left its storage yard before being 'cleaned'. Noting that subways were not the only trains available, some turned towards freight trains, which have since maintained a significant following in the US (Chalfant and Prigoff, 1987; *Videograf*, 1989–1994; Ferrell, 1998; Austin, 2001; Gastman *et al.*, 2006; Felisbret, 2009; Gastman and Neelon, 2010).

Conclusion: globalisation and street art

The major new developments after the subway trains were retaken by the MTA in New York City were the globalisation of graffiti art and the tentative (in the 1990s) alliances between individual graffiti artists and artists working in the emerging forms of street art. As mentioned above, graffiti art had already spread outwards from Philadelphia and New York City, and new and innovative scenes had appeared in San Francisco, Los Angeles and in several European cities by 1985. These local scenes have continued to proliferate, and with the advent of the World Wide Web, formed a network allowing graffiti artists to view works and communicate with fellow artists across the planet. Styles and innovations are no longer place-based; a Boston graffiti artist's work could reflect influences from artists living in Mumbai. Although street art has important early connections to New York City, this movement developed in a much more geographically dispersed way (Schwartzman, 1985). Street art opened a new career path for some graffiti artists, and several of the graffiti artists after 1990 moved quickly to producing paste-ups, glyphs, murals and 'legal walls' and gallery works that broadened and moved away from the imagery and main foci of graffiti art (Bengtsen, 2014). For many scholars, critics and artists, graffiti art has become a subgenre of street art.

Despite the remarkably rapid globalisation of graffiti art, New York City retains an iconic aura as the original spot of this long-lived art movement, which began before 1970. In this global context, New York City also enjoys a major reputation among those trying to control the illegal aspects of the art, although its anti-graffiti efforts are often covered under a broader umbrella of 'broken windows' policing (Vuchic and Bata, 1989; Kelling and Coles, 1996). By the 1990s, there was a noticeable flow of graffiti artists from all over the planet traveling to New York City to record themselves illegally painting 'clean' trains (Kirkpatrick, 1996; 'The Invasion of the Euro-Taggers', 1997). New York City anti-graffiti policing officials and advisors consulted with the anti-graffiti officials of other major cities. The long-standing tensions between graffiti art and its foes in the 1990s can perhaps best be encapsulated in the 'raids' made by the New York City police on several fine arts galleries in the city, where graffiti and street artists held (legal) shows to gain the attentions of an international art market (Siegal, 2000). The dialectic between artistic innovation, the claiming of a 'right to the city', and the dogged policing of its illegality continue to inform, and perhaps raise the prices and the costs, of graffiti art.

References

Anonymous. (1977). 'Fume Fears Halts Graffiti Work'. *New York Times*. 1 November: 64.
Anonymous. (1980). 'Graffiti Solvent Put Into Sewers Illegally'. *New York Times*. 22 August: B4.
Anonymous. (1997). 'The Invasion of the Euro-Taggers'. *New York Times*. 19 January: SM12.
Austin, J. (2001). *Taking the Train: How Graffiti Art Became an Urban Crisis in New York City, 1970–1990*. New York: Columbia University Press.
Beat Street. (1984). Lathan, S., director. Orion Pictures.
Becker, H. (1982). *Art Worlds*, 2nd edn Berkeley, CA: University of California Press.
Bengtsen, P. (2014). *The Street Art World*. Lund: University of Lund Press.
Brooks, M. (1997). *Subway City: Riding the Trains; Reading New York*. New York: Rutgers University Press.
Butterfield, F. (1988). 'On New York Walls, the Fading of Graffiti'. *New York Times*. 6 May: 1+.
Campos, R. (2012). Graffiti Writer as Superhero. *European Journal of Cultural Studies*, 16(2): 155–170.
Castleman, C. (1982). *Getting up: Subway Graffiti in New York*. Boston: MIT Press.
Cavalieri, P. (2011). *From the Platform: Subway Graffiti, 1983–1989*. Atglen, PA: Schiffer Publishing.
Cesaretti, G. (1975). *Street Writers: A Guided Tour of Chicano Graffiti*. Los Angeles: Acrobat Books.
Chalfant, H. and Cooper, M. (1984). *Subway Art*. New York: Thames and Hudson.
Chalfant, H. and Prigoff, J. (1987). *Spraycan Art*. New York: Thames and Hudson.
Chidakel, D. (1976). 'Fighting People's Art in N.Y.C'. *Science for the People*. November: 19.
Cooper, M. (2010). *Name Tagging*. Brooklyn, NY: Mark Batty Publishing.
Dwyer, J. (1989). 'Graffiti-Free Era Comes at a Cost'. *New York Newsday*. 11 May: 6.
Ehrlich, D. and Ehrlich, G. (2007). 'Graffiti in Its Own Words'. *New York Magazine*, 3 July. Available online at: http://nymag.com/guides/summer/17406/ (accessed 6 June 2014).
Farrell, S. and Pape, C. (2010). *Stay High 149*. Berkeley, CA: Gingko Press.
Fedorchak, V. (2005). *Fuzz One*. New York: Testify Books.

Feiner, J. and Klein, S. (1982). Graffiti Talks. *Social Policy*, 12(3): 47–53.

Felisbret, E. (2009). *Graffiti New York*. New York: Abrams.

Ferrell, J. (1998). Freight Train Graffiti: Subculture, Crime, Dislocation. *Justice Quarterly*, 15(4): 587–608.

Ferrell, J. and Weide, R. (2010). Spot Theory. *City*, 14(1–2): 48–62.

Gablik, S. (1984). *Has Modernism Failed?* New York: Thames and Hudson.

Gastman, R. and Neelon, C. (2010). *The History of American Graffiti*. New York: Harper Collins.

Gastman, R., Rowland D. and Sattler, I. (2006). *Freight Train Graffiti*. New York: Abrams.

George, N., Banes, S., Flinker, S. and Romanowsk, I. (1985). *Fresh: Hip Hop Don't Stop*. New York: Random House.

Glazer, N. (1979). On Subway Graffiti in New York. *The Public Interest*. 54: 209–217.

Greenberg, M. (2008). *Branding New York: How a City in Crisis Was Sold to the World*. London: Routledge.

Hager, S. (1984). *Hip Hop: The Illustrated History of Break Dancing, Rap Music, and Graffiti*. New York: St. Martin's.

Hager, S. (1986). *Art after Midnight: The East Village Scene*. New York: St. Martin's.

Harvey, D. (2007). *A Brief History of Neoliberalism*. London: Oxford University Press.

Hazlehurst C. and Hazlehurst, K. (1998). Gangs in Cross-Cultural Perspective. In C. Hazlehurst and K. Hazlehurst, (eds) *Gangs and Youth Subcultures: International Explorations* (pp. 1–34). New Brunswick, NJ: Transaction.

Hinton, J. and Kohl, H. (1972). *Golden Boy as Anthony Cool*. New York: The Dial Press.

Kelling, G. and Coles, C. (1996). *Fixing Broken Windows*. New York: Free Press.

Kirkpatrick, D. (1996). American Graffiti: These Tourists Visit and Vandalize. *Wall Street Journal*. 22 August: B1.

Kofman, E. and Lebas, E. (1996). Lost in Transposition – Time, Space and the City. In E. Kofman and E. Lebas, (eds and Trans.) *Writings on Cities: Henri Lefebvre* (pp. 3–60). London: Blackwell.

Lefebvre, H. (1968). The Right to the City. In E. Kofman and E. Lebas, (eds and Trans.) *Writings on Cities: Henri Lefebvre* (pp. 147–59). London: Blackwell.

Levitt, H. (1965, 1987). *In the Street: Chalk Drawings and Messages, New York City, 1938–1948*. Durham, NC: Duke University Press.

Ley, D. and Cybriwsky, R. (1974). Urban Graffiti as Territorial Markers. *Annals of the Association of American Geographers*, 64(4): 491–505.

Macdonald, N. (2001). *The Graffiti Subculture: Youth, Masculinity and Identity in London and New York*. New York, Palgrave.

Miller, I. (2002). *Aerosol Kingdom: Subway Painters of New York City*. Jackson, MS: University Press of Mississippi.

New York Times Editorial Staff. (1980). 'Bombing New York'. 19 October: E20.

New York Times Editorial Staff. (1981a). 'Seeds of Lawlessness', 7 August: A22.

New York Times Editorial Staff. (1981b). 'Suzy and Red vs. The Graffiti Painters'. 16 September: A26.

Phase 2 and Schmidlapp, D. (1996). *Style: Writing from the Underground*. Terni, Italy: Stampa Alternativa.

Powers, S. (1999). *The Art of Getting Over: Graffiti at the Millennium*. New York: St. Martin's.

Schjeldahl, P. (1973). Graffiti Goes Legit-But the 'Show-Off Ebullience' Remains. *New York Times*, 16 September: 147.

Schwartzman, A. (1985). *Street Art*. Garden City, NY: Dial Press.

Sheon, A. (1976). The Discovery of Graffiti. *Art Journal*, 36(1): 16–22.

Shuterlan P. (2004). *Autograf: New York City's Graffiti Writers*. New York: PowerHouse Books.

Siegal, N. (2000). 'Exhibition Become Opportunity for Arrest'. *New York Times*. 10 October: B4.

Snyder, G. (2009). *Graffiti Lives: Beyond the Tag in New York's Urban Underground*. New York: New York University Press.

Stewart, J. (1989). 'Subway Graffiti: An Aesthetic Study of Graffiti on the Subway System of New York City, 1970–1978'. (dissertation, New York University).

Style Wars. (1983). Silver, T. and Chalfant, H., directors. Public Art Films.

Thompson, M. (2009). *American Graffiti*. New York: Parkstone International Press.

Videograf. [video magazine] (1989–1994). Weston, C. and Turner C., editors. Videograf Productions.

Vuchic, V. and Bata, A. (1989). US Cities Lead Fight Against Graffiti. *Railway Gazette International*. January: 39–41.

Wild Style. (1982). Ahearn, C., director. First Run Features.

Wilson, J.Q. and Kelling, G. (1982). The Police and Neighborhood Safety: Broken Windows. *Atlantic Monthly*, March: 29–38.

18

"Boost or blight?"[1] Graffiti writing and street art in the "new" New Orleans[2]

Doreen Piano

Introduction

Pulled toward the economic drive to revitalize its urban center in the years after the levees breached during Hurricane Katrina in 2005, city officials in New Orleans are not only taking extreme measures to eliminate its criminal elements, but also addressing "quality of life" issues. Complaints made by citizens are often legitimate, especially in neighborhoods struggling with excessive blight, illegal dumping, and crime, but the adverse effects have been harsher penalties and stricter regulation of urban cultural practices such as graffiti and street art, music and performance.[3]

As these social and economic shifts occur, particularly within a post-Katrina environment, activists, artists, scholars, and long-term residents are raising questions about who gets to occupy, reside, and claim "the right to the city" (Mitchell, 2003). The adoption of the city's Master Plan (www.nola.gov/city-planning/master-plan) by City Council in 2010 along with a surge of "new arrivals" post-Katrina have contributed to social and economic changes described by Klein (2007) as "disaster politics."[4] The scale of flooding across the New Orleans' region that resulted in loss of life, a widespread diaspora, and overwhelming property loss also severely compromised the city's infrastructure, leading to diminished law enforcement, the disruption of city services, and the closing of most businesses, city offices and services, and educational institutions for an extended period of time. The storm, as locals call it, cleaved the city's historical timeline into a pre- and post-Katrina New Orleans.[5]

Before the storm, responses to graffiti writing and street art were typical of other urban environments where it was viewed as being "out of place" (Keith, 2005), "a spectacle of filth" (Conquergood, 2004), involving what Ferrell (1993: p. 37) describes as a "war of the walls." David (2007) describes the political aspects of street art in New Orleans as "visual resistance" (p. 233), a term that captures relations of power among graffiti producers, their products, and the effects of their actions (p. 233). Since the late 1990s, anti-graffiti vigilante Fred Radtke (aka the Gray Ghost) and his non-profit 501(c) corporation Operation Clean Sweep (www.operation cleansweepnola.com) with the endorsement of the City of New Orleans and neighborhood and business associations have attempted to enforce a "zero tolerance policy" (David, 2005: p. 225). Since 2009, more punitive laws have been passed at the state level, one specifically directed at the defacement of historic buildings. Radtke's imprint–buffed grey, pink, and blue walls – are found all over the city; some of his buffing of Katrina-related street art and commissioned murals were controversial and covered by local media. However, attempts to eliminate graffiti and street art by enforcing stricter penalties, encouraging neighborhood anti-graffiti abatement programs and sanctioning the actions of Radtke have been largely unsuccessful and graffiti writing remains not just active but growing throughout the city.

With the flow of young so called "new arrivals" into the city, street art such as stencils, wheat paste posters, tags, and stickers is commonly found in areas where they reside. Additionally, street artist Banksy's high-profile visit to New Orleans in 2008 initiated a stream of national and international street artists into the city. Moreover, neighborhoods still recovering from Katrina's floodwaters are prime spots, especially interiors. Despite the city's commitment to eliminate blight, graffiti crews, well-known street artists, and local and travelling writers all have made creative use of, what one graffiti crew, the Charles Gang, hashtags on Instagram as "floodwaste."

Graffiti writing and street art in the aftermath of Hurricane Katrina

The aftermath of Katrina changed the urban landscape of the city psychically and physically. Financial obstacles, mold-infested houses, and the challenges of rebuilding prevented the return of many locals. Aspects of urban life that had been taken for granted – accessibility, convenience, mobility – were replaced with a looming question: when would things return to normal? During a time when officials were debating whether or not to celebrate the 2006 carnival season due to the loss of lives, displaced citizens, and a shortage of law enforcement personnel, hurricane graffiti highlighted the storm's remnants and refuse, recasting private and commercial property as a canvas in which to represent an overwhelming and incommensurable collective loss.

In their analysis of images during the 2004–2005 Gulf Coast storm season, Alderman and Ward (2008) categorized hurricane graffiti into seven overarching themes that include historicizing the storm by writing on plywood, thus providing "a historical archive" of survival and resilience; expressing defiance, particularly personifying hurricanes; marking territory and imposing order through anti-looting messages; using humor as a form of escape and stress relief; incorporating prayer, both before a storm and afterwards, and deploying political commentary. These same themes were documented in photographs of graffiti that I took in New Orleans after Katrina. Many thousands more exist online and in photography books (Varisco, 2005; Misrach, 2010). According to Saul (2008), while humor was noticeably absent in the national media during the crisis, within the city, "static displays," revealed a humorous viewpoint. One in particular, written in diary form, the narrative, hand-painted on three plywood boards nailed into the façade of a carpet store on Lower St. Charles Avenue in the Garden District with its references to New Orleans cuisine, aggressive humor, and Mardi Gras illustrated a fierce regionalism as well as a survivor's resilience (See Figure 18.1).

Hurricane graffiti is not stylized nor is it implicitly illegal; often it is found on personal property, or in the case of New Orleans, on flooded houses and abandoned vehicles that became part of a post-Katrina landscape. Personal messages were directed at neighbors, insurance companies, and the hurricane (Donnie and I R OK, I Knew We Should've Moved to Denver, and I Survived Betsy but Katrina was a Bitch), angry and defiant messages directed at government (Screw You, Nagin, We Made our own Plan), and messages directed at and about the city (Viva New Orleans,

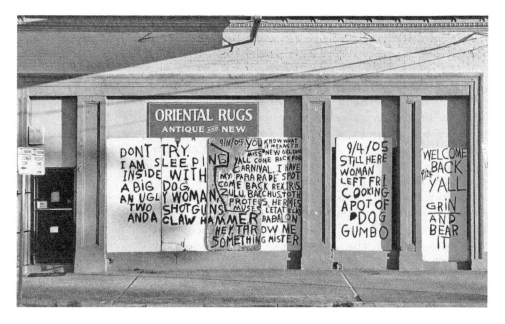

Figure 18.1 Hurricane graffiti in New Orleans, 2005 © Doreen Piano

New Orleans, America's No. 1 City) were prevalent during this time. Many responded to ongoing local events such as Mayor Ray Nagin's "Chocolate City" speech on MLK Day in 2007 that caused an outcry.[6]

During the recovery, controversies surrounding street art and graffiti became part of larger debates about the future of the city. In late September 2005, Mayor Nagin established the Bring New Orleans Back (BNOB) commission that would play a significant role in envisioning a new New Orleans. By early 2006 with the recommendations of the Urban Land Institute to shrink the city's footprint, (meaning heavily flooded areas or those with "green dots" would be converted into green space unless a neighborhood could make a good case for its viability) (Campanella, 2008: p. 346), residents living in these areas were enraged and eventually the map was tabled. Although not directly related, street artists fight for self-expression on the street (See Ehrenfeucht, 2014) paralleled civic debates over urban space, especially in relation to thousands of still displaced residents trying to return and rebuild. At this time, graffiti writers such as Harsh, Grubs, and Old Crow were active in desolate neighborhoods. Local writer Harsh often wrote on the back of billboards that advertised services to help with the recovery.

In an interview with *Times-Picayune* art critic Doug MacCash (2009), artist Skylar Fein claimed that Harsh's tag accurately depicted the "spectacular destruction" after the storm by commenting on the current climate in the city. He describes this period as "the golden age of HARSH." Other New Orleans' taggers' names (EVAK, RISK, and SANK) also reflected the city's post-Katrina vulnerability and destruction. In more populated neighborhoods, artist Rex Dingler's signs that conveyed upbeat messages to residents were targeted by Radtke, whose inability to discern legal from illegal street art led to his arrest for painting over a commissioned mural in 2008.[7] A few years later, Radtke would be accused of buffing a mural used in a rap video and destroying a commissioned mural (MacCash, 2011b).[8]

Radtke's vigilantism inspired Banksy to depict a grey-haired white man holding a paint roller in several of his New Orleans' stencils (www.banksystreetart.tumblr.com/tagged/new%20orleans).

In one, a man is painting over sunflowers, a possible reference to Dingler's optimistic signs or to the sunflowers that had blossomed in the months after the storm. Ostensibly, Banksy's visit on the third anniversary of Hurricane Katrina intended "to make a comment on the state of the clean-up operation" (quoted in Gill, 2008). His stencils elicited numerous articles, opinions, and discovery maps in local media for weeks afterwards.[9] The positive reception to his stencils may have been due to his status as an international street artist and his understanding of the city's continuing struggles to rebuild. Many stencils critiqued government's lack of response and the broken levee system while also incorporating the city's iconography (a boy playing a trumpet, a brass band, a refrigerator). In the *Times-Picayune*, MacCash pleaded with Radtke to "let these particular pieces survive" (2008b) while his anti-graffiti colleague, James Gill, conceded, "it is certainly of much higher quality than the graffiti that Radtke has been blotting out" (2008). Locating Banksy stencils that had not been stolen or painted over gave residents an opportunity to see how devastated some neighborhoods such as the Ninth Ward still were. Stencil art, as Truman (2010) points out, is capable of reflecting local concerns at the same time it connects "with broader cultural notions of resistance and change" (pp. 6–7). According to many residents, journalists, and cultural commentators, Banksy's stencils effectively communicated the disastrous effects of the flooding within a global context.

Graffiti and street art in and beyond the French Quarter

By 2010, New Orleans had re-established itself as a primary tourist destination, its high rating in travel magazines illustrating that the city was recovering, at least in the city's central tourist districts. Historic neighborhoods along the Mississippi were revitalized by a surge of new residents, many of them artists. Homeless and subcultural youth such as modern hobos, crusties, and Quarter rats also flocked to the city after Katrina, finding the lack of regulation and high density of blighted housing amenable for squatting. In early 2010, a devastating fire in an empty warehouse that killed eight young people exposed this relatively hidden demographic.[10] While difficult to tell whether these new populations have contributed to graffiti culture, tags, slaps, and wheat paste posters appear in areas near popular bars, clubs, and restaurants where young people hang out.

In the French Quarter, tags and stickers appearing on doorways, trash cans, street signs, sidewalks, and an occasional wall, most of it described as "aesthetically low-grade," (Nolan, 2011) is buffed quickly. More elaborate pieces and burners are found in "cutty" areas (sites that are isolated, sometimes dangerous) where there is less pedestrian or vehicular traffic, typically in industrial areas and neighborhoods in the north and east of the city still devastated by the floodwaters. Closer to the central areas of town, graffiti is found near railways, drainage canals, and underneath bridges. One writer known as Paws describes New Orleans as a small enough city for writers to be "all city" rather than certain crews being confined to specific areas (www.tumblr.com/tagged/paws-graffiti). Many crews and writers work the same terrain that also include permission or free walls, and interiors of empty high rises, and the upper stories of commercial buildings, abandoned hospitals and schools.

Compared to the vigilant anti-graffiti campaigns in and around the French Quarter, many low-income, predominantly African-American neighborhoods are not as heavily policed. Many of these neighborhoods are lacking amenities such as functioning street lights and nicely paved roads, have high concentrations of blighted properties, and in many cases are impaired by violent crime, raising a question about the city's uneven distribution of safety and quality-of-life issues. The high visibility of graffiti in these neighborhoods can either reinforce the negative implications associated with these neighborhoods or they can act to beautify desolate urban areas, calling attention to the city's neglect.

The high percentage of blighted properties after Katrina has led many graffiti writers to use interiors.[11] Interiors grant writers more time to create complex pieces, deflecting accusations of graffiti as "visual pollution" (Keith, 2005). Interiors also counter a prevailing notion that graffiti offers writers an avenue for "asserting their *place* in the city" (Austin, 1998: p. 243). They challenge this concept by providing more intimate audiences. As street artist MRSA (borrowing his tag from the flesh-eating bacteria) observes, "The only people who see them are other graffiti writers and they stay there a really long time" (Fein, 2011). Additionally, with the rise of social media apps used by graffiti writers, urban explorers, and graffiti chasers (i.e. photographers), artists and writers gain prestige through the circulation of images that have broader, intersecting audiences. The appropriation of interior spaces can be hazardous in New Orleans where many houses and buildings haven't been touched since floodwaters made them uninhabitable. Many are termite-ridden, rotted, and covered in hazardous materials. However, despite these dangers, they offer relative seclusion from law enforcement and buffing vigilantes. Interior locations or attractive spots in desolate neighborhoods are found through informal social media networks that allow travelling writers and crews to work alongside local ones, creating complex collaborations.

Another outlet for graffiti writers and street artists to display their work is on legal walls. In his research, Kramer (2010) observes that in New York City some graffiti writers do not perceive their relationship to society as "one marked by discordance" (p. 240). In fact, a substantial group of graffiti writers view their work as community oriented (Kramer, 2010: p. 249). Local businesses

Figure 18.2 Interior of an abandoned school, New Orleans, 2013 © Doreen Piano

often hire writers for larger pieces on their businesses. Additionally, because New Orleans has a history of custom lettered signage (Woodward, 2014), street artists who move between legal and illegal spots are not that extraordinary. While some may see permission walls as co-opting the cultural form through appeasement, as Kramer's research suggests, permission walls offer opportunities for participation in society (p. 240) and dispel fears of incarceration or fines. Permission walls also offer collaboration among artists. As graffiti writer Paws notes, "writers get along really well and have fun together on various commissions and free walls" (www. tumblr.com/tagged/paws-graffiti). Unfortunately, even when writers are given permission, their work can be destroyed. Operation Clean Sweep has been held responsible for buffing several commissioned works.

In a thought-provoking online discussion about Brandan Odums' mural-like portraits of African-American artists, intellectuals, and activists, MacCash (2014c) poses the question: "If graffiti helps lend the grit that implies authenticity, could graffiti play an ironic role in boosting property value?" For some graffiti advocates, permission walls or legal graffiti diminish the political effects of the form while others view it as a positive force for economic development in urban areas. For example, while restoring the defunct Rice Mills Lofts in Bywater, developer Sean Cummings retained graffiti on exposed walls in some units and collaborated with artist Skylar Fein to create a permission wall of shipping containers on the perimeter of the site. In an interview (MacCash, 2012), Cummings and Fein discuss how they view the wall as a perfect fit for the Bywater neighborhood while also re-directing the public's attention about graffiti's outlaw status toward its legitimacy. Admitting that his buildings have been tagged illegally, Cummings dispels the oddity of "being in cahoots with graffiti artists" (MacCash, 2012) by claiming these kinds of projects can appease those ostensible antagonisms.

In a similar vein, developer Lex Kelso opened a recently acquired warehouse for a one-night exhibit titled "Bombthreat," organized by Skylar Fein, representing graffiti artists from all over the city. In November 2014, after discovering Odums was utilizing the property illegally, developer Bill Thomason provided the space of an abandoned low-income high rise known as the Woodlands in Algiers for Exhibit Be, the international biennial art show known as Prospect.3, a one-day event that showcased numerous local and international artists (http://brandanodums.com/be). All of the artists involved, including local, national, and travelling writers, were encouraged to create their best work, which became part of the Prospect.3 International Art Show. As a testament to Odums' work and street art in general, over 2500 people attended the exhibit on its opening day. While these recent moves may not diffuse tensions among graffiti writers, property owners, and city officials, they create "the spaces required to develop the aesthetic possibilities of graffiti" (Kramer, 2010: p. 251).

Major writers and crews[12]

It is difficult to grasp the number of writers/street artists/taggers working in New Orleans. In an interview with Skylar Fein (2011), MRSA notes that the number of tags has increased exponentially since 2009. Writing about graffiti before the storm, David (2007) focuses on the political aspects of street art in residential and tourist areas and the debate over public space inspired by Radtke's vigilantism. His ethnographic work mainly focused on cartoon-like images. However writers such as Old Crow, TARD (known more recently as Fat Kids from Outer Space), MRSA, and members of TM (Top Mob) such as Harsh, Meek, Bugs, Sank, and Evak were writing before the storm hit. In fact, a recent downtown event celebrated Top Mob's thirtieth year of being a crew in New Orleans. In 2008, Banksy and Swoon visited the city, placing their work around the city. Many of them were destroyed, some were stolen, and a few still remain. Other high profile visits by internationally recognized street artists such as Rone, MTO and Reader have brought more media attention to the street art scene.

At the time of writing, several graffiti crews are active in New Orleans: TM (Top Mob), VRS (Very Real Shit), QNA (Quest N Adventure), DTB (Doing Things Better), 2F (Too Funky), and Hip Kids. The Bay Area, Charles Gang (aka Charles Mafia, Charles Cartel), who stayed in the city for six months in 2014, left behind a treasure trove of elaborate pieces, raising the bar for local writers. The crew members, especially Uter, Meck, and Dvote often collaborated with local writers during their stay. Sharing walls regardless of crew affiliation is common, perhaps because the scene is quite small and locations are accessible. Other writers and crews who have come for short stays include OYE (Open Your Eyes), a small crew whose high profile member Reader (also tags as Boans and Bonafide) painted "rollers" spelling out READ on abandoned businesses around the city starting in 2009. Reader also uses tags, icons of an open book often with skulls, and X's, along with stickers saying "Read More Books". His work is often seen with Reverend and You Go, Girl (known for his decrepit looking hand and a woman's face with cat's eye glasses and a large nose) and is reportedly well received by more than graffiti advocates according to Brian Knowles, who claims that his work "runs for longer because of the positive message" (www.juxtapoz.com/graffiti/read-more-books-238472346235). The controversial tagger Gay for Pay whose tag on private property as well as dumpsters and street signs was condemned by many for its perceived homophobia (see Fein, 2013a); additionally the Bourghog Guild whose RIP tags acknowledged dead artists also created a stir by intentionally tagging over a Banksy.

Many New Orleans' writers remain letter-based such as members of TM, some combine lettering with images such as Old Crow and You Go, Girl and others (Tard, MRSA, Paws) create elaborate, often fantastical, brightly colored figures. Elsie, Freya, and Yenta have each constructed distinctive women's faces. Elsie's figures are particularly haunting and ethereal while Freya relies on an anime aesthetic with a face that constantly changes moods, often frowning or glaring. In 2014, Wrdsmith's stencils of positive messages on top of an old school typewriter, San Francisco stencil artist Jeremy Novy's playful queer and koi fish stencils and Wren's animal wheat paste posters have appeared in downtown neighborhoods.

In recent years, more women appear to be involved in graffiti (Freya, Elsie, Yenta, Flea, Wren, Swoon), some are artists using the street as a public space for displaying their work. Others involved in graffiti are men in their twenties to late thirties of varied racial/ethnic backgrounds. The preponderance of young white men in graffiti culture explored by Monto *et al.* (2012) certainly holds true in New Orleans with many writers identifying with an "outlaw masculinity" that "values willingness to offend, rebelliousness, and risk-taking" (Monto *et al.*, 2012: p. 273). However, even among Anglo writers, varied forms of masculinity should be viewed as existing on a spectrum. For example, Tard, a member of Fat Kids from Outer Space, describes the crew name as "part of the whole retard thing, special needs, weirdness . . ." (Minksy, 2014). Writers/artists of color are also present in New Orleans, particularly African American artist Brandan Odums whose work in abandoned housing projects (the original Project Be) garnered local attention (Fein 2013b; MacCash 2013b).

Many graffiti and street artists move between the gallery and the street. In New Orleans, MRSA had a one-man show at Antenna Gallery, Ken Nahan, a street artist has stickered one-way street signs and exhibited his work in galleries, and visiting artists Caledonia "Swoon" Curry constructed a sculpture at New Orleans Museum of Art (NOMA) and also displayed her elaborate paste-ups around town and at the Dithyrambalina (www.dithyrambalina.com) an experimental music box now closed that was located in the Bywater in 2011. Odums participates in several

New Orleans Jazz and Heritage Fests as artist-in-residence and conducts workshops at universities and schools throughout the city. Odums sees his role as a street artist in terms of a collaborative one that involves the surrounding community. When interviewed about his "illegal" work, Odums has said: "I noticed after Katrina so much blight and physical signs of indifference in communities, and I had the responsibility as an artist to use my art to transform the space" (Hasselle).

The politics of preservation: local responses to graffiti culture

While nicknames for New Orleans such as the Big Easy and the City that Care Forgot may convey a permissive, carefree attitude, local authorities, neighborhood associations, historic preservationist groups, business organizations, and law enforcement all work in tandem to safeguard the city's historical uniqueness which include determining what kinds of cultural forms and practices can exist, or as the director of the Vieux Carre Commission (VCC) says: it's "not about keeping things looking pretty but addressing what's appropriate to character and quality" (Foster, 2011). Since the 1920s when elite white women campaigned to preserve a small section of the French Quarter (Stanonis, 2006), New Orleans' tourist economy has rested on a notion of its timelessness. When graffiti appears in the French Quarter, it is scorned by many. For example, in 2012, extinguisher graffiti by Erase North discovered on two abandoned buildings known to jazz aficionados as having significant historical value ("four of them are listed on the National Register of Historic Places") (Eggler, 2012) raised an outcry. Many condemned not just the graffiti writer but blamed the city for leaving the building in a state of disrepair so as to be "threatened with demolition" (Eggler, 2012). In a "stranger than fiction" New Orleans' twist, the graffiti was removed with a particular kind of paste designed to minimize damage to bricks, accompanied by a Voodoo Priestess's chanting, and music by the Treme Brass Band (Eggler, 2012).

Predictably, news media reports and op-eds about graffiti invoke the "broken windows" theory (Nolan, 2011; Hourglade, 2012). After a Bourbon Street shoot-out on Halloween night in 2011 that resulted in fatalities, the *Times-Picayune* reported the NOPD were cracking down on graffiti writers despite an attempt by the police superintendent to reduce minor arrests (Nolan, 2011). Tourists interviewed by local media reveal alarm or dismay when seeing graffiti in the French Quarter.

Typically, graffiti abatement programs have been handled (in co-ordination with the city government) by the private sector such as Radtke's Operation Clean Sweep or neighborhood associations, but in a post-Katrina climate, the city has hosted beautification days focused on eliminating graffiti and harsher penalties have been imposed. Additionally, bars and street musicians have been subjected to fines for violating noise ordinances. These actions are similar to the containment of illegal activities (graffiti included) that occurred in New York City as public spaces became privatized during the Giuliani era (Dickinson, 2008). Working in tandem with law enforcement are neighborhood associations (See Hourcade, 2012; MacCash, 2014b) and well-known residents who see graffiti as marring the city's "authentic"qualities: Chris Rose, author of *One Dead in Attic* (the title refers to a famous X-code), upbraided graffiti writers as "petulant, post-adolescents" (2011) and temporary resident/professor at Johns Hopkins, S. Frederick Starr has called for the city to designate a graffiti czar (2014).[13] Additionally, NOLA Ready, a digital communication service that sends emails of criminal activities, often includes videos of graffiti writing suspects posted on YouTube. Some street artists and performers are also hostile toward graffiti placed in the French Quarter as their economic well-being is yoked to the perception of an unchanging city. In 2010, several throw-ups discovered close to Café

Du Monde prompted this response from a performer: "To lose it all (history) because of something like this? It detracts from it [the French Quarter] tremendously" (OCSNO, 2010).

In local media, Times-Picayune art critic Doug MacCash views graffiti as an urban art form that reflects the city's complex history. In a column written five years after Banksy's visit, MacCash tracks down the surviving stencils, commenting on what he finds along the way. "If you wander 2013 New Orleans searching for Banksy's, you'll find a landscape in flux."[14] Even though MacCash describes himself as "ambivalent" toward traditional tagging, claiming it is "more antisocial than artistic" (2009), he dedicates frequent columns to debates surrounding illegal art and to visiting and local street artists. He has written effusively about Swoon's stencils, Reader's graffiti signage, and the Love signs nailed to telephone poles around the city in 2014. On the other hand, MacCash makes his preferences clear. For example, he has referred to Harsh's tags as boring and also distinguishes street art from tagging: "Tagging pristine property for grins seems mindlessly mean" (MacCash, 2013b). When street art is a "prank," it justifies the illegality of the act) Guzzled signs (www.guzzled.org) posted after the Gulf Oil spill.

As an art critic, MacCash reads street art within an aesthetic/intentionality distinction instead of a legal/illegal binary. Not content to review art relegated to conventional spaces, he often uses his columns to create a dialogue about the creative uses of public space, some of it illegal. He allows for multiple points of view that include detractors, proponents, citizens, and artists, utilizing the comments' section on the online version of his columns or Twitter to pose questions and RT readers' responses. Often he hosts live chats for residents and artists to discussing street art and graffiti. For example, after writing about Odums' work, MacCash (2013b) pleaded for the space to be cleaned up and opened for the Prospect.3 international art show in 2014 (2013b). Even though he admitted to the work's illegality, he observes that "no one was harmed and no property was damaged" (2013b). And in fact through coincidence or wish fulfillment, Odums and other street artists had their work displayed during Prospect.3.

In addition to MacCash's columns, artist Skylar Fein writes about graffiti culture for *NOLA Defender* (www.noladefender.com), often interviewing graffiti writers and unabashedly promoting graffiti as a significant art movement. In his online manifesto *Why We Write*, Fein challenges the Gray Ghost (Fred Radtke) claiming that he is also involved in illegal activities: "The question is not who is right – the question is who will win?" For his 2009 solo art show "Youth Manifesto," at the NOMA, Fein set up a figurative duel between Harsh and the Grey Ghost by juxtaposing a very large, blinking HARSH tag in front of a window on the second floor of the museum with a much smaller installation of a Gray Ghost tag, the T awkwardly lying on the ground. The opposing tags were set up as super heroes, thus, blurring the distinction between what was legal and illegal.

Further research

While site-specific case studies of graffiti and street art are able to capture the particulars of a city's location, local writers, proponents and detractors, as Appadurai (1996) argues, the global cultural economy must be viewed in terms of its "disjunctures," made up of varying flows that are overlapping and unpredictable. The documentary *Bomb It* (2007) revealed that graffiti is a global phenomenon that functions on a very local level. In recent years, photo-sharing and micro-blogging sites such as Flickr, Tumblr, and Instagram have played a role in facilitating graffiti and street art cultures. Lewisohn observes that the Internet makes street art more accessible (2008: p. 143). Sites such as ArtCrimes (www.graffiti.org), Endless Canvas (www.endlesscanvas. com), The Wooster Collective (www.woostercollective.com), and FatCap (www.fatcap.com) offer digital spaces for discussions, posting photographs, and learning about graffiti culture. During the initial recovery period, New Orleans had a steady flow of visiting street artists such as Banksy and Swoon who entered local debates about property claims, public space, and disaster (Ehrenfeucht, 2014). During the storm, images of hurricane graffiti circulated through numerous photo-sharing and news media sites providing an alternate view of the crisis. Even before the storm, David (2007) argues that the Internet held potential for political street art to be "a possible recruitment tool" (248) in New Orleans.

Given the number of street artists and graffiti crews visiting the city since the storm, future research may focus on how graffiti writers use social media to exhibit their work and attract a following. For some artists, writers, and crews, "knowing their place" (Austin, 1998) may be less about their right to a particular geographic locale and more about accessing and exchanging information with other writers and graffiti aficionados.[15] Street artist, Wrdsmth has been using the hashtag #wrdsmthinnola to make his location known and to foster a treasure hunt for those interested in seeing his work. Following specific hashtags on Instagram can lead to finding burners and pieces done in interiors that might be inaccessible or in unknown locations. The use of Instagram to promote one's work to larger audiences fosters informal networks among street artists, photographers, graffiti writers, and urban explorers. It also has become an essential tool for researching subcultures that demand secrecy and anonymity. Social media apps generate networks of circulation for images that can act as a substitute for the subway system's "alternative economy of recognition and prestige" (Austin, 1998). Tied to other fluid subcultures such as modern hobos and urban explorers, graffiti crews, and writers utilize digital communication to exhibit their work and make connections with others in addition to leaving visual traces that mark their journeys.

Notes

1 This phrase is taken from the title of a live chat hosted by Doug MacCash (2013c).
2 The author is indebted to Laura Carroll, Lisa Costello, Renia Ehrenfeucht, Skylar Fein, Erin Henley, Gerard Hauser, Doug MacCash, and Jeffrey Ian Ross for their feedback during the writing of this chapter. All inaccuracies are the responsibility of the author.
3 Harsher penalties for graffiti writing passed through state legislation in 2008 with maximum fines up to $10,000 and up to ten years in prison. In 2010, a law passed that punished people caught defacing historic buildings. Additionally, citations related to sound ordinances have increased under Mayor Landrieu's administration.
4 In *The Shock Doctrine*, Klein defines this term as "orchestrated raids on the public sphere in the wake of catastrophic events" (4).
5 See Jed Horne (2006) and Jordan Flaherty (2010) for reliable accounts of the aftermath of Hurricane Katrina written by local journalists. See Fussell (2007) for an assessment of population changes within New Orleans Parish one year after the storm. Her analysis points to a substantial reduction of African-American residents and a growing Latino population. This trend was confirmed in the 2010 US Census findings analyzed by The Data Center (Plyer, 2010).
6 Former Mayor Ray Nagin's comment that New Orleans should return to being a 'chocolate city' inspired outrage by mostly white residents who perceived it as critical of an increased white population.
7 See Ehrenfeucht (2014) for an in-depth discussion of the controversy surrounding Dingler's street signs.
8 See Winkler-Schmit (2009) for questions regarding there being more than one Gray Ghost. Radtke himself has claimed that some of the gray-painted blocks haven't gone far enough.
9 For local and national coverage of Banksy's 2008 visit, see Bloom (2008), Gill (2008), MacCash (2008b), MacCash (2013c), Smyk (2011), Spera (2008).
10 See Morton (2012) who provides an in-depth look at this tragedy, focusing on several of the victims.
11 Since Mayor Landrieu took office in 2010, his administration has launched a Fight against Blight Initiative. See The Data Center's Benchmarks for Blight for an analysis of blighted properties that range from habitable without occupancy to inhabitable based on USPS information collected in 2010. Available at www.datacenterresearch.org/reports_analysis/benchmarks-for-blight/

12 The author wishes to acknowledge Skylar Fein whose understanding of local graffiti culture contributed to this section's accuracy.

13 The City of New Orleans relies on Operation Clean Sweep, neighborhood associations, and property owners (who have thirty days to remove graffiti after its appearance before being cited) to eliminate graffiti.

14 An attempt to chisel off "Girl with Umbrella," was thwarted by neighboring residences of the property who reported suspicious activity at the stencil's site (NoDefStaff, 2014). Ironically, the police were involved in apprehending the vandals.

15 Initial observations about Instagram as preferential to Flickr or other photo-sharing sites may have to do with its more private interface.

References

Alderman, D. & Ward, H. (2008). Writing on the Plywood: Toward an Analysis of Hurricane Graffiti. *Coastal Management*, 35(1): 1–18.

Appadurai, A. (1996). *Modernity at Large*. Minneapolis, MN: University of Minnesota Press.

Austin, J. (1998). Knowing Their Place: Local Knowledge, Social Prestige, and the Writing Formation in New York City. In Austin, J. & Willard, M.N. (Eds) *Generations of Youth: Youth Cultures and History in Twentieth Century America* (pp.240–252). New York: New York University Press.

Bloom, J. (2008). Banksy Hits New Orleans. *The New York Times*. Available online at: www.nytimes.com/2008/08/29/arts (accessed June 20, 2014).

Campanella, R. (2008). *Bienville's Dilemma: A Historical Geography of New Orleans*. Lafayette, LA: Center for Louisiana Studies.

Conquergood, D. (2004). Street Literacy. In Gere, A. & Flood, J. (Eds) *Handbook of Research on Teaching Literacy Through the Communicative and Visual Arts* (pp. 354–375). New York: MacMillan.

David, E.A. (2007). Signs of Resistance: Marking Public Space Through a Renewed Cultural Activism. In Stanczak, G.M. (Ed.) *Visual Research Methods: Image, Society, and Representation* (pp. 225–254). Thousand Oaks, CA: Sage Publications.

Eggler, B. (2012). New Orleans jazz Landmarks on Rampart Street Scrawled with Graffiti. *The Times-Picayune*. Available online at: www.nola.com/crime/index.ssf/2012/03/new_orleans_jazz_landmarks_on.html (accessed June 22, 2014).

Ehrenfeucht, R. (2014). Art, Public Spaces, and Private Property along the Streets of New Orleans. *Urban Geography*, 3(5): 965–979.

Fein, S. (n.d.). *Why We Write*. Available online at: http://skylarfein.tumblr.com (accessed September 28, 2012).

Fein, S. (2011). Skylar Fein Talks with MRSA. *NOLA Defender*. Available online at: www.noladefender.com/category/tags/skylar-fein (accessed July 10, 2014).

Fein, S. (2013a). Gay for Pay Speaks. *NOLA Defender*. Available online at: www.noladefender.com/content/ga45y-p67ay-speaks (accessed July 10, 2014).

Fein, S. (2013b). Inside Project Be: Slamming the Door on New Orleans' Black Power Graf. *NOLA Defender*. Available online at: www.noladefender.com/content/in23side-pr56oject-be

Ferrell, J. (1993). *Crimes of Style: Urban Graffiti and the Politics of Criminality*. New York: Garland.

Ferrell, J. (1995). Urban Graffiti: Crime, Control, and Resistance. *Youth and Society*, 27(1): 73–92.

Flaherty, J. (2010). *Floodlines: Community and Resistance from Katrina to the Jena Six*. Chicago, IL: Haymarket Books.

Foster, M. (2011). Vieux Carre Commission Protects French Quarter. *Boston.com*. Available online at: www.boston.com/news/nation/articles/2011/11/23/vieux_carre_commission_protects_french_quarter (accessed May 5, 2014).

Fussell, E. (2007). Constructing New Orleans, Construcing Race: A Population History of New Orleans. *Journal of American History*, 94(3): 846–855.

Gill, J. (2008). A Brush with Greatness, or a Blot? *The Times-Picayune*. Available online at: http://blog.nola.com/jamesgill/2008/09/a_brush_with_greatness_or_a_bl.html (accessed July 10, 2014).

Horne, J. (2006). *Breach of Faith: Hurricane Katrina and the Near Death of an American City*. New York. NY: Random House.

Hourcade, S. (2012). Graffiti Reduction: A New Priority for the BNA. *Bywater Neighborhood Association Newsletter*, May, p. 7.

Keith, M. (2005). *After the Cosmopolitan: Multicultural Cities and the Future of Racism*. New York: Routledge.

Klein, N. (2007). *Shock Doctrine: The Rise of Disaster Capitalism*. New York: Picador.

Kramer, R. (2010). Painting with Permission: Legal Graffiti in New York City. *Ethnography*, *11*(2): 235–253.

Lewisohn, C. (2008). *Streetart: The Graffiti Revolution*. New York: Abrams.

MacCash, D. (2008a). Vandalism or Art? The Decades-Old Struggle Between Graffiti Producers, and those Who Seek to Prevent it Has Flared Again. *The Times-Picayune* Available online at: http://blog.nola.com/dougmaccash/2008/07/vandalism_or_art.html (accessed September 15, 2008).

MacCash, D. (2008b). A Celebrated Clandestine Artist Leaves His Mark on New Orleans' Streets. *The Times-Picayune*. Available online at: http://blog.nola.com/dougmaccash/2008/09/british_artist_takes_graffiti.html (accessed September 15, 2008).

MacCash, D. (2009). Artist Skylar Fein Discusses New Orleans Graffiti. *The Times-Picayune*. Available online at: http://videos.nola.com/times-picayune/2009/09/artist_skylar_fein_discusses_n.html (accessed June 15, 2014).

MacCash, D. (2011a). Appearing and Disappearing Graffiti Murals in New Orleans. *The Times-Picayune*. Available online at: www.nola.com/arts/index.ssf/2011/08/appearing_and_disappearing_gra.html (accessed August 9, 2011).

MacCash, D. (2011b). Graffiti Writer Turned Legitimate Muralist Frustrated by Gray Overpainting. *The Times-Picayune*. Available online at: www.nola.com/arts/index.ssf/2011/10/graffiti_writer_turned_legitim.html (accessed June 15, 2014).

MacCash, D. (2011c). 'Bombthreat,' a Graffiti-Style Group Show Takes Place Saturday in New Orleans. *The Times-Picayune*. Available online at: www.nola.com/arts/index.ssf/2011/10/bombthreat_a_graffiti_group_sh.html (accessed October 25, 2011).

MacCash, D. (2012). Developer Sean Cummings Builds a Legal Graffiti Wall in Bywater. *The Times-Picayune*. Available online at: http://videos.nola.com/times-picayune/2012/02/developer_sean_cummings_builds.html (accessed March 6, 2014).

MacCash, D. (2013a). Street Artists Strike in French Quarter. *The Times-Picayune*. Available online at: www.nola.com/arts/index.ssf/2013/08/guzzled_guerilla_street_art_si.html (accessed August 18, 2013).

MacCash, D. (2013b). Allow the Public to Visit Brandan Odums' 'Project Be' Graffiti Masterpiece. *The Times-Picayune*. Available online at: www.nola.com/arts/index.ssf/2013/09/allow_the_public_to_visit_bran_1.html (accessed September 11, 2013).

MacCash, D. (2013c). Boost or Blight? Live Chat on Monday About Brandan Odums' Graffiti Masterpiece. *The Times-Picayune*. Available online at: www.nola.com/arts/index.ssf/2013/09/the_marignybywater_irony_does.html (accessed July 15, 2014).

MacCash, D. (2014a). LOVE Signs on the Streets of New Orleans Call for Kisses, Reader Says. *The Times-Picayune*. Available online at: www.nola.com/arts/index.ssf/2014/06/love_signs_have_appeared_on_th.html (accessed June 21, 2014).

MacCash, D. (2014b). Anti-Graffiti/Pro-Graffiti Argument Alive in Mid-City, Website Reports. *The Times-Picayune*. Available online at: www.nola.com/arts/index.ssf/2014/07/anti-graffiti_pro-graffiti_arg.html (accessed June 23, 2014).

Minksy, D. (2014). Fat Kid from Outer Space: An Interview with NOLA Graffiti Artist Tard. *Anti-Gravity Magazine*. Available online at: www.antigravitymagazine.com/2014/07/fat-kid-from-outer-space-an-interview-with-nola-graffiti-artist-tard (accessed July 15, 2014).

Misrach, R. (2010). *Destroy This Memory*. New York: Aperture.

Mitchell, D. (2003). *The Right to the City: Social Justice and the Fight for Public Space*. New York: Guilford Press.

Monto, M.A., Machalek, J., & Anderson, T.L. (2012). Boys Doing Art: The Construction of Outlaw Masculinity in a Portland, Oregon, Graffiti Crew. *Journal of Contemporary Ethnography*, *42*(3): 259–290.

Morton, D. (2012). A World on Fire: Life and Death in a New Orleans Squat. *The Boston Review*. Available online at: www.bostonreview.net/BR37.1/danelle_morton_new_orleans_squat_fire.php (accessed February 2, 2012).

Moye, D. (2010). Katrina + 5: An X-Code Exhibition. Available online at: www.southernspaces.org/2010/katrina-5-x-code-exhibition (accessed June 15, 2014).

New Orleans Convention and Visitor Bureau. (n.d.). *City and CVB Awards*. Available online at: www.neworleanscvb.com/press-media/press-kit/city-cvb-awards/ (accessed June 24, 2014).

NoDefStaff. (2014). Unindentified Attempt to Move Banksy 'Girl with Umbrella'. *NOLA Defender*. Available online at: www.noladefender.com/content/unindentified-quartet-attempt-move-banksys-girl-umbrella (accessed June 15, 2014).

Nolan, B. (2011). New Orleans Officials, French Quarter Groups Work to Wipe out Graffiti in an Effort to Wipe out Crime. *The Times-Picayune*. Available online at: www.nola.com/politics/index.ssf/2011/11/new_orleans_officials_french_q.html (accessed June 15, 2014).

Piano, D. (2006). Writing the Ruins: Rhetorics of Crisis and Uplift after the Flood. *Rhizomes: Cultural Studies in Emerging Knowledge* (13). Available at: www.rhizomes.net/issue4/piano.html. (accessed June 25, 2014).

Plyer, A. (2010). What Census 2010 Reveals about Population and Housing in New Orleans and the Metro Area. Available online at: www.datacenterresearch.org/reports_analysis/census-2010.

Reckdahl, K. (2012). UNITY Showcases Priest's Portrait of Forlorn Child. Available online at: www.nola.com/politics/index.ssf/2012/06/unity_building_showcases_pries.html (accessed June 1, 2012).

Rose, C. (2011). Chris Rose: French Quarter Graffiti. Available online at: www.projectnola.com/the-news/news/42-fox-8/168225-chris-rose-french-quarter-graffiti (accessed September 27, 2012).

Smyk, B. (2011). Adventures in Art: The NOLA Street Art Tour. *Nolavie*. Available online at: www.nola.com/nolavie/index.ssf/2011/07/adventures_in_art_the_nola_str.html (accessed June 15, 2014).

Stanonis, A.J. (2006). *Creating the Big Easy: New Orleans and the Emergence of Modern Tourism 1918–1945*. Athens: University of Georgia Press.

Starr, S.F. (2014). Widespread Graffiti on Public Structures Reads Like City Tolerates Lawlessness. *The Lens*. Available online at: http://thelensnola.org/2014/01/14/widespread-graffiti-on-public-structures-reads-like-city-hall-tolerance-for-lawlessness (accessed May 20, 2014).

U.S. House of Representatives. (2006). *A Failure of Initiative: The Final Report of the Select Bipartisan Committee to Investigate the Preparation for and Response to Hurricane Katrina*. Washington, DC: US Government Printing Office.

Varisco, T. (2005). *Spoiled*. New Orleans: Tom Varisco Designs.

Winkler-Schmit, D. (2009). Is There More than One Gray Ghost in New Orleans? *The Gambit Weekly*. Available online at: www.bestofneworleans.com/gambit/is-there-more-than-one-gray-ghost-in-new-orleans/Content?oid=1257083 (accessed June 5, 2014).

Woodward, A. (2014). Sign Language. *The Gambit Weekly*. June 17, pp. 16–19.

WWL-New Orleans. (2010). Fred Radtke, Operation Clean Sweep New Orleans Has Hotline to Report French Quarter Graffiti. Available online at: www.youtube.com/watch?v=1tGtS3h9Usc (accessed May 21, 2014).

19

Pop culture and politics
Graffiti and street art in Montréal

Anna Wacławek

Signature graffiti worldwide

By the early 1980s, as the New York Style infiltrated European graffiti scenes, an incredibly large network of writers was forming. Writers in a number of cities in England, Germany, France and Spain, which already had graffiti scenes unconnected to hip-hop, began to employ the American style. As London's FADE 2 explains: 'Graffiti in this country has come like a model, an airplane model. It's come here already built. Graffiti in America has taken years to develop, all the styles like your wildstyle and bubble lettering. Over here we haven't added anything to it apart from brushing up on a few techniques' (Chalfant and Prigoff, 1987: p. 60). Indeed, in the early days many European writers were outright copying the graffiti they had encountered in films and photographs from the United States as a way to practice and develop their own techniques. While many were quick to incorporate the New York Style into their already existing practices, others acknowledged it simply as an alternative to their own approach. In England, for example, where many writers in places such as Bristol and London picked up on the New York Style, others, influenced by the punk rock scene, continued to write political graffiti, which led to a highly evolved graffiti scene specialising in stencils.

In 1987, Chalfant and Prigoff reported in *Spraycan Art* that writers in Paris painted primarily in vacant areas throughout the city (1987: p. 70). The aesthetics of graffiti writing as it existed in New York City did not grab hold of Parisian writers' imaginations for many years; only a handful of active writers employed that style during the 1980s. However, by the end of the decade, *'le graff s'est imposé comme LE phenomene culturel de la jeunesse'*[1] (Lemoine and Terral, 2005: p. 38). Graffiti exploded in concurrence with the French rap music movement of the 1990s. A similar scenario occurred in Montréal.

While the city of Montréal was not devoid of graffiti prior to hip-hop's invasion, it took until the 1990s for the scene to truly take form. Since the 1960s, Montréal had a history of socio-politically relevant graffiti, which appeared throughout the city's centre and its boroughs. This non-stylised form of graffiti writing was executed by any number of non-affiliated youth, and addressed national and local politics, namely: Québécois nationalism; Bill 101; socio-economic issues; racism; and First Nations issues. It was only by the end of the 1980s that several small collectives of graffiti aficionados influenced by the New York graffiti style began to write signature graffiti.

According to Montréal-based film producer/director/writer Pablo Aravena, today Montréal is 'one of the most painted cities in North America' (Pablo Aravena quoted in Knelman, 2007, R1). The great number of legal walls throughout the city offer persuasive evidence for this claim, as do the immense popularity of Montréal-based international festivals, such as Under Pressure[2] and the support of local contemporary galleries like the esteemed Yves Laroche Gallery.[3] The signature graffiti movement is alive and well in the city, and writers are increasingly employed by businesses to render their logos. In conjunction with the active writing scene, a number of street artists take part in the creation of Montréal's alternative cityscape. Aside from Montréal's street art pioneer, Roadsworth, artists such as Stikki Peaches, MissMe and Whatisadam (WIA) typify the local scene.

The Montréal scene

Legibly written, politically motivated graffiti most often gives voice to issues relevant to the citizens of a particular place. In Montréal this mode of self-expression – albeit it being most often anonymous – has been popular since the 1960s. It is not surprising that in a city like Montréal where language politics reigns supreme as a cultural marker, the types of graffiti that initially dominated the cityscape in the 1960s were connected to issues of the protection and sovereignty of Québécois culture, including language, and therefore were political in nature. Slogans, calls to action, and the expression of disdain via legible phrases – written anonymously – prevailed as the graffiti of choice in a city that has long aimed to control the language used in public signage. The issues that resonated at the forefront of Montréal's socio-political identity proved recurrently meaningful to those citizens who would take it upon themselves to publicly write unsigned slogans. First Nations, gender, nationhood, language and sovereignty issues spearheaded the political graffiti scene.

The question as to why writing evolved as a subculture in Montréal comparatively late, as compared to other major North American cities, is, according to Louise Gauthier, answered politically. The author stipulates that cultural distinctiveness and sovereignty are the main socio-political issues that shaped Montréal's graffiti landscape and delayed the evolution of signature graffiti (Gauthier, 1998: p. 100). In the 1960s, as the concept of nationhood become more succinctly defined through language in Québec, among other factors, the shift to safeguard francophone culture became an aggressively political act. As the number of those in favour of separatism increased, partly as a reaction to Pierre-Elliott Trudeau's (Canada's charismatic Liberal Party Prime Minister from 1968 to 1979, and again from 1980 to 1984) institution of Canada's bilingualism, debates surrounding Québec's identity intensified to the point of violence. The radical political group, Front de liberation du Québec (FLQ), established in 1963 during a period of industrial modernisation, is best-known for the 1970 October Crisis, when the FLQ committed a series of terrorist acts that led Trudeau's government to invoke the War Measures Act during peacetime. The aftermath of the October Crisis resulted, by the mid-1970s, in the Parti Québecois' official call to strengthen Québec's identity as culturally distinct. This era of political upheaval motivated much of the political graffiti that inundated the cityscape.

In the years that followed, numerous political events directly related to the issues of language laws as well as cultural distinctiveness for Québec's francophone population resulted in many public declarations, which often took the form of graffiti. The Charte de la langue française (more popularly known in anglophone contexts as Bill 101), passed by the Québec National Assembly to address the perceived issue of deculturation, was one such provocateur that motivated Montréal citizens to make manifest their views by writing directly on city walls. Bill 101's implementation in 1977 was followed by Bill 178 in 1988. Bill 178, or the 'French only'

Bill, mandated that all public signage in Québec must be written in French only. This law provoked varied reactions, from fervent support to outright dismissal.

Other contentious socio-political issues were also debated in the public sphere through writing. Personal opinions both in favour of and in opposition to any given debate appeared on public walls throughout the city. Graffiti referring to First Nations peoples, gender and gay rights, religion, anarchy and revolution, for example, proliferated within the urban sphere. This myriad of impassioned debates notwithstanding, Québec's contested sovereignty as well as the issue of language reigned as ongoing public dialogues for over a decade. Appearing in all manner of places, written in French, English or both, the often-anonymous graffiti specific to Montréal politics dominated the scene until, in the early 1990s, signature graffiti writing began transforming the visual language of the cityscape.

In the 1980s, Zilon was by all accounts the most recognised graffiti writer in Montréal, making work that hung in the balance between political and signature graffiti. Not firmly attached to either of these two traditions, his characteristically rendered images of faces are easily identified because of their style, which has enabled the artist's work to be recognised without the writing of a name, or a written message. While signature graffiti did make an appearance in Montréal circa 1983–1984, with writers such as Akira and Flow (a.k.a. Checker T) getting their names up, the scene did not burgeon at that time in any sustained way.

Spurred on by trips to NYC, the culture of hip-hop, as well as tourism, the second wave of Montréal graffiti materialised in a more pronounced way in the early 1990s with writers like Flow, Timer, Stack and Sike at the helm, establishing crews. The DownTown Crew (DTC), Smashing All Toys (SAT) and The Hard Crew (THC) did graffiti in the city around 1994, and the practice of signature graffiti writing in Montréal became an ongoing part of the city's landscape. Since writing already had an established international history by the time it boomed in Montréal, it therefore comes as no surprise that local styles developed swiftly, having a thirty-year history to build upon.

Over the years the Montréal graffiti scene has certainly produced its share of writing kings including Sake, who is respected by other writers for his focused work ethic and complete dedication to writing; Castro, whose work is highly visible when navigating the city; Stack, revered for his smooth style and skills, Seaz, member of TA and SAT crews, as well as a spokesperson and dedicated activist; Bez, who manipulates official city signage to create his own; Stare, who appropriates spaces of visual commerce (e.g. billboards, and/or storefront canopies/windows) to advertise his moniker as a sort of brand; Omen, who bridges traditional graffiti writing and street art with his own brand of unique aerosol portraiture; and many others such as Akira, Zek, Fluke and Monk-e.

The shift from political to signature graffiti is significant for numerous reasons, specifically in terms of message, composition, perpetrators and impetus – in other words, the divergent answers to the questions of who, what, when, where and why. While political graffiti is disseminated by males and females from potentially varied age groups, like many of the graffiti subcultures that subside internationally, Montréal's early signature graffiti scene was largely composed of young men who quickly organised themselves into crews. Although writers hail from dissimilar neighbourhoods, and socio-economic as well as cultural backgrounds, their shared activity, writing graffiti, becomes a unifying, albeit competitive, venture.

In short, the politicised messages that for decades had become commonplace within the public sphere of Montréal declined in number and were largely replaced by the culture of self-representation through graffiti. This change essentially meant that graffiti in Montréal shifted from being primarily political in terms of message to being political in terms of the action of writing itself – an action that for the writers themselves is one of empowerment. In her study of Montréal graffiti, Louise Gauthier explains that although signature graffiti's appearance in the city is part of the general trend of globalisation, it also responds to the need of young people to carve out an image of themselves, which, as subsequent anti-graffiti campaigns demonstrated, proved much more 'dangerous' than the protest phrases the city was accustomed to (Gauthier, 1998: p. 85).

The thriving scene expanded considerably through the congregation of writers in a handful of discrete places such as the Redpath Sugar Company factory in Pointe-Saint-Charles (known as The Point, Point-Saint-Charles is *Le Sud-Ouest* borough of Montréal), the nine million square feet that make up the city's deserted Turcot train yards, and the TA (Team Autobot) wall founded by Seaz in 1995. Montréal's abandoned buildings – especially large factories or warehouses such as the Redpath – provided writers with physical and psychological space, and thus these sites became pivotal in both building and sustaining a scene. From the mid-1990s until 1999 when it was slotted for redevelopment, Redpath was instrumental in the sustenance and development of Montréal's graffiti scene. This setting continues to resonate as a cultural marker in the city's writing history, and as a place of apprenticeship, development of personal style and stronghold of activity, proving the vibrancy of the local scene.

The massive, abandoned Turcot train yards (in west-end Montréal, bounded by the neighbourhood *Nôtre-Dame-de-Grace* (NDG), Highway 20 and the neighbourhood of St. Henri) later become another significant site for the culture of writing. An immense graffiti 'museum' which displays all writing elements from tags to large-scale pieces, the Turcot yards, like Redpath before it, is a sort of sacred site for writers in that its walls relay the history of the movement and evoke a collective consciousness. Additionally, a huge wall that runs under the Ville-Marie expressway (what Seaz named the TA Wall) was another site that quickly gained momentum when writers were expelled from Redpath. In Montréal, architectural structures such as the Redpath and the Turcot Yards are among the most culturally meaningful and venerated sites for writers. Not only places of congregation, these sites, partly because of their distance from the city's core, also functioned as sorts of laboratories for graffiti production.

The case of Roadsworth

In 2001 the artist known as Roadsworth began spray-painting stencils on city roads. He fabricates his stencils with specific locations in mind, and employs simplicity of visual representation to create meaningful images. Roadsworth's aim is not merely to use the street as a canvas, but to interweave and integrate his designs in and around the already existing road markings, which works to make people question the language of a city. By using the same paint colours as that of official infrastructural markers, Roadsworth's work remains within the confines of the city's language, but also breaks its visual monotony.

Roadsworth relies on the structure of the urban terrain as a necessary condition for the conception and production of his work. The artist's road stencils are typically attachments to or alterations of road signage and other physical road features, such as crosswalks, parking spaces, sewer-hatches and parking metres. His work can thus be read as specific to the sites of the road that prescribe certain behaviours in the city: stop, turn, park, yield, cross and so on. By juxtaposing his stencilled creations next to road signs, the artist proposes a different interpretation of signs and symbols most pedestrians and drivers are accustomed to. Thus, the language of the city is an indispensable prerequisite for his practice, which folds the site into its significance so completely that experiencing the work and the site becomes one and the same.

Shortly after starting his work, he was arrested in 2004, and as a result local radio, television and newspapers engaged the public in debating this criminalisation of an art form. The public conversation that followed Roadsworth's arrest succinctly illustrates street art's story in Montréal, a story that by all accounts involves three main players: individuals, institutions and the media. The Montréal street art scene did not spawn directly from an international graffiti connection, meaning that it is not made up of graffiti writers turned street artists as is sometimes the case internationally. In general, and unlike the local graffiti scene, it did not challenge the general public with overtly politicised messages, nor did it fight for credibility within the urban sphere. Instead, by the time street artists became active in Montréal, the international street art movement had already gained notoriety. Banksy and Shepard Fairey were more well-known; collectors, museums and galleries were interested in showcasing street work; and documentary films as well as the Internet had already informed the world of the phenomenon. In short, as opposed to the signature graffiti movement which revolutionised the city's visual landscape, street art practices were somewhat more gently inserted into localised settings.

Roadsworth is best known for his stencils in the Plateau and Mile End neighbourhoods of Montréal, applied directly onto roads using the same yellow and white paint used for official street marking. Some of his more popular works include: the fashioning of a zipper out of existing double lines on asphalt roadways, thus inviting city dwellers to undo their predetermined ideas about what does and does not belong in the public sphere; the alteration of pedestrian crossings into huge boot prints, which dwarf the surrounding area implying that the street ultimately belongs to pedestrians; and loudspeakers, inspired by prison speakers because they tell people what to do, much like advertising. These stencils, assumed by some Montréalers to have been commissioned by the city, brought 'some life onto Montréal's otherwise drab and potholed Plateau streets' (Lejtenji, 2006), and were overwhelmingly well received by the neighbourhood's residents.

On 29 November 2004, Roadworth's reign as Montréal's best-known stencil artist became precarious when he was caught while stencilling one of his pieces. Suddenly, the subtle images that had 'quietly aroused the imagination of passers-by', thrust the artist into the limelight when media reports of his arrest became public (Boudreau, 2006). The official explanation for Roadsworth's arrest was that his work represented a 'breach of public security' (Flannery, 2005). From a purely legal standpoint, his work has been argued to pose a safety hazard because his imagery is not found in the driver's handbook, and could thus confuse drivers. The artist was charged with fifty-three counts of mischief, a $265,000 fine (CDN), and possible banishment from the city for three years. Following his arrest, disputes about the role of art in public spaces ensued with 'intellectuals, city officials, lawyers, artists and art fans debating the rights and responsibilities – not to mention penalties – guerrilla street artists can expect' (Lejtenyi, 2004). After a great deal of pressure from Montréal citizens, including an online letter-writing campaign to 'save' the artist organised by Chris Hand of Zeke's Gallery, Roadsworth was finally offered a deal by the city on 17 January 2006, just minutes before his hearing. The artist accepted a conditional discharge – meaning no criminal record – and a massive reduction in the number of mischief charges from fifty-three to five. He was sentenced to serve eighteen months of probation during which he could not use stencils or spray-paint without the city's approval. He also had to pay $250 and serve forty hours of artistically-motivated community service.

The street art scene – individuals

Like the culture of graffiti writing, when street art practices began appearing in Montréal's cityscape, the international street art movement was in full effect. What remains unique about the Montréal street art scene, perhaps directly connected to its late emergence, is that official cultural channels, such as major art institutions, support it. The city-wide debate sparked by the Roadsworth affair encouraged others to participate in street art production. The scene itself is: largely localised within the Plateau Mont-Royal neighbourhood; supported by major institutions such as the Montréal Museum of Fine Arts (MMFA), summer festivals such as the Mural public art festival, and local galleries such as Station 16 and the Yves Laroche Gallery; and is characterised by the work of collectives, A'Shop and En Masse, as well as a handful of individual artists. In short, in distinct opposition to the local graffiti scene, the street art narrative in Montréal is one of cooperation between people, institutions and the media.

Having played an integral role in Roadsworth's criminal case, French and English television, radio and print media continues to support street art production. Conversely, the opposite continues to be the case for graffiti writing. Montréal street artists tend to favour working within a bohemian neighbourhood, the Plateau, known for its trendy shops, relaxed party atmosphere as well as musical, visual and performative artistic expression. It comes as no surprise then that both galleries dedicated to street art display are located in or adjacent to this neighbourhood, that the Mural public art festival takes place on St. Laurent boulevard, a street known locally as 'The Main', and that street artists disseminate the bulk of their works in the streets of a neighbourhood accessed daily by pedestrians.

Street artists MissMe, Stikki Peaches and WIA all work primarily with wheatpastes – (affixing artwork to surfaces with a mixture of flour and water) a preferred medium for artists operating outdoors in a city plagued by an unforgiving winter. Similarly, they all employ styles that reference music, film and North American material culture – in short, popular culture. Their work is therefore accessible not only by virtue of where it is displayed but also thanks to its often-recognizable iconography. Akin to street art practices worldwide, Montréal artists connect with their audiences through imagery that ignites a sense of familiarity, message and cleverness.

Often the political becomes personal in portraits as in this case whereby the artist, herself a jazz singer, aims to highlight historical fact so as to illuminate contemporary present with her portrait series. MissMe's series of jazz singers is one such powerful testament. She explains:

> If music was a religion: these would be my saints. I, as a jazz trained singer, have a deep love for jazz music and its social and historical implications. That is why I have decided to draw them as classical orthodox style icons, as I like the contrast of that classical style and the streets I put them in. I believe most of these women (Sarah Vaughan, Billie Holiday, Nina Simone, Josephine Baker) are either very little known or not known at all . . . (in terms of) their music or social battles (personal and political). Most kids our days, ignore all about the importance of Jazz musically as well (in today's music). I always try to add meaningful details to my saints. For example: Nina Simone has the Black Power symbol on her necklace as she played a very important role in the Civil rights movement in the 1960s. As for my Saint Billie Holiday, she is holding a scroll with the first words of the Strange Fruit poem. She was the very first one to sing LIVE on radio that extremely powerful and political piece in 1939. Takes strength. Takes courage. Takes a political vision. She was not only that beautiful lady that sang the blues with a flower in her hair. Jazz, in these times, was the voice of an oppressed group of people and we often forget how unglamorous all of it really was.[4]

By layering her portraits with numerous levels of meaning, some of which speak directly to the artist's own sense of self as part of a Jazz history, MissMe is able to translate these women's stories both as they played out in history and as they resonate with young people today. What is more, with her portraits MissMe speaks to two of Montréal's points of pride: its history of political activism and its endorsement of artistic expression. The portrayal of musical giants who have battled for acceptance and persevered as instruments in the face of oppression resonates with a society fighting for recognition as a distinct voice. Moreover, the indubitable influence of these individuals in history speaks to Montréal's own sense of joy at playing host and motherland to some of the world's best-known talent.

Montréal has other unique examples of street art. 'What if Art Ruled the World?' is a tagline question posed by an artist recognised widely for his mash-ups of characters such as 'BatBond' – a tantalising fusion of Batman and James Bond – which suggests we all participate with our own reply. Stikki Peaches' life-sized portraits of popular characters that are often narratives within narratives succeed in the public sphere because of their sleek reinterpretation of vigilante, rebellious, tough and seductive personalities. Known as an effervescent, sexy, cultural mecca, Montréal prides itself on its reputation as a lively, historically-rich metropolis. With his imagery, Stikki Peaches accesses the very essence of the city. Wheatpasted full-body interpretations of iconic male cinematic characters function, within the cityscape, as a counterbalance to MissMe's typically female, musical saints. Whereas Stikki Peaches merges two characters as a playful amalgamation of pop culture references, the iconographical details in MissMe's portraits serve to recount personal stories fraught with historical fact. Both artists' focus on the real or imagined portrait succeeds within a mass-mediated world where the lines between fact and fiction are often blurred.

The trend of mashing-up cultural references is also employed by WIA, another artist who favours wheatpasting to produce images which allude both to the natural world (namely via the depiction of wild North American animals), and the popular (especially as experienced through material culture). Best-known for his psychedelic depictions of the famed Québec maple syrup can, WIA both extends a nod to Warhol's legacy of animating material objects of mass pro-duction, and pays tribute to a symbol of local pride, which is available widely in tourist gift shops. Interested in depicting comic book inspired imagery that fuses human torsos with animal heads, and in creating unexpected narratives, WIA's forte is in referencing Canadian or specifically Québécois cultural markers to entice nostalgia. His recent depictions of Montréal Canadian hockey players, for example, appeared on city streets during heated playoffs and appealed to Montréalers as a public show of support for the local team.

The street art scene – collectives

Officially launched in 2009, A'Shop is a production company and artist-run collective specialising in painting all manner of objects and diverse indoor/outdoor spaces, yet they are especially revered for their large-scale legal murals. Given the group's wide range of expertise and multiple combined years of experience writing graffiti and painting murals, it is no surprise that they are sought after and their work is widely admired. Their most successful projects have included colourful murals spanning entire building facades whereby the narrative represented directly relates to the neighbourhood in which it appears. For example, their 2011 mural dubbed 'Our Lady of Grace' painted in Montréal's NDG neighbourhood incorporates landmarks familiar to its residents framed within an elaborate art nouveau inspired natural setting. As participants in the 2013 Mural festival the collective painted a hip elderly lady positioned within the Plateau's streets signalling that street art is a community affair – one that all ages can benefit from.

Less of a formal collective and more of an ongoing collaborative project, En Masse is the epitome of a collective artistic vision. Artists from diverse backgrounds have shared in the production of En Masse's collaborative murals, which are easily identified as theirs in the cityscape by virtue of their distinct black and white colour-scheme, and intermingled, jumbled, 'busy' appearance. The palette being the only unifier in their productions, En Masse's murals, which tend to cover every inch of available space, are extremely rich in narratives and intertwined representation.

Aside from combining the efforts of multiple individuals to produce a unified vision, A'Shop and En Masse share a dedication to facilitate community workshops and other pedagogical initiatives. Moreover, both collectives take on corporate and other commissioned projects, and both partner with the city of Montréal in the creation of community-building projects. In other words, these organisations are instrumental in fostering the city's general admiration of street art.

Institutions

Yves Laroche's founding vision since 1991 has involved a dedication to showcasing the avant-garde in contemporary art. While graffiti and street art are but two of the genres Laroche's commercial gallery displays, the space is widely recognised as a proponent of alternative art production. This formal enterprise has recently gained competition in the form of a less formal commercial outfit, Station 16, and a pop-up graffiti gallery, Fresh Paint. Station 16, initially solely a silk-screen print shop, but later a point of display for local and international street art talent, officially opened its print gallery space in conjunction with the launch of the Mural festival in 2013. Situated on The Main, the storefront gallery is perfectly positioned to entice Plateau residents, many of them artistically-inclined young professionals, to purchase affordable limited-edition street art prints. Supportive of local talent, in its short time on the scene, Station 16 has proven a valuable contributor to the community and market for this type of artistic production in every respect. The gallery's exhibition openings are routinely packed with local artists eager to support a growing scene already intertwined with international support. Furthermore, the relatively inexpensive prints allow younger audiences to collect art produced by emerging talent.

In contrast to both Station 16 and the Yves Laroche Gallery, Fresh Paint is a vastly different space in terms of function, display and impetus. The gallery opened up spontaneously in a temporarily abandoned space scheduled for refurbishment. Operated by the organisers of the Under Pressure festival, the haphazard space is quite literally taken over by art. As opposed to using traditionally formal display tactics, Fresh Paint employs a grittier, less stylised mode of display – one that mimics how graffiti or street art might exist on city streets. Its rotating exhibitions allow artists to cover any available space with their work, thus creating a wholly enveloping experience, where one can quite literally be surrounded by art on the floor, walls and ceiling.

Together, these exhibition spaces offer Montréalers the gamut of experiences relative to graffiti and street art indoors. Additionally, major institutions such as MMFA and Musee d'art contemporain de Montréal (MAC) have shown their support and advocacy for street art production. For example, En Masse was invited to paint the enormous closing room in the Big Bang!: Creativity is Given Carte Blanche exhibition at the MMFA (6 November 2011 – 22 January 2012), which allowed visitors to relax on bean bags and absorb the totality of the images. Later, the MMFA invited En Masse back to the museum to paint their newly renovated 'family lounge'. Furthermore, MAC ex-director, Marc Mayer, was instrumental in publicly supporting Roadsworth during his criminal trial and appeared in a documentary film that chronicled the artist's case in order to defend his cause.

Festivals

Montréal's first graffiti writing convention, Aerosol Funk, was organised in 1996 by Seaz. He went on to become a spokesperson for graffiti in Montréal urging people not to associate it with gang activity. Later that same year, Seaz teamed up with fellow writer Flow to produce the first national graffiti festival in Canada, Under Pressure (UP). Twenty-three graffiti writers participated in the event, which aimed to 'contradict the negative reputation that graffiti was getting from the city, who was trying to scare the public using local media'.[5] With participants from Ottawa, Toronto and Vancouver, UP proved that the Montréal graffiti scene is part of a greater national and international movement, and almost twenty years later the festival is still going strong.

The perseverance and enthusiasm of Sterling Downey and other members of the graffiti-rooted graphic design company, Urban X-Pressions, who organised the event, eventually bore fruit as evidenced by the massive success of UP in the coming years. As an annual international festival, UP provides an arena that unites writers belonging to different crews from around the world, and gives them the ability to paint together in a decriminalised community setting. By creating an engaging atmosphere and mounting the exhibitions in accessible venues, UP organisers are working to expose the public to current graffiti trends, familiarising them with the skill and creativity involved in this public expression. Showcasing the work of innovative and talented writers in an urban setting, graffiti art becomes less alienating to the general populace and gains credibility and respect from those who perceive it simply as vandalism.

By 2001, this hip-hop festival had grown to be one of the largest events of its kind in North America featuring over one hundred graffiti writers from all corners of the globe, thirty DJs and MCs, numerous breakdancing crews and most importantly an estimated five thousand spectators (Lamarche, 2002).

Festivals like this offer important opportunities for artists and audiences alike. In the safety of daylight, spectators have the rare opportunity to witness the creation of graffiti pieces and admire the hardship of working with spray paint as a medium. The writers themselves are able to pick up pointers from their international compatriots, and feed off each other's expertise. The event generates a definite sense of community among writers; however, graffiti's competitive drive does not cease to exist as these artists continue to compete for fame.

The Mural public art festival had its first edition in 2013 – again, a late inauguration for a festival that celebrates local and international street art production, yet it has already made a huge impact on audiences. Organised by LNDMRK, a local marketing and creative solutions company that liaises between artists and businesses, this festival is ideally situated on The Main to benefit from maximum pedestrian interaction. Organised to coincide with The Main's annual street sale, whereby the street is closed off to vehicle traffic to create a party atmosphere allowing vendors, bars and eateries to operate directly on the street, the timing of the festival is highly effective and creates hype. In fact, the 800,000 visitors to Mural in 2013 have secured LNDMRK a Grand Prix du tourisme québécois. In 2014, twenty additional murals were added to the twenty painted in 2013 by local and international artists, making St. Laurent boulevard a veritable street art gallery.

Conclusion

Montréal has reacted – and continues to react – to international graffiti and street art practices in a way that echoes what is going on globally. While criminal charges for individuals convicted of vandalism associated with graffiti have severely intensified, street art practices are generally more accepted and even supported by cultural institutions and the media. Moreover, as is often the case elsewhere, the work of street artists is routinely criticised by graffiti writers. Although writers are active all over the city and street artists tend to localize their practices within trendy, bohemian, pedestrian-heavy areas, graffiti writers continue to do what they do best, which is disrupt the cleaner, more institutionalised, more conformist iconography of street artists in diverse locales including abandoned post-industrial sites and other venues of decay. While writers are not exactly competing for space with street artists, they do continually re-assert their displeasure with street art's popularity by covering over their work with new layers of paint. That is to say, Montréal's writing culture is not affected by street art's popularity in the sense that writers continue to do what they've always done: to get their names up, anywhere and everywhere, without permission and without compromise.

Reflecting on the future of the Montréal urban art scene, local artist Omen argued that its fate will follow that of every alternate culture in any give city, with the outcome of 'corporate sponsorship and branding towards youth culture'. He continues:

> there are a lot of writers here that are still doing the true culture of graffiti: live in the streets and not on the web. They are the real "artists". This is not a Montréal Phenomenon. It is universal. The galleries will get the walls for the street artists and the writers will take them. And the world turns.[6]

The fact that Montréal's graffiti scene developed comparatively late has had no effect on the skills its constituents display or its permeation throughout the cityscape. Alive and well, Montréal's graffiti scene (although considerably more active in the warmer summer months) continues both to signal its presence throughout the metropolis and its arteries, and to push the boundaries of execution and visual disruption.

Notes

1   'Graffiti has imposed itself as *the* cultural phenomenon for youth' (My translation).
2   Under Pressure is both a bi-yearly magazine and the name of an international graffiti convention, www.underpressure.ca.
3   See www.yveslaroche.com. The urban gallery thrives on the showcasing of work by established and emerging underground and cutting edge graffiti, tattoo, comic, pop, illustration and surrealist artists.
4   Personal correspondence by email, 29 September 2013.
5   Urban X – Pressions: Visual Chaos from Grafic Dictators. Web Page. Available: www.urbanx-pressions.com. *Urbanx-pressions* invited graffiti writers from across Canada, as well as popular DJs such as Kid Koala and DJ A-Track, in the hopes of creating a kind of graffiti convention for writers and for the general public.
6   Personal correspondence by email, 9 April 2014.

References

Boudreau, L. (2006). The New Beautiful City: A Divided Highway. *Spacing Publications*; available online at http://spacing.ca/art-roadsworth.htm (accessed 22 September 2014).
Chalfant, H. and Prigoff, J. (1987). *Spraycan Art*. London: Thames and Hudson.
Flannery, C. (2005). Art on the Road Fails to Appeal to Montréal Officialdom. *Circa Art Magazine*; available online at www.recirca.com/artnews/396.shtml (accessed 14 December 2005).
Gauthier, L. (1998). *Writing on the Run: The History and Transformation of Street Graffiti in Montréal in the 1990s*. Ph.D. Dissertation. New York: New School for Social Research.
Knelman, J. (2007). Graffiti Goes Six-Figure Legit. *Globe and Mail*. Saturday, 4 August.
Lamarche, B. (2002). Les artistes de la bonbonne a l'oeuvre – Le Graffiti aux Foufs; available online at www.ledevoir.com/culture/arts-visuels/6603/les-artistes-de-la-bonbonne-a-l-oeuvre-le-graffiti-aux-foufs (accessed 22 September 2002).

Lejtenyi, P. (2004). Roadsworth Busted. *Mirror*, *20*(25); available online at www.Montréalmirror.com/2004/120904/front.html (accessed 3 January 2006).

Lemoine, S. and Terral, J. (2005). *In Situ: Un panorama de l'art urbain de 1975 a nos jours*. Paris: Editions Alternatives.

20

The battle for public space along the Mapocho River, Santiago de Chile, 1964–2014

Rodney Palmer

Introduction

Urban artists in the southern cone of South America habitually use combative language that expresses their intention *tomar* or to 'take' public space. For example, for Kat (aka Nekonekoteko) and Fede (aka Blablabuto), organisers of the radically alternative SABA (Street Arte Buenos Aires) urban art signifies taking the streets, reclaiming what is yours . . . an 'attack' on public space'.[1] The artists known as t.h.e.i.c. of Colectivo Licuado of Montevideo (www.colectivo licuado.com) and Henruz of Santiago (www.henruz.blogspot.com, www.henruz.com) have conversed about how they like 'to take a place', Henruz putting the rhetorical question: 'To take a space from what? . . . from nothingness, from publicity, from party political propaganda'.[2] This is a much more serious agenda than the humorous personal rivalries of ripostes and counter-ripostes between graffiti writers on city walls, such as that between the late King Robbo and Banksy in London, which characterise much street art in the Anglophone northern hemisphere.

While all the above-cited comments about taking public space – in the case of these graffiti artists painting walls and other surfaces in the street – were made in 2013, in Chile walls have been the vehicle for protest art for over a century. As Alejandro Mono Gonzalez (http://monogonzalez.blogspot.com) of the emblematic communist muralist collective, the Brigada Ramona Parra (BRP), has explained: 'It is customary for the Chilean left to occupy public space since the foundation of the Chilean Communist Party in 1912: That is to say before the movement of Mexican muralism began.'[3] This is one reason why it irritates Gonzalez that histories of Chilean street art begin with Mexican muralism; the other is that while most Mexican murals were painted indoors, most Chilean murals have been in the open air.

Such an historical perspective is not surprising coming from the founder of Chile's greatest (but by no means only) collective of political propaganda muralists. It is more surprising coming from young *graffitero* Coas: 'Here in Chile since the birth of the Communist Party there have always been artistic expressions in the street, the first of which was political muralism.'[4]

The abyss between political muralism and graffiti

Political *Brigadas* of muralists started to define themselves as such in the 1960s and their relationship to hip hop graffiti that began to appear in Chile from the 1980s has not been straightforward. According to protagonists from both sides, Mono González and Gustavo Arias (aka Lalo of the hip hop band Nueva York) there was an 'abyss' ('abismo') between the two subcultures and it is only since around 2008 there has been a convergence between political muralism and graffiti. Both sides recognise the enormous rift of the 1980s and 1990s. González explained in 2012:

> There was a period, and it is very important to say so, and to recognize that it was a period, a product of the dictatorship, that there was a cultural vacuum in which there was an abyss between the brigadistas and the *graffitero*. That is only recently in the last three or four years there has arisen a sort of re encounter between the *graffitero* and the muralist in which there is respect and recognition between one and the other. There started to be mutual recognition around the time of the centenary of the birth of Salvador Allende in 2008. Today the Open Sky Museum of San Miguel is very important because we have managed to bring *graffiteros* and muralists together.[5]

In a separate interview given in the same place on the same date, Arias indicated:

> Until four or five years back there was quite a big abyss between brigade muralism and graffiti. It must be understood that brigadism has to do with the political world; and that there are local elections in Chile in 2012 and also presidential elections next year, in which many brigades who are not necessarily muralists but are merely propagandists, set about occupying walls and in this occupation of walls often they do not respect what is continually painted on the street; and I refer not only to graffiti but also to muralism itself, mural art. That is in that battle-machine, if you are in the street and see things by political propaganda brigades is when this abyss is produced, and there is resentment that many people from the political parties come and cover up what s there with mere letters and propaganda for their candidate. It doesn t matter which candidate or who does it, no distinction needs to be made, because all candidates work in the same way, and this is pretty annoying to we who made the street scene, whether *graffiteros* or muralists. And fundamentally and constantly ever since the graffiti scene emerged, which is from the 1980s that it took off, there is this abyss. Now with Mono and with people who were part of the first phase of brigade muralism, brigadist as he calls it, and who also understand that there is an art behind graffiti, there has been this coming together. But at times such as this they alienate you once more, that is, it is not something that is absolutely exhausted. That is there is a good vibe with Mono, there is a good vibe with other authors of murals that are more classic, as they call it, more permanent, and the graffiti world, but the estrangement is not something that has completely come to an end.[6]

It is noteworthy that both González and Arias consider that the abyss between their respective subcultures was all but total until about 2007. In 2007, many would have agreed with a celebrated Chilean graffiti writer s perception that the BRP were anachronistic, embodying 'a different politics for a different time'. At about the same time, however, many second wave Chilean street artists expressed their admiration of the BRP (Palmer 2008: p. 60).

The best twenty-first-century example of individual street artists' energies fusing into a revolutionary collective is UMLEM (Unidades de Muralistas Luchador Ernesto Miranda: Units of Muralists Fighter Ernesto Miranda). Miranda had helped found the Chilean MIR (Movimiento de Izquierda Revolucionaria: Movement of the Revolutionary Left) in 1956 (Salinas 2013). MIR is still active in its own right and its libertarian revolutionary ideology is one of the models for UMLEM. UMLEM has grown beneath the radar and is now more widespread in Chile than any political muralist collective, baring only the BRP, has ever been, with eighteen affiliated groups almost the length of Chile from the southern island of Chiloe, to Tocopilla and Arica in the far north of Chile (Palmer 2011: pp. 153, 157).

UMLEM was born on 11 September 2003, at a commemoration of the thirtieth anniversary of the military coup in Chile, Talcahuano, the port contiguous with Chile's second city Concepción, an early heartland of their murals (Palmer 2008: p. 47). In their own words:

> The reasons that motivated their founding were . . . that we were a group of male and female comrades who had hitherto been painting individually and within different aesthetic tendencies all however related to street art and moreover trying to deliver a message that would help to raise awareness through painting . . . The process which drives us to develop a particular aesthetic has its roots in the historical recovery of the Latin American muralist tradition, including the Ramona Parra Brigades, but also constructing our own aesthetic as a means of creating something new, together with the libertarian Project that we have been building for ten years now.[7]

UMLEM murals use planar colours within a black outline of the classic style of BRP muralism, and their style is further characterised by a spectrum limited to black, white and a range of reds and pinks – an anarchist palette, UMLEM's libertarian project being informed by Bakuninian anarchism and its Latin American off shoots such as the FAU (Federación Anarquista Uruguaya: Uruguayan Anarchist Federation). UMLEM's distinctive style is also recognisable by its infantile figures, intended to be accessible to all. We will in due course come across a specific example of a context for UMLEM's libertarian project.

Widely recognised protagonist of the Chilean street art scene, Cekis, acknowledges that he still remembers the political murals of the BRP and other Brigadas,

> which made a strong impression on me when I was a boy. I think the opportunity to help fill in a part of the design on a political mural forged in me a small but significant hope that someday I would be able to do it on my own in a different context.
>
> (Ruiz 2011: p. 136)

Cekis is however adamant that street painting since 1990, influenced by contemporary western culture, is completely different from political mural painting; until the 2000s, in terms of actual intention the only thing that the brigades and muralists really had in common was to occupy public space.

Confluences

González has good reason to emphasise the importance of the Open Sky Museum of San Miguel, which is indeed a phenomenal coming together of muralists and graffiti writers and their target audience, resulting in the transformation of an entire neighbourhood (www.elmostrador. cl/cultura/2013/12/12/como-el-arte-salvo-a-una-poblacion-de-desaparecer).

Open Sky Museums such as that at San Miguel are important points of arrival for the Graffiti Mural. The Graffiti Mural is a twenty-first-century phenomenon of large-scale figurative murals that knowingly combine graffiti's irreverence with muralism's social content. The South American 'Graffiti Mural' has been developed in Sao Paulo, Santiago de Chile and Buenos Aires since around 2000, and shortly thereafter in Bogotá, Lima, Asunción and Montevideo. The 'Graffiti Mural' connotes large figurative walls by accomplished graffiti writers, some of them professionalised and the walls they paint willingly lended; however most of the strongest graffiti murals in Chile are on illegally appropriated walls, preferably ones easily visible by locomotive and pedestrian traffic.

Chilean propaganda Brigadas such as the BRP and Brigada Chacón calculated viewer numbers from buses, cars and the pavement and chose their walls accordingly in order to address a relatively mass audience (Castillo and Vico 2011; Sandoval 2001). These considerations are evolved in the sophisticated communication strategy of the graffiti mural, as Chilean conceptual street artist Claudio Drë explains: 'Each work has a particular intention, on the basis of which one looks for the place in which to situate the piece. One analyses: Physical context, size, spatial situation, automotive routes, pedestrian traffic, distance, visibility, typographic shape when incorporating letters, etc. Often the wall might have elements around it which can be made good use of, to accentuate or emphasise the point that is being made.'[8]

A nice fusion of aspects of *Brigadista* principles and the freedom of graffiti is Santiago's Brigada Negotrópica, formed by three siblings. 'Negotrópica' is their own neologism; of no fixed meaning. Since 2008 Negotrópica has painted unauthorised walls, and authorised murals, partly characterised by thick black outlines are handled with comic-strip agility, often in defence of animals. Tegri specialises in cats, especially tigers, in particular the Bengalese tiger, Pampa, murdered in Santiago's zoo. The Brigada Negotrópica are equally comfortable participating at graffiti events and in collective brigade murals.

A significant confluence of recent years has been the institutional facilitation of public space in Santiago's metro to individuals more accustomed to painting illegally on the street. Emblematically, Eugenio Heiremans (1923–2010), director of the Hospital del Trabajador on Parque Bustamente, enabled Mono Gónzalez to realise a wrap-around mural for Parque Bustamente metro station. Gonzalez and Heiremans friendship was unusual. Jorge Pintó, director of MetroArte recalls that Heiremans was politically exactly the opposite of the Communist González. Those present at the unveiling of Gónzalez mural were struck that, without either of them abandoning their principles or changing sides, Heiremans and González could only find good things to say about each other, which felt to impartial viewers like 'the start of a social accord'.[9] A further measure of the conciliatory nature of MetroArte public art program is that Raúl Zurita, best known for his involvement in the clandestine CADA (Colectivo Acciones deArte: Art Actions Collective), of which more shortly, was in 2009 writing in terms of stations as like embraces and as the new cathedrals (Las Nuevas Catedrales 2009). The bonhomie is starting to extend to graffiti writers as well. There have been obstacles to inserting graffiti art in Chile's metro system, but in 2011 Cekis was invited to put a mural-sized work on temporary display in the Quinta Normal metro station, home also to Roberto Matta's Verbo América. Cekis's work is still there (Palmer 2015: pp. 187–189). In some contexts, there are steps on both sides to bridge the polarisation in Chilean culture since the early 2000s. In others, there is no letting go of the memory of Pinochet s dictatorship; and, in the cause of undoing some of Chile's marked social injustices, there are public spaces that are taken over and over again.

The Mapocho

The best Chilean example of a public space to be taken and occupied is the stretch of the Mapocho river that runs through central Santiago. For at least half a century, the lateral walls of the Mapocho have been a battleground between political and then also graffiti murals on the one side, and authoritarian obliterations in grey on the other.

All murals and other interventions here discussed were or are on the river's northern bank, which broadly speaking can be compared to the Rive Gauche of the Seine in Paris, the South bank of the Thames in London, the Trastevere bank of the Tiber in Rome: being like all of the above the other side of the river from Santiago's main political and financial institutions, and, like the Rive Gauche, incorporating Santiago's bohemian quarter – Bellavista. The northern bank of the Mapocho hosts a fluctuating underclass population. Of course, murals painted on the north bank of the Mapocho are viewed from the South – at a distance easily visible both by pedestrians and from vehicles, the Mapocho being narrower than the Tiber, let alone the Thames or the Seine. The local municipalities along the river as its runs from east to west through central Santiago are: Upstream to the east Providencia on both sides, downstream to the west: Recoleta to the north and Santiago Centro to the south.

Murals became a main propaganda medium in support of Salvador Allende's presidential campaign of 1964; the biggest and most effective of these were those on the breakwaters of the Mapocho, by the artists Luz Donoso, Carmen Johnson, Hernan Meschi and Pedro Millar downstream and downtown opposite Santiago's *Vega Central* market, Gertrudis de Moses photographs of which are reproduced in Eduardo Castillo Espinoza's masterly book on twentieth-century Chilean art and politics (Castillo 2006: pp. 71–73). The protagonists of the murals of 1964 realised, in Luz Donoso's words, that beyond the murals themselves the best propaganda was to be there, painting. [10] They considered the texts in the finished mural at the Mapocho to be less significant than its imagery. Nonetheless, the textual content, on Chilean history and the politics of its mineral resources from the 1886–1891 presidency of Jose Manuel Balmaceda onwards, can be judged to have been effective propaganda in the medium term. Its largest and most legible legend raised the growing cause of the Nationalisation of Copper ('La Nacionalización del Cobre') that would be achieved by Salvador Allende in 1971.

Propaganda *Brigada* painting diversified during the 1970 presidential campaign, for instance the socialist Brigada Elmo Catalan (BEC) formed in July 1970. From Allende's election in September 1970 and during the following three years of the Unidad Popular government, the Banks of the Mapocho were extensively painted with figurative representations of the Chilean left's ideals. In 1970, Luz Donoso, Pedro Millar and Hernan Meschi, together with Gregorio de la Fuente and José Balmes of the Universidad de Chile and others returned to the breakwaters of the Mapocho to paint a mural equating Allende with José Martí (Bellange 2012: p. 60).

The most celebrated mural dating from the Unidad Popular government is *The First Goal of the Chilean People* (*El Primer Gol del Pueblo Chileno*), coordinated in November 1971 by Roberto Matta and members of the BRP at the then swimming pool of the underprivileged Santiago suburb of La Granja. However, as Eduardo Castillo has observed, the most visible product of Matta s collaboration with the BRP colleagues was the mural painted by Matta, Mono Gonzalez, Juan 'Chin-Chin' Tralma and others at the start of 1972 stretching 450 metres along the central mid-town stretch of the Mapocho from the height of the bohemian district of Bellavista to the museum of Bellas Artes, to mark the fiftieth anniversary of Chilean Communist Party. The mural assimilates Pablo Neruda's verbal power and Matta's surrealistic figures and the BRP motif of an extended – in this case fifty metre-long – arm, in an ideographic *brigadista* mural in the classic BRP style of profiles and symbols outlined in black (Castillo 2006: pp. 118–131).

Following the coup of 1973, in which Salvador Allende was overthrown by General Augusto Pinochet, all walls on the Mapocho were covered up with grey paint and *The First Goal of the Chilean People* obliterated beneath sixteen layers of paint (but, amazingly, the latter was largely restored between 2005 and 2007).

For the first decade or so artistic resistance to the military regime was mainly underground – in clandestine printed matter. Opponents of the regime started to organise themselves. 1983 is considered year zero of open resistance to the dictatorship. 1983 saw the formation of the Marxist Leninist guerrilla group FPMR (Frente Patriotico Manuel Rodriguez) which would realise attacks on Pinochet's regime including an attempt to assassinate Pinochet in 1986: FPMR was listed as a terrorist organisation by the US State Department until 1999 when FPMR's armed activity ceased (although as we shall see FPMR's militant propaganda interventions continue). The Mapocho was the chosen site of a key moment in the emergence of public resistance. At 2.30 pm on 23 September 1983, members of CADA and other participants including Luz Donoso and Pedro Millar with experience of painting the Mapocho in the 1960s, unfolded from the northern bank of the Mapocho, on the stretch by the *Vega*, four canvases with the chaacters 'N', 'O' and '+', and a revolver, plainly insisting on no more summary executions by the regime (Figure 20.1). In her essay of an intercontinental geographical scope that dwarfs this one, Cecilia Braschi has accentuated the participatory nature of the 'NO +' action (Braschi 2013: p. 184).

The fearless rejection of the regime in such a highly visible place proved to be contagious. From then on, during the rest of 1983, 1984 and succeeding years, the slogan 'NO +' would proliferate on Santiago's walls. CADA's 'NO +' action retched things up by explicitly incorporating the active participation of the community so much so that 'it became the communal slogan of the anti-dictatorial community, as Robert Neustadt pointed out in his book *CADA Día* (Neustadt 2012: p. 68). The same book reports many assertions by members of CADA of their realisation of the part of the NO + slogan in helping to bring Chile's military rule to an end. Diamela Eltit of CADA observed, 'All the protest marches towards the end of the Dictatorship, without exception, were led by banners saying "No +"';[11] for her fellow CADA activist, Raul Zurita, 'NO +' began in 1983 and 'did not end until the defeat of Pinochet in

Figure 20.1 CADA, *NO +*, Santiago de Chile 1983 (photo Jorge Brantmeyer)

the plebiscite of 1989.[12] Alas the background to the success of the NO campaign against Pinochet, of CADA s 'NO +' and also of the roots of its emblem, the rainbow, in Chilean psychedelic graphics of 1967–1973 (Castillo and Vico 2011; Larrea 2008; Vico and Osses 2009), are both overlooked in Pablo Larrain s otherwise tolerable film *No: la película* (Chile, 2012) that recreates the *NO* campaign.

The refrain 'NO +' would recur post plebiscite and post-dictatorship and continue to be a *leitmotif* in campaigns against the repression of Chile's largest indigenous population and against profiteering education in Chile, including abroad in stencil interventions in Montevideo in 2012 by the Uruguayan CEIPA (Centro de Estudiantes del Instituto de Profesores Artigas), 'NO +' represión a estudiantes en chile, to return to twentieth-century Santiago de Chile: In the mid- to later 1980s, the Colectivo BRP , Chin-Chin and a new generation including Carolina del Rio and Beto Pastene emerged. Their clandestine murals on the Mapocho would last for a day or so before being concealed. By the later 1980s resistance to the military regime became increasingly visible, in 1989 the plebiscite was won and by the start of 1990 *brigadistas* the BRP and the BEC felt sufficiently empowered openly to make *bajadas* or group descents down wooden ladders to the banks of the Mapocho: The BRP did so in January 1990 to paint a mural celebrating sixty-eight years of the Chilean communist party. More significant than the mural itself was the action of a large group of people openly taking to the banks of the Mapocho for the day, an action that would soon thereafter be emulated by the BEC (Castillo 2006: p. 152).

Since 1990, the Mapocho, especially its down- to mid-town stretches, has once again become the stage for left-wing propaganda murals. Unsanctioned political murals of the 2000s included:

- 2004: A BRP mural in support of Gladys Marin's efforts to overturn laws introduced by Pinochet, excluding radical and indigenous groups from the political process (Palmer 2008: pp. 62–63; Palmer 2011: p. 127).
- 2006: A BRP mural to mark Fidel Castro's eightieth birthday.
- 2007: A mural by Communist party members from underprivileged communes in southern Santiago, in memory of Salvador Allende (Palmer 2008: p. 21; Palmer 2011: p. 127).

Unsanctioned political propaganda murals on the Mapocho are not the exclusive preserve of the Communists or of left-wing parties. In 2008, a mural was painted at the Mapocho in support of the abortive presidential campaign of the maverick philanthropist Leonardo Farkas (http://commons.wikimedia.org/wiki/File:Farkas_mural.JPG). Fittingly the mural was well upstream and uptown of the stretch of the river chosen by CADA, BRP and other radical groupings – by the Purísima bridge, the main bridge leading to Santiago's bohemian Bellavista district, and just by Santiago's pivotal Plaza Baquedano. The Purísima bridge is also the point at which three communes meet: Central Santiago to it southwest; lower-middle class Recoleta; and its east, straddling both banks, relatively uptown Providencia.

In the 2000s the Mapocho continued to be a favoured place for graffiti. In 2006, a little further uptown of the Purísima bridge, in Providencia commune, the Chilean graffiti crew, DVE (*De la Vieja Escuela*: of the Old School/*Deskiziada Vida Escritora*: Unbridled Writing Life) realised their masterpiece, of an imaginary *Mapocho Navegable*: Navigable Mapocho (Figure 20.2a). It combined distinctive contributions in painting by Grin (the illusionistic architecture), Cekis (the larger figure in the boat) and Sick aka 888 (the boat itself and the floating buoys in the river) with Nicole's reflective mosaic mainly composed of shattered glass. In 2008, Grin returned to paint the Providencia stretch of the Mapocho opposite the Baquedano park with the aesthetic and humorous mural of a young woman in G-string only reading, as though on a beach (www.grin.cl; youtube.com/watch?v=5YHb4KkvxmQ); incidentally the very well

Figure 20.2a DVE Crew, 'Navigable Mapocho', Santiago de Chile 2006 (photo 2008)

Figure 20.2b DVE Crew, 'Navigable Mapocho', Santiago de Chile, erasure 2011 (photo 2011)

executed mural develops the theme of commenting on what the Mapocho is not, by imagining what it might be, even though its aim is not to make any point, but to entertain.

In 2007, just downstream of the *Purísima* bridge on the Bellavista stretch of the northern bank, Piguan, with Desoo, contributed a hedonic mural in which Piguan's contribution was a multi-eyed figure of a type recurrent in *santiaguino* street art (www.flickr.com/photos/piguan; Palmer 2008: p. 117).

In 2009, in the midtown stretch opposite the Bellas Artes museum, another graffiti master-piece was added to the Mapocho: The seventy-five-metre-long Pobreza material/Riqueza spiritual (Material poverty/Spiritual wealth) by the *santiaguino* duo Aislap (www.flickr.com/photos/aislaponer) (Figure 20.3a).[13]

In 2010 two more remarkable graffiti murals on the breakwaters of the Mapocho were created, relatively upstream on the Recoleta stretch of the river opposite Santiago central commune, Saile and Grin produced an extensive production of pictorial and architectural illusionism (www.Saile.cl; Palmer 2011: p. 127). In December 2010, inspired by the Aislap, Saile and Grin walls of the preceding year, Piguan revisited and improved the same stretch he had painted in 2007, this time accompanied by Bus. On a coloured background, economically and ecologically realised in water-resistant *látex*, Piguan and Bus portrayed women: Piguan evolving further the motif of faces with multiple sets of eyes – and indeed noses (Palmer 2011: p. 127).

In January 2011, the above-mentioned Aislap, Saile-Grin and Piguan-Bus graffiti murals on the stretch of the Mapocho opposite the Santiago commune were all buffed in brutally unaesthetic grey. The blanking was purportedly done to provide a neutral background for the Chile a la Luz light art projection of murals from the Bellas Artes stretch of the southern bank onto the surface of the river and its northern bank: Despite the latter being blank, the projected images were illegible. In the 2010s, any art that depends on using large amounts of electricity is misguided; while technically skilful use of low technology rollers, brushes and latex is proven the best medium for painting the Mapocho.

Allegedly, the buffing was done by the local government of Santiago central's commune . . . even though the murals themselves were on the opposite Recoleta stretch of the northern bank. The stretch embellished by Saile and Grin was left brutally ugly; the iconoclasts failed entirely to erase the memory of Aislaps's 'Material Poverty Spiritual Weath', the top of the head and the bottom of the foot of which survived (Figure 20.3b).

The previous occasion that large stretches of wall painting on the breakwaters of the Mapocho had been erased was in 1973, when Pinochet's military regime blanked a big, visually interesting BRP wall. A year into Chile s first right-wing government since Pinochet, the strong anti-cultural echo was most unfortunate: 'Horrible', in the words of Pablo Aravena, maker of the film *Next: A Primer on Urban Art* (Canada/France 2005), and in recent years involved in developing *Chile Estye*, a documentary film on urban art in Chile (www.youtube.com/watch?v= b5jEH8Knl-4) and the eponymous web page (www.facebook.com/chileestyle): The coolest portal to hip Chilean graffiti and street art.

The catalogue to the Piñera-backed *Chile a la Luz* venture declared 'It is important for us to take over the city, its parks and rivers' (*Chile a la Luz* 2012: p. 46): A sentiment which it can safely be said is the common ground of all those vying for visibility (or erasure) public space. By the time the *Chile a la Luz* catalogue was printed in 2012, it was clear that the erasures were not limited to the bank opposite the Santiago municipality, but a more sinister 'graffiticide', DVE's Navigable Mapocho, nowhere near where *Chile a la Luz* was projected, but upstream of the Bellas Artes from in Providencia, having also been erased later in 2011 (Figure 20.2b). The erasure of DVE's Navigable Mapocho clearly gave the lie to the claim that the preceding obliterations were solely to provide a backdrop for *Chile a la Luz* or the work of the Santiago Centro Municipality alone. The graffiticide of 2011 focused political and hip-hop collectives on taking over the Mapocho breakwaters anew.

Piñera's government of 2010–2014 will be remembered by many for the student protests of 2011 to 2013 on *educación*, especially *educa$ión* that is profiteering further education (Banda and Navea 2013; Tironi 2011). Education also became a main topic of Chilean street art. Against such a polarised background, neither political nor graffiti collectives were going timidly to accept authoritarian buffing of their work on the Mapocho. In 2012, political collectives and political brigades started to appropriate the Mapocho's walls again. It was noticeable that graffiti murals occupied stretches of the breakwater hitherto the preserve of propaganda paintings

Figure 20.3a Aislap 'Material Poverty/Spiritual Wealth', Santiago de Chile 2009

Figure 20.3b Aislap 'Material Poverty/Spiritual Wealth', Santiago de Chile 2009, erasure 2011 (photo 2011)

and vice versa: A further indication, it might be argued, of the convergence of graffiti with political muralism. To mark the centenary of the founding of their party a broad spectrum of Chilean communists combined to paint a largely figurative mural of many parts – as many as in any mural since the BRP mural of 1972 – on the Recoleta bank, pretty much opposite the Bellas Artes (http://noticias.terra.cl/chile/comunistas-pintan-mural-historico-en-ribera-del-rio-mapocho; Palmer 2015: p. 176).

In the same year, the duo Agotok (2012) and the collective Los Oberoles (The Overalls) combined to paint the figure on enormous clothed but barefooted skeleton *El Alambre* (The Wire) on the Vega stretch of the Mapocho (Figure 20.4). Certainly, *El Alambre* is very specific to its site down on the Mapocho, as Ago and Tok explained in March 2013:

Tok: The Wire is about life on the Wire. In street terms a bloke who's in a bad way, who's destitute, who lacks the basics . . .

Ago: who has no shoes . . .

Tok: is said to be on the wire. If you are on the wire you are precarious. In a way the people who live down on the Mapocho live this life. They come up. They steal. They look for drugs and alcohol. An extreme life, surviving in the street with nothing, homeless, living under a bridge. So the skeleton represents that you are metaphorically resting, sleeping, with dogs by its side, and the Overalls did the 'I see, hear, say nothing' . . .

Ago: . . . the reaction of passers-by to common people.[14]

Also in 2012, colour returned to the stretch of the Mapocho just upstream of the Purísima bridge, with a degree of alternative institutional support. In February, Piguan painted a mural with the backing of 'The Museum of Urban Art' (http://tmoua.org/) – a worldwide organisation in which South American street art, by Chileans Inti and Los 12 Brillos, and Argentines Jaz and Nazza Stencil, features very prominently. Later in the same year, as part of the event 'Hecho en Casa' (www.facebook.com/pages/Hecho-en-Casa-Festival, www.hechoencasa.cl), vibrant colour returned to the part of Mapocho breakwater where DVE's 'Navigable Mapocho'

Figure 20.4 Agotok with Los Oberoles: 'The Wire', Santiago de Chile 2012

had been obliterated by grey the previous year, in the form of Chileans LRM and Charquipunk and Peruvian Elliot Tupac s vibrant *Equilibrio* production (Lord K2 2015, p. 97; Palmer 2015, p. 177). Tupac left the Word 'Equilibrio' by way of reference to the Peruvian 'Equilibrio Festival de Arte Urbano y Medioambiente en espacios públicos', in which Charquipunk would participate in 2013: A sequence of events typical of self-curated street art events of the 2010s that empower the collective occupation of public space in a sequence of places. Tupac's *Equilibrio* also became popular with santiaguinos on its own terms.

In 2013 it seemed likely that the Mapocho might be on course for being gentrified as a cycling route and/or an open-air museum. In one noteworthy instance, by dint of a double negative, the riverbank was in 2014 sanctioned as a site of urban art. In the main, however, far from being gentrified in 2014 the northern bank is as combative as ever and the site of occupations of public space by *Brigadistas, graffiteros,* Santiago's underclass and revolutionary and separatist protest groups. The double negative, a marker in the transformed social position of graffiti artists, came in October 2014 when the mayor of Providencia groveled to Elliot Tupac, to apologise for her employees having buffed his *Equilibrio* as having been a mistake (www.t13.cl/noticia/actualidad/borran-mural-del-grafitero-elliot-tupac-en-el-rio-mapocho).

The intended target of the buffing was presumably the adjacent protest wall paintings in support of the hundred homeless people and their supporters who had, on 11 June 2014, taken the section of the breakwaters of the Mapocho either side of the *Purísima* Bridge. (http://eldesconcierto.cl/debajo-del-puente-el-movimiento-de-pobladores-demanda-una-mesa-social-desde-las-riberas-de-la-pobreza). Special police groups with teargas attempted to disperse them (www.ahoranoticias.cl/pais/metropolitana/pobladores-protestan-en-ribera-del-rio-mapocho.html). However by mid-August the *toma y okupa* (taking and occupation) was well entrenched and supported by an UMLEM mural (Figure 20.5). Just as for communist muralists on the Mapocho in the 1960s a main aim was to be seen painting there, so for anarchic-libertarian groups in the 2010s more than the mural itself, the propaganda is primarily the occupation of the river bank; where in 1990 the BRP and BEC made their *bajadas* to the Mapocho for a day, the MPL (*Movimiento Pobladores en Lucha*: Movement of Settlers in Battle), supported by UMLEM and others, camped there for months.

Probably the most trenchant protest mural at the Mapocho in 2014 was that commemorating the Mapuche martyr Matias Catrileo (1985–2008) with the uncompromising legend 'WE ARE NOT CHILEANS/WE ARE MAPUCHE/FREE MAPUCHE COUNTRY' (Figure 20.6).

Remarkably, in 2014 the Mapocho is more taken over by anarchist-revolutionary propaganda murals than ever (http://muralesdelconosur.blogspot.com/): For instance, the prominent stretch of the northern bank immediately in front of the *Vega* being occupied by a long mural with big portraits of FPMR activists, Cecilia Magni and Raúl Pellegrin, both killed by Pinochet's regime in 1988, naming suspects for their murder and calling for them to be brought to justice. In October 2014, a group of Brigadista painting collectives, among them the BEC, Brigada Laura Moya, Muralistas Pablo Vergara (MPV) and Brigada Negotrópica, met further downstream to paint murals commemorating forty years since the assassination of Miguel Enriquez, ex-secretary general of MIR (Salinas 2014: pp. 11–47).

In 2007 Brigadista murals seemed anachronistic to many graffiti writers; their main common ground the occupation of public space, both strands of street art remained socially marginal; and the northern bank of the Mapocho one of the locations from which they could project themselves, from an underground position, to a wide audience in central Santiago. Since then political and hip-hop street art have cross-pollenated in the graffiti mural (Palmer 2011: pp. 22–23; Palmer 2015: p. 16) to render the perception at the start of the 2000s, of collective *brigadista* art being

Figure 20.5 Housing protest featuring UMLEM mural, Santiago de Chile 2014

Figure 20.6 We are not Chileans we are Mapuche, Santiago de Chile 2014

anachronistic, itself an anachronism. Concomitant with this harmonious convergence, *brigadista* and graffiti murals have together become socially acceptable: Notably in the San Miguel Open Sky Museum and in Santiago s metro system. In contrast to the social accord of such officially sanctioned projects, the perennial resurgences on the Mapocho's bank of politically subversive actions and wall paintings continue to be on chronically polarised Chile's ideological frontline.

Notes

1 Email to author, 1 August 2013: 'el arte urbano significa tomar las calles, reclamar lo que es tuyo . . . un "ataque" al espacio público'.

2 Triangular conversation, Santiago de Chile, 13 August 2013, between Henruz, t.h.e.i.c. and Fitz of Colectivo Licuado, t.h.e.i.c: 'me gusta tomar un lugar'; Henruz '¿Tomar el espacio público de qué? . . . de la nada, de la publicidad, de la propaganda política partidaria'. Note that t.h.e.i.c. is an acronym for 'the happy end is coming'.

3 Mono González, interview with author, Santiago de Chile, 1 October 2012: 'es el costumbre de la izquierda Chilena de ocupar espacio público data desde la fundación del Partido Comunista chileno en el 1912, vale a decir antes que inició el movimiento de muralismo mexicano'.

4 Coas, interview with author, Santiago de Chile, 5 December 2012: 'Acá en Chile desde cuando nació el PC así hay siempre expresiones artísticas en la calle, la primera el muralismo politico'.

5 González, Santiago, 1 October 2012: 'Hubo un tiempo, y es super importante decirlo, y reconocer que fue un tiempo, producto de la dictadura que hubo un vacio cultural, en donde había un abismo entre los brigadistas con el graffitero. O sea recién hace algunos tres años o cuatro años se ha ido produciendo como un re encuentro entre el graffitero y el muralista en donde hay un respeto y reconocimiento uno con otro. Empezó a haber un reconocimiento por allí para el centenario de Allende [2008]. Hoy en día es muy importante el Museo a Cielo Abierto en San Miguel porque hemos logrado juntar graffiteros con muralistas'.

6 Gustavo Arias, Santiago de Chile, 1 October 2012: 'Hasta cuatro, cinco años atrás había un abismo bastante grande entre muralismo de brigadas y el graffiti. El brigadismo hay que entender que tiene a ver con el mundo político. Y en esta época por ejemplo este año hay elecciones acá en Chile, el próximo año también hay elecciones de presidente, donde muchas brigadas que no necesariamente son muralistas pero que son solamente propagandistas, salen a ocupar los muros, y en este ocupar los muros muchas veces no respetan lo que se hace en la calle eternamente; y no me refiero solo al graffiti sino también al muralismo como tal, el muralismo arte. Así que en esa batalla-maquina muchas veces si eres de la calle y ves en la calle cosas de las brigadas políticas de propaganda, es cuando se produce este abismo, y donde se siente de que mucha gente de los partidos políticos vienen y tapan con letras no más y con propaganda del candidato. Da lo mismo cual candidato, quien lo haga, no hay que hacer distinción, porque todos candidatos trabajan igual, y eso a la gente quien hicimos el mundo de la calle, sea graffiteros o del muralismo, nos molesta bastante. Y a la raíz, eternamente de que apareció el mundo del graffiti, que es del 80 y algo en adelante que inició a partir el tema, que hay este abismo. Ahora con el Mono, y con gente que estuvo en la primera etapa que fue el muralismo de las brigadas, brigadista que lo llama él, y que entienden también que hay un arte detrás del graffiti, se ha producido este acercamiento. Pero en épocas como esta también te vuelven a ajenar, o sea no es algo que está totalmente estancado. O sea hay buena onda con el Mono, hay buena onda con otros autores del mural más clásico, como se lo llama, más permanente, desde el mundo del graffiti, pero no es algo que está totalmente acabado'.

7 Email from liaison personnel of UMLEM Santiago to the author, 30 December 2013:

Las Unidades Muralistas Luchador Ernesto Miranda nacieron el 11 de septiembre del 2003 en Talcahuano en una conmemoración del 30° Aniversario del golpe militar. En sus propias palabras: 'Las razones que motivaron su fundación fueron . . . que éramos un grupo de compañeros y compañeras que pintábamos desde antes de manera individual y bajo distintas tendencias estéticas pero todas relacionadas con el "street art" y además intentando entregar un mensaje que permitiera concientizar a través de la pintura . . . El proceso que nos impulsa a crear una estética particular tiene sus raíces en el rescate histórico de la tradición muralista latinoamericana, incluyendo las Brigadas Ramona Parra, pero además construyendo estética propia como forma también de crear algo nuevo, junto al proyecto libertario que vamos construyendo ya desde hace 10 años.'

8 Claudio Drë, written interview, December 2012:

Todo dependerá de las intenciones y el concepto. Cada obra posee una intención particular de existir, a partir de ello, se buscará el lugar idóneo para situar esta pieza de Arte. Se analizará el contexto físico, tamaño, situación espacial, recorrido automotriz, tráfico de las personas, distancia, visibilidad, tamaño tipográfico en caso de incorporar letras, etc. Muchas veces el muro puede poseer elementos a su alrededor los cuales se pueden aprovechar de mejor forma para acentuar o dar mayor énfasis a lo que se quiere plantear.

9 Pintó, interview, Santiago de Chile, 4 November 2013, 'el principio de un acuerdo social en Chile'.
10 Castillo 2006, p. 70: 'nos dábamos cuenta que la mejor propaganda era estar ahí, pintando'.
11 Neustadt 2012, p. 173: Diamela Eltit: 'Todas las marchas finales durante la dictadura, todas sin excepción, iban encabezadas por pancartas diciendo "No +".'
12 Neustadt 2012, p. 138: Raúl Zurita: 'no terminó sino con la derrota de Pinochet en el plebiscito de 1988'.
13 Tok: 'El Alambre habla de la vida en Alambre. En dicho popular un tipo que está mal, que está en la miseria, que le falta lo básico.

Tok: se dice que está en el alambre. Si estás en el alambre, estás precario. En cierta forma la gente que vive abajo en el Mapocho vive esta vida. Suben. Roban. Buscan drogas y alcohol. Bajan. Es una vida en el alambre. Una vida extrema, sobrevivir en la calle sin nada, sin techo, vivir abajo un puente. Entonces la calavera representa que estás metafóricamente descansando, durmiendo, con algunos perros al lado, y los Oberoles hicieron el "No veo, no escucho, no hablo" . . .

Ago: . . . la diferencia entre la gente transeúnte y de la común corriente'.

References

Agotok (2012). Moreno, P. and Villa, S.: *Agotok: Graffiti y Muralismo from Santiago de Chile*, Santiago de Chile: Potoco Discos.

Banda, C. and Navea, V. (2013) (eds). *En Marcha. Ensayos sobre arte, violencia y cuerpo en la manifestación social*, Santiago de Chile: Adrede Editora.

Bellange, E. (2012). *El Mural como Reflejo de la Realidad Social en Chile*, Santiago: Editorial Universidad de Santiago de Chile.

Braschi, C. (2013). 'Re-signifier l'espace de l'art en Amérique Latine. L'expérience du C.A.D.A.' *Au nom de l'art Enquête sur le statut ambigu des appellations artistiques de 1945 à nos jours*, Paris: Publications de la Sorbonne, pp. 171–186.

Castillo, E. (2006). *Puño y Letra: Movimiento social y comunicación gráfica en Chile*, Santiago de Chile: Ocho Libros.

Castillo, E. and Vico, M. (2011). *Cartel chileno 1693–1973*, 4th edn, Santiago.

Las Nuevas Catedrales (2009). *Las Nuevas Catedrales*, Santiago: Metro de Santiago.

Lord K2 (2015). *Street Art Santiago*, Atglen, PA: Schiffer Publishing.

Neustadt, R. (2012). *CADA día: la creación de un arte social*, Santiago de Chile: Editorial Cuarto Propio.

Palmer, R. (2008). *Street Art Chile*, London/Corte Madera CA: 8 books/Gingko Press.

Palmer, R. (2011). *Arte Callejero en Chile*, Santiago de Chile: Ocho Libros.

Palmer, R (2015). *Murallas del Cono Sur*, Santiago de Chile: Ocho Libros.

Ruiz, M. (2011). *Nuevo Mundo: Latin American street art*, Berlin: Gestalten.

Salinas, S. (2013). *Las Tres Letras: Historia y Contenido del Movimiento de Izquierda Revolucionaria*, Santiago de Chile: RiL.

Salinas, S. (2014). *Memorias de la Militancia en el MIR*, Santiago de Chile: RiL.

Sandoval, A. (2001). *Palabras escritas en un muro: el caso de la Brigada Chacón*, Santiago de Chile: Ediciones del SUR.

Tironi, E. (2011). *¿Por qué no me quieren? Del Piñera way y la rebelión de los estudiantes*, Santiago de Chile: Uqbar ediciones.

21

London calling

Contemporary graffiti and street art in the UK's capital[1]

Jeffrey Ian Ross

Introduction

After New York City, London[2] is perhaps the second most renowned epicenter in the world for graffiti and street art. Many factors explain this situation, including numerous art schools, galleries, museums, auction houses, and art critics; a large creative class of people who serve as a catalyst for this kind of work; a vibrant youth culture; and easy access to other international centers of graffiti and street art.

First, there are no fewer than seven major art schools in London that are well attended by local and international students: Courtauld Institute of Art, Goldsmiths, University of London, Royal Academy, Royal College of Art, Slade School of Fine Art, and University of the Arts London. The city has one of the largest concentrations of major galleries and museums, both private and public, in the art world. These include Tate Britain, Tate Modern, the National Gallery, Saatchi Gallery, and the Design Museum. Moreover, numerous advertising agencies, and interior design and architecture firms are also located in London.

Second, hand in hand with these elite institutions, is the fact that London has long had a strong creative class (e.g. Florida, 2014), and it would seem logical that professionals tied to the art, design, museum, and gallery world would also promote new developments in their field.

Third, since the 1950s, London has nurtured a vibrant youth and protest subculture (e.g. Hall & Jefferson, 1976/1993; Brake, 2013). This has been reflected in the growth of well-known and publicized deviant and/or counterculture groups, such as the Mods, Rockers, and Punks. These youth sub- and countercultural movements either developed in tandem or separately from those that emerged in other major urban centers, such as New York City or Paris (Skelton & Valentine, 1998). Other subcultural developments include a Do It Yourself movement, and Grime Culture, which have had various impacts on graffiti and street art in London.

Finally, in many respects, London is a gateway to the rest of Europe for American graffiti and street artists who wish to engage in their craft outside of North America. In fact, there are numerous stories of U.S. based graffiti/street artists who came to London and teamed up with London-based writers and artists as part of their journey to fame and/or notoriety. The city presents minimal barriers for American graffiti and street artists in terms of language and contacts. In fact, it has been and still is a fertile ground for this kind of activity. The brief review above does not seek to suggest a causal theory of graffiti/street art in London, but to provide an outline of some of the contributing factors in explaining what occurs in this context.

Contemporary places and spaces where graffiti and street art are located

According to Schacter (2013),

> London is vast and each area has its own character and aesthetic in relation to graffiti; for example some districts in the 1990s had a really evil edge. The graffiti was raw – separate letters, ultra-legible, with double outlines so that it stood out even more. It was not about who was the most 'up' but about who was the most aggressive.
>
> (p. 150)

More specifically, there are a handful of locations where there is a disproportionate amount of graffiti and street art. In these areas the councils (i.e. local government units) no longer remove this work because they feel overwhelmed by the sheer number and the perception that this work creates economic and cultural benefits. "One finds artists at work; fanatics on the hunt, serendipitous locals, and tourists using their phones to record pieces they have come across. Three principal locations in London are Camden, East London, and Leake Street in Waterloo" (www.ravishlondon.com/londonstreetart, downloaded April 19, 2015). There are logical reasons why these areas attract a disproportionate amount of graffiti and street art.

Camden is a magnet for street art for three primary reasons: "A community of counterculture artists and musicians, including punks and alternative rockers," "[infrastructure:] It boasts a plethora of railway lines, bridges, canals, and old decaying buildings, prime street art estate. Street artists love these places because they can put their work up without being caught; and for the street artist it is morally acceptable to 'brighten up' a neglected building," and "Camden likes to celebrate the street artist by ripping them off! Because street art, in itself or by design, often gives the finger to the man; so it's no surprise to see market traders flogging the more notorious pieces reproduced on t-shirts and canvas for its counter-cultural clientele. Street art is welcome in Camden!" (www.ravishlondon.com/londonstreetart/)

With respect to East London, graffiti and street art are concentrated around "the Boroughs of Hackney and Tower Hamlets . . ., Shoreditch, Brick Lane and Spitalfields" (www.ravishlondon.com/londonstreetart/). Starting in the 1990s, due to the abundance of vacant low-rise buildings, artists, designers, and musicians became attracted to West Hackney and Shoreditch. Included among the up and coming artists were Tracy Emin and Damien Hirst. Their presence in this area served as a catalyst for other like-minded individuals.

"The integrity of the artistic community was and has been strengthened, like many artistic communities, by being juxtaposed with a community of considerable wealth, the City of London, to the south." This, in turn, led to the establishment of graphic design studios, interior designers, architects offices, and galleries (www.ravishlondon.com/londonstreetart/).

> Many of the galleries and businesses in Shoreditch have seen the attraction of, and benefits to be gained from, showing and commissioning art on the outside of their buildings. This has helped cement Shoreditch's place as the spiritual home of street art in London, and has attracted artists from all around the world, some of whom are invited, and some come of their own accord to put works up.
>
> (www.ravishlondon.com/londonstreetart/)

Shoreditch is considered by some to be

> dowdy, and despite the wealth, activity, and creativity, provides a smorgasbord of abandoned
> buildings, railway lines and wasteland car parks, upon which artists feel more than happy
> to mount their work . . . The streets are patrolled by bloggers, writers, and photographers,
> who record, sort, categorize, and analyze the works on the internet, with the vigor and
> detail of a gallery show handbook.
>
> (www.ravishlondon.com/londonstreetart/)

Shoreditch's days may be numbered as a haven for graffiti and street art as the area may be
a victim of geography and economics. It is nestled beside London's financial district, which is
slowly expanding and in need of new and close real estate. Although the financial crisis of 2007
has temporarily halted this expansion, when the economy improves, land and rental prices will
likely increase thus making it difficult for the artistic community to sustain itself. "Maybe . . .
the artists will shuffle, fearful and yet faithful, untidily, a bit more northwards and a bit more
eastwards, or maybe the scene will dissipate" (www.ravishlondon.com/londonstreetart/).

Finally Leake Street and Leake Street Tunnel, Waterloo, in South London is another popular
spot for graffiti and street art. Here, a disused railway tunnel just behind Waterloo Train Station
is a popular place for graffiti and street art. Leake Street became a hive for street artists and
graffiti artists after Banksy organized a street art festival [called the "Cans Festival," a play on
the juxtaposition of the Cannes Festival and aerosol/spray cans] there in Spring 2008.

> Shortly thereafter, local authorities designated the tunnel as a legal wall for graffiti and street
> art (www.ravishlondon.com/londonstreetart/). This location is where some of the best
> writers and artists in London frequent the walls, which are now painted every day. The
> tunnel hosts the annual 'Battle of Waterloo,' organized by 'Chrome & Black' (the best
> place in London for graffiti art resources), and many other graffiti jams. It has become one
> of the last legal halls of fame in London, yet its future is uncertain.
>
> (Epstein, 2014)

Pieces do not last long on Leake Street though. According to Ellsworth-Jones (2012), "The
pressure for legal space to paint is so intense that most pieces in Leake Street usually only stay
for a week or two, often less, before another artist comes and paints over them" (p. 43).

The legal context

In 1971, the Criminal Damage Act was passed in the U.K. It made graffiti illegal: "One English
council, Harrogate Council, classes it as 'somewhere between willful littering and vandalism'"
(Harrogate Borough Council, n.d.). Authorities can charge the artists/writers with criminal
damage or with being equipped to cause criminal damage. If convicted, the perpetrator typically
pays a fine and/or performs some sort of community service. When police officers encounter
someone who is doing illegal graffiti or street art, they can give them a fixed penalty notice
(a ticket), and the recipient has the right to contest this charge in court.

Despite the illegal nature of graffiti, not all U.K. councils follow the same policies in terms
of graffiti and street art enforcement and abatement. Some councils have spent very large sums
of money each year, cleaning graffiti. In 2002, the cost of cleaning graffiti in London alone was
estimated to be 100 million GBP (Anonymous, 2002). This included about 7 million GBP for

"scrubbing the walls of schools, hospitals and businesses," and transport companies expending 6 million GBP "removing daubings from buses and trains" (Anonymous, 2002).

The policy of the London Borough of Hackney is that "we can't make a decision as to whether something is art or graffiti. [We remove it as] the government judges us on the number of clean walls we have" (Daniell, 2011: p. 458). "Other councils 'tolerate' some graffiti" (p. 458). This kind of ambiguity regarding the place of graffiti and street art existed on the streets, too. According to Schacter, "Getting up illegally for the sake of getting up vs. getting up for the sake of drawing attention to your gallery show; a traditional graffiti letterform aesthetic vs. a pop art image-based aesthetic, often as a stencil or paste-up" (2013: p. 151). Typically graffiti that is sexist or racist is removed (Anonymous, 1986).

According to Epstein (2014),

> The legal/tolerated halls of fame in London are a testing ground for graffiti writers. This is where they can invest time to develop their styles and techniques . . . These halls are the birthplaces of many, very adept and talented graffiti writers and artists. Sadly though, most of these spaces are not protected in the interests of the art, but being neglected by local councils, or eyed-up by greedy developers circling the skyline of London. Despite protests from local artists and residents, these important spaces are being redeveloped into sterilized play-spaces, privatized housing, and desolate car parks.

The existing scholarship

Although a handful of books that include numerous photographs of graffiti and street art in London have been published (e.g. Perry, 1976; Epstein, 2014), a sustained scholarship on this subject has not been produced. For example, a Home Office study of vandalism in estates (Wilson, 1978) touches on graffiti as vandalism but does not examine this activity in any great detail. Alternatively, Ekblom (1988a), in a report on graffiti in the London Underground, based on situational crime prevention techniques and other suggestions, identified a series of preventive measures that could be implemented to reduce the amount of this kind of activity.

Even Macdonald's excellent groundbreaking book, *The Graffiti Subculture: Youth, Masculinity, and Identity in London and New York* (2001), is ostensibly slim on analysis of the graffiti scene in London, focusing instead on the dynamics among graffiti writers and situated in the subculture literature, as opposed to analyzing the diverse graffiti scene in the U.K. capital.

One of the earliest and most notable semi-systematic studies on graffiti in London was the 2002 report commissioned by the London Assembly, titled *Graffiti in London*. This investigation, chaired by Andrew Pelling (Conservative representative from Croydon Council), considered the causes and impact of graffiti. Divided into nine parts, the report examined the roles of parents, businesses, law enforcement, courts, and news media outlets on graffiti. In order to produce the report, the team gathered testimony from twenty-eight individuals, including graffiti writers/artists and representatives of government organizations. They also reviewed written evidence.

Much of the knowledge obtained was rudimentary by today's scholarly standards, including the portrayal of the types of people who do graffiti and the dangers inherent in its commission. The 102-page report's key findings were that magistrates (judges) are reluctant to deliver sentences that would act as a deterrent (p. 22). At that time, there was a belief that categorizing graffiti as a local offense would not assist in the proper government response. Proposals included a U.K. wide ban on the sale of spray paint to minors, acceptable behavior contracts, and the enhanced use of CCTV. The report highlighted the development of the Local Government Act of 2000, which "provides local authorities with new powers to promote or improve the economic, social, and environmental well-being of their area" (p. 28). Most of the recommendations pointed towards greater cooperation among various entities both in the public and private sectors.

The report made thirty-three recommendations to be enacted by different bodies, including the mayor, London Assembly, and utility companies. The report emphasized the fact that at the time there were thirty-three boroughs in London and that there was considerable diversity in their approaches to graffiti, including expenditures.[3] In other words, there was no consistent citywide method addressing graffiti.

Despite its presence, for reasons that are really unknown, few scholarly pieces on graffiti and street art in London have been written. Alvelos (2004) analyzed a series of case studies drawn from research that the author conducted between 1997 and 2001 on graffiti on the streets of London:

> The cases studied challenge a prevailing socio-cultural myth – one that regards graffiti's contemporary urban version as a subcultural form of expression, still autonomous, still rebellious, an outlaw enterprise still very much sheltered from outside influences or interference. The scenario is actually increasingly rare.
>
> (p. 181)

He describes how some advertising campaigns, in their pre-launch phases, used graffiti (or more specifically street art) elements to pique passerby curiosity regarding new products and services, as in the release of certain musical CDs. "Graffiti was indeed the first stage in the promotional activities that anticipated the product's actual launch. It was to act as a quasi-subliminal teaser, that rarely revealed the product in question" (p. 183). Alvelos also notes how graffiti has been adopted by other creatives in the promotion of various cultural products (i.e. plays, movies, books, magazines, websites, computer games, etc.) (p. 184).

Four years later, Dickens (2008) reviewed the Finders Keepers street art group, which during the 2000s was a rough assemblage of street artists who decided to hold an event where found objects would be re-crafted and displayed publicly in the Shoreditch neighborhood of London. When this "street theatre" like event ended, the people in attendance were allowed to take the objects with them when a whistle was blown. Other scholarship includes Schacter (2008) who examined the loose connections among graffiti artists, gallery owners, and the public. More specifically he was interested in how certain pieces of graffiti and street art in London achieved legitimacy and were eventually protected by the community.

In sum, a comprehensive history of graffiti and street art in London is largely unwritten. What we find instead is a preponderance of sections, in large format books, on the subject of graffiti and street art, which primarily include photographs with minimal textual discussion and/or analysis of the city's graffiti/street art culture. Much of the written commentary that does exist, however, is superficial if not ephemeral, and this also applies to the handful of similar smaller books focusing exclusively on London (e.g. MacNaughton, 2006; 2007; 2009; Frank Steam156 Malt, 2013). Also prominent are books offering guided walking tours of graffiti and street art in London or, more specifically, locations where Banksy's art may be found (e.g. Bull, 2011). Another interesting book is *The Lost Boyz: A Dark Side of Graffiti* (2011), written by Rollins, which is a confessional-style autobiographical book done by a London-based graffiti writer during the 1980s. Again the insight about graffiti and street art in London is not comprehensive.

More common are news articles published in the mainstream papers. Additionally from 1992 to 2012, a U.K. magazine called *Graphotism*, that featured images of graffiti, was produced. It started in a London-based retail shop that sold different types of spray paint and markers (Keegan, 2012). Not only did it feature images and stories about graffiti in London, but it also included work in locations around the world.

Method

Beyond a traditional literature review, a variety of research methods are available to gain a better sense of the history and contemporary status of graffiti and street art in London. Although a deeper examination of this important subject matter is warranted through interviews with graffiti artists/writers, agents of social control, council politicians, municipal police, curators and art critics, shopkeepers and other property owners, as well as with residents who have lobbied for and against graffiti and street art in their neighborhoods, this additional research is not possible at this time. Given resource constraints, in addition to the scant scholarly literature sources, this current examination is limited to and drawn from online websites and newspaper articles. Numerous newspapers cover London. In order to construct as comprehensive a picture as possible of graffiti and street art in London, a search was done of all articles published in the *Times* between January 1, 1980 and December 31, 2014 that mentioned graffiti and/or street art.[4] The majority of these articles referred to arrests and sentencing of individuals who were caught engaging in graffiti and street art. Although other news sources were occasionally used, one might legitimately argue that a more detailed picture might have been obtained if the universe had been expanded to more newspapers, however resource constraints prevented the writer from doing so. In scouring the web, there are also many sites offering or providing tours of graffiti and street art in London. Run by enterprising individuals, these businesses allow tourists to see the famous pieces of London graffiti artists. Others provide lists of graffiti and street artists and feature some of their work. This work was also examined.

Notable London-based graffiti and street artists

Over the past four decades, a handful of iconic London-based graffiti and street artists have defined the body of work in this city. Almost every collection of photographs on graffiti and street art has a section featuring individuals who work in London.[5] Although the criteria for inclusion are not articulated, the cast of characters includes, but is not limited to Solo One, Banksy, King Robbo, and EINE. Below is a brief review of these four individuals.

Solo One

Noteworthy among the contemporary street artists working in London has been Boyd Hill (aka Solo One). He began his career as a street artist in 1999 by placing his tag on post office labels and applying the stickers to all manner of surfaces throughout London (Alvelos, p. 187). "Recognizing the graffiti sticker trend's potential as a marketing medium, Boxfresh [an urban underwear clothing brand], launched a series of stickers whose design resembled that of the Post office stickers use by Solo One" (p. 187). In 2001, Boxfresh signed a deal with Solo One to have his moniker appear on their stickers. In this manner, the act of vandalism had come full circle with the artist's work now being co-opted by a mainstream capitalist organization (Schacter, 2013: p. 153).

Banksy

Originally from Bristol (located in Southwest England), the elusive Banksy started out doing graffiti and soon moved to street art, specializing in stencils. Not confined to Bristol, he extended his work to other locations both inside and outside the United Kingdom, such as the United States (e.g. New York City, New Orleans, Los Angeles, etc.) and other places around the world (e.g. Bethlehem, the West Bank, etc.) where his work has attracted a considerable amount of political controversy. The images of Banksy are synonymous with London. Over the years, he and/or the organization he created (Pest Control) have produced a number of books, such as *Wall and Piece* (2006). He was also the director of the movie *Exit Through the Gift Shop*. There appears to be as much interest in his elusiveness as in his work. There have been numerous Banksy sittings. Part of the importance of Banksy has forced North London council workers, who normally remove graffiti, to actually touch up ones that are attributed to him. According to *The Times*, "A list of all the paintings on walls by Banksy has been given to Islington Council's head of environment to stop them being painted over by cleanup teams. Some paintings are even being repaired after vandals have attacked them" (Anonymous, 2007). Banksy has also received his share of criticism. From 2009 to 2010, a very public and controversial dispute between Mike Robertson (aka King Robbo), a London-based graffiti writer, and he captured the attention of many keen graffiti/street art watchers (Ellsworth-Jones, 2012: pp. 51–52). The story eventually became the subject of a documentary, *Graffiti Wars: Banksy vs Robbo* (2011). Until that point, Robbo claimed to have had a twenty-five-year career as a graffiti artist and had winded down his career, until one day he met Banksy in a bar and they had a physical altercation. This was soon followed by Banksy purposely painting over one of Robbo's iconic pieces in Camden Town. Robbo started retaliating and altered some of Banksy's pieces. During the movie, there are interviews with various public works officials and workers over how street art is somehow privileged and graffiti is not. During this time period, Both Banksy and Robbo had wide-ranging support from fans. Robbo then held an exhibition of his work at the Pure Evil Art Gallery in Shoreditch and received a major commission to do a large graffiti-style silhouette of actress Zoë Kravitz in Berlin, for the premiere of her movie *Yelling to the Sky*. Shortly after the movie was shot, Robbo sustained a head injury and fell into a coma. Similar to Robbo's arguments, Banksy has received his fair share of criticism from graffiti and street artists alike for lacking talent.

Not content with simply doing his work on the city streets, Banksy (with the assistance of collaborators) has managed to affix his work on the walls of major galleries (e.g. Tate Modern) and museums (e.g. British Museum). Called incursions, these have taken a considerable amount of planning and the involvement of confederates who are on the lookout when these installations occur. Banksy's work, which is occasionally sold at auction, has fetched high prices. In one 2007 newspaper report, "A work by Banksy sold at auction for 288,000 GBP" (Collings, 2008).

King Robbo

For twenty years, Mike Robertson (aka King Robbo), described as "a founding father of London's street art scene in the Eighties" (Freeman, 2014), had a prolific career as a one of London's more prominent graffiti writers. During this time, he successfully kept his identity secret. He was known for creating iconic pieces that were placed on hard to reach places, including the sides of numerous canals in Camden. In 2009, despite apparently having been retired for close to a decade and working as a cobbler, he got involved in the famous battle with Banksy. This led to a resumption of his activities and eventually a handful of international commissions. The beef with Banksy was eventually settled amicably, but in April 2011, Robbo was found unconscious in front of his house on the street. He was placed in an induced coma, and he passed away in August 2014.

EINE

During the 1980s, Ben Flynn (aka EINE) became interested in hip-hop culture. He dropped out of school and started doing graffiti after seeing books on New York City subway art. EINE moved out of his parents' house and eventually got a job working for an insurance company. During this twelve-year period of absolutely hating his job, he spent a considerable portion of his spare time doing graffiti on trains, being arrested multiple times, and being forced to pay numerous fines (Godwin, 2013). During this period, he chalked up "about twenty arrests and seven convictions for graffiti vandalism" (Ellsworth-Jones, 2012: p. 6). Shortly before news footage showing him and some friends painting a train hit the media, he quit his job and found another one managing a bar in Shoreditch, where he met other graffiti and street artists (Godwin, 2013). He transitioned to becoming Banksy's printer, focusing on stencil and screen-printing techniques (Godwin, 2013). EINE is best known for his huge letters spray painted on shopkeepers' doors.

Since then, EINE has achieved more mainstream respectability, so much so that in 2010, one of his paintings was acquired by Prime Minister David Cameron, as a present for his first visit to the American President Barack Obama. "Eine was now famous, his prices went up and at a show he held in San Francisco, every piece was sold" (Ellsworth-Jones, 2012: p. 7). In 2014, EINE, who has since relocated to San Francisco, was invited to paint a wall in Rikers Island jail and on West Broadway in New York City (Anonymous, 2014).

A brief history of contemporary graffiti and street art in London

No formal history of graffiti and street art in London exists. Regardless, graffiti and street art in London predate the importation of hip-hop culture from the United States (e.g. Fleming, 2001; Daniell, 2011). These creative endeavors seem to function as a regular pressure valve to the street politics of the past twenty years. From slogans supporting the outlawed Irish Republican Army (IRA) terrorist organization to those specifically backing IRA hunger striker, Bobby Sands, a considerable amount of political graffiti is located on the streets, buildings, and canals around London. Not restricted to above ground locations, we have also seen some of this work in the London Tube/Underground (HMPS Department of Transportation, 1986). Perry Roger's book *The Writing on the Wall: The Graffiti of London* (1976), illustrated with black-and-white photographs, for example, is one of the earliest books to document the numerous unauthorized written slogans that have been painted on London's walls. Another example of this kind of book was Jac Charoux's book, *London Graffiti* (1980), which also contained both black and white photographs, but color ones too of pithy statements.

Most written accounts suggest that the origins of contemporary graffiti in London date back to the "New York City Rap Tour" which came to this city in 1982.[6] Others note the influence of American books like Cooper and Chalfant's *Subway Art* (1984), and Chalfant and Prigoff's *Spraycan Art* (1987), and movies, such as *Wild Style* (1983), that were making their way around youth circles during this time (Ellsworth-Jones, 2012). As the popularity of graffiti increased, so did the number of individuals who wished to experiment by writing and painting on different surfaces, including the London Tube and various walls around the city.[7]

By 1987, the London Transport, which is the former name of the organization for managing the London Underground (subway or tube), railways, and bus service estimated "that the cost of removing graffiti in 1986–1987 could amount to as much as £500,000" (Anonymous, 1987a).

Also in that year John Joporo, aged eleven, died as a result of being dragged underneath a London Tube train. It was alleged that he was trying to place his tag on a train (Anonymous, 1987b). In November 1987, a fire occurred in King's Cross Underground that led to the death of thirty-one individuals. One of the popular theories was that a fireball was enhanced by the cyanide gas that is produced when anti-graffiti paint burns (Dawe, 1989).

In 1989, the federal government unveiled "Special Action Squad," a plan to appoint a teacher at each public school who would be responsible for reducing vandalism, arson, and theft (Tytler, 1989). Although no fixed amount was estimated for graffiti, "The official cost of damage to schools is £49 million a year but local officers believe it is closer to £100 million" (Tytler, 1989). Also in 1989, the London Union of Youth Clubs convened a multipurpose "Graffiti Art" event at the South London Art Gallery. It was intended to "provide a more informed and positive response by the authorities and to limit the danger to those young people who risk death and criminalization in their attempts to express their creative illegality" (Holloway, 1989: p. 2). This event included a discussion among the artists, and "representatives of the police, British Railway Transport Police, and London Transport" (Coffield, 1991: p. 65).

In 1991, *The Times* reported on the increased amount of graffiti in London including the underground (the subway system). In an article it mentioned how "Since 1987, five teenagers have been killed while daubing [s]logans on trains. Graffiti damage to London Underground property is estimated at £5 million a year" (Dynes, 1991). The article adds, "Chris Connell, the British transport police inspector who heads the ten-man anti-graffiti unit, says that the hard core of graffiti writers, believed to number some sixty individuals, 'are highly organized, well equipped, and prepared to take terrible risks to get their tag displayed on London Underground trains.'" He adds,

> Catching them can take years. Each time a tag appears on a train or wall it is photographed and indexed, providing the police with a geographical range of the writer's activities, and dossier of damage that frequently amounts to £50,000 by the time the case comes to court. Nocturnal stake-outs are mounted, and occasionally the perpetrators are caught.

Other seemingly bizarre episodes occurred.

In March 1993, Declan Rooney, twenty, who along with other individuals was "involved in causing damage to London Underground trains estimated to have cost hundreds of thousands of pounds," was, instead of being imprisoned, was simply fined £1,500, and was placed on probation for a year. The judge in handing down the sentence stated "You have already cost the community very dear. With court appearances, the investigation and the damage, you have cost literally hundreds of thousands of pounds. It is not in the public interest that the community should pay even more money by putting you in custody" (Hidalgo, 1993).

During the early 2000s there were numerous selected stories about graffiti appearing on London walls, statues, and public monuments before, during, and after public protests. By 2002 the cost to clean up graffiti in London was reported to be a hundred million pounds (Anonymous, 2002). In 2001, an unnamed fifteen-year-old youth was convicted of stabbing to death an eighteen-year-old member of a rival graffiti writing crew for having defaced his graffiti. This incident, among others, served to further demonize individuals who were engaging in graffiti (Anonymous, 2001).

In 2003 the Labour government, under the leadership of Tony Blair, attempted to "declare a war on graffiti and dog mess" (Charter, 2002). In their attempts to improve the quality of life for citizens of the U.K., they developed "A Partnership between the council, police, fire brigade and community groups [which] aims to stamp out anti-social behavior by pooling resources and through a hotline to report incidents" including graffiti (Charter, 2002). Also in 2003, the

Home office, in conjunction with Crimestoppers, through "The Name That Tag campaign" offered a £500 reward for information leading to the arrest and conviction of any of the twelve most prolific individuals whom they identified as engaging in a disproportionate amount of graffiti in the London Tube and on buildings (Bjortomt, 2003). No evaluations of the program could be found. Meanwhile the London Underground started to publicize the specialized cameras that it was using to catch graffiti writers in the Tube. According to the reports "They are triggered by motion and give vandals an audio warning that they have been photographed" (Anonymous, 2004). In May of that year, Mayor Ken Livingstone, with the assistance of the other "twenty-seven borough police commanders" announced that they would be recruiting shopkeepers to volunteer not to sell spray paint to teenagers. The plan was met with criticism as selling spray paint was not illegal (Anonymous, 2003).

In 2005, in a sort of twist of fate, local graffiti artists objected to an advertising campaign spearheaded by Saatchi & Saatchi, a well-known advertising company that involved illegal spray-painting in different communities in public spaces.

> As part of a £20 million campaign for a new Brazilian spirit[,] they are spray-painting graffiti images on walls and buildings in the East End of London as a way to reach young consumers immune to conventional advertising. But the campaign appears to have backfired. Real street graffiti artist have begun taking 'direct action' against the interlopers.
>
> (Malvern, 2005)

In 2006, "nine men from south London, aged between eighteen and twenty-five, were charged with conspiracy to commit criminal damage after a seven-month British Transport Police (BTP) investigation. It is alleged the men committed 120 graffiti offences over two years . . . Robert Lee, a south-London writer known as Ribz, was jailed for three and a half years in December last year despite having 'retired'" (Addley, 2007).

By 2007, with the increasing acceptance of some graffiti and street artists, U.S.-based Shepard Fairey displayed his work at various London galleries, including a major exhibition called Nineteeneightyfouria at the StolenSpace gallery (Blackburn, 2007). Meanwhile periodic reports of deaths of young men doing graffiti were reported in the news. In January 2007, twenty-one-year-old Bradley Chapman (tag name Ozone) and nineteen-year-old Daniel Elgar were killed by a Tube train at Barking rail depot (Addley, 2007).

Continuing along this trend, in Spring 2008, the Tate Modern (one of the most respected museums of modern art in the world) held a "survey of street art," with works placed on the exterior of this museum. The surfaces were "covered with six towering works of Street Art, all around fifteen metres high" (Lewis, 2008). This work was done by a group of well-known international artists, including fail, Blue, Nunca, Os Gemeos, and Sixeart. Noticeably absent was work by Banksy (Falconer, 2008) (www.tate.org.uk/whats-on/tate-modern/exhibition/street-art) (www.news.bbc.co.uk/1/hi/entertainment/7419861.stm). Questions arose about why Banksy's work was not present, and when questioned, Cedar Lewisohn, the curator of the special exhibition, stated: "We wanted to bring international Street Artists to London, whose work the British public couldn't normally see. Banksy's work is very familiar to people in London." A more nuanced response why Banksy was not presenting was given by a source close to Banksy. He originally said that he was never asked, then later stated that the reason why Banksy was not participating was because automobile manufacturer Nissan sponsored the exhibition, as if to imply that the introduction of commercialism was crass, and had somehow tarnished the show.

In 2009, as previously mentioned, the clash between Banksy and Robbo reached a crescendo with both individuals defacing each other's work. As written, the conflict ended in a mutual truce.

In 2010, as selected pieces of graffiti and street gained a growing acceptance among some members of the public, it was not uncommon that situations like this would occur. Banksy biographer, Ellsworth-Jones describes a community meeting he attended in Hackney, where the residents were debating the merits of maintaining a huge painting of a rabbit by Roa, a Belgian street artist, that was affixed to the side of a wall of a recording studio (2012: pp. 5–6).

In 2011, Daniel Halpin (aka Tox), "known as the 'king of taggers,' was convicted of seven charges of criminal damage, and jailed for twenty-seven months. Halpin, twenty-eight, had spent ten years travelling the country painting his tag,. . . on trains, bridges, tunnels, stations" (Gillespie, 2013). Halpin was arrested as part of "BTP Operation Misfit, which claimed to have identified their tags . . ." He "claimed he was the victim of imitators. . . . [and] . . . had 'retired' in 2005 after a career defacing buses, trains, bridges, and walls earned him a string of asbos, which he largely ignored, and community service orders" (Davies, 2011). At his trial, testimony was given by retired and well-respected graffiti artists regarding their opinions and the authenticity of Halpin's tags (Davies, 2011).

Starting in 2011, with increasing public acceptance of graffiti and street art, newspaper articles started to suggest that graffiti and street art had become pretty mainstream. Jonathan Jones, writing in *The Guardian* (2011), opined,

> Street art is so much part of the establishment that when David Cameron spoke about this summer's riots, he was photographed in front of a bright and bulbous Oxfordshire graffiti painting . . . The efforts of and all the would-be Banksys' have so deeply inscribed the 'coolness' of street art into the middle-class mind.
>
> (Jones, 2011)

He adds,

> Maybe there was a time when painting a wittingly satirical or cheekily rude picture or comment on a wall was genuinely disruptive and shocking. That time is gone. Councils still do their bit to keep street art alive, and so confirming that it has edge. But basically it has been absorbed so deep into the mainstream that old folk who once rallied at graffiti in their town are now more likely to have a Banksy book on their shelves.
>
> (Jones, 2011)

Despite this trend, just before the 2012 Summer Olympics, the city of London and other governmental agencies (e.g. Hackney and Tower Hamlet councils) started to "clean up the city" by removing (painting over) certain graffiti- and street art-laden walls. There were also allegations during this time that there was an enhanced crack down on graffiti and street artists with suspects being routinely stopped, questioned, and in some cases, arrested (Allen, 2012; Jones, 2012). Frequent newspaper stories, like the one written by Jones, suggested,

> This week a graffiti painter – who claims he only works on legally sanctioned projects – was among several individuals banned from Olympic venues and London public transport, in a preemptive police strike against supposed threats to public order on the eve of the London Olympiad.
>
> (Jones, 2012)

Alternatively, in June 2012, two months before the start of the Olympics, Shepard Fairey was invited to create a mural, "his largest ever . . . a 138 ft. stencil encouraging free speech, at the London Pleasure Gardens" (Curtis, 2012).

In a semi-ironic twist of fate, shortly after the Olympics ended, some communities actively recruited graffiti and street artists to resume their work. Near the Olympics site, there was a flurry of commissioned graffiti activity. Much to the chagrin of local graffiti artists, like Sweet Tooth, the Legacy List Charity commissioned four pieces of work from international graffiti artists. A representative of the organization claimed, "We unashamedly wanted to showcase the best international artists and transform this part of the canal into a destination for street art" (Wainwright, 2013).

Beginning in 2013, news reports started surfacing about the death of graffiti. One article reported, "Painting names on buildings, trains, and buses used to be the preserve of teenagers, working at night and dodging security guards and police to daub their 'tags.' However, increased security . . . has led to a marked decline. According to figures from the British Transport Police . . . graffiti incidents fell by 63 percent between 2007 and this year [2013]" (Gillespie, 2013). The story mentioned an elusive study by Defra, the environment ministry, which claimed "a drop in graffiti." The article quotes Keegan Webb, "founder of The London Vandal, a graffiti blog and online shop, [who]said those who wanted to create graffiti in its 'true' form, without permission or special arrangements, now had to travel abroad" (Gillespie, 2013). As a result, there is more emphasis on galleries as places where graffiti artists may have their work displayed.

> But it is not just increased security and heavy penalties that are curbing the illegal graffiti artists; many of the early exponents have grown older and moved on. The younger generation . . . appears to have been lured away by computer games and iPads, which may not offer as much creativity but do not carry the threat of arrest either.
>
> (Gillespie, 2013)

The article, which quotes graffiti artist Solo One, states,

> graffiti was not declining but moving in different areas. It has changed "there is clearly in creativity [among young people] because they are mainly locked into online gaming," he added. It was really popular in the 1980s, when people were doing it as teenagers, but we are a lot more controlled now. If you look at estates [Britain's term for public housing] in the 1990s, they look like something out of Hungary. Many of the people who used to do it went on to careers in graphic design or music that still incorporated elements of it, but in terms of rebellious culture there is not as much of that, because we have been so tamed as a society.
>
> (Gillespie, 2013)

As part of the general public backlash, in 2013 Blakewill and Harris published *Wanksy: Interpreting a Graffiti Virtuoso* (Blakewill & Harris, 2013). The book, primarily consisting of color photographs, accompanied by short descriptive text, attempted to disparage and ridicule graffiti they encountered on the streets by suggesting that this kind of work is rudimentary.

Backing up these contextual factors, in April 2014, Yougov, a worldwide internet-based market research company, released the results of a recent poll it conducted, the results of which did not surprise most Londoners and indicated that, "The British public has . . . come a long way in their view of graffiti . . . a resounding three-to-one margin (66 percent to 22 percent), people now think graffiti can be considered as 'art.'" The accompanying post on the website stated: "In a separate question, only a third (34 percent) say 'all graffiti is vandalism' while the majority (58 percent) accept that 'some graffiti is acceptable.'" When specifically focusing on London, the author points out that "People in London, are almost split on graffiti (23 percent like it and 28 percent dislike it), while people elsewhere in Britain are much more likely to have a negative opinion of it" (Jordon, 2014).

Finally, in December 2014, the Graffiti Sessions, a three-day event, sponsored by the Graffiti Dialogues Network at Central Saint Martins (University of the Arts London), the UCL Urban Laboratory, and Southbank Centre, occurred. Its purpose was to "identify new horizons for future city strategies on graffiti and street arts and opportunities and challenges for evolving creative practice, towards places that are both safe and sociable." It also aimed to confront "deep-rooted preconceptions and speculation that have until now limited the progress of both policy and practice related to street art and graffiti." The format included "talks, workshops, and panel debates," featuring well-known and respected scholars, activists, and graffiti writers and street artists (http://graffitisessions.com/about). In many respects, this event both confirmed and symbolized the academic respectability of the study of graffiti and street art in London and elsewhere, and reinforced that this topic and practice had finally achieved a semi-respectability as an art form and as a method of political communication that can no longer be ignored.

Conclusion

Over the past four decades, the volume and creativeness of graffiti and street art in London have been simply amazing, but for reasons that are not clear, the scholarly coverage and analysis of this subject matter is highly selective and in need of further research. This chapter has attempted, in a small way, to shed some light into the history and main individuals, locations, and themes connected to graffiti and street art in London, in order to spur other researchers to do a more intense study of this rich but fading and often ephemeral urban visual content.

Notes

1   Special thanks to Christopher Brees-Rostveit for research assistance, and Rachel Hildebrandt, Ronald Kramer and Aaron Z. Winter for comments.
2   For purposes of clarification, this chapter focuses on graffiti and street art in Greater London. This encompasses the City of London, Inner London (consisting of 12 boroughs), and Outer London (comprised of 20 boroughs) (*London Government Act*, 1963).
3   The report writers extrapolated that at the time, the boroughs spent close to 7 million GBP combating graffiti.
4   A similar, but less intensive review of articles published on the British Broadcasting Website was also conducted.
5   Table of London based graffiti and street artists included in international anthologies:

Graffiti Writer/Street Artist	Art in the Streets (Deitch, et al., 2011)	The World Atlas of Street Art and Graffiti (Schacter, 2013)	Graffiti World: Street Art from Five Continents (Ganz, 2009)
Banksy	x		x
CEPT		x	
EINE		x	
GOLD PEG		x	
INKIE			x
Malcolm McLaren	x		
Adam Neate			x
PETRO		x	
ROUGH			x

6   The only available documentation of this event I could find was on the French-language Wikipedia page which states that it was part of a

> world tour (Paris, Lyon, Belfort, Mulhouse, Strasbourg, London, Los Angeles) organized by radio Europe 1 in 1982 and presented for the first time a non-American audience of graffiti -ARTISTS, the DJ scratching, the break dancers, the rappers, and Double Dutch. Participants included: Phase 2, Futura 2000, Dondi, Afrika Bambaataa, Grandmaster D.ST the Rock Steady Crew, Rammellzee, Buffalo Girls, and their manager Kool Lady Blue, promoter of the project with Bernard Zekri, a journalist for the magazine Actuel and Jean Karakos, leader of the label Celluloid. Entertainment was provided by Alain Maneval.
> ((http://fr.wikipedia.org/wiki/New_York_City_Rap) downloaded April 25, 2015)

7   London is also the home of active knitting graffiti/yarn bombing practitioners (Greenwall, 2012), and of Paul Moose, who engages in negative graffiti by cleaning dirty, sooty, and grimy walls to make attractive images.

References

Abel, E.L. & Buckley, B.E. (1977). *The Handwriting on the Wall: Towards a Sociology and Psychology of Graffiti*. Greenwood, CT: Greenwood.

Addley, E. (2007). Blood on the tracks, *The Guardian*, January 20, www.theguardian.com/uk/2007/jan/20/ukcrime.prisonsandprobation (downloaded May 12, 2015).

Allen, D.A. (2012). A round-up of retired graffiti artists for the London Olympics? *New Statesmen*, July 18, www.newstatesman.com/blogs/lifestyle/2012/07/round-retired-graffiti-artists-london-olympics (downloaded April 6, 2015).

Alvelos, H. (2004). The desert of imagination in the city of signs: Cultural implications of sponsored transgression and branded graffiti. In Ferrell, J., Hayward, K., Morrison, W. & Presdee, M. (eds) *Cultural Criminology Unleashed*, (pp. 181–191). London: The Glass House Press.

Anonymous. (1986). Parliament: Graffiti and the councils, *The Times*, December 18, (downloaded April 27, 2015).

Anonymous. (1987a). Parliament: Graffiti cost, *The Times*, April 23, (downloaded April 6, 2015).

Anonymous. (1987b). Graffiti death warning, *The Times*, December 17, (downloaded April 6, 2015).

Anonymous. (2001). Gang artist, 15, convicted of manslaughter, *The Times*, February 10, (downloaded April 27, 2015).

Anonymous. (2002a). Graffiti costs Londoners £100m, *BBC News*, May 7, http://news.bbc.co.uk/2/hi/uk_news/england/1972248.stm (downloaded April 25, 2015).

Anonymous. (2002b). Graffiti headache, *The Times*, May 7, (downloaded April 27, 2015).

Anonymous. (2003). Mayor launches graffiti war, *BBC News*, May 13, (downloaded May 1, 2015).

Anonymous. (2004). Vandals in frame, January 27, (downloaded April 27, 2015).

Anonymous. (2007). Council gives graffiti a helping hand, *The Times*, November 7, (downloaded March 9, 2015).

Anonymous. (2014). Prime Minister David Cameron's favourite graffiti artist Ben Eine hits New York, *London Evening Standard*, February 10, (downloaded January 28, 2015).

Banksy. (2006). *Wall and Piece*. London: Random House.

Blackburn, V. (2007). Poster boy with a difference, *The Times*, October 20, (downloaded April 27, 2015).

Blakewill, M. & Harris, J. (2013). *Wanksy: Interpreting a Graffiti Virtuoso*. West Sussex, England: Summersdale.

Bjortomt, O. (2003). Symbol for pound, reward to halt graffiti vandals, *The Times*, November 21, (downloaded April 27, 2015).

Brake, M. (2013). *Comparative Youth Culture: The Sociology of Youth Cultures and Youth Subcultures in America, Britain and Canada*. New York: Routledge.

Bull, M. (ed.). (2011). Banksy Locations & Tours Volume 1: A Collection of Graffiti Locations and Photographs in London, England. PM Press.

Chalfant, H. & Prigoff, J. (1987). *Spraycan Art*. London: Thames & Hudson.

Charoux, J. (1980). *London Graffiti*. London: WH Allen.

Charter, D. (2002). Labor targets dog mess and graffiti as new battleground, *The Times*, December 27, (downloaded April 27).

Coffield, F. (1991). *Vandalism & Graffiti: The State of the Art*. London: Calouste Gulbenkian Foundation.

Collings, M. (2008). Banksy's ideas have the value of a joke, *The Times*, January 28, (downloaded March 9, 2015).

Cooper, M. & Chalfant, H. (1984). *Subway Art*. New York: Macmillan.

Curtis, N. (2012). London best for street art, says obama poster creator, *London Evening Standard*, June 29, (downloaded June 28, 2015).

Daniell, C. (2011). Graffiti, calliglyphs and markers in the UK. *Archaeologies: Journal of the World Archeological Congress*, 7(2), 454–476.

Davies, C. (2011). Tox tagger faces prison term after jury decides his street art in plain vandalism: Feted author of graffiti attacks 'is no Bansky' 26-year-old was caught on CCTV in London and Paris, *The Guardian*, June 8, (downloaded January 28, 2015).

Dawe, T. (1989). Scientists gagged at seminar on King's Cross fire, *The Times*, May 31, (downloaded April 27, 2015).

Deitch, J., Gastman, R. & Rose, A. (eds) (2011). *Art in the Streets*. New York: Skira Rizzoi.

Dickens, L. (2008). 'Finders keepers': Performing the street, the gallery and the spaces in-between. *Liminalities: A Journal of Performance Studies*, 4(1), 1–30.

Dynes, M. (1991). An underground art form where death tags along, *The Times*, August 24, (downloaded April 27, 2015).

Ekblom, P. (1988a). "Combatting Vandalism to Public Services: The case of graffiti on London Underground trains," Report of TVS and British Telecom Conference. 1988 Combatting Vandalism to Public Services. British Telecom.

Ellsworth-Jones, W. (2012). *Banksy: The Man Behind the Wall*. New York: St. Martin's Press.

Epstein, J. (2014). *London Graffiti and Street Art: Unique artwork from London's Streets. LDN Graffiti*. London: Ebury Press.

Falconer, M. (2008). Graffiti on the gallery, *The Times*, May 17, (downloaded March 9, 2015).

Fleming, J. (2001). *Graffiti and the Writing Arts of Early Modern England*. Philadelphia, PA: University of Pennsylvania Press.

Florida, R. (2014). *The Rise of the Creative Class – Revisited: Revised and Expanded* (revised edn). New York: Basic Books.

Frank Steam 156 Malt. (2013). *London Street Art*. Årsta, Sweden: Dokument Press.

Freeman, S. (2014). Stairs fall that killed graffiti star 'King Robbo' still a mystery. *London Evening Standard*, December 5, (downloaded January 28, 2015).

Ganz, N. (2009). *Graffiti World: Street Art from Five Continents* (2nd edn). New York: Harry N. Abrams.

Gillespie, J. (2013). Graffiti artists mourn heyday of spray, *The Sunday Times*, November 17, (downloaded January 28, 2015).

Glass, R. (1988). Graffiti transforming look of London underground subway, removal costs soars, *Los Angeles Times*, June 12, p. 1.

Godwin, R. (2013). Ben Eine: The man who sprayed Selfridges, *London Evening Standard*, June 25, (downloaded January 28, 2015).

Greenwall, D. (2012). Guerrilla knitters stitch up London; A secret knitting gang is 'tagging' the capital with woolly artworks, *The Times*, March 28, www.standard.co.uk/lifestyle/london-life/ben-eine-the-man-who-sprayed-selfridges-8672414.html (downloaded January 28, 2015).

Hall, S. & Jefferson, T. (eds) (1976/1993). *Resistance Through Rituals: Youth Subcultures in Post-War Britain*. New York: Routledge Press.

Hidalgo, L. (1993). Graffiti vandal 'too costly to jail,' *The Times*, March 6, (downloaded April 27, 2015).

HMPS, Department of Transportation. (1986). Crime on the London Underground: Study Report.

Jones, J. (2011). Street art is dying – and its our fault, *The Guardian*, August 25, (downloaded January 28, 2015).

Jones, J. (2012). London 2012: The graffiti clampdown is like Versailles versus the sans-culottes, *The Guardian*, July 20, (downloaded January 28, 2015).

Jordon, W. (2014). Graffiti is an art form, say public, yougov, https://yougov.co.uk/news/2014/05/01/graffiti-is-an-artform-say-public/ (downloaded April 24, 2015).

Kaderabek, L. (2013). Off the Walls: The Constellations of Interconnected Practices Regarding the Street Art Ecosystem in Shoreditch and the Medium Instagram. Ph.D. Dissertation submitted in partial fulfillment of the requirements for the degree of MSc Digital Anthropology (UCL) of the University of London, University College London, Department of Anthropology.

Keegan, (2012). Graphotism closes its doors, *London Vandal*, June 25, http://blog.thelondonvandal.com/2012/06/graphotism-closes-its-doors-shuts-down/ (downloaded January 14, 2015).

Lewis, B. (2008). No it's not Banksy . . .: Wicked!, *Evening Standard*, May 23, www.standard.co.uk/goingout/exhibitions/no-its-not-banksy-7406738.html.

London Assembly. (2002). Graffiti in London. Report of the London Assembly Graffiti Investigative Committee. (Chair Andrew Pelling).

London Handstyles and Chapman Brothers. (2009). *London Handstyles*.

Macdonald, N. (2001). *The Graffiti Subculture: Youth, Masculinity and Identity in London and New York*. New York: Palgrave.

MacNaughton, A. (2006). *London Street Art*. New York: Prestel.

MacNaughton, A. (2007). *London Street Art 2*. New York: Prestel.

MacNaughton, A. (2009). *London Street Art Anthology*. New York: Prestel.

Malvern, J. (2005). Graffiti artists pour scorn on Saatchi's street art campaign, *The Times*, May 23, (downloaded March 9, 2015).

Perry, R. (1976). *The Writing on the Wall: The Graffiti of London*. London: Elm Tree Books/Hamish Hamilton.

Rollins, J. (2011). *The Lost Boyz: A Dark Side of Graffiti*. Sherfield Gables, UK: Waterside Press,

Schacter, R. (2008). An ethnography of iconoclash. An investigation into the production, consumption and destruction of street-art in London. *Journal of Material Culture*, *13*(1), 35–61.

Schacter, R. (2013). *World Atlas of Street Art and Graffiti*. New Haven, CT: Yale University Press.

Siddique, H. (2006). Patterns of crime: Graffiti in the London Borough of Hackney. Unpublished Undergraduate Thesis, University of Kingston, London.

Skelton, T & Valentine, G. (eds). (1998). *Cool Places: Geographies of Youth Cultures*. New York: Routledge.

Tytler, D. (1989). Schools to appoint teachers to fight vandalism, *The Times*, March 8, (downloaded April 27, 2015).

Wainwright, O. (2013). After the Olympics, even the graffiti is gentrified, *The Guardian*, August 7, (downloaded January 28, 2015).

Whitney, C.R. (1988). New plague for London: Graffiti tags, *New York Times*, October 13, p. a9. (downloaded April 15, 2015).

Wilson, S. (1978). Vandalism and 'defensible space' on London housing estates, In Clarke, R.V.G, (ed.) *Tackling Vandalism* (pp. 41–85). Home Office Research Study No. 47. London: Her Majesty's Stationary Office.

22

Graffiti and street art in Paris

David Fieni

Introduction

Since the early 1980s, multiple factors have coalesced to make Paris and its suburbs one of the most active and dynamic centers of urban graffiti and street art in the world. In order to understand this progression, this chapter explores the rise of Parisian graffiti and street art in the context of the historical transformations of French society and cultural production in combination with

Figure 22.1 Rue Dénoyez, Paris. An important center of graffiti and street art inside the city of Paris © the author

the globalization of France, both in terms of the influx of immigrants and cultures of immigration, but also the influence of graffiti and hip-hop cultures from outside the hexagon, or mainland France.

It should be noted at the outset that one of the key elements that has structured the practice of graffiti writing and street art in the Paris region is precisely the geographic and demographic situation of Paris proper in relation to its *banlieues*, or suburbs, many of which have become home to populations who had immigrated from France's former colonies in the aftermath of the collapse of the French empire. In many ways, the *banlieue* has functioned as a gateway through which much graffiti and street art first entered the country, at first under the influence of the New York scene. From these nerve centers on the periphery of the French capital, graffiti spread inwards to the center, becoming more visible (Paris being a city with a multi-billion dollar tourist industry) while also influencing, and coming into contact with, the rich cultural history of this cosmopolitan city where the artistic traditions of salons, galleries, and museums have long existed alongside more spontaneous expressions of popular sentiment.[1]

Graffiti and street art are forms of expression that are typically undertaken with the understanding that they will be erased or painted over. In order to reconstruct their history, researchers must therefore consult a unique kind of archive, one consisting of photos and videos of graffiti, alongside interviews with writers and readers of street art. In the case of Paris, there are two sources in particular that have compiled the oral histories, photographs, and videos of the birth of the local scene. *Paris Tonkar*, a 1991 book written by Tarek Ben Yakhlef and Sylvai Doriath, and the film, *Writers: 20 Years of Graffiti in Paris*, a 2004 full-length documentary directed by Marc-Aurèle Vecchione. While the ephemeral nature of graffiti and street art determines the contours of its cultural history, the importance of visibility and fame within the graffiti community determines the locations of its particular form of geography. In addition to these two milestones, the 2007 film *Bomb It!* includes voices of a group of inhabitants of the *banlieue*, who insist that graffiti started in these suburban ghettos, and was later exported, so to speak, to the center of Paris, in order to "tear up" the city. American graffiti artist Futura 2000 also gives a shout-out to the *banlieue*, when he dates the emergence of a full-fledged movement in "Paris and the suburbs" (Vecchione, 2004). Most of the recorded documentation of the movement, however, focuses almost exclusively on work that was done in Paris proper. In this early period, there is little or no distinction made between graffiti and street art as two distinct genres. Yet while figures who would come to be associated with the street art scene, such as Blek le Rat and Space Invader, began producing their work at the same period as those working in a more explicitly New York influenced style, more documentation of the New York style graffiti from this early period exists than for street art.

Despite the difficulty of establishing how the relationship between suburb and city center operated in the early days, the pioneers of graffiti in Paris tell a story that is clear in terms of the importance of New York City and the influence of seminal writers such as Taki 183 in the early 1970s. One of the key players at the emergence of the Paris scene was Bando (Phillip Lehman), who tagged with a number of crews in the 1980s and 1990s, but remains most closely associated with "Crime Time Kings" (CTK), and has been credited with being the first person to write graffiti in the New York style in the city of Paris. As he tells it, Bando went to New York City in 1981 or 1982, where he met and started tagging with local writers (Vecchione, 2004).

In the next several years, tags, throw-ups, and pieces start to appear at a variety of locations within the city: Along the quays of the river Seine, on walls lining vacant lots, and at construction sites. Perhaps the most important of these centers of activity was the work site on the grounds of the Louvre museum, where I.M. Pei's glass pyramid, commissioned by President

David Fieni

François Mitterrand in 1984 and completed in 1989, was under construction. This site offered budding writers a vast unguarded surface to write on at the center of the city, within eyeshot of tourists and Parisians alike, in the shadow of the former royal palace turned epicenter of France's artistic patrimony. Privileged sites such as the fences lining the Louvre Pyramid under construction were likely to have facilitated the formation of crews of writers and the development of uniquely Parisian styles of graffiti.

From the beginning, graffiti in Paris was a cosmopolitan practice, bringing together writers from New York, France, and other parts of Europe. Any attempt to name the most important or visible graffiti artists from this first period (roughly 1983–1990) will necessarily be incomplete and biased. *Paris Tonkar* lists no fewer than seventy-seven crews, along with the pseudonyms (tags) of the individual writers, all prefaced with the following caveat: "This is not an exhaustive list, especially since several *Graffeurs* are in many groups at the same time" (Ben Yakhlef & Doriath, 1991: p. 122). Nonetheless, a number of tags, names, and crews have come to be synonymous with the development, excitement, and influence of these early days. As Bando meets and collaborates with Shoe, an artist from Amsterdam who became part of USA (United Street Artists) crew, and French writer, Mode2, starts tagging with a British crew, TCA (The Chrome Angelz), work that was at first an imitation of New York style first comes to distinguish itself, and then begins to influence and motivate graffiti in other European cities.

In Paris, as in other cities where hip-hop was taking root throughout the 1980s, graffiti was often linked to a broader repertoire of youth cultures that also included styles of clothing, music, and dancing. While the birth of hip-hop can be traced specifically to the Bronx, and more generally to black and minority groups in the U.S., Paris was quick to emerge as a second center of hip-hop culture on the world stage. Around the same time that Bando and others were importing New York graffiti styles to Paris, the "New York City Rap Tour" came to Europe, making stops in both London and Paris. The tour featured an impressive slate of rappers and DJs, such as Afrika Bambaataa and Rock Steady Crew, but also graffiti artists Futura 2000, Phase 2, Ramelzee, and Dondi. One of the French DJs who had been largely responsible for first disseminating hip-hop in France, Sidney Duteil, the son of immigrants from Guadeloupe, would, two years later, in 1984, host the first television program devoted entirely to hip-hop music and culture, H.I.P. H.O.P. As one commentator has remarked, the difference between how hip-hop developed in the U.S. versus France was that it cultivated in New York as a relatively "unmediated" form of culture, whereas in France it was an import, and a mass-produced one at that, marketed in the form of cassette tapes and packaged tours (Charry, 2012: p. 5). While this may be largely true in terms of music and fashion, graffiti, because of its very nature as an underground and usually illegal activity, remained an important element of hip-hop culture that strongly resisted the market forces at play in its global dissemination.

Graffiti and street art?

Both *Paris Tonkar* and *Writers* focus on hip-hop graffiti to the exclusion of what is now often recognized as the semi-independent category of street art. On one level, this distinction is significant. If graffiti is all about the letter, then the rise of street art as a distinct mode of public art is notable for its abandonment of typographical experiments and its focus on the image. In a recent video interview with Blek le Rat (Xavier Prou), the "father of stencil graffiti," Blek narrates his compulsion to work on walls as a "need" he "cannot express in words" (Silver, 2014). Such a statement might seem to affirm the distinction between graffiti and street art. One problem with this kind of categorization, however, is that Blek le Rat claims to also have been influenced by New York graffiti of the 1970s (along with the large-scale human painted

290

figures of the Canadian public artist, Richard Hambleton). Both hip-hop graffiti and street art continue to flourish in Paris, often on the same walls as each other. It is also important to point out that it was and is quite common for hip-hop graffiti in Paris to juxtapose stylized letters of the writer's name or crew with figures drawn from comics, film, or pop culture. On the other hand, more image- or figure-based work also relies often enough on words, whether the signature of the writer/artist, or a longer text.

In order to situate graffiti and street art in their shared social and geographical context in the city of Paris as closely related if not identical modes of graffiti (in the general sense of the term), we can examine the competing styles of two of the major crews from the 1980s who were working in a more hip-hop oriented style (BBC and TKC), alongside two major figures in the world of Parisian stencil graffiti: Blek le Rat and Miss.Tic. BBC (Bad Bad Crew), whose members included Skii, Ash.2, Jon, and Jay, privileged the form of the name as part of the overall look of a piece, in which the relationship between letter and non-letter was fluid and integrated. CTK, featuring Bando, Boxer, Senz Sign, and Squat, on the other hand, tended to focus on the readability of the letters, which were often notable for their strong outlines and bold colors. American photographer and documentarian of graffiti, Henry Chalfant articulates the overall difference between the new Parisian styles and the New York styles that inspired graffiti writers in France, saying that "while they got their base from New York graffiti, they immediately transformed it into something different." Chalfant attributes what he calls "art school style" to the early graffiti in the city of Paris, specifying that "the color-sense was all different [than that of graffiti in New York]," as was the "technique and rhythm of the line" (Vecchione, 2004). Japanese animation and comic book style in general are clear influences on the painted figures and characters of French graffiti in this period. Hip-hop style graffiti in Paris have thus long blurred the line between "graffiti," as something that primarily experiments with the shape and volume of letters, and "street art," as a play of figures and images, of lines and colors.

Cited by renowned British street artist Banksy as a major influence, Blek le Rat started putting up stencils of rats around the city of Paris in 1981, about the same time as the work of the first taggers, graffiti writers, and crews first appeared. Preferring the term "urban art" to "graffiti," Blek grew up in a well-off family, the son of an architect, in the posh Paris suburb of Boulogne. While Chalfant's "art school style" might not apply to Blek's work, Prou did in fact attend art school and also studied architecture. His work thus represents an encounter between New York style graffiti and the long history of art and architecture, and especially the radical or even utopian tradition of art and art criticism, on the continent. He tells us that he began by painting rats, his signature emblem, for two reasons: First, he says, they are "the only free animal in the city," outnumbering the human population of Paris two-to-one. "Rat" is also an anagram of the word "art" (Silver, 2014). A hooded man in the shadows holds out a hand as if asking for change, a figure sleeps on the ground beside a dog, Leonardo's David holds a semi-automatic rifle, a ballerina suspended on a concrete wall dances in a blue tutu: These are among the life-sized stencils of human figures Blek has now painted on walls worldwide. Perhaps most notable is his stencil of a man in a dark suit and sunglasses carrying large suitcases in each hand: "The man who walks through walls." This piece, which features Blek's head and Buster Keaton's body, and which functions as a figure for the artist himself, expresses the desire for mobility and the revolt against enclosure that all graffiti share.

A rare instance of a highly visible woman graffiti artist, Miss.Tic has also been painting illegally in Paris since the mid-1980s. A self-described "cerebral libertine,"[2] her work most often features a dark-haired pochoir (stencil) avatar of herself, usually in provocative poses, staring at the viewer, bent over, or lifting the hem of her skirt, alongside lyrical or aphoristic stenciled text. "À Lacan ses lacunes," reads one such piece – "Lacan's gaps are his own" – a playful way of turning the supposed lack that characterizes the feminine in some accounts of psychoanalysis back at the men who theorized it. "I have *frissons* tattooed on the skin of my memory," "I leave to desire," "The abuse of pleasure is excellent for your health," are a few of Miss. Tic's texts, which combine the wit of a one-liner with the mindful provocation of a zen koan. Combined with images that both evoke a third-wave feminist celebration of sexuality and riff on stylized glamour advertisements, Miss. Tic's work carves out a space for a highly iconoclastic feminist critique in this capital of fashion.

Figure 22.2 Belleville neighborhood, Paris. Stencil (pochoir) by Miss Fuck, "I hate the world"
© the author

Without elaborating a full-blown argument about why hip-hop graffiti and so-called street art in Paris should be discussed in relation to one another instead of in isolation, one may nonetheless affirm the value of categorizing graffiti (in the general sense of the term) as an illegal act. While a focus on illegality may certainly be used as "an essential support beam for the theoretical claims being advanced by the author" or obfuscate the graffiti writer's desire for "integration" into the larger society or a "conventional" lifestyle (Kramer, 2010: p. 237), an emphasis on illegality does tell us a great deal about the positioning of the writer at the moment of writing in relation to the regimes of private and public property, of media and advertising, and how a desire for visibility and mobility makes graffiti writing worth the risk of arrest. Beyond the ethnographic specificities one may collect by interviewing members of a crew such as CTK, or the aesthetic analysis of a piece by Miss.Tic or Blek, exists the common gesture of re-inscribing or re-coding public space. Thus, while street art may tend to be informed by the history of so-called high-art, and while it is often done by individual auteurs, it is counter-productive to over-emphasize the aesthetic axis at the expense of the juridical one.[3] A similar critical tactic could of course be deployed for hip-hop graffiti: In their own emphases on criminality or oppositionality, critics should avoid simply reinforcing the criminalization of such work by the police, and should instead actively seek out the fluid beauty and avant-garde grotesque of the psychogeographical sublime that is graffiti.

It is precisely because the walls of a city offer a common workspace for people from diverse backgrounds, whether they prefer being called writers, graffiti writers, *graffeurs*, *graffeuses*, urban artists, public artists, bombers, or situationists, that critics should take care not to isolate styles and authors based on categories of analysis pertaining to class or ethnic identity, but should instead consider the diversity within the larger phenomenon of writing and painting on such walls. In the case of writers from France, marginalization of communities based on ethnic or religious affiliation exists alongside the Republican ideal of the abstract citizen. Parisian graffiti can be seen as a vivid illustration of the tension between these two poles of public life in France. On one hand, a tag, throw-up, or a piece can be understood as a reterritorialization of urban or suburban space, a way of inscribing identity, specificity, and the temporalities of bodies moving in space into a what Michel de Certeau has called the homogeneous space of the abstract modern city (de Certeau, 1988: pp. 117, 121): A place cleansed of the heterogeneous mess of bodies and memories, of desires and interdictions. On the other hand, unauthorized illegal writing and art in public allows graffiti and street artists to experiment with identity, anonymity, and pseudonymity. A wall is a place where what matters is what a body can do, specifically with spray paint, pens, stickers, stencils, tiles, pieces of a rubik's cube, or other materials, not what it looks like or where it came from.

Contagion and criminalization

While the term "viral culture" is most often used in contemporary discourse to describe the speed and reach of digital cultural production, graffiti can be said to have pioneered many aspects of this phenomenon. The fact that the practice of hip-hop graffiti from New York made a stop in Paris on its way to becoming a worldwide phenomenon itself demonstrates how graffiti participated in what Jeff Ferrell has notably called a "world politics of wall painting" (Ferrell, 1995) long before the internet would accelerate its viral spread. Graffiti begets other graffiti. As the writers and artists who create them tend to do so out of sight of the public eye, graffiti can create what we might call a viral effect, as letters and images seem to appear suddenly throughout a city as if created by invisible hands. A wall that was blank in the evening is now covered with colors and lines.

In Paris, this viral spread of graffiti accelerated throughout the 1980s, which results in a concomitant escalation of police enforcement, perhaps most notably seen in the notorious tagging (or graffiti "bombing") of the Louvre metro station in 1991 and police and news media reaction (discussed below). The spread of graffiti in Paris is increased by what graffiti artists see as a wildly disproportionate police response. Not too far from the Louvre Pyramid was the construction site around the Stravinsky Fountain at the Pompidou centre: The first was one of Mitterrand's *grands projets*, and the second a joint venture between the city of Paris and the national Ministry of Culture. These two projects, which involved modernizing France's cultural heritage for the new generation, and which were designed with younger tastes in mind, provided the platform, literally and inadvertently, for graffiti art to flourish in the city of Paris. From these sites, graffiti spread to many others: Metro trains and regional RER trains, as well as train yards and tunnels.

It was the area in the northeastern part of Paris, near the Stalingrad metro station, where the tenth *Arrondissment* (or Borough) meets the nineteenth Arrondissement, that provided the next true nerve center for graffiti writers in the city. From approximately 1982 to 1993, the vacant lots in this area came to be known as the "Hall of Fame" of graffiti in Europe. Such a designation indicates the roles that geography, nationality, and cultural specificity played and continue to play in the nomadic and transnational art of graffiti. Whereas a designation such as "francophone" is often used to designate literature written in French from writers who are either not French or not of French extraction, the location of Paris as a site for graffiti art, or a specific location such as Stalingrad, functions in a very different way. The vacant lots of Stalingrad provided writers with a combination of the visibility and the anonymity offered by the French capital.

A watershed moment in the history of graffiti in the center of Paris proper occurred on the night of May 1, 1991, when the Louvre-Rivoli metro station, "among the most beautiful" in the city, according to Pascale Manzagol, the newscaster who reported on the event the following evening, was covered in tags overnight. The media coverage of this event captured (and perhaps even manufactured) some of the public uproar over this event, with interviews with commuters and public officials. At the same time, these news reports helped promote the fame of the writers and of the very practice of graffiti writing itself. One young man interviewed at the station provided a close-reading of one tag, which the camera relayed to viewers: "La RATP [the company in charge of regional public transportation in the Paris area]: Qui sème le vent récolte la tempête," a reference to Hosea 8.7 from the Old Testament: "They sow the wind, and they will reap the whirlwind." A moment later, a middle-aged woman is arguing angrily with the young people, calling them "dogs," as they ask her whether cutting off a hand or a head would be a more appropriate punishment.[4] *Paris Tonkar* includes a mini-manifesto about the discourse of criminalization that reaches a head with this event. Signed by the writer OENO, of the VEP crew (Vandales en puissance, or "Vandals in Power"), beside the words "DISSIDENCE GRAPHIQUE," the rant begins by citing the supposed price of the clean-up: "500,000 fr[anc]s. What a bargain! So many zeros for our newspaper hungry for a scoop and a spectacle. In any case, why question these figures, since they come from such a respectable institution as the RATP!" (Ben Yakhlef & Doriath, 1991: p. 39).

OENO's manifesto articulates the double-bind that graffiti makes palpable for many:

> Either graffiti is the mirror that reflects the malaise of young people, or you just have to wait for society to evolve . . . or maybe we're just simply bad. If that's the case, then tremble – for graffiti is just the beginning. This is the dawn of destruction.
>
> (Ben Yakhlef & Doriath, 1991: p. 39)

The Louvre station would be bombed again in January 1992, magnifying the fame of the writers involved while also increasing police surveillance of highly visible locations, such as centrally-located metro stations, and increased penalties for those caught "defacing" public or private property.[5] The viral nature of this event is clear in the dialectic of prohibition, media attention, and the explosion of graffiti that followed. The viral effect continues to this day, a fact that becomes clear when one watches the YouTube clip where this news report is today viewable online, as it is in fact an advertisement for a book of graffiti images, *Descent Interdite*, about graffiti in the Paris metro.

The Paris police expressed their response to the repeated attacks on the Louvre station as a desire to maintain the city center as a "clean" and unmarked space, free of what RATP director Christian Deplaces called the "scribbling" of the taggers. The graffiti writers' work thus demonstrated a direct challenge to this regime of urban neutrality and hygiene, and the graffiti themselves often commented on the fact that their task in the larger order of urban signs is that of an intervention aimed at disturbing the spatial ordering of the French city as decreed from above, and at bringing the margins into the center, the very heart of Paris. At the same time that this new insistence on protecting the city center against the so-called contagion of what was perceived as uncivil behavior, French urban policy also turned its attention to the banlieue as a "troubled" locale in need of special attention from the technocratic penal state. Mustapha Dikeç sums up the overall trend of the spatialization of social policy in terms of a form of neoliberalism of urban policy:

> Neoliberal strategies deployed in cities, it has been argued, sharpen socioeconomic inequalities and displace certain groups from cities, whose presence in the city is deemed undesirable . . . Urban neoliberalism is deeply concerned with imposing a certain 'social landscape' on the city. The third issue follows from the [socioeconomic and sociospatial manifestations of neoliberalism], and involves new and aggressive strategies of policing and surveillance aimed at particular groups and particular spaces (mostly city centres), criminalization of poverty, and the increased use of the penal system.
>
> (Dikeç, 2006: p. 63)

French urban policy in the 1980s and 1990s can thus be seen as a set of "substantially spatial practices that produce spaces of intervention (or containment), although the discursive articulations of such spaces and the modes of legitimization vary depending on established political traditions, as do forms of neoliberalization and state restructuring" (Dikeç, 2006: p. 77). The effort to keep the Louvre station free of "scribbling" thus represents one element of France's contribution to the European penal state and the work of taggers and writers an explicit act of direct action committed against the rapid spread of this apparatus in France.

Official response to graffiti and street art

Article 322–321 of the French Penal Code, created in 1994, is most often used to punish acts of graffiti and street art in Paris. The law imposed a 25,000 FF fine (roughly equivalent to 3,700 USD) for "tracing inscriptions, signs, or drawings, without prior authorization, on facades, vehicles, public thoroughfares, or urban street furniture or fixtures," provided the damage is not severe.[6] For more severe acts of vandalism, that is, for "destruction, degradation, or deterioration" of property belonging to someone else, the penalty is a two-year prison sentence and a fine of 200,000 FF (roughly equivalent to 40,000 USD). In addition to the existing law and criminal penalties, politicians from different levels of government have reacted to graffiti and street art. During the 2002 deliberations in the French Senate, regarding the price of graffiti removal, Senator Alain Gournac articulated his concerns with graffiti and the effect of graffiti culture on public life in the Ile-de-France region and France's national self-image. Gournac spoke of the "sad spectacle of the facades of our public and private buildings," saying that tags "eat away at our cities and harm our environment, the image of our country, and its morale."[7]

The numbers cited in these deliberations affirm that from 1998 to 2000, the RATP paid a minimum of 26 million euros per year for graffiti removal and prevention, whereas the national railroad company, the SNCF, paid a minimum of 15 million euros in the Paris region. Other sources cite vastly different sums, ranging from 6 million euros per year for cleaning SNCF trains, to 50 million euros per year for the all graffiti-related costs for the RATP.[8] While it can be difficult to obtain accurate numbers for the cost of graffiti removal in a given locale, one may compare this 41 million euro price tag for graffiti cleaning on Parisian public transportation cited in the above Senate deliberations to the 4.5 million euro cost of graffiti removal within the city itself.[9] It is also worth noting that Paris is often cited as being the only city that pays for the cost of cleaning graffiti from private property (Michot, 2012).

As of 2012, Paris contracted three companies for this task, which has become an increasingly specialized industry employing over forty so-called "tag hunters" (Michot, 2012). Korrigan, one such company detailed in a 2012 article in *Le Figaro*, is based in the municipality of La Corneuve, which was one of the hotbeds of the banlieue riots of 2005, and also a center of graffiti in the Paris region. While the Département of Seine-Saint-Denis, where La Corneuve is found, provides funds for graffiti clean-up comparable to those of Paris proper,[10] it is nonetheless symptomatic of the relationship between the suburban margin and the urban city center: Writers from the banlieue go into Paris to write; Paris hires a company from the banlieue to erase the writing; Paris thus serves as a self-erasing canvas.

La Corneuve, one of many banlieue neighborhoods categorized by the French government as "sensitive," also played a special role in the events leading up to the 2005 riots. In the aftermath of the shooting death of an eleven-year-old boy, then minister of the interior, Nicolas Sarkozy visited in June, 2005, and proceeded to tell inhabitants and the media that "beginning tomorrow, we will clean out this project [cité] with a Kärcher," equating policing of the area with the cleansing of graffiti done by Kärcher high-pressure water cleaning machines used by companies like Korrigan.[11] Combined with Sarkozy's comments from later that year, where he called residents of the banlieue "scum" (*racaille*), a rather explicit position had emerged, further exacerbating tensions between the local and national authorities and the banlieue youth, largely of immigrant origins.[12]

Aesthetics and illegality

At the same time that graffiti in Paris has been viewed as a symptom of brute criminality and lawlessness, as a sign of the decay of French civilization, the encroachment of a kind of "visual pollution" (in the words of François Dagnaud, the Mayor's "Assistant in Charge of Cleanliness") from the margins into the city center, it has also, of course, been viewed as a practice at the cutting-edge of art, writing, design, and activism. To explore graffiti and street art in the contexts of galleries, literature, cinema, and pop culture at large is to remove it from the world that gave birth to it and from which its meanings derive, but also to view it from a different angle and open up its tangled lines and often opaque meanings. Graffiti artist Delta articulates the relationship between aesthetics and illegality in graffiti by affirming that writers "have to be a lot more original on a legal wall" (Vecchione, 2004). In other words, whether on the street or in a gallery, graffiti exists on a continuum in which risk and originality determine the prestige value of a particular piece.

Before work done in France was to achieve the recognition that accompanies being displayed in a Paris art gallery, it was primarily New York artists who were featured in these spaces.

Following his appearance in the previously mentioned 1982 Rap Tour, graffiti artist FUTURA 2000 was perhaps the first graffiti artist to have a solo gallery show in Paris, in 1983 at the Yvon Lambert Studio.[13] By comparison, Jean-Michel Basquiat, the celebrated New York City artist whose work borrowed elements from graffiti, would not have a solo show in the city until January 1987, at the Galerie Daniel Templon, after having shown his work in cities around the world. Graffiti thus entered Paris art galleries before Basquiat's work did. New York transplant JonOne followed suit with a series of shows beginning in 1991. As French street art developed its own audience, so did its visibility in the gallery scene in Paris, which grew exponentially to comprise over sixty galleries featuring street art and graffiti, which now constitute approximately 10 percent of all galleries in the city.[14] With the global reputation of street artists like Banksy, graffiti and street art have continued their ascent into the world of *haute culture*, for better or worse, which also exacerbates the tension between simpler tags and more elaborate pieces and instances of street art.

A kind of apotheosis occurred in 2009 and 2010, as two major exhibitions of graffiti art took place in Paris: *Né dans la Rue* at the Fondation Cartier for Contemporary Art in 2009, and *Le Tag au Grand Palais* in 2010. The later exhibit can be seen as a moment when graffiti in Paris came full circle: Whereas the movement began on the makeshift walls and barriers around the construction site at the Louvre, it had now entered the hallowed halls of a historical monument, Le Grand Palais built as a crowning achievement of French culture and industry for the 1900 Universal Exposition. The work of Thomas Hirshcorn, a Swiss artist working in Paris, represents what can be perhaps be seen as a more adventurous instance of placing graffiti-style writing and messaging into a museum setting. His free 2014 exhibit at the Palais de Tokyo, *La Flamme Éternelle*, was built from an enormous maze of recycled automobile tires (evoking a new kind of barricades for an age of planetary self-consumption) and featured a range of interactive projects, in which participants could freely create posters, write, draw, and sculpt the exhibit itself, creating the kind of open-ended, interactive space that so much graffiti already imagines in the real spaces of the contemporary city, where the specter of private property and policed public domains continually collide. The exhibit was draped with large cloth banners that featured spray-painted slogans left deliberately unfinished, inviting visitors to collaborate by finishing them: "PEOPLE BEFORE PROFITS! NO TO."[15] It evoked the history of unauthorized popular expression in the French capital, from the 1789 Revolution, to the 1871 Commune, to May 1968. Instead of ripping graffiti out of its context, Hirschorn's *Eternal Flame* invited the public to participate in the creative spirit of popular revolt, at the same limit where street art and illegal graffiti inscribe their signs.

In addition to its temporary home in the street, subway, gallery, and museum, graffiti and street art in France continue to find a place in cinema and literature. The number of French films and written fiction where graffiti makes a cameo is too great to list here, but a brief discussion of a few examples can elucidate important aspects of how graffiti functions in the larger cultural imagination in France. *La Haine* (Hate) (1995) and *Banlieue 13* (2004) illustrate two contrasting ways that graffiti has been used in French cinema. *La Haine* begins with documentary footage of riots, and then cuts to a main character, Saïd, tagging the back of a police van with his name/ tag and the words, "Fuck the police." Other scenes in the film show the young characters from the projects using spray paint to interact with their environment and counteract official messages that clash with their lived experience. *Banlieue 13*, on the other hand, is a sensationalistic comic-book style film in which the banlieue that police have deemed the most dangerous has been walled in and surrounded by checkpoints. While the film vividly depicts the spatial marginalization and political abandonment of this community by the French government, it also mainly uses graffiti as a backdrop that signifies crime, lawlessness, and a dystopian future.

Published in 1983, Mehdi Charef's *Tea in the Harem* tells the story of a group of young men growing up in a poor, working-class housing project in a banlieue of Paris. Beyond using graffiti as a symptom of delinquency or a sign of social decay, Charef's novel in many ways can be said to model itself on the act of writing graffiti itself. Just as he uses the term "concrete" as a metonymy for the drab milieu of the housing project itself, graffiti appears in the novel in a way that parallels Charef's very writing, as the characters echo the uncensored, frequently misogynistic language of the graffiti in the novel.

Figure 22.3 Rue de Tolbiac, Paris. Side by side paste-ups by Moyoshi and Levalet © the author

The current state of graffiti and street art in the French capital

From its origins in the early 1980s, where it appeared in clusters at selected locations in Paris and environs, graffiti and street art have become a ubiquitous feature of the urban landscape in neighborhoods throughout the city and throughout France. Parisian graffiti and street art could perhaps be most aptly characterized by its innovation of technique and a diversity of materials. Figures who emerged out of the early scene, such as Lokiss and Nasty, have gone on to become legendary figures in the world of graffiti. The list of well-known street artists is long, and the current chapter only provides the space for a small number of those who deserve to be named: Jeff Aerosol and Speedy Graffito, two masters of stencil graffiti, contemporaries of Blek le Rat; Space Invader (or just "Invader"), perhaps the most iconic of all Parisian street artists, who uses ceramic tiles and other materials, such as pieces of Rubik's Cubes, to create video game style "invasions" of cities worldwide; Jérôme Mesnager, whose evocative human figures animate walls around Paris and beyond; Dja'louz and Septik, who continue to experiment with geometrical forms; El-Seed and l'Atlas, whose groundbreaking work transforms Arabic calligraphy and arabesque designs in public space; and many other established and emerging names, such as Monsieur Chat, Seth, Levalet, Mygolo 2000, who have all radically transformed the visual terrain of Paris.

While the rise of street art has by and large made graffiti more respectable and accepted by the French public, the conflict between what is considered vandalism and what can be said to constitute art continues. While millions of euros are spent in the region on cleanup and prevention, many municipal government officials have embraced street art. Jérôme Coumet, mayor of the thirteenth Arrondissement in the southeastern part of the city, has been a notable advocate and promoter of public graffiti and street art projects. Among these projects was the Tour 13, which opened up an entire building set for demolition to graffiti writers and street artists, and ballots sent to residents that allowed them to vote for one of several proposed compositions in their neighborhood.[16] Today, those interested in exploring the graffiti and street art of the city can book tours through sites like undergroundparis.org. Among the most active sites today are the Rue Denoyez (near the Belleville metro station) and Les Frigos (near the Mitterand National Library site). But as the French public and their elected officials continue to disagree, at times vehemently, about what constitutes crime and what constitutes creativity, many of the most innovative and powerful works of this hotly debated form of expression can only be found online.

Notes

1 For a view that contrasts the North American "black ghetto," as a marginalized space where race plays the determining role, with the *banlieue*, where class is the key distinguishing factor, see Wacquant (1992; 2007). For a recent, opposing view, which seeks to revive the term and concept of the "ghetto" for a sociological analysis of the French banlieue, see Lapeyronnie (2008).
2 www.liberation.fr/portrait/2005/11/17/une-femme-mur_539317
3 Kramer's (2010) notion of analyzing graffiti as a complex practice that occurs along two axes, a juridical axis and an aesthetic one is a useful tool for understanding graffiti, provided one avoids identifying more supposedly "sophisticated" forms of graffiti and insisting on reading them through an aesthetic lens, and/or identifying so-called "lower" forms and reading through the lens of illegality and lawlessness.
4 www.youtube.com/watch?v=hlW5i8ELEpw. Accessed November 6, 2014. The book in question is *DESCENTE★INTERDITE: Graffiti dans le métro Parisien*, by Karim Boukercha.
5 http://fresques.ina.fr/jalons/impression/fiche-media/InaEdu01205/la-station-de-metro-louvre-est-recouverte-de-tags.html

6 www.legifrance.gouv.fr/affichCodeArticle.do;jsessionid=56B5DB136FEC502BF68EBBFDE641CB79.
   tpdjo10v_1?idArticle=LEGIARTI000006418258&cidTexte=LEGITEXT000006070719&categorieLien
   =id&dateTexte=20011231. Accessed November 11, 2014.
7 www.senat.fr/questions/base/2001/qSEQ01101139S.html. Accessed November 11, 2014.
8 www.leparisien.fr/une/les-tags-un-fleau-qui-17-03-2005-2005787083.php#xtref=http%3A%2F%
   2Fwww.google.com%2Furl%3Fsa%3Dt%24rct%3Dj%24q%3D%24esrc%3Ds%24source%3Dweb%24cd
   %3D25%24ved%3D0CD0QFjAEOBQ%24url%3Dhttp%253A%252F%252Fwww.leparisien.fr%252Fun
   e%252Fles-tags-un-fleau-qui-17-03-2005-2005787083.php%24ei%3Da9toVJ3-EIuoNsizgfgM%24usg%
   3DAFQjCNGdv76wvhcLa6XfciNZsQJIoUh9Bw%24sig2%3DKPELWUONxBH401_2wzxS_w%24b
   vm%3Dbv.79142246%2Cd.eXY. Accessed November 11, 2014.
9 www.lefigaro.fr/actualite-france/2012/09/04/01016-20120904ARTFIG00564-45millions-d-euros-
   le-cout-du-nettoyage-des-tags-a-paris.php. Accessed November 11, 2014.
10 www.ville-la-courneuve.fr/4_evenement/even.php?id=2234
11 www.europe1.fr/politique/on-va-nettoyer-au-karcher-la-cite-273835
12 For a more in-depth discussion of Sarkozy's comments in the context of French urban policy and
    French attitudes towards immigrant youth cultures, see Fieni, 2011.
13 www.artnet.com/artists/futura-2000-lenny-mcgurr/biography
14 www.bloomberg.com/news/2014-03-26/how-overprotective-paris-became-the-center-of-street-
    art-.html
15 The slogans were left unfinished, inviting visitors to collaborate by finishing them.
16 www.tourparis13.fr/#/fr/teaser. Accessed December 8, 2014.

References

Ben Yakhlef, T. & Doriath, S. (1991). *Paris Tonkar*. Paris (53 Av. de Ségur, 75007): F. Massot et R. Pillement.
Besson, L., Morel, P. Naceri, B., Belle, D., Raffaelli, C. & D'Amario, T. (2006). *Banlieue 13*. Los Angeles, CA: Magnolia Home Entertainment.
Boukercha, K. (2011). *DESCENTE★INTERDITE: Graffiti Dans le Métro Parisien*. Paris: Broché.
Charef, M. (1989). *Tea in the Harem*. Trans. Ed Emery. London: Serpent's Tail.
Charry, E. (2012). (Ed.) *Hip Hop Africa: New African Music in a Globalizing World*. Bloomington: Indiana University Press.
De Certeau, M. (1988). *The Practice of Everyday Life*. Berkeley and London: University of California Press.
Dikeç, M. (2006). Two Decades of French Urban Policy: From Social Development of Neighbourhoods to the Republican Penal State. *Antipode*, *38*(1), 59–81.
Ferrell, J. (1995). The World Politics of Wall Painting. In Ferrell, J. & Sanders, C. (eds) *Cultural Criminology*. (pp. 277–294) Boston: Northeastern University Press.
Fieni, D. (2010). What a Wall Wants, or How Graffiti Thinks: Nomad Grammatology in the French Banlieue. *Diacritics*, *40*(2), 72–93.
Hack, S. (2014). How Overprotective Paris Became the Center of Street Art. *Bloomberg.com*, March 28, 2014.
Kramer, R. (2010). Painting With Permission: Legal Graffiti in New York City. *Ethnography*, *11*(2), 235–253.
Lapeyronnie, D. (2008). *Ghetto urbain. Ségrégation, violence, pauvreté en France aujourd'hui*. Paris, Robert Laffont, Series: Le monde comme il va.
Michot, A. (2012). À Paris, le nettoyage des tags coûte 4, 5 millions d'euros, *Le Figaro*, September 5.
Rossignon, C., Cassel, V., Kounde, H., Taghmaoui, S., Foster, J., Vincendeau, G., & Gavras, C. (2007 [1995]). *La Haine: Hate*. Director approved special ed.; widescreen format (1.85:1). [Irvington, N.Y.]: Criterion Collection.
Silver, L. (2014) Legendary Street Artist Blek Le Rat Tells His Story on the Streets of New York City, www.complex.com/style/2014/10/blek-le-rat-tells-his-story-on-the-streets-of-new-york-city. Accessed November 1, 2014.
Vecchione, M. (2004). *Writers: 1983–2003, 20 Ans de Graffiti à Paris*. Resistance Films.
Wacquant, L. (1992). Banlieues françaises et ghetto noir américain: de l'amalgame à la comparaison. *French Politics and Society*, *10*(4), 81–103.
Wacquant, L. (2007). *Parias urbains. Ghetto, Banlieues, Etat. Une sociologie Comparée de la Marginalité sociale*. La Découverte, series: La Découverte/Poche.

23

From Marx to Merkel

Political muralism and street art in Lisbon[1]

Ricardo Campos

Introduction

Lisbon, the Portuguese capital, is a relatively small city when compared to most of the other ones included in this collection. This city spreads over an area of 84 km², and its population of approximately 548,000 inhabitants[2] has been steadily decreasing over the last years,[3] in contrast with the demographic growth in the surrounding areas. The Lisbon Metropolitan Area (LMA) is comprised of eighteen municipalities and accommodates over three million people. Thus, it would be misleading to focus strictly on the city of Lisbon, forgetting the vast network of interconnected localities within which it exists, and the hundreds of thousands of people that pass through them on a daily basis.

Therefore, a discussion of graffiti in Lisbon should inevitably be more concerned with understanding the elements of mobility and interconnection between districts than with determining fixed geographical territories and boundaries. The graffiti found in Lisbon is nourished by a creative energy that transcends its physical borders, since most writers and crews acting in the city originally come from neighboring areas. In fact, graffiti crews frequently consist of writers living in different districts.

I have studied graffiti in the LMA for the last decade. My research began in 2004, when I started my PhD in Anthropology. Since then I have witnessed great transformations in this field of activity, especially regarding public representations of this phenomenon, as reflected in the portrayals conveyed by the media and public entities. However, this chapter does not intend to focus exclusively on the North American-inspired graffiti made in Lisbon during this period. I decided upon an approach that seeks to emphasize the distinctive aspects of the different informal pictorial expressions that have marked mural painting (both legal and illegal) in Lisbon over the last decades, and which ultimately are responsible for establishing a unique historical and symbolical heritage. Lisbon's informal and vernacular mural art bears specific traits that deserve being singled out. This chapter describes the historical evolution of these expressions in Lisbon, analyzing the social, cultural, and urban impact of these changes.

Before the emergence of North American-inspired graffiti, the post-revolutionary period of the 1970s in Lisbon was marked by the appropriation of the public wall to support group paintings with a strong political and ideological element. The disappearance of this form of artistic expression in a way coincided with its replacement by graffiti, a transnational visual language that asserted itself during the decade of 1990 and has remained part of the urban landscape ever since. These visual expressions were visible not only on the city walls, but also on trains and subway carriages. The spread of illegal graffiti in the 2000s slowly generated a public reaction of displeasure, particularly as a consequence of the street bombing in Lisbon's central and historical districts. This form of expression was considered as a kind of urban blight. Subsequently, the city council adopted a more restrictive policy, launching a graffiti removal program that exerted an overall increased control over graffiti.

In recent years, two phenomena are noteworthy. On the one hand, the non-sanctioned, unofficial political mural produced by graffiti-writers and street artists has emerged as a result of the severe economic and social crisis affecting Portugal. While the last couple of decades were characterized by the explosion of a kind of artistic language that was in no way linked to our muralist history, the severe economic and social crisis of the last few years has favored a mild resurgence of the somewhat forgotten political murals. The most curious thing is that these new samples somehow combine elements of both periods, insofar as being political in content, and thus recovering the legacy of the 1970 decade, they are mostly made by artists connected to the graffiti community. On the other hand, we have recently witnessed the official acclamation and legitimation of many Portuguese street artists, promoted by public entities, cultural entrepreneurs, museums, and art dealers. In recent years Lisbon city council has decided to support various street art initiatives, which is bound to place the city among the main street art production sites in Europe.

Marx on the wall

For most of twentieth century, Portuguese political life was constrained by a dictatorship that lasted nearly five decades and left an indelible mark on Portuguese society and its political dynamics. The Salazarist regime[4] took over in 1933 and remained in power until the "carnation revolution"[5] on April 25, 1974.[6] This event was the culmination of the regime's gradual process of deterioration and the growing dissatisfaction felt by a majority confronted, among other things, with a colonial war that seemed both endless and helplessly lost. This colonial conflict, fought on several fronts of the so-called "ultramarine provinces"[7] (Angola, Guiné-Bissau, and Mozambique), consumed enormous financial and human resources, including forcing thousands of young Portuguese men to war.

Following the political repression, censorship, and persecution of the Salazarist government, the April revolution (1974) and the institution of a democratic regime gave way to a short period of instability marked by extreme political activity. The streets were a witness to this political vitality.[8] During this time, public demonstrations, organized by the different political parties, occurred on the streets, and the streets served as a background for the various forms of political propaganda developed during that time. The city walls played a very significant role in these events. The walls became one of the main devices of political communication,[9] and were used by both right and left wing parties, although predominantly by the latter. During this period, the Portuguese left was fragmented into several parties of varying scope, and almost all of them used mural painting as a channel of political and ideological communication.

The iconography used in these forms of propaganda alluded to revolution and to the existing ideological context, inspired by the prevalent socialist ideals at the time. Marx, Lenin, and Mao were familiar faces often displayed along with other figures representing social or professional groups, such as the people, the proletariat, or the peasantry (see Figures 23.1–23.3). These murals

Figure 23.1 MES mural © Arquivo Municipal de Lisboa, Colecção Neves Águas

Figure 23.2 UDP mural © Arquivo Municipal de Lisboa, Colecção Neves Águas

Figure 23.3 PCTP mural © Arquivo Municipal de Lisboa, Colecção Neves Águas

were generally group works that were often executed with the aid of artists.[10] While many of these murals were relatively complex and well-structured compositions from a formal point of view, in some cases the works displayed a naïf and vernacular character. For over a decade, these works were a present feature of Lisbon's cityscape. However, the murals have gradually disappeared due to the official entities' inability to comprehend their historical and cultural value.[11] The lack of any effort to preserve these works has nevertheless not prevented them from remaining in the collective imagination and memory of all those inhabitants of Lisbon who were fortunate enough to witness their existence.

Winds of modernity: MTV, hip-hop, and spray-can art

After four decades of an isolationism that was actively sought by the old regime, entrance into the European Economic Community in the decade of 1980, and the subsequent economic growth it brought, helped to transform Portuguese society, especially in major urban centers that were naturally more cosmopolitan and open.[12] The increasing consumer spending power was accompanied by a growing interest in North-American popular culture propagated through cultural industries. The icons of Anglo-Saxon popular culture, particularly those of North-American origin, gradually occupied center stage in the imagination of Portuguese youth. This generation grew up watching American MTV and blockbuster movies. In an increasingly globalized world, Lisbon youth cultures of that period imitated the same groups found elsewhere (i.e. punks, goths, headbangers, skinheads, rappers, etc.). The initial graffiti in Portugal emerged in the wake of these economic and cultural shifts, introduced by a hip-hop culture that was taking its first steps.

The first expressions of a hip-hop culture created and developed in Portugal appear at the beginning of the 1990s decade, as a consequence of the globalization that spread this cultural movement beyond the North-American borders (Fradique, 2001; Simões et al., 2005). Rap is probably the most visible manifestation of a movement that expanded in Portugal during that period.[13] Graffiti came into the scene of the greater Lisbon area in the Oeiras district[14] (Moore, 2010). One of the first crews to appear around this area was the Criminal Assassins Crews (CAC)– and included the writers Mistik, Spin, Safari, and Gizmo. Another important crew to emerge a few years later was known as Paint Rackin Mafia (PRM), formed by Wize, Kase, Saxe, Youth, and afterwards Lis One (Mosaik).[15] In the mid-1990s, graffiti had already spread through various LMA districts, but mainly in three main areas:[16] Cascais, Sintra, and South Bank (Moore, 2010). Besides the names mentioned above, other important writers from this period include Yssuk, Dojo, Uber, Mind, Ster, Prat, Hedo, Opse, Hope, Play, Spot, Eith, Sin, Cab, Revolt, Darko, Resh, Roket, Tape, Time, Dose (Byzar), Seux, Rote, Art, Kreyz. The graffiti from this period is mostly a replication of the North-America tradition (Campos, 2010). First, it reproduces the methods, techniques, and imagery, and second it perpetuates the values, modes of action, and vocabulary of North-American graffiti.

We find a combination of the "ludic" dimension (Campos, 2010, 2013b) with the sense of risk, competitiveness, and adrenalin. It is an activity driven by the search for status among peers, obtained by means of a risky and illegal practice: tag dissemination. This community is constituted by youths acting, as McDonald (2011) proposes, with an aim to develop a "moral career."[17] Such a career is built on the basis of the quantity and quality of the works produced. However, a practical and symbolical distinction is established between two graffiti genres. For these writers, graffiti is divided into the legal and illegal kind. The former involves legal or semi-legal mural paintings,[18] more complex from the pictorial construction point of view, generally known as Hall of Fame. The later implies "bombing" actions, such as tagging and throw ups. Despite the dichotomy in this field, the LMA writer community actually presents us with a wide variety of attitudes, since we find those adopting both modes of action, while others concentrate uniquely on one of those fields. Certain crews specialize in particular forms of action, mastering the execution of graffiti on trains in a given train line, for example, or developing artistic graffiti styles bearing a distinctive pictorial language.

Some events[19] organized during this period not only show that the dissemination process was in significant expansion, but also give the first indication that the more aestheticized trend of graffiti was attracting admirers from outside the community, and was starting to be acknowledged as culturally valid by public entities such as local councils.[20] Despite the hesitant start, by the end of the decade, the graffiti writer's community was vibrant, diversified, and dynamic.

From vandalism to "artification"

The end of the 1990s and the beginning of 2000s are marked by an explosion of illegal graffiti and the multiplying of writers and crews working in the Lisbon Metropolitan Area. Connected to the proliferation of graffiti is the fact that this phenomenon never featured in the national or local political agenda. In other words, albeit its negative public representations (conveyed for instance in the media), the phenomenon did not draw enough political attention so as to generate the enforcement of integrated policies to fight or contain graffiti. Therefore, unlike in other countries, there were no public "demonization" campaigns portraying graffiti as a public and urban hazard. The relative tolerance of this movement by authorities created the conditions for the burgeoning of a very active community that spread throughout the LMA in the period of a decade.

During this time, the number of writers increased and the competition among them was substantially intensified, leading to the creation of well-defined territories (both geographical and stylistic). Train lines were dominated by different crews, which protected their sphere of action, sometimes triggering conflicts between writers and crews regarding the negotiation of borders (Campos, 2010). Even though train painting is symbolically an important field of expertise for a writer, given its dangerous nature, it is not unanimously practiced. Besides the physical risks involved in missions targeting trains, this kind of action is also subject to close surveillance by police authorities and private security systems. The subway network, due to its reduced public visibility and the high degree of difficulty in execution, is even less targeted by graffiti writers. However, train and subway painting are considerably significant from the symbolical point of view, and are crucial towards establishing reputation and prestige among LMA graffiti writers.[21] Unlike the more limited train-bombing, street-bombing spread throughout Lisbon's cityscape, finding several hot spots, such as the Bairro Alto district.[22]

This was also the period during which some of most relevant LMA writers (e.g. Mosaik, Odeith, Nomen, Ram, etc.) built a name for themselves. The result is an increasing number of complex walls of fame executed by the best writers from this time. The first cases of commissioned work also date back to this period and with them the vague hope of a professional career for some writers. The existence of private and public commissions, combined with the visibility gained by some of these murals and the consolidation of a circuit of regular festivals,[23] are indicators of a shift, not just within this specific cultural field, but also in the social representations that it projected.

Therefore, the twentieth century ends with the unmistakable signs of a new outlook on graffiti, in terms of the reassessment of its cultural and aesthetic value. I believe that this period marks the beginning of a phase that involved the questioning of graffiti and its boundaries. New conceptions of informal, illegal, and non-commissioned aesthetic expressions, such as "post-graffiti" and "street art," also gained increasing prominence during this period, seeming to hint that the "old graffiti" was changing. In other words, the distinguishing lines between "art" and "vandalism," "legal" and "illegal," become blurred. The so-called "artistic graffiti"[24] comes gradually closer to legitimate artistic forms. There are a few factors that can be identified as justifying such a change. First, we have what we might call endogenous reasons. From these, on the one hand, the growing number of actors in an increasingly competitive field, which in turn led some to specialize in artistic graffiti and obtain prominence in that area; and on the other hand, the gradual opening up of the field, and what it implied in terms of a certain degree of "miscegenation" between graffiti and other forms of expression.[25] However, there are other exogenous factors that should be noted. During the 2000s, there was a growing interest worldwide in graffiti and other so-called urban art forms (e.g. stickers, stencils, posters, etc.). International media gave increasing coverage to artists, whose works thus obtained public recognition and legitimacy within the art world, including its market. The significance of this phenomenon extends to the growing number of books and publications that seek to portray graffiti and urban art as legitimate artistic forms (Manco, 2002, 2004; Ganz, 2004; Bou, 2005; Lazarides, 2008; Stahl, 2009). It's actually remarkable that the sections dedicated to graffiti and urban art nowadays found in major bookstores are usually next to the art and design sections. All of these endogenous and exogenous circumstances had an impact on national media, which started to portray graffiti and street artists in a different light.

If on the one hand graffiti and street art is a global phenomenon, as demonstrated by the celebration of a number of street artists by some of the most renowned artistic institutions worldwide (e.g. Foundation Cartier,[26] Tate Modern,[27] Los Angeles Museum of Contemporary Art,[28] Centro Cultural de Belem,[29] etc.), on the other hand some local characteristics derive from the particular dynamics of individual cities. Lisbon provides an especially interesting case study in this respect. The opening of the first Urban Art Gallery (GAU) and the Crono project[30] are two relevant examples, for what they represent in terms of reassessing the role played by urban art within this city.

The GAU is the first example of a project that gave integrated and consistent support to urban art in Lisbon (Câmara, 2014). Curiously, its birth was deeply connected to a set of political measures taken by the local authorities with the aim of fighting graffiti in Lisbon's historical districts (Campos, 2009). As compensation for a plan to control and erase graffiti from the city's historical center (Bairro Alto), in 2008 the city council (CML) created the capital's first Urban Art Gallery in a public space (see Figures 23.4 and 23.5). To that end, the CML invited a number of artists and graffiti writers. The gallery is still active and organizes an annual exhibition featuring a guest artist together with a selection of artistic projects chosen by a jury that is appointed by the city council. The GAU project has diversified its activity, most notably through its urban art inventory project. This survey is extremely significant insofar as it reveals public recognition on the part of official entities of the artistic and cultural relevance of the different forms of non-institutional graffiti and urban art found in the city of Lisbon. Meanwhile, throughout the last

Figure 23.4 Urban art gallery, artists Pedro Zamith and Vanessa Teodoro © José Vicente | DPC | CML 2012

Figure 23.5 Urban art gallery, artist Miguel Januário © José Vicente | DPC | CML 2013

years, the GAU has been supporting several other projects and strengthening the bonds with the local artistic community (including both graffiti writers and street artists).

In its turn, the Crono project, which took place between 2010 and 2011 with the support of the city council, was among the most significant events due to its pioneering way of giving a new perspective to urban art in Lisbon. This effort, organized by Alexandre Farto – Vhils, Pedro Neves – Uber (both actively involved in the graffiti scene for many years) and Angelo Milano, sought to bring to Lisbon some of the most prominent international names in street art to produce large scale works in the facades of several buildings (see Figures 23.6 and 23.7). The list of invited artists included names such as Blu, Os Gêmeos, Sam3, Ericailcane, Lucy Mclauchlan, Brad Downy, Momo, Arm Collective, etc.

The proliferation of artistic achievements resulting from this support for legal and commissioned forms of intervention, brought an unexpected visibility to Lisbon, attracting the attention of some international media. For that reason, similarly to what has been occurring elsewhere, graffiti in Lisbon has undergone a process of "artification." According to Shapiro:

> Artification designates the transformation of non-art into art. It emerges from a complex effort that produces change in the definition and status of people, of objects and activities. Far from corresponding to merely symbolic changes . . . artification rests on very concrete foundations . . . Thus artification is the resultant force of a combination of processes – practical and symbolic, organizational and discursive – by which people agree to identify an object or an activity as art.
>
> (2013: pp. 20–21)

Figure 23.6 Crono project, artist Ericailcane © Ricardo Campos

Figure 23.7 Crono project, artist Sam3 © Ricardo Campos

Figure 23.8 Underdogs project, artists How and Nosm © José Vicente | DPC | CML 2013

Figure 23.9 Underdogs project, artists VHILS and Pixel Pancho © José Vicente | DPC | CML 2013

Artification was followed by the "commodification" of graffiti, now also perceived as a decorative art that could be used in projects of urban regeneration or embellishment. The development of this economic niche has provided a livelihood and a certain degree of professionalization for some graffiti writers and street artists, who develop their street work while continuing to invest in a more conventional artistic career.[31] Therefore, major spray painted murals or other commissioned street artworks are currently promoted in Lisbon, and are clearly validated as a legitimate form of public art. This has been possible thanks to the valuable contribution of several privately funded events and citizen initiatives, among which projects such as the Ephemeral Museum,[32] Dedicated,[33] Undergdogs,[34] or Wool[35] deserve to be singled out. This proliferation of initiatives reflects not only this field's vitality, its creativity, and strong international connections, but also a clear position on the part of local policies for the promotion of these urban forms of expression. The fact that it has become a political option over the last years has had strong impact on Lisbon's urban network and visual cityscape.

The economic dimension cannot be ignored either, especially when we realize that these art forms have merited the attention of international media, thus promoting the city and its tourism. This phenomenon is equally present in local business enterprises that exploit this patrimony, such as some touristic tours created in recent years by small businesses or individuals with connections to this field.

The politicization of graffiti in times of crisis

Recent years, marked by the deep economic crisis and growing discredit of the political elite in Portugal, have witnessed the reemergence of political murals. The Portuguese government's request for international economic assistance in 2011, and the arrival of the international team of advisors appointed to oversee the implementation of the program, also known as the Troika (a term that alluded to the three organizations involved in the process: IMF, ECB, and EC), lead to severe austerity policies that resulted in the dramatic growth of unemployment rates and salary cut downs affecting most of the population. This context prompted the rise of several popular demonstrations and protest movements, to a great extent inspired by similar phenomena in other European countries, in the wake of the international financial crisis. The transnational movement "Occupy," the Spanish "Indignados" movement, and the vigorous demonstrations witnessed in Greece, were also reflected in the Portuguese context. One of the largest demonstrations ever seen, occurred in 2012,[36] and curiously was not organized by political parties or union movements, but by a citizens association that, not accidentally, went by the name of "Damn the Troika." Such an atmosphere of strong civil mobilization and political protest seems to have encouraged the mild resurgence of mural art forms of a political nature.

Despite not bearing the same weight on the urban landscape as it did during the 1970s and 1980s, this format of visual communication is noteworthy for the symbolical role it has played. The murals and street art projects that have been cropping up are completely different from the works produced in the post-revolutionary period. To begin with, the first major difference has to do with the setting and authorship. While the post-revolutionary mural was produced within the framework of political party propaganda and evidenced a clear ideological connection, the current version is completely different. These political demonstrations are generally illegal[37] and are generated outside the sphere of the political parties,[38] by isolated individuals or groups that are not involved in the political life. This is a new phenomenon, and the acute crisis seems to have created the need for political involvement as the expression of an active citizenship. A number of murals that are characterized by their criticism of the current situation and a satirical portrayal of the political elite, especially those political parties that have governed Portugal over the last decades, started to appear in the Lisbon area (see Figures 23.10–23.12). These forms of

Figure 23.10 German chancellor Angela Merkel with the Portuguese PM and the minister of foreign affairs

Figure 23.11 "The law of the strongest" – depicting current Portuguese PM, Pedro Passos Coelho

Figure 23.12 "Pray for Portugal" © José Vicente | DPC | CML 2013

expression belong to a long tradition of unauthorized and transgressive manifestations of a vernacular nature, which aim to strike against power (and its representatives) and resort to satire and slander as communicational formats (Balandier, 1980). The return of this kind of work indicates that the streets and its walls, despite being politically dormant during times of relative political appeasement and socio-economic well-being, continue to be a privileged backdrop for symbolical confrontations. They are the media, par excellence, for civil demonstrations, and particularly for those who have no access to other channels of communication and political expression.

Conclusion

In the post-revolutionary period following the Carnation Revolution of 1974, Lisbon city walls became the repository for numerous political murals painted by a wide variety of political parties, particularly of the left wing persuasion. At the time, mural painting, using Marxist and Maoist iconography, was a socially accepted way of political communication, and dominant throughout the urban visual landscape. These murals slowly vanished, giving way to American-inspired graffiti. Driven by a globalized hip-hop culture, particularly present in the media, tags, throw-ups, and masterpieces, gradually acquired a significant place in the Lisbon metropolitan area.

The first examples of graffiti in the Lisbon metropolitan area appeared almost two decades after their emergence in the U.S.A. This phenomenon's feeble beginning during the last decade of the twentieth century gave way to a boom of graffiti in the first decades of the twenty-first century, a fact which can be explained by the absence of strict anti-graffiti laws on the part of authorities. As a matter of fact, despite the condemnation of these practices in public discourse (in the media and among the political elite), described as acts of vandalism, an integrated plan to fight the phenomenon was never put in place. In its absence, the number of young people joining this world multiplied, as so did the crews acting in the Lisbon metropolitan area.

This situation set the foundations for the development of a strong community, with a creative and well sustained dynamic.

The first attempt at developing a policy of graffiti abatement and cleaning was enforced in one of Lisbon's most legendary historical districts, the Bairro Alto. The plan, which was started in 2008, also became a historical bench mark for the Lisbon graffiti and street art movement, insofar as it started the development of a strong policy of commissioned urban art. This institutional encouragement to urban art constituted a turning point in the way graffiti-writers and their works were considered from then on. The condemnation of illegal graffiti is accompanied by an increasing public taste for the so-called "artistic graffiti" (legal or semi-legal), present in murals of extreme chromatic and figurative complexity. Many of these graffiti-writers are elevated to the category of artists, legitimated by the media, the art market and official institutions.

Many writers from the initial generation continue to be fairly active (e.g. Nomen, Odeith, etc.), but other names have established a reputation since (e.g. Ram, Vhils, Mais Menos, Smile, Pariz, Aka, Corleone, Add Fuel, Paulo Arraiano, Mais Menos, etc.), some of whom made their entrance into the street art world from other artistic fields (e.g. Kruela or Paulo Arraiano).

We are currently witnessing a process of "artification" of graffiti and the less transgressive urban art forms, which involves both a legitimation of these artistic languages and their authors, and a promotion of their works. Thus, the recognition of aesthetic value is followed by the cultural, urban, and economic value that this kind of work can bring to the city. In this way, certain forms of urban art become connected to processes of urban rehabilitation and gentrification in a number of Lisbon districts, through public strategies of urban embellishment promoted by local councils. Contrasting with this commodification of urban art, we find the persistence of certain niches that can be described as belonging to the world of "transgressive aesthetics" (Campos, 2013a), involving forms of dissidence (political, ideological, etc.) or transgression (illegal use of city space for tag dissemination). In recent years, the emergence of examples of political mural art that revive the memory of the revolutionary muralist tradition, which marked Lisbon's walls during the decades of 1970–1980 has occurred. The economic and social crisis that has been felt shows that, in times of social unrest, the streets and the walls continue to be a haven for popular expression and protest.

In sum, urban art in Lisbon over the last years is distinguished for its great vitality and diversity. If on the one hand, a universe strongly linked to a more "purist" graffiti of the North American tradition continues to exist, on the other hand, a more hybrid artistic field, legitimated and supported by different instances, has also developed. These two spheres are not antagonistic, quite on the contrary. They are closely linked, making it sometimes hard to include a work within rigid boundaries, since the limits that distinguish graffiti from urban art and public art are increasingly permeable and brought into question.

Notes

1 This research was financed by the Fundação para a Ciência e a Tecnologia, project «PEst-OE/SADG/UI0289/2014. I would like to express my very great appreciation to Silvia Câmara and Miguel Moore for their valuable and constructive suggestions.
2 According to information from the 2011 census (National Statistical Institute).
3 According to the 2011 census, between 2001 and 2011 Lisbon lost approximately 17 thousand inhabitants (National Statistical Institute).
4 Authoritarian regime headed by António de Oliveira Salazar, also known as "Estado Novo" (New State).
5 Revolution carried out by junior military officers. This revolution occurred with almost no bloodshed, since there was little resistance from the power in place or the military who remained faithful. The

military that rebelled were received with carnations by the people of Lisbon, thus the name "carnation revolution."

6 In fact, Salazar stepped down from power in 1968, but the so-called "New State" lasted until 1974 under the leadership of Marcelo Caetano, who succeeded Salazar during this last period.

7 War lasted between 1961 and 1974.

8 Before the revolution, walls were also occasionally used to voice political watchwords and slogans, through writings that were severely punished by the political police of the time.

9 The relevance of the political mural dates back to the 1917 Bolshevik revolution, and was equally important during both the Mexican revolution and the Chinese Cultural Revolution.

10 One particular characteristic of these murals was that they were mostly executed by ordinary citizens, party militants with no artistic training. The murals were usually executed collectively, by groups of political militants with diverse artistic skills.

11 Today there's a strong consensus about the relevance played by these murals, not only due to their historical significance, but also their cultural and aesthetical singularity. Official entities, academic elites and the art world view these extinct murals as examples of "popular art" produced during a specific period of our history. A clear example of their importance was the recently promoted action "40 anos, 40 murais" (40 years, 40 murals) on the occasion of the fortieth anniversary of the carnation revolution celebration (April 2014). This action consisted in the production of 40 murals that revived the memory, iconography and style of the old murals. Some of these paintings were faithful reproductions of famous murals while others were original works.

12 Corresponding, for example, to a great influx of immigration, mainly from Portuguese-speaking African countries during the decade of 1980.

13 Even though breakdance became fairly popular during this period, with the existence of competitions and projection in the media.

14 More precisely in the area of Carcavelos. The emergence of graffiti appears to be linked to the presence of foreigners passing through Portugal responsible for transmitting this practice, as in the case of the writer of French origin Kazar, who painted in this area between 1988 and 1989 (Moore, 2010; Grácio et al., 2004).

15 In 1994, an interview with some writers from this crew for the Portuguese music journal *Blitz*, brought great national visibility to graffiti, which was clearly in expansion. Between 1997 and 1998 two journals specialized in graffiti are created, *D'Outros Tipos* in 1997 and *Filthy* in 1998, reflecting the growth of this community and the potential audience for this kind of subject matter.

16 All of them in the Lisbon Suburban area.

17 A career based on social value and prestige, without any kind of economic or professional compensation.

18 The formal "legality" of the act is not especially relevant in this case, given that this classification applies to the execution of murals in authorized sites (either expressly authorized by the rightful owner, or in its absence, at least socially tolerated).

19 Gallery exhibitions and graffiti shows.

20 That is the case of the "Graffiti Oeiras" competition, which started in 1994, or of the "First International Graffiti Festival" occurred in 1999, both organized by the Oeiras Town Hall. The former became a referential event, bringing together members of this community every year.

21 Two factors explain why train painting is a highly relevant and prestigious achievement for the writer First, train painting is a dangerous and demanding activity. It is risky because train yards are protected by strong security systems, posing a challenge to the specific physical and strategic skills of graffiti writers and crews. Second, train painting is connected to the origins of North American graffiti, particularly in New York City, and as such it is an essential part of the historical memories and mythology. Therefore, succeeding in painting a train brings the kind prestige and notoriety among peers and connoisseurs that is highly valued by practitioners of this art form.

22 Historical neighborhood in the Portuguese capital's downtown area. Besides being a widely popular tourist destination, for decades it has been known for its intense cultural and bohemian activity, and its active nightlife.

23 Graffiti shows and competitions in Oeiras, Seixal etc.

24 This is a term often used by graffiti writers to describe large and complex mural paintings (wall of fame). These works are valued for their aesthetical qualities (not for the risk and transgression involved) and require high level of technical skills on the part of its authors. Normally these works are executed collectively and in some cases with prior permission.

25 Some of the writers most acknowledged for their artistic work attended art school or have a career in art, design or illustration.
26 Born in the Streets – Graffiti Show, 1999.
27 *Street Art* Show, 2008.
28 Art in the Streets show, 2012.
29 Os Gémeos solo show, 2010.
30 Equally relevant due to the mark it made in the process of graffiti legitimation in the national context, were the different shows put up by the members of the Leg Crew, under the name Visual Art Performance, which started in 2005.
31 Many street artists develop parallel artistic careers of a more conventional nature (illustration, design or painting, etc.) which ensure them greater financial stability and allow a more sustainable management of their career.
32 Although extinguished in the meantime, this was a pioneering project in creating the first open space ephemeral museum in 2008, in one of Lisbon's most emblematic locals for its nightlife and existing graffiti and street art: the Bairro Alto. For a more detailed description of this neighborhood's dynamics see Campos (2009).
33 It started by being a shop selling graffiti and street art related material. Meanwhile it promoted an intense activity towards the legalization of spaces for Portuguese and foreign writers to paint on.
34 Founded in 2010, Underdogs is a Lisbon based international platform of artists connected to urban art. It organizes various gallery and street art shows.
35 Founded in 2011, this project is based outside of Lisbon. It started merely as an urban art festival in Covilhã (a town in Portugal's central region), but has become very active developing partnerships and events related to street art forms in Lisbon and elsewhere (especially noteworthy was the organization of a show of Portuguese artists in Paris in 2013).
36 The growing economic crisis in Portugal led citizens on to the streets though out the country with huge demonstrations having taken place on October 15 and November 13, 2012.
37 The first examples of these political murals emerged unexpectedly and were illegal. More recently, however, several political murals were painted with the support of Lisbon Municipality and other entities to celebrate the fortieth anniversary of the Portuguese revolution. Nevertheless, the murals painted under the "40 years, 40 murals" project, had a celebrative leitmotiv and were not intended to be critical to the contemporary political class.
38 Although we still find some instances of political murals being executed occasionally by left-wing political parties.

References

Aurélio, D. (1999). Mitos, murais e muros, *Camões – Revista de Letras e Culturas Lusófonas*, 5(0), 83–89.
Balandier, G. (1980). *Le pouvoir sur scène*. Paris: Fayard.
Bou, L. (2005). *Street Art*. Barcelona: Instituto Monsa Ediciones.
Caldeira, A. & Marques, C. (2009). *Os murais de Abril*, CML: Lisboa, CD-ROM.
Câmara, S. (2014). An Inventory Methodology in Urban Art: Concepts, Criteria and Norms. In C. Sarmento & R. Campos, (eds), *Popular and Visual Culture. Design, Circulation and Consumption* (pp. 219–234). Newcastle-upon-Tyne: Cambridge Scholars Publishing.
Campos, R. (2009). On Urban Graffiti: Bairro Alto as a Liminal Place. In *Brighenti*, A.M. (ed.), *The Wall and the City* (pp. 135–151). Trento: Professional Dreamers.
Campos, R. (2010). *Porque Pintamos a Cidade? Uma Abordagem Etnográfica ao Graffiti Urbano*. Lisboa: Fim de Século.
Campos, R. (2013a). A Estetização da Transgressão no Âmbito da Cultura Visual e Popular Urbana. In C. Sarmento (ed.), *Entre Centros e Margens: Textos e Práticas das Novas Interculturas* (pp. 151–164). Porto: Afrontamento.
Campos, R. (2013b). Graffiti writer as superhero. *European Journal of Cultural Studies*, 16(2), 155–170.
Ganz, N. (2004). *Graffiti World – Street Art from Five Continents*. London: Thames & Hudson.
Lazarides, S. (2008). *Outsiders. Art by People*. Century: London.
Macdonald, N. (2001). *The Graffiti Subculture. Youth, Masculinity and Identity in London and New York*. Hampshire: Palgrave Macmillan.

Manco, T. (2002). *Stencil Graffiti*. London: Thames & Hudson.

Manco, T. (2004). *Street Logos*. London: Thames & Hudson.

Moore, M. (2010). Intro. In Underdogs, *Underdogs* (pp. 4–17). Lisboa: Vera Cortes Agência de Arte.

Shapiro, R. (2012). Avant-Propos. In R. Shapiro & N. Heinich (eds), *De l'artification. Enquêtes sur le passage à l'art* (pp 20–21). Paris: EHESS.

Stahl, J. (2009). *Street Art*. Cologne: H.F. Ullmann.

24

The field of graffiti and street art in post-January 2011 Egypt

Mona Abaza

Introduction

A number of generalizations have been made about the emergence of graffiti in particular and the arts in general in post-January Egypt, one of which is to be seen as a novel and unprecedented phenomenon in Egypt. This sudden gaze towards revolutionary street art could be interpreted as part of the Western euphoria in analyzing the Arab spring as an ahistorical unprecedented and sudden revolt. While the January revolution mesmerized the world through the impact of the velocity of information, through the fascinating circulation of images and photography, and the unprecedented usage of social media, mobile phones, and the role satellite channels, such analyses that focused on the Facebook revolution often ignored the long cumulative history of political struggles, demonstrations, and numerous protests that took place prior to 2011.

The same could be said about the long established traditions in the field of art and culture in the Arab World. The field of graffiti, much like the underground and alternative music scene was already quite vibrant in various Egyptian cities well before the revolution. For example, graffiti, together with the alternative or underground scene of young musicians, expressing multifarious and varied musical trends in the city of Alexandria were handled with great sensitivity in the award winning film of Ahmed Abdallah, *Microphone*, which was completed in 2010 just before the revolution. Since 2011, newspaper articles, exhibitions, talk shows, and installations have all focused on clandestine street art and artists.

However, what makes a difference is the fact that the Tahrir effect (so named because this is perceived to be the epicentre of the revolution) led to the explosion of the arts in public to create a novel understanding of public performances, like chanting, grieving, protesting, and communicating through redefining the role of public space. Tahrir opened a myriad of possibilities through a conjunction of an emerging public visibility of an unprecedented powerful visual culture (Abaza, 2013: pp. 88–109) associated with a new configuration of what Mitchell calls "the rhetoric of space" (Mitchell, 2012: p. 11). These transformations teach us that one of the main material transformations of the city of Cairo since January 2011 has been precisely over the fascinating art and tactics of squatting of public spaces.

While it would be unfeasible to provide a comprehensive study on the field of Egyptian street art here, this chapter provides a snapshot about the main trends. A large number of graffiti

Figure 24.1 Gate of the American University in Cairo, Mohammed Mahmud Street. Captured September 3, 2012. Mock Plaque in blue written on it: The Street of the Eyes of Freedom. Underneath is written: entrance forbidden to the dogs of the Ministry of Interior. Top left. Graffiti Nefertiti with gas mask by artist El-Zeft. On the left side: For the memory of Mohammed al-Durra who passed away on August 30, 2000, during the Palestinian intifada. © the author

artists who participated at the beginning of the revolution have argued that they used street art with the intention of occupying the street during the demonstrations and the violent confrontations with the police forces. Shortly said, graffiti was perceived as a performative act of resistance. The artists goal was to mark a territory and be present during the battles and urban wars that kept on multiplying as time went by. The drawings on walls and streets faithfully narrated the rapid and unfolding political events that occurred during the past three-and-a-half years. Several walls in cities like Alexandria, Port Said, and Cairo witnessed then countless graffiti accompanied with poems, insults against the ancient regime, jokes, as well as famous sayings, quite often expressed in reversals and satire. Mock plaques and reinvented names were painted on the streets, such as the street of the "eyes of freedom" or the street of the Martyrs" to designate the Mohammed Mahmud Street that witnessed various battles, after that cement blocks, as buffers were erected by the army and so many protesters lost their lives and eyes.

The graffiti and murals portrayed the battles and killings against the police forces. These also portrayed the numerous martyrs of the revolution who kept on growing in size through time, gender, and sexual harassment, as well as biting satire about the unfolding political events. They exposed the lies of the successive regimes through, time and again, reversals. The hardships of the poor and street children were portrayed too. Graffiti constantly made mocking portraits of the army and the politicians of the ancient regime.

It is not only the murals' aesthetic appeal that has captured the imagination of many observers, but also how they exemplify a fascinating fusion between a variety of cultural artistic traditions that portray Egypt's rich history, namely Pharaonic, popular Islamic, and contemporary traditions. They all reinvent, adapt to, and adopt universal schools of painting, adding a fascinating "Egyptian twist" to express – sometimes humorously – the spirit of rebellion and resistance. Moreover, a myriad of symbols derived from either mass culture like superman and superwoman with reversals, to borrowings from Banksy s graffiti, often accompanied with Arabic slogans and text messages such as "no to military rule," or simply by drawing the word "no" and a thousand times "no" in different calligraphic forms by art historian Bahia Shehab.[1] And adding the following words: "You can crush the flowers but you cannot delay spring." Graffiti equally extensively referred to the long and established tradition of Egyptian cinema. Celebrated iconic Egyptian films, famous actresses like late Souad Husni and Nadia Lutfi and even belly dancers, were portrayed to narrate women's struggles, oppression, and sexual harassment. It is no coincidence that Alaa Awad, who resides and works as an assistant professor of art in Luxor, earned his fame in the field of street art through reproducing sceneries from ancient Egyptian Pharaonic temples. His murals, which were all whitewashed in 2012, (after him insisting on "fixating the walls" by adding a transparent layer of paint that would hinder whitewashing of the wall). This was undertaken through the assistance and financial support of the administration of the American University, upon Alaa Awad s request. These portrayed ancient Egyptian funeral rituals and demotic calligraphy to mourn the fans of the Ultra Ahli football club who were massacred in Port Said in 2012.

Similarly, female artist Hanna al Degham who spends her time living between Berlin and Cairo painted another wonderful realist mural (that disappeared once again in 2012) portraying the hardship of the poor. She illustrated the critical shortage of Butagaz bottles,[2] which were being sold on the black market, affecting the poor more than ever during the acute shortage in winter 2012. Mira Shehadeh, an artist and Yoga teacher, painted another powerful mural on one the erected Supreme Council for Armed Forces (SCAF) walls in the area of Mohammed Mahmoud Street. Her mural portrayed a clearly terrorized woman surrounded by hundreds of sexual harassers, carrying knifes, symbolizing the serial public gang rapes that took place in Tahrir in 2012–2013.

While Ammar Abu Bakr s who is a highly prolific muralist, became famous for painting over dimensional fantastic portraits. He often shifted in styles ranging from resorting to Islamic symbols like the *buraq*,[3] and to reproducing traditional murals of the returning Hajjis (those who go to the pilgrimage), popular in the countryside, to Quranic calligraphy to counteract the Islamists by combating them on their own ground, to portrayals of police soldiers in demonstrations. However, Abu Bakr constantly borrows from a myriad of Western and non-Western traditions. For instance, he recently painted the Mohammed Mahmud Wall in pink to ponder about the complex relationship between the people and the army, while remaining satirical. Abu Bakr states that his recent wall was inspired from Andy Warhol.[4]

It is possible to classify the Cairene graffiti into basically two forms: stencils and murals. For stencils, Kaizer and Ganzeer where at the start of the revolution and later al-Zeft, the rising stars in the Egyptian graffiti scene. To my understanding Kaizer and Ganzeer are highly cosmopolitan in the way they manipulate symbols. They mainly use stencils. Al-Zeft, a graduate from the German University in Cairo, faculty of engineer, has drawn the famous Nefertiti with the gas-mask that turned a success to be replicated in numerous performances and posters in Europe, like for example by Amnesty International. Ganzeer is a graphic designer by training who is fluent in English. You need to look at Ganzeer s "Mask of freedom," (to be found on his website), to realize that he will be soon internationally acclaimed.[5] Examine Kaizer s graffiti of Snow White carrying a gun, (which is surely culled from Banksy) to realize that these are, I think, Middle class youngsters who have had a Western education or are at ease with Western culture. They play very well with reversals as well as with cosmopolitan dissident culture. Ganzeer,

Figure 24.2 Alaa Awad Ancient Egyptian funeral © the author

Figure 24.3 Ammar Abu Bakr and Ganzeer © the author

was arrested with two other artists in May 2011. The arrests made him even better known for his daring drawing of a huge tank standing in front of a cyclist carrying a large tray of bread over his head. He also posted a sticker of the "Mask of Freedom," which must have infuriated the SCAF (Ganzeer, 2011, 2012). But this was not the end. Between May 20–21, 2011, Ganzeer launched a successful campaign that he called "The Mad Graffiti Week," which was picked up and resulted in hundreds of anonymous graffiti that filled the city (El Hebeishy, 2011). Ganzeer and Kaizer clearly differ from Alaa Awad and Ammar Abu Bakr who are the products of the local national university with a more "classical" training in the faculty of the arts. Because of the degeneration of the national education system, teaching art has turned to be quite rigid and uninventive. Alaa Awad lives in Luxor and is himself a teacher at the faculty of arts. He does not for instance speak English. He paints murals wonderfully, rather than stencils that portray his traditional or "classical" training in the academy of the arts.

After January 2011, Keizer has attracted considerable attention from the press for his powerful images combining direct and witty slogans. What grabbed me most is a statement in Arabic: "If you are not part of the solution, you are part of the problem." His sardonic portraits of former pro-Mubarak Minister of Antiquities Zahi Hawass were accompanied by statements such as "traitor to the Pharaohs." As for the famous actor Adel Imam, who expressed anti-revolutionary sentiments in January 2011, Keizer drew a portrait of him, followed by the comment, "Raahet Alyak ya Zaim" ("You have missed the bandwagon, leader"). The former

Figure 24.4 Graffiti by Kaizer, gate of the Ahli Club, Zamalek: "The meaning of life is that you give it (to life) a meaning" (June 8, 2012) © the author

323

Minister of Interior Habib al-Adly's portrait is accompanied by a rhyming sentence: "Adl al-Nahaārdah ya Adly" ("Justice today Adly"), playing on the words Adl (justice) and Adly (derived from the word for justice). His jokes are short and to the point.

The powerful and heart-breaking drawing of a martyr in the form of a winged angel stands in stark contrast to the previous three graffiti. It appeared on the wall of the Ahli club in Zamalak, following the massacre of the Ultras Ahli fans of Port Said in February 2011. Kaizer complements his graffito with the following sentence: "The meaning of life is that you give it (to life) a meaning." The Sad Panda is another piece of graffiti found all over the city. It became famous with the following slogan: "al-mushiñr mikhallıni hazın akthar" ("the general makes me even sadder").

Satire, laughter, and mourning

The January 2011 revolution in Egypt conveyed two strong conflicting and yet parallel emotions. On the one hand, the extraordinary courage of the people who no longer feared to confront police vehicles, tear gas, bullets, and the blatant brutality of the Mubarak regime, and who suffered a horrendous death toll during the first days of the revolution, symbolized an epical moment in street battles against a ruthless dictatorship. On the other hand, these moments were followed by the occupation of Tahrir Square that caught world attention through the chanting, slogans, biting text messages, irony, spontaneous jokes, and irreverent sense of humor that Egyptians are famous for.

The revolution was obviously not merely about irony and laughter. The unfinished revolution, marked by a scar that was deepening by the day through the toll of martyrs, killings, disfiguring, conscious mutilation, and torturing of young bodies, and humiliating and raping of women in public. The years 2011 and 2012 witnessed the dramatic massacres of Abbasiyya, the Balloon incidents, the Maspero and Port Said massacres, the Mohammed Mahmud Street episode I (2011) resulting in the killing of more than seventy protesters, the incident of the Cabinet and the burning of the *Institut d'Egypte*, the Mohammed Mahmud Street episode II (2012) and the death of a young man called Gika. Violent confrontations around the presidential palace were sparked by forcing a referendum on the "boiled" constitution, a popular expression that symbolized the maneuvers of the Muslim Brothers to implement a highly controversial constitution. This time, armed militias of the Muslim Brothers violently attacked anti-Morsi protesters, resulting in more deaths. As a result of these incidents, themes of disappeared young martyrs, mothers of victims, and disfigured and tortured bodies took up a major space in the graffiti landscape.

Street art portrayed these paradoxical and diametrically opposite emotions (such as satire, irony, insults, death, martyrdom, and pain) are closely intertwined in artistic expressions. Large murals and stencil graffiti multiplied in numerous Egyptian cities to narrate stories, to play with humor, or to simply display insults and sheer anger against the symbols of authoritarianism and the violence perpetrated by the army and police forces. The fantastic murals that appeared around Tahrir Square, in particular on Mohammed Mahmud Street, bear witness to the bloody battles that took place during November 2011 and caught the attention of the international media.

The murals conveyed epic visual scenarios of the battles between the police, the armed forces, and the thugs paid by the "ancient regime" on the one side, and the revolutionaries on the other side. They also depicted martyrs of the revolution who appear as ghosts and angels, forceful women who are shown as fighters facing hordes of soldiers and police on their own, injustices, and the dreams of young people for a better future.

Figure 24.5 Written on top of the graffiti, reality is even uglier (November 13, 2012)
© the author

The street of the eyes of freedom/The martyrs street

Since 2012, Mohammed Mahmud Street, also known as *sharei' uyuun al-hurriyyah* (the street of the eyes of freedom) or the martyrs street, became an iconic space. The street was discovered by numerous photographers and passersby, not only for its mesmerizing graffiti and murals, but also for the curiosity it has raised; for the remembrance of the martyrs who were killed there; for journalists who still want to investigate the violent events that took place around that area during the course of the past year and follow-up on how the quarter is coping with the barricades and walls erected by security forces; for its dwellers who suffered not only from skirmishes but also the use of lethal and tear-gas by anti-riot police during successive clashes; for its popular cafés juxtaposing the murals; and, last but not least, for those who still remain nostalgic about popular life around the old campus of the American University in Cairo (AUC).

In the aftermath of clashes between protesters and security forces that took place between November 19 and 24, 2011, Mohammed Mahmud Street witnessed the erection of a cement block-stones-wall that cuts it in the middle and separates it into two different areas. It also witnessed the destruction of this same wall in February 2012 by the revolutionaries and residents who at the time were engaged in similar confrontations with security forces. It later witnessed the construction of more walls and barriers that blocked various side streets leading to the main parallel Sheikh Rehan Street, the location of the monumental Ministry of Interior, currently protected by tanks and wired checkpoints.

Of greater importance, during the entire year of 2011, the wall of the old campus of AUC witnessed fantastic mutations and transformations of graffiti on weekly bases, epitomized in a constant war that entailed the painting of walls. The same street also witnessed a constant erasure and whitening of the walls by both the authorities as well as painting over previous drawings by the graffiti painters. Much attention has been drawn to the mesmerizing appearance, disappearance, and reappearance of the numerous faces and portraits of the martyrs of the revolution on the walls of the city of Cairo.

After the February 2012 Port Said massacre of the fans of the Ahli Ultras, even more publics came to interact with the space of the street after the appearance of many new martyr portraits on the walls. The street was transformed into a memorial space, a shrine (a *mazaar*) to be visited and where flowers could be deposited.

Martyrs

Words on walls

"haq al-shuhada fi raqabatina"
The martyrs' right are on our neck
Plaque 94

"matinsuuch haqqui"
Don't Forget my right
Plaque 93

"iw'u fi huugat al-kalaam . . . damm al-shahiid tinsuh"
In the midst of the bursting words, don't you ever forget the blood of the martyrs."
Plaque 91

– Extracted from Maliha Maslamani (2013: pp. 90–91)

Al-qassas al-qassass darabu ikhwatna bil russass
Avenge, avenge the martyrs; they have shot bullets on our brothers and sisters.

Haq al-shuhada lissah magaash, damm al-shuhada mish bibalaash
The right of the martyrs did not arrive (was not collected); the martyrs' blood is not for nothing.

"Ya nigiib Huquhum ya nimuut zayuhum"
We either get their right (blood) or die like them.

– Slogans chanted in the streets

Since 2011, numerous massacres, killings, and obvious violations of human rights were perpetrated by the successive post Mubarak regimes (Abaza, Global Dialogue, May 2013). This occurred at the same time as a mesmerizing public culture of protest through highly well-organized marches and demonstrations, violent confrontations, and violent urban wars. Egyptians were confronted with an unprecedented escalating violence that was building into a "collective trauma" over how to come to terms with the frightening number of very young victims, of mutilated bodies, and even more of blinded protesters. A collective trauma, which has resulted in that, today mourning mothers, who have lost their children, are gaining public visibility in the media by the day. Thus, martyrdom was becoming a public concern. It is no longer the poor man's concern, since violence and murders have touched upon middle class children. This is so new, since Khaled Said, the good looking middle class young Alexandrian, was turned into the iconic martyr exactly because of the diffusion via Internet of his face, tortured and fractured by the police officers; this face is one of the iconic symbols that were used in the Facebook campaign that triggered the January demonstrations.

This explains why there is a kind of perseverance in the act of commemorating the martyrs, collectively, in a multiplicity of ways, through displaying large size photographs of the tortured and dead bodies such as those of the protesters who were brutally tortured at the Presidential Palace in Heliopolis in December 2012. A large number of these photographs have been displayed in Tahrir Square and in the marches. To the contrary, President Morsi continuously praised the efforts of the officers when they continued in crescendo to display brutality, while twenty-one civilians were sentenced to death for the Port Said massacre (Kandil, www.lrb.co.uk/v35/n06/hazem-kandil/deadlock-in-cairo, March 21, 2013). This has left the street with mounting anger growing by the day. *Al-Quassaas*, justice for the blood of the martyrs, remains thus the major unfulfilled demand of numerous parents and friends of martyrs.

The wall of the American University in Cairo in Mohammed Mahmud Street has become iconic by constantly appearing on television, especially on private ONTV channel as symbolizing the stage of the ongoing revolutionary events, so that the epicenter has shifted from Tahrir Square to Mohammed Mahmud Street. The wall was then turned into the new Mecca of foreign tourists.

Then after the Port Said massacre in February 2012, a large billboard appeared on top of the entrance door of the Ahli Club on the residential Zamalek Island (located at a fifteen minutes' walk from Tahrir Square through the Kasr al-Nil bridge). In the middle of the billboard, a large script of the number seventy-two was encircled by the photos of the seventy-two martyrs who were massacred at the stadium. Then, the fences all around the Ahli club were repainted by huge impressive portraits of each single martyr.

The martyrs are represented in a multiplicity of ways. Often in the form of repertoires, with the sentence that keeps on appearing and disappearing with the graffiti, "Glory to the martyrs"

Figure 24.6 Mina and Emad Martyrs Sheikh Emad Effat (Muslim faith) who was killed in the incidents of Mohammed Mahmud I and Mina Daniel (Christian faith) killed in the Maspero massacre, symbolizing Muslim–Christian solidarity (April 2013)

al-magd lil shuhada` and *al-Quassaas*, to avenge the blood of the martyrs. Through these repertoires a kind of a conversation with the martyrs is meant to be engaged. For example, underneath the portraits the following sentence appears "I pray God, may you be happy where you are."

Khaled Said, killed in Alexandria, Azharite Sheikh Emad who was killed in Mohammed Mahmud Street, and Mina Daniel, a Copt killed in the Maspero events in October 2011, have become iconic heroes who keep on appearing and reappearing in multiple metamorphosed ways. The depiction of the martyrs as winged angels is recurrent. The murals of the Ahli Ultra fans that were drawn immediately after the massacre in Mohammed Mahmud Street were filled with many angels dressed in short and ultra Ahli outfits.

The numerous victims of the fans of Ultras Ahli of Port Said and young martyr Gika killed on Mohammed Mahmud Street in 2012 all appear, disappear, and reappear on the walls as if they were repertoires (especially the repetition of images of martyrs). Sheikh Emad Effat and Mina Daniel keep on appearing as pairs in multiple drawings. Sometimes they are holding each other`s hands, smiling in a position of victory. Here too one notes the size of both Sheikh Emad Effat and Mina Daniel kept on growing over time. Often their portraits are juxtaposing each other. They symbolize Egypt's religious unity as the Azharite Sheikh and young Coptic activist are united by martyrdom.

In November and December 2012, the wall was once again repainted, portraying more martyrs and Khaled Said's smashed, destroyed face appearing against a red background with a long series of disfigured martyrs. This series of portraits is remarkably powerful, or rather chocking through accurately conveying the destroyed and tortured young dead bodies. It was drawn by Ammar Abu Bakr. On top of the portraits is written: "If the picture still needs to be made clearer, Sir, then the reality is even uglier." Ammar Abu Bakr told me that Khaled Said s sister conveyed to him her disagreement at such a brutal portrayal of her deceased brother. She felt it was simply debasing the dead. Abu Bakr's point of view is that to bluntly expose brutality is the most pervasive way of confronting public with reality. Thus, it still remains the most effective way of conveying a message. It is a conscious counter-portrayal to the smiling good-looking face of the Khaled Said stencil that is accompanied with the play of words "Khaled mish Said" "Khaled is not happy."

Nevertheless, despite continuous erasures, the martyrs continue to occupy a prominent place on the walls of Cairo, as the main subject matter in the graffiti. Another prominent subject matter concerns gender issues, such as sexual harassment or the so-called blue bra incidents.[6] Gender also figures centrally in the iconography of martyrdom itself, which explains why graffiti is drawing so much the attention of feminists. For example, the long Egyptian tradition of funerary rituals, of mourning and excessive weeping, or what could be called a local culture of death, mainly perpetrated by women, is wonderfully depicted in the murals. The mothers of the martyrs keep on appearing and reappearing on the walls. *Gowayya shahiid, Inside me is a Martyr*, by Heba Helmi (2013) is among the most recent publications on graffiti, once again dedicated to the martyrs of the revolution.

Commodification is (for sure) coming[7]

If one undertakes a Google search with the keywords "graffiti Egypt," about 4,340,000 results will emerge. If one searches the same keywords on Youtube one gets 1,500,000 results.[8] The immediate impression one gets not only from the Internet, when following the cultural scene in Cairo since January 2011, is that nothing has become more popular and fashionable among foreign and Egyptian journalists, documentary film makers than produce Youtube videos, articles for both Arabic newspapers and the international press, reports, and documentaries about Egyptian street art.

I would even dare say that Egyptian graffiti is the next most globally appealing art, widely circulated after the powerful universal effect of birds eye shot of Tahrir Square. Graffiti images internationalized the Egyptian revolution as well, in selling an appealing counterculture. Nothing became more fashionable than flying into Cairo as a journalist or a documentary filmmaker, to be aided by local fixers,[9] and produce a film on graffiti. As evidence, hundreds of Youtube documentaries have been recently overflowing the market.

In my capacity as a sociologist at AUC, I have never been so much solicited on regular bases for the past three years by countless students, artists, Western graffiti artists, journalists, and academics, asking me for either providing helpers, translators, research assistants, addresses, and names of graffiti painters or ideas about the topic.[10] The question to be raised is then why such an interest today in graffiti from the West? Why is it for example that much less studies are undertaken on social movements, the role of the army, or political parties in the Egyptian revolution? Is not the study of graffiti easier to research, rather than dwelling in the complexity of *longue durée* studies, to circuit the confusion of a counter-revolutionary moment? Possibly then, foreign journalists, Western young academics and pundits focused intensively on graffiti, perhaps because it is less demanding intellectually? This leads me to raise the question, is this interest mainly because it is visually a highly appealing art? Or is it because quite often, many such readings are undertaken at the expense of neglecting the paramount significance of text messages, insults, the play with words, satire, poems, puns, which appeared on all the walls of the city from the first days of the revolution that accompanied graffiti.

Yet as both, Amr Shalakani (2014) and Sherief Gaber (2013) argued, while the Western press focused on graffiti, most of the time it actually ignores often the semiotics accompanying it. Often jokes and insults reveal a local twist hard to be decoded by foreigners. Egyptian artists have not only genuinely developed an innovative own style, but the walls turned to be the pulse of the unfolding events narrated with symbols and codes, quite often, mainly understood by those following closely politics.

It is difficult to oversee the element of commercialization of the revolution. On the other hand, the commodification of revolutionary art evidently reveals paradoxes and tensions among artists, in addition to frictions between the street artists and the gate keepers of cultural production such as curators, foreign donors in the domain of art and culture, and foreign cultural centres wanting to promote once again revolutionary art. Not only foreign donors became at a certain point important players in the promotion of what is marketable art in the West, equally too, is the noticeable phenomenon of booming elitist galleries discovering how lucrative revolutionary art can turn to be.[11]

Conclusion

Kirsten Scheid interprets the discourse about the marveling of the "awakening of revolutionary art" as going parallel with a perpetrated orientalist perception that is emptying Arab history from the long and complex tradition of political anti-colonial struggles. These novel politics of culture are the reverse side of a yet disguised neo-colonial policy of what Scheid labels once again as a "humanitarian intervention that minimizes and limits how victimized people may come to participate in global politics" (Scheid, www.jadaliyya.com, August 31, 2012). Scheid, just as Nancy Demerdash (www.brismes.ac.uk), and myself (www.e-ir.info/2013/10/07/) point to the growing and quite often far from innocent role of the curators, funders, and gatekeepers of revolutionary art as the everlasting profiteers in the neo-liberal art market. Scheid laments the fact that art is being promoted at the expense of denying the despicable economic conditions of bare survival in the Arab world and thus obfuscating the entire role of foreign funding as a corrupting element. Second, the "awakening" discourse remains silent, for instance, on the way the long tradition of contemporary modern Iraqi art, including the pillage of antiquities after the American invasion, has been intentionally denied. According to Scheid,

> In fact, many of the lesser-known Iraqi artists who remained inside the country after 1991 turned to reproducing nineteenth-century Orientalist paintings. They had discovered a new souvenir market for the diplomatic and humanitarian delegates who desired to bring home images of a nargileh-drugged, bed-ridden populace, whose siege the same delegates effectively supported by keeping it on a *'minimal* life-support' system.
>
> (www.jadaliyya.com, August 31, 2012)

The expanding field of the producers of the knowledge on graffiti, over and above the controversies among graffiti painters themselves, seem to be two highly sensitive and yet quite fascinating spheres to study the process of the commercialization, of earning fame and social capital for artists and of the labelling of what is considered to be "revolutionary art" in international markets. One is tempted to speculate that post January street art, in general however, the entire field of art is turning to be a highly competitive bread winning domain for photographers, publishers, foreign donors, and foreign cultural centres located in Egypt, as well as being quite attractive for the workers in the cultural sphere.

Alone the fact that graffiti artists have received so much attention from the Western media raises questions about whether the community of street artists have developed a sufficient critical awareness regarding the effect of the "culture industry" on the emerging street art scene. Whether the artists have been able to raise pertinent questions regarding self-perception of belonging to an underground scene, that is being co-opted in the art market.

Numerous publications on graffiti and the revolution have come out.[12] However, as a first impression, each newly published book seems to perhaps intentionally or un-intentionally ignore the cumulative process of knowledge of previous works, books, and articles in the field. Similarities in depicting one and the same motive like take for instance the "buraq," is repeatedly referred in each new book on graffiti without referring to the previous published texts on exactly the same and identical murals. It is also possible to observe numerous repetitions in the accompanying texts explaining the artists work. Moreover, for example, it is worthwhile pointing to three recently published excellent Arabic books. First, *Walk Talk* (2012) edited by Sherif Borai, second Heba Helmi's *Inside me is a Martyr* (2013), and third Maliha Maslamani *Graffiti of Egyptian Revolution* (2013). All three remain perhaps less lavish in the quality of paper and print compared to the English works, but which function parallel to the English publications, yet to be hardly acknowledged in the Anglo-Saxon world.

Often too, and at the expense of infuriating some, the English publications still remain as coffee table books. They seem to dismiss various rich analyses easily traced in previous writings published in academic journal and websites. Significant bloggers who made major contributions through keeping a thorough chronology of street art since the start of the revolution such as the excellent work of Soraya al-Morayef's *suzeeinthecity* (http://suzeeinthecity.wordpress.com/), once again, are not properly acknowledged in these publications. Here the lack of knowledge of Arabic language from the part of the mass of flocking researchers, journalists, and film makers, a lacunae which often goes as consciously understated in academic theses and works, is worth reflection on once again the nature of expertise and scholarship.

The ongoing internal battle for social justice and the respect of human rights, the two main reasons that triggered the revolution remain still unaccomplished. Let aside the internal ego struggles among artists and/or struggles with curators, street art has been undergoing a new phase of curtailment. This is happening with the massive campaign led by the Sissi military regime, after ousting President Morsi who belonged to the Muslim Brotherhood and him becoming President to "clean up" the city from street vendors. Thus restoring "order" is part and parcel of eliminating the poor and the "riff raff" (according to those in power), whitewashing the walls, closing down street cafés, police patrolling the centre of town, and maintain military public visibility (tanks and soldiers in town) on alert for possible demonstrations. One wonders if street art has not lost altogether momentum since the walls of Mohammed Mahmud Street remained unchanged for quite some time.

Notes

1 See Bahia Shehab's TED talk on painting calligraphy. "A Thousand Times No," www.ted.com/talks/bahia_shehab_a_thousand_times_no (accessed December 13, 2014).
2 Natural gas used for cooking and heating homes.
3 The *Buraq* is a mythological creature that is half-animal and half-human with wings. The body has often been described as representing a half-mule, half-donkey. In some Islamic traditions the *Buraq* is figured with the head of a woman, while in some paintings it appears with a male head. Earlier Islamic references do not seem to define the human element of the head. The *Buraq* is famously known as the creature that is said to have transported the Prophet Muhammed from Mecca to Jerusalem and back on the night of the "*Israa and Meraj*" (the night journey). Associated with flying and defiance of gravitation, the Buraq is often viewed as a symbol of freedom and liberation. (Mona Abaza The Buraqs of Tahrir www.jadaliyya.com/pages/index/5725/the-buraqs-of-tahrir) accessed November 2014.
4 Personal communication with Ammar Abu Bakr September 2014.
5 Unfortunately, Ganzeer has left Egypt recently, following a significant exodus of intellectuals and human rights activists who feared for their lives after the two recent draconian anti-demonstration law and the law curtailing the activities of the NGOs.
6 On December 20, 2011, a veiled female protestor was beaten, dragged, and stripped of the clothes by soldiers in Tahrir Square. The photographs taken while she was dragged, stampeded with the soldiers shoes, revealed her blue bra and the jeans she was wearing under her *abaya* (a cloak). The female protester with the blue bra, turned to be another icon of the revolution, resulting to painting all the walls of the city with blue bras graffiti.
7 The title is a reference to Huda Lutfi s painting "Democracy is Coming" 2008, (http://arttattler.com/archivehudalufti.html) and Lara Baladi s installation of a huge iron Chastity Belt, exhibition titled "Freedom is Coming" in Townhouse Gallery, Cairo, December 1, 2013–January 8, 2014.
8 Numbers according to the author's search carried out on July 26, 2014.
9 Fixer is a term used for local journalists or helpers to foreign journalists who assist them in writing the story. Obviously, there are numerous stories about the unequal relationship between fixers and foreign journalists. Fixers end up being the unacknowledged heroes and sometimes victims in the making of stories. For example see the article of Andrew Bossone "The Thankless Work of a Fixer," www.cjr.org/reports/the_thankless_work_of_a_fixer.php?page=all (accessed December 13, 2014).
10 I consciously avoid here the systematic tracking of the biographies, and works of the street artists, who have been by now widely advertised and diffused in Websites and in the international press. Suffice here to mention the most prominent names which can be easily googled such as: Ganzeer, al Teneen, Kaizer, Ammar Abu Bakr, Alaa Awad, El- Zeft. Female artists: Hanaa Degham, Aya Tarek, Mira Shehadeh, Salma al Tarzi, less famed but remaining very interesting artists are Charles Aql and Amr Gamal, Ahmed Naguib, Mohammed Khaled, El Mozzah.
11 Only the upper class residential island of Zamalek witnessed, as never before, a boom in galleries amounting to nineteen galleries.
12 Including Maslamani, (2013); Helmi, (2013); Gröndhal (2013); Tarek (2014).

References

Websites

Abaza, M. "An Emerging Memorial Space? In Praise of Mohammed Mahmud Street," March 10, 2012. www.jadaliyya.com/pages/index/4625/an-emerging-memorial-space-in-praise-of-mohammed-m (accessed October 10, 2012).

Abaza, M. "The Revolution s Barometer," June 12, 2012. www.jadaliyya.com/pages/index/5978/the-revolutions-barometer (accessed June 20, 2013).

Abaza, M. "The Dramaturgy of a Street Corner," January 25, 2013. www.jadaliyya.com/pages/index/9724/the-dramaturgy-of-a-street-corner (accessed February 20, 2013).

Abaza, M. "Intimidation and Resistance, Imagining Gender in Cairene Graffiti," June 30, 2013 (Appeared also in Ahramonline). www.jadaliyya.com/pages/index/12469/intimidation-and-resistance_imagining-gender-in-ca (accessed July 30, 2013).

Abaza, M. "The Violence of the Counter-Revolution," *Global Dialogue*, Volume 3, May 3, 2013. http://isa-global-dialogue.net/the-violence-of-counterrevolution-disfiguring-mutilating-and-denuding-in-egypt/ (accessed June 3, 2013).

Al-Jazeera English channel. "Artists Use Graffiti to Tell Egypt Revolution Stories," n.d. www.youtube.com/watch?v=K1f1BqkpiCY; (accessed October 30, 2013).

Anonymous. "Graffiti Artists as Protestors in Egypt," n.d. www.youtube.com/watch?v=b4NmSByn3AQ; (accessed October 30, 2013).

Baladi, L. "Freedom Is Coming," *Townhouse Gallery*, December 1, 2013–January 8, 2014. www.thetownhousegallery.com/exhibitions/past/freedomiscoming (accessed February 8, 2014).

Barsoum, M. "Cairo s Street Vendors Left Weary After Government Relocation Move," August 24, 2014. http://english.ahram.org.eg/NewsContent/1/64/109120/Egypt/Politics-/Cairos-street-vendors-left-weary-after-government-.aspx (accessed October 30, 2014).

Bossone, A. "The Thankless Work of a Fixer," n.d. www.cjr.org/reports/the_thankless_work_of_a_fixer.php?page=all (accessed December 13, 2014).

Demerdash, N. "Consuming Revolution: Ethics, Art and Ambivalence in Arab Spring," *BRISMES*, n.d. www.brismes.ac.uk/nmes/consuming-revolutionethics-art-and-ambivalence-in-the-arab-spring#1. On the commodification of graffiti See my article "Mourning, Narratives and Interactions with the Martyrs Through Cairo s Graffiti." www.e-ir.info/2013/10/07/mourning-narratives-and-interactions-with-the-martyrs-through-cairos-graffiti/ (accessed October 30, 2014).

Egypt Graffiti, Sawra, Revolution graffiti, Ahmed Abdel Moneim. n.d. www.youtube.com/watch?v=jzUWf95FAOc (accessed October 30, 2014).

El Hebeishy, M. "Mad Graffiti Weekend Storms the Egyptian Capital," *Ahram Online*, May 23, 2011. http://english.ahram.org.eg/NewsContent/5/25/12720/Arts–Culture/Visual-Art/Mad-Graffiti-Weekend-storms-the-Egyptian- capital.aspx (accessed April 15, 2012).

Gaber, S. "Beyond Icons: Graffiti, Anonymous Authors and the Messages on Cairo's Walls," December 3, 2013. http://cairobserver.com/post/68890839257/beyond-icons-graffiti-anonymous-authors-and-the (accessed August 15, 2014).

Ganzeer. "Things I ve learned from the Mask of Freedom," *Rolling Bulb*, June 7, 2011. http://rollingbuib.com/postl6290244674lthings-ive-learned-from-the-mask-of-freedom (accessed April 15, 2012).

Ganzeer. *Blog Ganzeer*, 2012. http://ganzeer.blogspot.co.uk/ (accessed May 5, 2012).

Kandil, H. "Deadlock in Cairo," *London Review of Books*, March 21, 2013, www.lrb.co.uk/v35/n06/hazem-kandil/deadlock-in-cairo (accessed October 30, 2013).

Lutfi, H. "Democracy Is Coming," 2008. http://arttattler.com/archivehudalufti.html (accessed October 30, 2013).

Maat el Seer ma'al Fanaan. July 6, 2014. www.masralarabia.com/ (accessed August 3, 2014).

Maat al-Sirr ma'a al-Fanaan. "The Secret Is Dead with the Artist," 26 July, 2014. (accessed August 1, 2014).

The Mohammed Mahmoud Incidents. August 12, 2014. http://ar.wikipedia.org/wiki/أحداث_شارع_محمد_محمود (accessed October 30, 2014).

Shehab, B. "A Thousand Times No," *TED*, n.d. www.ted.com/talks/bahia_shehab_a_thousand_times_no (accessed December 13, 2014).

Scheid, K. "On Arabs and the Art Awakening: Warnings from a Narcoleptic Population," *Jadaliyya*, August 31, 2012. www.jadaliyya.com/pages/index/7149/on-arabs-and-the-art-awakening_warnings-from-a-nar (accessed October 30, 2014).

Books

Abaza, M. (2013). Cairo Diary: Space-Wars, Public Visibility and the Transformation of Public Space in Post-Revolutionary Egypt, in Berry, C., Harbord, J. & Moore, R.O. (eds), *Public Space, Media Space*, (pp. 88–109). London: Palgrave Macmillan.

Borai, S. (eds). (2012). *Wall Talk: Graffiti of the Egyptian Revolution*, Cairo: Zeitouna.

Gröndhal, M. (2013). *Revolution Graffiti, Street, Art of the New Egypt*, Cairo: The American University in Cairo Press.

Helmi, H. (2013). *Gowayya Shahiid, Inside Me Is a Martyr*, Cairo: Dar al-ain lil-nashr.

Maslamani, M. (2013). *Graffiti of Egyptian Revolution*, Beirut: Arab Centre for Research and Policy.

Mitchell, W.J.T. (2012). Image, Space, Revolution: The Arts of Occupation, *Critical Inquiry*, 39(1), 8–32.

Salem, H. & Taira, K. (2012). Al-Thawra al-Dahika: The Challenge of Translating Revolutionary Humor, in Mehrez, S. (ed.), *Translating Egypt's Revolution*, (pp. 183–212). Cairo. The American University in Cairo.

Shalakani, A. (2014). The Day the Graffiti Died, *London Review of International Law*, 2(2), 357–378.

Tarek, A. (2014). Arab Women and Street Art, in Stone, D. K & Hamdy, B. (eds), *Walls of Freedom: Street Art of the Egyptian Revolution*, (pp. 218–220). Berlin: From Here to Fame.

25

Wall talk

Palestinian graffiti

Julie Peteet

Introduction

Two graffiti pieces on the Israeli separation wall slicing through Abu Dis, a Palestinian village on the edge of Jerusalem, catch the eye: "From Warsaw ghetto to Abu Dis ghetto" and "Welcome to Soweto" and resonate with multiple audiences – international, Palestinian, and Israeli. This graffito pointedly encapsulates Palestinians' understanding of the wall and their socio-spatial location in relation to it. They graphically render an historical awareness that draws on the power of comparison across time and space. Palestinian graffiti, street art, and murals, what can be referred to as the "writing on the walls" (Peteet, 1996), have been constantly in motion, appearing and disappearing; painted or written over, they document and index changing events and sentiments on the ground in Palestine. Significantly, they encompass the voices and imaginations of both local and international writers/artists and thus speak to a multiplicity of audiences. Indeed, this was dramatically captured in the May 25, 2014 photo of Pope Francis gently touching his forehead and right hand to the wall in Bethlehem framed by red graffiti: "Free Palestine" and "Bethlehem looks like Warsaw ghetto."

This chapter examines two periods in the life of graffiti and street art in Palestine: the first intifada, the popular uprising (1987–1993) against the Israeli occupation of the West Bank and the Gaza Strip beginning in 1967, and the graffiti and street art that have accompanied the second, or 2000 al-Aqsa, intifada and the construction of the separation wall beginning in 2002. Although graffiti, street art, and murals occur in Palestinian locales at a distance from the wall that speaks to an internal audience, this chapter focuses more on the numerous and highly visible graffiti and street art of locals and foreigners dotting the separation wall.

These two periods also implicate fairly distinct spaces as tableaus for murals, street art, and graffiti: the ordinary stone walls of homes and businesses during the first intifada and the separation wall emblematic of the past decade in Palestine. Before delving into the writing on the walls, I briefly describe the Israeli policy of closure and the wall which are the context and the medium for post-2000 graffiti and street art. Along with over 500 checkpoints, a draconian permit system that regulates Palestinian mobility, and a segregated road system, the wall enacts the policy of closure. Launched in March 1993, closure refers to Israeli restrictions on the movement of Palestinian goods, labor, and people into Jerusalem, between the Gaza Strip and the West Bank, between them and Israel, and most devastatingly and tellingly, between Palestinian communities in the occupied West Bank. For Palestinians, the results have been geographic fragmentation, economic devastation, immobilization, social fracturing, and a deep sense of isolation (Peteet, 2016). Closure spatializes the distinction between Palestinians and Jewish Israelis and clears Palestinian land for new Jewish settlements. In short, closure fragments and miniaturizes Palestine and facilitates stringent control over access to the space of Palestine by *Palestinians*, while forging spatial contiguity and mobility for Israelis.

Combining architectural simplicity and modern technology, the wall is a spectacle, performance, and symbol. Israelis refer to it as "the security fence" or "the separation barrier." Palestinians call it "the wall" (*al-jidar*) or the "apartheid wall" and, more bitterly, apropos its incarceratory nature, forming "a prison without a roof." The bare prefabricated slabs of upright concrete blocks snake through cultivated and populated areas, punctuated by prison-like watchtowers and firing posts. At nearly 25 feet high and at an estimated 700 kilometers in length, it is significantly longer and higher than the 12-kilometer-long, 8-foot high Berlin Wall. Thousands of acres of Palestinian agricultural land were confiscated and tens of thousands of trees were uprooted to construct the wall. In places, it extends up to 14 miles into Palestinian territory. It draws a unilateral border that includes large blocks of settlements on the Israeli side, prevents a territorially contiguous Palestinian state, and separates villages from their agricultural lands and from each other. Indeed, the wall dissolves the West Bank into a multiplicity of dis-contiguous enclaves.

Graffiti can be a potent medium of communication especially in an arena of conflict such as Palestine/Israel where the authority to represent and access to media are vastly disparate. As a form of cultural production and communication, it may be a universal medium and communicative act with origins millennium old, as evidenced in pre-historic rock art. In the two historical periods to be reviewed, graffiti has been both a mode of communication and political commentary on Israeli settler-colonialism and occupation, whether by Palestinians, or more recently, by a transnational cadre of supporters. Each period has engendered qualitatively different forms of graffiti and murals. Painted on a distinct and highly charged surface, targeted to multiple audiences, the act of writing on the wall *(al-jidar)* has been taken up by foreign supporters; this is not to overlook the continued taking to the walls by Palestinians in villages and camps well away from the separation wall.

As a public "literacy act" (Hanauer, 2011: p. 305), the writing on the walls compels questions as to its aims and efficacy. What are they and can they be assessed? Often depicted as a transgressive medium, it provides a counter-discourse, by turns comparative, satirical, mocking, warning, and plaintive, a challenge to dominant narratives and an appeal made by the often marginalized and voiceless. Yet, graffiti and street art on the Israeli separation wall occur on a space built by the occupier. Is this reclamation of space a turning of the wall back on itself? Is it a refusal to normalize the wall? Or is it a beautification and commodification of what should remain stark and ugly?

Graffiti and street art are often deemed "illegal" or of an "illicit" nature; this may be an instance where the structure, the actual physical mechanism of power, the wall, limits and shapes the contours of the resistance it generates. In the U.S., they are widely considered acts of vandalism because they are drawn without permission on private or public property (Ross & Wright, 2014: p. 177); Palestinian graffiti, street art, and murals were forbidden by Israeli military orders that govern daily live in the West Bank. With the Oslo Agreements[1] and the Palestinian Authority's (PA) assumption of quasi-authority in limited areas of the West Bank, Israeli censorship eased; with the redeployment of Israeli troops from major Palestinian towns, graffiti's legal status is now rather ambiguous. In the context of an illegal occupation, and more recently a separation wall deemed illegal by the International Court of Justice, positioning graffiti as vandalism or an illegal act seems nothing short of irrelevant. Indeed, how illegal can it be to daub graffiti on a wall that is itself illegal?[2]

In Palestine, graffiti joins a historically broad constellation of actions to respond to and challenge occupation ranging from protests, petitions, general strikes, uprisings, civil disobedience, hunger strikes, stone throwing, legal action, popular music and art, armed struggle, and the Boycott, Divestment, and Sanctions (BDS) movement, among others. With the consolidation of the Israeli occupation and the doubling of settlers in the occupied West Bank in spite of the Oslo Agreement, and the impossibility of a state in the fragmented territory of what remains of Palestine, one can detect a Palestinian shift to combating normalization of the status quo, pursuing membership in UN organizations, and encouraging the BDS. In this atmosphere, it could be argued, the communicative dimension of graffiti lessened. Yet graffiti remains in the roster of resistant tactics Palestinians have had recourse to over several decades. It continues to serve as a form of documentation and voice of Palestinian opinion and sentiment but increasingly writing it and visits to view its more elaborate forms have become an act of solidarity by international visitors with those under occupation. In writing on the wall, an unmediated narrative landscape of dissent, anger, solidarity, and mourning has crystallized. Thus in registering a written and visual rejection of the normalization of incarceration behind a concrete wall, graffiti can be understood as constituting a form of political action or intervention.

So, who is the audience for Palestinian graffiti? Several publics come to mind: international, Israeli, and local. A Palestinian public has waned as the graffiti no longer delivers messages or directives as it did in the first intifada; Israelis seldom encounter wall graffiti except in certain stretches of the wall in Jerusalem. Much of it is directed to an international network of supporters and the journalists who photograph it (see Bishara, 2013). The contemporary context of graffiti and its meaning is best conceptualized by situating it in the shifting topography and structural mechanisms of a colonial occupation and resistance

Graffiti of the first intifada: the writing on the walls

During the first intifada, or uprising against the occupation of the West Bank and Gaza, often dubbed a "war of stones," the main Palestinian weapon, graffiti was a "print weapon" (Peteet, 1996: p. 139). Thus, stone was both "weapon and medium," recording domination and simultaneously intervening in it (ibid.: pp. 141–142). Written on the stone walls of Palestinian homes and businesses, it was ubiquitous and written mainly in Arabic. In an era of simpler communications technology (no cell phones, email, Internet, or social media), and heavy censorship, graffiti announced strike days and issued directives for action. I conceptualized them as "interventions in a relation of power" because they were a communicative component of a mass uprising (ibid.). They conveyed messages and "directed, informed, commemorated, provided critical commentary, and could be a diagnostic of occupation tactics" (ibid.: p. 152). "No taxes without representation," written during the tax revolt in the Palestinian town of Beit Sahour aptly captures all of these functions. It directed and supported the refusal of an occupation practice and in doing so, forged a relationship with the Palestinian community in the project of resistance. For Palestinians, graffiti affirmed resistance: "The intifada continues" as well as indexed a historical event. In the contested terrain of Palestine, graffiti also cleverly claimed place and inscribed memory of it, embodied in the expression: "1948 + 1967 = all Palestine."

Graffiti tags were primarily done by political organizations such as Hamas, Fatah, the Popular Front for the Liberation of Palestine (PFLP), or the United National Leadership (UNL), an underground coalition of political groups that directed the uprising. Graffiti used in this zone of protracted conflict, like gang graffiti elsewhere, also serves as territorial markers of these various political entities. As a component of the Israeli pacification campaign against the uprising, graffiti and graffiti writers elicited a swift response from the occupying Israeli military authorities. Declared illegal, graffiti was often blackened out in a war of words and those caught writing could be beaten and/or detained and charged with a criminal offense.

The street art of closure: writing on *the wall*

"Free Palestine," "No Wall," "No to the racist separation wall," and "Stop the wall," are scribbled repetitively on the separation wall in English. "CAPTIVATING," painted in large black capital letters, each letter filling one of the concrete slabs that together compose the wall, is a witty play on words. The imposing wall itself is visually captivating and those behind it are captive. Like the ordinary stone walls of homes and businesses in the first intifada, the materiality of the wall is simultaneously the context and the medium. Much of the substance of graffiti is commentary on the wall itself. Akin to prisoners laboriously scratching names, dates, and messages on the concrete walls that confine them, the structure of imprisonment is also the medium of protest.

Similar to the first intifada, contemporary graffiti, street art, and murals signal a refusal to acquiesce and to normalize the abnormal. As a riposte to enclosure's mammoth and imprisoning wall, they can be considered an intervention in a relation of power. However, this work departs in significant ways from the writing on the walls during the first intifada. Distinctions between these two periods involve questions of location (walls and now *the wall*), visibility, risk, temporality, message or content, language, audience, and response. This section explores these continuities and changes.

To Palestinians, the wall is ugly and menacing, a monstrosity exemplified in the graffito, "wall=horror." Yet this iconic device of separation, isolation, and subjugation at once inspires artistic expression and serves as a communicative tableau. On its stark slabs, foreigners and Palestinians daub graffiti and paint elaborate murals. Eye-riveting, often highly colorful and woeful as well as satirical, an array of graffiti and murals protest, state opinions, offer analysis and commentary, and express solidarity. Scrawled across the wall in a multitude of languages, this public blackboard is a medium for polysemic political commentary, its stone slabs the canvas on which is registered anger, hope, dreams, defiance, political stances, and grief of both Palestinians and foreign supporters.

In this atmosphere of separation and immobilization, graffiti no longer performs as it once did. During the first intifada, writing graffiti was hedged with the danger of being caught by the occupying military forces. In that context, it was an act of civil disobedience. With separation of Israelis and Palestinians by closure, which entails severe restrictions on Palestinian mobility, few Israelis come into contact with graffiti. There are a few areas where graffiti appears on the wall as it runs along roads traveled by Israelis such as the road south east to the Allenby Bridge and the Dead Sea. Stark commentary was evident in the single word "Ghetto" neatly stenciled in large angular black script every couple of hundred feet on the wall along this otherwise blank canvas. Furtiveness and risk were involved in painting on a road traveled by Israelis. With greater visibility to Israelis comes more risk. However, in large part, Israelis seldom see most graffiti as it is out of their direct line-of-sight.

With closure and enclavization, graffiti has been increasingly written by non-Palestinians in solidarity with them and directed to the world outside. In more urban areas such as Jerusalem, and at sections of the wall easily accessible to visitors, Arabic is now accompanied by a cacophonous polyglot of English, Spanish, French, etc. At heavily trafficked sites with fairly easy access, the wall serves as an international bulletin board where visitors leave commentary and messages.

Once a highly local medium, and part of an internal Palestinian conversation, graffiti and street art now have acquired a transnational quality. The vivid Palestinian street art of the first intifada, located in neighborhoods not generally on the path of tourists or journalists, have now been re-fashioned by a cohort of international street artists for the separation wall. It should be noted that wall graffiti and street art have received considerable attention from journalists and solidarity groups (Bishara, 2013: p. 237). Some of the most widely photographed and circulated are by those by the internationally acclaimed street artists such as Banksy and Blu; their works are readily available on numerous websites. Graffiti and the murals have become an objectified, conscious, commoditized form of cultural production, often drawn by well-known artists and those who come to read and photograph them. For 30 Euros, a Netherlands based website called www.sendamessage.nl will arrange for a message to be written on the wall; a photo of the message is then sent to the purchaser who can then circulate it. Sometimes they are messages of support; other times they are personal gimmicky messages such as a marriage proposal written on the wall. Graffiti by-proxy is form of commodification but with the gloss of a non-profit. Proceeds go towards overhead and then to aid communities negatively affected by the wall. Many Palestinians find the conflation of art, suffering, and revenue problematic, to say the least.

Graffiti pieces were once temporally short-lived, often fleeting images, hastily scrawled under cover of darkness and then painted over or erased within days or even hours. They now exist in a new temporal space of longevity, openly painted, where repetitive viewing renders them a colorful although eventually faded foreground to the wall.

Post-2000 writing on the wall constitutes an intervention in political action but more as commentary and a critical response than a means to propel direct action. It does not announce actions to be taken nor issue directives about strikes or demonstrations. New communication technologies such as social media, the cell phone, and the Internet ensure instant communication. Suggestive of moral stances and political positions, contemporary writing on the wall critiques Israel and the U.S., expresses outrage and solidarity, draws attention to human rights violations, compares the wall with apartheid South Africa and events in Jewish history, satirizes closure and mocks Israeli colonialism. Above all, it is a voice of rejection and a refusal to be silenced.

It is fairly easy to discern graffiti written by Palestinians. It includes expressions such as: "We have the same blood," which speaks directly to Israelis as do these bitter appeals to the humanity of Israelis: "You must be ashamed," and "Witness the Jewish Shame." "No for another Wailing Wall" speaks to Jewish religious tradition. All were daubed on the Israeli side of the wall in Jerusalem. Additional graffiti at a spot in the Abu Dis wall, where children had to climb over cement slabs to reach their now cut off schools in Jerusalem, include: "Children want to go to the schools," or "Who wants to be children in a jail." Highlighting the hardships imposed by the wall on children, these lamentations are diagnostic of a colonial cartography of cruelty and deprivation.

Graffiti no longer gives as much expression to national unity or reaffirms a relationship bet-ween a leadership and a populace as it did during the first intifada when many were signed by political organizations or the UNL. Orders or directives have been replaced by protest and political commentary with a good dose of satire. In villages and refugee camps, one can still see Palestinian-written graffiti and painstakingly painted murals depicting events in Palestinian history, poetry, and commemorations of nationalist days. It often references local, intra-Palestinian tensions and features posters of martyrs (those killed by the Israeli Defense Force). Yet there are instances when local graffiti spikes in appearance. With the 2012 hunger strike by Palestinian prisoners, protests spread throughout the occupied territories and among Palestinian communities in Israel. Prisoners come from all political factions and their plight can be a unifying factor among Palestinians; nearly all families have at least one member who has been through the prison system.[3] Graffiti in support of the hunger-strikers spoke to a Palestinian audience and echoed the graffiti of the first intifada when directives were issued and calls to action were prominent. Simple stenciled images of Khader Adnan, a well-known prisoner, with his bushy beard and round glasses, relied less on aesthetics, irony or even commentary but in their simplicity were a call for national solidarity and mobilization. The graffiti "#dying2live" in English under his stenciled face or "Freedom for Khader Adnan," were common in English and Arabic.

Handala, the ragged and forlorn iconic Palestinian refugee child appears frequently on the wall, in villages, and in camps. Created by Palestinian cartoonist Naji al-Ali, Handala symbolizes the Palestinian condition; he faces away from us, hands clasped behind his back as he patiently observes and waits for justice and return. Like the flag and the key either alone or in a clenched fist, Handala represents all Palestinians regardless of political affiliation. Handala can be spotted randomly on the wall and on the walls of homes and businesses. His now commoditized image can be found in jewelry, in posters, on stickers, on coasters, and coffee cups.

The wall is a main spot for solidarity visits or what is sometimes called "political or conflict tourism." At heavily trafficked sites with fairly easy access, the wall resembles an international bulletin board where visitors leave commentary and messages in protest and solidarity (see Bishara, 2013; Hanauer, 2011). For example, visitors pen messages of support: "Scotland Supports Palestine," "Seattle Supports Palestine," "Ireland Supports Palestine," "Norway Supports Palestine," "England Supports Palestine," and "Together in Stopping the Wall." Christian visitors have also left their messages: "Love God Love People" and "God leads us to Peace." A sense of plaintiveness is apparent in this French graffito: "*Ou est le monde?*" (Where is the world?")

Comparison is a prominent rhetorical device in graffiti in Palestine. For example, "This is an apartheid wall" is a common graffito. Thus, it is worth probing what sort of work comparison does. Evans-Pritchard dubbed the impulse to compare "one of the elementary processes of human thought" (1965: p. 13). Indeed, comparisons help make sense of the world. Comparison locates particular histories and forms of subjugation in more expansive fields of analysis. Comparison's power lies in its capacity to make things seem familiar (or different) by highlighting broad resemblances or approximations. Comparison draws on the logic of analogy as an empirical, cognitive and, it may be argued, an emotive, rhetorical device. Most importantly, comparison opens a space for shifting narratives in new directions. It can be disruptive of grand, in this case, national narratives. It can *work* to dislodge facile assumptions of Israeli exceptionalism. Invoking a named or highly resonant analogy or "cross-cultural juxtaposition" (Marcus & Fischer, 1986: p. 157), can open space for criticism. Likening Israel with apartheid familiarizes it. For example, "*Faisonstomberle murd'Apartheid*"("Let the Apartheid wall fall") draws upon the rhetoric around the fall of the Berlin Wall and declares the wall that separates Israel from Palestine a form of apartheid. Or, consider this comparison in black capital letters neatly painted on a splash of whitewash on the wall in Spanish: "Guernica 1937 . . . Palestina 1948 . . .?" invoking a comparison between the mass displacement of Palestinians in 1948 and the 1937 bombing of the Basque town of Guernica. Declaring things equivalents works to de-exceptionalize what can appear to be a unique and intractable situation.

This little comparative chestnut, on the Jerusalem wall in Abu Dis, draws upon local historical memory of particular instances of Israeli violence and Palestinian displacement. It lays out over fifty years of critical moments in Palestinian history, their encounter with colonialism and violence, and the beginning of the wall:

DeirYassin 1948
Sabra and Shatila 1982
Hebron 1994
Jenin 2000
Wall 2003

While replete with declarative comparisons such as: "Sharon = Nazi" and "From Warsaw ghetto to Abu Dis ghetto," comparison can also convey warnings: "Jerusalem is stronger than Apartheid," reminding that apartheid did fall eventually.

"We will return," hastily scribbled or stenciled in black block letters, is a frequently encountered graffito. Sometimes, it is accompanied by a drawing of a key, the symbol of homes in Palestine now destroyed or occupied by Israelis in 1948. It reiterates the Palestinian right of return and is reminiscent of the formulaic logic of that mathematical graffito from the first intifada: "1948 + 1967 = all Palestine" (Peteet, 1996: p. 149) in it evocation of place, time, and rights. Such a spatio-temporal formula carries tremendous meaning to Palestinians inside and outside Palestine. "Jerusalem is ours" captures presence and reaffirms a claim. Palestinian poet Mahmoud Darwish's famous line: "Write down, I am an Arab! . . ." boldly affirms rootedness and is a warning to those who usurped the land of Palestinian.

"A-Quds ilna" ("Jerusalem is ours") dots the wall near Jerusalem. A diagnostic of the intent of the wall to sever the West Bank from Jerusalem, it epitomizes Palestinian understanding of the intent behind the wall: separation, immobilization and fragmentation rather than the standard security arguments put forth by Israeli spokespersons. West Bank Palestinians are prevented from legally entering Jerusalem without a difficult to obtain Israel-issued permit. This graffito also affirms a Palestinian negotiating principal that East Jerusalem is to be the capital of a Palestinian state.

Palestinian voices on the wall can be detected in the register of "we" and "our": "Jerusalem – our land our capital" or "We will return" signaling presence, indigeneity, and a refusal to cede neither memory and historical consciousness, nor the internationally-sanctioned right of return. A graffito on the wall of a mosque in a town well away from the wall: "We will not forgive. We will not forget," ties together present and future.

There is little Israeli response to graffiti or street art, no rushing of jeeps full of soldiers to blacken it out and if possible arrest the authors as was common during the first intifada. Graffiti is no longer conceptualized as much of a security threat as in first intifada. With security in the West Bank out-sourced to the PA as part of the Oslo agreements, Israeli forces are not as engaged in preventing or erasing it or punishing those who take to the walls. Usually daubed on the Palestinian side of the wall, it is out of the visual range of Israelis. However, the threat of violence is ever present. For example, while drawing on the wall, an Israeli soldier stopped Banksy in an encounter in which guns were drawn and cocked.

It is worth briefly acknowledging Hebrew or Israeli graffiti, particularly with the discernible increase in anti-Arab graffiti and the "price tag" incidents and vandalism of Palestinian property by settler youth groups known as "Hilltop Youth." "Price tag"[4] references the retribution settlers say they will inflict on Palestinians for any curbing of settlement activity in the West Bank and Jerusalem by the Israeli government. The not infrequent Hebrew graffiti "Death to Arabs" was now accompanied by anti-Christian graffiti such as "Jesus is garbage" scrawled on a church in Jerusalem, especially in the run-up to Pope Francis' May 2014 visit. "Death to Arabs and Christians, and to anyone who hates Israel" "Transfer Now," "Arabs Out," and "Death to Arabs" have dotted the landscape for well over a decade.

Street art

While street art on the wall, often by well-known international street artists, attracts a global viewing, get off the well-trodden path and into villages and camps and street art also abounds. With a highly localized audience and themes, Arabic graffiti tagged by political organizations is commonplace as well. Street art depicting historical events are part of community efforts at crafting a landscape of memory and commemoration of a lost homeland and martyrs. In the camps, scenes of idyllic villages in Palestine are common; compositional elements also include the key, symbol of homes lost to Israel, the Dome of the Rock, the tree of life, maps of pre-1948 Palestine, the emblematic olive tree, and the Palestinian flag.

For renowned street artists such as Banksy, the location of their work is integral to what they want to convey. Thus the wall, that ugly scar on the landscape, is transformed into an artist's canvas. Banksy is quoted:

> The segregation wall is a disgrace. On the Israeli side it's all manicured lawns and SUVs, on the other side it's just dust and men looking for work. The possibility I find exciting is you could turn the world's most invasive and degrading structure into the world's longest gallery of free speech and bad art.[5]

Thus, his work combines humor and art to effect a visual denunciation of the wall and its dehumanizing effects. Banksy calls attention to the dehumanizing wall by making the viewer alert to the wall itself. The wall exceeds itself as a canvas and comes alive to speak its own horror.

Banksy's now well-circulated meta-linguistic image of a pig-tailed girl gracefully lifted to the sky by her handful of balloons on a string provides a striking backdrop to the massive Qalandia checkpoint that controls Palestinian movement between the north and the south. The stenciled image suggests the freedom to soar above the ugliness and repressiveness of the wall and a will to persevere. Another awe-inspiring mural depicts a child painting a white ladder rising up to the top of wall. Some of his black stencils speak to absurdity such as that in Bethlehem of a soldier checking the identity card of a donkey. Although a mocking of the Israeli insistence on surveillance of Palestinians and their incessant demands for identity documents and permits to the point of absurdity – even donkeys need identity papers – Palestinians painted over this mural thinking it was equating them with donkeys.

Others point to mobility as in a stencil of black and white figures either walking or riding an escalator up the wall. Below it is an over-sized bug toppling a series of dominoes that resemble the concrete slabs of the wall. Escape, mobility, and the inevitability of release from imprisonment behind the wall are common mural themes as is the desire for and denial of a normal life; in a trompd'oeil that peels away the wall to reveal a thicket of trees swaying over the blue lapping water of the beach while children play with toy pails and shovels among the rubble at the base of the wall. Images of escape draw our attention to the incarceratory nature of the wall. The wall has become thematic in other cultural and artistic venues as well. A watercolor by American artist Ellen O'Grady displayed at the exhibit, "Breaching the Wall," mounted by the Jerusalem Fund in Washington, D.C. in May 2011, somberly depicts a Bethlehem home and its car-repair business surrounded on three sides by the wall; the looming dark clouds allude to the devastation to come. A lone male figure, hands jammed in his pants pockets, stands forlornly on the street. The barbed-wire topped wall forms the backdrop against which the house, the lone-figure, and two stray cats are positioned. Palestinian artist Najat el Khairy's painting, "Wall, Return of the Soul," re-creates the floral, cross-stitch patterns of traditional Palestinian red, white and black embroidery on the wall's cement panels. The exhibit catalogue aptly frames the panels as engraving identity on the wall built on Palestinian land.

Wall aesthetics

The wall's two sides are markedly different in appearance. Each side displays a strikingly different set of visuals. The Palestinian side is filled with a disorderly array of street art and graffiti. In an attempt to minimize the behemoth wall's stark, grey appearance looming on the landscape, sections of the side visible to Israelis are adorned with colorful pastoral scenes of meadows, trees, and blue sky. Near the Gilo settlement, close to Bethlehem, for example, beautification is evident in the neatly landscaped horizontal dirt mound abutting the wall, planted with flowers, which diminishes the perception of its height and adds a splash of natural color. In other locales, a pastoral tableau of green fields, colorful flowers, and tidy white houses is part of a sanitizing aesthetic that masks the desolation on the other side. By late 2010, the wall in Bil'in, a Palestinian village whose lands have been confiscated by the Modi'in settlement, displayed this aesthetic. The Palestinian side was stark cement, while the Israeli side was painted with a brick terraced look in several shades of alternating brown, beige, and white, ironically mimicking the terraced landscape of Palestine. Parts of the wall in Jerusalem are painted in soft pastels, depicting a viaduct bordered by lush green fields and a vibrant blue sky. These aesthetic devices are conscious attempts to disguise walled separation and the harsh reality of a scarred terrain. According to Bishara,

> In a nod to Palestinians' mixed feelings about street art, the now oft-quoted exchange between Banksy and an elderly Palestinian man is worth reiterating:
>
> *Old Man:* You paint the wall, you make it look beautiful
> *Me:* Thanks
> *Old Man:* We don't want it to be beautiful, we hate this wall, go home.
> (quoted in Bishara, 2013: p. 244)

Such an exchange is not unusual. I have heard Palestinians, particularly older people insist that artists stop trying to beautify the wall. Some Palestinians think graffiti minimizes the seriousness of the wall. The Palestinian artist Ayed Arafah says, "I won't touch the wall with colors, it's an act of normalization or beautification. People come here now as though they are visiting the pyramids in Egypt, like they are visiting a tourist attraction" (quoted in Wiles, 2013).

The wall provides fodder for local humor. Jokes circulate about people being lifted over the wall with a crane. In this vein, humorous postcards entitled "The Palestinian Daily Olympics" depicted a young man pole vaulting over the wall; the flip side depicts the same young man running furiously from Israeli soldiers in a jeep. The graffito "Open Sesame," in large black stenciled letters, referencing Arabic/Persian literature and the international language of a children's TV show,[6] coveys imprisonment and the endless and unpredictable waiting that Palestinians endure as they wait for Israelis to let them pass through checkpoints or open the gates that will let them access their schools and agricultural lands. The graffito "CTRL-ALT-DELETE" indicates that irony is not in short supply either.

Conclusion

Once a form of resistance signaling "civil disobedience and a self-reflective moment" (Peteet, 1996: p. 145), contemporary Palestinian graffiti is less often a call to action and more an expression of solidarity and political commentary. The street art and graffiti unfold against the backdrop of a voice and perspective marginalized in the international arena.

As dystopic spaces, walled communities can be contradictory, fostering intimacy and creativity, as evidenced by street art, murals, and graffiti, as well as the isolation and despair the wall itself imposes. I use dystopia less to refer to a degenerative process and more to an exclusivist utopian project that spelled disaster for the indigenous population and transformed their terrain into dysfunctional, unsustainable places. Street art and graffiti have changed little about the wall except to bring it more forcefully into the consciousness of the world by those who use it as a find and those then observe, photograph, and circulate it as images. The commodification and entry of Palestinian wall art into global circuits links Palestine with other distant struggles against marginalization and subjugation. Ultimately, this crafting and circulation of words and images does open a space for conversation about the wall and its meaning. Yet the space on which these images are inscribed is a space not under the control of those who inscribe their words and images on it but of those who built it. In both moments discussed here (first intifada and post 2000), street art and graffiti have been constant reminders of the abnormality of everyday life under occupation and now closure. They shed some light on the policies of occupation and an expanding settler-colonial project. They draw attention to its de-humanizing aspect and the resilience and creativity of a subjugated people while refusing normalization. I wonder about the graffito: "Silence is complicity." Would an empty wall, a barren cement slab, devoid of human response, imply acceptance?

Notes

1   Oslo is a set of interim agreements hammered out between Israel and the PLO in 1993 and 1995, which set up the Palestinian National Authority (PNA or PA). They include protocols for security and economic relations and fragment the West Bank into Areas A, B, and C with differentiated levels of Israeli and Palestinian presence, control and responsibility. On the ground, realization set in that Oslo had simply garnered Palestinian acquiescence to relentless colonization and was ultimately an agreement to buy time for Jewish Israelis to further populate the West Bank. Relations between Israel and the PA would revolve around managing conflict.
2   The wall is widely recognized as a response to the impending demographic imbalance between Palestinians and Israelis and unilateral land grab. Israel touts the wall as a security device; however, a state's protection of its citizens must be within the bounds of International Humanitarian Law (IHL): that means the response to perceived security risks must be proportionate. In 2004, the International Court of Justice (IJC) ruled 14–1 that the wall constitutes collective punishment, causes disproportionate harm, is an acquisition of land by force, and violates the prohibition on changing status in occupied territory and thus violated IHL and human rights law. It ruled the wall must be dismantled and a resident whose land was confiscated be compensated. No sanctions were forthcoming from the US or the international community.
3   In the first decade of the new century the number of young males incarcerated was around 69,000. In over four decades of occupation, around 650,000 Palestinians have been arrested (Rosenfeld, 2011: pp. 3–4). Given the small size of the Palestinian population in the OPTs (1 million in 1967 and around 4.5 million in 2012), this is a phenomenally high rate of arrest, detention, and incarceration.
4   "Price tag" and "Hilltop Youth" are euphemisms for what Israeli writer Amos Oz referred to as "sweet names for a monster that need to be called what it is: Hebrew neo-Nazi groups" that "enjoy support of numerous nationalist or even racist legislators as well as rabbis . . ." "Amos Oz calls perpetrators of hate crimes 'Hebrew neo-Nazis'" *Haaretz* May 10, 2014 www.haaretz.com/news/national (accessed May 14, 2014).
5   "Banksy: A guerilla in our midst" *The Independent* August 6, 2005. (www.independent.co.uk/news/uk/this-britain/banksy-a-guerilla-in-our-midst accessed April 19, 2014)
6   The TV show Sesame Street in Arabic was entitled *iftah ya simsim* "Open Sesame" in English.

Julie Peteet

References

Bishara, A. (2013). *Back Stories. U.S. News Production and Palestinian Politics.* Stanford, CA: Stanford University Press.

Evans-Pritchard, E.E. (1965). The Comparative Method in Social Anthropology. In Evans-Pritchard, E.E. (ed.) *The Position of Women in Primitive Societies and Other Essays in Social Anthropology.* (pp. 13–36). New York: The Free Press.

Hanauer, D. (2011). The Discursive Construction of the Separation Wall at Abu Dis. *Journal of Language and Politics* 10(3): 301–321.

Marcus, G. & Fischer, M. (1986). *Anthropology as Cultural Critique. An Experimental Moment in the Human Sciences.* Chicago, IL: University of Chicago Press.

Peteet, J. (1996). The Writing on the Walls: The Graffiti of the Intifada. *Cultural Anthropology* 11(2): 139–159.

Peteet, J. (2016). *Space and Mobility in Palestine.* Bloomington, IN: Indiana University Press (forthcoming).

Rosenfeld, M. (2011). The Centrality of the Prisoners' Movement to the Palestinian Struggle against the Israeli Occupation: A Historical Perspective. In Baker, A. & Natar, A. (eds) *Threat: Palestinian Political Prisoners in Israel.* (pp. 3–24). London: Pluto Press.

Ross, J.I. & Wright, B. (2014). "I've Got Better Things to Worry about": Police Perceptions of Graffiti and Street Art in a Large Mid-Atlantic City. *Police Quarterly* 17(2): 176–200.

Wiles, R. (2013). Palestinian Graffiti: "Tagging Resistance." *Al-Jazeera* November 26, www.aljazeera.com/indepth/features/2013/11/palestinian-graffiti-tagging-resistnace (accessed May 20, 2014).

26

Graffiti/street art in Tokyo and surrounding districts

Hidetsugu Yamakoshi and Yasumasa Sekine

Introduction

The history of graffiti and street art in Japan, and Tokyo, in particular, is interesting and colorful. It is bounded by particular developments that occurred among the artists themselves, the community in which it appeared, and local government reactions. This chapter explains these developments including the Sakuragichō neighborhood as a "Street Art Sanctuary," one of the most important (but now dormant) locations for these activities.

In order to understand graffiti and street art in contemporary Japan, one must keep in mind that the country is regarded as a society that has already shifted from a "disciplinary society" to a "control society" (Deleuze, 1990). It is also seen as a post-modern "risk society," "surveillance society," and/or "dual society" associated with an audit culture, in which people tend to make rules by anticipating someone else's challenge in advance in order to avoid risks. That means that those who do not adopt a risk-avoidance strategy are expelled from mainstream society or are seen as deviant people who struggle to find a way to relate to society. In such a society, graffiti writers and street artists as practitioners face difficulties in imaging and finding meaningful connections with society, positively or even negatively. Thus, the essence of the graffiti-creativity of deviation would be forced to branch off when the connection to society is refused. As a result, the energy of the writer works within the subculture for the maintenance of the relationship with their companions, or it works outwardly to sublimate graffiti into art, the only alternative being to quit as a graffiti writer. The following discussion reviews the history of graffiti/street art in Japan from 1990s through the mid-2000 to present.

Growth of graffiti/street art and its regulation

Developing stage (until mid-2000)

Graffiti expanded in Japan among young people in the 1990s and with the large-scale graffiti exhibition called "X-Color/Graffiti in Japan" held in 2005, graffiti was popularized among the general public to some extent. An online search of *Asahi Shinbun* (one of the largest and most prestigious newspapers in Japan) for articles containing the keyword "graffiti" and "graffiti damage" from the 1970s to 2000 generates the matrix as shown in Table 26.1.

Table 26.1 The number of the articles containing the keyword "graffiti" and "graffiti damage" from the 1970s to 2000 by on-line search of *Asahi Shinbun*

Period	Key word	
	Graffiti	Graffiti damage
1970s	20	0
1980s	34	0
1990s	About 1500	126

The number of both keywords stayed low in 1970s and 1980s. However, they increased sharply in 1990s. This could mean that the amount of graffiti increased suddenly in the 1990s, or perhaps that people started paying attention to graffiti as a social problem in this period.

It was not until 1982 that the mainstream news media first considered graffiti not merely illegal activity, but as art (*Asahi*, June 26, 1982). Graffiti was seen as a leading-edge art scene at the time. In that context, in 1983, *Wild Style*, one of the most famous movies dealing with the graffiti scene in New York City, was released.

In Japan, writing graffiti without permission is illegal and the criminal law Article 260 (Damage to Buildings) or 261 (Damage to Property) can be applied. In those days, police regulation was not very strict, so everyone was able to write graffiti on walls inside and outside parks almost freely, even during daytime (*Studio Voice*, 2005: p. 38). Around 1995, the number of tags written by graffiti writers increased sharply (*Asahi*, November 21, 1995b). Around 1997, most of the street art on the wall of Sakuragichō changed to graffiti (*Studio Voice*, 2005: p. 38).

The great popularity of the graffiti movement was sustained by the influence of shops, magazines, and videos. In 1994, a graffiti shop named "Funk Crib" opened at Shimokitazawa, a district of western Tokyo known as a "town for young people." The shop played an important role in forming an early graffiti scene in Japan, because it not only sold items for doing graffiti like cans of spray paint, but also provided a place for exchange of information among the graffiti writers. A Japanese subculture fashion magazine *Fine* published articles explaining how to write graffiti. In 1999, *Kazemagazine*, the first all-graffiti magazine (which is still in publication), was issued by the writer KRESS. Another graffiti magazine, *HS magazine*, (also still in publication) was issued by the writer VERY in 2004. Other subculture magazines, like *Relax* and *Studio Voice*, featured graffiti sometimes, though they did not specialize in graffiti, rather treating it as one of the various youth subcultural activities.

Also, many graffiti images were shown in promotional videos for hip-hop songs. Many young Japanese people saw graffiti through these videos and even though they did not have enough graffiti writing knowledge, some practiced by themselves using trial and error.

In 1996, the first graffiti exhibition in Japan, "Graffiti Expo '96" was held. The program included an event called "Graffiti Art Discussion" in which the participants argued about the graffiti scene in Japan and famous graffiti writers such as KAZZ and TOMI-E were criticized by writers who were proud to call their own graffiti vandalism, classifying works by KAZZ and TOMI-E as commercial (Fujita, 1996: p. 32). However, KAZZ once explained in an interview with *Asahi Shinbun* that his motivation was not a desire to struggle for power or to send a message to society; rather, he just wanted to stand out and create masterpieces (*Asahi*, November 18, 1995a). In this sense, the criticism of his graffiti-writing seems to miss the point slightly.

As the amount of graffiti increased in society, the values and motivations of the graffiti writers were challenged on the issue of the illegality of street art and graffiti respectively. In 2005, however, a turning point in the Japanese graffiti scene occurred. During this year, a large-scale exhibition "X-Color/Graffiti in Japan Exhibition" (hereinafter called "X-Color") was held in Mito City, Ibaraki prefecture, located in the northeastern side of Tokyo. At this event, the organizers did not treat graffiti as an underground subculture or as vandalism. They introduced graffiti as a new form of artistic expression. Kenji Kubota, the curator of the museum, explained that the aim of the show was "to introduce the present scene of graffiti in Japan" and to demonstrate "what graffiti is." For this event, forty graffiti writers participated from all parts of Japan. During X-Color, in addition to the walls inside the museum, in order to change the negative image of graffiti among ordinary people, the management of the museum asked permission of local residents to use their walls as surfaces to paint graffiti on. The local citizens were happy to have their walls painted.

Saturated stage (after mid-2000s)

Since the mid-2000s, as more young people have taken up graffiti, the values of graffiti writers have diversified. Graffiti is no longer considered as part of an underground youth subculture anymore. The graffiti scene in Japan has reached its "saturated stage."

Before, only the graffiti that was done illegally was considered authentic. However, now it became common for graffiti writers to have exhibitions at galleries as artists do. For example, in 2009, the writer QP who participated in "X-Color" had a one-man show named "Oykotokyoykot" at a gallery in Shirokane, Tokyo.

At the same time, even famous graffiti writers did not stop doing illegal graffiti. It is not only because they are fascinated by doing graffiti illegally, but also because they think that illegal actions form their identity. Therefore, graffiti fans would most likely criticize someone who does not act on the street illegally and yet calls himself a graffiti writer. Thus, nowadays, writers show a keen interest in legal acts such as exhibitions and live painting demonstrations, but they still base their identity on illegal actions.

Many writers around Tokyo form and belong to "crews." The crews often make nocturnal raids for "bombing" their tags in downtown areas such as Shibuya, Harajuku, Shinjuku, and Ikebukuro in Tokyo. They also go to the western suburb of Tokyo where there is more space left for doing graffiti and they can spend more time to make a "piece," that is, more complicated and larger-scale graffiti designs without being bothered by the police. Usually after they have drawn a piece in the suburbs, writers post it on the web by using social network services like Tumblr or Instagram and share it with other writers. These social media connect writers even if they live far apart. Because of the development of internet technology, young people can easily access the latest scene of worldwide graffiti and then they can start their own career as a graffiti writer.

Styles of Japanese graffiti

Though this recent phenomenon improved the standard of Japanese graffiti, it has also brought a formalization of style. Here we will discuss two different reactions to this stylistic impasse. One is to seek a unique Japanese style of graffiti. For example, the writer DICE insists that Japanese people have to do graffiti written in Japanese and he usually uses katakana syllabaries to write his tags (Nagasawa & papier colle, 2007: p. 94). Occasionally, as in Figure 26.1, people will even write a tag written in kanji pictograms (see Figure 26.1). For other examples, the writer BEL×2 drew a Japanese monstrous being called a Youkai at "X-Color" and the writer SKLAWL is strongly influenced by Japanese Anime such as Gundam.

Figure 26.1 A tag "*Samurai*" written in the Japanese kanji pictograms (December 2003, photography taken by the author)

The other way involves expanding the styles of expression. Some of the graffiti writers feel bored by the formalized expression of graffiti and later on become street artists. For example, the street artist named JON JON GREEN says that he is interested in graffiti but at the same time, he feels it lacks uniqueness and seems boring (Nagasawa & papier colle, 2007: p. 79). During an interview with street artist Ōyama Enrico Isamu, he mentioned that we should not define graffiti as an illegal act, but that we needed to explore the way that graffiti had adapted through time. So he is further developing his idea of "post graffiti." In this idea, he is seeking an updated graffiti style which is not get involved in the consumerism but has a connection with the society.[1]

Ethnography of graffiti today in Tokyo

Where is graffiti found? Filling "the gap" of urban space

One of the most well-known places where graffiti has been located has been in Shimokitazawa, near Shibuya, Tokyo, where many trendy shops such as second-hand clothing stores, and night clubs attract young people (Yamakoshi, 2010). A contrast exists in this area between two adjacent areas – namely Kitazawa 2-chōme (city district), a commercial area, where many stores stand along the alley and where pedestrians enjoy shopping, and Daita 2-chōme, a quiet residential area. Despite the two areas being adjacent, far more graffiti is found at Kitazawa 2- chōme.

The most popular spot where graffiti is written is on the outside walls of stores. Much of this graffiti and tags tend to be written at spots concealed from pedestrians like drainage pipes and switchboard boxes. Other popular spots are public properties like telegraph poles, vending machines, bulletin boards, etc. At Daita 2-chōme, we can see graffiti and tags mainly on public properties and partly on the walls of old or abandoned private buildings. Graffiti writers prefer to put their tags on places of unclear ownership and on old places rather than on newly-built locations.

Motivation for writers: solidarity inside the crew

In 2010, during fieldwork in Chiba city, one hour away from Tokyo by train, Yamakoshi met a man named Takashi. Besides working for a hip-hop clothing store, Takashi also organizes a

Table 26.2 The comparison of the places where tags were written

The place where tag was written		Kitazawa 2-Chome (A)	Percentage (A)/(B)	Daita 2-Chome (C)	Percentage (C)/(D)
Stores	Walls	206	42.7%	1	3.7%
	Switchboards	38	7.9%	0	0%
	Drainage pipes	30	6.2%	0	0%
	The others	36	7.5%	1	3.7%
Total number of tags written on the stores		310	64.3%	2	7.4%
Apartment	Walls	4	0.8%	1	3.7%
	Switchboards	0	0%	0	0%
	The others	6	1.2%	0	0%
Total number of tags written on the apartment		10	2%	1	3.7%
Public telephone booth		7	1.5%	0	0%
Vending machines		37	7.7%	0	0%
Telegraph poles		14	2.9%	7	25.9%
Fire hydrant		13	2.7%	5	18.5%
Community bulletin board		28	5.8%	1	3.7%
carpark		34	7.1%	1	3.7%
the others		29	6.0%	10	37.0%
	合計	482(B)	100%	27(D)	100%

graffiti crew along with his friends. When Takashi was fourteen years old, he saw a hip-hop music promotional DVD and was impressed by the graffiti written on the wall in the background. The next day, he went to the general store to buy cans of spray paint. When he was a high school student, he was arrested for writing a tag on the wall of the police station at Chiba city. Afterwards he went to Sakuragichō, where he met KAZZ by chance. Greatly excited, he swore to produce even better works than KAZZ and become the best graffiti writer in the land.

At the end of 2010, Takashi organized a crew named "ESC." One of the members, Sōta, got to know Takashi through a social networking service. The other two members are Daisuke, who was working as a chef at an Italian restaurant, and a junior high school student Justin. They visited the shop where Takashi worked and got to know each other.

The values and purposes for doing graffiti are different from one writer to another, even within the same crew, but they do often go out together for bombing. Takashi explained about his feelings when he goes out bombing his tag. "Yeah, it's fantastic. I'm so concentrated; I often check where other writers' tags are written." Takashi also said that he wanted to get his name known by other writers. In fact, the perception of graffiti depends on each writer. One day Sōta said "When I go bombing, I am worried about someone informing the police so I often feel scared; I have never been excited." From his comment, it sounded as if he was not enjoying or did not feel excited about bombing. He added: "It's rather for myself. I want to write where I hang out, because I feel like my tags protect me." For a non-writer, it is not easy to understand his feelings. However, it is clear that we should not interpret the purpose of the graffiti writers simply as resistance to society.[2]

Figure 26.2 A piece by Japanese writer BLES from ESC crew (photo taken by BLES)

Figure 26.3 Other pieces written by Japanese writers (photo taken by BLES)

Hanging out with a crew member is one way to avoid the risk of being arrested. The story below is about a day in 2013 when Takashi took Sōta and Justin out to go graffiti bombing together.

> When we were writing on a wall near a downtown intersection, someone reported us to the police. I was still writing when Sōta told me the police was coming. I grabbed my backpack and we ran away. A few minutes later, about four police cars and three police motorcycles came . . . and also about five policemen on foot. I drew their attention and let Sōta and Justin ran away while I dashed to a nearby field. There was a kindergarten and a bus was parked there so I hid under the bus. After a few minutes, I called Sōta and asked him if he was OK. Sōta told me that he asked his mom to pick him up (laughs) . . . his mom was very understanding about the situation. Afterwards my mom called me on my phone, and scolded me: 'You did it again!' (laughs) I left my helmet and wallet in the glove compartment of my motorcycle parked near the crossroads. So the police identified me. Yeah, it was terrible. Later, I washed my hands to clean the paint off and went to the police station with Sōta to take my wallet back.

The incident described by Takashi sounds just like a movie scene. The police pressed Takashi and Sōta with questions, but since the police did not see the scene of the crime, the graffiti writers narrowly escaped being arrested. The interesting thing is that each member has a role inside of the crew. In their case, Takashi is a leader and he protected the other two members. The tension through the graffiti practice associated with this kind of self-sacrifice develops a strong sense of trust and bonding among the members (see Table 26.3).

The reaction from society

Starting in and around 1995, because of the increase of this type of art in Tokyo, the local government began to crack down gradually on graffiti. As a result, many graffiti writers in Tokyo scattered to outlying areas around Tokyo. In Japan, illegal graffiti or street art is rarely protected by the community or the local government even if it has a high level of art skill. Any graffiti tends to be erased without distinction. The tendency of exclusion accelerated toward the 2010s.

In 2010, the Office for Youth Affairs and Public Safety in the Tokyo Metropolitan Government released a booklet "Case Studies of Graffiti Removal" to promote the voluntary efforts (see www.metro.tokyo.jp/INET/OSHIRASE/2010/03/DATA/20k3h300.pdf#search). According to the document, graffiti ruins the appearance of the city and increases the number of criminal activities. It is important to remove graffiti as soon as possible when people find it.

Table 26.3 Profile of members from the ESC crew

No	Name	Age	Carrier	Occupation	Education	Family situation
1	Takashi	18	5 years	Shop assistant	University dropout	Living with his grandmother
2	Souta	18	5 years	University student	Currently under way	Living with his mother and younger brother
3	Daisuke	24	2 years	Cook	High school graduate	Living with his parents
4	Justin	16	2 years	Junior high school student	Currently underway	Living with his parents

The Tokyo Metropolitan Government recommended establishing community organizations in order to remove graffiti. Meanwhile they offered support like sending experts and supplies for graffiti removal. During the period from 2008 to 2010, the makeup of graffiti-removing teams was notable: Volunteers from among local residents accounted for 47 percent and far exceeded the 19 percent who were professional cleaners working for the local government, staff, and experts hired by the government, although the other 34 percent did not take any action. Moreover, ordinances to ban graffiti were enacted by some municipalities.

In Shimokitazawa, local residents made a voluntary group for the removal of graffiti in 2002 and they have been working at crime prevention activities. Setagaya Ward (the local authority) pays their expenses such as the cost of cleaning supplies. Their activities do not just involve cleaning up the town; they also have an event named "Shutter art in Shimokitazawa. "At this event, they ask art school students to paint on shop shutters to discourage graffiti.

On the other hand, some efforts for inclusion of graffiti are found. Since the 2000s, in order to protect high quality but illegal graffiti, a preservation movement has developed. The Nonprofit Organization KOMPOSITION launched a project named "Legal Wall." In this project, they offer the opportunity of activities to young street artists who have skill and the will to create but little or no chance to do so. KOMPOSITION negotiates with the government and local residents in order to get a wall where the artists can draw. After that, KOMPOSITION offers the artists a budget to cover their expenses for painting on the walls.

The first project was a wall inside Miyashita Park in Shibuya. It started in 2004, through negotiations with Shibuya ward office to get permission to use this wall as a "Legal Wall." However, it was not easy. Members of KOMPOSITION kept cleaning the park for a while. They finally got permission from the ward office, and street artists made a mural there.

In the same year, they also made a mural on a wall along the Shibuya River depicting a dragon god cleaning the water of the river. In 2006, they made a large scale legal mural called "Sakuragichō on the Wall" on the exterior of a commercial building in Yokohama. To date they have succeeded in creating more than fifteen works of legal street art. In 2014, however, KOMPOSITION announced that there would be no further projects. According to the group's representative, Motokazu Terai, their experiences had shown that these projects require a huge amount of effort to sustain. For example, when they made a mural along the wall of the Shibuya River, local residents objected that the color tone did not fit the surrounding environment. And in another case, the artist refused to submit a sketch in advance. Also, the cost of making the murals far exceeded their estimates. Artists seeking freedom of expression tend to have a different aesthetic conception to that of local residents. Also, some artists and writers suspect that KOMPOSITION is trying to trick and manipulate them for the benefit of the local government. The attempt of KOMPOSITION to build a bridge between the government and the artists leaves many problems and is currently stagnant.

Rise and fall of the "sanctuary" of the street art/graffiti

The symbolic way of examining the above-mentioned history of graffiti and street art in Tokyo is by looking at Sakuragichō in Yokohama city (a city adjacent to Tokyo), a mere 30 minute train ride from Tokyo. Not long ago, there existed a "Street Art Sanctuary" where artists gathered to collaboratively create a series of murals. Sakuragichō was one of the best places to find street art in Japan. A large wall which runs beneath the elevated railway and continues all the way to Yokohama station provides an excellent location for both street artists and graffiti writers to do their work. A famous street artist by the name of Rocco Satoshi was allegedly one of the pioneers of this place. Rocco started creating street art using chalks in the late 1970s.

Figure 26.4 Sakuragichō in 2003: along the street wall, a considerable amount of graffiti used to exist (December 2003, photography by the author)

Until the late 1980s, Rocco worked alone. It was after the late 1980s that other artists started to join Rocco, crafting their own art alongside his creations. Finally, this place was filled with artists' works and started to call a sanctuary of street art. The San Diego Contemporary Art Exhibition which was realized with the collaboration between artists from United States and Japanese held there in 1992. It was a symbolic event recognizing this street art sanctuary. This event was held for the 35 years anniversary of the sister-city relationship between San Diego city and Yokohama city. Artists from United States and Japan, as well as students of the local junior high school joined this event and made fifteen murals. The press reports helped to disseminate the image of the Art Sanctuary of Sakuragichō.

From the mid-1990s graffiti became dramatically more popular in Japan, and many writers, both Japanese and foreign, found their way to Sakuragichō to leave their work. People, therefore, began to refer to Sakuragichō as a "Graffiti Sanctuary," rather than a "Street Art Sanctuary." However, the development of graffiti was not appreciated by Rocco. He commented that "They looked all the same and there was no uniqueness," and "It seemed to be somewhat violent, and it even looked ugly (see www.rocco-zoo.com/column.html)."

However, in 2008 the local government finally banned all street art and graffiti from the "street art sanctuary" and expunged all the existing works. Around the mid-2000s, the local government started to overtly control the activities of street artists and graffiti writers, although the local

Figure 26.5 Sakuragichō in 2014. All the graffiti was removed, and demolition started in some parts of the wall (February 2014, photography by the author)

government had been concerned about the increase in graffiti since the mid-1990s. Their control methods changed from using art to combat graffiti, to complete removal. Before the complete removal, there were two notable incidents of control by using art. One was an event called "ART-16" held in 2004. This event brought Rocco, as well as a collection of other artists chosen by a contest, to paint over the illegally created graffiti, replacing it instead with a new, collaborative mural. Another was an event called "Sakuragichō on the Wall," held in 2007, in which KOMPOSITION cooperated with local artists to create a new mural on the wall.

Conclusion: rethinking the challenge of street again

In a present "control society," there is no doubt that embattled graffiti writers and street artists face difficulties in finding meaningful connections with society positively or even negatively. This means that urban streets are almost perfectly controlled by the administrative units such as a metropolitan government In other words, the street almost all lost its creative feature based on resistance, deviation, violence, and mobility, the code of which is different from the home-oriented code of decency. This stagnant situation has made graffiti writing in the street lead to involution. Where has streetness gone? In this connection, we once again need to remind the vivid 1990s' scene in which street art challenged against the controlling power and streetness was living.

In the 1990s, there were many cardboard houses made by homeless people in the underground shopping area of JR Shinjuku Station West Exit, following the collapse of the bubble economy in Japan. The Tokyo Metropolitan Government regarded cardboard houses as obstacles to pedestrians and made regular efforts to remove them.

In this situation, Také, an art school student at the time, got together with some friends to paint colorful illustrations on the walls of the cardboard houses. According to him, he did not have any conscious aim at the beginning of his action, but later realized that as the project progressed, the increasing number of paintings had started to enrich the atmosphere of the cardboard houses.

In 1996, the Tokyo Metropolitan Government forcibly removed the cardboard houses on the pretext that they impeded the construction of the moving walkway. They were moved to another square, also within the precincts of Shinjuku station (Mōri, 2009: pp. 155–157). The authorities also set up "Art objects" to prevent the re-construction of the cardboard houses. Reacting to it, Také placed other objects he had made over the existing "Art objects." But security guards removed them within a few hours. On August 19, 1996, he painted directly on the "Art objects," and got arrested for property damage. On February 7, 1998, a fire occurred at "the cardboard house village" and two people died. Using the fire as justification, the Tokyo Metropolitan Government removed all the cardboard houses from the square (Mōri, 2003: p. 172). Since then, most of the homeless people there have moved to other places.

In an interview with the magazine *Gendai Shisō* (*Contemporary Thought*), Také mentioned his memory of the government announcement on the removal of the cardboard houses that he heard at the underground shopping area of JR Shinjuku Station at the time. It said "We will remove the obstacles to return the street to how it should be." However, Také wondered "Originally the street has various functions like spending your time, people passing each other, meeting or chatting to stop and so on, doesn't it?" (Také & Ogura, 1997: p. 59). He believed that removing the cardboard houses was taking the area away from the original purpose of a street, rather than returning it to some kind of "original" condition.

It should be noted that this unique resistance of Také as a street artist happened just at the time when graffiti was becoming popular in Japan. The awareness that Také raised in the interview gets right to the kernel of the discussion about graffiti and street art. It tells that the distinction between illegal graffiti and legal art does not matter that much: What matters is the real aims of those practices and activities, which lie in the deeper dimension of what the street is.

As Také mentioned, the street inherently embodies hybridity. Since we are living in an era when there are no bright prospects in the movement to "reclaim the streets" and the neo-liberalist tendency towards "killing the street" is steadily gaining in strength (Davis, 1999), seeking the inherent nature of the street in terms of hybridity and ambivalence (Sekine, 2009; Salzbrunn & Sekine, 2011) may sound impossible and anachronistic. As Ferrell points out that the exclusionary controls and commercialization often destroy the history of alternative culture (Ferrell, 2002: p. 191). The contemporary society precisely because of that repressive direction, we must rethink deeply once again the features of the street. Thus, the necessity of rethinking and reclaiming the street is intensifying. The dilemma of current graffiti writers and street artists is our torn dilemma in general. There is an iron law that new creativities are born only in the liminal domain of predicament. To live the ambivalent process before asking for results or to uninterruptedly continue "becoming the street" (Sekine, 2014a, 2014b) is all we can do and should do from now on. The deep ambivalence of the death of street is the new starting point for reclaiming the street today. At that point, the core group of graffiti writers will have to hold onto the principle of illegal graffiti drawing.

Notes

1 Personal conversation November 9, 2009.
2 Personal conversation September 19, 2013.

References

Asahi Shinbun, online commercial database of the Asahi Shinbun. (June 26, 1982, Tokyo, evening edition). Machi ni Afureru Rakugaki Tagu: Wakamono no Sonzai Sengen, Tōkyō Monogatari (Overflowing graffiti tags: Declare of the existence by the youth? Tokyo story), (accessed January 18, 2014).

Asahi Shinbun, online commercial database of the Asahi Shinbun. (November 18, 1995a, Tokyo, morning edition). Kazz san Supurēkan de Gurafiti, Anohito Konomachi (Kazz, Graffiti by using spray can), (accessed January 20, 2014).

Asahi Shinbun, online commercial database of the Asahi Shinbun. (November 21, 1995b, Tokyo, morning edition). Gokusaishiki, Chikarazuyosa, Supīdo kan: Āto ni Natta Nyū Yōku no Rakugaki (Brilliant Colors, Vigour, Sense of Speed: Graffiti in NY as an Art), (accessed January 20, 2014).

Contemporary Art Center/Gallery, Art Tower Mito. (2005). X-COLOR/Graffiti in Japan Exhibition. Available at www.arttowermito.or.jp/xcolor/xcolor.html (accessed March 6, 2014).

Davis, M. (1999). Fortress Los Angeles: The Militarization of Public Space. In Sorkin, M. (ed.), *Variations on a Theme Park: The New American City and the End of Public Space*, (pp. 181–204). New York: Hill and Wang.

Deleuze, G. (1990). *Pourparlers: 1972–1990*, Paris: Les Éditions de Minuit.

Deleuze, G. (1992). *Kigō to Jiken: 1972–1990 nen no Taiwa*, Miyabayashi, K. (trans.), Tokyo: Kawade Shobo Shinsha.

Ferrell, J. (2002). *Tearing Down the Streets: Adventures in Urban Anarchy*, London: Palgrave Macmillan.

Fujita, T. (1996). *Tokyo Hip Hop Guide*, Tokyo: Ōta publishing.

Iida, Y. & Nango, Y. (2007). Gurafiti Raitā (Graffiti Writer). In Yoshimi, S. & Kitada A. (eds), *Rojō no Esunogurafī* (Ethnography on the Street), (pp. 207–284). Tokyo: SericaShobō.

Mōri, Y. (2003). *Bunka=Seiji: Gurōbarizēshon jidai no kūkan hanran* (Culture=Politics: Cultural and Political Movements in the Age of Globalization), Tokyo: Getsuyō-sha.

Mōri, Y. (2009). *Sutorīto no Shisō: Tenkanki tōshite no 1990-nendai* (Philosophy in the Streets: The 1990s as a Turning Point), Tokyo: NHK Publishing.

Nagasawa & papier colle, (2007). *Scratch on the Wall*, Tokyo: Space Shower Network.

Rocco Satoshi. (2010). Rocco's Official Website rocco-zoo.com. Available at www.rocco-zoo.com/column.html (accessed November 10, 2013).

Salzbrunn, M. & Sekine, Y. (2011). *From Community to Commonality: Multiple Belonging and Street Phenomena in the Era of Reflexive Modernization*, Seijo, Japan: Seijo University.

Sekine, Y. (2014a). "Street," *The Encyclopaedia of World Ethnic Groups*, (pp. 250–251). Tokyo: Maruzen Publishing.

Sekine, Y. (2014b). The Challenge of Street Anthropology (The Panel Presentation), IUAES Inter-Congress, (Makuhari, May 16, 2014)

Sekine, Y. (ed.) (2009). *Sutorīto no Jinruigaku* (An Anthropology of the Street), Volumes 1 and 2, Osaka, Japan: National Museum of Ethnology.

Snipe 1. (2005). Nihon no Gurafiti no Yoake (Dawn of Japanese Graffiti), *Studio Voice*, 360(12), Tokyo: Infas, 38–39.

Také, J. & Marukawa, T. (2003). Sakana o kakaeta Ebisu sama (The God Ebisu Holding a Fish), *Gendai Shisō* (Contemporary Thought), 10, Tokyo: Seidōsha, 139–145.

Také, J. & Ogura, M. (1997). Rojō Geijutsuka Také Junichiro-shi ni Kiku: Shinjuku Nishiguchi Danbōru mura yori (Interview with Také Junichiro: From the cardboard house village at JR Shinjuku Station West Exit), *Gendai Shisō* (Contemporary Thought), 25, Tokyo: Seidosya, 55–64.

Tokyo Metropolitan Government Office for Youth Affairs and Public Safety. (2010). *Rakugaki shōkyo katsudo jireishū* (Case Study Book on Graffiti Removal). Available at www.metro.tokyo.jp/INET/OSHIRASE/2010/03/DATA/20k3h300.pdf#search (accessed February 22, 2014).

Yamakoshi, H. (2010). Graffiti no "Katarinikusa": Nihon no Gurafiti Community o Keisei suru Kachikan no Kōzō (The Difficulties in Describing 'Graffiti': The Structure and Value of Japanese 'Graffiti'), *Seikatsugaku Ronsō* (Journal of Lifology), 18, 33–42.

27

Claiming spaces for urban art images in Beijing and Shanghai

Minna Valjakka

Introduction

Since the mid-1990s, intricate and ever-changing negotiation processes are shaping the spaces for urban art images in mainland China. The scenes and their developments vary from one city to another because of the impact of individual local and foreign creators of urban art images,[1] government officials, agents of contemporary art including, among others, gallery owners, art critics, art professors, and many other related features, such as local and international events. Rapid urban development has both created and destroyed sites for urban art images. Despite some accepted sites to paint, for many locals, creating any kind of urban art image is a short-term pastime, usually a part of student life. Most of the early pioneers have become occupied with their daily jobs and time to continue engagement on the streets is very limited. Some creators, such as art students, may only take part once or twice in authorized events by officials promoting their own understanding of acceptable forms (see e.g. China.org.cn 2013).

Regardless of the ephemerality of the images, sites, and creators, the aim of this chapter is to introduce the main characteristics of the phenomenon through case studies focusing on the scenes in Beijing and in Shanghai, and to suggest a framework beneficial for further research. When compared with the international trends that have defined the emergence and transformation of what is usually addressed as "graffiti" or "street art," we are able to pinpoint significant differences in terms of intentions, perceptions, reception, employment, and the art market in both Beijing and Shanghai. The focus of this chapter lies in these two cities in which I have followed the developments since 2006 through fieldwork periods, news and social media, interviews, personal communication, and observations in situ.

Examining urban art images in mainland China

Understanding the concepts of "graffiti" and "street art" varies greatly among scholars, media, officials, citizens, and the creators involved in these formats. Especially when we travel outside of the Euro-American cultural context, the meanings can be remarkably different. As art historian John Clark (1998: pp. 49–69) argues, in the context of modernity in Asian art, transferring art discourses from one cultural area to another is a highly restricted and complex receptive process. It is controlled by the needs of the receiving culture, and the adaptation also depends on varying modalities of transfer as well as the mediating culture. This kind of partial adaptation is visible in terms of the visual forms of self-expression in urban public space today: They may have new formats, intentions, and values based on the needs of the locals.

The habit to denote anything scribbled, written, drawn, smudged, or incised on any surface as "graffiti" usually ignores the obvious differences in style, format, materials, language, content, and intentions as well as variations in the understanding of the phenomenon, which depends on the socio-political and cultural contexts (Valjakka 2011). The risk in this approach is to disregard the richness and indigenous historical background of the visual phenomena. It is necessary to acknowledge that the Chinese language has different concepts for different formats of writing and/or painting in public, especially when it comes to indigenous formats: For instance, *shíkè* (石刻 "stone engraving"), *dàzìbào* (大字报 "big character poster"), or *nóngmín huà* (农民画 "peasant painting") painted mainly by peasants and workers especially during the Great Leap Forward (1958–1961), or *chāi* (拆, the character written by officials onto the houses doomed to be demolished) are not regarded as *túyā* (涂鸦 "graffiti") or *túyā yìshù* (涂鸦艺术 "graffiti art") in Chinese. The colloquial word *túyā* indicates "poor handwriting," "to scrawl" and is used also to refer to small children's doodling. Because of the negative connotations, the news media and those involved in *túyā* in the twenty-first century have often opted for *túyā yìshù* ("graffiti art") to create a more positive response.

Further elaborations, such as "ancient," "traditional," "gang," and "subway" graffiti can serve as useful concepts to elaborate the discussion to some extent in Euro-American cultural contexts but not necessarily outside of them.[2] The indigenous formats and the concepts used in the local language and how they are constantly changing, reveal the inherent interaction with the socio-political and cultural context in question. In other words, the concepts bear deep and complex cultural meanings and values that have an impact also on the development and reception of the contemporary formats. As an example, even today, *dìshū* (地书 "street calligraphy"), written with water and brush (or a sponge modified as a brush) is popular especially among elderly men. It is considered as a form of *shūfǎ* (书法, "calligraphy") which has been appreciated as a form of art before and above ink painting since the early centuries of the Common Era. This form is clearly different from *túyā* or *túyā yìshù* because of the materials, intentions, and evaluation criteria. To label this appreciated form of public writing as "graffiti" would confuse more than clarify.

To make a basic, although not unproblematic distinction, I suggest that "contemporary graffiti" be used for the new, international form of graffiti that emerged in East Asia in the late 1980s and in mainland China in the mid-1990s.[3] However, even this concept is not sufficient for a comprehensive approach on its own. Some Chinese involved with the phenomenon see graffiti and graffiti art as a form of *jiētóu yìshù* (街头艺术, "street art"), while others think that street art focuses on art and music performances on the street and *excludes* any kind of graffiti. For many, the concepts are interchangeable, but during the last couple of years, the Euro-American perception has been gaining ground that contemporary graffiti have to be based on writing, whereas murals with pictures represent street art.

In order to assist a more open-minded study which can take into account the changing understanding of the key concepts of this visual phenomenon in mainland China, I propose to use the broader concepts of "urban art images" and "creators of urban art images," without limitations of the format, content, style, or language employed (Chinese characters, transliteration of Chinese in *pīnyīn*, or Latin alphabets) in the images created today.[4] Inspired by James Elkins' (1999: pp. 82–89) suggestion of a trichotomy of an image as writing, notation, and picture, I define *urban art images* as creative action that leaves a visible imprint, even a short-lived one, on public urban space. They can include *numbers and writing* (in any language), *pictures*, and *three-dimensional objects and materials* – or any combination of these three.

Also, urban art images can be legal or illegal, commissioned or voluntarily made, resulting from private or collective actions. Focusing only on illegal actions would limit the understanding of the scene: The notion of "illegal" is complicated because some sites and formats are semi-illegal or even legal (Valjakka 2014). In addition, especially in Beijing, dates are also a relevant factor for the levels of illegality. Near to any major events or significant dates, such as October 1st (National Day), June 4th (Tian'anmen Incident), or political meetings, the city tightens the overall level of surveillance. This was seen with urban art images, too, during the Olympic Games in Beijing in 2008. As Jacob Dreyer (2012: p. 50) argues, "[i]n contemporary China, the most forceful language that the government can speak is the language of controlling urban space itself."

Claiming the space for urban art images in contemporary society is a continuous negotiation process between officials, media, companies, advertising, citizens, and the creators of urban art images. The creators devise standards and norms for the scene itself and they can deviate somewhat from the common social norms. Internal disagreements are unavoidable and influence the accepted formats, styles, identities, collaborations, etc. The circumstances fluctuate continuously and can vary greatly between cities even in one country. Roughly speaking, in mainland China, the majority of the urban art images – especially those easily visible to the general public – are apolitical in their content, because targeting the establishment would cause severe problems. Accordingly, urban art images are not necessarily anti-institutional, but they are still primarily non-institutional by virtue of having been created without institutional or organizational support.

The detailed study of the developments and the current status of the scenes of urban art images are only possible through a many-sided contextual analysis. Such analysis takes into account the other traditional and contemporary forms of public writing and visual arts in China, the nationality/ethnicity and agency of the creators of urban art images, as well as the site-responsiveness,[5] content, language, format, and style of urban art images. It also considers the changes in Chinese legislation concerning self-expression in public space, media, art markets, and the impact of Euro-American trends. Through this approach, the aim is to allow varying notions to exist and new formats to emerge within these two "umbrella" concepts. When writing about the individual creators, I will use the concepts preferred by the creators themselves.

Local premises of the Beijing scene

Contemporary graffiti was introduced in Beijing by contemporary artist Zhang Dali (张大力) in 1995. Zhang had started to create a profile of a bald-headed man already in Italy and continued to paint this figure in Beijing. In 1998, he further developed his idea of a spray-painted graffiti image; he decided to chisel holes shaped exactly like the bald-headed man onto the walls of partially demolished buildings. Together, these works constituted a series of artworks entitled *Dialogue* (对话 *Duìhuà*).[6] In an interview, Zhang explained that the profile originated from his own self-image but gradually transformed into an abstract concept of an empty man without identity. Zhang also emphasized that true graffiti requires the use of spray paint and that he can therefore be regarded as the pioneer in Beijing. It was not until the mid-1990s that spray paint could even be bought in mainland China. Zhang continued to make the spray painted profiles until 2005, when he decided to concentrate on other forms of contemporary art.[7] In December 2006, he nonetheless felt obliged to spray paint once more in Qianmen area, which was undergoing remarkable reform because of the forthcoming Olympic Games.[8]

Zhang said that he used three symbols to express his understanding and relationship with the city. The first of these symbols is the head, the second the AK-47, and the third reads as 18K.

Figure 27.1 Zhang Dali's *Dialogue*, 798 art district, Beijing, photographed in May 2007,
© Minna Valjakka

These reflect the changes and issues of Chinese society at the time: Money, violence and the residents' growing indifference (Zhang, interview in Crayon 2012). Although a groundbreaking form of art in the 1990s in China, contemporary graffiti was only one method of many for Zhang to express his ideas. In addition, he has not considered himself a graffiti artist but instead prefers to be defined as an artist adhering to extreme realism (极端现在注意 *jíduān xiànzài zhùyì*).[9] Despite his abundant oeuvre and significance in promoting an understanding of contemporary graffiti as art (see Valjakka 2011; Pan 2014), Zhang's impact on a new generation of creators has been limited.[10] Zhang has not been part of any crew nor has he actively interacted with other creators.

Still, another local pioneer in contemporary graffiti Li Qiuqiu admits that Zhang has influenced him to a degree. Li Qiuqiu, who today prefers to define himself as a street artist, started in 1996 mainly by spray painting pictures. For almost a decade, there were apparently no other active creators in Beijing than Zhang and Li. Around 1999–2000, Li started to use the tag name 0528. In 2006 he co-founded the Beijing Penzi crew (BJPZ) with MORE, SOOS, and ALS. Two years later, ZAK, QER, and CORW joined the team. BJPZ, one of the first known crews in Beijing, focused on both pictures and writing and developed a style that reflected their Chinese origins. The crew and the members were active for some years, but they are now kept busy by paid work and seldom have time to create on the streets.[11]

It was not until 2004–2007 that contemporary graffiti gradually started to become visible in Beijing. The growing presence of contemporary art and art districts facilitated the development and the establishment of some crews along with the emergence of other specific locations popular for painting. These areas include those in the vicinity of the Central Academy of Fine Arts, Wudaokou, Sanlitun, Renmin University, and China–Japan friendship hospital. Naturally, the attractiveness and accessibility of the walls have fluctuated during the years. At the moment, Jingmi Road (京密路) is the longest wall to paint safely, also during the daytime.

The Kwanyin Clan[12] graffiti art studio was established in June 2006 in the 798 art district in the northeast of Beijing by TIN, YUMI, QUAN, and JEV. A year later, the crew was joined by NAT, AP, KENO, VICA, JAK, and SCAV. The most active period lasted for three years, until 2009. The crew's primary aim was to develop a notion of Chineseness in contemporary graffiti. The perceptions became more diversified when more people joined the crew and the crew also started to explore ways of employing contemporary graffiti style in other visual arts including ceramics. Unfortunately, after the crew members graduated from university, the competitive everyday life in Beijing has forced the members to focus on their daily jobs in order to support their families.[13]

The Beijing scene has also benefited from people moving in from other cities. The four writers (写字人 *xiězìrén*) of the ABS crew[14] are originally from different cities around the Bohai Sea. SCAR (a.k.a. SMER), SEVEN, and ANDC come from Shijiazhuan; SCAR and SEVEN started to paint in 2004, while ANDC took up painting a year later. NOISE from Dalian started to paint in 2007, the same year when the four writers set up a crew. In 2010, the members moved to Beijing and established their first studio in the 798 art district in northeast Beijing. In 2012, the ABS crew opened a store named as "400 ML," to sell spray paint, and graffiti/street art-related books, and other related street gear. ABS also aims to promote acceptance of contemporary graffiti through events and happenings, such as "Meeting Neighborhood" (邻里相聚 *línlǐ xiāngjù*) and "Graffiti On" (涂鸦手稿交流活动 *túyā shǒugǎo jiāoliú huódòng*). Besides legal activities, the crew continues actively to bomb in the streets.[15]

Mainland Chinese creators commonly praise ABS as skillful and as one of the best-known current crews in mainland China. The crew members have their own strengths of writing and/or painting characters (公仔 *gōngzǎi*/人物 *rénwù*) and they have learned to collaborate to make the

Figure 27.2 ABS crew's winning piece at Wall Lords Asia in Taiwan, 2011, photo courtesy of ABS

best of their individual talents. ABS focus on artistically skillful, large works; they favor wildstyle but also employ comic and funky styles. Their skills have also been recognized more widely. In 2011, ABS won both the Wall Lords China competition in Chengdu and the Wall Lords Asia in Taiwan.[16]

Another currently active Beijing crew is KTS,[17] set up in October 2009 by MES and BOERS, who had started doing contemporary graffiti one year earlier. Shortly afterwards, the crew was joined by WRECK, who had taken up graffiti in 2009, and later by EXAS (a.k.a. SWE). All four old-school writers were either born or grew up in the capital. Instead of creating large pieces, KTS are mainly active in bombing (崩 *bēng*) in the Haidian district but consider the whole city as their playground and battlefield.[18] A fourth crew that has been influential during the past years in the capital is TMM ("The Marginal Man") set up by CLOCK and DIOS in

Figure 27.3 WRECK's throw-up, Beijing in April 2014, © Minna Valjakka

early 2011. Three other members, GAN, CAMEL and 525 soon joined. Three of the members are originally from Hubei, Hebei, and Guangdong.[19]

Despite the indigenous origins of the contemporary graffiti in Beijing, transcultural and national trends have obviously affected the scene. For instance, ZYKO, a German graffiti writer, first visited Beijing in 2006 and made it his home in 2009. ZYKO paints mainly alone and is currently working on his own style but also collaborates with locals and visiting foreigners. Another foreigner who was recently influential for couple of years on the scene, especially through active bombing, was AIGOR. Two other foreign graffiti writers who have more recently made their mark on the scene are SBAM, who arrived in 2012 and ZATO in 2013. ZATO has also been experimenting with writing in Chinese. Style-wise, according to ZYKO, the German CANTWO (a.k.a. CAN2) and the American REVOK from MSK crew as well as AWR crew from Los Angeles have had an impact on contemporary graffiti in Beijing. Both REVOK and CANTWO have also visited China, CANTWO on repeated occasions.

The impact of foreigners is growing to an extent, because during the recent years more short-term visitors have come to Beijing and interact with locals both in authorized and unauthorized activities. Some of the visitors such as American James Powderly, co-founder of Graffiti Research Lab (GRL) and one of the developers of laser graffiti, have tested the boundaries of the acceptable. In 2008, Powderly was working together with students for a Free Tibet in conjunction with the Olympic Games protests. One evening, in the outskirts of Beijing, the group was making laser stencils when they were detained for ten days and deported for disturbing the public order (see, e.g. Jacobs & Moynihan 2008). The message and the connection to pro-Tibet activities was too much for the officials although the medium itself, laser tagging, does not harm the buildings.

Internationality of the Shanghai scene

Shanghai's history as a semi-colonial city with international settlements makes it somewhat more international and accessible for foreigners even today. While urban art images came to Shanghai only around 2005–2007 – later than they did to Beijing – the Shanghai scene has been more international from the very beginning. The oldest of the known Shanghai crews is the Paint Every Night (PEN) crew, founded in 2005 by SAIL and Mr. Lan, both from Changsha, Hunan province. SAIL and Mr. Lan are still occasionally putting up their works, which represent their own unique styles, on the streets of Shanghai.

OOPS Crew, the best-known crew in Shanghai, represents the transcultural and transnational trends. Although it was set up in 2007 by Shanghainese Tin.G, REIGN and READ (a.k.a. HURRI), OOPS Crew evolved to include SNOW from Shanghai, KITE from Guangxi, AEKONE from Yangzhou, and two Europeans, STORM and DIASE.[20] The crew cultivates varying perceptions and self-identities in their work, but they are as a whole known for their elaborate pieces combining alphabets, Chinese writing and characters. Currently, many of the local members are occupied by their everyday work and seldom have time to paint. Street artist Tin.G started around 2006 and is the only female in this international crew.[21] She is one of the rare long-term female creators in mainland China – and one of the most acknowledged. Another female representative based in Shanghai, but originating from Guangzhou, is illustrator Popil, who around 2007 began to paint mainly with brush. Her current work focuses on legal commissions.[22]

The transcultural and transnational impacts are not limited to OOPS Crew. Numerous foreign creators have either visited Shanghai or lived there for a while shaping the scene. Short-term residents usually remain members of their original crews in their home cities and paint mainly

Figure 27.4 Tin.G's part of the collaboration with other members of Graffiti Girls crew in Meeting of Styles in Shenzhen in April 2014, © Minna Valjakka

as individuals when in Shanghai. Dezio from France, who has lived in Shanghai since 2006, has had a recognizable impact on the development of contemporary graffiti in the city. His works have exhibited playful yet skillful engagement with contemporary graffiti for around two decades. Dezio is known not only for his accomplished alphabets but also for his elaborated writing in Chinese, which he uses even for his own name (度西奥).[23]

In addition to the international creators, the Shanghai scene benefits from Moganshan Road (莫干山路), the long street leading to the M50 art and creative district. Despite occasional rumors that the wall along the road would be demolished (Shanghai Daily 2011) and the fact that a short stretch of it was actually torn down in December 2013 (Yao 2013), the wall has remained

Figure 27.5 Dezio's part of the collaboration with KEFLOUIS, at Moganshanlu, Shanghai, 2013, photo courtesy of Tom Dartnell

Figure 27.6 Shanghainese Mr. MORE's piece at Moganshanlu, Shanghai in April 2014,
© Minna Valjakka

a safe site to paint since 2007. In other areas in Shanghai, surveillance is tight and over painting
is quick. Some smaller walls and demolition areas have been popular too, but these tend to be
gone quickly.

Old-school writer FLUKE was active in Britain in the early 1990s, but stopped painting
around 1995. When he moved to Shanghai in 2010, he gradually started to write again. He is
still a representative of "Brighton style"[24] from the 1980s. FLUKE doubts whether there is
currently a contemporary graffiti scene in Shanghai at all. Only less than ten foreigners remain
active, such as Dezio, DIASE and FLUKE; many of the long-term locals are too busy with
their everyday lives to keep on painting. Not many newcomers are emerging, either, because
contemporary graffiti might not be that trendy anymore.[25]

Indeed, the popularity of creating urban art images has been decreasing. Based on my personal
observations and comments deriving from the creators in Shanghai, it appears that fewer people
are painting in public space. Although numerous small events, happenings, and exhibitions have
been organized in Shanghai, at least since 2007, they have not had a lasting impact. The public
in general and the audiences of contemporary art have remained uninterested in the trends of
street art and contemporary graffiti. Most recently, the French Magda Danysz gallery – known
for discovering some of the most famous international street artists and promoting their works
in Paris for years – opened a new gallery space in their own premises in Shanghai in 2012. The
gallery has hosted exhibitions for such international celebrities as Portuguese street artist Vhils,
French Miss Van, one of the first ladies painting on the streets in the 1990s, and French JR,
world famous for his black-and-white photographic portraits. From these, Vhils has left the
most enduring mark to the city: Two large works are permanently visible on the outer walls
of the gallery. While the exhibitions have drawn crowds, the local audience has not yet been
keen to purchase the works of international street artists. The gallery has not yet exhibited any
local or Chinese creators of urban art images. The promotion of Chinese and Asian creative
people, including street artists, is nevertheless the primary interest of NeochaEDGE, a
Shanghainese creative agency and their bilingual online magazine.[26]

Figure 27.7 One of the two portraits made by Vhils for Magda Danysz Gallery, Shanghai, photographed in April 2014, © Minna Valjakka

Challenges and characteristics

Opinions are split as to whether the scene is better in Shanghai or in Beijing. The development has been fluctuating in both cities, depending on, among others, the occasional tightening of surveillance, the changing circumstances in contemporary art scene, and changing numbers of active creators. However, more foreign creators are passing by or making the cities their home, at least for a while. The scenes have become increasingly international especially in recent years.

Transculturality and transnationality have been enhanced by crew members of different nationalities, living in these two cities or even across borders. The scenes remain small in both cities, but at the time of writing, Beijing has more bombing and tagging going up in the streets than Shanghai. Also, the locals are becoming more prominent in Beijing than in Shanghai.

Common perceptions of Beijing and Shanghai and of their contemporary art scenes are occasionally reflected in the comments of the creators of urban art images, too. Both Beijing and its contemporary graffiti are sometimes referred to as being closer to Chinese culture or as expressing "Chineseness," while Shanghai is seen as more commercial. Such statements are mere simplifications of the complex realities that relate to the individual creators' aims and intentions in shaping the scenes.

As AZEROX, a British old-school graffiti writer who has lived in Zhenjiang near Shanghai since 2004 has claimed, contemporary graffiti in China serves a different function than it did in Europe originally. Contemporary graffiti in mainland China is a form of escapism, afforded mainly by children from the middle classes or wealthier families. For many Chinese, it is a short-lived hobby; the creators may turn to something else within a year or two.[27] Similar thoughts have also been raised by ZATO in Beijing. There is little deep passion to do contemporary graffiti in mainland China today. Because few have the zeal to spend years mastering the skill of spray paint and because the level of competition is not high, the scene can even appear boring.[28]

Depending on the political and monetary value of the site where urban art images are made and on their content, creating unauthorized urban art images is basically seen as mischief; the punishments are seldom very strict. In addition, there are walls where one can paint safely. Despite this leniency, urban art images have not really spread among the youth in Shanghai and Beijing. What is strictly unacceptable is hitting the trains. Estimates on how many times locals or foreigners have aimed to mark the subways or trains in Beijing or in Shanghai vary, but it is not a very popular activity. A handful of foreign creators have also tried but have occasionally been caught and deported.

We need to bear in mind that the formation of a scene for urban art images not only depends on legislation, although the authorities' agency is no doubt a crucial factor. For instance, it is sometimes assumed in relation to European cities, that strict surveillance and zero tolerance will eliminate creative activities. Although strong policy will restrict the phenomena to certain extent, it seldom erases it completely. Another formidable factor is the tolerance and potential support to urban art images shown by the ordinary citizens: Whether they report the actions to the police or allow or even invite creators to paint their walls. While these two agencies obviously exert an influence, the core issue is the need of the creators. If they have no urge to create urban art images, the scene will not develop. At the same time, if the creators really wish to leave their marks on the public space, they will find a way to do so. Even if the surveillance is high, the options are many, from small stickers to semi-illegal and legal sites.

In addition to differences of class, brought up by AZEROX, the creators in mainland China differ from those in the early stages in Europe in terms of their level of education. Many of the creators have a background in arts or other related creative industries. This explains partially why hopes to develop creating urban art images into a profession have been so strongly visible in mainland China right from the start. For many creators, contemporary graffiti is indeed a form of art. Foreign creators in particular have voiced their disapproval of this artistic development and at times blame their Chinese peers for misunderstanding and/or misrepresenting the conventions of contemporary graffiti. However, we should not forget that even the early forms of graffiti were exhibited as an art form already in the 1970s and that it has been argued to represent the most important art movement of the late twentieth century (Austin 2001: pp. 6, 271). Similar increasing interest in legal commissions, forms that are usually considered as street art, and professional careers as artists has also been seen in Euro-American cities during the past couple of decades

Criticism of issues of style is expressed both by locals and foreigners. Chinese creators are technically very skillful, but not many of them are necessarily developing their own ideas in contemporary graffiti. Often they follow the trends inspired by foreigners, and some foreign styles easily become a fashion in China. For instance, around ten years ago 3D style caught on because American REVOK (Rime) from the MSK crew was one of the first contemporary graffiti celebrities idolized in China. Even today the majority of the styles echo the traditions of Euro-American scenes. Because of the numerous interactions and visiting German creators, the German styles have also had a fairly heavy impact on the Chinese scene, visible even today.

But should Chinese creators manifestly express their Chineseness? For a period, it was quite popular to employ either Chinese language or other visual references that were easily recognizable as Chinese, such as dragons, lanterns, and pandas. The notion shared by many Chinese creators is to keep developing and to venture beyond the easy option of adding Chinese visual references to their works. Some local creators aim to convey a sense of Chineseness by other means, such as composition. According to SCAR and ANDC from ABS crew, for instance, the aim is to express the quintessence of Chinese culture (中国文化的精髓 *Zhōngguó wénhuà de jīngsuǐ*).[29] The perceptions among the foreign creators swing from anticipation of seeing something original to emerge in China to arguments that using Chinese is an easy way of standing out. It is also argued that contemporary graffiti is a "Western game" and in order to be part of it, Chinese creators have to stick with the "Western conventions" including writing with Latin alphabets. If Chinese creators opt for Chinese, their target audience and competition will remain Chinese, while if they write in the Latin alphabet they are part of global competition. The past cannot be erased, and some also doubt if it is possible to create something completely new in the first place—especially as graffiti writers are expected to know the grammar of writing and how it has evolved. The aim for developing a personal style is nevertheless a mainstay of the global contemporary graffiti scene.

Conclusion

During the past ten years when I have been exploring the scenes of urban art images in mainland China, it has become evident that the circumstances, perceptions, and manifestations of urban art images change constantly both in Beijing and in Shanghai. Single events, art galleries, legislative changes, and the existence of semi-illegal walls may have a significant impact on how the scenes turn out. Every city in mainland China also has characteristics of their own, causing the scenes of urban art images to vary and fluctuate in different ways.

In general, as this brief introduction to the scenes of urban art images in Beijing and Shanghai scenes indicates, apolitical contemporary graffiti is tolerated to some extent. It is not regarded as a severe crime as long as the content is not assaulting or does not become too prominent. It is censored, and the formats and sites of visual expression are limited. The formats usually employed in international street art, such as wheat-pastes, stencils, and stickers, are rare in comparison to Hong Kong. One of the reasons given is that, for instance, wheat-pastes get cleaned up very quickly, as the authorities are concerned with any possible political implications of the messages.

As we know, similar to public space, information online or provided by news media in mainland China is under a certain degree of scrutiny, which also applies to urban art images. Some anti-governmental examples are occasionally discussed in the social media, but the clear majority of controversial actions are not. In order to truly research urban art images in mainland

China, one needs to adopt an approach that includes observations in situ and communication with the creators. If the researcher does not take to the streets, how can s/he examine the physical interaction of the urban art images within the city, that very interaction that is highly dependent on the interrelations, visibility, and accessibility of the sites?

Notes

1 Here, "creator" denotes anyone who is creating urban art images in urban public space. This will be explained in detail in the next section.
2 For an introduction the "ancient graffiti" of the Greek and Roman worlds, see Baird & Taylor, 2011. The main differentiation of "traditional" and "subway graffiti" was suggested by Stewart (1989), but he also employs further categories, such as "gang," "agnomina," "political," etc.
3 Cf. Valjakka 2011. As is elaborated in detail in the next chapter, contemporary graffiti emerged in Hong Kong already in the 1980s. However, as I have pointed out earlier (Valjakka 2011), it is important to remember that Hong Kong was governed by the British until 1997, so strictly speaking, contemporary graffiti in the People's Republic of China (PRC) starts with Zhang Dali.
4 For a more detailed discussion of the theoretical approach, see Valjakka 2015b, 2014; cf. Valjakka 2011.
5 In order to emphasize the actual interaction between the site, the work(s) and the creator(s), and the continuous impact of this interaction on the meaning of works, through visual dialogue (where one work is created as a response to an already existing one), I prefer using the concept "site-responsive" instead of site-specific. Valjakka, 2015b. Cf. Kwon, 2004/2002 and Bengtsen, 2013; Bengtsen, 2014, 134–135.
6 Zhang Dali, interview, June 20, 2008, Beijing. For images and more information, see Zhang (1999). Zhang Dali's works were first discussed in English in Wu, 2000; Marinelli, 2004 and Marinelli, 2009 but without contextualizing them with the emerging scene of urban art images in China. More recent approaches which examine Zhang in relation to "graffiti" in China are provided in Pan, 2014: pp. 139–145 and Bruce, 2010: pp. 105–115. Both articles, unfortunately, do not define or question what the authors mean with "graffiti." They also rely on information available online or in the media without consulting the creators directly. Illuminating as it may be, this kind of approach remains one-sided.
7 Zhang Dali, interview, June 20, 2008, Beijing, email correspondence July 27, 2014.
8 Zhang Dali, email correspondence, June 12, 2014. Cf. Zhang's interview in Crayon 2012.
9 Zhang Dali, email correspondence, July 27, 2014. The idea of "realism" in Chinese art departs from common Euro-American usage and has changed notably in relation to ideologies and trends during the twentieth century. The detailed complexity of "realism" cannot be explained here but in contemporary Chinese art, "realism" is not a specific mode of representation. It is not limited to format or method. It implies the aim of adhering to and reflecting the realities of life through art as the artists experience them.
10 ZYKO, graffiti writer from Europe, interview, Beijing, April 15, 2014.
11 The literal translation of the name Beijing Penzi (北京喷子) is "sprayer(s) of Beijing." Earlier, "pēnzi" was used as an equivalent for "writer," but currently "xiězìrén" is more common. Li Qiuqiu, interview, Beijing, April 17, 2014.
12 The name derives from the East Asian goddess of mercy, also known as bodhisattva of compassion. The current transliteration in pinyin is Guānyīn (观音).
13 NAT and TIN, interview, Beijing, April 17, 2014.
14 The first meaning of ABS is "active, brilliant, and significant." It also refers to the anti-lock braking system, implying the quest to keep things on track and to follow the original idea of graffiti.
15 SCAR, ANDC, and Wendy, Business Development Director of ABS crew, interview, Beijing, April 15, 2014. See also ABS crew's website www.abs-crew.com/ (accessed June 2, 2014).
16 Ibid. Wall Lords, is the largest graffiti battle in Asia, established by Hongkongnese XEME and SINIC. During 2008–2012 they organized annual contemporary graffiti competitions on national and international levels around Asia, including the Philippines, Singapore, Japan, South Korea, China, Indonesia, Malaysia, Thailand, and Taiwan.
17 Originally the name stood for Kill the Streets, but was later changed to mean, Keep the Smile.
18 WRECK, old school graffiti writer, email correspondence, July 29, 2014.

19 CLOCK, email correspondence, September 4, 2014.
20 HURRI, email correspondence, May 12, 2013.
21 Tin.G, email correspondence, June 15, 2013, interview April 20, 2015.
22 Popil, email correspondence, March 13, 2011.
23 DEZIO, interview, March 23, 2013.
24 "'Brighton style' is a loose term for a lettering style (typically semi-wildstyle with a lot of sharp edges) that was popular in the UK in the 1990s. A writer called She One (who has gone on to have quite a successful art/graffiti career) started developing it while living in the south coast town of Brighton and members of his crew DFM (Da Freeze Mob) such as Fire, Nema and Skore 204 later adopted it and developed it further. By the mid-1990s it was being copied by writers from other cities in the UK, but most would acknowledge the style as Brighton style" (FLUKE, email correspondence, September 18, 2014).
25 FLUKE, interview, April 12, 2014. Foreigners visiting Shanghai for a short term are too numerous to be mentioned here. For more information, see Dezio's interview in Sanada & Hassan, 2010, pp. 14–17.
26 For more information, see the agency's website http://edge.neocha.com/agency/ (accessed June 5, 2014)
27 AZEROX, interview, Shenzhen, April 12, 2014. FLUKE, too, expressed similar ideas. FLUKE, interview, April 12, 2014.
28 ZATO, interview, Beijing, April 17, 2014.
29 SCAR, ANDC, and Wendy, interview, Beijing, April 15, 2014.

References

ABS crew's website. (n.d). Available at www.abs-crew.com/ (accessed June 2, 2014).
Austin, J. (2001) *Taking the Train: How Graffiti Art Became an Urban Crisis in New York City*. New York: Columbia University Press.
Baird, J.A. & Taylor, C. (2011). Ancient Graffiti in Context: Introduction. In J.A. Baird and C. Taylor (eds), *Ancient Graffiti in Context* (pp. 1–17). New York & London: Routledge.
Bengtsen, P. (2013). Site Specificity and Street Art. In J. Elkins, K. McGuire, M. Burns, A. Chester & Kuennen, J. (eds), *Theorizing Visual Studies: Writing Through the Discipline* (pp. 350–353). New York: Routledge.
Bengtsen P. (2014). *The Street Art World*. Lund, Sweden: The Lund University.
Bruce, C. (2010). Public Surfaces Beyond the Great Wall: Communication and Graffiti Culture in China. *Invisible Culture*, (15), 102–153.
China.org.cn. (2013). Beijing unveils world's largest graffiti wall. April 24, 2013. Available at http://beijing.china.org.cn/2013–04/26/content_28656391.htm (accessed July 12, 2014).
Clark, J. (1998). *Modern Asian Art*. Honolulu, HI: University of Hawaii Press.
Crayon, L. (2012). *Spray Paint Beijing, Graffiti in the Capital of China*. (Documentary film.)
Dreyer, J. (2012). Shanghai and the 2010 Expo: Staging the City. In G. Bracken (ed.), *Aspects of Urbanization in China. Shanghai, Hong Kong, Guangzhou* (pp. 47–58). Amsterdam: Amsterdam University Press.
Elkins, J. (1999). *Domain of Images*. Ithaca, NY: Cornell University Press.
Jacobs, A. & Moynihan, C. (2008). 5 Americans are arrested for protest in Beijing. *The New York Times*, August 8, 2008. Available at www.nytimes.com/2008/08/20/sports/olympics/20china.html?pagewanted=print&module=Search&mabReward=relbias%3Ar&_r=0 (accessed June 3, 2014).
Kwon, M. (2004/2002). *One Place after Another: Site-specific Art and Locational Identity*. Cambridge, MA: MIT Press.
Marinelli, M. (2004). Walls of Dialogue in the Chinese Space. *China Information*, 18(3), 429–462.
Marinelli, M. (2009). Negotiating Beijing's Identity at the Turn of the Twentieth Century. In M. Butcher & S. Velayutham (eds), *Dissent and Cultural Resistance in Asia's Cities*, (pp. 33–52). London & New York: Routledge.
NeochaEDGE's website. (2014). http://edge.neocha.com/agency/ (accessed June 5, 2014).
Pan, L. (2014). Who is Occupying the Wall and Street: Graffiti and Urban Spatial Politics in Contemporary China. *Continuum: Journal of Media & Cultural Studies*, 28(1), 136–153.

Sanada, R. & Hassan, S. (2010). *Graffiti Asia*. London: Laurence King Publishers. (Includes video with a same title).

Shanghai Daily. (2011). Graffiti Artists Ponder Fall of the Wall. *Shanghai Daily*, August 2, 2011, B1–B2.

Stewart, J. (1989). *Subway Graffiti. An Aesthetic Study of Graffiti on the Subway System of New York City, 1970–1978*. PhD diss. New York University.

Valjakka, M. (2011). Graffiti in China – Chinese Graffiti? *The Copenhagen Journal of Asian Studies*. Special issue: *Art, Artists and Art Worlds in Asia, 29*(1), 61–91.

Valjakka, M. (2012). Kiinalaisen urbaanin taiteen kulttuurisidonnaisuus. [The cultural contextuality of Chinese urban art']. *Tahiti*, no.1. Available at http://tahiti.fi/01–2012/tieteelliset-artikkelit/kiinalaisen-urbaanin-taiteen-kulttuurisidonnaisuus/#Val25 (accessed June 5, 2014).

Valjakka, M. (2014). Contesting the Levels of Il/Legality of Urban Art Images in China. *Review of Culture, 45*, 96–118.

Valjakka, M. (2015a). Urban Art Images and the Concerns of Mainlandization in Hong Kong. In G. Bracken (ed.), *Asian Cities: Colonial to Global* (pp. 95–122). Amsterdam: Amsterdam University Press.

Valjakka, M. (2015b). Negotiating Spatial Politics: Site-responsiveness in Chinese Urban Art Images. *China Information*, Special issue on visual arts and urbanization. Guest editors: Meiqin Wang and Minna Valjakka. *29*(2), 253–281.

Wu, H. (2000). Zhang Dali's Dialogue: Conversation with a City. *Public Culture, 12*(3), 749–768.

Yao, M. (2013). Developer pulls down part of M50 graffiti wall, *Shanghai Daily*, December 13, 2013. Available at www.shanghaidaily.com/metro/Developer-pulls-down-part-of-M50-graffiti-wall/shdaily.shtml (accessed July 21, 2014).

张大力 Zhang, D. (1999). 张大力: 对话的拆. *Zhang Dali: Demolition & Dialogue*. Beijing: Courtyard Gallery.

28

Contesting transcultural trends

Emerging self-identities and urban art images in Hong Kong

Minna Valjakka

Introduction

Hong Kong[1] is transnational and transcultural by nature. The trends in visual and popular culture are constantly shaped by people and vogues flowing through the city. A key issue visible in all spheres of life is the balancing between two aims: How to be part of the international scene while also developing Hongkongnese self-identities (as citizens of Hong Kong) mirrored against the mainland Chinese as the "other." Differentiation from mainland China co-exists with interdependence and co-operation in many fields of culture, too. While the impact of foreign trends and creators of urban art images[2] has been significant in Hong Kong, one should not lose sight of original production, either. A case in point is the "King of Kowloon" (Tsang Tsou-choi, 1921–2007), a prolific writer of calligraphic texts on any surface in urban public space since the 1960s. As will be discussed, King and his oeuvre is an illuminating case of transforming perceptions and the inconvenience of Western definitions. He also illustrates how the development of urban art images differs from that in mainland China: His production spans decades of Hong Kong history, from British governance until 1997 to the city's particular status as a Special Administrative Region of the Peoples Republic of China. The socio-political and cultural context of Hong Kong has clearly had an impact on the emergence and development of the urban art images, including the variety in content and format as well as the varying levels of transculturality, concepts, acceptance, and employment for different purposes by institutions, city authorities, and even the police. Nonetheless, the vicinity of mainland China, and of the city of Shenzhen as Hong Kong's next-door neighbor, allows forms of collaboration with mainland Chinese creators in exhibitions and various events in particular, including the Meeting of Styles (MOS).

Adaptation of urban art images

A consensus regarding the definitions for "graffiti" and "street art" does not exist and is not foreseeable for the near future. Especially when these concepts are used in different and historically dependent socio-political and cultural contexts, their meanings are contested and altered. New styles and meanings are clearly visible in Hong Kong, where the different perceptions on the formats, contents, and materials of "graffiti" and "street art" have generated five broad groups in terms of self-identities: first, "graffiti writers," who are closest to the old-school definitions; second, "graffiti artists," who primarily but not solely use spray paint and writing but wish to emphasize the artistic process, placing more value on the pictures; third, "street artists," who mainly use formats other than spray paints; fourth, those who are fine with any of these three identities; and last, those who do not consider themselves part of the first three groups but would prefer to use other concepts, such as "spray painter," "mural artist," "mural painter," "artist," "street art maker," or just a "player" – or no definition at all. This last group is clearly the largest, and growing.[3]

Quite a few creators also change their primary format or use a variety of formats and/or mixed techniques throughout their oeuvre. Unsurprisingly, they find it even more challenging to identify with the two major concepts of "graffiti" or "street art." For instance, a Canadian Chinese PROSE a.k.a. Grayshades, who moved into Hong Kong in 2012, writes PROSE in his graffiti pieces but signs his black-and-white photograph stickers with Grayshades. For him, to be undefined feels the most suitable identity choice.[4]

I find it far more beneficial to examine the complex contemporary scene in Hong Kong through the broader concepts of "urban art images" and "creators of urban art images," rather than simply "graffiti" or "street art." "Urban art images" and "creators of urban art images" allow us to explore more open-mindedly what is happening today – without limitations of the format, content, style, or language employed in the works.[5] Inspired by James Elkins' (1999: pp. 82–89) suggestion of a trichotomy of an image as writing, notation, and picture, I define *urban art images* as creative action that leaves a visible imprint, even a short-lived one, on public urban space. They can include *numbers and writing* (in any language), *pictures*, and *three-dimensional objects and materials* – or any combination of these three.

Furthermore, urban art images can be un/authorized, resulting from private or collective actions. Focusing only on illegal examples would limit the understanding of the scene, as the notion of "illegal" is considerably complicated because some sites and formats are semi-il/legal or even legal (Valjakka, 2014). The majority of the creators in Hong Kong, including graffiti writers, are willing to accept legal commissions, as far as the emphasis in their oeuvre remains in unauthorized works. However, while urban art images are not necessarily anti-institutional, they are still primarily non-institutional: they are created without institutional or organizational backing, (i.e. without financial or material support). Through this approach, the aim is to allow varying notions to exist and new formats to emerge within these two "umbrella" concepts. When writing on the individual creators, I will use the concepts preferred by the creators themselves.

The King and his bequest

Tsang Tsou-choi (1921–2007), "the King of Kowloon," can be regarded as the pioneer in the history of urban art images in Hong Kong. Because of his materials, brush, and a mixture of black ink and paint, Tsang was rather a calligrapher than a graffiti writer. Even more importantly, he started before the new form of graffiti emerged in New York (Clarke, 2001: p. 177). Still, no definition really captures Tsang and his works (Vigneron, 2014: p. 315).

The main motivation behind Tsang's work was to declare that the land which had originally belonged to his family in Kowloon had been wrongly taken by the British government, but the ideological context of Tsang and his works has shifted remarkably since the handover in 1997. In the context of decolonization, visible first in visual arts, Tsang was transformed "into a signifier of a local" (Clarke, 2001: p. 183). Tsang and his works became an important part of the local identity building. In the wake of his deteriorating health and move into elderly care, Tsang started to write on paper and objects instead of public surfaces (see Lau, 1997; Chung, 2010). Gradually, his works were treated as contemporary art as well as re-employed for souvenirs. According to art critic Oscar Ho (2014), King and his work was betrayed in the end, and because his works were detached from the urban public space, his work gradually lost its meaning.

The protection of Tsang's last surviving works in public space as cultural heritage, gained media attention in 2013. One of the remaining examples was collected by the new museum for visual culture, M+ (e.g. Chow, 2012, 2013), while another is protected by plexiglass at the Tsim Sha Tsui Ferry Piers. Tsang also continues to command respect in the streets. Shortly after Tsang's death in 2007, European graffiti writers, MAIS and ORSEK, with a local graffiti writer JAMS created a commemorative piece close to Fotan metro station, including two facial portraits of Tsang.[6] The respect among the creators today derives from Tsang's substantial oeuvre and ability to connect with the city. Site-responsiveness was already important for Tsang, who modified the content of his writings according to the site (Valjakka, 2015a, pp. 99–105; see also Valjakka, 2015b).

There are clear differences in style, materials, format, content, and intention in the commemorative piece mentioned above and Tsang's own writings although they all emerged in public space in Hong Kong and are blandly labeled as "graffiti." Here, too, any deeper understanding of the richness of this visual phenomenon and its varying formats are rather obscured than clarified if the concept of "graffiti" is used to denote anything and everything scribbled, written, drawn, smudged, or incised on any surface – as it often is. The unfocused usage of "graffiti" ignores the obvious differences which primarily depend on the socio-political and cultural contexts, contents, and intentions (Valjakka, 2011). Further elaborations, such as "ancient," "traditional," "gang," and "subway" graffiti may serve as useful concepts to start a discussion.[7] However, Tsang represents indigenous, "traditional" forms of writing in public space, developed before and independently from the new, international form of "graffiti" which has its roots in putting up one's name with spray paints and marker pens as developed in the United States since the end of the 1960s. To make a basic, although not unproblematic distinction, I suggest that "contemporary graffiti" be used for the new, international form of graffiti which emerged in East Asia in the late 1980s. Nonetheless, contemporary graffiti remains only as one contested subcategory of urban art images in Hong Kong today. In the following, based primarily on intentions, materials, and stylistic motivations, I will explore the varying new forms of visual self-expression which started to emerge in Hong Kong in the 1980s.

Emerging scene

It is impossible to discuss all the local and foreign creators in this short introduction, let alone how they have contributed to the scene of urban art images. For instance, many creators have been active only briefly and established and/or joined in many crews successively and/or simultaneously. But what is characteristic for the Hong Kong scene is transculturality and transnationality, which occasionally even hinders clear definitions of the "local": crews have members from different nationalities and across borders, people have ethnically mixed backgrounds, and/or they were born elsewhere but have lived most of their lives in Hong Kong.

The first known examples of contemporary graffiti appeared in the early 1980s. In 1982, American based ZEPHYR, Dondi, and Futura from The Death Squad (TDS) crew were commissioned by Jeffrey Deitch, an art curator and dealer to paint in the I Club. Despite the difficulties of acquiring spray paints, they managed to paint the enormous space (Witten & White, 2001: pp. 160–161). At around the same time, a local television broadcast a video by The Clash, a British punk rock band, featuring Futura and his works. In 1983, THREE, a British citizen living in Hong Kong, started to write his SOS tag (the O crossed by diagonal lines) already before visiting the I Club, but he became even more inspired to continue to explore further when he saw the pieces of TDS. In the following years, a few other foreign teenagers made some tags too, but they remained scarce.[8] Some local contemporary graffiti apparently emerged in the late 1980s,[9] but no visual evidence nor detailed information has so far surfaced.

The contemporary graffiti gradually started to take root in the mid-1990s. International creators kept passing through Hong Kong or were invited to specific events by shops targeting younger customers, such as the now defunct BFD skateboard shop. For instance, the first subway train was bombed by German LOOMIT and CHINTZ in Kowloon Bay Yard in January 1996 on their stop-over to Australia.[10] The information was first published only in a German magazine, and most of the locals have been rather unaware of their input until recently.

The first local creators and crews known today also appeared in the mid-1990s. SYAN . . .[11] made his first graffiti pieces in France in 1990. His first piece in Hong Kong, however, dates from 1994. With 3DOM, REALM and SPOON, SYAN . . . established Chinese Evolution Aerosol (CEA) crew in 1997. They remained active all around the city for a few years. SYAN . . . still makes the occasional work both legally and illegally. He created his latest unauthorized work in Hong Kong in 2010.[12]

In 1998, a skateboarding team of several members started to bomb under the name of freeS. In 1999, three members from this team, KDG, GRIV, and GHOST 2 (KOSTWO) formed a crew, Fuck Da Cops (FDC) and were active around the city. Around 2000, two European

Figure 28.1 The first "ChinamanWall" by SYAN . . . in collaboration with MIST and TILT, in Mongkok, Hong Kong, June 2005. Photo courtesy of SYAN . . .

Figure 28.2 FDC repainted this throw-up to express their support to *the Occupy Central with Love and Peace* movement and for the first time ever, they added yellow color to highlight the letters. Yuen Long, Hong Kong, October 2014. © Minna Valjakka

graffiti writers, DOFI and CIE, were briefly part of the crew too. In 2002, KDG, GRIV, and GHOST 2 set up a shop, Dirty Panda, selling spray paints and other related materials. Recently, KDG has been taking care of the enterprise, promoting contemporary graffiti also through collaborations with local schools, institutions and youth centers. In around 2008, FDC was further joined by SICO and in 2010 by MCHKG.[13]

The early local creators also include KS (a.k.a. Kahs), who started around 1998/1999. For a short while he also had a crew, K7C. Today KS is more concentrated on arts.[14] One of the first females, ROSA, became involved around the same time, in 1999. She spent seven years abroad before returning to Hong Kong in 2010. She has since been exploring on wheat-pastes and stickers as CathLove and continuing contemporary graffiti under both names.[15]

The beginning of the twenty-first century

The turn of the century saw significant developments among new local and foreign crews and creators. The abundance of foreign creators makes it impossible to identify them all, and it is even more challenging to verify who has had an impact on the scene and how. Depending, for instance, on the duration of the stay, the media publicity, and the level and format of pursuits, the impacts of foreign creators vary greatly in terms of style, inspiration, collaboration, and pushing the scene forward. Some foreign visitors might not collaborate with the local scene so their effect remains limited and unmentioned. As an example, apparently a foreign graffiti writer, MORE, had made throw-ups in Hong Kong Island before 1997,[16] but whether he influenced anyone remains unclear.

In contrast, the impact of German graffiti writers, NECK and SEAK from CNSkillz crew is acknowledged although they visited only briefly in 2000. They were invited by the Warehouse Teenage Club, a non-profit youth center, which had started to promote new forms of youth culture and contemporary graffiti, to paint the wall of the center's basketball court in collaboration with SYAN . . .[17] In addition, the local creators usually name Eric Haze, PATROL, DILK, and Space Invader when asked which foreign short-term visitors have influenced them in the early phases.

It could be argued that anyone who has created urban art images in Hong Kong has been influential to an extent – at least by making the scene highly transcultural and transnational. Usually, however, those who decide to live in Hong Kong for some time have clearly more impact than the short-term visitors. The more influential creators include FlipOne, FLOW1, DANSK, and Selph. The level of the impact may not directly correlate with the length of the stay and/or it can also vary during the stay. This was the case, for example, with graffiti writer DOFI, who lived in Hong Kong in 2000–2013. During the first years he was very influential in the scene, but subsequent disagreements made him stop collaborating with other creators and focus on working with his own crew, The Wild Ones (T.W.O), established in 1995.[18]

Local crews and creators started to emerge in growing numbers, partly inspired by international names. For instance, four local females established the Bombing Never Stop (BNS) crew in 2000. After about a year, SWAMP, SMIRK, and REDY still continued, the latter two most actively. Before moving to Germany in 2011, REDY repeatedly painted with other crews and friends. So far she is the most long-term female graffiti writer in Hong Kong.

Figure 28.3 REDY's collaboration with Pest (TMD, New Zealand), 4Get and Mais (FHK, CLW) in Hong Kong, February 2015. Photo courtesy of REDY

In 2001, graffiti writer XEME became active and has continued ever since. Two years later, he and his peers, BASE and SHRUB, established the Kong Brotherhood (KB) crew, which is one of the most distinguished crews in Hong Kong because of its history, size, and presence. KB has had around fifteen members and at the time of writing involves XEME, FACTS, BASE, SINIC, and YUMOH, and – from mainland China – TOUCH, MOON, and GAS.[19] KB is the most active bombing and tagging crew in Hong Kong today. Of the crew members, XEME and YUMOH, a graffiti writer who started in 2008, are visible around the city through tags, throw ups, rollers, and stickers.

MICK (a.k.a. MIC) similarly started in 2001. During 2003–2007, he was an active all-city writer, and his name is still visible on the streets. In 2011, he also experimented with street art, putting up wheat-pastes based on Chinese New Year decorations. Currently, he is more focused on art on canvas, running a gallery, and preferring to define himself as a street art maker.[20]

Local graffiti artist Uncle also started on the streets in 2001. With PERS, he had a Start team for a couple of years. In 2009, he launched AfterWorkShop, which he currently maintains with his wife Rainbo from mainland China. He has recently focused more on commissioned works, such as murals.[21]

The first years of the twenty-first century left a visible mark on what is usually considered street art. THREE, who had been practicing art after graduating from university, returned to Hong Kong from Britain. In 1996, he decided to start creating in public space, drawing dozens of spirals in wet cement laid on the streets. At the time, however, there was no street art in Hong Kong, so whether THREE's spirals could be considered as street art remains questionable.

Figure 28.4 Piece by XEME in Yau Tong in spring 2014. Photographed in March 2014. Photo courtesy of HKstreetart.com

In 2002, THREE extended his oeuvre on the streets to small cement sculptures, stencils, and number threes made in metal, becoming part of the emerging street art scene.[22]

One of the local pioneers of street art, Start From Zero (SFZ), was established by Dom in 2000 and Katol soon joined in. SFZ has since become known for the variety of its works, including wheat-pastes, stickers, and stencils – some with a witty socio-political edge.[23] Another influential local artist is Big Mad (also known as BM 13177 and Otoss), who actively explored various formats during 2002–2012. One of Big Mad's trademark was a face drawn with one fluent line.

Around the same time, in 2002, MRM, British by birth but living in Hong Kong since 2000, started to write as FUSION. With local school friends RETRON, SHA, and MELLOW, he set up the Time 4 Change (T4C) crew the following year. Their involvement in street art was mainly inspired by SFZ and Big Mad. In 2005, however, MRM started to write MRMENA, the crew's name was changed to Freelance Urban Deco (FUD), and they got more involved with contemporary graffiti. MRMENA mainly maintained the crew alone during 2006–2008. In recent years he has expanded to commissioned mural paintings and art works.[24]

The past decade

The scene has fluctuated between revivals and regressions. Since 2005, it has grown especially vigorous thanks to new creators, events, institutional support, and competition among the crews and creators. For instance, in 2005 a local creator who prefers to be identified as a spray painter,[25] 4Get About It, who had returned from London the previous year, started to experiment with spray paints and hand-drawn stickers.[26]

Figure 28.5 One of the faces by BM still visible in Tai Hang, Hong Kong. Photographed in March 2015. © Minna Valjakka

Similarly, in 2005, a local crew SABCAT was established by JAMS, AMSON, DEVIL, and ZIM. SABCAT remained active until 2012, and was known especially for piecing. In 2011, Stay Home Son (SHS) got set up by DREAMS, HAMP, JAMS, and TAYE from Shanghai. A year later, Parent's Parents – which also seeks to build a brand – was established by JIMJIMJIMSON (a.k.a. AMSON), WONG TIN YAU (a.k.a. JAMS), CHRIS, and YSOO, one of the new women on the scene.[27] Both SHS and Parent's Parents are active today albeit in different ways.

Also in 2005, a French graffiti writer MAIS made Hong Kong his home and started to collaborate with both local and foreign writers. Soon, along with European SHOES, he joined a crew, Fuck Hong Kong (FHK), established by American CEME and European ORSEK in 2006–2007. Later, the European ASMO came along. The previously mentioned two locals, JAMS and AMSON, were also part of the crew for a short while.[28] Unsurprisingly, the name of the crew and some actions of the members have caused disagreement and misunderstandings. The opinion and intentions among the members vary even today, but according to MAIS, the name of the crew was to suggest displeasure with the normative society restricting, for instance, the usage of public space,[29] and the relative lack of culture in Hong Kong compared to other large international cities. FDC echoed the rebellious notions of MAIS' earlier crew in France, On détruit Montpellier (ODM, in Eng. "we destroy Montpellier"). It was not intended to have racist implications towards the locals although this is how it was interpreted.[30] Today, only MAIS and CEME of the crew's foreign members have stayed in Hong Kong, remaining active in their own, different ways.

Also the street art circles got new participants. In January 2005, Jay FC established ST/ART, a collective of around ten local and foreign creators: ★COM, C#, Graphic Airlines (GAL), Ping, KS1, Big Mad, Start From Zero (SFZ), and ESP including Dkoda, Selph, PHilfy, and Irie. ST/ART aimed to increase artistic value, strengthen skills and confidence of the artists and make art accepted in public space. By working together, they managed to launch the careers of some artists most active today, such as the above mentioned SFZ and Graphic Airlines (GAL),[31] formed by Tat and Vi in 2002. In 2006, GAL started to create stickers and wheat-pastes on the streets. Since then, they have become acknowledged for their original style, which emphasizes the "aesthetics of the ugly."[32]

Among the local graffiti writers and artists bubbling under, such names as DOVE (a.k.a. Dovetail), and ROES represent the most recent generation. Also many new foreign creators keep moving in, including Masa in 2008, and Mark Goss and Cara To (a.k.a. Caratoes) in 2013, who use different formats and add their own flavor to the multilayered scene. More recent visitors or short-term residents include, to mention a few, DRUIDE, UTAH and ETHER, BUCKET, JR, Kidult, Dface, Anthony Lister, PEAR, NASTY, EDGE, and Kaid Ashton.[33] Their actions vary from targeting the trains and streets in various formats to gallery exhibitions and participation in Art Basel, the world-known international art show.

The development of the scene is also reflected in new formats. Lenticulars[34] were introduced in spring 2013 by the American designer OBSRVR, who has lived in Hong Kong since 2010.[35] Another new format is urban knitting. Local Esther Poon got inspired by a workshop organized with Magda Sayeg in conjunction with her exhibition at a Hong Kong shopping mall in July 2012. Gradually, Esther continued, first through legal works but in February 2014, she started to put up unauthorized pieces, too.[36] In 2013, the street art scene was further strengthened, when two local females formed a street art crew, the Martians, to put up stickers and wheat-pastes.[37]

Despite these recent developments, the scene has remained relatively small. Estimates of active creators vary, but based on my own assessment of all formats of urban art images in 2013–2014, there were about thirty creators active in some ways, and more than fifty had moved away or

Figure 28.6 Urban knitting by Esther Poon, Sheung Wan, Hong Kong, September 2014. Photographed in October 2014. © Minna Valjakka

withdrawn. Without a doubt, some creators are still unknown to me. The ratio of locals to foreigners also keeps changing. Roughly estimated, in the early years of the twenty-first century, about half of the creators were locals, half non-locals. In 2012–2013, the relation slightly shifted in favor of the locals but it might be reversing at the moment.

Organizational and institutional collaborations

In order to support their activities, creators have found ways to form collaborations. One internationally common form of developing the scenes is to establish related publications. Since the end of the 1990s, the local media has repeatedly published on urban art images in Hong Kong, characterizing the work in both positive and negative terms (see, e.g. Pearl Channel, 2007). Despite continuous media interest and the growing use of social media and related websites, publications on any kind of urban art images remain surprisingly rare.[38] *Invasian*, a magazine of contemporary graffiti in Asia and urban culture, was launched in May 2008.[39]

One of the endeavors to enhance the development of and collaboration among the Asian graffiti community was Wall Lords, established by Hongkongnese XEME and SINIC. During 2008–2012 they organized annual contemporary graffiti competitions on national and regional levels around Asia, including the Philippines, Singapore, Japan, South Korea, China, Indonesia, Malaysia, Thailand, and Taiwan.

Two more recent attempts to invigorate the scenes locally in Hong Kong are MicroGalleries and HKwalls, which both highlight different formats. In 2013, without consulting the city officials, MicroGalleries organized two street art events: first in Tai Hang in April and second in Wan Chai in December. The local and international artists employed such varied methods as photographs, wheat-pastes, installations, and mini gardens.[40] In May 2014 and in March 2015, HKwalls, an annual street art and graffiti festival, has focused on creating on the walls and shutters with spray paints, brushes and markers.[41] Both events intend to continue in the future.

Hong Kong displays growing institutional interest in urban art images and their use for varying purposes, from advertisements to office decoration and crime prevention. Efforts to transform at least some formats of urban art images into acceptable forms of art through teaching, exhibitions, and commissions are made both by institutions and individual creators. For instance, the Warehouse Teenage Club has continued to organize workshops and collaborate to find legal walls. Two crews have been established in connection with this collaboration, Paint Da Wall (PDW) in 2003 and Graffiti Art Association (GAS) in 2006. In 2011, Warehouse also co-organized an exhibition with local and international artists (Tang, 2011).[42]

Three galleries have been supporting the local creators in the face of Hong Kong's tough and costly realities. Part-of Gallery, the first of these, was founded in 2008. One of the benefits is a large wall in the alley leading to the gallery – often painted in accordance with the exhibitions. The galleries of HAJI and Above Second opened in 2010 and have staged several exhibitions. Above Second also invites international names.[43] For instance, in spring 2013, they arranged a collaborative street art exhibition "Work in Progress" with Swire Properties, inviting Cyrcle, Vhils, Beastman, Cannonball Press, Rone, Victor Ash, and Meggs to give workshops and create on the walls in collaboration with local creators.

Private enterprises, too, continue to shape the scene. At the beginning of 2014, the French restaurant Bibo invited international names to create works for the premises. Among the arrivals was one of the pioneers of street art, French Space Invader, who also took the opportunity during his second trip to Hong Kong to place forty-eight works around the city, a process which he calls an invasion.[44] Some of his latest works were based on the American animated character from the 1970s, *Hong Kong Phooey*. To use American subject matter, trained in

Figure 28.7 French street artist, Hopare's contribution to the HKwalls in March 2015, Sheung
    Wan, Hong Kong. © Minna Valjakka

Hongkongnese kung fu, adds to the layers of transculturality in the Space Invader's oeuvre,
which has mainly focused on figures deriving from Japanese video games, Space Invaders and
Pac-Man. Unfortunately, the works were quickly removed, to the consternation of many citizens.

Issues of style

In the early years, the locals were eager to experiment and learn. They applied a mixture of
styles, using bubble letters, wildstyle, 3D, and so forth, depending on who visited Hong Kong
or whose work was accessible by other means. Despite transcultural trends, the locals have sought
to develop indigenous styles and, occasionally, even formats, such as wheat-pastings resembling

decorations used for Chinese New Year celebrations. However, there is nothing yet that could be defined as a recognizable "Hong Kong style." The reasons vary from the scene's small size and underdevelopment to commercialization and lack of collaboration. A factor which now to some extent hinders the development of an original style – not only in Hong Kong – is the prominence of the Internet and social media. An enormous amount of information is available online, and it is far easier to be inspired by new global trends than it was in the 1980s or 1990s. Currently, a clear majority of the creators in Hong Kong primarily aim to develop their own personal style, not a "Hong Kong style." In the works of some crews, the individual styles can merge into a crew style. Naturally, opinions of who is interesting and/or improving in terms of styles vary enormously among the creators.

Indigenousness in urban art images can be expressed in many different ways. One is to use the Cantonese language and to include and/or modify written Cantonese characters as part of the work or as one's tag. This is done, for instance, by SYAN . . . who has developed a method on dismantling and reconstructing the written characters by turning the angle of the writing process by 90 degrees to the left. Another popular method is to incorporate other visual references to the local society, politics, and culture, such as noodles, dragons, and local people. A third method would be to develop a style that goes beyond these visual references and to incorporate a notion of Hongkongness (i.e. the understanding of identity and unique cultural aspects which distinguish people in this territory from the mainland Chinese) to the content or composition. A fourth method is to use an indigenous format. As an example, since 2011, a local graffiti artist, RST2, has borrowed the banners of the political parties, spray painted them, and put up the remodified versions back on the streets.

Conclusion

The creators are not alone in traveling in and out of Hong Kong. Urban art images are also mediated in movies, magazines, on the Internet, and in the social media. These have all contributed to the emergence and current development of urban art images in Hong Kong. The flip side of this transculturality and transnationality is that although local creators and institutions work hard to develop the scene, international names remain more appreciated in galleries and commissioned works than the locals. This is partly because of a similar trend in the contemporary art scene: galleries rely on non-locals to bring in the profits. Furthermore, Hong Kong has become an essential site for the art market, coming close to New York and London. During the Art Basel in particular, organized annually since 2013, the city is filled with international art stars, including many famous creators of urban art images who tend not to miss the opportunity to put up their works on the streets. How much this will influence the scene is yet to be seen.

Another characteristic of the Hong Kong scene is the impermanence of the creators: both locals and non-locals move back and forth for study and work. In addition, creating urban art images is a short-lived fad for many local creators. The Hong Kong scene is often criticized by foreign graffiti writers for not being "hard-core" enough. For instance, there are also relatively few urban art images on trains or other forms of public transport in Hong Kong. What is becoming more popular instead is the bombing of trucks and vans that weave around the city. While many graffiti writers insist on the tradition of keeping it "real" through emphasis on illegality, bombing, and Latin alphabets, they might neglect differences caused by nationality/ethnicity, class, and socio-political and cultural contexts. For a Hong Kong writer in the twenty-first century, it cannot be *exactly* the same struggle as it was for the writers from poor ethnic minorities in the streets of New York in the 1970s. But does this inevitable difference, dependent on the socio-cultural and political circumstances, necessarily mean that the scene in Hong Kong is somehow worse or lower in quality? Is it becoming too commercial and legal? These value-loaded questions are causing much heated debate, but similar trends transforming the scenes and the growing popularity of street art forms are visible worldwide.

For the majority of the creators in Hong Kong, regardless of the specific form of expression – whether they focus on putting up their name or leaving a message – it is more about self-expression and style, interaction with the city and other creators combined with a rebellious notion. However, especially those who do not have a steady job, or do not want to have one, often seek to build a profession on their passion. The options include developing one's own brand with a focus on clothing and/or illustrations, organizing events, publishing, taking commissioned works, teaching, and developing an artistic career with exhibitions. Most of the creators I know would accept a commission, but the ways in which a work is created as well as its style and content obviously impact on how it is evaluated by the peers. A focus on only commissioned works is an open invitation for criticism. Street credibility with unauthorized actions is still a core value, no matter which format and identity are involved. Without a question, the locals and non-locals alike are increasingly interested in creating their own identities, perceptions, and adaptations.

Notes

1 Hong Kong refers usually for the whole area of Hong Kong Special Administrative Region, including the New Territories and Kowloon. Hong Kong Island is the southern, main island.
2 This concept will be explained in detail in the next section.
3 The information mainly derives from my fieldwork periods in 2012 (six weeks) and in 2013 (six months), which gave me the opportunity to follow up numerous events and activities, and meet and interview on several occasions dozens of active and non-active, local, and foreign creators and other actors related to the scene. I am greatly in debt to all who shared their time and insights.
4 PROSE a.k.a. Grayshades, interview March 18, 2013.
5 For a more detailed discussion, see Valjakka 2014, 2015b; cf. Valjakka 2011.
6 MAIS, email correspondence, August 23, 2013; JAMS, email correspondence, August 24, 2013; ORSEK, email correspondence, September 16, 2013; *South China Morning Post*, August 1, 2007.
7 For a discussion of the "ancient graffiti" of the Greek and Roman worlds, see Baird & Taylor 2011. The main differentiation of "traditional" and "subway graffiti" was suggested by Stewart 1989, but he also employs further categories, such as "gang," "agnomina," "political," etc.
8 THREE, interview, June 3, 2012.
9 Friendly, one of the founders of *Invasian*, interview, May 21, 2012. Since August 2011, Friendly have been in sole charge of the magazine.
10 LOOMIT, e-mail correspondence, January 23, 2012. See also *Bomber* (1996) 7(11). A window-down silver train, a challenging target to hit, took them about half an hour to complete. "A window-down" is painted below the windows of a train or subway car.
11 SYAN . . . prefers his tag name written with three dots and is known as MC Yan (MC仁) as a musician.
12 SYAN . . ., interview, March 13, 2013.
13 KDG, interview, March 25, 2013.
14 KS, interview, May 6, 2013.
15 ROSA a.k.a. CathLove, interview, March 20, 2013.
16 SYAN . . ., interview, March 13, 2013.
17 KDG, interview, March 25, 2013; Ellen Tang, interview, March 19, 2013. For more information on Warehouse Teenage Club, see their website, http://warehouse.org.hk/en/index.htm.
18 T.W.O. originally included DOFI, TOIK, and ZUCK. At the moment there are six international members. They all live in different countries: DOFI in Asia, CIE in Australia, AZEROX in China, BOSE in the USA, TOIK in Sri Lanka and ZUCK in Denmark. DOFI, interview, March 15, 2013.
19 XEME, interview, May 24, 2013.
20 MICK, interview, May 31, 2013.

21 Uncle, interview, Mar 14, 2013.
22 THREE, interview June 3, 2012. The first cross put up in public space at Hospital Road in December 31, 2002, was still there on March 1, 2013.
23 Dom and Katol, interview, April 18, 2013. See also Lanyon (2013). SFZ also has a clothing brand the products of which were available at their Rat's Cave shop until recently. The closing party of Rat's Cave was held on June 20, 2014.
24 MrM, interview, May 15, 2013.
25 As stated in the beginning, a growing number of creators wish to employ other self-definitions than "graffiti writer," "graffiti artist," or "street artist." "Spray painter" is one of the new identities.
26 4Get About It, interview, June 2, 2012.
27 JAMS, AMSON, and YSOO, interview, March 21, 2013.
28 MAIS, interview, June 17, 2012, email correspondence, June 7, 2014; CEME, interview, May 5, 2013.
29 As an example, the regulations for parks vary, but may forbid gambling, walking on the grass, skate boarding, playing ball, picking flowers, bicycling, walking dogs, feeding birds, sleeping on the bench, hawking, etc.
30 MAIS, interview, June 17, 2012, email correspondence, June 7, 2014.
31 Jay FC, interview, March 14, 2013. See also ST/ART's website: www.start.hk/index.html.
32 Tat and Vi, interview, June 6, 2012; March 21, 2013. See GAL's website, www.graphicairlines.com.
33 Banksy's works were exhibited in the Schoeni Gallery in May 2008, but whether he arrived in Hong Kong was not revealed and/or known by the gallery.
34 Lenticulars are a type of printing that enables the image to change depending on the viewer's perspective.
35 OBSRVR, interview, February 16, 2014.
36 Esther Poon, interview, February 15, 2014. See also Wong (2012).
37 The Martians, interview, March 16, 2013.
38 Two books aim to introduce the history in Chinese: Kuang (2011); Chang and Kao (2012).
39 For more information, see *Invasian's* website, www.invasianmagazine.com.
40 Kat Roma Greer, artistic director, interview, February 14, 2014. See also MicroGalleries' website, www.microgalleries.org. I also personally documented the event in Tai Hang.
41 See HKwalls' website, http://hkwalls.org.
42 Ellen Tang, interview, March 19, 2013.
43 Steve Yuen, interview, March 5, 2013; May Wong, interview, June 24, 2012; Michael Lee and Mini Choi, interview, June 3, 2013.
44 SYAN . . ., interview, January 2014. The first invasion took place in September 2001 with 19 invaders. See Space Invader's website, www.space-invaders.com/hk.html.

References

Baird, J.A. & Taylor, C. (2011). Ancient Graffiti in Context: Introduction. In J.A. Baird & C. Taylor (eds), *Ancient Graffiti in Context* (pp. 1–17). New York & London: Routledge.
Chang, T.K. & Kao, C.L. 張讚國 & 高從霖 (2012). 塗鴉香港: 公共空間, 政治與全球化 [*Graffiti Hong Kong: Public space, politics and globalization*]. Hong Kong: City University of Hong Kong Press.
Chow, V. (2012). King of Kowloon's graffiti to appear in new M+ museum. *South China Morning Post*, September 23, 2012. Available at www.scmp.com/lifestyle/arts-culture/article/1042583/king-kowloons-graffiti-appear-new-m-museum (accessed June 4, 2014).
Chow, V. (2013). King of Kowloon's graffiti art waits for salvation. *South China Morning Post*, January 30, 2013. Available at www.scmp.com/news/hong-kong/article/1138796/king-kowloons-graffiti-art-waits-salvation (accessed June 4, 2014).
Chung, J. (2010). *Kowloon King*. Hong Kong: Asia One.
Clarke, D. (2001). *Hong Kong Art. Culture and Decolonization*. Durham, NC: Duke University Press.
Elkins, J. (1999). *Domain of Images*. Ithaca, NY: Cornell University Press.
HKwalls' Website. (n.d). Available at http://hkwalls.org/ (accessed June 7, 2014).
Ho, O. (2014). The Betrayal of the King. *Artlink*, 34(1), 51–52.
Kuang, Y. (ed.) (2011). 塗鴉 [*Graffiti*]. Hong Kong: 上書局 UpPublications.
Lanyon, C. (2013). From small beginnings. *South China Morning Post*, March 10, 2013. Available at www.scmp.com/lifestyle/arts-culture/article/1186311/small-beginnings (accessed May 30, 2014).

Lau, K.W. (ed.) (1997). *The Street Calligraphy of Tsang Tsou Choi.* Hong Kong: Kin Wai's Workshop.

MicroGalleries' Website, Available at www.microgalleries.org/ (accessed May 30, 2014).

Pearl Channel. (2007). *Great Walls of China.* The Pearl Report. Hong Kong: Pearl Channel of Television Broadcasts.

South China Morning Post. (2007). Graffiti artists spray tribute to the late 'king of Kowloon.' August 1, 2007. Available at www.scmp.com/article/602541/graffiti-artists-spray-tribute-late-king-kowloon (accessed June 3, 2014).

Space Invader's Website. (n.d). Invasion of Hong Kong. Available at www.space-invaders.com/hk.html (accessed May 30, 2014).

Spalding, D. (ed.) (2014). *The King of Kowloon: The Art of Tsang Tsou Choi.* Bologna, Italy: Damiani. Available at www.start.hk/index.html (accessed June 8, 2014).

Stewart, J. (1989). Subway Graffiti. An Aesthetic Study of Graffiti on the Subway System of New York City, 1970–1978. PhD dissertation. New York University.

Tang, E. (ed.) (2011). *From Underground to Community.* Hong Kong: Warehouse Teenage Club.

Valjakka, M. (2011). Graffiti in China – Chinese Graffiti? *The Copenhagen Journal of Asian Studies: Art, Artists and Art Worlds in Asia,* 29(1), 61–91.

Valjakka, M. (2014). Contesting the Levels of Il/legality of Urban Art Images in China. *Review of Culture,* 45, 96–118.

Valjakka, M. (2015a). Urban Art Images and the Concerns of Mainlandization in Hong Kong. In G. Bracken (ed.), *Asian Cities: Colonial to Global* (pp. 95–122). Amsterdam: Amsterdam University Press.

Valjakka, M. (2015b). Negotiating Spatial Politics: Site-responsiveness in Chinese Urban Art Images. *China Information,* special issue on visual arts and urbanization. Guest editors: Meiqin Wang and Minna Valjakka, 29(2), 253–281.

Vigneron, F. (2014). King of Kowloon. In E. Lorenz and S. Li (eds), *Kowloon Cultural District—an Investigation into Spatial Capabilities in Hong Kong* (pp. 301–316). Hong Kong: MCCM Creations.

Warehouse Teenage Club's Website. (n.d.). Available at http://warehouse.org.hk/en/index.htm (accessed June 10, 2014).

Witten, A. & White, M. (2001). *Style Master General: The Life of Graffiti Artist Dondi White.* New York: ReganBooks.

Wong, H. (2012). Hong Kong got 'yarn-bombed.' *CNN Travel,* August 8, 2012. Available at http://travel.cnn.com/hong-kong/life/hong-kong-ladies-market-colorful-yarns-662553 (accessed June 4, 2014).

Part IV

Effects of graffiti and street art[1]

Jeffrey Ian Ross

Introduction

Although a respectable amount of research examines the causal dynamics of graffiti/street art, less scholarship systematically evaluates the reactions (including responses, consequences, and outcomes) to this phenomenon. To help remedy this shortcoming, this section of the *Handbook* incorporates chapters that review how the public, local/municipal politicians, law enforcement, businesses, moral entrepreneurs, and the private sector have responded to graffiti/street art. These responses include legal reactions, enforcement, abatement, removal, and diversion programs (e.g. mural projects).

Also important are the ways that the work of graffiti and street artists has been appropriated and commodified. This would include how cultural industries have integrated graffiti and street artists, imagery, and characters into movies and literary fiction, and how the news and social media depict graffiti and street art.

This section tracks the changing reactions to graffiti/street art, ranging from purely legal reactions to harm-reduction strategies and diversion programs through to more recent re-evaluations of particular graffiti/street art forms in the creative economy. In addition to a discussion of the tensions between legal and illegal graffiti/street art, this section explores a variety of strategies that have been used in the management of graffiti and street art in different international locations. Finally, it considers the ambiguous nature of the legal wall site and the ongoing art versus crime debate.

Overview of chapters

A total of seven chapters makes up this section, which begins with "How major urban centers in the United States respond to graffiti/street art," written by Jeffrey Ian Ross. This chapter examines how, in some larger cities, various actors, such as politicians, moral entrepreneurs, the Departments of Public Works, and Business Improvement Districts, have engaged in an array of abatement efforts. Some of these reactions include crackdowns on graffiti/street artists, while other responses are legalistic in nature, such as anti-graffiti ordinances (e.g. laws that force property owners to clean up after graffiti/street art, bans on the sale of spray paint to minors, etc.) and other methods of abatement. One important aspect of this phenomenon is the militarization of the response to graffiti. Finally, Ross discusses the uncertain effectiveness of these various interlinked responses.

This chapter is followed up by "New York City's moral panic over graffiti: normalizing neoliberal penality and paving the way for growth machines" by Ronald Kramer. This piece reviews the author's long-term research in New York City on the official responses to the graffiti writing culture. Drawing from a variety of documents, such as newspaper articles, political press releases, internal memos, and government reports, Kramer shows that the city's reaction to graffiti constitutes a form of moral panic and that the significance of this response can be understood through theoretical insights developed by urban sociologists. On this basis, Kramer argues that graffiti has become a symbolic and material site of contestation among social groups: Residents, real-estate developers, and public officials have competing conceptions of whose interests the urban environment should address. Conflicts over the meaning of graffiti manifest these social differences.

In "Stealing from the public: the value of street art taken from the street," Peter Bengtsen discusses the generally negative market reception of removed street artworks, and emphasizes the importance given by the market to the wishes of the artists, who often will not authenticate removed artworks. Cases where such artworks have been authenticated by artists and subsequently have sold underscore the importance of artists openly acknowledging a removed object as their work. The chapter argues that such an acknowledgement confirms not only that an artist has created the initial street artwork but also that it should be considered a work of art after the removal from its original site.

Although the market status of removed street artworks is currently largely reliant on statements from the respective artist, there is a continued effort to take down, restore and preserve artworks. The willingness to cover the great costs incurred from this practice suggest an expectation that more artists will eventually come to acknowledge the removed artworks as part of their oeuvre or that the emphasis now put on their statements will diminish in favor of other types of provenance. Further, the chapter points out the possible long-term benefits of preserving a certain number of street artworks and making sure that they become available to the public. However, it also acknowledges that removal entails a significant trade-off, as the original context often significantly adds meaning to the artwork.

In "How American movies depict graffiti and street art," Jeffrey Ian Ross analyzes both documentary and commercial films that depict, in whole or in part, graffiti/street art in terms of the actors and motifs used. He finds that there are a number of recurrent themes that perpetuate the myths connected to this subculture, including absentee parents (especially fathers), and the predominance of lower class and racial/ethnic perpetrators. Rarely do the movies move away from stereotypes and challenge their viewers to understand the range of individuals who engage in graffiti and street art.

In "Challenging the defense of graffiti, in defense of graffiti," Stefano Bloch examines some of the negative reactions to graffiti, specifically the ones that qualify as forms of moral panic and vigilantism, and explores some of the common defenses that speak to graffiti as an art form in need of sanctioned space. Relying on his personal experiences as a former Los Angeles-based graffiti writer and tapping into the social science literature that addresses what Bloch calls "stylized and systematic urban graffiti in the U.S. context," He touches on the contradictions inherent in interpretations of graffiti as vandalism. Unlike systematic criminalization, informal reactions to graffiti point to its power as both an effective aesthetic disruption and an affective act of defiance worthy of sometimes aggressive responses. Whereas legal criminalization targets a specific criminal act (i.e. vandalism) in a codified and proscribed way, moral panic, and vigilantism, like the production of graffiti itself, illustrate people's willingness to operate outside the confines of the State in an effort to exact innovative forms of justice, power, and socio-spatial order.

As graffiti/street art have gained in popularity and become a recognized commodity, a number of contextual arguments regarding their protection have been raised. Some scholars have focused on the protections available to private property owners, who are victimized by graffiti while being required by municipal ordinances to remove it, but who may wish to retain the art work under the free speech guarantees of the U.S. Constitution (Mettler, 2012). Alternatively, in "Does copyright law protect graffiti and street art?" Dan Schwender reviews the rights offered to artists under the copyright laws of the U.S. and discusses the laws' limitations regarding graffiti. The U.S. Copyright Act grants a bundle of limited, exclusive rights to original works of art fixed in a tangible medium. Its application to graffiti remains complex, in part, due to the varying definitions of "graffiti," which often include simple tags or short words and phrases that may not be protected. In addition, many works of graffiti/street art contain the work of other artists, such as a stencil of another's photograph, which may infringe on another's copyright, absent a finding of "fair use." Further, although the U.S. Copyright Act does not mention legality of creation as a precondition, the courts have not fully considered whether copyright covers art created by illegal conduct, and such recognition could create difficult property right issues, such as the prevention of a property owner from removing or altering a work from his property. Finally, graffiti artists would risk criminal and civil prosecution should they shed their anonymity by claiming copyright infringement. In short, the application of copyright law to illegal graffiti remains ambiguous and difficult.

Finally, Maia Morgan Wells' chapter, "Graffiti, street art, and the evolution of the art market," argues that graffiti's uncertain romance with the gallery world is nothing new. Almost from the very beginning of the modern graffiti subculture, the art world – at least at its margins – has taken notice. From the Razor Gallery show in 1972 to Patti Astor's Fun Gallery to the Times Square Show and Fashion Moda in the South Bronx, the gallery scene recognized this powerful new style almost upon inception, but it has taken over forty years for the genre to crystalize into the fine art phenomenon it is today. This essay focuses on the fault line between art and vandalism, exploring the nuances of the graffiti art world's canonization through a brief review of recent social science literature on the topic. From criminology to sociology of culture to urban studies, there is a wide body of work on graffiti as art. However, as this chapter argues, the extant literature leaves room for more depth of engagement concerning the complicated ways in which art worlds and graffiti relate to one another

Omissions

Although the chapters included in this section provide a respectable introduction to the effects of graffiti/street art, it would be useful to understand the *various businesses that have been established to make money from the offering of graffiti removal and remediation services* to municipalities and businesses. Alternatively, another related topic pertains to the subject of *how graffiti and street art is taught to students in different settings* (i.e. art colleges and universities), including both art and academic kinds of classes. These other topics might give us a fuller understanding of the effects of graffiti/street art.

Note

1   Special thanks to Stefano Bloch, Rachel Hildebrandt and Ronald Kramer for their comments.

Jeffrey Ian Ross

References

Mettler, M.L. (2012). Graffiti Museum: A First Amendment Argument for Protecting Uncommissioned Art on Private Property, *Michigan Law Review, 111*(2), 249–281.

29

How major urban centers in the United States respond to graffiti/street art[1]

Jeffrey Ian Ross

Introduction

Since the widespread emergence of graffiti/street art in the early 1980s, most municipalities in the United States have been forced to respond to this phenomenon. Although a considerable amount of graffiti falls into the category of tags that do not require a considerable amount of skill to create, increasingly there are other types of graffiti/street art, including throwies (i.e. throwups), pieces (i.e. masterpieces), and a variety of street art forms, that occupy large open and visible spaces in the urban community, and that require the artists to expend considerable resources in their creation.[2]

The majority of the graffiti/street art that appears in cities is placed on buses, subways, retail establishments, residences, walls, doors, lampposts, signage, retaining walls, bridges, and overpasses. Almost every type of surface imaginable (e.g. brick, concrete, glass, wood, plastic, and metal) can be the site of graffiti/street art.

Graffiti/street art elicit varying responses from both the artists/writers and the neighborhoods and cities in which the works appear.[3] These reactions differ widely and are sometimes contradictory (Gomez, 1993). Many politicians, members of the news media, and moral entrepreneurs, using a "broken windows" rationale (Wilson & Kelling, 1982; Ferrell, 1995; Halsey & Young, 2002), for example, argue that graffiti/street art may lead to other kinds of deviant and criminal activity, including the presence of street gangs. This argument suggests that neighborhoods and cities that experience graffiti/street art undergo a decline in the use of public transportation systems, a loss of retail sales, and a decrease in property values (Weisel, 2004). On the other hand, graffiti/street art may help bring color to an otherwise drab or austere part of a city, and therefore be perceived as a positive factor in the branding of that neighborhood with a sense of cultural uniqueness, which might even promote tourism (Ferro, 2014). Alternatively graffiti/street art and other kinds of public art have been perceived as an asset to the so-called creative cities movement, a perspective that by extension challenges previously held notions of graffiti/street art as deviant behavior (Zukin & Braslow, 2011; McAuliffe, 2012).

According to Taylor and Marais (2009),

> In addition to the countless hours and funds spent on removing tags, throw-ups, and pieces, considerable resources are also spent on a plethora of ad hoc reactive and proactive graffiti prevention measures. However, many of these measures have been adopted without a credible body of empirical evidence to either support or negate their effectiveness. In some instances, the initiators of these reactive and proactive measures draw support for their use from an associate body of literature pertaining to the prevention of other aspects of youth anti-social/criminal behaviour.
>
> (p. 59)

Regardless, the sums of money spent by municipalities on abatement are considerable. Although there is no single database or source that tracks the dollar value spent by cities, counties, or other governmental units, periodic newspaper reports have mentioned different, yet staggering amounts. One recent report places the amount that municipalities in the United States have spent on clean-up activities at $12 billion (Silver, 2013). More importantly, graffiti/street art has led to a number of challenges to the controlling, managing, abating, and removing of graffiti/street art. At the base of these efforts are numerous constituencies and methods, both proposed and implemented.

Before continuing, one must distinguish among important relevant terms and processes: abatement, removal, and deterrence. First, abatement concerns a multiplicity of activities designed to prevent, reduce, and remove graffiti/street art. Second, removal, on the other hand, is the attempt to eradicate graffiti/street art though power washing, sandblasting, scraping, chemical peel, or some other similar technique. Third, deterrence refers to legal methods designed to increase the costs to perpetrators of engaging in graffiti/street art, in the hopes of preventing individuals from participating in this activity again. It is also understood that,

> [m]ost current methods aimed at fighting graffiti vandalism are ineffective and demonstrate that it is time for a change in both law and policy. In response to the problem, cities and states have enacted legislation and adopted policies designed to prevent the purposeful destruction of property.
>
> (Gomez, 1993: p. 657)

She adds, "Many of these policies and laws, however, fail to reduce vandalism because they fail to address, and in fact often purposefully ignore, the reasons behind graffiti vandalism" (p. 657).

The unique challenges of responding to graffiti/street art for municipalities

Introduction

For politicians, Departments of Public Works, Business Improvement Districts, home and business owners, and community activists, not to mention law enforcement agencies, graffiti and street art pose a number of challenges. Rarely do cities utilize experts to develop a comprehensive response plan to graffiti/street art, one that is "inclusive, balanced, informed, and equitable" (Young, 2010: p. 101). Also less frequent are solutions that incorporate ideas from perpetrators about controlling graffiti (e.g. Brewer, 1992). Even if this does happen, as Young mentions, the hard work and rationales that go into crafting a draft abatement strategy (e.g. Melbourne,

Australia) might be ignored (or selectively utilized) by a city council when it determines unilaterally, or sometimes with encouragement from law enforcement and state governments, that the approach articulated in an inclusive strategy is too radical. In light of this complicated framework, this chapter reviews the most common difficulties encountered in responding to graffiti/street art.

Appreciating nuance

When responding to graffiti/street art, constituencies need to understand that each city has a slightly different graffiti/street culture. In Washington, D.C., for example, some of this culture has been celebrated in movies (e.g. *The Red Line, The legend of Cool "Disco" Dan*),[4] in books on local graffiti (Gastman, 2001), and in exhibitions in private and public galleries (Corcoran Gallery, Fall 2013 event). Moreover, certain local personalities can have an effect on framing the discussion. Roger Gastman, one of the most well-known graffiti impresarios in the country, originally from Bethesda, MD, (adjacent to Washington, D.C.) native, has had an effect on the growth and interpretation of graffiti in the District. One cannot ignore this legacy. More specifically, one must understand this legacy and respect it in order to manage its production (http://redlinedc.wordpress.com/).

It is also important to understand that in Washington, as in other large urban centers, graffiti/ street art is not simply limited to one neighborhood. A considerable amount of this activity can be found around 14th Street, U Street, Union Market, Georgetown, and in selected portions of the Metro's red line (especially between Fort Totten and Silver Spring, MD). Each of these neighborhoods has its own norms that must be considered in abatement attempts.

Managing different constituencies

One of the numerous problems that municipalities have faced is the managing of the different constituencies that are interested in graffiti/street art abatement. This group includes but is not limited to the residents who complain about the shade of the paint that the BID uses to cover over existing graffiti, private volunteer groups (such as environmental and community activists, and historical preservationists), politicians, employees, and managers for the DPWs and BIDs, and vigilantes who might harass and/or physically attack graffiti writers/street artists, or engage in abatement efforts themselves.

As previously mentioned, sometimes the news media (from the editorial staff to columnists) and community groups are worried that graffiti/street art is gang-related. This raises the possibility of a moral panic (e.g. Garland, 2008). When elites or agents of social control connect graffiti to gangs, this connection is often used to demonize graffiti/street art and the people who engage in this activity, not to mention art school students and teenagers whose outward appearances may make them look like they are part of this demonized subculture. As a result, unnecessary profiling and increased stop-and-frisk encounters may increase. According to Ferrell (2013),

> In both public pronouncements and day-to-day street policing, such campaigns have regularly conflated the various forms of graffiti under the general heading of gang activity and dangerous youth crime, in part as justification for more aggressive legal penalties for graffiti writing. As a result, public perceptions of graffiti have in many cases hardened, and arrests and convictions for graffiti writing have multiplied.

(p. 181)

Historical properties

In terms of the sites of graffiti/street art, numerous historical properties must be properly protected from potentially invasive or destructive abatement practices. For example, sometimes brown brick surfaces are chosen for graffiti, and the nature of this material makes removal difficult. The DPW and BID authorities, as well as private contractors, need to take into consideration that each type of surface must be treated individually. Occassionally the DPW, BID, and/or their subcontractors have painted over or used invasive solvents on graffiti laden walls that were historically significant, and that has resulted in the further and irrevocable destruction of the surface being freed of graffiti. These errors clearly indicate the necessity for them to co-ordinate with multiple political actors.

Gomez (1993) distinguishes four primary approaches that governments have used to "combat" graffiti: including "criminal prosecution and penalties," civil remedies directed against writers, actions used for their parents, and "prophylactic measures" (pp. 656–696). McAuliffe (2012), on the other hand, suggests that enforcement, removal, and engagement are the dominant responses by cities in their attempts to deal with graffiti. The first two reactions require coordination with municipal agencies including the police and DPWs, whereas the last involves the participation of the graffiti/street artists.

Costs

All alternatives are bounded by costs. Not all expenditures for graffiti/street art removal can be passed on to the perpetrators, their parents, or the targets of the graffiti/street art (Gomez, 1993). For example, some municipalities have decided to charge a tax on the sale of spray paint to defray the cost of abatement; however, not even an economic measure like this one can sufficiently deal with the removal of graffiti (ibid.).

Options/Solutions

Municipalities have at their disposal a wide range of responses and techniques, ranging from what might be called hard to soft reactions to address graffiti/street art. Many of these strategies, sometimes collectively subsumed under the label of "war against graffiti," often have unintended consequences that serve to either infuriate graffiti/street art practitioners and/or to increase the production of graffiti/street art. Some of the responses to graffiti/street art are diversion programs, while others are sanctions and/or ordinances. The reactions reviewed below are rank-ordered from least to most frequent in terms of their approximate use or frequency of occurrence.

Increasing meaningful youth programs

Some scholars (e.g. Gomez, 1993) have argued that if cities implement programs that engage youths, these will provide an alternative and creative outlet for them, minimizing gang activity and, in turn, graffiti. Unfortunately, not only do many of these initiatives conflate gangs with graffiti, but this proposition has not been tested in a systematic fashion in the graffiti/street art realm. Most of the evidence upon which these statements are drawn is from newspaper articles and not from rigorously conducted research. These programs and activities could equally provide a place for youth to meet and improve their artistic skills.

Vigilante actions

Not only are numerous private citizens (and the groups they do or may claim to represent) vocal regarding their displeasure of graffiti/street art, but some believe that they have the authority to take aggressive action against graffiti/street art in their communities and/or against the individuals who engage in this activity. These citizens do this by painting over instances of graffiti/street art, scraping it off surfaces, or intimidating and/or attacking the artists. In most cases, the private citizens think that the police, and the DPWs and BIDs are not doing a proper job at graffiti/street art abatement. The so-called "shadow buffers" – people who in the early hours of the morning use a scraping tool, a roller, or a spray can to cover up the graffiti/street art that has been placed at night – have become iconic figures in many municipalities. However, despite their efforts, they often fail to remove the stickers and posters on the wall surfaces, and simply paint over them. The entire process often results in a surface that looks less appealing.

One of the most well-known portrayals of the buffer culture is the documentary movie, *Vigilante Vigilante* (2010). The filmmaker depicted the activities of three prominent American buffers, including Jim Sharpe in Berkeley, CA, Fred Radtke in New Orleans, LA, and the infamous Jim Connolly in Los Angeles, CA. Given the long-term connection between tagging and gang activity, during the 1990s, graffiti artists/writers have also been attacked by gangbangers in selected locations. In Los Angeles and other cities, for example, graffiti artists have even been shot by citizens (Carrillo, 1995; Riccardi & Tamaki, 1995; see Bloch, this book).

Legal walls and murals

Many municipalities recognize that they cannot totally eradicate graffiti/street art. As an alternative, they have occasionally adopted a strategy where designated groups can manage the graffiti/street art activities, channeling them to locations where the artistic works might be seen as less of an eyesore and be more appealing to the different constituencies (e.g. Gomez, 1993; Kramer, 2010). Typically these spaces are protected locations managed by a city's public art department or an arts foundation. Former graffiti artists and/or arts professionals may even teach painting skills to youth. In order to be successful, these programs need to be implemented in a professional, systematic, and non-haphazard manner, promoted through proper advertising channels, especially social media. In short, these programs need to be credible (Craw *et al.* 2006). Legally sanctioned graffiti walls may be successful at deterring some graffiti and street artists from painting over the already-existing artwork. On the other hand, it may also serve as a location for other artists to paint over the existing work.[5]

Yet another alternative approach involves municipalities, DPWs, BIDs, and/or private businesses installing removable panels at or near locations that are frequently targeted. Also at construction sites, in order to minimize graffiti or the posting of bills on street dividers/partitions, the owners of these properties occasionally identify and clearly mark sections where graffiti is sanctioned. With proper incentives (e.g. awards/prizes based on creativeness, convened by mutually agreed-upon experts), graffiti and street artists can be encouraged to use these spaces to place their work. The panels might be removed at some point in time, and then displayed in other places, such as public or private galleries, or even auctioned off for charity. As these examples reveal, graffiti/street art should be an integrated part of the total public art strategy for a neighborhood.

Despite the seemingly positive impact of these kinds of practices, the limited scholarly research on this topic is less than heartening. Two studies from Western Australia question the effectiveness of these approaches. Craw *et al.* (2006) argue that although the establishment of legal walls minimizes graffiti in nearby locations, they do not completely eradicate it. Similarly Taylor and Marais (2009) suggest that sanctioned murals do not help minimize the existence of graffiti. Both studies do indicate, however, that legal walls reduce graffiti in the short term.

Advertising/anti-graffiti campaigns

Many municipalities have engaged in anti-graffiti advertising campaigns. In New York City, for instance, during the early 1970s, famed boxers Hector Comancho and Alex Ramos, baseball player Dave Winefield, and singer-songwriter and actress Irene Cara spread the perspective that doing graffiti was bad (Chronopolous, 2013: p. 113). This public-service program, called "Make your mark in society, not on society," featured billboards, subway advertising, and spots on television using images of and anti-graffiti quotes from the previously mentioned spokespersons. Similarly, in 1997, the City of Los Angeles distributed a children's coloring book titled *Kyle the Graffiti Fighting Bear*. Some of this advertising was planned in conjunction with tip lines, where members of the community could call a dedicated number to report graffiti in their neighborhood and any possible suspects. These programs sometimes offered a reward if a tip led to the successful prosecution of perpetrators (Schwada & Sahagun, 1992).

Covering extant graffiti/street art

Property owners, DPWs, and BIDs frequently paint over graffiti/street art. Numerous alternative methods have been used, ranging from "soap and water, to sandblasting, to chemical solvents, to lasers" (Gomez, 1993: p. 685). "The majority of these removal costs are spent removing tags" (Taylor & Marais, 2009: p. 58). Even when private contractors are hired, there is no guarantee that the work will be done properly and/or in a systematic fashion. Most BIDs deploy teams of individuals who, in addition to their duties of trash removal, snow removal, and leaf cleanup, paint over graffiti and, if possible, scrape off sticker art and posters.

In some communities, there is a perception that the failure to remove hate-related graffiti/street art will increase violence directed towards the group that is attacked (See Martin, this book). Sometimes abatement and removal is done by paid professionals, and at other times, there are volunteers who assist in this process (Tavares, 2014). DPWs and private contractors are often part of the clean-up process as well. According to Gomez (1993), another method of defraying costs is to develop various programs, such as the California Department of Transportation's Adopt-A-Wall program:

> Under this program, the Department encourages individuals to pick up the expenses of cleaning up walls along transportation routes, such as highways. Some cities and towns have sought to collect clean-up money either through imposing taxes on the sale of spray paint and markers or through tax donations.
>
> (pp. 687–688)

Hardening targets

One of the most common reactions to graffiti/street is for business owners and municipalities to "harden the targets." This can include the installation of physical security or increased human security. To begin with, as one of the multiple responses to the increase in graffiti/street art, barbed wire, razor, Constantine, and concertina ribbon fences are often installed where they did not already exist. Other measures include double fences with guard/attack dogs, if permissible, and the use of or an increase in security patrols to minimize the attacks by graffiti crews. Sometimes even surveillance cameras are installed. Most cities now have the ubiquitous barbed/razor wire zones surrounding their subway tracks and yards, and bus garages (Iveson, 2010). Municipalities may also use graffiti-resistant material in the construction of various surfaces, making them easier to clean and/or remove graffiti.

Target hardening against graffiti has had a long and colorful history. New York City's efforts have been chronicled by a handful of scholars and bear repeating.19

> The first anti-graffiti alliance (1971–1973) organized by the then-mayor of New York John Lindsay, was unsuccessful. The second attempt at the 'war on graffiti' (1980–1983) led by Mayor Edward Koch, however, resulted in a mass transposition of graffiti from subway trains to city walls.
>
> (Wacławek, 2011: p. 50)[6]

According to Wacławek, "The city's first attempt to eliminate subway graffiti failed primarily because the initial plan focused on repainting graffiti laden trains. This solution backfired for two important reasons" (p. 50). To begin with,

> repainting the trains provided graffiti writers with fresh canvases, thus creating new spaces on which they could paint. As writers painted these surfaces, the scale of their works increased dramatically. The culture's visual and social history had been erased, encouraging new attempts at fame and new competition for [status].
>
> (Wacławek, 2011: p. 50)

Second, . . . the task of removing graffiti was often imposed as a sentence on convicted writers. The idea that "buffing" or chemically removing graffiti could work as a punishment for writers was misplaced: instead of teaching young people a lesson, this clean-up sentence proved to be an excellent opportunity for graffiti writers to meet others from all over the city and make plans to paint together.

> (Wacławek, 2011: pp. 52, 54)

Given these dismal results, Koch and his administration tried to "implement a successful 'clean car programme,' which committed subway staff to clean the trains after each run" (Wacławek, 2011: p. 54). This was supplemented by installing two rows of fences around subway train depots, along with using guard dogs to protect the trains. Community leaders and citizens who talked to the news media about the "scourge" of graffiti on the trains further shored this approach. This strategy

> proved successful, making the second major attempt at getting rid of graffiti one that forever changed the writing culture in New York. The tactics used – guard dogs, video surveillance, a task force and razor fences – worked to deter writers from trains and back onto city walls.
>
> (Wacławek, 2011: p. 54)

Eventually, the MTA purchased new subway cars that had stainless steel and/or Teflon interiors, and exteriors from which it was easier to remove spray paint. Unfortunately, some of the chemicals that were applied to the graffiti slowly ate away at the surfaces of the trains, and the MTA was forced to replace many car windows.

Jeffrey Ian Ross

Increased patrols and surveillance

One of the typical responses to graffiti/street art is increased patrols and surveillance by both private security and local law enforcement and transit police, sometimes in coordination with citizen volunteers (Rainey, 1993; Rivera, 2008). These strategies, however, are resource-intensive responses. Even if a facility or location uses surveillance cameras, if a person or crew suspected of engaging in graffiti/street art is detected, then someone is ultimately required to respond to the situation, and if the response takes too long, the perpetrator/s will have fled. When the police are called, there is often a delayed response time, as most municipal police consider graffiti/street art to be a low-level/less serious enforcement action (Ross & Wright, 2014). Nonetheless, some municipalities have created specialized police task forces designed to respond to graffiti (Gomez, 1993; Iveson, 2010). In addition to closed circuit television (CCTV), which provides visual information to those who are monitoring the camera, some municipalities have explored the use of motion, audio, and vapor detection systems (that have been adopted from the military). These alert security officers and/or police when someone is engaging in graffiti/street art on monitored properties (Iverson, p. 120). These practices may be supplemented by vandalism hotline programs that provide financial rewards to citizens who report on individuals who engage this kind of activity (Schwada & Sahagun, 1992; Rainey, 1993).

Laws/ordinances/criminal penalties

According to Gomez (1993), "many cities first have sought to encourage more arrests and prosecutions of vandalism under criminal mischief, malicious mischief, intentional destruction of property, or criminal trespass statutes" (pp. 657–658). Convictions usually are accompanied by sanctions such as fines, jail sentences, community service, mandatory education classes, drivers' license suspensions, or delays in license application deadlines. Gomez (1993) argues, as do others, that these measures do not work (pp. 666–670).

Not only have criminal law remedies been applied to graffiti writers, but so too have civil remedies, including but not limited to civil trespassing and nuisance charges (Gomez, 1993: pp. 670–672). Another common part of the repertoire of responses has been involving the parents of the perpetrators through parental fines or setting in place "education, counseling, and cleanup" requirements (Gomez, 1993: p. 673).

Traditionally because of overcrowded dockets and because of perceptions among criminal justice practitioners that graffiti/street art is not a serious infraction (e.g. Gomez, 1993: p. 659; Ross & Wright, 2014), charges of this nature rarely come to court. "Convictions on graffiti-related charges are rare and sentences, if given at all, are short. Contributing to this effect is the fact that most writers are young and are tried as juveniles" (Gomez, 1993: pp. 659–660).

Some municipalities have introduced ordinances directed toward banning the sale and possession of graffiti-related materials. In many jurisdictions, it is illegal for retailers to sell spray paint to individuals less than eighteen years of age (Gomez, 1993; Gee, 2013). Alternatively, select cities have placed bans on the sales of felt tip markers over a particular size. In some instances, signs (similar to those which are used in the sale of alcohol) are posted to indicate that spray paint cannot be sold to people under a certain age and that these materials are to be carefully stored in retail establishments. Legislators believe that these procedures will minimize the theft of spray paint. Also, some jurisdictions have made it a misdemeanor to be in possession of "graffiti tools."

Despite their good intentions, these measures have had a minimal deterrent effect. Why? Graffiti writers are more likely to steal their materials from somewhere, than to buy them legally.

Other writers will simply resort to using other materials. Problems with respect to enforcement also plague this strategy. In terms of the age-related bans, just as with alcohol purchases, writers can often convince adults to purchase the materials for them.

Conclusion

This chapter has attempted to provide a comprehensive rendering of the range of efforts that municipalities and their citizens engage in when experiencing or contending with graffiti/street art. As in any kind of analysis, legislators, policy makers and practitioners must be cognizant of the unintended consequences of their responses, which are bounded by the perceptions of the seriousness of the problem and the various constituencies involved. The response is also predicated on the resources that the entities have at their disposal. If they have sufficient resources, then there are more options how they can deal with illegal graffiti/street art.

According to Tavares (2014), "Unfortunately, graffiti removal programs tend to be among the first to experience budget cuts in the wake of financial crisis" (p. 60). In her evaluation of graffiti removal programs in California cities, Tavares points out that by "practicing cost-savings strategies, staff is eliminated and positions are contracted out" (p. 60).

Unfortunately, no analytical studies exist that examine the relative effectiveness of these processes. In fact, it has been argued elsewhere that most of these measures have been of minimal deterrence value (Gomez, 1993). In general, the "war" against graffiti/street art is unwinnable. At the very least, municipalities can control discrete aspects of these activities and minimize their flow. However, they cannot completely eliminate or eradicate graffiti/street art, regardless of the extent of their efforts.

Notes

1   Special thanks to Stefano Bloch, Rachel Hildebrandt, and Ronald Kramer for their comments and Christopher Brees-Rostveit for research assistance.
2   Although important, this chapter does not review attempts to commodify graffiti and street art through its use in fashion, galleries, and museums.
3   Although important, this chapter does not review the system of self-policing among graffiti artists/writers. For a discussion of this see, for example, Docuyanan (2000).
4   For a review of *The Red Line*, see, for example, Rudansky (2013).
5   For a review of a legal wall in Adelaide, Australia, see for example, Halsey & Pederick (2010).
6   Alternative renderings of this story have been presented by Austin (2001) and Castleman (2011), among others.

References

Austin, J. (2001). *Taking the Train: How Graffiti Art Became an Urban Crisis in New York City*. New York: Columbia University Press.
Barnard, L. (2006). Graffiti abatement and management, *Law & Order, 54*(5), 115–117.
Brewer, D.D. (1992). Hip-hop graffiti writers' evaluations of strategies to control illegal graffiti, *Human Organization, 51*(2), 188–196.
Carrillo, L.A. (1995). Perspectives on the tagger shooting: How to kill a Latino kid and walk free. *Los Angeles Times*, November 27. http://articles.latimes.com/1995–11–27/local/me-7721_1_affirmative-action (downloaded May 1, 2015).
Carter, P. (2007). Pubica space: Its mythopoetic foundations and the limits of the law, *Griffith Law Review, 16*(2), 430–443.
Castleman, C. (2011). The politics of graffiti, in M. Forman & M.A. Neal (eds) *That's the Joint: The Hip Hop Studies Reader*. (pp. 13–22, 21–29) (2nd edn). New York: Routledge.

Jeffrey Ian Ross

Chronopolous, T. (2013). *Spatial Regulation in New York City: From Urban Renewal to Zero Tolerance*. New York: Routledge.

Craw, P.J., Leland, L.S., Bussell, M.G., Munday, S.J. & Walsh, K. (2006). The mural as graffiti deterrence, *Environment and Behavior, 38*(3), 422–434.

Dickinson, M. (2008). The making of space, race and place: New York City's war on graffiti, 1970-the present, *Critique of Anthropology, 28*(1), 27–45.

Docuyanan, F. (2000). Governing graffiti in contested urban spaces, *PoLAR: Political and Legal Anthropology Review, 23*(1), 103–121.

Ferrell, J. (1995). Urban graffiti: Crime, control and resistance, *Youth & Society, 27*(1), 73–92.

Ferrell, J. (2013). Graffiti, in J.I. Ross (ed.) *Encyclopedia of Street Crime in America*. (pp. 180–182). Thousand Oaks, CA: Sage Publications.

Ferro, S. (2014). Can graffiti be good for cities? *Fast Company*, January 20, 2014. (downloaded November 1, 2014).

Garland, D. (2008). On the concept of moral panic, *Crime, Media, Culture, 4*(1), 9–30.

Gastman, R. (2001). *Free Agents: A History of Graffiti in Washington, DC*. Berkeley, CA: R. Rock Enterprises and Soft Skull Press.

Gee, E. (2013). City walls can speak: The street art movement and graffiti's place in first amendment jurisprudence, *Effrey S. Moorad Sports Law Journal, 20*(1), 209–246.

Geason, S. & Wilson, P.R. (1990). *Preventing Graffiti and Vandalism*. Canberra, Australia: Australian Institute of Criminology.

Gomez, M.A. (1993). Writing on our walls: Finding solutions through distinguishing graffiti art from graffiti vandalism, *University of Michigan Journal of Law Reform, 26*(3), 633–707.

Halsey, M. & Pederick, B. (2010). The game of fame: Mural, graffiti, erasure, *City, 14*(1–2), 82–98.

Halsey, M. & Young, A. (2002). The meanings of graffiti and municipal administration, *Australian & New Zealand Journal of Criminology, 35*(2), 165–186.

Iveson, K. (2010). The wars on graffiti and the new military urbanism, *City: Analysis of Urban Trends, Culture, Theory Policy Action, 14*(4), 115–134.

Kan, K.H. (2001). Adolescents and graffiti, *Art Education, 54*(1), 18–23.

Kramer, R. (2010). Painting with permission: Legal graffiti in New York City. *Ethnography, 11*(2), 235–253.

McAuliffe, C. (2012). Graffiti or street art? Negotiating the moral geographies of the creative city, *Journal of Urban Affairs, 34*(2), 189–206.

Rainey, J. (1993). Surveillance teams to help fight graffiti, *Los Angeles Times*, 112, p. Al, June 2.

Riccardi, N. & Tamaki, J. (1995). Praise and insults for man who killed tagger. *Los Angeles Times*, February 4.

Rivera, J. (2008). *Vandal Squad: Inside the New York City Transit Police Department, 1984–2004*. New York: Powerhouse Books.

Ross, J.I. & Wright, B. (2014). I've got better things to worry about. Police perceptions of graffiti and street art in a large mid-Atlantic City, *Police Quarterly, 17*(2), 176–200.

Rudansky, A.K. (2013). Red line documentary takes deeper look at graffiti along the tracks in Northeast Washington. *Washington Post*, www.washingtonpost.com/local/trafficandcommuting/red-line-docu mentary-looks-behind-graffiti-along-the-tracks-in-northeast-washington/2013/03/09/d8fea62e-8805-11e2-98a3-b3db6b9ac586_story.html

Schwada, J. & Sahagun, L. (1992). Graffiti reward program nearly out of money. *Los Angeles Times*, 111, p. B3, August 11.

Silver, M.R. (2013). How cities can remove and deter graffiti and maximize cost recovery, *Western City, 89*, 11.

Snyder, G.J. (2006). Graffiti media and the perpetuation of an illegal subculture, *Crime, Media Culture, 2*(1), 93–101.

Tavares, S.S. (2014). California Graffiti Removal Programs: Benchmarking San José's Graffiti Abatement Program Against Best Practices in the Cities of Long Beach, San Diego, and Santa Ana. Master's Thesis. San Jose State University, CA.

Taylor, M. & Marais, I. (2009). Does Urban Art Deter Graffiti Proliferation? In *Urban Art and Graffiti Papers from the British Criminology Conference 9*, pp. 57–70.

Wacławek, A. (2011). *Graffiti and Street Art*. London: Thames & Hudson.

Weisel, D.L. (2004). Problem oriented guides for police; problem-specific guides series no. 9, Graffiti.

Wilson, J.Q. & Kelling, G. (1982). The police and neighborhood safety: Broken windows. *Atlantic Monthly*, March, 29–38.

Young, A. (2010). Negotiated consent or zero tolerance? Responding to graffiti and street art in Melbourne, *City, 14*(1–2), 99–114.

Young, A. (2012). Criminal images: The affective judgment of graffiti and street art, *Crime, Media, Culture, 8*(3), 297–314.

Zukin, S. & Braslow, L. (2011). The life cycle of New York's creative districts: Reflections on the unanticipated consequences of unplanned cultural zones, *City, Culture and Society, 2*(3), 131–140.

30

New York City's moral panic over graffiti

Normalizing neoliberal penality and paving the way for growth machines[1]

Ronald Kramer

Introduction

For the last forty years or so, political elites in New York City have been creating an image of graffiti writing (and street art) as a monolithic destructive force, one that invariably wreaks havoc upon the city's cultural, economic, political, and social wellbeing. Throughout the 1970s and 1980s, insofar as graffiti was overwhelmingly produced in an illegal manner, it is perhaps not surprising that this perspective gained currency. However, since the 1990s, a period in which graffiti writing culture increasingly sought legal avenues of expression and social acceptance, such an image is radically losing (or at least should be) whatever plausibility it was able to take for granted in the past. That the official discourse concerning graffiti is so out of step with historical trends suggests that political leaders are not interested in understanding writing culture, but in continuing to fuel a moral panic.

Stanley Cohen (1972) initially traced the idea of moral panic through an analysis of how powerful social actors, such as the mass media and agencies of social control, reacted to the "mods" and the "rockers," two British subcultures of the 1960s. Subsequently, Hall *et al.* (1978; 1976) and Goode and Ben-Yehuda (1994) offered accounts that were pitched at a more abstract, theoretical level. Despite their differences, these approaches all seem to agree that moral panics consist of discursive practices that profoundly misrepresent some kind of behavior, and that such negative portrayals pave the way for disproportionate responses. As is implied by these remarks, moral panics are usually steered by relatively powerful groups and are directed against those who occupy marginalized social locations.

Although there may be agreement on how to recognize a panic when it occurs, there is less agreement on what motivates powerful social groups to over-react to relatively inconsequential behaviors. According to Erikson (1966), for example, panics are motivated by the need to maintain social solidarity, but for Hall *et al.* (1978), panics are driven by the need to divert attention away from the crises of capitalism. Goode and Ben-Yehuda (1994) argue that various social groups may fan panics for a wide array of reasons.

In this chapter, I demonstrate that the official reaction to graffiti in New York City throughout the 1990s and into the twenty-first century is best understood as a moral panic. Following this, I suggest that particular economic and political interests currently drive powerful elites to over-react to graffiti. To explore these themes, I rely on an analysis of approximately 3,000 pages of documents consisting of newspaper articles from the *New York Times* and *Daily News*, and press releases, political memos, and archived material from the administrations of Mayor Giuliani and Mayor Bloomberg.

As neoliberalism ushered in growing economic inequalities, problems such as homelessness, unemployment, and underemployment became entrenched. In the United States and elsewhere, the state has responded to those who are more or less excluded from the economy in an extremely punitive manner (Wacquant 2009; Pratt & Eriksson 2013). In this context, I believe that graffiti operated as "gateway penality." That is, it provided an easy target that political elites could isolate and disparage in order to normalize punitive responses to the social problems that accompany neoliberal governance.

I also argue that, at the urban level, anti-graffiti rhetoric and practice currently serves the interests of landed capitalists, or what Logan and Molotch (1987) refer to as "growth machines." At the expense of using land to satisfy basic needs, growth machines ultimately seek to extract the maximum profit possible from how space is put to use. Particular strategies here include enticing corporations to locate their headquarters in the city, gentrifying neighborhoods and transforming the urban environment into a hospitable tourist destination for privileged social classes. As their discourse makes clear, political elites understand graffiti as a practice that threatens such interests and, as such, must be eradicated from the city.

"Folk devils" caught in a "spiral of signification"

According to Cohen (1972) and Hall *et al.* (1978), an essential ingredient of any moral panic is extremely negative portrayals of certain behaviors or events. Cohen conveyed this idea through his concept of "folk devils," which are created by the mass media through metaphor and symbolization. Similarly, Hall *et al.* (1978) developed the notion of convergence, a process in which benign behaviors and social groups are conflated with more threatening forms of social behavior. Convergences essentially push relatively harmless behaviors beyond societal thresholds of tolerance, thereby allowing room to rationalize draconian responses.

Anti-graffiti rhetoric has consistently painted graffiti writers as folk devils and, through various convergences, construed the practice as capable of bringing western civilization to its knees. While separating graffiti writers from humanity often involves portraying them as animals and psychologically defective individuals (Kramer 2009), the most common trope used to push graffiti into the realm of the "socially intolerable" involves drawing erroneous links between writing culture and violent forms of criminality.

One such image suggests that despite the disparity between misdemeanors and felonies, the proclivity to commit either type of offence will be found within the same "soul." The notion of a soul that harbors a broad spectrum of criminality is often conveyed allegorically. In an article looking at a series of crimes committed in one particular neighborhood in New York City, for example, we are first told about several incidents of violent crime including the "savage" beating of a transit police officer; the beating of an immigrant "to death with boards and pipes"; the "pummeling" of several navy officers; and a stabbing "outside a bar." We are also told about an act of arson in which a park building was burnt "to the ground." These crimes are then attributed to several youth groups within the neighborhood who, when a little less preoccupied with beating people to death, "seem to be mostly interested in drinking beer, occasional smoking of marijuana," and "scribbling graffiti." Despite the lack of evidence, park authorities assure us that the torching of the park building was committed by a group of teenagers angered by the fact that "the graffiti they inscribed on the park house was repeatedly being blotted out" (Kleinfield 1994).

When allegory and speculation are not used, inaccurate language will be favored. Generally speaking, the convergence most commonly used to make it seem as though there is no difference between graffiti writing and criminal activity of a more menacing nature works by erasing the distinction between *writing culture* and *gangs*.

This usually involves a failure to acknowledge the differences between "gangs" and "crews." In one article, for instance, we are told about "the *elaborate designs* of (-) gangs – which are also called posses and *crews*" (Brenner 1993). This seemingly simple and straightforward statement is false in more ways than one. First, to the extent that the notion of "elaborate designs" evokes what is known among graffiti writers as a "piece," it must be noted that "gangs" do not generally produce "pieces." Thus, what the first part of this statement does is take a practice from graffiti writing culture – "piecing" – and labels it as something produced by "gangs." Second, although some gangs may refer to themselves as "posses," they do not refer to themselves as "crews." The obverse of this is just as true: Graffiti writing "crews" do not refer to themselves as "gangs." The two cultural groupings each possess a unique historical lineage, pursue different activities, and engage in different practices. As such, they are distinct entities.

Some reports drop the subtleties altogether and simply claim that graffiti writers are becoming more "gang-like" and that one of the signs of this is a supposedly new inclination to act in a violent manner. We may be told about "ego-driven graffiti scribblers" who have "turned to violence" and now refer to themselves as "tag bangers" (Drummond Ayres Jr. 1994). Or about young graffiti writers who "carry a spray can in one hand [and] a gun in the other" (Terry 2000). "Tag bangers" may be young, or even "little tiny kids," but we must not be deceived about the threat they present. As one transit officer informs us: "I always loosen the holster strap on my gun before I move in [to arrest graffiti writers]. You never know what is going to happen these days" (Drummond Ayres Jr. 1994).

Much of this emotive rhetoric finds its "intellectual" counterpart in the broken windows thesis, which asserts that minor forms of disorder, if left unchecked, will invite serious forms of crime and that this will lead to a spiral of urban decline (Wilson & Kelling 1982). Since its rise to prominence in the late 1970s and early 1980s, the broken windows theory has utilized graffiti as one of the central indicators for its concept of disorder. As such, the theory provides much of the epistemic foundation for the anti-graffiti efforts orchestrated by officials in New York City. However, despite all the political faith in broken windows, the thesis remains surrounded by uncertainty.

Aside from the many contradictions within political rhetoric that suggest broken windows amounts to less than an accurate reflection of empirical conditions (Kramer 2010), social scientists working from within a variety of perspectives have also undermined the thesis. Sampson and Raudenbush (1999) emphasize the importance of "collective efficacy" for reducing crime. With the concept of collective efficacy, they suggest that to the extent a community works together to solve problems, they develop a sense of cohesiveness, and it is this that provides a defense against criminal activity. Harcourt and Ludwig (2006) have provided compelling statistical analyses that suggest different variables, such as fluctuations in crack markets and broader economic trends, are better able to account for the changes in rates of serious crime that many major U.S. cities saw throughout the 1990s. Other empirical studies find, at best, very limited support for the thesis (Taylor 2001; Corman & Mocan 2005; Worral 2006; St. Jean 2007; Snyder 2009).

Regardless of its known limitations, the broken windows thesis is cited approvingly by political elites and within the mass print media ad nauseam. On occasion, government publications have simply assumed the empirical validity of broken windows (e.g. Russell *et al.* 2002).

Exterminating graffiti: technology fetishism, prison, limits to private property

As theory on moral panics would lead us to expect, these overly emotive portrayals and pseudo-intellectual understandings of graffiti push it into a zone of criminality that rationalizes disproportionate responses from the state. According to Goode and Ben-Yehuda (1994: 38) the concept of moral panic rests on disproportionality and can be demonstrated in a number of ways. Given that the official reaction to graffiti is based on ideas concerning its social and economic ramifications, disproportionality can be said to exist when the (official) response to an activity is excessive in light of available empirical evidence concerning the objective harm caused by that activity.

Aside from the millions of dollars spent each year to combat graffiti, the excessive response to the phenomenon is evident in new policing strategies, the growing intensity of punishment for graffiti writing, and the sustained attempt to eradicate graffiti as an aesthetic category, even if this means clamping down on private property owners. This multi-pronged attack occurs even though there is little empirical support for the notion that graffiti will lead to serious crime and urban decline.

Reflecting the longstanding and seemingly unshakable faith in the power of technology to address "problems," catching graffiti writers took a "high-tech" turn during the 1990s. Inventors and scientists have worked, and continue doing so, to produce a variety of graffiti removal solutions and preventative coatings. Some of these efforts seem reasonable; others verge on the slightly absurd. For example, in 1996 city authorities considered the possibility of using a laser beam to remove graffiti. The laser beam in question was initially developed by the military for the purpose of shooting down enemy missiles (Browne 1996). In 1997, the MTA consulted NASA for advice on developing a "weapon" that would conceal scratches made in glass (Rutenberg 1997). Although the laser beam, at a cost of about $250,000, was a little beyond the budget allocated for graffiti removal, the NYPD do make use of technologies developed by the military to catch writers. These include night vision goggles and telescopes (Bennet 1992; James 1992; Hernandez 1993); long-range video and audio equipment (Krauss 1996); and infra-red/thermal imaging cameras (Donohue 2001; Rutenberg 2005).

As the NYPD's vandal squad, which consists of seventy-six police officers (Kelly 2005), continues to arrest writers, New York City's public officials have increasingly come to perceive imprisonment as an appropriate punishment for graffiti. To be sure, the idea of sentencing graffiti writers to prison dates back to the early 1980s when Mayor Koch recommended that a person convicted three times for writing graffiti be sentenced to five days in prison (Silver & Chalfant 1983). However, only recently has this idea entered the realm of practice as judges have come under growing pressure from political elites and community groups to sentence graffiti writers to prison.

When COST was arrested for graffiti vandalism and made to appear in court in 1995, at least one councilperson wrote the judge hearing the case a two-page letter urging that he be sentenced to prison. When the case was being heard, local council members and members of community groups attended wearing badges denouncing graffiti. Although COST escaped the sixty day jail sentence recommended by the prosecutor, he was sentenced to three years' probation,

Ronald Kramer

$2,180 in fines, psychological counseling and, finally, 200 days of community service, which was to be spent removing graffiti (Belluck 1995).

DESA, arrested several years before COST, was not so lucky. When word got out that he would be appearing in court, a "court watchers" group quickly formed. Consisting of approximately thirty members from a variety of civic associations, the group attended every one of his court proceedings and had every intention of flooding the courtroom on his day of sentencing (Onishi 1994). Dubbed the "$1 million vandal" by law enforcement officials, DESA was sentenced to one to three years in prison (Kocieniewski 1996; Donohue 2002). After serving four months in prison and eight months in a work-release program, he was paroled towards the end of 1995 (Donohue *et al.* 1996).

Upon hearing of KIKO's arrest, a City Councilperson, known for his dislike of graffiti, went to the print media and not only denounced him as a "punk," but labeled him one of the "most wanted graffiti vandals." Applying such a label to KIKO was very peculiar. While the name DESA did appear with enough frequency in the public spaces of New York City to warrant inclusion in the Vandal Squad's "most wanted" list of "graffiti vandals," the name KIKO did not. For example, Steve Mona, a now retired lieutenant who spent the last decade of his career as the head of the Vandals Task Force, when asked about KIKO, replied by saying that he had "never heard of him" (Gardiner 2007). Despite KIKO being, at best, a minor player within graffiti writing culture, after the aforementioned city council member pressured the district attorney handling the case to push for a prison sentence, and after he insisted – despite the judges objections – upon reading a victim impact statement before the court on sentencing day, KIKO was sent to Rikers Island for six months, put on probation for five years, and fined $25,000 (Gardiner 2007).

Taking on a life of its own, disproportionate reactions to graffiti have extended well beyond those who paint without permission. Since the early 1990s, the city has embarked on a quest to eradicate graffiti as an *aesthetic* category. Alongside the condemnation of legal graffiti, the city opposes commercial uses of the "graffiti look." Moreover, public officials have begun to explore avenues for penalizing those who can be held responsible for the presence of graffiti, or those who refuse to adopt the city's hostile anti-graffiti standpoint.

Political elites, for instance, have openly criticized places such as "5 Pointz," which was one of the few places in New York City where graffiti writers could paint with permission. It was a relatively large warehouse building located in Long Island City, a neighborhood of Queens, but was white-washed and shut down in late 2013 as the neighborhood continues to undergo gentrification (Buckley & Santora 2013).

Instead of seeing it as a place where individuals could express themselves freely and legally, or as a place that provides an outlet for those who might otherwise write graffiti in an illegal manner, one public official condemned "5 Pointz" as a place that feeds the "addictions of young 'graffiti vandals'" (Weir 1998) and suggested that allowing people to paint with permission is the equivalent of "sending candy thieves to work in a candy factory" (Ruiz 1998).

Similarly, public officials have expressed strong opposition to commercial uses of graffiti (e.g. hiring graffiti writers to paint store billboards; using graffiti-style aesthetics in advertising). Such opposition is usually based on the idea that turning graffiti into a legitimate enterprise somehow promotes illegal graffiti. As one police officer has said of "graffiti for hire": "We discourage it . . . if graffiti, even done with permission, is tolerated in one place, it tends to spread to other places where it is unwelcome. If people want to do some advertising, let them get a billboard" (police officer quoted in Marriott 1993).

Alongside this kind of condemnation, the city has also turned to penalizing owners of private property who fail, or refuse, to remove graffiti from their buildings. The logic under-pinning the aesthetic control of private property seems to be that property owners should be punished for failing to support the city in its mission to deny anyone and everyone the possibility of encountering graffiti within the urban environment. In December of 2005, Bloomberg announced the passing of a new law in a press release:

> Commercial property owners and owners of residential properties . . . will face a fine of up to $300 for failure to remove graffiti. These property owners will not face any penalty if they inform the City – through 311 – of the graffiti on their property and sign a waiver allowing the city to clean it.
>
> (Bloomberg 2005b)

Somewhat paradoxically, exercising the kind of power in question is, at least in part, legitimated by the abstract notion that private property is not to be "touched" or interfered with – as if it were somehow sacred. As Bloomberg once put it, "You do not have the right to go up to somebody's private property who doesn't want you there and exercise some mythical right of self-expression" (Bloomberg quoted in Saul 2002).

However, by the time the sacred nature of property is inscribed into law, as this piece of legislation makes unmistakably clear, some people do end up in possession of the practical right to walk up to somebody else's property and exercise that "mythical right of self-expression." Initially postulated as something that non-owners are not to interfere with, private property is reconceived as state property under this law. Rather than being protected from graffiti, it is exposed to the kinds of defacement preferred by those in authority.

Graffiti as "gateway penalty" to neoliberal punitiveness

Two previous studies have assumed that the moral panic concept could be meaningfully applied in analyzing responses to graffiti writing. The first, conducted by Ferrell (1996), was based on graffiti writing in Denver, Colorado and argued that city opposition to the practice was grounded in the need to reinforce public acceptance of the rights of the state to exercise authority over its subjects. The second was conducted by Austin (2001) and was based on graffiti writing in New York City throughout the 1970s and 1980s. Austin argued that official opposition to graffiti occurred in order to deflect attention and criticism away from capitalism during a period of crisis. These studies have the virtue of linking official reactions to graffiti to broader structural forces.

Following Ferrell and Austin, the state and economic trends are important for compre-hending responses to graffiti. Much recent scholarship characterizes the latter part of the twentieth century as one marked by the rise and entrenchment of neoliberalism. According to Wacquant (2009), neoliberalism can be understood as a new state formation that involves the further promotion of commodification, controlling the social body through public policy and prisons, and ideologies of personal responsibility. The consequences of neoliberalism include extreme social inequalities, high rates of underemployment, and the withdrawal of robust social welfare programs.

As this conceptualization intimates, instead of addressing poverty and inequality through public assistance, the neoliberal state has overwhelmingly supported punitive responses to deviance and those who fail to display docility. This is often rationalized by claiming that individuals are responsible for maintaining continuous employment and avoiding poverty, and by a culture that valorizes political elites who promise to be "tough on crime." In this context, I would argue that graffiti writing culture has many attributes that make it an ideal candidate to exploit for the sake of legitimizing the punitive tendencies of neoliberalism.

Graffiti writers appear to engage in a youthful activity that is governed by the pursuit of pleasure and enjoyment. Yet they are relatively powerless, lack access to communication channels that could explain their behavior, and operate within a long discursive and material history that denounces graffiti. As an inherently public act, society's members are often compelled to encounter the best and worst works of graffiti, which can foster resentment among middle classes and property owners, especially in a context where they are encouraged to perceive graffiti as a problematic practice.

Given these characteristics, it is no accident that graffiti remains a political issue and can be regarded as what I would refer to as a "gateway penalty." That is, a mode of behavior that appears to many as non-utilitarian, or lacking any social necessity; that is easily stigmatized due to the relative marginality of its participants, and therefore difficult to defend or portray in a manner that is sympathetic and compelling. Situated as such, it becomes a site where one can introduce and exercise the extremely punitive measures that are required to regulate the social problems that accompany exclusionary social orders (Pratt & Eriksson 2013) with relative impunity. Once such measures become normalized and routine, they can extend to other "objectionable" behaviors as they emerge.

The urban dynamics to panic: growth machines and the ideology of privatism

At the urban level, the response to graffiti is further fueled by growth machines. According to Logan and Molotch (1987), growth machines are loose coalitions that form between local political elites, landowners, corporate developers, and speculators (i.e. landed capitalists). What unites these actors is an interest in extracting the maximum profit possible from how land is put to use as opposed to using land for the satisfaction of relatively modest needs.

The growth machine relies on the ideology of privatism to ensure its smooth functioning. Privatism is an interrelated set of statements that seek to consecrate the following notions: When the public sector facilitates the flow of private capital by offering businesses tax incentives and providing them with necessary infrastructure, a better economic climate is created. This climate is good because it invites businesses to the city, which creates jobs and increases the tax base. With a greater pool of wealth, material gains will eventually "trickle-down" and all of the city's residents will benefit (cf. Logan & Molotch 1987; Squires 1996).

Thus, according to privatism, public-private partnerships can be considered an independent variable whereas the presence of stable business communities and better living conditions for city residents figure as dependent variables. Like privatism, anti-graffiti rhetoric claims that business communities and living conditions are dependent variables. However, instead of emphasizing public-private partnerships, anti-graffiti rhetoric claims that where graffiti is *present*, business and "quality of life" are adversely affected:

> [Graffiti] hurts business because it turns the street into a frightening place.
>> (Probation Commissioner Raul Russi
>> quoted in Bertrand 1997)

The consequences of graffiti include businesses relocating to other cities or states and tourists foregoing trips to NYC. When this occurs, New Yorkers lose jobs and economic opportunities, and the city loses revenue.

(Giuliani 1996)

The graffiti affects everyone's quality of life. It's ugly and it brings down property values.
(Coordinator of the 106th precinct Sal Petrozzino quoted in Lemire 2002)

Consistent with this logic, officials also claim that the *absence* of graffiti fosters stable business communities and creates an environment from which all of the city's residents benefit:

Last July, we launched a citywide campaign to clean up graffiti . . . Not only does that keep New Yorkers safe; it also helps sustain neighborhoods where people want to live and businesses want to locate and invest.

(Bloomberg 2003c)

. . . graffiti hurts neighborhoods both aesthetically and economically. To boost New York City's economy and create jobs, it's critical to create neighborhoods where people want to live and businesses want to locate and invest.
(Economic Development Corporation president Andrew Alper,
see Bloomberg 2003b)

Not only are we cleaning graffiti, we also send a message to people around the city that our neighborhood is a great place to live and raise a family.
(City Council member Eric Gioia quoted in Yaniv 2005)

These [anti-graffiti] initiatives not only improve the quality of life for New Yorkers, but show visitors that New York is a clean, responsible, vibrant city.

(Giuliani 1995b)

The similarities between anti-graffiti rhetoric and the ideology of privatism are obvious such that further comment is hardly necessary. It is, however, worth noting that statements like the ones (re)presented above are repeated by public officials with such a degree of regularity that it would be more than fair to say that what we see in anti-graffiti discourse is a constant redeployment of a few major "sound bites."

As noted, privatism's main role is to facilitate the functioning of growth machines (Logan & Molotch 1987). Previous research indicates that in cities where growth machines work towards the over-development of land, thereby inflating property values, those who are most disadvantaged include small property owners and renters (Zukin 1991); small business owners (Logan & Molotch 1987); low-income households (Massey & Denton 1993); and those who live around or below the poverty line (Smith 1996).

Building upon this kind of analysis, Neil Smith (1996) and Mike Davis (1990, 2002) have suggested that as over-development generates areas of concentrated privilege, the need to defend such enclaves also arises. This often translates into an over-policing of certain neighborhoods, the militarization of public space, and draconian uses of the law (See also Castells 1983; Parenti 1999). This suggests that where the economic strategies of growth machines meet their limitations, public officials will resort to the use of force.

That the Giuliani and Bloomberg administrations, like most city level political administrations, have often allowed the private sector to more or less determine how urban spaces will be put to use is no secret. However, in accordance with the critical analyses of urban sociologists, it becomes very difficult to accept the notion that "all New Yorkers benefit" (Giuliani 1995a; Bloomberg 2003a) from the arrangement between growth-machines and the state's punitive forces when, almost within the same breath, Bloomberg can state with some exuberance that

> Residential property values have appreciated by more than 80 percent over the last four years.
>
> (Bloomberg 2005a)

And,

> the percentage of [misdemeanor] defendants receiving jail sentences has increased 48 percent, with sentences of more than 30 days increasing 74 percent.
>
> (Bloomberg 2004)

Within less than a year of the previous communiqué, the progress being made concerning higher rates of imprisonment was noted:

> . . . the percentage of cases resulting in jail time has increased from 45 percent to 67 percent.
>
> (Bloomberg 2005a)

This would seem to suggest that when growth machines dominate the decision making process that ultimately determines how urban land will be utilized, not all New Yorkers benefit. As urban environments are re-created through these processes, from which some do stand to gain, many are displaced or, even worse, become entangled with the city's carceral complex. For anybody who is familiar with New York City, or has witnessed the changing social composition of neighborhoods such as Williamsburg, Brooklyn, over the last twenty or so years, the way in which space can be rapidly created anew will seem fairly obvious.

What may be less obvious are the mechanisms that make such changes possible. I have suggested that there is no relationship between graffiti and "disorder," or the economic and social vitality of a city. Instead of emphasizing visual factors, I suggested that a city's funda-mental social and economic structures are more likely to be determined by growth machines, which seek public approval and legitimacy through ideological means.

Seen in this light, many aspects of the moral panic over graffiti writing in New York City can be read as a variation on the ideology of privatism (Squires 1996) that ultimately serves the interests of growth machines. Anti-graffiti rhetoric, however, is a much more palatable version of privatism because it links efforts at crime reduction to the economic and social order of things. This rhetorical trope operates on the assumption, arguably correct, that people are more likely to support anti-crime initiatives than what may appear to be the public subsidization of private (or "big") business.

Conclusion

By focusing on representational practices and disproportionate responses, I have tried to demonstrate that the official reaction to graffiti in New York City constitutes a moral panic. I have also suggested that the rise of neoliberalism and the dynamics associated with urban growth machines can be understood as major driving forces of such a response.

My emphasis on neoliberalism is not necessarily at odds with the work of Ferrell and Austin, who have also explored the macro social forces behind official reactions to graffiti. Nils Christie once said of crime that it is a "limitless natural resource" that we can exploit as much, or as little, as we need (Christie quoted in Worrall 2002). I think something similar could be said of graffiti writing: It is a practice that can be exploited at different times, in different spaces, and for various reasons by powerful groups. This is because it opens up possibilities for an anti-graffiti rhetoric that, due to its malleability, is compatible with numerous political and economic climates.

Given the relative powerlessness of graffiti writers, it is easy to portray their culture as sinister and threatening, thereby turning them into scapegoats for many kinds of "crisis." As neoliberalism became entrenched, it developed extremely punitive policies to address its related social problems. Graffiti, and its intense criminalization, provided political elites with the type of fodder that allowed them to communicate and, more importantly, normalize the draconian penal policies of neoliberalism.

Some of these dynamics are further reflected when one considers reactions to graffiti at the urban level. Here, again, we see powerful players dominate the meaning that is given to graffiti. Within the urban context, anti-graffiti rhetoric mirrors privatism. Not only does this adversely affect graffiti writers, it also works against the interests of that portion of city residents who seek to *live* in urban communities rather than exploit them for economic gain. This follows from the power of anti-graffiti rhetoric to hook residents on supporting what appear to be rational, anti-crime initiatives while camouflaging how such rhetoric simultaneously serves the interests of landed capital, which essentially commodifies urban space thereby minimizing the ability of marginal social groups to remain within the city.

Note

1   Special thanks to Jeffrey Ian Ross for thoughtful comments and feedback on this chapter. This chapter builds upon my article "Moral panics and urban growth machines: Official reactions to Graffiti in New York City, 1990–2005." *Qualitative Sociology, 33*(3): 297–311, 2010.

References

Austin, J. (2001). *Taking the train: How graffiti art became an urban crisis in New York City.* New York: Columbia University Press.

Belluck, P. (1995). Graffiti maker 'Cost,' a prankster to some but a criminal in the law's eyes, is sentenced. *New York Times,* June 29, B3.

Bennet, J. (1992). A new arsenal of weapons to tag graffiti artists. *New York Times,* September 27, Section 4, p. 2.

Bertrand, D. (1997). Graffiti vandals unpainting the town. *Daily News,* May 21, Suburban, p.1.

Bloomberg, M.R. (2003a). Mayor Michael R. Bloomberg delivers 2003 state of the city address. January 23, Press Release # 024–03.

Bloomberg, M.R. (2003b). *Mayor Bloomberg updates citywide graffiti cleanup initiative.* July 16, Press Release # 195–03.

Bloomberg, M.R. (2003c). Making our city stronger neighborhood by neighborhood. July 20, Public Address.

Bloomberg, M.R. (2004). Mayor Michael R. Bloomberg announces historic crime reduction in 2004. December 13, Press Release # 345–04.

Bloomberg, M.R. (2005a). Mayor Bloomberg discusses crime reduction strategies at Citizen's Crime Commission breakfast. May 2, Press Release # 168–05.

Bloomberg, M.R. (2005b). *Mayor Bloomberg signs legislation to fight graffiti.* December 29, Press Release # 486–05.

Brenner, E. (1993). Combating the spread of graffiti. *New York Times,* May 30, 1993.

Browne, M.W. (1996). Laser weapon obliterates graffiti, not missiles. *New York Times*, April 21, Section 1, p. 36.

Buckley, C. & Santora, M. (2013). Night falls, and 5Pointz, a graffiti mecca, is whited out in Queens. *New York Times*, November 19.

Castells, M. (1983). *The city and the grassroots: A cross-cultural theory of urban social movements.* Berkeley, CA: University of California Press.

Cohen, S. (1972). *Folk devils and moral panics: The creation of the mods and the rockers.* London: MacGibbon & Kee.

Corman, H. & Mocan, N. (2005). Carrots, sticks and broken windows. *Journal of Law and Economics*, 48(1): 235–266.

Davis, M. (1990). *City of quartz: Excavating the future in Los Angeles.* London: Verso.

Davis, M. (2002). *Dead cities and other tales.* New York: The Free Press.

Donohue, P. (2001). Transit cops' camera turning up the heat. *Daily News*, May 10, p. 17.

Donohue, P. (2002). Cops: Graffiti king back, infamous tagger's 'DESA' moniker spotted. *Daily News*, January 14, p. 10.

Donohue, P., Marzulli, J., & Jamieson, W. (1996). New brush with the law, cops sign off graffiti artist again. *Daily News*, January 19.

Drummond Ayres Jr., B. (1994). In a city of graffiti, gangs turn to violence to protect their art. *New York Times*, March 13, Section 1, p. 20.

Erikson. K. (1966). *Wayward puritans.* New York: Wiley.

Ferrell, J. (1996). *Crimes of style: Urban graffiti and the politics of criminality.* Boston, MA: Northeastern University Press.

Gardiner, S. 2007. KIKO was here. *The Village Voice*, February 28, p.16.

Giuliani, R.W. (1995a). *Mayor Giuliani kicks off adopt-a-highway maintenance provider program.* March 23, Press Release # 124–95. From Giuliani Papers, Office of the Mayor, Folder Title: March 1995. Location: Folder # 16511; Roll # 60276 (NYC Municipal Archives).

Giuliani, R.W. (1995b). *Mayor Giuliani removes graffiti from Queensborough Bridge.* July 10, Press Release # 375–95. From Giuliani Papers, Office of the Mayor, Folder Title: Anti-Graffiti Task Force—Executive Order. Location: Folder # 4676 (NYC Municipal Archives).

Giuliani, R.W. (1996). *NYC (anti-graffiti) technology expo '96.* Brochure found in Giuliani Papers, Office of the Mayor, Folder Title: Police Department—Graffiti. Location: Folder # 0141; Roll # 60696 (NYC Municipal Archives).

Goode, E. & Ben-Yehuda, N. (1994). *Moral panics: The social construction of deviance.* Oxford: Blackwell.

Hall, S., Critcher, C., Jefferson, T., Clarke, J., & Roberts, B. (1976). Some notes on the relationship between the societal control culture and the news media, and the construction of a law and order campaign. In S. Hall & T. Jefferson (eds) *Resistance through rituals: Youth subcultures in post-war Britain* (pp. 75–81). London: Hutchinson.

Hall, S., Critcher, C., Jefferson, T., Clarke, J., & Roberts, B. (1978). *Policing the crisis: Mugging, the state, and law and order.* New York: Holmes & Meier Publishers, Inc.

Harcourt, B.E. & Ludwig, J. (2006). Broken windows: New evidence from New York City and a five-city social experiment. *University of Chicago Law Review*, 73(1): 271–320.

Hernandez, R. (1993). Police scope out night writers. *New York Times*, October 3, Section 13, p. 12.

James, G. (1992). Goggles brighten dark subway. *New York Times*, April 10, B2.

Kelly, R. (2005). The NYPD strategic approach to stopping graffiti vandalism. *The Police Chief*, August, 72(8): np. Alexandria, VA: International Association of Chiefs of Police (accessed online March 14, 2014: www.policechiefmagazine.org/magazine/index.cfm?fuseaction=display_arch&article_id=667&issue_id=82005).

Kleinfield, N.R. (1994). Bay Ridge begins to fear its youth. *New York Times*, October 5, B2.

Kocieniewski, D. (1996). One year later: New canvas, same 'tag.' *New York Times*, January 19, B2

Kramer, R. (2009). *A social history of graffiti writing in New York City, 1990–2005.* Yale University, CT: Unpublished doctoral dissertation.

Kramer, R. (2010). Moral panics and urban growth machines: Official reactions to graffiti in New York City, 1990–2005. *Qualitative Sociology*, 33(3): 297–311.

Krauss, C. (1996). Decoding graffiti to solve bigger crimes: Police experts identifying gangs, feuds, drugs and personal signatures. *New York Times*, October 4, B1.

Lemire, J. (2002). Graffiti kids tagged out, cleanup tied to lower crime. *Daily News*, June 3, Suburban, p. 1.

Logan, J.R. & Molotch, H. (1987). *Urban fortunes: The political economy of place*. Los Angeles, CA: University of California Press.

Marriott, M. (1993). Too legit to quit. *New York Times*, October 3, Section 9, p. 8.

Massey, D.S. & Denton, N.A. (1993). *American apartheid: Segregation and the making of the underclass*. Cambridge, MA: Harvard University Press.

Onishi, N. (1994). Finally, that's all he wrote. *New York Times*, November 20, Section 13, p. 10.

Parenti, C. (1999). *Lockdown America: Police and prisons in the age of crisis*. London: Versoe.

Pratt, J. & Eriksson, A. (2013). *Contrasts in punishment: An explanation of Anglophone excess and Nordic exceptionalism*. London: Routledge.

Ruiz, A. (1998). Graffiti phactory fights vandal tag. *Daily News*, April 20, Suburban, p. 4.

Russell, J.S., Kennedy, E., Kelly, M., & Bershad, D. (2002). *Designing for security: Using art and design to improve security*. New York: Guidelines from the Art Commission of the City of New York.

Rutenberg, J. (1997). A window of opportunity: TA tests 'scratchiti' weapon. *Daily News*, August 21, p. 7.

Rutenberg, J. (2005). Task force renews fight on graffiti in the city. *New York Times*, January 14, B6.

Sampson, R.J. & Raudenbush, S.W. (1999). Systematic social observation of public spaces: A new look at disorder in urban neighborhoods. *American Journal of Sociology*, 105(3): 603–637.

Saul, M. (2002). Mike vows to rub out graffiti all over town. *Daily News*, July 11, Suburban, p. 1.

Silver, T. & Chalfant, H. (1983; re-released 2004). *Style wars*. Los Angeles, CA: Public Art Films.

Smith, N. (1996). *The new urban frontier: Gentrification and the revanchist city*. London: Routledge.

Snyder, G. (2009). *Graffiti lives: Beyond the tag in New York's urban underground*. New York: New York University Press.

Squires, G. (1996). Partnership and the pursuit of the private city. In S.S. Fainstein & S. Campbell (eds) *Readings in urban theory* (pp. 207–229). Cambridge, MA: Blackwell.

St. Jean, P.K.B. (2007). *Pockets of crime: Broken windows, collective efficacy, and the criminal point of view*. Chicago, IL: The University of Chicago Press.

Taylor, R.B. (2001). *Breaking away from broken windows: Baltimore neighborhoods and the nationwide fight against crime, grime, fear, and decline*. Boulder, CO: Westview Press.

Terry, D. (2000). Cleaning graffiti-scarred areas, a wall at a time. *New York Times*, October 20, A18.

Wacquant, L. (2009). *Prisons of poverty*. Minneapolis, MN: University of Minnesota Press.

Weir, R. (1998). Wall hits a patron of graffiti. *New York Times*, February 15, Section 14, p. 10.

Wilson, J.Q. & Kelling, G.L. (1982). Broken windows: The police and neighborhood safety. *Atlantic Monthly*, 249(3): 29–38.

Worrall, A. (2002). Rendering women punishable: The making of a penal crisis. In P. Carlen (ed.) *Women and punishment: The struggle for justice*. (pp. 47–66). Cullompton: Willan.

Worrall, J.L. (2006). The discriminant validity of perceptual incivility measures. *Justice Quarterly*, UK 23(3): 360–383.

Yaniv, O. (2005). Spray and wash in Sunnyside. Trailer patrols nabe to quickly KO graffiti. *Daily News*, August 3, Suburban, p. 2.

Zukin, S. (1991). *Landscapes of power: From Detroit to Disney World*. Berkeley, CA: University of California Press.

31

Stealing from the public
The value of street art taken from the street

Peter Bengtsen

Introduction

Since the early years of the twenty-first century, street art has come to be a ubiquitous part of the urban landscape of major cities as well as smaller towns around the world. Initially unsanctioned and often illegal, street art has steadily gained popularity and acceptance, and an economy has been built around the phenomenon, with, for example, organized street art tours and curated street art festivals becoming increasingly commonplace.

Street art is placed in public space (or at least what is perceived by many as public space). Its content is often easily understandable and frequently relies on figurative subject matter and references to popular culture. In addition, street art commonly entails using mediums different to the somewhat stigmatized freehand spray painting of traditional graffiti. These are reasons that street art has managed to engage a wide audience spanning from members of a general public that would not normally set foot in an art gallery and rarely visit museums to a demographic of young urban creatives and seasoned art enthusiasts.

In the wake of the growing interest in street art, since around 2007 well-known art auction houses like Sotheby's and Christie's have regularly been including in their contemporary art sales studio work by artists who first became known for working in the street, and in February 2008 the less established art auctioneer Bonhams held its first auction entirely dedicated to so-called *urban art*. While this term is sometimes taken to be synonymous with street art, it is also commonly used to describe commercial art products made by artists who are in some way associated with the street art world (Bengtsen, 2014). Being labeled an urban artist does not necessarily entail actually having done work as a street artist. Antony Micallef, for example, is an artist who was – at least for a while – discussed as an urban artist solely because of his association with the Lazarides gallery in London. Until 2008, Lazarides represented Banksy, perhaps the most famous creator of street and urban art. Other artists who have been placed in the urban art category include Takashi Murakami and Chiho Aoshima who were part of an early show of urban art entitled *Spank the Monkey*, which ran at the Baltic Centre for Contemporary Art in Gateshead, U.K. from the fall of 2006 to the beginning of 2007 (Vincentelli, 2006). Murakami and Aoshima, however, are traditionally more closely associated with the Japanese art movement Super Flat (Murakami, 2000).

The early successes of auctions featuring urban art – however vaguely that category was defined – garnered quite a bit of press coverage which in turn led to a further popularization of both urban and street art, and helped establish a veritable urban art market (see, e.g. Dickens, 2009; Derwanz, 2013). This market, to a large extent, exists online and caters to a partly new art buying public. As I have pointed out elsewhere, this creates numerous problems. Since this art seems to speak to people who otherwise have had no deep interest in – and therefore possess little knowledge about – art and the wider art market, it has also established a partly new customer base which relies heavily on the expertise of art dealers in relation to questions about value and authenticity and which is therefore easy to manipulate and exploit (Bengtsen, 2012).

This chapter will primarily focus on a more experienced faction of urban art enthusiasts who in many cases have been following the urban art market since its inception. Many of these aficionados imbue with importance a perceived connection between urban artworks and the street. A connection that can be established, for example, by replicating existing street artworks, using spray paint, incorporating paint drips and/or using found materials in studio works. Interestingly, these same people are often critical when it comes to the trade in actual street artworks that have been removed from the street (Bengtsen, 2014). Although a number of such objects have been put on the market in recent years, they are for the most part currently perceived not as collectable artworks, but rather as worthless both in an artistic and monetary sense. There are, however, also competing discourses, which highlight the potential future value of removed and preserved street artworks.

The removal of street artworks with a view to sell adds new dimensions to an already complex field of social and legal issues associated with graffiti and street art. In relation to the creation of graffiti, in the late 1970s sociologist Nathan Glazer contended that the subway rider in New York City

> is assaulted continuously, not only by the evidence that every subway car has been vandalized, but by the inescapable knowledge that the environment he must endure for an hour or more a day is uncontrolled and uncontrollable, and that anyone can invade it to do whatever damage and mischief the mind suggests.
>
> (Glazer, 1979)

The latter part of this quote subsequently appeared in the famous essay "Broken Windows," which introduced the highly contentious *broken windows theory* and vilified graffiti further (Wilson & Kelling, 1982). Joe Austin (2001) gives a comprehensive account of the way that graffiti was constituted as a social problem in New York City from the late 1960s onwards.

In recent years, the focus on issues like vandalism and trespassing in relation to the creation of street artworks and the social or political implications of the criminalization of the practices of street art (Dickinson, 2008; Young, 2014) have been augmented by other concerns. While Alison Young (2012) shows that graffiti is often considered a "serious" offence by the judicial system regardless of the actual damage done, Ian Edwards (2009) argues that this has become more complicated since, in the specific case of Banksy, the defacement can actually add monetary value to the property it is conducted on. The popularization of street art has seemingly also had other effects: In a court case from 2014, a judge reportedly heard that the nineteen-year-old defendant could be "the next Banksy" because of his stencil paintings in the street. Due to his artistic endeavors, the defendant was spared a jail sentence despite having thirty-one prior convictions. It is interesting to note that the defendant was not arrested on suspicions of doing graffiti, but of stealing an iPhone (Jones, 2014).

The changing status of street art can be related to the increasing commercial success of some artists' studio output, which bleeds over into the perception of both monetary and artistic worth in relation to their street work. This change, described well by Mary Elizabeth Williams (2013), is gradually creating a situation where some street art is no longer described as vandalism, but instead as *attracting* vandalism: People who object to the commodification may seek to paint over or otherwise destroy the art, while others may attempt to remove it for its potential commercial value, destroying property in the process. In the latter case, the act of theft may also come into play.

With the increasing value of street artworks, questions of securing street art as intellectual property are also increasingly prevalent (Lerman, 2013; Smith, 2014), although it falls without the scope of the present chapter to further explore these issues.

Street art removed from the street: a few cases

In the fall of 2006, Mexican director Alfonso Cuarón's dystopian film *Children of Men*, based on the novel by P.D. James, introduced to its audience a not-too-distant future where human beings have seemingly lost the ability to procreate. As a result, hopelessness reigns and society has all but broken down, giving way to a brutal and totalitarian state. At one point, the film's protagonist, Theo, visits Battersea Power Station in London, which has been turned into one of the last bastions of human history and culture: It now serves as a repository for some of the dying world's most renowned artworks.

Slavoj Žižek, in a commentary of the film, has pointed out the absurdity in the creation of such a place, observing that the artworks collected there "are deprived of a world, they are totally meaningless because what does it mean to have a statue of Michelangelo or whatever? It only works if it signals a certain world. And when this world is lacking, it's nothing" (Žižek, 2006). As Theo arrives at this so-called *Ark of the Arts*, a large cut-out section of a wall with a rendition of Banksy's stencil painting *Kissing Coppers* is standing in the middle of the entrance hall. This suggests that in the year 2027 – when the film takes place – this street artwork is considered to be among the most prominent artistic masterpieces ever produced. An interesting point here is that the painting depicted in the film is not created on canvas or another traditional and movable medium, but rather on a wall. This suggests that it is not meant to resemble a studio artwork by Banksy, but rather one that has been removed from the street. This can be seen as a subtle indication that the artist's street work may prove more important in an art historical sense than the commercial work.

When *Children of Men* was released in 2006, the idea that removed street artworks might one day be preserved and displayed in this manner seemed almost comical. In the years since the release of the film, however, the practice of removing, preserving and exhibiting street artworks by Banksy and a number of other artists has become increasingly commonplace as prices for the artists' studio work have gone up. A prolific example is the exhibition *Stealing Banksy?* which opened in the basement of the ME London Hotel on The Strand in central London in April 2014.

On display at *Stealing Banksy?* were eight paintings allegedly by Banksy that had been removed from their original locations and were to be auctioned off at the end of the show. Estimates ranged from £100,000 for a stencil painting on a piece of plywood of a police officer to £500,000 for a stencil painting on a wall of two kids playing with a red "No Ball Games" sign. The latter painting had been cut into three sections, presumably to reduce the total weight of the piece (Figure 31.1). In the show was also a painting on canvas entitled *Brace Yourself*, depicting the grim reaper riding in a bumper car, which was not for sale. In addition, a specially produced newspaper called *The Banksy Bugle*, which served as a catalogue for the show, advertised a ninth street artwork not actually on display: the so-called *Liverpool Rat*, a giant mural which was painted on the side of a pub in Liverpool in 2004.

Stealing Banksy? was not the first exhibition to display and attempt to sell multiple street artworks allegedly created by Banksy. In August 2011, an exhibition in Southampton, New York – jointly arranged by Bankrobber Gallery and Keszler Gallery – featured two large murals originally painted in the Palestinian part of Bethlehem in 2007 as well as four other street artworks that had been removed from the streets of Los Angeles, New Orleans, London, and Brighton.

Banksy publicly denounced both the Southampton exhibition and *Stealing Banksy?*. In relation to the latter, the artist's website published a statement that the exhibition had "been organised without the involvement or consent of the artist" and added the tongue-in-cheek comment that Banksy "would like to make it clear – this show has nothing to do with me and I think it's disgusting people are allowed to go displaying art on walls without getting permission" (Ellis-Petersen, 2014; Vincent, 2014).

Banksy is so far the only artist who has had (unauthorized) exhibitions entirely dedicated to what are claimed to be his removed street artworks, and he remains by far the most obvious example when discussing artists whose work is taken off the street and put on the art market. However, similar removals and attempted sales of a number of other artists' work are in fact

Figure 31.1 The so-called *No Ball Games* mural as displayed at *Stealing Banksy?*, April 2014.
Photo © Peter Bengtsen

taking place. For example, four stencil paintings on metal from the streets of Berlin, ostensibly by the New York-based artist collective Faile, went under the hammer and sold at Fine Art Auctions Miami in February 2014. The same auction saw the apparent sale of a heavily restored rendition of Banksy's *Kissing Coppers* – the image also featured in *Children of Men* – which was removed from the outer wall of a pub in Brighton. Two other street artworks painted in New

Figure 31.2 Stencil paintings by Faile and Bast in Brooklyn, New York City, 2011. Photo ©
Peter Bengtsen

York City in October 2013 and attributed to Banksy failed to sell (Major Street Art Auction Catalogue, 2014; Rushmore, 2014). Other artworks by Faile have been removed and sold. In January 2011, Faile and the Brooklyn-based artist Bast, created a cluster of thirteen stencil paintings on a large metal-plated door in Williamsburg, Brooklyn (Figure 31.2). The whole door was eventually taken down and the plating cut into smaller pieces. In the period March–June 2012, nine of the individual stencil paintings were put up for sale on eBay with eight pieces actually selling at prices ranging from $460 to $1,144.

Even though they are difficult to remove in one piece, several street artworks by the French artist Invader have also been taken down and put on the market in recent years. Invader has become famous within the street art world for creating and adhering to street walls tile mosaics that replicate or paraphrase characters from the late 1970s arcade video game, *Space Invaders*. More recently the artist has also begun to incorporate other characters in his work, although the *Space Invaders* game remains central to his oeuvre.

An example of a removed Invader street artwork is a large mosaic of a princess on a background of numerous white space invaders (Figure 31.3). It was put up on Orchard Street in New York City in October 2013 and was promptly removed by the building's owner (Litvak, 2013), who has claimed that he is "going to hold on to it and cherish it" (Turco, 2013a). Although this particular piece has thus apparently not been put on the market, a number of other artworks supposedly by Invader have been removed and offered up for sale through galleries, eBay, or Internet forums dedicated to street art.

Figure 31.3 Mosaic by Invader on Orchard Street, New York City, 2013. Photo © Mark Miller

Views on removals and a discourse of stolen artworks

There is a clear tendency for graffiti and street art enthusiasts and practitioners to consider the removal of and trade in artworks from the street as both problematic and antithetical to the ethos of graffiti and street art. In an interview following the removal of the Orchard Street mosaic in late 2013, Invader responded to a question about his feelings towards property owners that take his artworks down:

> If it is because [they don't] like it, that's ok. If it's to sell it on eBay or to put it in [their] living room, that doesn't make me happy. Street pieces are made for the street and for the people in the street to enjoy them.
>
> (Turco, 2013b)

In a similar vein, the British artist Eine has stated that street artworks are

> not painted to be sold a few years later . . . This is one reason I don't sign my street stuff, and, like other artists, would never authenticate it – it's not made to be sold, but to be enjoyed.
>
> (Shaw, 2012)

The issue of authentication brought up by Eine is central to the status on the art market of removed street artworks and will be discussed in the following section. In addition to those who legally remove artworks from their own property, there have been numerous examples of street artworks being taken without permission. In some instances, artworks removed in this manner potentially fall into the category of stolen property. Although no criminal convictions on the count of theft have so far been made, the removal in February 2011 of a street artwork attributed to Banksy often referred to as *Sperm Alarm* led to a case in which the defendant, Leon Lawrence, was convicted of attempting to convert criminal property (Daily Mail, 2012).

It should be noted that irrespective of whether the art is considered stolen property in a formal sense, many street artists, as well as street art enthusiasts and urban art collectors, on principle find it inappropriate to remove and trade in art from the street (Bengtsen, 2014). There is a strong notion that street art is ephemeral and should remain on the street until it disappears "naturally" (e.g. being whitewashed, destroyed by elements, or gone over with other art). Removal with a view to collect or sell is not considered natural or acceptable, and even legally-removed street art is often described as having been stolen from the public for which it was intended and to which it – in a moral sense – rightly belongs. This is a quite pervasive discourse in the worlds of street art and urban art, and one that is also hinted at in the title of the *Stealing Banksy?* exhibition.

The authentication and authenticity of street artworks

The negative stance taken by many artists towards the removal of their artworks from the street influences the status of these works on the art market. It is a fundamental notion when trading in art that it is important to be able to substantiate the origin and authenticity of an artwork since this may significantly increase market interest and the work's monetary value. If an artist or an artist's representative is unavailable or unwilling to authenticate an artwork, establishing good provenance (e.g. dating, assembling a list of previous owners, and appearances in exhibitions and auctions and collecting paperwork attesting to the artwork's origin) becomes paramount, since "[d]eterminations about the authenticity and value of paintings and other art objects are largely made based on the provenance of the work" (Carter, 2007: p. 76).

As suggested by Eine, when it comes to work taken from the street, many artists will not provide formal authentication. Other provenance is therefore important and often consists of visual documentation of the relevant work in its original context and during the removal process. In addition, any direct or indirect acknowledgement by the artist of having created the artwork can be put on record. For example, when an image of a street artwork appears on Banksy's website, this is taken by many as circumstantial evidence that Banksy created it. Although indirect, such recognition by the artist is usually the most persuasive indicator of genuineness available.

At the 2011 show of removed street artworks attributed to Banksy in Southampton, the organizers had to rely heavily on the above-mentioned types of provenance, since none of the artworks had been authenticated by the artist's authentication company, Pest Control. The same was the case at *Stealing Banksy?*. Of the nine removed street artworks for sale at the 2014 show, only one – a 2.4 by 9.95 metres painting originally created on the side of a semi-trailer – had been given a certificate of authenticity by Pest Control. Even though many of the artworks at these two shows were being presented with relatively convincing provenance information, none of them sold.

The lack of sales may in part be explained by factors such as the high estimates the artworks had been given, their restored state, and in some cases their size and weight which would present a potential buyer with significant logistical challenges. However, the lack of sales were also partly caused by the fact that establishing good provenance is often perceived as insufficient by the art market when it comes to removed street artworks. One reason for this is that street artworks are created – and often embedded – in a specific context, and their meaning can change quite drastically when they are removed from their original site. In relation to works of such a site-specific nature, authenticity is not tantamount to simply establishing their origins beyond reasonable doubt.

The context of street artworks can at times be of a specific geographical or socio-political nature. Italian artists Blu and Ericailcane's large-scale oil-and-environment-themed mural painted in Stavanger, Norway in 2010 and Banksy's famous murals created on the Israeli separation wall in 2005 are examples of this. However, the ever-present and fundamental relationship of any street artwork to the street must also be considered. The street constitutes a site beyond, and perhaps in opposition to, the ideological and economic constraints of an established and elitist art world which Miwon Kwon has observed is seeking to "*actively* disassociate the space of art from the outer world" (2002: p. 13). The street as a site creates a direct connection between art and lived life and thus plays a fundamental role in establishing the meaning of street artworks. Therefore, even if it is possible to remove an artwork from its original location without breaking it in the physical sense, embedding that work in the context of the art market or an art institution could still damage or destroy it conceptually and, for that reason, monetarily (Bengtsen, 2013). In addition, street artworks in the same area often feed off and add meaning to each other. As a result, even street artworks that may initially appear relatively self-contained can become increasingly site specific over time as they are gradually embedded in a network of meaning together with other artworks.

The site specific nature of street art is one reason that the intentions and views of the artist are currently being taken so seriously by the art market. In relation to Banksy, contemporary art expert Lock Kresler from Christie's London has stated that the auction house "will not sell anything removed from the street because it's something the artist isn't happy with, so we try to abide by the wishes of the artist" (Corbett, 2011). A certificate or other direct acknowledge-ment from the artists or his/her representative of a removed artwork's authenticity is taken to be important not just because it confirms whether the artwork in question was originally created by the relevant artist, but also because it is indicative of whether the removed object should be considered an artwork in its current form. This focus on the potentially changed status of the removed object in the eyes of the artist – and the risk that the object might eventually be publicly denounced as a fake – may in part explain why work has failed to sell even if it has been removed legally and has reasonably good provenance.

In addition to the more conceptual issues related to site specificity, the removal of street artworks and the lack of official recognition by artists of such removed objects also raise a practical concern about the risk of buying outright fakes. In a statement on his website in April 2014, Invader commented on the trade in artworks attributed to him which have ostensibly been removed from the street:

> The Space Invaders I put up in the street aren't signed and are made from readily available mosaic tiles, which [make] them easy to copy. A mosaic that has been removed from its original site loses all value as it can no longer be distinguished from a reproduction.
>
> One of the techniques used by illicit dealers is to destroy the Space Invader in situ, then recreate it using new mosaic tiles which they artificially age. The copy is then offered for sale as an original. Sometimes several copies of the same piece are made. Examples regularly come up on eBay.
>
> (Invader, 2014)

Similarly, in September 2008, Pest Control issued a statement that they do not authenticate street artworks and that Banksy would "encourage anyone wanting to purchase one of his images to do so with extreme caution" (Pest Control Office, 2008). This was seen by many as a hint that five street artworks coming up for auction at Lyon & Turnbull at the time might be fake and is believed to be a major reason that none of these artworks sold.

While the lack of sales of removed artworks is becoming less clear-cut as some do seem to sell privately or at auction, many collectors still appear to be adhering to the negative stance taken by artists in relation to the removal and sale of street artworks. In the few cases where larger artworks removed from the street have ostensibly sold, the lack of transparency on the art market means that there is a lot of skepticism among collectors and street art enthusiasts and there is speculation as to whether a reported sale is genuine or a ruse to attempt to drive up prices and demand for other street artworks the same seller or his/her associates may have in stock. By way of example, in a discussion thread from July 2014 about the alleged sale of a car door with part of a stencil painting attributed to Banksy, a member of the *Urban Art Association* – one of the most prolific internet forums dedicated to the discussion of and trade in urban art and street art – commented:

> The piece did not sell. The article you are thinking of states it received an offer of 145k USD (I do not believe that personally). It did not meet the reserve which I believe was 200k USD. This was back in [February 2014]. . .the same piece was still for sale as of about two months ago by [Keszler], the same person who listed it in the Miami Auction, for 185k USD.
>
> Knowing [Keszler] I would be [. . .] shocked if he had an offer of 145k and passed. That's just a quote drummed up by his PR person to try and generate interest in the piece.
>
> ("AFR1KA," 2014)

Alternatively, some artists do sometimes authenticate street artworks, and this can change fundamentally the attitude of prospective buyers towards the relevant artworks. An example of this can be found in the responses to a post on *Urban Art Association*, where a collector advertises for sale a removed street artwork by Faile. The sales post reads as follows:

> I'm selling my original Faile on wood. This piece was originally a street piece in Brooklyn. It was removed by the person I purchased it from (who claimed it was on a building being torn down, etc., the usual story). I'm not one to buy pieces taken from the street, however, I contacted both members of Faile before purchasing the piece and was provided with full authenticity, as well as their blessing to go ahead and purchase the piece as an original. I will include this correspondence with the piece as provenance.
>
> ("solar77," 2008)

Unlike in other cases on *Urban Art Association* and similar forums where removed street artworks have been offered for sale, the responses from other members contain no critical comments. Instead, many members express their interest in the artwork. There are several factors that may have contributed to this outcome. The seller is clearly aware of the dominant negative discourse surrounding the removal and sale of artworks from the street. He begins by making clear that the artwork was taken down by someone else, thereby absolving himself of any direct involvement in the removal. He invokes the common notion among street art enthusiasts that removing artworks from condemned buildings is somewhat acceptable since it can be perceived as an act of rescuing artworks that would otherwise have disappeared from the street anyway. Highlighting the exceptional nature of the sale by stating that he would not normally trade in removed artworks, the seller also explains that he contacted Faile and received their approval before buying the painting. The significance of the artists having recognized and authenticated the artwork "as an original" and of the promise that documentation of this will be provided to the buyer is reflected in the response from one member that the artwork "is a beauty and well done on getting the official nod of approval before buying it" ("Ged," 2009). This case exemplifies the emphasis put on the views of the artist by collectors, as this particular removed street artwork is perceived by the forum community as an authentic Faile not only because the artists made it, but also because they are said to have acknowledged its status as an artwork in its current state.

Possible benefits of removing street art from the street

After *Stealing Banksy?* ended with no sales in April 2014, The Sincura Group, who organized the show, published a statement. They claimed that

> many of the pieces displayed were not actually available for sale. Furthermore, those artwork [sic] made available had strict caveats placed on them – that upon purchase they would be put back on public display and that the proceeds from any sale would benefit local charities.
>
> (*Stealing Banksy?* website, 2014)

In the statement, it was further asserted that the whole event had been a test to assess the viability of establishing in central London a museum dedicated to removed street artworks. While it still remains to be seen if such a museum is in fact underway, the idea itself feeds into an existing argument for the possible long-term benefits connected to the preservation of street art – an argument that challenges the prevalent view among street artists, street art aficionados, and collectors that the removal of artworks from the street is necessarily negative. An example of this alternative argument can be found in the following post from the online art discussion forum *The Artchival*:

> you need a certain percentage captured from the wild in order to save for posterity, like a breeding program for an endangered species, but in this case breeding scholarship and continued interest in the genre. I'd think things would be far less interesting, for example, if all the Haring subway drawings had been left & lost, if we didn't have vintage NYC subway windows and doors, full of a generation of tags, in private collections, and museums, if all we had left of KAWS bus-stop distortions were old photographs, etc., etc.
>
> There is a preservation aspect that I appreciate.
>
> ("Mose," 2012)

Though, as suggested in the above-cited forum post, there may be beneficial long-term consequences of the removal and preservation of street artworks, these are often disregarded in public discussions among street art enthusiasts. Co-editor of the influential book *Beyond the Street: The 100 Leading Figures in Urban Art*, Patrick Nguyen, observes in an email

> the knowledge [among street art aficionados] that recognizing any grey area or validity to the salvaging argument will simply serve to justify the removal of further street pieces. Street art enthusiasts are thereby discouraged from engaging in open and honest debates on the matter.[1]

Although the argument that the removal and preservation of a certain number of street artworks may in time prove to be beneficial is still not widely accepted among street art practitioners and enthusiasts, there does seem to be a growing awareness – perhaps fueled by pragmatic resignation to the fact that street artworks *are* being removed regardless of anyone's feelings about the matter – of the potential benefits of preservation. These benefits include having access to a more complete overview of certain artists' body of work and allowing future museum goers and researchers to study samples of actual street artworks from the early twenty-first century rather than only photographs and other forms of documentation. However, since the preservation argument hinges on at least some removed street artworks in time becoming accessible to the public, it is significantly challenged by the fact that these street artworks have so far ended up in the hands of private collectors or in the stocks of galleries.

Conclusion

Among street artists and street art enthusiasts, there is a widespread idea that street artworks are ephemeral and site specific, and that they are meant for the public and should be allowed to remain in their original location until they are destroyed or gradually disappear. With the increasing prices commanded by commercial studio work by some of the artists who are also known for their work in the street, however, in recent years the removal of and trade in street artworks has become increasingly commonplace.

The market reception of removed street artworks has generally been negative. The market puts a lot of emphasis on the wishes and opinions of the artists, who often will not authenticate removed artworks. Cases where removed artworks have been authenticated by artists and subsequently have sold underscore the importance of artists openly acknowledging a removed object as their work. By doing so, they confirm not only that they have created the initial street artwork but also that it should be considered a work of art after it has been removed from its original site.

While the status of removed street artworks on the art market is currently very much reliant on statements from the respective artist, the continued effort to take down, restore, and preserve artworks at great cost suggests that some expect either that more artists will eventually come to acknowledge the removed artworks as part of their oeuvre or that the emphasis now put on the artists' statements will diminish in favor of other types of provenance.

The negative stance towards the status of removed street artworks is also being challenged by the preservation argument, which focuses on the long-term importance of preserving a certain number of street artworks and making sure that they become available to the public. However, even if artworks become accessible to the public, their removal, restoration, and preservation in an art institution entails a significant trade-off in terms of the loss of their original context, which often adds meaning to the artworks. Since street artworks are in essence site specific, the shift to the context of the museum may significantly alter how the artworks are perceived, and in some cases deprive them of meaning. Although market forces may be chipping away at it, the dominant public stance among street art enthusiasts and sellers of urban art can – for the moment – be summed up by paraphrasing Slavoj Žižek's observations about the masterpieces of art collected at Battersea Power Station in the film *Children of Men*: Street artworks removed from the street are deprived of their context, they are totally meaningless because what does it mean to have a street painting by Banksy or whatever? It only works in a certain context. And when this context is lacking, the artwork is nothing.

Note

1   Email correspondence with P. Nguyen (February 10, 2013).

References

"AFR1KA." (2014). Post on *Urban Art Association*, July 28, 2014. Available at http://banksyforum. proboards.com/post/1234514/thread (accessed July 31, 2014).

Austin, J. (2001). *Taking the Train: How Graffiti Art Became an Urban Crisis in New York City*. New York: Columbia University Press.

Bengtsen, P. (2012). Den förlorade etiken. *Sydsvenska Dagbladet*, October 18, 2012, B5. Available at www.sydsvenskan.se/kultur–nojen/den-forlorade-etiken/ (accessed July 18, 2014).

Bengtsen, P. (2013). Site Specificity and Street Art. In J. Elkins, K. McGuire, M. Burns, A. Chester, & J. Kuennen (eds), *Theorizing Visual Studies: Writing Through the Discipline* (pp. 250–253). New York & London: Routledge.

Bengtsen, P. (2014). *The Street Art World*. Lund, Sweden: Almendros de Granada Press.

Carter, R.G.S. (2007). Tainted Archives: Art, Archives, and Authenticity. *Archivaria*, 63(Spring), pp. 75–86.

Corbett, R. (2011). Pest Control Stymies Keszler Gallery Sales. *artnet.com*, October 12, 2011. Available at www.artnet.com/magazineus/features/corbett/keszler-banksy-10–12–11.asp (accessed July 31, 2014).

Daily Mail. (2012). Art Thief Who Tried to Sell a Banksy on eBay: Vandal Ripped 'Sperm Alarm' Graffiti From London Hotel Wall and Auctioned it for £17,000. *Mail Online*, September 13, 2012. Available at www.dailymail.co.uk/news/article-2202752/Art-thief-tried-sell-Banksy-Sperm-Alarm-graffiti-piece-17–000-ripped-wall-outside-London-hotel.html (accessed July 29, 2014).

Derwanz, H. (2013). *Street Art-Karrieren: Neue Wege in den Kunst- und Designmarkt*. Bielefeld, Germany: Transcript Verlag.

Dickens, L. (2009). *The Geographies of Post-graffiti: Art Worlds, Cultural Economy and the City*. Unpublished PhD thesis, University of London.

Dickinson, M. (2008). The Making of Space, Race and Place: New York City's War on Graffiti, 1970–the present. *Critique of Anthropology*, 28(1), pp. 27–45.

Edwards I. (2009). Banksy's Graffiti: A Not-so-simple Case of Criminal Damage? *The Journal of Criminal Law*, 73(4), pp. 345–361.

Ellis-Petersen, H. (2014). Banksy Works Go Under Hammer In Auction Criticized by Artist. *The Guardian*, April 24, 2014. Available at www.theguardian.com/artanddesign/2014/apr/24/banksy-works-auction-london-hotel (accessed July 22, 2014).

"Ged." (2009). Post on *Urban Art Association*, January 1, 2009. Available at http://banksyforum.proboards.com/post/450631/thread (accessed July 31, 2014).

Glazer, N. (1979). On Subway Graffiti in New York. *Public Interest*, 54(Winter), pp. 3–11.

Invader (2014). Don't Be Fooled! Blog post, April 3, 2014. No longer accessible.

Jones, C. (2014). 'The Next Banksy': Graffiti Artist Spared Jail After Court Told of His Street Art Talent. *Wales Online*, August 11, 2014. Available at www.walesonline.co.uk/news/wales-news/the-next-banksy-graffiti-artist-7595535 (accessed August 24, 2014).

Kwon, M. (2002). *One Place After Another. Site-Specific Art and Locational Identity*. Cambridge, MA: The MIT Press.

Lerman, C. (2013). Protecting Artistic Vandalism: Graffiti and Copyright Law. *N.Y.U. Journal of Intellectual Property and Entertainment Law* 2 (295), pp. 295–337.

Litvak, E. (2013). Space Invader Reportedly Arrested Overnight on Orchard Street. *The Lo-Down*, October 31, 2013. Available at www.thelodownny.com/leslog/2013/10/space-invader-reportedly-arrested-overnight-on-orchard-street.html (accessed July 29, 2014).

Major Street Art Auction Catalogue. (2014). Available at www.liveauctioneers.com/catalog/50889_major-street-art-auction/page1?rows=80 (accessed July 28, 2014).

"Mose." (2012). Post on *The Artchival*, December 7, 2012. Available at http://artchival.proboards.com/post/67379/thread (accessed July 31, 2014).

Murakami, T. (2000). *Super Flat*. Tokyo: Madra Publishing Co., Ltd.

Nguyen, P. & Mackenzie, S. (2010). *Beyond the Street: The 100 Leading Figures in Urban Art*. Berlin: Gestalten.

Pest Control Office (2008). Archived version of Pest Control Office website available at https://web.archive.org/web/20080927130058/www.pestcontroloffice.com/whatispco.html (accessed July 29, 2014).

Rushmore, R.J. (2014). Results: Street Works by Banksy, Kenny Scharf and More at Auction. *Vandalog*, February 18, 2014. Available at https://blog.vandalog.com/2014/02/street-works-by-banksy-and-more-at-auction/ (accessed July 28, 2014).

Shaw, A. (2012). Banksy Murals Prove to Be An Attribution Minefield. *The Art Newspaper*, February 16, 2012. Available at www.theartnewspaper.com/articles/Banksy-murals-prove-to-be-an-attribution-minefield/25631 (accessed July 22, 2014).

Smith Cathy, Y.N. (2014). Street Art: An Analysis Under U.S. Intellectual Property's "Negative Space" Theory. *Journal of Art, Technology and Intellectual Property Law*, 24 (259), pp. 259–293.

"solar77." (2008). Post on *Urban Art Association*, December 31, 2008. Available at http://banksyforum.proboards.com/post/450476/thread (accessed July 31, 2014).

Stealing Banksy? Website. (2014). Available at http://stealingbanksy.com/ (accessed May 7, 2014, statement no longer online).

Turco, B. (2013a). Invader Reportedly Arrested on the Lower East Side. *Animal*, October 31, 2013. Available at http://animalnewyork.com/2013/invader-reportedly-arrested/ (accessed July 29, 2014).

Turco, B. (2013b). From the Streets to the Stratosphere: An Interview with "Space Artist" Invader. *Animal*, November 4, 2013. Available at www.animalnewyork.com/2013/streets-stratosphere-interview-space-artist-invader/ (accessed July 29, 2014).

Vincent, A. (2014). Banksy condemns 'disgusting' Stealing Banksy exhibition on opening day. *The Telegraph*, April 24, 2014. Available at www.telegraph.co.uk/culture/art/art-news/10785417/Banksy-condemns-disgusting-Stealing-Banksy-exhibition-on-opening-day.html (accessed July 22, 2014).

Vincentelli, A. (Ed.) (2006). *Spank the Monkey*. Berlin: Die Gestalten Verlag.

Williams, M.E. (2013). Part I: Who Owns Street Art? *Center for Art Law*, March 25, 2013. Available at http://itsartlaw.com/2013/03/25/part-i-who-owns-street-art/ (accessed August 21, 2014).

Wilson, J.Q. & Kelling, G.L. (1982). Broken Windows: The Police and Neighborhood Safety. *The Atlantic*, March. Available at www.theatlantic.com/magazine/archive/1982/03/broken-windows/304465/ (accessed August 24, 2014).

Young, A. (2005). *Judging the Image*. London: Routledge.

Young, A. (2012). Criminal Images: The Affective Judgment of Graffiti and Street Art. *Crime, Media, Culture*, 8(3), pp. 297–314.

Young, A. (2014). *Street Art, Public City: Law, Crime and Urban Imagination*. New York & London: Routledge.

Žižek, S. (2006). Commentary on *Children of Men* DVD. Available at www.youtube.com/watch?v=pbgrwNP_gYE (accessed July 25, 2014).

32

How American movies depict graffiti and street art[1]

Jeffrey Ian Ross

Introduction

Since the turn of the last century, films, movies, and cinematic productions have become powerful methods of explanation and interpretation of contemporary phenomena. Not only can this medium assist viewers to understand these phenomena, but it can also influence and/or reinforce their opinions. Films establish expectations for the audience and often reflect dominant stereotypes (Monaco, 1977). They also promote and reinforce myths and misconceptions about people and activities, and may affect policy responses (Rafter, 2006, 2007; Rafter & Brown, 2011). In short, movies are conduits for framing issues that are dominant in social and political arenas (Yar, 2010; Welsh *et al.*, 2011).

Since the advent of contemporary graffiti (i.e. post 1970s), numerous films have used graffiti/street art as backdrops or individuals who engage in graffiti/street art as characters to tell a story, while other movies have attempted to chronicle graffiti/street art and practitioners in different locations. These films, both fictional (also referred to as commercial, feature-length, Hollywood, and popular) and documentary, may contain images of graffiti and street art, as well as interviews with the individuals who either engage in or respond to this activity. Not only have many of these films been screened at movie festivals and local theatres, but they have also been available through television programing and various content providers on the World Wide Web. Despite the improved access to this medium, we do not have a good understanding of the information and themes that these movies have presented and portrayed, and to what extent they have been a reflection of reality or have created and/or perpetuated myths.

In order to correct this imbalance, this chapter analyses fictional/commercial and documentary movies that have been produced on graffiti/street art.[2]

Method

A thorough search of the internet was performed in order to identify English-language, American-made movies that disproportionately focus on graffiti and street art.[3] Once the films were selected, the researcher asked scholars and other experts who specialise in this subject matter if they could add to his working list of movies. While not all movies added by the experts focused predominately on graffiti and street art,[4] or were easily accessible, the investigator was able to narrow down a manageable viewing list, and he then systematically watched these movies, paying careful attention to identify prevalent themes.

From 1979 to 2014, approximately twenty-two full-length English-language, American-made[5] films depicting graffiti and/or street art and artists/writers[6] were identified (Ross, 2015). Of this total, seven are fictional accounts (see Table 32.1), and fifteen are documentaries (see Table 32.2).[7]

Once a potential theme was identified, the researcher established it as a category, and looked for its prevalence in all of the other movies. An attempt was made to watch these films in a chronological fashion. By viewing these films in this manner, the investigator hoped to witness the evolution of depictions of graffiti and street art. In some cases, it was necessary to watch these movies several times to better understand, categorise, and contextualise them. Finally, by limiting the framework to popular (i.e., relatively easily accessible) films and documentaries, the analysis was made more manageable.[8]

Table 32.1 Fictional/commercial films on graffiti/street art

Dreams Don't Die
Wild Style
Bomb the System
Against the Wall/Quality of Life
The Graffiti Artist
Transit
Gimme the Loot

Table 32.2 Documentaries on graffiti/street art

Stations of the Elevated
Graffiti Verite 1
Piece by Piece
Infamy
A Rash: Of Graffiti
Just to get a Rep
Next: A Primer on Urban Painting
Tatscru: Mural Kings
Bomb It
Alter Ego
Beautiful Losers
Bomb It 2
Sly Artistic City
Vigilante Vigilante
The Legend of Cool "Disco" Dan

Discussion

Fictional films about graffiti/graffiti artists/writers

Introduction

Seven fictional movies featuring graffiti/street artists and themes were reviewed for this study: *Dreams Don't Die* (1982); *Wild Style* (1983); *Bomb the System* (2002); *Against the Wall/Quality of Life* (2004);[9] *The Graffiti Artist* (2004); *Transit* (2004); and *Gimme the Loot* (2012).[10] The movies were analysed based on three categories: Characters, settings, and themes, and the quality of the movies was also taken into consideration.

Characters

Graffiti writers shoplift, especially spray paint
Some of the graffiti writers engage in petty crimes, like shoplifting (e.g. food) and jumping turnstiles into the subway. To support their graffiti habit and sometimes to make extra money, most of the graffiti artists steal spray paint. In *The Graffiti Artist*, along with skateboarding and graffiti writing, Nick and Jesse shoplift spray paint and steal fruit from street vendors and shopkeepers. In *Quality of Life/Against the Wall*, Curtis and a friend invent a complicated ruse in order to distract the shopkeeper in order to steal spray paint. In *Gimme the Loot*, the movie begins with a major spray paint heist and closes with Sofia assisting Malcolm steal flowers. This kind of activity is consistent with scholarly research on the criminal activity of graffiti artists (Taylor *et al.*, 2012), which suggests that stealing spray paint is both part of the initiation and maintenance process of graffiti crews.

The primary characters come from lower socio-economic backgrounds
The majority of the main characters come from poor socio-economic circumstances. In *Dreams Don't Die*, Danny comes from a working-class family, where his mother is trying to make ends meet. In *The Graffiti Artist*, Nick lives by himself and leads a hermit-like existence where he has little food in his fridge, shoplifts food, and does not have much money on hand. In *Transit*, Ritchie lives in a small, modest house with his mother. In *Against the Wall*, although Mikey's father runs his own small business, he is not rich by any means. In *Gimme the Loot*, based on their street talk and the final scene, we know that Malcolm and Sofia come from a lower socio-economic status. In the end, Malcolm goes home to his mother's apartment building, which appears to be in the projects. None of the protagonists are middle class, or come from the suburbs or from families of means. The class differences between graffiti writers and outsiders are highlighted in various scenes. For example, in *Wild Style*, Raymond meets gallery owners at a party who talk to him condescendingly. The partygoers are comparatively well dressed, disproportionately white, and show minimal interest in graffiti. A similar situation occurs in *Gimme the Loot*, when Malcolm spends time with Jenny and her college-educated friends, and they talk down to him.

Graffiti artists/writers are primarily young males from selected races/ethnicities
The movies typically feature males as graffiti artists/writers, and women (mothers and girlfriends) are relegated to secondary roles. This gendered rendering of the graffiti world is consistent with early findings (Macdonald, 2003). One exception is *Wild Style*, in which Rose, Raymond's graffiti-writing girlfriend, plays a very minor role. In *Gimme the Loot*, Sofia is paired with Malcolm and is an equal, if not more dominant, graffiti partner. Finally, Alexandra, who is Anthony "Blest" Campo's love interest in *Bomb the System*, is a street artist who unsuccessfully tries to convince him to join her in a cross-country street art adventure.

To these movies' credit, the protagonists span a number of races. Some are white, like Danny (*Dreams Don't Die*), Curtis and Mikey (*Against the Wall*), and Anthony "Blest" Campo (*Bomb the System*). Alternatively, other primary graffiti writers are Hispanic, like Raymond (*Wild Style*) and Ritchie (*Transit*). Finally, Malcolm and Sofia in *Gimme the Loot*, and Justin "Buk 50" and his brother Kevin "Lune," Anthony's two crew members in *Bomb The System*, are African American. There are no Asian or American-Indian graffiti writers featured in these movies.

Finally, all of the protagonists are young (i.e. teenagers), with few of them older than their mid-twenties. None of the perpetrators are middle-aged. This runs counter to Kramer's work (2010) on post graffiti, which reveals how graffiti, especially that which currently exists in New York City, is created by individuals from all age groups.

Graffiti writers engage in graffiti primarily for fun and to build their reputations
In almost all of the films reviewed, the writers engage in graffiti primarily for fun, the thrill of the experience, and/or to build or maintain their reputations as skilled players. This is reflected in the dialogue and actions of the protagonists, and this is why the majority of the writers become upset when their graffiti is buffed over or crossed out by rivals. In *Transit*, Ritchie is worried about his graffiti being crossed out by rival graffiti crews, and this leads to a battle (i.e. competition) with a rival graffiti crew. In *Gimme the Loot*, Sofia's graffiti is crossed out by a rival crew and this bothers her considerably.

Most graffiti artists have one or more absentee parents
In the majority of the films, parents do not appear, are not mentioned, or provide minimal supervision of their teenagers/young adults. In *Dreams Don't Die*, Danny's mother works long hours in a sweat shop. Although she knows of his graffiti activity and even warns him that he will be arrested, she needs to work extra hours to pay the bills, thus she is not home when he returns from school. In *Transit*, we briefly see Ritchie's mother twice: When she warns him that is going to get killed, and in the final scene, as she grieves his death. In *Against the Wall*, although Mikey's father is present, we learn that his mother has left. In contrast, we never hear about or see Mikey's friend Curtis's parents. In *The Graffiti Artist*, we find out that Jesse has a mother, because apparently she has sent him money to visit her. In *Gimme the Loot*, although Malcolm's mother periodically calls him on his cell phone and he steals flowers to celebrate her birthday, we never see either Malcolm or Sofia's mother. Blest's mother (*Bomb the System*), like Ritchie's mother, has lost a graffiti-writing son to gun violence and warns her other sons against following in their brother's footsteps.

Most of the fathers of graffiti artists are either absent or "missing in action"
In the majority of the movies, the fathers are either absent or they are not emotionally engaged. In *Dreams Don't Die*, Danny goes home and observes his "good for nothing" father, who is lying on a bed smoking a cigarette and watching television with beer in hand. Later, it is implied that his father beats Danny's mother. In *Against the Wall*, although Mikey's father runs a painting company and is quite authoritarian in his treatment of his son, no mention is made of Curtis having a father. In *Transit*, we do not see Ritchie's father, but he does have a mother and a girlfriend who warn him that he will be shot. The lack of a father is evident in *Bomb the System*. Although Blest's mother is concerned for his son, his father is never mentioned.

Authority figures occasionally provide or suggest a path out of the graffiti lifestyle
In *Dreams Don't Die*, Danny is caught by Banks, an African-American police officer, while he is painting on the subway platform. Banks offers to introduce him to a man who might help

him get a paid job as an artist. In *Transit*, an unnamed African-American college recruiter encourages Ritchie to fill out an application for art school in order for him to improve his artistic abilities and make a living by doing this. In *Against the Wall*, even though Mikey has a father, he comes under the more direct influence of Dino, an older friend, who works in a Buddhist temple. This relationship provides him with spiritual guidance in escaping the graffiti lifestyle and dealing with Curtis's death.

Settings

Settings are limited to a handful of well-known big cities on either the West or East Coast
Whereas *Against the Wall*, *The Graffiti Artist* and *Transit* take place in West Coast locations, respectably San Francisco, Seattle and Los Angeles, *Dreams Don't Die, Wild Style, Bomb the System* and *Gimme the Loot* are shot in New York City. Other large cities with thriving graffiti scenes, including Washington, DC, Chicago, Philadelphia and New Orleans, are absent from these movies.

Targets of graffiti

In the movies reviewed, graffiti is usually placed/written on subway trains, subway platforms, freight trains, police cars, rooftops, sides of buildings, walls and metal roll-down doors for retail businesses. Other places include phone booths, bus shelters and metal trash dumpsters. With the exception of Sofia in *Gimme the Loot*, who occasionally places a United States Postal Service mailing label sticker with her tag on a couple of places, and Alex in *Bomb the System*, there is little street art done by the characters in the movies.

Themes

The primary themes in these movies concern: The soundtracks; characters' fears of selling out; and rivalries among graffiti artists/crews.

Soundtracks

Soundtracks help to locate the films during a period in contemporary American history. Most of the movies rely on rap and/or hip hop music played in the background. The only exception to this is *Gimme the Loot* where the majority of the music is rhythm and blues, with the occasional gospel piece mixed in. *Wild Style* uses overly dramatic music, and it often seems like the film is more of a celebration of rap artists than graffiti. In *The Graffiti Artist*, the soundtrack is dominated by electronic music based on Indian tabla music. In *Bombing the System*, the soundtrack is punctuated with Indian music, including Bollywood, during a scene in a nightclub.

Displaying graffiti in galleries means that the artist/writer has sold out and/or been co-opted

In some of the movies, the protagonists confront the possibility that they could stop doing graffiti and could assume more legitimate/legal jobs or careers, especially through ceasing street-based graffiti activities and displaying of their work in galleries.[11] In *Dreams Don't Die*, Danny does not want to "sell out," but he eventually gets a job as an apprentice graphic artist. In *Wild Style*, the notion of joining a union of graffiti artists is proposed to Raymond, but he is not interested. Danny is also introduced to a bunch of "squares" at a party, including the director of acquisitions at the Whitney Museum of American Art, who does not take kindly to him. In *The Graffiti Artist*, Jesse suggests to Nick that he send photographs of his graffiti to a magazine called *Underground Productions* and try to have his work shown in a gallery. Nick says that he wants no part of this. In *Bombing the System*, Hazer, who was friends with Blest's dead brother and at whose place Blest is staying, reveals that he is ready to display his work at a gallery. Blest, however, refuses to follow his example.

Jeffrey Ian Ross

In short, for these protagonists, going legitimate is one of the most dreaded consequences to befall a graffiti artist and speaks of co-optation and/or selling out.

Rivalries among graffiti writers and crews frequently occur.
In order to keep the viewers engaged, the majority of the movies depict rivalries among individual graffiti writers and/or crews. *Wild Style*, for example, shows the rivalry between two graffiti crews. In *Gimme the Loot*, Malcolm and Sofia are up against the Westside Crew. In *Transit*, Ritchie's West Coast Kings is challenged by the ABC Crew. This leads to the deaths of the ABC leader and Ritchie.[12]

The characters, places and themes embodied in these movies reinforce stereotypes about graffiti writers and the conditions under which they operate. The films neglect the conclusions of contemporary research that are more nuanced with respect to who the perpetrators are, their motivations and the kinds of challenges they face in their lives.

Quality of the movies

Most of the characters, scenes and stories (or selected aspects of each) are unrealistic.
One of the most important issues that these movies can be criticised on is the degree to which they are a reflection of reality they are. Although they are understood to be works of fiction, in order to be believable, they must include substantial elements of reality. Unfortunately, many of these films undermine their legitimacy by including numerous unrealistic aspects as enumerated below. These movies fall short in their depictions of characters, scenes and stories.

Many of the *characters* appear caricature-like. In the movie *Wild Style*, from his clothing to his speech, Kirk, the juvenile drug dealer, bears little relation to actual drug dealers. He is seen being driven around town in a chauffeur-driven limousine while he does small-time drug deals and shoots at people from the comfort of this car. Similarly, in *Bomb the System*, from the food they eat to their dialogue, NYPD officers Cox and Shots appear to be caricatures of corrupt New York City police officers.

Stories
Some of the movies have gaps in the storylines, introduce questionable scenes or pose logical contradictions. In *Wild Style*, the movie moves from one scene to another without much logical sense. In *Dreams Don't Die*, a senior NYPD detective allows Danny to look through a police file on a suspected criminal. Although this may have been permissible during the 1970s, today it would certainly compromise the integrity of a police investigation. In *Against the Wall*, it is unclear why Lisa would hang out with someone with as few professional prospects as Curtis. In *The Graffiti Artist*, although Nick does not have any money, he is able to afford an apartment, and survive on shoplifting. Not once does he go to a homeless shelter or a public food line, or use food stamps for food. Additionally, although Nick is initially locked up, when he gets out of prison, he still has an apartment. Although Nick takes pictures with a disposable camera and the police take Polaroid photographs, it is unclear why in 2004, the year the movie was shot and ostensibly set in, no cell phones or digital cameras seem to be in use. In *Transit*, just in case the viewer cannot figure out that the men interrogating Ritchie are police officers, one of them eats a doughnut. Although Ritchie lives with his mother in a modest house and qualifies for a financial aid scholarship, he somehow has money to rent a studio. At the end of *Transit*, when Ritchie is shot, the sequence looks very unrealistic. In *Gimme the Loot*, Malcolm goes to a basement "headquarters" underneath a bodega in the Lower East Side run by two middle-class, university-educated, small-time pot dealers. It hard to imagine, that individuals like this would be putting small amounts of pot into bags and selling them.

434

Scenes
In *Transit*, toward the end of the movie there is a fist fight between Ritchie and Alex while the ABC crew watches. The fight is poorly choreographed. This flaw is exacerbated by the sound that does not sync with the punches. In the majority of the movies, many of the most unrealistic scenes surround criminal activities.

Most of the films appear amateurish
A little more than half of the films (i.e. *The Graffiti Artist*, *Bomb the System*, *Against the Wall/ Quality of Life* and *Gimme the Loot*) received awards at various film festivals. Despite these accolades, many of the films looked very amateurish in terms of acting and production values. This is embodied in the poor and/or forced acting, the transitions from one scene to another, the lack of authentic costumes, the poor sound and lighting quality and the choice of the angles and shots. Most of these difficulties can perhaps be explained because these movies probably depended on students and friends or acquaintances to play the parts, rather than professionals. Sometimes it even sounds like the actors forgot their lines because they hesitate in the delivery.

In terms of production values, although the fictional films may have a documentary feel, it is not clear why. This is reflected in the quality of the pictures and sound. Even though the grainy video, which occurs when film is shot at night under street, poor and/or minimal lighting conditions, may add to the authenticity and artistry of the films, it is also a reflection of the low budget that these films had. Both the amateurishness and the uneven story lines are probably connected to the relatively meagre budgets that were allocated for these movies.

Summary

It may be too early to suggest that there is a genre of graffiti films. However, the graffiti movie may be a subgenre of the modern day gangster films, like *Boys in the Hood*, *Warriors* etc. (Berman, 1992; Przemieniecki, 2005). Despite the obvious acts of vandalism that the graffiti writers engage in, there is little discussion about the criminal component of their actions. In many respects, the graffiti writers are portrayed as anti-heros or Robin Hoods (Campos, 2013).

Although some of these treatments of graffiti are accurate reflections of reality, there are numerous exceptions in the actual practice of graffiti (i.e. how graffiti writers engage in their craft), many of which have been identified in the scholarly literature. For example, although there are thriving graffiti (not to mention street art) scenes in New York City, Los Angeles, Seattle and Portland, almost every big city in the United States has a graffiti subculture. Each has different norms and key players. Thus to suggest that it only exists in the settings used in the fiction movies reviewed here is a bit narrow. Graffiti artists engage in graffiti for a number of reasons beyond fun and/or building a reputation (Taylor *et al.*, 2012). Moreover, the notion that graffiti writers have one or more absentee parents – primarily fathers who are either absent or "missing in action" – does not bear out in the academic literature. Finally, while many graffiti artists accede to the belief that displaying their work in galleries is a form of selling out or being co-opted, no empirical research indicates that this is a widespread perception. Similarly, there are usually no authority figures who come around to suggest or provide a path out of the graffiti lifestyle. These last points are perhaps better understood to be part of the myth-creation process surrounding the practice of graffiti and graffiti artists that has been formed by the wider dominant society. Indeed, the field of graffiti studies is at a rudimentary level. As more scholarly research and knowledge accrues, we can better critique these films and suggest ways that they differ from reality. This information should be communicated to parents, social workers, the news media, municipal politicians, departments of public works personnel and criminal justice practitioners, so that they can better understand and respond to graffiti and those who engage in this practice.

Documentaries

For the purposes of this analysis the documentary genre consists of films with nonfictional content, the intent of which is instruction or the capturing of a part of the historical record. Full-length documentaries usually run between 45 and 95 minutes in length. In addition, numerous short films (i.e. "shorts") (e.g. *Atlas: Los Angeles Graffiti Documentary* (2005) and *MUTO*, a wall-painted animation by BLU) documenting graffiti and street art have been made.

Many of these are accessible via YouTube or Amazon Prime, or third-party websites. The focus of this analysis, however, is on the longer and, in most cases, better known and easily accessible full-length movies. Thus the researcher has excluded what appear to be mostly unnarrated, self-produced/vanity home-style movies.[13]

In sum, the documentaries on graffiti/street art included in this review were all made between 1980 and 2012. Since the majority of these movies have been reviewed in other venues, this paper is not meant to be a collection of reviews. It seeks, however, to interpret their content and approach to their subject matter.

In general, documentaries on graffiti and street art can be placed into three categories: Movies focusing primarily on one graffiti/street artist and/or a particular graffiti crew; films that feature graffiti/street art in one particular location; and movies covering graffiti in different locations throughout the United States or around the world. The following is a brief review of the films using these categories.

A considerable amount of resources have been invested in the shooting, editing and directing of these movies. It was no easy feat to track down many of these individuals who spent a considerable portion of their lives engaging in graffiti/street art and evading detection. Also, in many cases, these documentaries required the directors and their crew to travel to both domestic and foreign places to capture the footage they wanted. This introduced additional logistical challenges. The conditions under which some of the films were shot, evidenced by grainy video and night shots under street, poor and/or minimal lighting conditions, is testimony to the directors' perseverance. It was also very resource intensive to track down the archival footage and photographs that were included in some of the films.

In the main, the documentaries on graffiti/street art are informative and professional looking. This is noticeable in the range of subject matter that most of these films cover, the editing and the quality of the shots. Viewers get to see inside the world of graffiti/street art and the people who do this sort of thing. The audience learns about how and why graffiti artists/writers are attracted to this activity, as well as the process of graffiti/street art, the difficulties between various writers/artists, and the work of anti-graffiti activists and vigilantes. These interviews and images are accompanied by music that is disproportionately drawn from the hip hop and/or rap genres.

The audience is presented with a considerable amount of time-lapse photographs and grainy colours, and the interviewees' faces are frequently pixelated to disguise the identity of the artists/writers. Time-lapse photography shows graffiti artists and crews installing new pieces on walls or other surfaces and/or how the walls/surfaces have changed over time as different writers/artists have placed their graffiti/street art there. Over the thirty-five-year period these movies span, the films reflect an increasing technical sophistication. In an indirect manner, most of these films attempt to confront popular myths and misrepresentations of graffiti writers and street artists as lacking respect for private property and as mindless anarchists. Some of these movies are very good at pointing out the hypocrisy of various situations. For example, in *Vigilante*

Vigilante, the buffers who go around town painting over graffiti are also committing vandalism. We also learn about how public space has been increasingly taken over by corporations advertising their goods and services, and how this has an effect on the urban visual landscape.

On the downside, these movies can be criticised for a number of reasons. First, although tags, throw-ups, pieces and paste-ups are identified, rarely are the differences among the various types of graffiti/street art explained to the viewer in an easily digestible manner. Nor are the advantages and disadvantages of these various techniques explained to the audience.

Second, while the majority of movies review graffiti artists and the graffiti/street art scene in big cities, both in the United States and elsewhere, other large cities with thriving graffiti/street art scenes, including Cairo, Shanghai and Toronto, are absent from these films. With the exception of some footage in South Africa, none of the movies touch upon graffiti/street art in Africa and the Middle East. Also underrepresented are places in Asia.

Third, with notable exceptions (e.g. *Exit Through the Gift Shop*, *Vigilante Vigilante*, *The Legend of Cool "Disco" Dan*), most of the documentaries resemble each other mainly because they repeat the same information, interview the same graffiti writers and street artists, dwell on the same kinds of issues and rarely go beyond these themes/tropes. We learn about the history of graffiti/street art, the major players, debates regarding whether it is art or simply vandalism and if this activity is still legitimate once the principle activity is moved from the streets to the gallery. The viewer of these films may ask what new information each new movie offers. Overall, these films sort of run together and get a little boring because they are so similar. With each new documentary movie, it becomes a case of diminishing returns. The films tend to repeat the same basic information without presenting any new interpretations and/or theories. In short, it does not seem like the directors did their homework by reviewing the other movies that were produced before embarking on their own films. To the directors'/producers' defence, it may very well be that at the time that many of these movies were produced (mid-2000s), the other films may not have been as widely accessible as they are today. Perhaps these movies were primarily playing in the independent film festival circuit.

Fourth, most of the narratives lack an argument and/or easily identifiable chronology. Some of the films (e.g. *Bomb It 2*) seem to simply be collections of vignettes with no central argument or point. They bounce around from one location to another, and from one graffiti/street artist to another. In some cases, the movies defy logic in terms of the choice of why certain cities and themes are included. For example, in early scenes of *Next: A Primer on Urban Painting*, we see shots of a spray paint manufacturer, but there is no logical reason why these are included. Other than the fact that graffiti had its historical origins in New York, and the movie starts and ends with shots of graffiti in that city, the viewer is not certain what the director's intent was in this case.

Finally, although a handful of the graffiti/street art documentaries also interview citizens, law enforcement and politicians about their reactions to graffiti and street art in their cities, almost all of the movies disproportionately rely on interviews with the artists/writers. Nonetheless, these individuals appear to be one-dimensional caricatures. Interviews with politicians, anti-graffiti activists and law enforcement officers seem tacked on like an afterthought. The almost singular approach to interviewing graffiti writers and street artists unnecessarily privileges the perpetrator's voice, placing them on pedestals and portraying them, in some cases, as super heroes (Campos, 2013).

It would have also been helpful to interview scholars of graffiti/street art to get a sense how they interpret this activity, and, with the exception of *Style Wars*, the families and loved ones of the graffiti/street artists to understand how they feel about this activity. The films fail to integrate the contemporary scholarly research on graffiti/street art that is more nuanced with respect to who the perpetrators are, their motivations, and the kinds of challenges they face in their lives.

Because of these drawbacks, many of these movies provide superficial analyses of their subject matter.

Conclusion

Feature length movies and documentaries that focus on graffiti/street art are important on varying levels. There is a wealth of information that has been captured and translated to the viewer.

That being said, in some respects, it would be more interesting for viewers to learn about how graffiti artist/writers and street artists go about making choices with respect to the types of images, paint, colours and methods of application and location. Other questions could include: What was their intent and meaning for the piece, if there was one at all? How much, if any, planning went into the pieces that they created? These sorts of questions are not answered well in the documentaries produced in this field.

Additional insights might have been drawn about these films if the investigator had interviewed the writers, directors, producers and/or graffiti/street artists featured in these movies. At the very least, the researcher could have asked questions about the rationales behind their productions. However, the investigator did not have the appropriate resources, nor did he think that the additional information would contribute much value to the findings presented here. This study only included English-language, American-made movies. Additional insights about the film medium may have been drawn and/or different results may have been achieved if foreign documentaries had also included in the review. However, this would have required a higher level of resources than the researcher had.

Over time, and in conclusion, these movies tend to repeat basic information and themes (i.e. the terms, the illegality of graffiti/street art, and well-known individuals who engage in graffiti). This constant repetition serves as the biggest encumbrance to this body of work in moving beyond superficial analyses and portrayals to more complex situations.

Notes

1 This chapter builds upon Ross (2015).
2 It would be useful to include fictional movies on street art, however, the researcher could not locate any.
3 As of this writing, the website www.graffitimovies.weebly.com, lists 206 films on the subject matter of graffiti, most of which are uploaded to that site. On closer examination, many of these movies are self-produced "home movies" of minimal quality. Moreover, many of these films do not appear to have a distinguishable narrative.
4 For example, only a small portion of *Beat Street* deals with graffiti, and the movie *Getting Up: Contents Under Pressure* is an animated movie connected to a computer game that uses graffiti.
5 Since most of the films were produced in the United States, it makes sense to focus on this type of film.
6 The researcher uses the term "graffiti writer/artist" interchangeably throughout this chapter.
7 Some may question the exclusion of *Exit Through The Gift Shop*, *Robbo v. Bansky*, and *RASH*. These films, however, are foreign-produced films.
8 Given that the origins of graffiti and street art are American, an argument might be made for the importance of movies that originate from the United States.
9 For reasons unknown to the writer, this movie has been released with two different titles.
10 In all likelihood, there are numerous movies made by film students that are of a fictional nature; however, the ones reviewed here are well known and have, in some, respects achieved a cult status.

11 Closely related to this trend is the graffiti writer who despite his attempts to go straight, has friends who pull him back into the game. For example, in *Transit*, Shifty encourages Ritchie to continue writing, despite being on parole and his inclination to stop.

12 My comment is not to dismiss the importance of conflict in a graffiti writers' career (e.g. Snyder, 2011), but to question the dominance of this element and why it is included in almost all of these films.

13 These films include, but are not limited to, Cope2 – Kings Destroy; 5 AM Part 1; 5 AM Part 2, State Your Name and Fuckgraff #1.

References

Berman, S.J. (1992). View at your own risk: Gang movies and spectator violence. *Loyola of Los Angeles Entertainment Law Journal, 12*: 477–507.

Campos, R. (2013). Graffiti writer as superhero. *European Journal of Cultural Studies, 16*(2): 155–170.

Kramer, R. (2010). Painting with permission: legal graffiti in New York City. *Ethnography, 11*(2): 235–253.

Monaco, J. (1977). *How to Read a Film*. New York: Oxford University Press.

Przemieniecki, C.J. (2005). Gang behavior and movies: Do hollywood gang films influence violent gang behavior. *Journal of Gang Research, 12*(2): 41–71.

Rafter, N. (2006). *Shots in the Mirror: Crime Films and Society* (2nd edn). New York: Oxford University Press.

Rafter, N. (2007). Crime, film and criminology recent sex-crime movies. *Theoretical Criminology, 11*(3): 403–420.

Rafter, N.H. & Brown, M. (2011). *Criminology Goes to the Movies: Crime Theory and Popular Culture*. New York: New York University Press.

Ross, J.I. (2015). Graffiti goes to the movies: American fictional films featuring graffiti artists/writers and themes, *Contemporary Justice Review, 18*(3): 366–383.

Snyder, G.J. (2011). *Graffiti lives: Beyond the Tag in New York's Urban Underground*. New York: New York University Press.

Taylor, M.F., Marais, I., & Cottman, R. (2012). Patterns of graffiti offending: Towards recognition that graffiti offending is more than 'kids messing around'. *Policing and Society: An International Journal of Research and Policy, 22*(1): 152–168.

Welsh, A., Fleming, T., & Dowler, K. (2011). Constructing crime and justice on film: meaning and message in cinema. *Contemporary Justice Review, 14*(4): 457–476.

Yar, M. (2010). Screening crime: Cultural criminology goes to the movies. In K.J. Hayward & M. Presdee (eds), *Framing Crime: Cultural Criminology and the Image*, (pp. 68–82). London: Routledge.

33

Challenging the defense of graffiti, in defense of graffiti

Stefano Bloch

Introduction

In my decade long career as an active graffiti writer in Los Angeles during the 1990s, I witnessed some of the most rampant criminalization and disproportionate violence ever committed against writers in the United States. Beginning in 1991 with the first well-publicized arrest of Chaka, the notorious tagger (Anima, 1991; Sahagun, 1991), followed by local news coverage of the "graffiti scourge" and the hugely popular Fox's "Front Page" undercover exposé on so-called "tag-bangers" (combination of "tagger" and "gang banger") in 1993, everyday citizens across the city were made acutely aware of the supposed violence committed by graffiti writers that accompanied writing on walls. As a result of the conflation between vandalism and violence, politicians and law enforcement called for increased abatement and far stricter penalties for graffiti writers.

Writing one's name on surfaces around the city, which was once treated by law enforcement as an infraction, or misdemeanor charge at worst, began in the 1990s to be treated as a felony-level assault on the city.[1] Whereas New York City politicians and police officials beginning in the 1980s argued that graffiti was a "quality of life" issue, in Los Angeles graffiti went from being identified as "indigenist glyphs" (Latorre, 2008) and "barrio calligraphy" (Sanchez-Tranquilino, 1995; Chastanet, 2009) beginning in the 1940s, to being seen by some as a matter of life and death.

In 1992 the homicide rate in Los Angeles rose to an all-time high, with over 1,200 murders citywide, including 53 killings directly related to the L.A. Riots. Gang membership was also at its peak, as was the proliferation in the number of graffiti writers and "tagging crews." The justified fear and rampant paranoia people felt during this violent era, which even among graffiti writers is known as the "Dark Days,"[2] contributed to the idea that all forms of graffiti, particularly when done illegally and lacking in colorful imagery, legible lettering, and apparent artistry, was evidence of a brutal demarcation of property.

Whereas gang members have in fact traditionally used graffiti in addition to violence to lay claim to territory, writers use graffiti (or non-gang related "tagging") to gain personal fame, challenge abstract notions of authority, and nonviolently assert their fleeting presence over a wide geographical area.

The easy conflation of the two distinct street-based subcultures could not be more distorted. For gangs – a group for whom territorial demarcation is part of their *raison d'etre* – tagging presents a vivid existential challenge. So threatening was non-gang graffiti to turf integrity in the gang-ridden streets of Los Angeles during the early 1990s, the Mexican Mafia purportedly issued a "green light" on taggers (Phillips, 1999).[3] The edict allowing for the killing of taggers regardless of their race was passed down from the *veteranos* in the California State prisons to the "pee-wees" on the streets that were responsible for violently maintaining the integrity of the *barrio* and its drug trade. Like members of aggressive home owners' associations, real estate agencies, and chambers of commerce, especially in economically fragmented places like Los Angeles (Davis, 1990), gang members are highly aware of the challenge that graffiti presents to territorial control and declared authority over place identity.

By the 1990s, violence committed by gang members against graffiti writers became all too personal as it began to take the lives of some of my best friends and writing partners. Skesk was beaten to death and Cycle was shot and killed by members of the infamous Mara Salvatrucha (MS) gang. My closest friend and first writing partner with whom I would go "all-city" during the first years of the decade was Efren "Tolse" Barbosa. He was shot at close range by a member of the Pacoima 13 gang. In none of these cases was the victim "mistaken for a gang member" as local media accounts would have it (Miller and Ha, 1999). In each case he was killed because he was a graffiti writer.

But it was the killing of a writer by a vigilante in 1995 that attracted the most news media attention due in part to the added component of "victim-precipitated" inter-race violence.[4] Ceasar Rene "Insta" Arce was shot in the back as he ran away after having written his name on a freeway underpass in the San Fernando Valley. His killer, William Masters, was celebrated and congratulated by members of the local community and law enforcement as a "hero," "do-gooder," an "observant neighbor" and a "white knight" (Riccardi & Tamaki, 1995; Phillips, 1999), for combating graffiti and the "Mexican skinheads" who did it (Carrillo, 1995). Masters was not criminally changed for Insta's death, but was sentenced to thirty days of community service, removing graffiti, for a misdemeanor conviction for carrying a concealed and loaded firearm in public (Hernandez, 1995).

Insta's killing marks a significant turning point in L.A.'s most violent era. By the end of the decade a gang truce had been brokered between the notorious Bloods and Crips gangs, and the green light on taggers had been rescinded. Homicide rates would begin their steepest and longest plummet in city history, and by 1997 the district attorney could no longer aggregate individual misdemeanor offenses to form a felony charge. The period also marks the very beginning of a cultural change in the way Angelenos appear to have begun viewing graffiti as more of a quality of life infraction than a violent crime akin to drive-by shootings, thereby relocating it into the more acceptable realm of low-level urban offenses. This change in perception may have been spurred by an increased use of graffiti in mainstream marketing, media, and in the production of local creative capital by the turn of the century (Baudrillard, 1993; see also Alvelos, 2004). Just as it had once been associated with hip-hop culture in New York, it was becoming seen as part of hipster culture in L.A..

In neighborhoods like Echo Park – a traditionally Chicano/a and bohemian district in Los Angeles (Hurewitz, 2007) – graffiti, which was once seen as evidence of a strong gang presence, began to be seen as indicative of artsy lifestyles and fashionably transgressive sensibilities (Bloch, 2012a). Part of this shift is the result of graffiti increasingly being understood as produced by white, art-school educated, middle-class, suburban, men and women possessing high degrees of distinctive social, economic, and cultural capital (Bourdieu, 1984, 1986; Lasley, 1995). The turn away from conflating graffiti with gang activity also resulted in a name change.

Graffiti in some of its more acceptable forms began to be called "street art," a less portentous term than "post-graffiti," which had been in use in academic circles since the efforts to gallerize graffiti in New York City in 1983 (Janis, 1983; Dickens, 2008). Both terms, however, speak to the fact that graffiti, which is typically seen as a cryptic form of text produced with spray paint and markers, was being included with stenciling, stickering, and wheatpasting, which the general public could more easily decipher and interpret as an elevated form of creative industry and focused talent, which, as street artist Shepard Fairey puts it, is no-less "integrated with the texture of the street" (Manco, 2002: p. 103; see also Dickens, 2010; McAuliffe, 2012).

By 2004 in Echo Park, where the Los Angeles Police Department's militarized CRASH (Community Resources Against Street Hoodlums) units once patrolled and often brutalized suspected taggers and gang members alike, "art openings" for graffiti writers and street artists were becoming common. In fact, Banksy, the world's most well-known street artist (Banksy, 2006; Young, 2014), had his first U.S. show in a space I had been criminally charged for writing on less than ten years earlier. On the night of his opening, formerly suburban residents who had once feared the likes of urban graffiti writers were mingling with them, even asking for "autographs" and taking pictures. For those of us in the graffiti community nothing had changed except for how we were being received in such spaces and social situations. The performative and street-based practice of doing graffiti was just as perilous as it had always been, especially given the difficulty in accessing and marking infrastructure (Austin, 2001), but the superficial aesthetic of graffiti was being displaced and warmly embraced. The newfound acceptance and increased celebrity did not sit well with me. Only when contested and unrestrained did I feel that graffiti had something to say.

Deeply superficial perspectives[5]

At 6 am on December 31, 1996, just before the California State Legislature's prohibition on aggregating vandalism misdemeanors to form a felony charge would go into effect, Detective Jerry Beck and the Los Angeles Police Department's "Community Tagger Task Force" raided my family's North Hollywood apartment. My ailing mother, 13-year-old brother, and 6-year-old sister with her tight curls and flower-patterned night gown were ordered at gun point by Detective Beck to lay on the living room floor as a dozen heavily armed and armored officers and accompanying civilian volunteers tore through every room. They left once they had collected what they considered incriminating evidence sufficient to charge me with a felony by linking me to a string of misdemeanor vandalism offenses: as itemized in the complaint, a set of colored pencils, a school folder with "various markings adorning it," and a shoe box with "graffiti monikers scrawled across it." I pled guilty to individual misdemeanor charges to avoid an enhanced 2-year prison sentence being offered by the District Attorney.

In the years preceding my arrest I had faced less-coordinated challenges to my tenure as a graffiti writer, though from the perspective of a generally timid teenager each confrontation with anti-graffiti "heroes," vigilantes, gang members, and cops alike was equally as frightening as well as validating of graffiti's import.

What each type of anti-graffiti zealot has in common with those they pursue, arrest, and sometimes kill is a deep respect for and understanding of the potentially transformative power of graffiti. To be preoccupied with the seemingly superficial appearance and personal demarcation of the built environment relies on the type of spatial consciousness and action that Lefebvre (2003) understood as revolutionary. It may be those who are morally panicked and outraged by its presence who recognize that graffiti is a form of transgression and contestation that forces us to outright question, or at least consciously think about, moral geographies (Cresswell, 1996;

McAuliffe, 2012) and what Edensor (2005) calls "authoritative spatialization" – or the normative spatial codes and dominant ideological structures that are manifested in and on public space. So challenging is graffiti to the dominant sense of order, as Iveson (2007) points out, municipalities have even gone so far as to wage wars on graffiti that rely on the type of rhetoric and militarization of police and public space typically reserved for anti-terrorist campaigns.

Part of the reason graffiti is understood as a challenge to authoritative spatialization is due to how it reveals the contradiction of urban space seen and treated as a commodity with exchange value as well as a collective resource with myriad use values. For Lefebvre (1991) and others (Harvey, 2001), this contradiction is inherent in the capitalist production of space. However, to use Foucault's (1986) terminology, the continued production of a more "heterotopic," or diverse and mutually contestative, space is possible, but only through what constitute "deviant," "anti-social," and "criminal" acts committed against existing spatial manifestations of power.

The resulting disorderly and anarchic system of producing space engenders another kind of order for Lefebvre (1991, 2003). That is, a logic and order arising from a non-hierarchical, unplanned, and practiced city, which lends itself to the fight for spatial justice (Soja, 1996, 2010). For Lefebvre, refiguring the dominant organization of space must be accomplished in the street, materially, with the use of "bulldozers and Molotov cocktails" (1991: p. 56), or symbolically whereby the street becomes a

> place for talk, given over as much to the exchange of words and signs as it is to the exchange of things. A place where speech becomes writing. A place where speech can become 'savage' and, by escaping rules and institutions, inscribe itself on walls.
>
> (2003: p. 19)

While far from constituting terrorist acts or engendering an immediate or recognizable overthrow of the capitalistic, hierarchical, and planned city system, from a spatial perspective graffiti is after all, and should be, illegal. It is the act of illegally occupying and writing on infrastructure that defines graffiti as such. Graffiti signifies the presence of a person acting "out of place" by making a personalized claim for space, which rebukes conventions for private property, the rule of law, standards regarding the appropriate appearance of infrastructure, and mores regarding acceptable public behavior (Bloch, 2012b). To accost, hunt down, and even violently attack those who illegally paint on walls is to preserve a system whereby only those who legally own, oversee, or pay may lawfully enter, alter, or personalize the seemingly superficial appearance of the city.

Concurring with those who adhere to the philosophy of the Broken Windows theory (Kelling & Wilson, 1982), graffiti is in fact transformative. If allowed to "stay up," the unsanctioned graffiti mark provides evidence of a community that is oblivious to, ambivalent about, permissive, or even encouraging of socio-spatial transgression wrought against the *status-quo* of law, order, and ownership. While graffiti is certainly superficial in what it is literally and materially appending to surfaces, its perceived effect on moral, normative constructions of space is deeply profound. To defend graffiti as not being worthy of such extrapolation would be to render the power of authoritative spatialization moot. Such a move would have consequences for critical understandings of hegemonic power and ideological structures (Althusser, 1971; Gramsci, [1971] 1996).

Below I provide examples of how it is, perhaps counter intuitively, the defense of graffiti that may be most effective at abating graffiti and rendering it meaningless as a potentially transformative socio-spatial act. It is not those who aggressively confront graffiti who lack an understanding of its potential to challenge dominant socio-spatial forms of order and control, but rather, I argue, it is those who celebrate graffiti as an "art form" and advocate for "permission walls" without regard for its spatial context who may be unwittingly diluting its strength. As Iveson (2007: p. 135) puts it, "legal graffiti projects reinscribe a respect for private property relations, and the consequent control by owners over the appearance of public space in which they are located."

Within the large literature on graffiti that recognizes it as a systematic, stylized, and personalized form of illegal wall writing by members of a geographically dispersed, though socially cohesive subculture (e.g. Kurlansky *et al.*, 1974; Castleman, 1982; Ferrell, 1996; Macdonald, 2001; Young, 2014), there have in fact been those who focus more explicitly on the spatiality of this modern urban phenomenon.

In one of the first accounts of graffiti as distinct from overtly political, personal, or gang-affiliated wall writing, Ley and Cybriwsky (1974) distinguish "loner" graffiti writing from other forms of wall writing by mapping its spatial diffusion across Philadelphia and pointing to local "graffiti king" Corn Bread's disregard for bounded territoriality. For Ley and Cybriwsky, modern graffiti is distinct from earlier forms of wall writing because of its placement and prolificacy more than its aesthetic aims or the personal motivations behind its production.

Cultural criminologist Jeff Ferrell (1996) understands graffiti as a visual expression of anarchic action taken against and engendered by the spatial controls and physical partitioning of activities put upon urban inhabitants by policy makers, property owners, law enforcement, and other dominant communities. Graffiti writers need not be conscious of the socio-spatial or political transgression taking place since it is the prohibition and reaction it precipitates that, according to Bataille (Foucault, 1977; see also Suleiman, 1990: p. 75), is revealing of and challenging to normative socio-spatial boundaries. It is here, in considering writers' intentionality, that graffiti as transgression is clearly distinct from graffiti as deliberate, overtly politically motivated, or articulable contestation (Ferrell, 1996, 2001, 2012).

Continuing with his project to spatialize graffiti, in his article with Weide (Ferrell & Weide, 2010), Ferrell investigates in deep ethnographic fashion the physical placement of graffiti, providing situated spatial analysis of graffiti's engagement with the urban environment through the categorization of the "spots" that writers access and select to showcase their work (see also Austin, 2001). Each category – "audiences and visibility," "longevity and durability," "availability and competition," and "seriality and accumulation" – focuses on the importance of placement above all else. As in Borden's (2001) work on skateboarding, innovative "spot" selection is crucial to an actor's identity and status within a spatially-consciousness subculture, which is often glossed over in traditional subcultural studies that understate the deep intricacies of space (Hall & Jefferson, ([1976] 1993).

But it has been Cresswell (1996) who has developed the clearest link between the illegality of graffiti and its physical placement. He asserts that graffiti is criminalized for its transgression against moral landscapes, thereby signaling "inappropriate geographical behavior." The source of graffiti's criminality, he argues, "lies in its being seen . . . and in the subversion of the authority or urban space" (p. 58). For Cresswell, and recently for Young (2014), the almost universal anxiety, disgust for, and rampant criminalization of graffiti reveals the complex "common sense" workings of the form, function, and appearance of the urban environment. As Young (2014: p. 145) puts it, unauthorized wall writing and street art "makes its own space, not as a partitioned, permitted, semi-tolerated activity, but as an emergent, auto-poietic practice, a de-territorializing tactic that exposes the multiple boundaries and borders of the propertied cityscape."

Challenging the common defenses of graffiti

Informed by these and other writings in addition to my own practice and spatial perspective as an active graffiti writer for over a decade, I now introduce cursory challenges to four widely articulated defenses of and supportive rhetorical approaches to graffiti that appear in everyday discourse, popular writings, and within the academic literature. I initiate this argument in an effort to provoke conversation and to identify graffiti's most powerful attribute as a marker and producer of alternative urban spatialities. I do so not to romanticize or justify graffiti as a counter-moralizing act or service consciously performed in the interest of forwarding social or spatial justice, but to argue that regardless of writers' intentions, graffiti reveals the otherwise unseen geographical boundaries and deeply-held aesthetic sensibilities that most people take for granted and sometimes actively and even violently defend.

There should be legal spaces for graffiti

By advocating for legal walls and sanctioned spaces, supporters are contributing to the confinement of graffiti, thereby reducing it to an aesthetic product rather than a productive aspect of public urbanism.

Legal and semi-legal walls and "yards" have long been important to graffiti writers looking for a place to meet and practice their styles. But suggesting that legal walls would be an appropriate substitute for existing expanses of city space, or that legal spaces would help reduce unwanted graffiti elsewhere, is uninformed from a writers' perspective. Even when afforded sanctioned public spaces, such as the Art Wall in Venice, California, or any number of tacitly tolerated yards such as the recently redeveloped Five Points in New York City and Belmont Tunnel in the Westlake District of Los Angeles, graffiti writers do not shirk at the opportunity to simultaneously produce graffiti elsewhere. The notion that legal or semi-legal spaces help to reduce less desirable graffiti has not been sufficiently supported by anecdotal or statistical evidence (Shobe & Banis, 2014).

Legal spaces also force graffiti writers to engage with and be beholden to local government and property owners – two groups to whom writers have traditionally been antagonistic. Furthermore, such a relationship robs graffiti of its autonomy and subcultural legitimacy. Asking for permission is a deathblow to a subculture bent on the improvisational, aggressive, and individualistic marking of space.

While, as Halsey and Young (2002), Snyder (2009), Kramer (2010a), McAuliffe (2013), and others show, there exists a subset of graffiti "artists" who transition into legal, municipally sanctioned, "subcultural careers" and primarily paint legal walls, the argument that legal walls succeed in satisfying graffiti writers' artistic desires minimizes the complexity and importance of what it means to pursue a politically and spatially transgressive graffiti career in the first place. Such a focus on "career opportunities," the "professional path," and the use of the problematic concept of the "life course" (Snyder, 2009) posit the desire to maturely and gainfully create art as a predominant motivator for doing graffiti over the concerted desire to occupy and demarcate space for a variety of less practical and profit-oriented reasons. McAuliffe and Iveson (2011) and MacDiarmid and Downing (2012) are correct to problematize the strict legal/illegal binary and emphasize how graffiti writers who do seek out and rely on legal spaces actually drift between legal and illegal involvement, which challenges the notion that the "professional path" out of the graffiti subculture is smooth and unidirectional, even when desired.

Stefano Bloch

There should be art programs for graffiti writers

Similar to the culturally enervating effects of spatial confinement, government financing and private support for arts programs weaken graffiti through economic legitimization and conservative frameworks for expression. Advocating for confined, funded, and bureaucratically structured art programs neglects the fact that graffiti is more than a visual art. Graffiti is a performative art practiced by those who are not merely frustrated artists looking for "creative outlets," but as Halsey and Young (2006: pp. 276–277) put it, it is "an *affective* process that *does things* to writers' bodies (and the bodies of onlookers) as much as to the bodies of metal, concrete and plastic, which typically compose the surfaces of urban worlds" (emphasis in original). Such a perspective is, indeed, in need or further attention and elaboration (Campbell, 2012).

Within the context of the cultural economy of cities, securing proper – i.e. legal – spaces for graffiti may in fact help package it for easy and profitable consumption in exactly the way so-called neoliberal place makers and profiteers desire. Such a fear of the loss of legitimacy for graffiti through its relocation and cooptation was common in New York City during the late 1970s and early 1980s. In his criticism of the gallerization and rebranding of graffiti as "Post-Graffiti" (Janis, 1983), Lachmann (1988) drew a distinction between what was being painted on the subways and streets at the time and what was being brought into the space of the gallery. He advocated for unsanctioned and spontaneous graffiti, and against the market sterilization of graffiti, which was accompanied by the destruction of "writers' benches" and the "value of pursuing artistic, deviant, or any activity with others" (p. 249). Further, despite support for municipal art programs, many graffiti writers insist that "graffiti and the art world have incompatible and irreconcilable ideological strategies, and that they should exist as separate spheres" (Dickens, 2008: p. 7).

Scholars have also argued that legal spaces and arts programs provide more time and resources for composition, thus allowing graffiti writers to paint to their full potential, thereby making it more aesthetically appealing. As with spatial confinement, arts program-based graffiti is often that which is easily consumed and superficially celebrated as "authentic," despite the objective loss of context. Furthermore, the notion that arts education contributes to an aesthetically superior form of graffiti often relies on metaphors that suggest that graffiti writers "evolve" from producing simplistic tags to painting sophisticated pieces under supportive conditions. While such assumptions are supported by the fact that some graffiti writers do transition into careers in arts-related professions based on their subcultural status and fostered talents (Snyder, 2009), the fact is graffiti writers actually showcase expanded repertoires as they develop their skill set on the street. As legendary graffiti writer and artist Mear One put it,

> I might blow you away with a mural that takes me all day to paint, but on my way home I'm still gonna catch tags the whole way. You might even hire me to come paint a 'beautiful' mural over that 'ugly tagging' that 'somebody' 'scribbled' on your wall.[6]

Graffiti is art

Evoking graffiti's artistic appeal posits "ugly" graffiti – i.e. illegible, monochromatic, out of place – as less desirable than colorful, legible, "beautiful," and properly placed graffiti based on subjective criteria, and therefore positions some types of graffiti as less worthy of occupying space. Such binary reductionism justifies the hatred of some graffiti, which, by extension, is used as justification for the hatred of "some types" of graffiti writers based on age, class, level of educational attainment, race, and ethnicity.

Graffiti is not a crime

Positing that graffiti is not a crime differs slightly from the unrealistic argument that graffiti should be legal. While the former argument appeals to graffiti as, perhaps, a decontextualized art form, the latter speaks to forms of graffiti that, due to their placement, fall under the category of vandalism, but apparently should not. While it is true that some incarnations of graffiti are in fact not a crime, graffiti as vandalism is.

In general, however, proponents of the legalization of graffiti are employing an unrealistic normative framework that is, to use Estlund's (2014: p. 118) playful concept, "hopelessly aspirational." But instead of challenging the argument for legalization on the grounds that it is unrealistic, I ask that we shift our attention from that "utopian project" to ask to what degree graffiti, as an act of transgression or contestation, is effective at challenging people's conceptualization of existing moral geographies.

Regardless of how effective graffiti is at forcing people to acknowledge the presence and power of moral geographies, the unsanctioned mark does reveal the occurrence of a trespass in both normative spatial and social terms (Young, 2014). The conflation of the spatial and the social in determining low-level crime is frequent even when law enforcement is dealing with "victimless" offenses, or what criminologist call "public-order crimes" in which participants consensually take part and for which there is no immediate or direct threat to potential victims. Trespassing and most forms of vandalism, loitering, disorderly conduct, and other spatially-conceived crimes are generally non-violent, but nevertheless may elicit high-levels of social ostracism, physical banishment, aggressive policing strategies, and occasionally incarceration, thereby limiting individuals' right to the city. Controlling behavior through the imposition of moral geographies in and across a bounded territory or neighborhood is a prevalent law enforcement tactic. So-called "place-based policing" (Weisburd et al., 2008), which derives in part from the logic of the Broken Windows theory, understands quality of life crimes as clustering in particular deviant and disorderly spaces and committed by "disreputable, obstreperous, and disorderly people" (Harcourt, 2009: p. 31; see also Kelling & Wilson, 1982).

Regardless of the hotly contested issue of spatial policing within the social sciences (Herbert, 1997; Mitchell, 1997; Herbert & Brown, 2006; Crawford, 2010), the presence of graffiti still suggests that someone has acted out in a way that does not jibe with socio-spatial norms and conventions for appropriate behavior. Graffiti in this way is in fact disorderly as it challenges top-down notions of orderly behavior.

Conclusion

Most convincingly challenging my position that graffiti should not be defended are the graffiti writers themselves who are often quoted in academic texts and popular media outlets advocating for legal spaces, decriminalization, and increased arts education. The profusion of such opinions in scholarly writings is the result of how some academics and journalists in the field access particular types of entrenched graffiti writers who may be aligned with non-profit arts organizations or are part of, or firmly on a career path toward, the legitimate private arts sector.

In major centers of graffiti activity – Los Angeles, New York, London, Paris, Berlin, Rome, São Paulo, Buenos Aires, and Melbourne for example – there appear oft-quoted unofficial spokespersons speaking for the cohesive though loose-knit global graffiti community. Many of these *de facto* spokespeople contend with harsh criticisms coming from the general public, law enforcement, members of the business community, property owners, mural organizations, and "urban arts" educational non-profits. To counter myriad existential challenges to graffiti/street art, or merely to advocate for their own vested interest in seeing greater tolerance for and nuance in the definition of graffiti (McAuliffe & Iveson, 2011; MacDiarmid & Downing, 2012), these spokespersons adhere to a narrow perspective that consists of calls for decriminalization, legitimacy, permission, and ultimately legality.

While some call for increased tolerance as part of a desire for social justice and respect for diversity, in many cases such advocacy works in the interest of the promotion of privately owned graffiti apparel and "artist spray paint" shops, "how-to" graffiti art and mural classes, private mainstream art careers, and "urban art" galleries that cater to presumably law abiding consumers of a safe graffiti aesthetic.

Those who rely on entrenched writers as respondents may be at pains to include a diversity of opinions given the difficulty that "outsiders" face in accessing the more prolific or radical members of an elusive criminal subculture (Adler & Adler, 1987).[7] Whereas in popular media the focus often falls on internationally known graffiti "artists" who have "made it," or presumably "made it out" – Keith Haring, Basquiat, Barry Mcgee, and others – in the academic literature the focus often falls all too easily on those who actively network and legally self-promote.

Finding and accessing respondents in the field has ranged from "asking art dealers and collectors for the names of 'graffiti artists' " (Lachmann, 1988: p. 233) and making contact at an art opening with " 'writers' who were organized into a marketing agency" (Rahn, 1999: p. 22), to "simply call[ing] the number" graffiti writers had written on the legal murals they had painted (Kramer, 2010a, p. 241) and approaching graffiti writers at "legal writing events" (MacDiarmid & Downing, 2012: p. 610). In his "rewriting of subcultural resistance" and ethnography of graffiti writers' successful "career paths," Snyder (2009: p. 22) admits that he gained access to the graffiti community, or "got in," in part by dressing in "the latest hip hop fashions."

While each of these pooling examples appears appropriate given the difficulty in making contact as an outsider-researcher, what is missing from the data is the perspective on the legality/illegality of graffiti belonging to those writers who are more guarded or even hostile to the notion of discussing and justifying their illicit practice. Furthermore, in addition to being more likely to advocate for legal spaces for doing graffiti "art," the community of entrenched graffiti writers tend to be disproportionately affluent, formally educated, white, male, and as Brewer (1992) puts it, "mature," which provides a minority of writers with the privilege of speaking on behalf of the majority. As Brewer (1992: p. 189) bluntly explains, when making contact he distinguishes between taggers and "elite writers," or those who "tend to be older and more experienced as writers, possess more maturity for systematic interviewing tasks, and have greater awareness of traditional and alternative strategies to control illegal graffiti."

While some graffiti writers may articulate a well-rehearsed position for the legalization or decriminalization of doing graffiti for a variety of personal reasons that range from their political standpoint to self-preservation, outsiders who do the same may be inadvertently arguing for the demise of a practice, performance, and aesthetic for which they may otherwise advocate. Mainstreaming graffiti by bringing it under the banner of legitimacy removes one of the most visibly transgressive and contestative acts from the public sphere. Such an act further relegates subversive, creative, and bottom-up uses of space to the margins, as those with identifiable "skill," "talent," proper motivation, and legal spatial literacy contribute to the reinforcement of socio-spatial parameters issued from the top-down.

Notes

1   While several high profile graffiti writers have faced long prison sentences for vandalism, these individuals were most often also facing other charges for weapons and drug violations and typically had prior arrest records. While I do not want to downplay the disproportionate criminalization and

incarceration of graffiti writers that has in fact occurred, I also think it would be dishonest to suggest that long jail sentences issued for vandalism alone have been the norm. In fact, in the face of moral panics, overzealous policing, and impetuous district attorneys (Kramer, 2010b), judges have been slow if not reluctant to issue harsh sentences for graffiti vandalism. As Halsey and Young (2006: p. 290) point out in their study, "an important distinction needs to be made here between *crimes committed in order to write illegally*, as against *other crimes* committed by those who happen, at certain times, to write illegally."

2   Personal interview, Wisk, July 4, 2013.

3   Personal communications, 1994–2014.

4   In some cases, victims are seen as a major contributor to a criminal act (Wolfgang, 1957) and are believed to have contributed to their own victimization as a result of direct provocation, a failure to reasonably protect themselves, or as result of their appearance or membership in a group that could reasonably be seen as placing them in harm's way. Criminologists refer to this as "Victim Precipitated Homicide," which has often been used to justify the killing of taggers or to suggest that such an action was a matter of self-defense on the part of the perpetrator.

5   I borrow the term "deeply superficial" from political street artist Robbie Conal and his description of the importance placed on and extracted from outward appearances in Los Angeles.

6   Personal interview, Mear One, April 24, 2014.

7   For applicable discussions on "edgework," or ethnographic field work among dangerous and marginal populations, the homeless, sex workers, drug dealers, graffiti writers, and gang members, see Ferrell and Hamm (1998).

References

Adler, P.A. & Adler P. (1987). *Membership roles in field research*. Thousand Oaks, CA: Sage.

Althusser, L. (1971). Ideology and ideological state apparatuses (notes towards an investigation). In *Lenin and philosophy and other essays* (p. 127).

Alvelos, H. (2004). The desert of imagination in the city of signs: Cultural implications of sponsored transgression and branded graffiti. In Ferrell, F., Hayward, K., Morrison, W. & Presdee, M. (eds), *Cultural criminology unleashed* (pp. 181–192). London: Glasshouse.

Anima, T, (1991). "Prosecutors await 'Chaka' report." *Los Angeles Times*, May 4.

Austin, J. (2001). *Taking the train: How graffiti art became an urban crisis in New York city*. New York: Columbia University Press.

Banksy. (2006). *Wall and piece*. New York: Random House.

Baudrillard, J. (1993). Kool killer, or the insurrection of signs. *Symbolic exchange and death* (pp. 76–86). London: Sage.

Bloch, S. (2012a). *The changing face of wall space: Graffiti-murals in the context of neighborhood change in Los Angeles*. Ph.D. dissertation. Minneapolis, MN: University of Minnesota.

Bloch, S. (2012b). The illegal face of wall space: Graffiti-murals on the Sunset Boulevard retaining walls. *Radical History Review*, *2012*(113), 111–126.

Borden, I. (2001). *Skateboarding, space and the city: Architecture and the body*. London: Bloomsbury Academic.

Bourdieu, P. (1984). *Distinction: A social critique of the judgment of taste*. Cambridge, MA: Harvard University Press.

Bourdieu, P. (1986). The forms of capital. In Richardson, J. (ed.), *Handbook of theory and research for the sociology of education* (pp. 241–258). Westport, CT: Greenwood.

Brewer, D.D. (1992). Hip hop graffiti writers' evaluations of strategies to control illegal graffiti. *Human Organization*, *51*(2), 188–196.

Campbell, E. (2012). Transgression, affect and performance: Choreographing a politics of urban space. *British Journal of Criminology*, *53*(1), 18–40.

Carrillo, L.A. (1995). "Perspectives on the tagger shooting: How to kill a Latino kid and walk free." *Los Angeles Times*, November 27.

Castleman, C. (1982). *Getting up: Subway graffiti in New York*. Cambridge, MA: MIT Press.

Chastanet, F. (2009). *Cholo writing: Latino gang graffiti in Los Angeles*. Årsta, Sweden: Dokument Press.

Crawford, C.E. (2010). *Spatial policing: The influence of time, space, and geography on law enforcement practices*. Durham, NC: Carolina Academic Press.

Cresswell, T. (1996). *In place-out of place: Geography, ideology, and transgression*. Minneapolis, MN: University of Minnesota Press.

Davis, M. (1990). *City of quartz: Excavating the future in Los Angeles*. London: Verso.

Dickens, L. (2008). Placing post-graffiti: The journey of the peckham rock. *Cultural Geographies, 15*(4), 471–496.

Dickens, L. (2010). Pictures on walls? Producing, pricing and collecting the street art screen print. *City, 14*(1–2), 63–81.

Edensor, T. (2005). *Industrial ruins: Space, aesthetics and materiality*. Oxford: Berg.

Ferrell, J. (1996). *Crimes of style: Urban graffiti and the politics of criminality*. Boston, MA: Northeastern University Press.

Ferrell, J. (2001). *Tearing down the streets: Adventures in urban anarchy*. New York: Palgrave Macmillan.

Ferrell, J. (2012). Anarchy, geography and drift. *Antipode, 44*(5), 1687–1704.

Ferrell, J. & Hamm, M.S. (eds) (1998). *Ethnography at the edge: Crime, deviance, and field research*. Lebanon, NH: University Press of New England.

Ferrell, J. & Weide R.D. (2010). Spot theory. *City, 14*(1–2), 48–62.

Foucault, M. (1986). Of other spaces. *Diacritics, 16*(1), 22–27.

Foucault, M. (1998). A preface to transgression. In J. Faubion (ed.), *Aesthetics, method and epistemology* (pp. 69–87). New York: New Press.

Gramsci, A. ([1971] 1996). *Prison notebooks*. New York: Columbia University Press.

Hall, S. & Jefferson, T. (eds) ([1976] 1993). *Resistance through rituals: Youth subcultures in post-war Britain*. New York: HarperCollins Academic.

Halsey, M. & Young, A. (2002). The meanings of graffiti and municipal administration. *Australian & New Zealand Journal of Criminology, 35*(2), 165–186.

Halsey, M. & Young, A. (2006). 'Our desires are ungovernable': Writing graffiti in urban space. *Theoretical Criminology, 10*(3), 275–306.

Harcourt, B.E. (2009). *Illusion of order: The false promise of broken windows policing*. Cambridge, MA: Harvard University Press.

Harvey, D. (2001). *Spaces of capital: Towards a critical geography*. London: Routledge.

Herbert, S. (1997). *Policing space: Territoriality and the Los Angeles police department*. Minneapolis, MN: University of Minnesota Press.

Herbert, S. & Brown, E. (2006). Conceptions of space and crime in the punitive neoliberal city. *Antipode, 38*(4), 755–777.

Hernandez Jr., E. (1995). "Valley man who killed tagger gets probation." *Los Angeles Times*, November 9.

Hurewitz, D. (2007). *Bohemian Los Angeles and the making of modern politics*. Los Angeles, CA: University of California Press.

Iveson, K. (2007). *Publics in the City*. Oxford: Wiley-Blackwell.

Iveson, K. (2010). The wars on graffiti and the new military urbanism. *City, 14*(1–2), 115–134.

Janis, S. (1983). *Post-graffiti*. Printed gallery material. New York.

Kelling, G.L. & Wilson, J.Q. (1982). Broken windows: The police and neighborhood safety. *Atlantic Monthly, 249*(3), 29–38.

Kramer, R. (2010a). Painting with permission: Legal graffiti in New York City. *Ethnography, 11*(2), 235–253.

Kramer, R. (2010b). Moral panics and urban growth machines: Official reactions to graffiti in New York City, 1990–2005. *Qualitative Sociology, 33*(3), 297–311.

Kurlansky, M., Naar J. & Mailer, N. (1974). *The faith of graffiti*. New York: Praeger.

Lachmann, R. (1988). Graffiti as career and ideology. *American Journal of Sociology, 94*(2), 229–250.

Lasley, J.R. (1995). New writing on the wall: Exploring the middle-class graffiti writing subculture. *Deviant Behavior, 16*(2), 151–167.

Lefebvre, H. (1991). *The production of space*. Oxford: Blackwell.

Lefebvre, H. (2003). *The urban revolution*. Minneapolis, MN: University of Minnesota Press.

Ley, D. & Cybriwsky, R. (1974). Urban graffiti as territorial markers. *Annals of the Association of American Geographers, 64*(4), 491–505.

MacDiarmid, L. & Downing, S. (2012). A rough aging out: Graffiti writers and subcultural drift. *International Journal of Criminal Justice Sciences, 7*(2), 235–253.

Macdonald, N. (2001). *The graffiti subculture: Youth, masculinity and identity in London and New York*. New York: Palgrave Macmillan.

Manco, T. (2002). *Stencil graffiti*. New York: Thames Hudson.

McAuliffe, C. (2012). Graffiti or street art? Negotiating the moral geographies of the creative city. *Journal of Urban Affairs, 34*(2), 189–206.

McAuliffe, C. (2013). Legal walls and professional paths: The mobilities of graffiti writers in Sydney. *Urban Studies, 50*(3), 518–537.

McAuliffe, C. & Iveson, K. (2011). Art and crime (and other things besides . . .): Conceptualising graffiti in the city. *Geography Compass*, *5*(3), 128–143.

Miller, T.C. & Ha, J. (1999). "1 Killed, 2 Hurt in Chain of Gang Shooting." Los Angeles Times, January 25 (Downloaded April 20, 2015).

Mitchell, D. (1997). The annihilation of space by law: The roots and implications of anti-homeless laws in the United States. *Antipode*, *29*(3), 303–335.

Phillips, S.A. (1999). *Wallbangin': Graffiti and gangs in LA*. Chicago, IL: University of Chicago Press.

Rahn, J. (1999). Painting without permission: An ethnographic study of hip-hop graffiti culture. *Material Culture Review*, *49*(1). (http://journals.hil.unb.ca/index.php/MCR/article/view/17784/19059).

Riccardi, N. & Tamaki, J. (1995). "Praise and insults for man who killed tagger." *Los Angeles Times*, February 4 (Downloaded November 1, 2014).

Sahagun, L. (1991). "Tagger 'chaka' agrees to clean up graffiti." *Los Angeles Times*, April 24 (Downloaded September 21, 2014).

Sanchez-Tranquilino, M. (1995). Space, power, and youth culture: Mexican American graffiti and Chicano murals in East Los Angeles, 1972–1978. In Bright, B.J. & Bakewell, L. (eds.), *Looking high and low: Art and cultural identity* (pp. 55–88). Tucson, AZ: University of Arizona Press.

Shobe, H. & Banis, D. (2014). Zero graffiti for a beautiful city: The cultural politics of urban space in San Francisco. *Urban Geography*, *35*(4), 586–607.

Snyder, G.J. (2009). *Graffiti lives: Beyond the tag in New York's urban underground*. New York: NYU Press.

Soja, E.W. (1996). *Thirdspace: Journeys to Los Angeles and other real-and-imagined places*. Oxford: Blackwell.

Soja, E.W. (2010). *Seeking spatial justice*. Minneapolis, MN: University of Minnesota Press.

Suleiman, S.R. (1990). *Subversive intent: Gender, politics, and the avant-garde*. Cambridge, MA: Harvard University Press.

Young, A. (2012). Criminal images: The affective judgment of graffiti and street art. *Crime, Media, Culture*, *8*(3), 297–314.

Young, A. (2014). *Street art, public city: Law, crime and the urban imagination*. London: Routledge.

Weisburd, D., Bernasco, W. & Bruinsma, G. (eds) (2008). *Putting crime in its place*. New York: Springer.

Wolfgang, M.F. (1957). Victim precipitated criminal homicide. *Journal of Criminal Law Criminology & Police Science*, *48*(1), 1–11.

34

Does copyright law protect graffiti and street art?

Danwill D. Schwender

Introduction

Mainstream culture's recent embrace of graffiti and street art has raised some of these artists' awareness of copyright law. For example, when Fiat ran a television commercial featuring Jennifer Lopez driving past a Bronx wall containing a mural by TATS Cru (a group of former illicit taggers who now create art for such well-known names as Coca-Cola, Nike, and Beyoncé), the artists sought to stop the advertisement based on copyright infringement and, ultimately, settled the dispute (Kaplan, 2011). Similarly, artists whose works adorned New York's international graffiti mecca "5 Pointz" initiated a copyright lawsuit against the warehouse owner in an attempt to prevent its demolition (Holpuch, 2013). Additionally, as art galleries and museums continue to collect graffiti and street art, artists have found themselves targeted by forgers, such as the graffiti artist John Perello (aka JonOne) who recently sued a Paris gallery for selling forgeries (Childs, 2014). Copyright law provides these artists a mechanism to profit from, and protect, their works by granting limited, exclusive rights to reproduce, distribute, publicly display, and create derivative works and, for certain works, the rights to attribution and integrity.

This chapter focuses on the application of United States' copyright law to public art, street art, and graffiti art. Definition of these art forms has varied over the years (Lewisohn, 2008; Danysz & Dana, 2010) and may have special legal definitions for criminal enforcement.[1] For purposes of this chapter, the following definitions apply: Public art includes an assortment of commissioned or authorized art forms, including paintings, murals, architecture, sculpture, and performance art that is free for the public to observe, and this chapter focuses only on paintings and murals (Wacławek, 2011: p. 65). Street art encompasses stencils, stickers, and posters affixed to surfaces and objects without the property owner's permission (Ross, 2013: p. 392). Graffiti art refers to words, figures, and images drawn on surfaces without the property owner's authorization (Ross, 2013: pp. 180–181).

The public has constantly struggled with the boundaries of art and the privileges offered to artists and, therefore, the above definitions are important. Few people question the application of copyright to works produced by artists for museum and gallery display. As such, the publishers of any art reproductions in books, movies, or posters, must obtain permission from the copyright owner or risk a lawsuit for copyright infringement. This includes works by renowned artists Keith Harring, Jean-Michel Basquiat, Barry McGee, and Banksy, who all obtained fame through graffiti and street art. Application of copyright to street art and graffiti, however, remains inconclusive, largely due to the illegality of the art's creation.[2] But, whether vandalism or art, many of these artists have gained acceptance in galleries and museums and found their works commercialized by others without permission. The pressing question, therefore, is whether the illegality involved in creating these works should prohibit an artist from obtaining or enforcing copyright for that work.

What is copyright?

Art by its very nature is intangible. A mural can exist in only one place, but anyone can relatively easily reproduce its expression in books, posters, advertisements, and films for mass distribution. To protect this form of intellectual property, most countries grant limited, exclusive rights to artists, known as copyrights.

Copyright emerged from the protection for publishers upon the invention of the printing press. Prior to the printing press, an elaborate system of censorship and control over scribes existed in England (from whom the U.S. based much of its law). To maintain control and censorship over the mass publication of literature with the printing press, England created a publishing monopoly under the Licensing Act of 1662. After this law lapsed, England granted authors of books the exclusive right to copy their literature for a fixed term under the Statute of Anne in 1710. Upon expiration of the copyright term, a work would fall into the "public domain" – for all to use freely. The underlying theory for copyright assumes creators require an economic incentive to create, absent which culture and society would suffer from a lack of production of cultural works (Landes & Posner, 1989; Nimmer, 2014).

Although England's law only protected the copying of books in 1710, other uses such as translations and derivative works were later added. Eventually, copyright expanded to protect other types of creations, including maps, musical compositions, and paintings. There is no "international copyright" that will automatically protect an author's works throughout the world. But, international trade brought about intellectual property treaties, such as the Berne Convention for the Protection of Literary and Artistic Works (1886), which requires that a member country extend the same treatment to the works of nationals of other member countries as are enjoyed by its own citizens. The Berne Convention also obligates member countries to adopt minimum standards for copyright protection. Today, approximately 170 countries have joined the Berne Convention, including the U.S.

In the U.S., the United States' Constitution provides Congress authority "to promote the Progress of Science and useful Arts, by securing for limited times to authors and inventors the exclusive right to their respective writings and discoveries" (U.S. Constitution, art. 1, § 8, cl. 8). Congress utilized this power to enact copyright law and, as with England, it expanded slowly.[3] It now encompasses all "original works of authorship fixed in any tangible medium of expression" (Copyright Act, §102(a)). For works that meet this definition, the Copyright Act grants: (1) The right to reproduce the work; (2) The right to prepare derivative works; (3) The right to distribute duplicates of the work to the public; and (4) For certain works, the right to display or perform the work publicly[4] (Copyright Act, §106). Only the artist, or those deriving their rights through the artist, can rightfully claim ownership of copyright in a work[5] and the rights are limited in time, generally life of the author plus seventy years.[6] The copyright owner may exclusively, or non-exclusively, transfer or license these rights in bulk, or separately, as desired.

The U.S. also grants certain works of "visual art" created after June 1, 1991 two "moral rights" (often referred to as *droit moral*): (1) The right to attribution, and (2) The right to integrity (VARA, 1990). These rights support "society's interest in the preservation of works of artistic merit; and the artist's economic self-interest in preservation of his or her own works so as to enhance his or her reputation as an artist" (Pollara, 2003). VARA specially defines "visual art" to include a painting, drawing, print, or sculpture, existing in a single copy or in a limited edition of 200 copies or fewer. VARA specifically excludes works made-for-hire and "any poster, map, globe, chart, technical drawing, diagram, model, applied art, motion picture, or other audio-visual work." An artist's moral rights only last for the life of the author and they cannot be transferred or licensed, though they may be waived.

The right of attribution includes: (1) The right to demand the artist's name be used in conjunction with a display of the artist's work; (2) The right to prevent use of an artist's name as the author of a work that she did not create; and (3) The right to prevent use of the artist's name as the author of her own work "in the event of a distortion, mutilation, or other modification of the work which would be prejudicial to his or her honor or reputation" (VARA, 1990).

The right of integrity includes: (1) The right to prevent intentional distortion or other modification of a work that would prejudice the artist's honor or reputation; and (2) The right to prevent destruction of a work of "recognized stature." An integrity violation does not result from modifications due to "the passage of time or the inherent nature of the materials." Nor does a violation occur due to "modification of a work of visual art which is the result of conservation, or of the public presentation" unless caused by gross negligence (VARA, 1990). Therefore, a museum may choose how to light, frame, and place a work, but may not physically modify it.

Recognizing the potential conflict between an artist's moral rights and the rights of real property owners, exceptions to VARA exist for works incorporated in a building. For works that can be removed without destroying or modifying the art, the building owner must make a good faith effort to notify the artist of the intended removal and allow the artist ninety days to either remove the work on his own or pay for its removal. When a work cannot be removed without damaging the art, however, the artist has no right to integrity and no right to prevent use of his name with the damaged work if the artist consented in writing to the possible modification of the work due to removal (Copyright Act, §113(d)).

In the U.S., the fact that graffiti and street art are publicly displayed does not relegate the works to the public domain or provide others a license to make use of the art, other than by viewing it.[7] For example, Peter Rosenstein authored a book of photographs of graffiti entitled "Tattooed Walls" (Rosenstein, 2006). Neither Rosenstein nor his publisher obtained authorization from the artists prior to publication of the book. As a result, they had to settle with numerous artists who complained of the unauthorized use, including TATS Cru (Gonzalez, 2007).

However, as discussed below, these art forms face three potential hurdles in obtaining and enforcing copyright: (1) They must contain the requisite originality; (2) Their moral rights may be limited due to their irremovable nature; and (3) Their illegality may limit or prevent their protection entirely.

Does U.S. copyright law encompass public art, street art, and graffiti?

To enjoy the benefits of copyright, an artistic work must be an (1) original (2) work of authorship (3) fixed in a tangible medium. Public art, street art, and graffiti easily meet the latter element as the works are normally affixed to building walls, subway cars, billboards, or some other tangible object within the public's view. The temporary nature of the works due to removal or destruction does not negate this because a work need only be sufficiently permanent to permit it to be perceived for a period of more than a transitory duration either directly or with the aid of a machine (Nimmer, 2014, §2.03[B]).

Additionally, most public art, street art, and graffiti fall within the definition of "work of authorship," which includes pictorial, graphic, and sculptural works among its non-exhaustive list. The statute's definition, however, expressly excludes "words and short phrases such as names, titles, and slogans; familiar symbols or designs; [and] mere variations of typographic orna-mentation, lettering or coloring . . ." (Copyright Act, §202.1). Therefore, tags and simple throw-ups are likely excluded from protection. For example, New York graffiti artist Michael Tracy painted a roller-skate and the graffiti-styled words of "Skate Key" on a roller-skating rink at the owner's request. Upon Tracy's application for copyright registration, the Copyright Office registered the roller-skate drawing (Tracy, 1980), but denied registration to the "Skate Key" work (see Tracy, 1988).

Tags and throw-ups may also lack originality. This element requires that a work be independently created by the author and possess at least a minimal degree of originality (Nimmer, 2014, §2.01). Each individual work need not "promote the arts" to merit protection, but the work must have a scintilla of creativity to meet the low threshold of originality. Similarly, a "work may be original even though it closely resembles other works so long as the similarity is fortuitous, not the result of copying" (Feist, 1991: p. 345). Generally, the more elaborate the work, the more likely copyright will protect it. Therefore, tags and throw-ups that simply indicate a name and place with minimal artistic nuances may not contain sufficient creativity. Whereas, works with characters, landscapes, portraits, or written statements, such as graffiti "pieces" and "masterpieces," likely meet the test of originality.

The U.S. Copyright Office, for example, granted registration to graffiti artist Daniel Reece for his graffiti-styled drawings of the word "Dip" (Reece, 1972). Standing alone, however, each element of Reece's work would unlikely qualify for copyright protection: (1) The word "dip" is an unprotected word or short phrase; (2) The use of stylized graffiti lettering is an unprotected variation of typographic ornamentation or lettering; (3) The use of certain color schemes is an unprotected variation of color; (4) The use of geometric shapes, such as circles, squares, or stars, to ornament the "i" in "Dip" is an unprotected use of common symbols; and (5) The use of certain background colors and shadowing to the word "Dip" are unprotected variations of color (Reece, 2011). But, when Reece sued Marc Ecko Unlimited for copyright infringement over use of graffiti-styled "Dip" works in the videogame "Getting Up: Contents Under Pressure," the court recognized that "the form of the lettering at issue is arguably central to the artistic expression of particular words" in graffiti art and, therefore, analyzed these elements for possible copyright infringement. The court reviewed the degree of abstraction, the connectivity, the relative size, and the two- or three-dimensional appearance of the letters (Reece, 2011: p. 28). Notably, the court did not deny Reece's claims as excluded under the "work of authorship" definition or for lack of originality. Nonetheless, the court ultimately ruled the videogame's works lacked any substantial similarity to Reece's works to warrant a finding of infringement due to differences in color, shadowing, letter shapes and styling, use of geometric shapes and backgrounds, and spacing.

In short, public art, street art, and graffiti with sufficient originality should meet the threshold requirements of copyright. However, as discussed in more detail below, VARA adds additional restrictions before an artist can enjoy the benefits of moral rights.

Does VARA protect public, street, and graffiti art?

VARA does not grant rights to all works of art. First, VARA excludes stickers and posters and, therefore, most street art (as defined for this chapter) do not enjoy moral rights.

Second, some artists may have difficulty proving the work has "recognized stature" for the right to prevent destruction (Bougdanos, 2002; Barnett, 2013). VARA does not define "recognized stature," but the courts hold it requires "(1) that the visual art in question has 'stature,' i.e. is viewed as meritorious, and (2) that this stature is 'recognized' by art experts, other members of the artistic community, or by some cross-section of society" (Carter, 1994: p. 325; Kwall, 1997).

For example, in *Hanrahan v. Ramirez* (1998), a group of neighborhood children painted a mural on the side of a liquor store with the owners' approval. Three years later, the storeowners painted over half of the mural with an advertisement for the store. The artists sued under VARA. The court found the artists to be of "recognized stature" because the piece won a national contest and enjoyed local and national support. Therefore, the court awarded the artists $48,000 and ordered the restoration of the mural.

In contrast, the court in the case of 5Pointz struggled to find recognized stature in many of the artists' works. The artists highlighted the popularity of 5Pointz as a whole and that certain artists had gained gallery and national attention, but had difficulty illustrating particular works at 5Pointz that had gained national "recognition" (Cohen, 2013). Due to such difficulties, some courts and scholars have called for a lower threshold using community opinion and public interest or removal of the restriction entirely (Martin, 1999; Robinson, 2000; Jones, 2005).

Third, graffiti may be considered "site-specific art" and at least one court has held that VARA does not protect site-specific works (Phillips, 2006). Essentially, for site-specific art, the location of the art is an integral element of the work such that the art is destroyed if moved from its original site (Phillips, 2006; Nordby, 2007; Garson, 2001). Whether incorporation of the "street" in graffiti is essential to the work remains inconclusive among scholars (Riggle, 2010; Bengtsen, 2013). Certainly, some works of graffiti may be site-specific due to placement on a particular building, but this conclusion could differ between viewers and artists.

Moreover, this strict interpretation of VARA to site-specific art has been questioned because VARA does not explicitly, or impliedly, exclude site-specific art. Additionally, relocating site-specific art does not necessarily destroy the work. Further, the "building exception" to VARA suggests that VARA includes site-specific art. Also, an artist's moral rights can be violated in ways that do not implicate the work's location or manner of public presentation, such as modification of the work and the right of attribution (Nordby, 2007; Norton, 2008/2009; Cascio, 2009; Spotts, 2009; Kelley, 2011).

Regardless, a tension remains between an artist's right to use public space and the public's right to that space. While few would deny an artist the right to paint as he chooses, does an artist have the right to compel the public to accept and display his works by placing them without permission? The next section summarizes the debate on whether street and graffiti artists should enjoy the benefits of copyright given their unauthorized placement.

Does copyright protect illegally created works?

Although many works of street and graffiti art meet the requirements for copyright protection, their illegality creates an equitable and social concern. As a result, the application of copyright to illegally created works remains inconclusive.[8]

At least one court has raised the issue of illegality in relation to graffiti and copyright. In *Villa v. Pearson Education, Inc.* (2003), graffiti artist Herman Villa (aka "UNONE") sued the publisher of a Tony Hawk skateboarding videogame strategy guide. Villa claimed the guide infringed his rights to reproduce and distribute his work. The court avoided ruling directly on whether Villa could copyright an illegally created work, but stated *in dicta* that whether copyright protects graffiti "require[s] a determination of the legality of the circumstances under which the mural was created" (Villa, 2003: p. 3). This statement caused some commentators to highlight illegality as a potential defense to copyright infringement (Keller & Cunard, 2005; Smith, 2005; Schwender, 2008).

In contrast, the court in *Reece v. Marc Ecko Unlimited* (2011), described earlier, did not address the issue of illegality in ruling on Reece's copyright infringement claims. A similar ruling came in *Mager v. Brand New School* (2004) concerning street art. Damian Mager's stylized eyeball stickers adorned many of New York's billboards before covering the eyes of Carson Daly in a television commercial without authorization. Mager sued and the court noted the stickers placed across the city may have been without authorization and by people other than Mager, but did not weigh that potential illegality in its ruling.

Landowners' strong real property rights also complicate the application of moral rights to graffiti and street art. Again, the courts' guidance is contradictory. In *English v. B.F.C. & R. East 11th Street LLC* (1997), a group of artists turned an empty city lot into a garden and public art space with a number of outdoor murals. When the city sold the lot to a private developer who intended to demolish the building, the artists sought to prevent the destruction of their works under VARA. The court held that VARA does not apply to artwork illegally placed on the property of others when such artwork cannot be removed from the site in question. The court reasoned that enforcing artists' rights in irremovable art placed on a building without consent "could effectively freeze development of vacant lots by placing artwork there without permission" and would contradict the property rights of owners under the Constitution. A number of other cases have reached the same conclusion in applying state moral rights (see, e.g. Botello, 1991).

In *Pollara v. Seymour* (2003), the court noted that the decision in *English* (1997) only applied to works that could not be removed without destruction. In *Pollara*, artists illegally placed a banner constructed on an individual frame on the property of the Empire State building in preparation for a protest by a public interest group. The banner was easily removed without harm to the art. Although the court found VARA did not apply in this situation because it considered the banner an advertisement excluded from VARA, the court did state: "[T]here is no basis in the statute to find a general right to destroy works of art that are on property without the permission of the owner" (Pollara, 2003: p. 396 n.4).

With limited and varied court decisions on the issue, whether illegality of creation prevents application of copyright to street art and graffiti altogether or limits artists' moral rights remains unclear. Perhaps as a result of the lack of precedent, many copyright treatises fail to mention graffiti at all (Brown & Denicola, 2002; Nimmer et al., 2006; Demarsin et al., 2009; Stokes, 2011; Goldstein, 2014; Nimmer, 2014) or simply mention its status as criminal without a discussion of the effect of illegality on copyright (Feldman et al., 1986; Lerner & Bresler, 2005).

Yet, some scholars have addressed the issue (Smith, 2005; Morgan, 2006; Rychlicki, 2008; Schwender, 2008; Sandifer, 2009; Davies, 2012; Grant, 2012; Seay, 2012; Lerman, 2013; Roundtree, 2013). Several of these academics have analogized illegality of creation to copyright cases regarding illegality of content (Schwender, 2008; Davies, 2012; Grant, 2012; Lerman, 2013), such as works of obscenity, where the courts have also struggled to find uniformity (compare Mitchell, 1979; Jartech, 1982 with Devil Films, 1998). These commentators argue that copyright should protect illegally created works because: (1) The Copyright Act remains neutral and nothing in the Act renders these works any less worthy of copyright; (2) The courts have historically disapproved of copyright restrictions; (3) Judges should not be determining public morality and artistic merit; (4) Congress did not authorize an "unclean hands" defense (i.e. a plaintiff may not use the court to benefit from his wrongdoing) to copyright infringement claims; (5) Application of an unclean hands defense could fragment application of copyright to street art and graffiti based on the varying laws and morals of the individual states; and (6) Denying copyright would add little to the existing arsenal of weapons against street art and graffiti (Schwender, 2008; Lerman, 2013).

Granting street art and graffiti the benefits of copyright also raises a number of unanswered questions. Would granting copyright protection increase vandalism or possibly incentivize artists to create more legal works rather than illegal ones? Would the Copyright Office be able to distinguish between commissioned, legal murals and illegally placed works when determining whether to register a work? Should VARA exclude unauthorized works or limit the moral rights offered to such works? Would protection under VARA cause graffiti artists to sue other graffiti artists for damages? (Schwender, 2008; Lerman, 2013).

A number of scholars also argue against copyright in its entirety, as to all forms of art (for a review of arguments see Vaidhyanathan, 2001 and DeLong, 2002) and a few commentators argue that graffiti's cultural norms and natural rights sufficiently protect their work (Davies, 2012; Roundtree, 2013). Roundtree (2013) particularly notes the similarity of graffiti norms to copyright in that "getting up" acts as registration, a custom against copying exists but allows for fair use, pseudonyms are a right to attribution, and prohibition of partial paint-overs and preservation of recognized works are similar to a right to integrity. In this sense, copyright may be unnecessary in the world of graffiti, but does this adequately protect street artists and graffiti artists in the commercial world?

To this end, a few commentators highlight that these artists create their works not for financial reward, but as acts of rebellion against the law for street credibility, fame, and recognition (Morgan, 2006; Davies, 2012; Grant, 2012; Roundtree, 2013). Additionally, some academics theorize application of copyright to street art and graffiti could stifle creativity and note that graffiti culture flourished and evolved on its own without assistance of copyright. Davies (2012) also fears that copyright enforcement could rob graffiti of its transgressive power and political significance.

On the other hand, merely providing the opportunity for copyright protection and financial gain does not mean that every artist will enforce the protection or solicit their works. But, should an artist wish to enforce his copyright, he should be aware that others are entitled to certain fair uses of his work. A short discussion of fair use and appropriation art follows.

Infringement, fair use, and appropriation art

To prove copyright infringement requires proof of (1) ownership of a valid copyright, and (2) copying of original elements of the work. Copying contains two components: (1) Copying, and (2) Unauthorized appropriation (Feist, 1991; Nimmer, 2014, §13.01). But, the Copyright Act grants *limited* rights in works of art – not an absolute monopoly. Artists' rights are balanced in two important ways with the freedom of speech, the ability to build on another's work, and the public's interest in a vast culture of the arts to use and explore.

First, copyright only protects the "expression" of a work of authorship, not its "idea" – this is known as the idea/expression dichotomy (Copyright Act, §102(b); Nimmer, 2014, §2.03). For example, copyright does not protect the idea to paint a woman sitting in a chair, but it does protect the particular expression in an actual painting of a woman sitting in a chair.

Second, the Copyright Act expressly permits "fair use" of copyrighted works for news, teaching, criticism, and the transformation of another's work into something new and different

(Copyright Act, §107). Such an opportunity for fair use "has been thought necessary to fulfill copyright's very purpose, 'to promote the Progress of Science and useful Arts'" (Campbell, 1994: p. 575; McEneaney, 2013). Thus, the "fair use doctrine" prevents the rigid application of copyright law in such a manner that creativity is stifled and it prevents encroachment upon the freedom of expression protected by the First Amendment.

In making a fair use determination, the courts weigh: (1) The purpose and character of the use, including whether such use is of a commercial nature or for nonprofit educational purposes; (2) The nature of the copyrighted work; (3) Whether the amount and substantiality of the portion used in relation to the copyrighted work as a whole is reasonable in relation to the purpose of the copying; and (4) The effect of the use upon the potential market for, or value of, the copyrighted work (Campbell, 1994).

Direct copying for such purposes as art criticism, education, and news, therefore, does not normally violate copyright. However, the line between an infringing derivative work and fair use in the arts can be tricky[9] and the difference between wrongful appropriation and legal appropriation often turns on the transformative nature of the subsequent work under the first fair use factor (Fisher et al., 2012). A work is transformative if it alters the original piece sufficiently to create a new expression, meaning, or message. The more transformative the new work, the less significant are the other fair use factors (Campbell, 1994).

For example, Derek Seltzer created a poster called "Scream Icon" and placed it on a wall in Los Angeles. The music group Green Day incorporated the image, without permission, into a collage of other posters and graffiti in a video backdrop used at live concerts. In Seltzer's copyright lawsuit, the Court found the changed use and placement conveyed "new information, new aesthetics, new insights, and understandings that are plainly distinct from those of the original piece." As such, the court held Green Day's "new" work was transformative and not infringing (Seltzer, 2013).

On the other hand, street artist Thierry Guetta (aka Mr. Brainwash), featured in the Banksy produced movie, *Exit Through the Gift Shop*, used a photograph of the music group Run DMC by Glen Friedman without authorization in four separate works, including a simplified stencil depicting the three members of Run DMC. Friedman sued and the court found Guetta copied almost all of the photograph without significant transformation except use of a different medium. Therefore, the court ruled Guetta's use infringed on Friedman's copyrighted photograph (Friedman, 2011).

As these cases suggest, appropriation art has flourished in the street art and graffiti worlds. The public, art critics, and academics have enjoyed a great narrative over appropriation art, which has expanded greatly due to technological advances and the Internet. But, the basic point here is that street and graffiti artists should analyze the transformative nature of any new work that appropriates another's art as its base and that simply copying works into a new medium is likely insufficient transformation to avoid copyright infringement.

Conclusion

Copyright law provides a mechanism for artists to seek compensation for their artistic endeavors by providing the right to reproduce, distribute, display, and make derivative works. Without considering illegality, original works of street art and graffiti generally meet the threshold requirements of copyright eligibility and copyright owners may enforce these rights. Under VARA, copyright also grants artists of particular works of "visual art" the ability to demand attribution for their works and to prevent their works from modification or destruction. VARA, however, likely excludes most street art from these benefits because street art (as defined for this book) includes the expressly excluded works of stickers and posters. And, many graffiti artists may have difficulty showing their works have obtained the "recognized stature" required to prevent destruction. But, all of these rights may be unenforceable or severely limited due to the illegal nature of the art's creation. The case law on this issue, however, is limited, contradictory, and provides minimal guidance to artists of these genres.

Additionally, street and graffiti artists must weigh the risk of losing anonymity, possible criminal prosecution, and potential civil lawsuits before deciding to enforce their copyrights. Although seeking compensation from commercial infringers may prove profitable (e.g. Tracy won $65,000 for Skate Key, Inc.'s unauthorized uses), street culture and the norms of graffiti provide an arena that may be ill-suited to copyright. Imagine well known and respected graffiti and street artists King Robbo and Banksy fighting in the courts over monetary damages rather than reputations and street credibility in their recent graffiti war (Fuertes-Knight, 2013).

In the end, graffiti artist Eye Six probably said it succinctly:

> This graffiti art is vulnerable to direct public response in ways that city administered 'public' art is not . . . [G]raffiti writers make no claims as to protecting, preserving, or profiting from their public art. They own and control their throw ups and pieces less than they simply expose them to public appreciation (or condemnation).
>
> (Ferrell, 1996: pp. 174–175)

Notes

1 For example, California Penal Code section 594 defines graffiti as "any unauthorized inscription, word, figure, mark, or design that is written, marked, etched, scratched, drawn, or painted on real or personal property."

2 For example, California criminalizes the act of graffiti, the possession of materials used for graffiti artwork with the intent of defacing property, and the sale of spray-paint to anyone under eighteen (California Penal Code §§594-594.2, 640.6-640.7). States without specific anti-graffiti laws may still prosecute graffiti artists under laws prohibiting trespass, destruction of private property, nuisance, or mischief.

3 The U.S. passed a resolution in 1783 recommending the several states to enact protections to authors or publishers of books. The first federal copyright act in 1790 protected authors of books, maps, and charts. Congress expanded copyright to include paintings, drawings, chromolithographs, and statues in 1870. The Copyright Act of 1909 expanded protection to "all the writings" of an author.

4 Many countries grant similar rights, although some do not confer a display right and many grant stronger moral rights (*droit moral*) and offer resale rights (*droit de suite*) (Nimmer, 2014, §17.09). In the U.S., only California offers a resale right (California Civil Code, §986).

5 In the U.S., copyright in a work becomes the property of the artist immediately upon creation. When multiple artists jointly create a work, all of the co-artists own the copyright unless there is an agreement to the contrary. For works created as part of a periodical or other collective work, the copyright in each particular work falls first to each separate contributor and is distinct from the copyright for the collective work as a whole. Under the work-for-hire doctrine, however, copyright ownership starts with the person who hired the artist and the employer, not the employee, holds the copyright. Registration is not necessary to own these rights, but registration provides the court jurisdiction over an infringement lawsuit and the right to statutory damages, attorneys' fees, and costs of suit if the owner prevails at trial (Copyright Act, §113(3)).

6 For works created after January 1, 1978, the term of protection continues for the artist's lifetime (or the last surviving artist of a co-authored work) plus seventy years. For works done anonymously or under a pseudonym, the term extends for the lesser of ninety-five years from first publication (i.e. the distribution, or offer of distribution, of copies of a work to the public) or 120 years from the date of its creation unless the artist identifies herself in the registration records of the Copyright Office. Moral rights last for the life of the author only. All of these rights end upon expiration of the term and the work then falls into the public domain for all to use.

7   An exception is made for the photographing of architectural works in buildings, but not for art (Copyright Act, §120(a)). Some countries, however, allow the photographing and commercial use of photographs of publicly displayed art (see, e.g. Copyright, Designs and Patents Act, 1988, c. 48, sec. 62 (U.K.)).

8   For example, Alexandre Veilleux, aka Alex Scaner, seeks $45,000 in damages in a recent lawsuit he filed against the television station Radio-Canada and the production company Production Aetios Inc. for use of his graffiti in the opening scenes and advertisements for the show "30 Vies." Sébastien Pigeon, vice-president of legal affairs for Aetios, stated:

> The judge will have to decide whether someone who creates a work illegally like that can then benefit from the protection of the Copyright Act to demand payment . . . Everyone knows the adage that crime doesn't pay; he committed an act that is not permitted by the law and is trying to profit from it afterwards.
>
> (Hamilton, 2014)

9   Compare artist Jeff Koons' mixed-media artwork using images from an advertisement that the court found not infringing (Blanch, 2006) with Koons' painting based on an everyday couple's family portrait where the court found infringement (Rogers, 1992). In the recent case of Cariou vs. Prince (2013), the court found placing purple guitars and eyes on photographs of Rastafarians sufficiently transformed the works such that fair use precluded copyright infringement. For further reading, Fisher *et al.* (2012) analyze the litigation between street artist Shepard Fairey and the Associated Press over the Obama Hope poster and provide a fine primer on fair use, appropriation art, and copyright.

References

Barnett, G. (2013). Recognized stature: Protecting street art as cultural property. *Chicago-Kent Journal of Intellectual Property*, *12*, 204–216.

Bengtsen, P. (2013). Beyond the public art machine: A critical examination of street art as public art. *Konsthistorisk Tidskrift/Journal of Art History*, *82(2)*, 63–80.

Bougdanos, M. (2002). The Visual Artists Rights Act and its application to graffiti murals: Whose wall is it anyway? *New York Law School Journal of Human Rights*, *18*, 549–575.

Brown, R. & Denicola, R. (2002). *Copyright; unfair competition, and related topics bearing on the protection of works of authorship* (8th edn). New York: Foundation Press.

Cascio, V. (2009). Hardly a walk in the park: Courts' hostile treatment of site-specific works under VARA. *DePaul Journal of Art Technology & Intellectual Property Law*, *20*, 167–197.

Childs, C. (2014). Fake graffiti reach courts as forgeries on market increase. *The Art Newspaper Issue 254*. Available at http://old.theartnewspaper.com/articles/Fake-graffiti-reach-courts-as-forgeries-on-market-increase/31634 (accessed May 31, 2014).

Danysz, M. & Dana, M. (2010). *From style writing to art: A street art anthology*. Rome, Italy: Drago Arts and Communication.

Davies, J. (2012). Art crimes?: Theoretical perspectives on copyright protection for illegally-created graffiti art. *Main Law Review*, *65(1)*, 27–55.

DeLong, J. (2002). Defending intellectual property. In A. Thierer & W. Crews (eds), *Copy fights* (pp. 17–36). Washington, DC: Cato Institute.

Demarsin, B., Schrage, E.J.H., Tilleman, B., & Verbeke A. (eds) (2009). *Art & law*. Oxford: Hart Publishing.

Feldman, F., Weil, S., & Biederman, S. (1986). *Art law: Rights and liabilities of creators and collector*. Boston, MA: Little, Brown.

Ferrell, J. (1996). Crimes of style: Urban graffiti and the politics of criminality. *Journal of Criminal Justice and Popular Culture*, *3(4)*, 98–101.

Fisher, W., Cost, F., Fairey, S., Feder, M., Fountain, E., Stewart, G., & Sturken, M. (2012). Reflections on the hope poster case. *Harvard Journal of Law & Technology*, *25(2)*, 243–338.

Fuertes-Knight, J. (2013). King Robbo exclusive interview: My graffiti war with Banksy. *Sabotage Times*, October 3. Available at http://sabotagetimes.com/people/king-robbo-exclusive-interview-my-graffiti-war-with-banksy/#_ (accessed May 27, 2014).

Garson, F. (2001). Before that artist came along, it was just a bridge: The Visual Artists Rights Act and the removal of site-specific artwork. *Cornell Journal of Law & Public Policy*, *11*, 203–244.

Gonzalez, D. (2007). Walls of art for everyone, but made by not just anyone. *New York Times*, June 4. Available at www.nytimes.com/2007/06/04/nyregion/04citywide.html?pagewanted=all&_r=0 (accessed August 5, 2014).

Grant, N. (2012). Outlawed art: Finding a home for graffiti in copyright law. *Expresso*. Available at http://works.bepress.com/nicole_grant/1 (accessed May 27, 2014).

Hamilton, G. (2014). Artist sues after TV show films Montréal building that he had tagged with graffiti. *National Post*, July 28 (Canada). Available at http://news.nationalpost.com/2014/07/28/artist-sues-after-tv-show-films-montreal-building-that-he-had-tagged-with-graffiti/ (accessed August 5, 2014).

Holpuch, A. (2013). New York graffiti mecca 5 Pointz will likely 'come down', judge says. *The Guardian*, November 8. Available at www.theguardian.com/world/2013/nov/08/5-pointz-graffiti-come-down-judge (accessed May 31, 2014).

Jones, C. (2005). Site-specific art parks on moral ground: Distilling old whine in new battles over The Visual Artists Rights Act. *Computer Law Review & Technology Journal*, 9, 355–391.

Kaplan, D. (2011). Fiat settles claim with Bronx graffiti artists over J. Lo ad. *New York Post*, November 30. Available at http://nypost.com/2011/11/30/fiat-settles-claim-with-bronx-graffiti-artists-over-j-lo-ad/ (accessed May 31, 2014).

Keller, B. & Cunard, J. (2005). *Copyright law: A practitioner's guide*. New York: Practicing Law Institute.

Kwall, R. (1997). How fine art fares post VARA. *Marquette Intellectual Property Law Review*, 1(1), 1–64.

Lerman, C. (2013). Protecting artistic vandalism: Graffiti and copyright law. *New York University Journal of Intellectual Property & Entertainment Law*, 2, 295–338.

Lerner, R. & Bresler, J. (2005). *Art law: The guide for collectors, investors, dealers, and artists* (3rd edn). New York: Practising Law Institute.

Lewisohn, C. (2008). *Street art: The graffiti revolution*. New York: Abrams.

McEneaney, C. (2013). Transformative use and comment on the original: Threats to appropriation in contemporary visual art. *Brooklyn Law Review*, 78, 1521–1551.

Morgan, O. (2006). Graffiti – who owns the rights? (working paper). *Social Science Research Network*. Available at http://ssrn.com/abstract=929892 (accessed May 27, 2014).

Nimmer, M., Marcus, P., Myers, D. & Nimmer, D. (2006). *Cases and materials on copyright and other aspects of entertainment litigation including unfair competition, defamation, privacy* (7th edn). Newark, NJ: Matthew Bender.

Nordby, R. (2007). Off of the pedestal and into the fire: How Phillips chips away at the rights of site-specific artists. *Florida State University Law Review*, 35, 167–192.

Norton, A. (2008/2009). Site-specific art gets a bum wrap: Illustrating the limitations of the Visual Artists Rights Act of 1990 through a study of Christo and Jeanne-Claude's unique art. *Cumberland Law Review*, 39, 749–784.

Riggle, N. (2010). Street art: The transfiguration of commonplaces. *Journal of Aesthetics and Art Criticism*, 68(3), 243–257.

Robinson, C. (2000). The 'recognized stature' standard in the Visual Artists Rights Act. *Fordham Law Review*, 68(5), 1935–1976.

Rosenstein, P. (2006). *Tattooed walls*. Jackson, MS: University Press of Mississippi.

Ross, J.I. (2013). Street art. In J.I. Ross (ed.), *Encyclopedia of street crime in America* (pp. 392–393). Thousand Oaks, CA: Sage Publications.

Roundtree, A. (2013). Graffiti artists "get up" in intellectual property's negative space. *Cardozo Arts & Entertainment Law Journal*, 31, 959–993.

Rychlicki, T. (2008). Legal questions about illegal art. *Journal of Intellectual Property Law & Practice*, 3(6), 393–401.

Sandifer, S. (2009). Unauthorized and unsolicited: Is graffiti copyrightable visual communication? *John F. Kennedy University Law Review*, 12, 141–150.

Schmalz, K. (1983). Problems in giving obscenity copyright protection: Did Jartech and Mitchell Brothers go too far? *Vanderbilt Law Review*, 36, 403.

Schwender, D. (2008). Promotion of the arts: An argument for limited copyright protection of illegal graffiti. *Journal of the Copyright Society of the USA*, 55(2–3), 257–282.

Seay, J. (2012). You look complicated today: Representing an illegal graffiti artist in a copyright infringement case against a major international retailer. *Journal of Intellectual Property Law*, 20, 75–86.

Smith, S. (2005). Copyright ownership and transfer. In *Patents, copyrights, trademarks, and literary property course handbook series no. 830, Advanced seminar on copyright law* (p. 29). New York: Practicing Law Institute.

Spotts, L. (2009). Phillips has left VARA little protection for site-specific artists. *Journal of Intellectual Property Law*, 16, 297–322.

Stokes, S. (2011). *Art and copyright*. Portland, OR: Hart Publishing.

Vaidhyanathan, S. (2001). *Copyright and copywrongs: The rise of intellectual property and how it threatens creativity.* New York: New York University Press.

Wacławek, A. (2011). *Graffiti and street art.* New York: Thames and Hudson.

Walmesley, J. (2005). In the beginning there was the word. In Baker, A. Rose, & C. Strike (eds), *Beautiful losers: Contemporary art and street culture* (pp. 193–207). New York: D.A.P./Iconoclast.

Legal citations

Berne Convention for the Protection of Literary and Artistic Works. (1886). 828 U.N.T.S. 221 ("Berne Convention").

Blanch vs. Koons, 467 F.3d 244 (2006).

Botello vs. Shell Oil Co., 280 Cal. Rptr. 535 (1991).

California Civil Code (Lexis 2014).

California Penal Code (Lexis 2014).

Campbell v. Acuff-Rose Music, Inc., 510 U.S. 569 (1994).

Cariou vs. Prince, 714 F.3d 694 (2013).

Carter vs. Helmsley-Spear, Inc., 861 F. Supp. 303 (1994).

Cohen vs. G & M Realty L.P., Case No. 13-CV-5612 (E.D.N.Y. 2013).

Copyright Act of 1976, 17 U.S.C. §§ 101–1332 (Lexis 2014) ("Copyright Act").

Copyright, Designs and Patents Act 1988 (U.K.).

Devils Films, Inc. vs. Nectar Video, 29 F. Supp. 2d 174 (1998).

English vs. B.F.C. & R. East 11th Street LLC, 1997 U.S. Dist. Lexis 19137 (S.D.N.Y. 1997).

Feist Publications, Inc. vs. Rural Telephone Service Co. Inc., 499 U.S. 340 (1991).

Friedman vs. Guetta, 2011 U.S. Dist. Lexis 66532 (2011).

Hanrahan vs. Ramirez, 1998 WL 34369997 (1998).

Jartech, Inc. vs. Clancy, 666 F.2d 403 (1982).

Kelley vs. Chicago Park District, 635 F.3d 290 (2011).

Mager vs. Brand New School, 78 USPQ 2d 1389 (2004).

Mitchell Brothers Film Group vs. Cinema Adult Theater, 604 F.2d 852 (1979).

Phillips vs. Pembroke Real Estate, Inc., 459 F.3d 128 (2006).

Pollara vs. Seymour, 344 F.3d 265 (2003).

Reece vs. Marc Ecko Unlimited, 2011 U.S. Dist. Lexis 102199 (2011).

Rogers vs. Koons, 960 F.2d 301 (1992).

Seltzer v. Green Day, Inc., 725 F.3d 1170 (2013).

Tracy vs. Skate Key, Inc., 697 F. Supp. 748 (1988).

United States Constitution.

Villa vs. Pearson Education, Inc., 2003 U.S. Dist. Lexis 24686 (2003).

Visual Artists Rights Act of 1990, 17 U.S.C. §106A (Lexis 2014) ("VARA").

Copyright registrations

Reece, D. (created 1972). Dip. Reg. No. VAu001035632/2010–06–01.

Tracy, M. (created 1980). "Skate-key" logo. Reg. No. VAu000081120/1985–07–29.

35

Graffiti, street art, and the evolution of the art market

Maia Morgan Wells

Introduction

The visual expression of graffiti has come a long way from its roots in the streets of New York and Philadelphia. Just like tagging evolved from single-stroke signatures to colorful whole-car productions[1] in the early 1970s, the outsider art form is now evolving beyond its rebellious origins to form the aesthetic and ideological backbone for a growing fine art category. Usually labeled with the catch-all category Street Art, the phenomenon represents the first style-driven genre development in the contemporary art market since Pop Art.[2] Street Art mixes the art, social relationships and economics of graffiti writers – and by extension, designers, muralists, urban sculptors, and collage artists – with an intricate collection of institutional and individual supporters. This intertwining of art worlds ends up constituting a fully-fledged "art world" as the fastest growing style category in Post-war contemporary art.

Graffiti, and by extension Street Art, are now the pillars of a pluralistic art category based in the aesthetic of the streets, an expressive subculture and art style not fully engaged in the social sciences literature. The art world perspective adds another dimension to the existing criminological perceptions (Lachmann 1988; Ferrell 1995a, 1995b), subcultural studies (Macdonald 2001), and ethnographic accounts of the lives of graffiti writers (Snyder 2009). This chapter first presents a set of definitions clarifying my particular use of "Graffiti" and "Street Art," as labels applied in the art world context. Then, we move into an overview of Graffiti's infusion into in the art world and explore implications for artists' careers and the evolution of the art market.

Art world definitions: graffiti and street art

In the professional art world, the terms "Graffiti" and "Street Art" have taken on different meanings than perhaps practitioners in the street would have them represent, creating a definitional tension that warrants a separate explanation of how the terms are (re)created in a context beyond the streets. Though this handbook has provided definitions of the terms "graffiti" and "street art," this chapter provides further specification in the circumstances of professionalization and the art market. In detail, the way these terms are used in the art market indicate a distinct category linked to the business of culture that is different from the use of graffiti and street art as criminological or subcultural categories.

From the eyes of its practitioners in the streets, "graffiti" is a culture. It is a way of engaging with the world as a rebel and a creative outsider. In the street world, graffiti is about making claims of public wall space through the application of one's tag or piece (i.e. "getting up"), and in the purist definition, it is focused solely on letters and never for sale. The art world use of "Graffiti" (capitalized here to provide a short-hand way to distinguish its use in particular contexts from its general or street use) is distinctly a *market category*, and strays from the cultural definition primarily in its disengagement with the core element of illegal production. Whereas illegality is central to the existing colloquial (and even academic) definition of graffiti, it is removed from the conversation in most art world transaction contexts.[3]

As a rapidly growing niche in contemporary art, the definition of "Graffiti" is fluid, but generally rests on two key elements. The first element involves the internal aesthetics of the artwork in question. If the piece focuses on the creative manipulation of letterforms in the form of an individual moniker or crew name, executed as a burner or throwie, it is, "Graffiti." However, a painting could also be classified as such when does not use letters per se, but perhaps uses the stylistic elements of traditional urban street graffiti. The abstraction of proper letters has been compared to Cubism.[4] The highly subjective classification of a painting as "Graffiti" can also include graphic elements like the b-boy style characters in the old school hip hop aesthetic.[5] A canvas could be composed of layers of colors, images, tags, and slogans in a collage format, or even mimic letter manipulations, even if the gestures do not add up to actual letters. Any or all of these things might be called "Graffiti" in a market context.

The second piece of the definition goes beyond the aesthetic elements within each piece, and asks whether an artist's biography may help to define particular works or artists as Graffiti. Curators or collectors may ask, "Did the artist learn his craft outside of art school?" "Did she grow up in tough circumstances?" "Did he write graffiti on the subways and walls of New York City?" For many participants in the Street Art world, if the answers to these questions are in the affirmative, the artist's expression could be considered Graffiti, even if it had little to do with the Wildstyle lettering and egotistical bravado that typically characterizes it on the streets. If a particular artist has ties to the social circles of graffiti, or operates in the public sphere, creating or placing works illegally, that person might be classified along with the category, even if they were never necessarily a writer.[6]

This definitional element evokes the idea of the "outsider artist" (Ardery 1997; Bowler 1997), wherein the *who* about an artist matters as much or even more than the *what*. And, as the art form has evolved both within and outside of the formal art world, the inclusion or exclusion of particular stylistic elements *as* Graffiti, and their acceptance *as art* has evolved as well. It is important to understand these definitions as subjective and fluid within the context of interaction. There are plenty of artists whose work is classified as "Graffiti" who are White, female or who hold MFA degrees; in other words, they don't fit the art world biographical stereotypes of graffiti producers. However, this discussion presents the *typical* or common ways art world professionals discuss Graffiti and its artists.

Advocating for a more careful definitional process is important, because sometimes the gallery, museum, and even academic world mislabel art and artists as Graffiti, to the chagrin of those participants who feel like the cultural stewards and innovators of a movement that is deeply impassioned about authenticity. Two prominent mislabeling examples come in the enthusiastic touting of 1980s art world darlings Jean-Michel Basquiat and Keith Haring as "Graffiti Artists" in gallery announcements, the trade press, and mainstream media coverage of the budding urban art scene of the time. Although both men did ply their skills on the streets of New York City,

Figure 35.1 Saber "Base Elements." Mixed media on canvas, 2011. Reprinted courtesy of Saber One and Opera Gallery, NYC

neither ever engaged in the defining practice of "getting up." Neither ever concentrated on the manipulation of letters in a tag or burner of their own names, and neither were part of the inner-sanctum of the urban street graffiti subculture. This is not to take away from the genius of their art, of course, but a more appropriate label might be "street-influenced art," "urban art," or even, plainly, Pop Art, in Haring's case. These examples illustrate the need for a more nuanced and culturally sensitive approach to genre definition.

Moving to our second clarification, we now extend to the discussion of the term "Street Art." In the most straight-forward sense, street art is art that is made or affixed *illegally* to a surface *in the streets*. The definition seems simple on its surface, but gets complicated when the art moves from the street context to the gallery. In the art world version of the definition of Street Art, the mediums of collage, printmaking, photography, stenciling, and even sculpture blend with a DIY ethos of rebellion, satire, sarcasm, boasting, and activist themes, to constitute a graffiti-influenced, creative culture that is now loosely referred to in the art world as Street Art. This term is an art world catchall for outsider art forms that share a certain youthful, urban creative sensibility, whether tattoo art, wheatpasted[7] digital prints, satirical stencils, or 3D sculptures illegally welded to the corner signpost. As the stylistic innovations of *the streets* have become increasingly established inside the formal art world, the labels of Graffiti and Street Art tend to refer not only to concrete elements of *what* and *who* and *where* of how art is produced, but also to an *ethos* of youth, rebellion and outsiderism. The following section explores the development of this ethos through a brief discussion of important moments in the genre's history.

Graffiti in galleries: a brief history

Initiation

Though it started as a youthful pursuit with simple, one-line hits[8] on train interiors and was mostly seen as vandalism, the perception of graffiti as art grew as the complexity of pieces on trains increased (Austin 2001). Many graffiti historians note the importance of the *New York Times* (1971) coverage of Taki 183 in spreading the trend throughout the New York transit system. As an increasing number of teenagers added their own twist to what they saw on the subways, competition ignited rapid stylistic innovation. Before long, the subculture of writing developed its own conventions of letterform, style, shape, images, references, color, even production materials and constituted a fledgling "art world" of its own (as defined in Becker 1982). The progression of graffiti's visual aesthetic accelerated with the blank canvases (i.e. clean trains) provided by the city's first "war on graffiti" in 1972, and after many trains were whitewashed, larger and even more elaborate styles flooded the transit system. The emergence of roll down gates for businesses after the destruction suffered in the riots and looting during the 1977 blackout in New York City, and increased pressure to move away from trains led to a spillover of artists from the underground to the streets, painting handball courts, gates and walls with elaborate, multi-colored and visually accessible pieces. This more stationary way of creating graffiti art allowed different reactions and perspectives to emerge, and even more elaborate styles and content.

Around the same time early graffiti stars like Lee Quiñones and Futura 2000 entered this ego-centered street milieu, outsiders like Martha Cooper, Henry Chalfant, Hugo Martinez, and Stefan Eins captured the work in amazing photos and created early support institutions (like galleries) that provided some of the most creative early writers and artists with a different outlet and inspiration. These key early figures achieved the first art world fame for the subculture, and served to move the style forward in many aspects, both visually and culturally. For example, in 1972, New York University sociology student Hugo Martinez started UGA, he says, "as a collective that provided an alternative to the art world" and opened up an opportunity for "redefining the purpose of art." UGA hosted a group show of its members at Razor Gallery in 1973, some say the first gallery show for Graffiti.

In 1978, Stefan Eins, and partner Joe Lewis, opened Fashion Moda gallery, an artists' "anti-space" in the South Bronx, and quickly became the institutional center of the uptown Graffiti Art scene. It was in the cocoon of Fashion Moda that artists like Crash and Daze honed their art world chops, and some of the first collectors started forming affinities for this new expression. In these early years, as galleries like Razor (NYC) and Medusa (Rome, Italy) began showing Graffiti Art, there was a group of writers who ended up at the center of the first wave transition from the early years into the Graffiti explosion of the 1980s. Early on, Lee Quiñones became one of the most important figures, and along with Futura 2000, SEEN and others, Quiñones continued to execute breathtaking works in public spaces, and, by 1980, reached a pinnacle of style by subcultural aesthetic standards. This artistic development, coupled with increasing pressure from a city government focused on stopping vandalism and increased interest from the formal art world, led graffiti and its practitioners into the gallery scene, filling a void left by the waning popularity of Pop Art.

1980s explosion

In the 1980s, New York's Lower East Side saw the proliferation of multi-disciplinary arts events and a tightly knit social scene revolving around creativity, parties, and drugs. Like Abstract

Expressionism in the 1940s, or the beat poets and social activists of the 1960s, the Graffiti movement blossomed within a specific, subversive social scene (Crane 1989). The Mudd Club and Danceteria (dance clubs) were hotbeds of expression and the perfect context for the growing relationships of street graffiti to innovators of the art market like Patti Astor and Diego Cortez. In addition, sympathetic supporters (or, more cynically, keen marketers) corralled artists into collectives producing art for display and sale (e.g. Esses Studio collective and the Soul Artists).

At the end of 1980, CRASH curated the pivotal, "Graffiti Art Success for America" show at Fashion Moda, and by the spring of 1981, Graffiti started to gain cultural traction in the art scene. LEE, who was later covered frequently in mainstream media as positive coverage of graffiti peaked through the early 1980s, was the star of this early era of the commercialization of graffiti. He was in almost every group show, from 1981's "New York/New Wave" at PS1, curated by Mudd Club co-founder Diego Cortez, to "Beyond Words" at the Mudd Club (Curated by Fab 5 Freddy & Futura), which also featured works by Daze, Lady PINK, Rammellzee and Keith Haring. Only a few months after "New York/New Wave," Patti Astor founded the Fun Gallery on the Lower East Side with help from arts-educated friends like Mary-Anne Monforton, and it wasn't long before the art of the street had taken over as the hottest new aesthetic in visual art (and music).

The first major wave of Graffiti inside the formal art world was driven by the New York gallery scene (primarily on the Lower East Side), and the European art market (primarily concentrated in Denmark, France, and the Netherlands at the time) where it gained its first museum acceptance. Though there had been a few shows featuring Graffiti art in the 1970s, the early 1980s brought in the hype, and the style was packaged as the young, wild expression of untrained outsider artists. Major collectors, media outlets, and institutions began to show support, but even though graffiti became a pop culture phenomenon, it was not yet recognized as a form of high art, at least not in the United States.

In 1982, over two-dozen canvases, along with early photography from Cooper and Chalfant, were shown as part of an exhibition on graffiti at the University of California, Santa Cruz. The reception on the West Coast made the artists feel like celebrities. The same year, back on the Lower East Side, 51X Gallery opened just two blocks away from Fun Gallery, and expanded not only the availability, but also the content of Graffiti Art. It was with 51X, for instance, that Dondi extended his visual repertoire toward more abstract and "atmospheric" pieces in his 1982 show, "The Ugly Man" (Witten and White 2001). By 1983, the art form had taken root in the European market, gaining most of first museum acceptance there as well. The show simply titled "Graffiti" at the Boymans-Van Beuningen in Rotterdam (1983) featured the second-generation stars who became Graffiti's first wave of professional artists: BLADE, SEEN, Futura, CRASH, QUIK, NOC, and LEE, and the same show spread the formal appreciation of Graffiti first to the Groninger Museum, and then to the Stedelijk in Amsterdam and across Denmark's Lousiana Museum in 1984. Museum acceptance in Europe was one of the key factors in Graffiti's early canonization.

A few creative masters arose from this early stage, and learned to play the art game well, pushing the boundaries of subject matter, style, and modes of production, and developing the business savvy and social mannerisms that allowed them to move into the art world. One of the key factors for the success of any art form is the artists' ability to play the game well, or to get representation who can help them navigate the system. Many of graffiti's early pioneers never got the recognition they deserved inside the art world, because their expressions weren't easily packaged for the market (i.e. they were mostly on trains), and their personalities, or cultural capital (Bourdieu 1986) prevented smooth business dealings. My interviews with Graffiti artists and writers at all levels (along with five years of original ethnographic data) suggest that success

Figure 35.2 The iconic "Hotel Amazon" painting by DAZE. Acrylic on canvas, 1988. Reprinted courtesy of Chris "Daze" Ellis and the Museum of the City of New York

inside the art market is not much different for street-based artists than it is for any other contemporary artist – you have to play the game to make it, and those who can't play the game well, because they don't understand the interactional rules of business, or perhaps are trying to stay too "street," get left behind despite crucial contributions to the creative and cultural conventions of the genre.

DIY and the seeds of "street art"

By the mid-1980s, the first Graffiti Art craze died out as an art world fad. It was marketed as a novelty, and behaved as one, fizzling when bandwagon interest waned. Graffiti was eliminated from New York's subway system by a tenacious transit authority using new cleaning technologies, and only the die-hard writers continued to focus on art (and tagging) in the streets (Kramer 2009). Essentially, the artistic underground moved west, and California emerged as a hotbed of development for what would later become Pop Pluralism (Rose 2004; Neelon 2012). As children of Generation X came of age, disillusioned with formerly idealistic hippie parents who had settled for the suburbs and finding an outlet in punk, skateboarding and, later hip hop, a DIY ethic developed, and incorporated classic graffiti and its art world form, Graffiti, as one of many influences.

Comic books, illustration, and graphic design had a huge influence on the 1990s art, seeping into the works of the era's stars like Mark Gonzales and Barry McGee (Rose 2004). What built up around them was an entirely autonomous production and distribution system for art, one that mirrored the alternative gallery system of 1980s Pop and Graffiti Art, but, in its conventions, even more objectively separated. New York was still covered in graffiti in the 1990s, but it definitely wasn't the darling of gallery elite any longer. Curator and filmmaker Aaron Rose explicitly cites graffiti as a major aesthetic and energetic influence in the founding of his Alleged Gallery in New York in 1992. Just like the Fun Gallery and 51X a decade before, Alleged Gallery became the epicenter of a new art world – the world of DIY.

> We had our own network and distribution that existed completely outside of the [mainstream] art world. What was happening in all these small galleries was new, full of passion and, more important than anything, it was ours!
>
> (Rose 2004: 39)

Beyond the DIY art world, commercial projects and commissioned murals sustained many traditional graffiti artists still working in the original styles and media during this time. Staying true to their roots in aerosol art, BG183, Nicer and Bio formed TATS CRU out of Bronx, NY in 1997 and carved a niche for themselves as the kings of the commissioned mural. Before the end of the 1990s, they had worked with huge corporations like CocaCola, and learned business acumen that has helped them build their crew into a sought-after commercial art outfit to this day. Many other artists and writers expanded into digital art, graphic design, and even commercial product design for high-end vinyl toys and apparel (e.g. Ewok 5MH, Ces, Wise). The expansion swirled with influences from tattoo culture, skateboarding, and punk rock, and the west coast influence of DIY fused with the outsider ethos of street graffiti to constitute a larger field of cultural production (Bourdieu 1983) wherein new stars like Barry McGee, Margaret Kilgallen, Shepherd Fairey and Steve "ESPO" Powers emerged. Pushing the aesthetic and social boundaries of Graffiti, the 1990s wave of outsider cultural producers paved the way for the more inclusive "Street Art" genre that we know today.

The post-Banksy art market

One of the most important artists in recent art history is British street artist and painter, Banksy, who plays with the establishment through his subversive, witty content and innovative production contexts. Garnering the highest auction prices in history for street-influenced art, Banksy has turned the art world on its head, and he seems – at least publically – to find that fact hilarious. In 2003, for example, after gaining record sums for pieces like *Ballerina with Action Man Parts* ($160,000 approx.) and *Bombing Middle England* ($170,000 approx.), Banksy posted a photo of a room full of people bidding on a picture that read, "I Can't Believe You Morons Actually Buy This Shit." Love him or hate him, Banksy has opened the door for the final countdown to the full acceptance of Graffiti and Street Art *as fine art* in the world's most prestigious institutions.

For all the hype surrounding Banksy, a less-recognized set of artists is doing amazing work without as much fanfare, and the fine art world has taken significant notice. As the genre has continued to mature, institutional support has grown past the initial few outsider art galleries and has now infiltrated the blue chip art world of Chelsea (the center of New York's art market), the Museum of Modern Art and the European auction market. As of 2014, there have been several major museum retrospectives for some of the genre's top artists, blue chip signings of some of the most innovative artists of the streets and publically listed secondary sales of works in the style of Graffiti and Street Art. The art market for Graffiti and Street Art has even extended to unorthodox sales fields wherein illegally placed public art works are cut out of concrete walls, or removed from doorframes and sold in the legitimate art market. Today's art world stars, including newer artists like Banksy, Faile, Swoon, Bast, Kaws, and Saber, DIY darlings like McGee, Fairey, and ESPO, as well as first-wave mainstays like Futura, Daze, LEE, and Crash continue to lead the evolution of content and inspire new institutional configurations. What's clear is that "the streets" has become a valuable notion within mainstream contemporary art, and has infused the white walls of high art with very colorful progression into the new and youthful.

Discussion

The social context in which street graffiti emerged was very different than the social context of art and arts consumption today. In the late 1960s and 1970s, the art world could not have been further removed from the impoverished Black and Brown youth who ruled the streets of New York (Austin 2001). Art was something for the rich and generally thought of as out of reach for the youth of the ghetto (DiMaggio & Powell 1983). Abstract Expressionism ruled the elite world of visual art, and it took education and breeding to understand its artists and paintings (Crane 1989). However, after the proliferation of television and later the Internet, arts access and creativity has now gained exposure among a much wider audience. Popular and fine arts are mixing in ways never before seen, and the art market has changed as a result.

As the distinction between high and low art faded (cf. Peterson & Kern 1996; Sullivan & Katz-Gerro 2007; Bellavance 2008; Van Eijck & Lievens 2008), a number of factors had to come together for Graffiti and Street Art to gain acceptance in the art world. First of all, it may just be that the generation who grew up when street culture first entered the mainstream consciousness – those who were in their teens and twenties in the 1980s and 1990s – are now in their thirties and forties, an age group that controls creative production for the most part, especially in design and technology. They are also significant art collectors and influential figures in the world of finance. The kids who grew up during the short lived burst of Graffiti's art world glory in the 1980s saw the aesthetic, often coupled with hip hop, in advertising on the streets, and in backgrounds for videos on the fledgling music network MTV. This generation identified with the rebellious, fun nature of Graffiti (and graffiti), and later may have followed the outsiders of contemporary art into the DIY scene. Many important figures in the contemporary art world (e.g. Jonathan LeVine, Aaron Rose, George Benias, Sean Corcoran) cite youthful affinities with the graffiti aesthetic as a motivating factor for their continued involvement. Though no systematic data is available, the collectors, organizers, and main institutional supporters of Street Art seem, by and large, to come from this generation of babies born in the late 1960s–1970s, and they are now controlling the marketplace.

Another important factor is the Internet. The availability of art and photos online has had multi-dimensional effects on the art market, specifically for Graffiti and Street Art. The effect of this technology was obvious within the subculture, because it allowed writers from all over

Figure 35.3 Example from Banksy's 2013 *Better Out Than In* residency in New York City. Author's photo. Image used with permission of Pest Control

the globe to learn styles and techniques from each other (see Austin 2001; Snyder 2009 for detailed explanation), but what concerns us here is the effect it had upon the art form's canonization. The Internet allowed for those outside of the culture to access its cultural products, and facilitated an entirely new way to buy art. It is via Internet outlets like Dirty Pilot that the market for high-end vinyl toys and inexpensive prints emerged. In addition to new distribution channels and new product types, technology has offered an entirely new way for audiences to engage with art and artists. Banksy's 2013 *Better Out Than In* "residency" in New York, for example, could not have happened with such an incredible impact on art audiences as well as the general public without the social media photo-sharing platform Instagram.

This "residency" on the streets of New York had hundreds of spectators trekking all over the City to find each of the thirty pieces the artist claimed to have placed in different boroughs and advertised through his BanksyNY.com website and Instagram account. The project bypassed the usual art world channels and took the work direct-to-public, shattering usual arrangements of property rights, providence, and authentication of works when property owners opted to cover some of the illegal stencils with Plexiglas to prevent vandalism, and even cut out portions of brick and concrete walls or removed doors containing Banksy pieces in order to auction them to the highest bidders. In the traditional auction or gallery context, transferring such unauthenticated work is unheard of. Now, people are clamoring to get a piece of Street Art history, even though Banksy's "Pest Control" (a pseudo-agency/management entity) refuses to authenticate street works. This refusal to provide authentication indicates at least some loyalty on Banksy's part to the ethos of the streets – that this public artwork is not meant for the market. One of the most significant developments in the professional progression of Graffiti and Street Art is the impact the styles have made on the institutional structures of the art world, illustrated in this example by new ways of seeing and selling art.

As the art form progresses and its practitioners mature, two distinct professional pathways have emerged for Graffiti-related artists. One set of elite artists has begun to infiltrate the formal art world. At the top are artists like KAWS who is represented by Chelsea's blue chip Mary Boone Gallery, but these cases are only the tip of the iceberg. Many Graffiti and Street Artists have now gained international recognition and representation by small and large galleries in major art cities. Opera Gallery (SEEN, Saber, Faile, Bast), Copro Nason (Shag, Mis Van), Jonathan LeVine (Tara McPherson, Pose, Invader), and others lead the primary market for Graffiti and Street Art, while secondary market drivers like Christie's and Sotheby's have developed entire Street Art divisions. Artists from the old school (Daze, Lee, Sharp, Lady Pink) and new school (Os Gemeos, ESPO, Revok, Barry McGee) have gained recognition from museum institutions (e.g. MoCA in Los Angeles, The Whitney in New York City), marking the legitimation, once and for all, of this incredible style. Graffiti's entrance into the art world opened a door for an entirely new set of professional options for budding artists. Before Graffiti, very few artists, if any, sidestepped the traditional pathway of art school – MFA – gallery representation – success. Now, aspiring artists from all corners of the globe have started to create images in the streets, bypassing the institutional pathways of formal art and going direct-to-audience. Snyder (2009) traces many of these career paths and provides an extension to the thinking of both, the Birmingham School of subcultural studies as well as the post-subculture scholarship of Muggleton and his contemporaries (Muggleton 2000; Muggleton & Weinzierl 2003).

What is next is not exactly clear, but some gallerists have predicted a shift away from the simple stencil and wheat paste works of artists like Banksy and Shepherd Fairey back to single-authored, original paintings in oil and acrylic as art audiences crave authenticity in production. However, it is important to remember that because of the importance of the "ethos of the streets," there may never be a full integration of Graffiti into the formal art world, because the authenticity so craved within the genre – its main location of value – must continue to be derived from the illegal placement of works in public places and the reputation that results for the artists. Without "the streets," the excitement of the style is compromised. On the other hand, perhaps artists who have already gained enough street cred to last them a lifetime – like Banksy, Saber, Revok, Faile, Cope 2, Indie, and many more – can continue to evolve within the formal art world without risking imprisonment or worse by working in the streets. It is certainly an area ripe for exploration.

Notes

1 "Whole-car production" is a subcultural term within graffiti that means the artists covered an entire subway car from top to bottom and end to end with a colorful "production" of work including main lettering, background, and accents – often including characters.
2 Pop Art is a style that emerged in Britain in the 1950s and gained traction in the New York art world in the 1960s with artists like Andy Warhol, Roy Lichtenstein, and Jasper Johns.
3 This statement is based on over five years of qualitative research on the business of graffiti and the formation of the street art genre conducted by the author.
4 Cubism is an early twentieth century art movement whose most famous representative was painter, Pablo Picasso.
5 The "old school hip hop aesthetic" as used here consists of the colorful imagery used early in the development of the street graffiti style in New York City. This can include, but is not limited to, brightly colored "bubble letters," comic book style characters, and references to hip hop culture including breakdancers, also known as "b-boys."
6 "Writer" is what most purist graffiti practitioners prefer to be called.
7 Wheatpasting is a street art technique wherein a digitally printed image is affixed to a public surface with a special long lasting wheat glue mixture.
8 "Hit" is early slang for the "tag" or signature of a writer.

References

Ardery, J.S. (1997). " 'Loser Wins': Outsider Art and the Salvaging of Disinterestedness." *Poetics* 24(5): 329–346.
Austin, J. (2001). *Taking the Train: How Graffiti Art Became an Urban Crisis in New York City*. New York: Columbia University Press.
Becker, H.S. (1982). *Art Worlds*. Berkeley, CA: University of California Press.
Bellavance, G. (2008). Where's High? Who's Low? What's New? Classification and Stratification Inside Cultural 'Repertoires'. *Poetics* 36(2): 189–216.
Bourdieu, P. (1983). The Field of Cultural Production, or: The Economic World Reversed. *Poetics* 12(3–5): 311–356.
Bourdieu, P. (1986). The Forms of Capital. In J. Richardson (ed.) *Handbook of Theory and Research for the Sociology of Education* (pp. 241–258). New York: Greenwood Publishing Group.
Bowler, A.E. (1997). Asylum Art: The Social Construction of an Aesthetic Category. In V.L. Zolberg & J. Maya (eds) *Outsider Art: Contesting Boundaries in Contemporary Culture* (pp. 11–36). Cambridge, MA: Cambridge University Press.
Crane, D. (1989). *The Transformation of the Avant-garde: The New York Art World, 1940–1985*. Chicago, IL: University of Chicago Press.
DiMaggio, P. & Powell, W. (1983). The Iron Cage Revisited: Institutional Isomorphism and Collective Rationality in Organizational Fields. *American Sociological Review* 48(2): 147–160.
Van Eijck, K. & Lievens, J. (2008). Cultural Omnivorousness as a Combination of Highbrow, Pop, and Folk Elements: The Relation Between Taste Patterns and Attitudes Concerning Social Integration. *Poetics* 36(2): 217–242.
Ferrell, J. (1995a). Style Matters: Criminal Identity and Social Control. In J. Ferrell & C. Sanders (eds) *Cultural Criminology* (pp. 169–189). Boston, MA: Northeastern University Press.
Ferrell, J. (1995b). Urban Graffiti: Crime, Control, and Resistance. *Youth & Society* 27(1): 73–92.

Kramer, R. (2009). *A Social History of Graffiti Writing in New York City, 1990–2005*. New Haven, CT: Yale University.

Lachmann, R. (1988). Graffiti as Career and Ideology. *American Journal of Sociology 94*(2): 229–250.

Macdonald, N. (2001). *The Graffiti Subculture*. New York: Palgrave Macmillan.

Muggleton, D. (2000). *Inside Subculture: The Postmodern Meaning of Style*. Oxford: Berg.

Muggleton, D. & Weinzierl, R. (2003). *The Post-subcultures Reader*. Oxford: Berg.

Neelon, C. (2012). *Delusional: The Story of the Jonathan Levine Gallery*. New York: Ginko Press.

New York Times. (1971). Taki Spawns Pen Pals. July 21, p. 37.

Peterson, R.A. & Kern, R.M. (1996). Changing Highbrow Taste: From Snob to Omnivore. *American Sociological Review 61*(5): 900–907.

Rose, A. (2004). *Beautiful Losers: Contemporary Art and Street Culture*. San Francisco, CA: DAP.

Snyder, G.J. (2009). *Graffiti Lives: Beyond the Tag in New York's Urban Underground*. New York: New York University Press.

Sullivan, O. & Katz-Gerro, T. (2007). The Omnivore Thesis Revisited: Voracious Cultural Consumers. *European Sociological Review 23*(2): 123–137.

Witten, A. & White, M. (2001). *Dondi White: Style Master General: The Life of Graffiti Artist Dondi White*. New York: HarperCollins.

Glossary[1]

Adbusting   A type of "culture jamming" where individuals or groups purposely distort the advertised message of a business or corporation to create a different, sometimes humorous, message. This can be done by adding or subtracting words or images. Usually done with signs and billboards, but can be done with videos (e.g., posted on the World Wide Web).

Battles   Lyrical, musical, physical, and/or artistic competitions. Prevalent in hip-hop culture.

Bombing   The prolific writing of one's tag. Bombing usually involves saturating a given area with a large number of one's "tags" and/or "throw-ups" (aka "throwies") (see this glossary). Often regarded as an important avenue for achieving recognition among other graffiti writers.

Broken windows theory   Explanation for crime causation developed by George Kelling and James Q. Wilson that argued that low levels of neighborhood blight (e.g., broken windows, abandoned or boarded up houses and vehicles, lawns with grass uncut) including graffiti are magnets for more serious deviancy/crime (e.g., drug sales, robberies, gang activity).

Buffing   The removal or covering of graffiti and street art, usually by state agencies. Buffing graffiti may take various forms, such as the removal of paint/ink with power washers and chemical solutions. It may also involve painting over graffiti.

Burner   A graffiti piece that is regarded as high quality. To "burn" is to outdo the work of others.

Can control   The ability to control and manipulate a spray paint can and tip/nozzle in various ways, thereby being able to produce aesthetic effects, such as color gradients, flares, and thin/clean lines.

Characters   A term used to describe pictorial elements of graffiti works, especially renditions of creatures or personas. Characters are often used in conjunction with elaborate pieces of a graffiti writer's name/tag, and often incorporate gestures that draw the viewer's attention to the name.

Clean car program   A New York City subway program that took trains out of service if they had graffiti on them. During this time, subway staff cleaned trains after each run hoping that this practice would cut down on graffiti.

Commodification   To monetize something, often by making it widely available for popular consumption.

Crew   Graffiti artists/writers who usually paint together. They serve different roles in the construction of elaborate murals and pieces. Not only do crew members paint together, but also they often socialize together. Crews may live geographically close together or they may live in different cities and countries and periodically assemble to work together.

Culture jamming   Disruption, distortion, subversion, and/or damage to publicly displayed cultural artifacts/icons/signs, including advertising, to create a different sometimes humorous or mocking message. Includes re-configuring logos, images, etc. Some of the messages that are attacked can be religious, political, or cultural, and not necessarily those produced by a business.

Discretion   Decisions made by criminal justice practitioners to invoke the law/criminal sanction. In the case of police, it includes the decision to stop, question, search, arrest, and to use force against a suspect.

Electric shadows   Outlining silhouettes of ordinary urban elements such as traffic lights and mailboxes (developed during the 1990s).

Etching techniques   "The act or process of making designs or pictures on a metal plate, glass, etc., by the corrosive action of an acid instead of by burning" (graffiti like technique used on windows of subway cars in NYC during the 2000s. www.nytimes.com/2006/04/25/nyregion/25mta.html?_r=0).

Go citywide/all city   "Denotes writers' success at spreading and maintaining their graffiti throughout an urban area" (Ferrell, 2013, p. 181).

Go nationwide   Placing graffiti on vehicles (e.g., freight trains), to send ones work throughout the country (Ferrell, 2013, p. 181).

Graffiti   Typically refers to words, figures, and images that have been written, drawn and/or painted on, and/or etched into or on surfaces where the owner of the property has NOT given permission. (More detailed definition is provided in the introductory chapter of the book.)

Hand skills   The ability to control a marker, spray can, or paintbrush effectively in order to accomplish an aesthetically pleasing tag.

Hand style   The aesthetic "look" of a graffiti writer's tag/signature. among graffiti writers, it tends to be used in an evaluative manner. For example, someone may be said to have a "good" hand style, or a "bad" hand style. The former would suggest the graffiti writer could produce an aesthetically pleasing tag; the latter would suggest the graffiti writer is inexperienced and lacks style.

Hip-hop   A youth cultural movement, originating in the African American neighborhoods (especially the Bronx) in New York City during the 1970s. It is popularly believed to be characterized by rap music, emceeing/deejaying, dance (especially break dancing), and graffiti.

King   A graffiti artist/writer who is more experienced, skilled, and respected by other graffiti artists/writers.

Knitting graffiti   Wrapping public objects such as statues, bike racks, lamp posts, parking meters, etc. with knitted yarn. (Also known as yarn bombing).

Latrinalia   Graffiti placed on bathroom stalls.

Liminal   Threshold, a space of ambiguity, disorientation, and forgotten site/place.

Moral panic   Disproportionate action taken by the public, politicians and/or mass media against a "deviant" situation or individual.

Murals   Large paintings on walls, sides of buildings etc. where the artist/s have been given express permission by the owner, and/or has been commissioned to do the piece (e.g. the work of Diego Rivera). Often depicting historical and/or religious events, themes, individuals, etc.

Nation of Graffiti Artists (NOGA)   Started in 1974 and tried to promote graffiti artists and decriminalize graffiti. Set up workshops to help graffiti artists.

Paste-up (wheat-paste)   Paper containing art work (i.e., text, images, etc.) that is affixed to a surface by applying a coating of a solution made of flour and water to the backing.

Pieces (short for "masterpieces")   Large, colorful, elaborate, detailed, and stylistically intricate rendering of letters and images. Pieces require a greater amount of time and expertise to create than "throw-ups" and "tags". (Usually deserving of more respect from other graffiti artists/ writers).

Post graffiti   The name given to the conversion of graffiti from an illegal urban action to a legal canvas art (e.g. Dickens, 2008).

Public art   Includes "a vast assortment of art forms and practices, including murals, community projects, memorials, civic statuary, architecture, sculpture, ephemeral art (dance, performance theatre) . . . can be experienced in a multitude of places – parks, libraries, public squares, city streets, building atriums, and shopping centres" (Wacławek, 2011, p. 65). Like graffiti and street art it is free for the public to see. Unlike street art, public art is legal (permission has been given), and frequently commissioned.

Quality of life crimes   Includes graffiti, public gambling (e.g., three-card monti), pick-pocketing, etc. A term popularized by Ed Koch, New York City Mayor from 1978 to 1989.

Stencils   A piece of cardboard or plastic where images and/or letters are cut out, requiring the street artist to simply paint over via brush or spray paint and the image is left on the surface.

Stickers   Paper with adhesive backing (often mailing labels) that are affixed to surfaces. The stickers may have the artist's tag written on it, or contain an image that was reproduced on the sticker.

Street art Stencils, stickers, and artistic/noncommercial posters that are affixed to surfaces where the owner of the property has NOT given permission for the individual to place them on it. Can include words, figures, images and/or a combination of these.

Tag Quickly written name/moniker of the graffiti artist/writer. Typically do not use their real name and use their street/code name instead.

Tagging the heavens "Illicitly writing graffiti atop a building or freeway overpass, and imparts status due to the difficulty and visibility of the spot selected" (Ferrell, 2013, p. 181).

Throw-ups (also known as throwies) Style of graffiti that first started to appear in New York City. Produced with spray paint, throwies spell out a graffiti writer's name in bubble-style letters. These letters are usually produced and filled in quickly with a single color, and then outlined with a second color of paint. Throwies may also be done with a single can of paint, in which case the graffiti writer will produce a quick series of letters. In the more recent history of graffiti, throwies have increasingly come to be recognized as a distinct and valuable part of a graffiti writer's repertoire, often leading to the production of multi-colored throw-ups. Compared to masterpieces, throw-ups are often regarded as "quick pieces intended to be painted in a prolific manner much like tags." Unlike masterpieces, throw-ups allow graffiti writers to cover more surface area relatively quickly.

Tips, caps or nozzles Part of spray can where paint comes out. They can be modified to allow for varying the thickness of lines. Since the early 2000s specialized tips have been produced and made available for purchase by graffiti artists.

Tools of trade Instruments/equipment that graffiti artists use to express their art, such as markers, spray paint, spray-can tips, etc.

Toy An inexperienced and unskilled graffiti writer/artist who does not garner much recognition or respect for their work.

Train graffiti Graffiti that is done inside subway trains. Later progressed to the outside of subway trains, freight trains, and passenger trains.

United Graffiti Artists (UGA) Group started in 1972 to help writers with creativity and make graffiti legal and profitable.

Urban ethnography A qualitative research method that relies on close observation and descriptive analysis. When conducted properly it is a more systematic and self-reflective approach to gathering and interpreting data than used by the news media. Conducted in an urban environment, thus the use of the modifier "urban."

Vandalism "The intentional destruction or damage of public or private property" (Breen, 2013, p. 437).

Vigilante An individual who takes the law into their own hands, and/or in some case acts out beyond the confines of the law to enact a personal sense of "justice." (They assume the various roles and duties of members of the criminal justice system . . . but they also often go beyond what is permitted by the justice system.)

Wildstyle   Energetic pieces of graffiti with interlocking, highly stylized and often cryptic lettering.

Writing style   The letter style, colors, originality, and intricacy of graffiti.

Note

1   Special thanks to Stefano Bloch, Ronald Kramer, and Minna Valjakka for their comments. The reader should keep in mind that because of regional/geographical differences, these terms and definitions may vary in how they are used and applied.

Chronology[1]

50,000–12,000 BC, (Upper Paleolithic Era) Lascaux caves in southwestern France contain wall paintings.

700 BCE–500 CE Graffiti appears in Graeco-Roman culture.

1930 Brassaï photographs graffiti in Paris.

1930s Origins of Hobo graffiti.

1932, Mexican muralist David Alfaro Siqueiros paints his *América Tropical* on an exterior wall above Los Angele's *Placita Olvera*. The controversial mural is quickly whitewashed, but with its use of color and placement inspires a *Chicano/a* mural and graffiti movement beginning in the 1970s.

1940s American servicemen stationed in Italy write and/or carve the iconic "Kilroy was Here" tag in places they stayed.

1940s, Shoeshin boys in Los Angeles' original plaza write their names on walls with shoe polish, giving rise to *Cholo* (aka Mexican-American gang) based writing, or *placas*.

1960s, Darryl McCray, aka Cornbread, tags locations in Philadelphia.

1970s, Graffiti appears on subways in New York City.

1970s, Chaz Boroquez, a local gang member and creator of the *senior suerte* icon—a black fedora-wearing *calavera*—paints stylized roll-calls and his character on freeway and flood channel retaining walls through LA's eastside districts.

1971, Article about Taki 183 appears in the *New York Times*.

1972, Founding of United Graffiti Artists in New York City.

1973, Graffiti starts to appear with increasing frequency in the streets of New York City.

1973, Opposition to graffiti amongst New York City's political elite and within the mass media emerges.

1974, The publication of David Ley and Roman Cybriwsky's "Urban Graffiti as Territorial Markers" in the *Annals of the Association of American Geographers*.

1974, Founding of Nation of Graffiti Artists (NOGA) in New York City.

1979, Graffiti artists Lee Quinones and Fab 5 Freddy work displayed in Rome gallery graffiti.

1982, Stencils by Blek le Rat, appear in Paris.

1982, Craig Castleman's *Getting up: Subway graffiti in New York* is published.

1983, Movie *Wildstyle*, directed by Charlie Ahern, first fictional movie using graffiti as backdrop is is released.

1983, PBS Documentary *Style Wars* is released.

1984, *Subway Art* by Martha Cooper and Henry Chalfant published.

1984, Movie *Beat Street*, directed by Stan Lathan, is released.

1984, Graffiti writers in Los Angeles such as Wisk One bomb the backs of freeway signs (called "heavens") in anticipation of the city's hosting of the Summer Olympic Games

1985, Fashion Moda art gallery in the Bronx has first show specializing in graffiti.

1987, Los Angeles-based graffiti writer Power publishes the graffiti magazine *Can Control*.

1987, *Spraycan Art* by Henry Chalfant and James Prigoff published.

1989, New York City subway officially declared "graffiti free."

1989, LA Graffiti writer Chaka goes "all city," producing an estimated 10,000 tags with is bold and legible writing style. His arrest the next year makes national news.

1990, Banksy, working as part of DryBreadZ (DBZ) crew starts doing graffiti in Bristol, UK.

1992, *Fox Television*'s "Front Page" broadcasts an undercover exposé on "daredevil taggers" and "tag bangers" in Los Angeles (erroneously conflating "taggers" with "gang bangers")

1994, one of the first public websites, *ArtCrimes.com* launches as a global database for pictures of graffiti

1995, Rudolph Gulliani, New York City Mayor, establishes Anti-Graffiti Task Force.

1995, Graffiti festival "Paint Louis" begins in St. Louis, Missouri attracts graffiti artists from around the world.

1996, Jeff Ferrell publishes *Crimes of Style*, first ethnographic academic book covering graffiti.

2000s, semi-legal painting locations and meccas for graffiti writers and street artists in Los Angeles (Belmont) and New York City (5Pointz) are shut down and commercially developed.

2008, Shepard Fairey, street artist behind the OBEY Giant sticker campaign, designs iconic Hope poster for Barak Obama's first Presidential Campaign.

2008, Tate Modern, Art Museum in London, holds "Street Art" Exhibition.

2010, Banksy produced documentary *Exit Through the Gift Shop*, released.

2011, The Museum of Contemporary Art in Los Angeles hosts *Art in the Streets*, the first major survey of American graffiti and street art.

2014, John Robertson (aka King Robbo), London based graffiti artist who has iconic fued with Banksy dies.

Note

1 Special thanks to Stefano Bloch, Ronald Kramer, and Rod Palmer for comments and providing additional events.

Index

UK and US spelling used in this index. 'n' refers to end of chapter notes.

Made in the USA
Monee, IL
27 January 2021